HISTORICAL PERSPECTIVES:
A Reader & Study Guide
Volume II, Sixth Edition

HISTORICAL PERSPECTIVES:
A Reader & Study Guide
Volume II, Sixth Edition

DOUG CANTRELL

BARBARA D. RIPEL

Abigail Press   Wheaton, IL 60189

Design and Production: Abigail Press
Typesetting: Abigail Press
Typeface: AGaramond
Cover Art: Sam Tolia

HISTORICAL PERSPECTIVES:
A Reader & Study Guide
Volume II, Sixth Edition

Sixth Edition, 2012
Printed in the United States of America
Translation rights reserved by the authors
ISBN 1-890919-70-5   978-1-890919-70-2

Contents in Brief

Contents

Chapter Twelve

RECONSTRUCTION: The Turning Point That Never Turned

From April 1861 to April 1865 Americans fought the most devastating war in the nation's history. The American Civil War produced thousands of casualties on both sides. When the conflict ended in the Spring of 1865, the United States faced the daunting task of reconstructing the nation. Wounds to the nation sustained during the war had to be treated and bound so that the healing process could begin. The ultimate goal of reconstruction was to develop a political process that could restore the defeated Confederate states to a normal constitutional relationship with the victorious Union. Before Reconstruction could be completed, however, numerous questions had to be settled. Who would control the Reconstruction process— Congress or the president? Would the South be punished for leaving the Union? Should political and military leaders within the former Confederate states be stripped of their property and citizenship? Should they be imprisoned for treason? What about the ex-slaves freed as a result of the war? Should they be given property? Should the Federal government establish schools in southern states to teach blacks how to read? Should ex-slaves be given citizenship and the right to vote? What kind of government should ex-Confederate states have and who should control those governments? Should southern whites be disenfranchised? What kind of economic and labor system should develop in the South following the Civil War? These and other issues produced much controversy within the nation from 1865 until 1877.

Many of the difficulties the nation faced during the Reconstruction process resulted when Congress and the president could not compromise on the many questions Americans had to wrestle with during Reconstruction. Unlike Abraham Lincoln who was assassinated shortly after the Civil War ended, Andrew Johnson was not willing to compromise. Johnson, who ironically was a southern Democrat, stubbornly insisted that the president should control Reconstruction and that former pardoned Confederate leaders be allowed to head state governments in the South. Conflict between Johnson and Congress reached a boiling point when southern states enacted Black Codes that virtually re-enslaved blacks. Radical Republican members of Congress who wanted to punish Southerners for secession were not willing to tolerate Johnson's pardon of ex-Confederate leaders and their attempt to restrict the freedom of southern blacks. Radical Republicans fought back by creating the Freedman's Bureau and passing bills granting Civil Rights to former slaves. When Johnson vetoed Radical Republican legislation, the fight between the executive and legislative branches of government intensified. Radical Republicans eventually gained enough power in Congress to impeach President Johnson and give Congress control of the Reconstruction process. Although impeachment did not result in Johnson's removal from office, his power was weakened, and he became a lame duck and lost the ability to influence Reconstruction.

Within the South governments were established under terms of the Reconstruction Acts, which divided the former Confederacy into five military districts and sent federal troops as an occupying force into each district. Governments in each southern state were controlled by the Republican coalition comprised of "carpetbaggers" from the North, southern "scalawags," and ex-slaves. Although the alliance between these groups was fragile, from 1867 to 1877 they engineered much social and political change in the South. Black males were given the right to vote, a system of public schools was established for the first time in the South, public hospitals and insane asylums were built, and roads and railroads were rebuilt.

Most southern whites, however, resented changes wrought by the Republican Coalition governments because taxes were imposed to pay for schools, hospitals, and roads and because ex-slaves were, for the first time, allowed to participate in the political process. Terrorist groups such as the Ku Klux Klan arose to resist reforms instituted by the Republican coalition governments. A particular target of white terrorists was the newly enfranchised black. Night riders dressed in robes often threatened, intimidated, whipped, and lynched African Americans to prevent them from voting. Corruption also hurt efforts of Republican Coalition governments to affect change within the South. Southerners generally perceived Reconstruction governments as existing to exploit people defeated in war. Southern resistance to Reconstruction coupled with conservative attitudes within the North about property rights meant that land redistribution to former slaves would not occur. Consequently, southern blacks faced economic difficulty and had to become sharecroppers to support themselves.

As Reconstruction progressed, many reforms were repealed or ignored. Even though the Fifteenth Amendment guaranteed blacks the right to vote, southern states, once the Democratic Party regained control of governments, disenfranchised blacks through poll taxes, literacy tests, and Grandfather Laws. Disenfranchisement became possible after Feminists, who previously had supported black rights, became disenchanted when Congress refused to grant women voting rights in the Fifteenth Amendment and after many Radical Republicans in the North died. The northern population, beset by an economic downturn, lost interest in Reconstruction, which ended as a result of controversy in the 1876 presidential elections. Under terms of the Compromise of 1877, southern Democrats agreed to support the election of Republican Rutherford B. Hayes in return for an official end to Reconstruction and the removal of federal troops from South Carolina, Louisiana, and Florida. Within the South a rigid system of racial segregation known as Jim Crow was put in place by legal statutes, which were upheld by numerous Supreme Court decisions.

IDENTIFICATION: Briefly describe each term.

Abraham Lincoln

Ten Percent Plan

Thirteen Amendment

Fourteenth Amendment

Andrew Johnson

Tenure of Office Act

Reconstruction Acts

Radical Republicans

Thaddeus Stevens

Black Codes

Freedman's Bureau

Edwin Stanton

Ku Klux Klan

Sharecrop System

Charles Sumner

Rutherford B. Hayes

Samuel Tilden

Civil Rights Act of 1875

Elizabeth Cady Stanton

Carpetbaggers

Scalawags

Credit Mobilier Scandal

Susan B. Anthony

Election of 1876

Compromise of 1877

Jim Crowe

New South

THINK ABOUT:

1. Had political corruption not have been pervasive throughout the United States, would Reconstruction have turned out differently? Why or why not?

2. How might American History been different if former slaves had been given sufficient land on which to farm?

A LETTER "TO MY OLD MASTER," c. 1865

Slaves freed by the Civil War relished their new found freedom and did not want to return to a life of bondage. Most ex-slaves wanted to make a better life for themselves and their families. Jourdon Anderson, a former Tennessee slave, answers a letter from his old owner asking Anderson and his family to return to his previous master's farm as a wage laborer. Anderson clearly states in the letter to his old master exactly how he feels about slavery and how it compares to his new life as a free wage laborer in Nashville.

TO MY OLD MASTER, COLONEL P.H. ANDERSON, BIG SPRING, TENNESSEE

Sir: I got your letter, and was glad to find that you had not forgotten Jourdon, and that you wanted me to come back and live with you again, promising to do better for me than anybody else can. I have often felt uneasy about you. I thought the Yankees would have hung you long before this, for harboring Rebs they found at your house. I suppose they never heard about your going to Colonel Martin's to kill the Union soldier that was left by his company in their stable. Although you shot at me twice before I left you, I did not want to hear of your being hurt, and am glad you are still living. It would do me good to go back to the dear old home again, and see Miss Mary and Miss Martha and Allen, Esther, Green, and Lee. Give my love to them all, and tell them I hope we will meet in the better world, if not in this. I would have gone back to see you all when I was working in the Nashville Hospital, but one of the neighbors told me that Henry intended to shoot me if he ever got a chance.

I want to know particularly what the good chance is you propose to give me. I am doing tolerably well here. I get twenty-five dollars a month, with victuals and clothing; have a comfortable home for Mandy—the folks call her Mrs. Anderson—and the children—Milly, Jane, and Grundy—go to school and are learning well. The teacher says Grundy has a head for a preacher. They go to Sunday school, and Mandy and me attend church regularly. We are kindly treated. Sometimes we overhear others saying, "Them colored people were slaves" down in Tennessee. The children feel hurt when they hear such remarks; but I tell them it was no disgrace in Tennessee to belong to Colonel Anderson. Many darkeys would have been proud, as I used to be, to call you master. Now if you will write and say what wages you will give me, I will be better able to decide whether it would be to my advantage to move back again.

As to my freedom, which you say I can have, there is nothing to be gained on that score, as I got my free papers in 1864 from the Provost-Marshal General of the Department of Nashville. Mandy says she would be afraid to go back without some proof that you were disposed to treat us justly and kindly; and we have concluded to test your sincerity by asking you to send us our wages for the time we served you. This will make us forget and forgive old scores, and rely on your justice and friendship in the future. I served you faithfully for thirty-two years, and Mandy twenty years. At twenty-five dollars a month for me, and two dollars a week for Mandy, our earnings would amount to eleven thousand six hundred and eighty dollars. Add to this the interest for the time our wages have been kept back, and deduct what you paid for our clothing, and three doctor's visits to me, and pulling a tooth for Mandy, and the balance will show what we are in justice entitled to. Please send the money by Adam's Express, in care of V. Winters, Esq., Dayton, Ohio. If you fail to pay us for faithful labors in the past, we can have little faith in your promises in the future. We trust the good Maker has opened your eyes to the wrongs which you and your fathers have done to me and my fathers, in making us toil for you for generations without recompense. Here I draw my wages every Saturday night; but in Tennessee there was never any pay-day for the Negroes any more than for the horses and cows. Surely there will be a day of reckoning for those who defraud the laborer of his hire.

In answering this letter, please state if there would be any safety for my Milly and Jane, who are now grown up, and both good-looking girls. You know how it was with poor Matilda and Catherine. I would rather stay here and starve—and die, if it come to that—than have my girls brought to shame by the violence and wickedness of their young masters. You will also please state if there has been any schools opened for the colored children in your neighborhood. The great desire of my life now is to give my children an education, and have them form virtuous habits.

Say howdy to George Carter, and thank him for taking the pistol from you when you were shooting at me.

FROM YOUR OLD SERVANT,
JOURDON ANDERSON

HOW WELL DID YOU UNDERSTAND THIS SELECTION?

1. How did Anderson feel about slavery?

2. How did Anderson feel about his former owner?

3. Does Anderson intend to accept the offer to return to his former home?

4. How did ex-slaves generally feel about freedom?

After it became clear that the South had lost the Civil War and that slavery would end, southern state legislatures passed numerous laws that were a thinly veiled attempt at reinstituting slavery. These Black Codes, as the statutes were called, denied ex-slaves basic rights that southern whites enjoyed. Despite their intent, white Southerners maintained that the Black Codes were necessary to keep order in southern society and protect black rights.

The Black Code of
St. Landry's Parish, 1865

Whereas it was formerly made the duty of the police jury to make suitable regulations for the police of slaves within the limits of the parish; and whereas slaves have become emancipated by the action of the ruling powers; and whereas it is necessary for public order, as well as for the comfort and correct deportment of said freedmen, that suitable regulations should be established by their government in their changed condition, the following ordinances are adopted, with the approval of the United States military authorities commanding in said parish, viz:

SECTION *1. Be it ordained by the police jury of the parish of St. Landry,* That no negro shall be allowed to pass within the limits of said parish without a special permit in writing from his employer. Whoever shall violate this provision shall pay a fine of two dollars and fifty cents, or in default thereof shall be forced to work four days on the public road, or suffer corporeal punishment as provided hereinafter.

SECTION *2. Be it further ordained,* That every negro who shall be found absent from the residence of his employer after 10 o'clock at night, without a written permit from his employer, shall pay a fine of five dollars, or in default thereof, shall be compelled to work five days on the public road, or suffer corporeal punishment as hereinafter provided.

SECTION *3. Be it further ordained,* That no negro shall be permitted to rent or keep a house within said parish. Any negro violating this provision shall be immediately ejected and compelled to find an employer; and any person who shall rent, or give the use of any house to any negro, in violation of this section, shall pay a fine of five dollars for each offence.

SECTION *4. Be it further ordained,* That every negro is required to be in the regular service of some white person, or former owner, who shall be held responsible for the conduct of said negro. But said employer or former owner may permit said negro to hire his own time by special permission in writing, which permission shall not extend over seven days at any one time. Any negro violating the provisions of this section shall be fined five dollars for each offence, or in default of the payment thereof shall be forced to work five days on the public road, or suffer corporeal punishment as hereinafter provided.

SECTION *5. Be it further ordained,* That no public meetings or congregations of negroes shall be allowed within said parish after sunset; but such public meetings and congregations may be held between the hours of sunrise and sunset, by the special permission of writing of the captain of patrol, within whose beat such meetings shall take place. This prohibition, however, is not intended to prevent negroes from attending the usual church services, conducted by white ministers and priests. Every negro violating the provisions of this section shall pay a fine of five dollars, or in default thereof shall be compelled to work five days on the public road, or suffer corporeal punishment as hereinafter provided.

SECTION *6. Be it further ordained,* That no negro shall be permitted to preach, exhort, or otherwise declaim to congregations of colored people, without a special permission in writing from the president of the police jury. Any negro violating the provisions of this section shall pay a fine of ten dollars, or in default thereof shall be forced to work ten days on the public road, or suffer corporeal punishment as hereinafter provided.

SECTION *7. Be it further ordained,* That no negro who is not in the military service shall be allowed to carry fire-arms, or any kind of weapons, within the parish, without the special written permission of his employers, approved and indorsed by the nearest or most convenient chief of patrol. Any one violating the provisions of this section shall forfeit his weapons and pay a fine of five dollars, or in default of the payment of said fine, shall be forced to work five days on the public road, or suffer corporeal punishment as hereinafter provided.

SECTION 8. *Be it further ordained,* That no negro shall sell, barter, or exchange any articles of merchandise or traffic within said parish without the special written permission of his employer, specifying the articles of sale, barter or traffic. Any one thus offending shall pay a fine of one dollar for each offence, and suffer the forfeiture of said articles' or in default of the payment of said fine shall work one day on the public road, or suffer corporeal punishment as hereinafter provided.

SECTION 9. *Be it further ordained,* That any negro found drunk within the said parish shall pay a fine of five dollars, or in default thereof shall work five days on the public road, or suffer corporeal punishment as hereinafter provided.

SECTION 10. *Be it further ordained,* That all the foregoing provisions shall apply to negroes of both sexes.

SECTION 11. *Be it further ordained,* That it shall be the duty of every citizen to act as a police officer for the detection of offences and the apprehension of offenders, who shall be immediately handed over to the proper captain or chief of patrol.

SECTION 12. *Be it further ordained,* That the aforesaid penalties shall be summarily enforced, and that it shall be the duty of the captains and chiefs of patrol to see that the aforesaid ordinances are promptly executed.

SECTION 13. *Be it further ordained,* That all sums collected from the aforesaid fines shall be immediately handed over to the parish treasurer.

SECTION 14. *Be it further ordained,* That the corporeal punishment provided for in the foregoing sections shall consist in confining the body of the offender within a barrel placed over his or her shoulders, in the manner practiced in the army, such confinement not to continue longer than twelve hours, and for such time within the aforesaid limit as shall be fixed by the captain or chief of patrol who inflicts the penalty.

HOW WELL DID YOU UNDERSTAND THIS SELECTION?

1. What effect on black freedom did the Black Code of St. Landry's Parish have?

2. What was the real intent of the Black Codes?

3. How would newly freed slaves have felt about the Black Codes?

4. How would northern whites have felt about the Black Codes?

5. How would Radical Republicans have perceived the Black Codes?

Following the Civil War blacks newly freed by the Thirteenth Amendment faced economic hardship in southern states. Radical Republicans and other Northerners believed one solution to black economic problems was land redistribution. The idea was to confiscate property owned by former Confederate leaders and large plantation owners and break it into small parcels that would then be given to ex-slaves. While this idea appealed to Radical Republicans, such as Congressman Thaddeus Stevens, other Americans thought it violated long held views on property ownership. The following brief selections represent the views of a Radical Republican Congressman, the New York Times and a former slave in Arkansas.

From a speech by THADDEUS STEVENS, 1865
Published in the Congressional Record

We especially insist that the property of the chief rebels should be seized and appropriated to the payment of the national debt, caused by the unjust and wicked war they instigated [started] .... There are about 6,000,000 of freedmen in the South. The number of acres of land is 465,000,000. Of this those who own above 200 acres each number about 70,000 persons, holding in the aggregate—together with the states—about 394,000,000 acres. By forfeiting the estates of the leading rebels the government would have 394,000,000 of acres besides their town property, and yet nine-tenths of the people would remain untouched. Divide the land into convenient farms. Give, if you please, forty acres to each adult male freedman. Suppose there are 1,000,000 of them. That would require 40,000,000 acres, which deducted from 394,000,000 leaves 354,000,000 acres for sale. Divide it into suitable farms, and sell it to the highest bidders. I think it, including town property, would average at least $10 per acre. That would produce $3,540,000.

The whole fabric of southern society must be changed and never can it be done if this opportunity is lost. Without this, this government can never be, as it has never been, a true republic.... How can republican institutions, free schools, free churches, free social intercourse exist in a mingled community of nabobs [men of wealth and high position] and serfs [tillers of the land]? If the South is ever made a safe republic let her lands be cultivated by the toil of .. free labor....

Nothing is so likely to make a man a good citizen as to make him a freeholder. Nothing will so multiply the production of the South as to divide it into small farms. Nothing will make men so industrious and moral as to let them feel that they are above want and are the owners of the soil which they till.... No people will ever be republican in spirit and practice where a few own immense manors and the masses are landless. Small and independent landholders are the support and guardians of republican liberty.

NEW YORK TIMES, July 9, 1867:

[Land confiscation] is a question not of humanity, not of loyalty, but of fundamental relation of industry to capital; and sooner or later, if begun at the South, it will find its way into the cities of the North.... An attempt to justify the confiscation of Southern land under the pretense of doing justice to the freedmen, strikes at the root of property rights in both sections. It concerns Massachusetts as much as Mississippi.

A Conversation between a Freedman and a General at Fort Smith Arkansas
Reported by the JOINT CONGRESSIONAL COMMITTEE ON RECONSTRUCTION, 1867:

FREEDMAN: Sir, I want you to help me in a personal matter.
GENERAL: Where is your family?
FREEDMAN: On the Red River.
GENERAL: Have you not everything you want?

FREEDMAN: No sir.

GENERAL: You are free!

FREEDMAN: Yes sir, you set me free, but you left me there.

GENERAL: What do you want?

FREEDMAN: I want some land; I am helpless; you do nothing for me but give me freedom.

GENERAL: Is not that enough?

FREEDMAN: It is enough for the present; but I cannot help myself unless I get some land; then I can take care of myself and my family; otherwise I cannot do it.

HOW WELL DID YOU UNDERSTAND THIS SELECTION?

1. What did Congressman Stevens propose?

2. Who would have favored Stevens' plan? Who would have opposed it?

3. Is Stevens correct when he maintains that land redistribution would strengthen both democracy and the southern economy? Why or why not?

4. Why does the *New York Times* oppose land confiscation and redistribution? Is the argument correct? Why or why not?

5. How did the recently freed blacks see the issue of land confiscation and redistribution?

Most ex-slaves entered freedom in an illiterate condition. Laws regulating slavery in the Old South prohibited masters from teaching slaves how to read or write because whites feared literate slaves might question the morality of slavery and organize a revolt against their white masters. After the Thirteenth Amendment ended slavery, blacks needed to learn how to read and write in order to survive economically. Blacks also realized that education offered them opportunities for upward social mobility and could open a world to them that illiterate slaves could not imagine. The following passages provide insight on the importance of education for the freedmen.

Dedicated Teachers, Determined Students, 1869

RALEIGH, N.C., FEB 22, 1869

It is surprising to me to see the amount of suffering which many of the people endure for the sake of sending their children to school. Men get very low wages here—from $2.50 to $8 per month usually, while a first-rate hand may get $10, and a peck or two of meal per week for rations—and a great many men cannot get work at all. The women take in sewing and washing, go out by day to scour, etc. There is one woman who supports three children and keeps them at school; she says, "I don't care how hard I has to work, if I can only   Sallie and the boys to school looking respectable." Many of the girls have but one decent dress; it gets washed and ironed on Saturday, and then is worn until the next Saturday, provided they do not tear it or fall in the mud; when such an accident happens there is an absent mark on the register.... One may go into their cabins on cold, windy days, and see daylight between every two boards, or feel the rain dropping through the roof; but a word of complaint is rarely heard. They are anxious to have the children "get on" in their books, and do not seem to feel impatient if they lack comforts themselves. A pile of books is seen in almost every cabin, though there be no furniture except a poor bed, a table and two or three broken chairs.

MISS M. A. PARKER, In *American Freedman, April 1869*

SYDNEY ANDREWS quoted in the Joint Report on Reconstruction, 39th (U.S.) Congress, 1st Session, 1866:

Many of the negroes ... common plantation negroes, and day laborers in the towns and villages, were supporting little schools themselves. Everywhere I found among them a disposition to get their children into schools, if possible. I had occasion very frequently to notice that porters in stores and laboring men in warehouses, and cart drivers on the streets, had spelling books with them, and were studying them during the time they were not occupied with their work. Go into the outskirts of any large town and walk among the negro inhabitants, and you will see children and in many instances grown negroes, sitting in the sun alongside their cabins studying.

CAPTAIN C. M. HAMILTON in a letter to the Office of the Adjutant General in Washington, D.C., 1866:

The night school has been frequently disturbed. One evening a mob called out of the school house, the teacher, who upon presenting himself was confronted with four revolvers, and menacing expressions of shooting him, if he did not promise to quit the place, and close the school. The freedmen promptly came to his aid and the mob dispersed.

About the 18th or 19th of the month, I was absent ... when a formidable disturbance took place at the school. The same mob threatened to destroy the school that night, and the freedmen, learning this, assembled... at their place of instruction in a condition of self-defense.

I understand that not less than forty colored men armed to protect themselves, but the preparation becoming known to the *respectable, rowdies,* they only maneuvered about in small squads, and were wise enough to avoid a collision.

HOW WELL DID YOU UNDERSTAND THIS SELECTION?

1. What value did Blacks place on education?

2. What problems did southern blacks face when trying to go to school?

3. Why did southern whites want to prevent blacks from learning how to read and write?

4. Why were blacks adamant about education?

5. How did blacks respond when confronted with "respectable rowdies"?

WOMEN'S RIGHTS V. BLACK RIGHTS

Prior to the Civil War, advocates for women's rights generally supported abolition of slavery. After the war, however, the alliance between women's rights advocates and former abolitionists who now supported black rights splintered over suffrage. Feminist, who had put aside their push for suffrage to affect abolition of slavery, expected the right to vote to be extended to both blacks and women. After it became clear that many advocates for black suffrage did not favor extending the franchise to women, feminists became disenchanted and less enthusiastic in their support of black suffrage. The following selections explore the dispute between feminists and advocates for black rights over universal suffrage.

A petition drafted after the Civil War by ELIZABETH CADY STANTON and SUSAN B. ANTHONY, leaders of the women's movement and also abolitionists:

To the Senate and House of Representatives in Congress Assembled:
The undersigned citizens of the State of _____ earnestly but respectfully request that in any change or amendment of the Constitution you may propose to extend or regulate Suffrage, there shall be no distinction made between men and women.

Letter to Susan B. Anthony from abolitionist and advocate of suffrage for ex-slaves GERRITT SMITH, December 30, 1868

My Dear Susan B. Anthony: I this evening received your earnest letter. It pains me to be obliged to disappoint you. But I cannot sign the petition you sent me. Cheerfully, gladly can I sign a petition for the enfranchisement [granting the right to vote] of women. But I cannot sign a paper against the enfranchisement of the Negro man, unless at the same time woman shall be enfranchised. The removal of the political disabilities of race is my first desire, of sex my second. If put on the same level and urged in the same connection, neither will be soon accomplished. The former will very soon be, if untrammeled by the other, and its success will prepare the way for the other.

A Response by Elizabeth Cady Stanton

[Gerritt Smith] does not clearly read the sign of the times, or he would see that there is to be no reconstruction of this nation, except on the basis of Universal Suffrage, as the natural, inalienable right of every citizen to its exercise....

As the aristocracy of this country is the "male sex" and as Mr. Smith belongs to the privileged order, he naturally considers it important, for the best interests of the nation, that every type and shade of degraded, ignorant manhood should be enfranchised, before even the higher classes of womanhood should be admitted to the polls.

This does not surprise us. Men always judge more wisely of objective wrongs and oppressions, than of those in which they themselves are involved. Tyranny on a southern plantation is far more easily seen by white men... [in] the north than the wrongs of the women of their own households....

Again, Mr. Smith refuses to sign the petition because he thinks that to press the broader question of "Universal Suffrage" would defeat the partial one of "Manhood Suffrage"; in other words to demand protection for women against her oppressors would jeopardize the black man's chances for securing protection against his oppressors. If it is a question of precedence merely, on what principle of justice or courtesy should woman yield her right of enfranchisement to the Negro? If men cannot be trusted to legislate for their own sex, how can they legislate for the opposite sex, of whose wants and needs they know nothing! It has always been considered good philosophy in pressing any measure to claim the uttermost in order to get something .... Henry Ward Beecher advised abolitionists, right after the war, to demand "Universal Suffrage" if they wished to secure the ballot for the new made freedmen. "Bait your hooks," said he, "with a woman and perhaps you will catch a Negro." But their intense interest in the Negro blinded them, and they forsook principle for policy. In giving woman the cold shoulder they raised a more deadly opposition to the Negro than any we had encountered, creating an antagonism between him and the very element most needed, especially in the South, to be propitiated in his behalf...

... There is no other ground on which to debate the question. Every argument for the Negro is an argument for woman and no logician can escape it....

Although those who demand "Women's Suffrage" on principle are few, those who would oppose "Negro suffrage" from prejudice are many, hence the only way to secure the latter is to end all this talk of class legislation, bury the Negro in the citizen, and claim suffrage for all men and women as a natural, inalienable right.
- ELIZABETH CADY STANTON, January 14, 1869

"Being Persons, Then, Women are Citizens"

Though the words persons, people, inhabitants, electors, citizens, are all used indiscriminately in the national and State constitutions, there was always a conflict of opinion, prior to the war, as to whether they were synonymous terms, but whatever room there was for doubts, under the old regime, the adoption of the Fourteenth Amendment settled that question forever in its first sentence:

All persons born or naturalized in the United States, and subject to the jurisdiction thereof, are citizens of the United States wherein they reside.

The second settles the equal status of all citizens:

No state shall make or enforce any law which shall abridge the privileges or immunities of citizens of the United States; nor shall any State deprive any person of life, liberty, or property without due process of law; nor deny to any person within its jurisdiction the equal protection of the laws.

The only question left to be settled now is: Are women persons? I scarcely believe that any of our opponents will have the hardihood to say that they are not. Being persons, then, women are citizens and no State has a right to make any new law, or to enforce any old law, which shall abridge their privileges and immunities. Hence, every discrimination against women in the constitutions and laws of the several States is today null and void, precisely as is every one against Negroes.
- SUSAN B. ANTHONY, November 1872

HOW WELL DID YOU UNDERSTAND THIS SELECTION?

1. Why did Gerritt Smith and other advocates of Black suffrage refuse to support suffrage for women?

2. How do feminists like Elizabeth Cady Stanton view the issue of suffrage?

3. What does Susan B. Anthony argue regarding women's suffrage?

4. Why did women's rights advocates become less enthusiastic about black rights?

5. Were feminists justified in splitting with former abolitionists? Why or why not?

BLACKS AND RECONSTRUCTION: THE WHITE SOUTHERN PERSPECTIVE

Most white Southerners saw the Reconstruction era as a time period in which blacks, drunk with new-found power, lorded it over the oppressed white population. The reality, of course, was far different. Blacks never had real power in any state and were very moderate in their demands and votes. Albion Tourgee was a Northerner who served as a judge in the South, propelled by idealism. He was eventually disillusioned by the level of resistance to rights for freed people he found among southern whites. Thomas Dixon's bestselling novel, **The Clansman,** *reflected the attitudes of southern whites. (It later became the basis for the popular movie,* **Birth of a Nation,** *which was instrumental in disseminating negative images of black-actions in Reconstruction.) The final document in this segment relates the experiences of a black man who gained some measure of authority during Reconstruction.*

From the Novel, *A Fool's Errand*
By the "carpetbagger," Albion Tourgee (1879)

When the second Christmas come, Metta wrote again to her sister:

"The feeling is terribly bitter against Comfort on account of his course towards the colored people. There is quite a village of them on the lower end of the plantation. They have a church, a sabbath school, and are to have next year a school. You can not imagine how kind they have been to us, and how much they are attached to Comfort.... I got Comfort to go with me to one of their prayer meetings a few nights ago. I had heard a great deal about them, but had never attended one before. It was strangely weird. There were, perhaps, fifty present, mostly middle-aged men and women. They were singing in a soft, low monotone, interspersed with prolonged exclamatory notes, a sort of rude hymn, which I was surprised to know was one of their old songs in slave times. How the chorus came to be endured in those days I can not imagine. It was—

13

'Free! free! free, my Lord, free!
An' we walks de hebben-ly way!'

"A few looked around as we came in and seated ourselves; and Uncle Jerry, the saint of the settlement, came forward on his staves, and said, in his soft voice, "'Ev'nin', Kunnel! Sarvant, Missus! Will you walk up, an' hev seats in front?'

'We told him we had just looked in, and might go in a short time; so we would stay in the back part of the audience.

"Uncle Jerry can not read nor write; but he is a man of strange intelligence and power. Unable to do work of any account, he is the faithful friend, monitor, and director of others. He has a house and piece of land, all paid for, a good horse and cow, and, with the aid of his wife and two boys, made a fine crop this season. He is one of the most promising colored men in the settlement: so Comfort says, at least. Everybody seems to have great respect for his character. I don't know how many people I have heard speak of his religion. Mr. Savage used to say he had rather hear him pray than any other man on earth. He was much prized by his master, even after he was disabled, on account of his faithfulness and character."

From the Novel, *The Clansman*
By Thomas Dixon Jr. (1905)

At noon Ben and Phil strolled to the polling-place to watch the progress of the first election under Negro rule. The Square was jammed with shouting, jostling, perspiring negroes, men, women, and children. The day was worm, and the African odour was supreme even in the open air....

The negroes, under the drill of the League and the Freedman's Bureau, protected by the bayonet, were voting to enfranchise themselves, disfranchise their former masters, ratify a new constitution, and elect a legislature to do their will. Old Aleck was a candidate for the House, chief poll-holder, and seemed to be in charge of the movements of the voters outside the booth as well as inside. He appeared to be omnipresent, and his self-importance was a sight Phil had never dreamed. He could not keep his eyes off him....

[Aleck] was a born African orator, undoubtedly descended from a long line of savage spell-binders, whose eloquence in the palaver houses of the jungle had made them native leaders. His thin spindle-shanks supported an oblong, protruding stomach, resembling an elderly monkey's, which seemed so heavy it swayed his back to carry it.

The animal vivacity of his small eyes and the flexibility of his eye-brows, which he worked up and down rapidly with every change of countenance, expressed his eager desires.

He had laid aside his new shoes, which hurt him, and went barefooted to facilitate his movements on the great occasion. His heels projected and his foot was so flat that what should have been the hollow of it made a hole in the dirt where he left his track.

He was already mellow with liquor, and was dressed in an old army uniform and cap, with two horse-pistols buckled around his waist. On a strap hanging from his shoulder were strung a half-dozen tin canteens filled with whiskey.

From—*The Autobiography of JOHN ROY LYNCH,*
an ex-slave appointed justice-of-the peace in Natchez, Mississippi at age 22
(he later was elected a three-term congressman)

[A] case of some significance that came before me was that of a white man that I knew unfavorably and well. He had cursed, abused, and threatened the life of an inoffensive old colored man on account of a misunderstanding over a small business transaction. Upon the complaint of the colored man, a warrant was issued for the arrest of the party against whom the complaint was made. When he was brought before the court and the charges had been read to him and he was asked whether or not he was guilty as charged, he seemed to be somewhat surprised. "Why," he remarked, "do you mean to tell me that it is a crime for a white man to curse a nigger?" "Yes," the court replied. "It is a crime for a white man to curse a Negro as it is for a Negro to curse a white man." "Well," he exclaimed, "that's news to me. You certainly must be mistaken. If there is such a law, I never heard of it." The court then handed him the code and told him where he could find the section bearing upon the point at issue and requested him to read it for himself, which he did.

When he had finished, he exclaimed in a somewhat subdued tone: "Well, I'll be damned." The court then admonished him that if that remark should be repeated, he would be committed to the county jail for contempt of court. He quickly apologized and assured the court that no disrespect was intended. He said that he could not deny having used the language set forth in the affidavit, but he hoped the court would not be severe because he did not know and did not believe that in using that language he was violating any law. Since it was his first offense, he was let off with a fine of five dollars and costs which he promptly paid. It was the first and only time he was brought before me.

HOW WELL DID YOU UNDERSTAND THIS SELECTION?

1. Compare and contrast the different views about Reconstruction in the three selections?

2. Which view is the most truthful? Why?

3. Was the judgment against the white man who cursed the black man fair? Why or why not?

4. How had life changed for blacks and whites in the South?

As the decade of the 1870s progressed, Americans lost interest in Reconstruction. One by one, states in the former Confederacy were "redeemed" as governments controlled by white Democrats replaced Republican Coalition governments after federal troops were withdrawn. By 1876 only three southern states: Florida, South Carolina, and Louisiana, remained under Reconstruction. Residents of northern states paid little attention as terrorist groups such as the Ku Klux Klan directed violence at blacks and their Republican supporters to prevent black participation in the political process. Black rights were pushed off the political stage by governmental corruption and an economic downturn that beset the North. In 1877 Reconstruction officially ended as a result of the Compromise of 1877, a deal to settle the disputed presidential election of 1876 by removing federal troops from Florida, Louisiana, and South Carolina and ending Reconstruction in those states. By 1877 all southern states had been "redeemed" and the South was firmly in the hands of Democrats who opposed black rights.

An excerpt from the speech of black Congressman Richard Harvey Cain of South Carolina on the floor of the House in support of the Civil Rights Act of 1875.

All we ask is that you, the legislators of this nation, shall pass a law so strong and so powerful that no one shall be able to elude it and destroy our rights under the Constitution and laws of our country. That is all we ask....

We do not want any discriminations to be made. If discriminations arc made in regard to schools, then there will be accomplished just what we are fighting against. If you say that the schools in the State of Georgia, for instance, shall be allowed to discriminate against colored people, then you will have discriminations made against us. We do not want any discriminations. I do not ask any legislation for the colored people of this country that is not applied to the white people. All that we ask is equal laws, equal legislation, and equal rights throughout the length and the breadth of this land.

[Another congressman] says that the colored men should not come here begging at the doors of Congress for their rights. I agree with him. I want to say that we do not come here begging for our rights. We come here clothed in the garb of American citizenship. We come demanding our rights in the name of justice. We come, with no arrogance on our part, asking that this great nation, which laid the foundations of civilization and progress more deeply and more securely than any other nation on the face of the earth, guarantee us protection from outrage. We come here, five millions of people—more than composed this entire nation when it had its great tea-party in Boston Harbor, and demanded its rights at the point of a bayonet—asking that unjust discriminations against us be forbidden. We come here in the name of justice, equity, and law, in the name of our children, in the name of our country, petitioning for our rights.

Source: Congressional Record, 43rd Cong., 1st session, Vol. II, pg. 1

Political Terrorism by the Ku Klux Klan
Testimony by Harriet Hernandez

The following account by Harriet Hernandez, a former slave of Spartanburg, South Carolina, describes how the Klan used threats and violence to intimidate black Republican voters in the region. It is excerpted from her testimony in December 1871 before a congressional committee appointed to investigate Klan activities.

Question: Did the Ku-Klux: ever come to your house at any time?
Answer: Yes, Sir; twice.
Q.: Go on to the second time....

A.: They came in; I was lying in bed. Says he, "Come out here, Sir; Come out here, Sir!" They took me out of bed; they would not let me get out, but they took me up in their arms and toted me out—me and my daughter Lucy. He struck me on the forehead with a pistol, and here is the scar above my eye now. Says he, "Damn you, fall!" I fell. Says he, "Damn you, get up!" I got up. Says he, "Damn you, get over this fence!" And he kicked me over when I went to get over; and then he went to a brush pile, and they laid us right down there, both together. They laid us down twenty yards apart, I reckon. They had dragged and beat us along. They struck me right on the top of my head, and I thought they had killed me; and I said, "Lord o' mercy, don't, don't kill my child!" He gave me a lick on the head, and it liked to have killed me; I saw stars. He threw my arm over my head so I could not do anything with it for three weeks, and there are great knots on my wrist now.

Q: What did they say this was for?

A: They said, "You can tell your husband that when we see him we are going to kill him."

Q: Did they say why they wanted to kill him?

A: They said, "He voted the radical ticket, didn't he?" I said, "Yes, that very way."

Q: When did your husband get back after this whipping? He was not at home, was he?

A: He was lying out; he couldn't stay at home, bless your soul

Q: Has he been afraid for any length of time?

A: He has been afraid ever since last October. He has been lying out. He has not laid in the house ten nights since October.

Q: Is that the situation of the colored people down there to any extent?

A: That is the way they all have to do—men and women both.

Q: What are they afraid of?

A: Of being killed or whipped to death.

Q: What has made them afraid?

A: Because men that voted radical tickets they took the spite out on the women when they could get at them.

Q: How many colored people have been whipped in that neighborhood?

A: It is all of them, mighty near.

Source: Report of the Joint Select Committee to Inquire into the Condition of Affairs in the Late Insurrectionary States (1872)

Excerpts from the original draft of the South Carolina 1876 Democratic party campaign plan formulated by ex-Confederate general MARTIN W. GARY

[It is decreed] That the Democratic Military Clubs are to be armed with rifles and pistols and such other arms as they may command. They are to be divided into two companies, one of the old men, the other of the young; an experienced captain or commander to be placed over each of them. That each company is to have a first and second lieutenant. That the number of ten privates is to be the unit of organization. That each captain is to see that his men are well armed and provided with at least thirty rounds of ammunition. That the Captain of the young men is to provide a Baggage wagon in which three days rations for the horses and three days rations for the men are to be stored on the day before the election in order that they may be prepared at a moment's notice to move to any point in the County when ordered by the Chairman of the Executive Committee....

Every Democrat must feel honor bound to control the vote of at least one Negro, by intimidation, purchase, keeping him away or as each individual may determine, how he may best accomplish it....

Never threaten a man individually. If he deserves to be threatened, the necessities of the times require that he should die. A dead Radical is very harmless—a threatened Radical or one driven off by threats from the scene of his operations is often very troublesome, sometimes dangerous, always vindictive [vengeful]....In the month of September, we ought to begin to organize Negro [Democratic] clubs, or pretend that we have organized them.... Those who join are to be taken on probation and are not to be taken into full fellowship until they have proven their sincerity by voting our ticket.

HOW WELL DID YOU UNDERSTAND THIS SELECTION?

1. Why was it important that Congress pass the Civil Rights Act of 1875?

2. Why did the Ku Klux Klan fight Reconstruction with violence, threats, and intimidation? Why were these tactics successful?

3. What did Democrats in the South generally favor?

AFTER RECONSTRUCTION

*The promise of Reconstruction did not last in the South. Black hopes for full American citizenship, equal protection under the law, and the ability to participate in the economy on a level field were not realized. The Supreme Court in cases such as **Plessy v. Ferguson** and **Berea College v. Kentucky** upheld state laws requiring racial segregation, which allowed southern state legislatures to impose a rigid system of racial segregation throughout the former Confederacy known as Jim Crow. Black leaders such as Federick Douglass quickly realized that political and economic gains blacks had made during Reconstruction were being reversed after the Democratic Party gained control of southern state governments. In a speech made to a black convention meeting in Louisville, Kentucky in 1883, Douglass addresses racial discrimination and calls for an end to Jim Crow segregation.*

Address to the Louisville Convention (1883)
FREDERICK DOUGLASS

Born on American soil in common with yourselves, deriving our bodies and our minds from its dust, centuries having passed away since our ancestors were torn from the shores of Africa, we, like yourselves, hold ourselves to be in every sense Americans, and that we may, therefore, venture to speak to you in a tone not lower than that which becomes earnest men and American citizens. Having watered your soil with our tears, enriched it with our blood, performed its roughest labor in time of peace, defended it against war, and at all times been loyal and true to its best interests, we deem it no arrogance or presumption to manifest now a common concern with you for its welfare, prosperity, honor and glory ...

It is our lot to live among a people whose laws, traditions, and prejudices have been against us for centuries, and from these they are not yet free. To assume that they are free from these evils simply because they have changed their laws is to assume what is utterly unreasonable and contrary to facts. Large bodies move slowly. Individuals may be converted on the instant and change their whole course of life. Nations never. Time and events are required for the conversion of nations. Not even the character of a great political organization can be changed by a new platform. It will be the same old snake though in a new skin. Though we have had war, reconstruction and abolition as a nation, we still linger in the shadow and blight of an extinct institution. Though the colored man is no longer subject to be bought and sold, he is still surrounded by an adverse sentiment which fetters all his movements. In his downward course he meets with no resistance, but his course upward is resented and resisted at every step of his progress. If he comes in ignorance, rags, and wretchedness, he conforms to the popular belief of his character, and in that character he is welcome. But if he shall come as a gentleman, a scholar, and a statesman, he is hailed as a contradiction to the national faith concerning his race, and his coming is resented as impudence. In the one case he may provoke contempt and derision, but in the other he is an affront to pride, and provokes malice. Let him do what he will, there is at present, therefore, no escape for him. The color line meets him everywhere, and in a measure shuts him out from all respectable and profitable trades and callings. In spite of all your religion and laws he is a rejected man.

He is rejected by trade unions, of every trade, and refused work while he lives, and burial when he dies, and yet he is asked to forget his color, and forget that which everybody else remembers. If he offers himself to a builder as a mechanic, to a client as a lawyer, to a patient as a physician, to a college as a professor, to a firm as a clerk, to a Government Department as an agent, or an officer, he is sternly met on the color line, and his claim to consideration in some way is disputed on the ground of color.

Not even our churches, whose members profess to follow the despised Nazarene, whose home, when on earth, was among the lowly and despised, have yet conquered this feeling of color madness, and what is true of our churches is also true of our courts of law. Neither is free from this all pervading atmosphere of color hate. The one describes the Deity as impartial, no respecter of persons, and the other the Goddess of Justice as blindfolded, with sword by her side and scales in her hand held evenly between high and low, rich and low, white and black, but both are the images of American imagination, rather than American practices.

Taking advantage of the general disposition in this country to impute crime to color, white men color their faces to commit crime and wash off the hated color to escape punishment. In many places where the commission of crime is alleged against one of our color, the ordinary processes of law are set aside as too slow for the impetuous justice of the infuriated populace. They take the law into their own bloody hands and proceed to whip, stab, shoot, hang, or burn the alleged culprit, without the intervention of courts, counsel, judges, juries, or witnesses. In such cases it is not the business of the accusers to prove guilt, but it is for the accused to prove his innocence, a thing hard for him to do in these infernal Lynch courts. A man accused, surprised, frightened, and captured by a motley crowd, dragged with a rope about his neck in midnight-darkness to the nearest tree, and told in the coarsest terms of profanity to prepare for death, would be more than human if he did not, in his terror-stricken appearance, more confirm suspicion of guilt than the contrary. Worse still, in the presence of such hell-black outrages, the pulpit is usually dumb, and the press in the neighborhood is silent or openly takes side with the mob. There are occasional cases in which white men are lynched, but one sparrow does not make a summer. Every one knows that what is called Lynch law is peculiarly the law for colored people and for nobody else. If there were no other grievance than this horrible and barbarous Lynch law custom, we should be justified in assembling, as we have now done, to expose and denounce it. But this is not all. Even now, after twenty years of so-called emancipation, we are subject to lawless raids of midnight riders, who, with blackened faces, invade our homes and perpetrate the foulest of crimes upon us and our families. This condition of things is too flagrant and notorious to require specifications or proof. Thus in all the relations of life and death we are met by the color line.

While we recognize the color line as a hurtful force, a mountain barrier to our progress, wounding our bleeding feet with its flinty rocks at every step, we do not despair. We are a hopeful people. This convention is a proof of our faith in you, in reason, in truth and justice our belief that prejudice, with all its malign accomplishments, may yet be removed by peaceful means; that, assisted by time and events and the growing enlightenment of both races, the color line will ultimately become harmless. When this shall come it will then only be used, as it should be, to distinguish one variety of the human family from another. It will cease to have any civil, political, or moral significance, and colored conventions will then be dispensed with as anachronisms, wholly out of place, but not till then. Do not marvel that we are discouraged. The faith within us has a rational basis, and is confirmed by facts. When we consider how deep-seated this feeling against us is; the long centuries it has been forming; the forces of avarice which have been marshaled to sustain it; how the language and literature of the country have been pervaded with it; how the church, the press, the play-house, and other influences of the country have been arrayed in its support, the progress toward its extinction must be considered vast and wonderful....

We do not believe, as we are often told, that the Negro is the ugly child of the national family, and the more he is kept out of sight the better it will be for him. You know that liberty given is never so precious as liberty sought for and fought for. The man outraged is the man to make the outcry. Depend upon it, men will not care much for a people who do not care for themselves. Our meeting here was opposed by some of our members, because it would disturb the peace of the Republican party. The suggestion came from coward lips and misapprehended the character of that party. If the Republican party cannot stand a demand for justice and fair play, it ought to go down. We were men before that party was born, and our manhood is more sacred than any party can be. Parties were made for men, not men for parties.

The colored people of the South are the laboring people of the South. The labor of a country is the source of its wealth; without the colored laborer today the South would be a howling wilderness, given up to bats, owls, wolves, and bears. He was the source of its wealth before the war, and has been the source of its prosperity since the war. He almost alone is visible in her fields, with implements of toil in his hands, and laboriously using them to-day.

Let us look candidly at the matter. While we see and hear that the South is more prosperous than it ever was before and rapidly recovering from the waste of war, while we read that it raises more cotton, sugar, rice, tobacco, corn, and other valuable products than it ever produced before, how happens it, we sternly ask, that the houses of its laborers are miserable huts, that their clothes are rags, and their food the coarsest and scantiest? How happens it that the land-owner is becoming richer and the laborer poorer?

The implication is irresistible that where the landlord is prosperous the laborer ought to share his prosperity, and whenever and wherever we find this is not the case there is manifestly wrong somewhere....

Flagrant as have been the outrages committed upon colored citizens in respect to their civil rights, more flagrant, shocking, and scandalous still have been the outrages committed upon our political rights by means of bull-dozing and Kukluxing, Mississippi plans, fraudulent courts, tissue ballots, and the like devices. Three States in which the colored people outnumber the white population are without colored representation and their political voice suppressed. The colored citizens in those States are virtually disfranchised, the Constitution held in utter contempt and its provisions nullified. This has been done in the face of the Republican party and successive Republican administrations....

This is no question of party It is a question of law and government. It is a question whether men shall be protected by law, or be left to the mercy of cyclones of anarchy and bloodshed. It is whether the Government or the mob shall rule this land; whether the promises solemnly made to us in the constitution be manfully kept or meanly and flagrantly broken. Upon this vital point we ask the whole people of the United States to take notice that whatever of political power we have shall be exerted for no man of any party who will not, in advance of election, promise to use every power given him by the Government, State or National, to make the black man's path to the ballot-box as straight, smooth and safe as that Of any other American citizen....

We hold it to be self-evident that no class or color should be the exclusive rulers of this country. If there is such a ruling class, there must of course be a subject class, and when this condition is once established this Government of the people, by the people, and for the people, will have perished from the earth.

Source: *The Life and Writings of Frederick Douglass*, Philip Foner, ed., vol. IV (1955).

HOW WELL DID YOU UNDERSTAND THIS SELECTION?

1. Summarize the main points of Douglass' speech.

2. What are the primary problems Douglass observes after Reconstruction?

3. What does Douglass think can be done to solve the problems blacks face?

SELF TEST

MULTIPLE CHOICE: Circle the correct response. The correct answers are given at the end.

1. Ex-slaves were granted citizenship by the
   a. Thirteenth Amendment.
   b. Fourteenth Amendment.
   c. Fifteenth Amendment.
   d. Sixteenth Amendment.

2. What did the Thirteenth Amendment do?
   a. Prohibit slavery in all states and territories.
   b. Grant blacks citizenship.
   c. Establish due-process of law.
   d. Give ex-slaves the right to vote.

3. What were Black Codes an attempt to do?
   a. Give blacks full and equal rights with whites.
   b. Allow blacks to participate fully in the political process.
   c. Establish a system of free public schools for blacks in the South.
   d. Limit black rights and ensure that blacks remained in a servile position in southern states.

4. Why was President Johnson impeached?
   a. Because he violated the Tenure of Office Act.
   b. Because he was often drunk and disorderly in public.
   c. Because he was a southern Democrat.
   d. Because he wanted to cede control of Reconstruction to Congress.

5. After Reconstruction ended, most blacks in southern states earned their living through
   a. Teaching.
   b. Carpentry.
   c. Sharecropping.
   d. Working for the government.

6. The greatest failure of Reconstruction was
   a. The failure to alter significantly the economic and social structure of southern states.
   b. The failure to grant blacks citizenship.
   c. The failure to extend the franchise to blacks.
   d. The failure to adequately punish Southerners for treason.

7. What did the Supreme Court authorize in the *Plessy v. Ferguson* case?
   a. Integrated schools in southern states.
   b. Racial segregation mandated by state law.
   c. The right of blacks to vote.
   d. The right of blacks to attend schools alongside whites.

8. The legalized system of racial segregation established by legislative statutes that engulfed the South after Reconstruction was called
   a. The Black Codes.
   b. Jim Crow.
   c. The Black System.
   d. Ku Kluxism.

9. Carpetbaggers, Scalawags, and ex-slaves banded together into the _____ and were able to control governments in southern states during Reconstruction.
   a. Ku Klux Klan.
   b. New Democrats.
   c. Bourbon Democrats.
   d. Republican Coalition.

10. Why did Congress refuse to confiscate plantation lands and redistribute it to former slaves during Reconstruction?
   a. Because southern blacks already had land.
   b. Because this idea was opposed by the head of the Freedman's Bureau.
   c. Because Andrew Johnson opposed the plan and vetoed the legislation Congress passed giving blacks plantation land.
   d. Because most Congressmen believed in laissez-faire capitalism.

Answers: 1-b; 2-a; 3-d; 4-a; 5-c; 6-a; 7-b; 8-b; 9-d; 10-d

ESSAYS:

1. Why did Congress and the president disagree over Reconstruction? What effect did their conflict have on Reconstruction?

2. How did Reconstruction change southern economic and social life?

3. Identify the most important accomplishments of Reconstruction.

4. Discuss the most significant failures of Reconstruction?

5. Overall, what impact did Reconstruction have on the United States? On the South? On blacks?

6. What happened after Reconstruction ended in the South?

OPTIONAL ACTIVITIES: (Use your knowledge **and** imagination.)

1. Pretend that your history class is the U.S. Senate during the impeachment trial of President Johnson. Conduct the trial as the Senate conducted it. What verdict did the class reach?

2. You are a southern Scalawag during Reconstruction. Explain to a southern Democrat why you joined the Republican Party after the Civil War.

3. You are a New South Advocate. Write a newspaper editorial that expresses your economic views after the Civil War.

WEB SITE LISTINGS:

Harper's Weekly – America's Leading Magazine During Reconstruction
  http://www.harpweek.com

Library of Congress
  http://lcweb.loc.gov/exhibits/africa/intro.html
  http://memory.loc.gov/ammem/aaohtml/exhibit/aopart5.html
  http://scriptorium.lib.duke.edu/collections/african-american-women.html
                                    /franklin/af-am-mss.collections53.html

Many Specific Events
  http://www.channelone.com/fasttrack/ushistory/1800-1877/

Primary Sources including a Black Code and Sharecropper's Contract
  http://longman.awl.com/history/activities_16_20.htm

Report of the Joint committee on Reconstruction
  http://odur.let.rug.nl/~usa/usa.htm

Making of America – hundreds of articles and books in search
  www.hti.umcih.edu/m/moagrp
  http://moa.cit.cornell.edu/moa

Chapter Thirteen

INDUSTRIALIZATION

America's Industrial Revolution kicked into high gear about 1880. For the next forty years everything about the United States changed, including government, society, politics, work, and, most of all, the economy. The machine age embodied optimism and opportunity. Technological adaptation of existing devices, such as the steam engine and the sewing machine, as well as new discoveries and inventions in electricity, chemistry, physics, engineering, manufacturing, and agriculture, enabled the United States to move to the forefront of industrial nations. No people were more inventive and innovative than were Americans during this time. Between 1790 and 1860 the U. S. Patent Office granted a total of 36,000 patents. In 1897 alone it granted 22,000; by 1920, it had granted about 1.4 million patents.

Despite the optimism, industrialization did not proceed without problems. Cities experienced tremendous growth. Areas that before the Civil War had been, at best, small towns became bustling metropolitan areas almost overnight. New buildings had to be built, police forces enlarged, fire brigades created, streets enlarged, and new neighborhoods to house the growing population had to be constructed. Mayors and city councils sometimes struggled to find financing to pay for these projects.

Workers also experienced problems. Before the Industrial Revolution most products sold in the United States were produced by craftspeople working in shops near their houses. They set their own hours and worked when they had orders to fill. Mechanization changed methods of production, destroying time-honored crafts, such as glass-making and iron molding, and subjecting workers to rigid schedules and repetitive routines they had never before experienced. Although mechanization created new jobs, it also produced low wages because most machines were labor saving devices that enabled fewer workers to produce more products. This created a situation workers had never experienced—unemployment and low wages. Workers responded by organizing unions such as the Knights of Labor and the American Federation of Labor. Their goals were generally to improve the lives of workers and eliminate evils like child labor.

Imperialism also came with industrialization. In 1898 the United States acquired its first overseas colonies and fought a war of seven years duration to prevent the Philippine Islands from gaining independence. Many Americans believed imperialism sullied America's reputation around the world and protested against it. Despite the protests, industrialists demanded that the United States acquire colonies so they could market products to additional populations.

Racism and Jim Crow segregation continued to play a prominent role in the South. Efforts by African Americans to overcome the racism, prejudice, and discrimination that were part of their everyday life generally centered on education. African-American leaders hoped that an educated population would be able to surmount racial barriers that white society had erected. Unfortunately, this was not reality.

IDENTIFICATION: Briefly describe each term.

Joseph Pulitzer

William Randolph Hearst

Andrew Carnegie

John D. Rockefeller

J. Pierpont Morgan

Cornelius Vanderbilt

Henry Huntington

Leland Stanford

Robber Barons

Standard Oil of Ohio

James Duke

Thomas Edison

Alexander Graham Bell

Vertical Integration

Horizontal Integration

Sherman Silver Purchase Act

Sherman Anti-Trust Act

Interstate Commerce Act

Queen Liliuokalani

Spanish-American War

Rough Riders

Emilio Aguinaldo

Gospel of Wealth

Ida B. Wells

Theodore Dreiser

Jacob Riis

Knights of Labor

Chinese Exclusion Act

Haymarket Square Bombing

American Federation of Labor

Mary Harris "Mother" Jones

Pullman Strike

Booker T. Washington

W.E.B. Du Bois

Women's Suffrage Movement

Lucy Stone

Susan B. Anthony

Elizabeth Cady Stanton

Francs Willard

Jane Addams

THINK ABOUT:

1. How did the Industrial Revolution change America? Could historians argue that modern America began with the Industrial Revolution? Why or why not? If not, when did modern America begin? What characteristics are part of modern America?

2. How did imperialism and the Spanish-American War change American foreign policy? What impact throughout the twentieth century did the Spanish-American War and imperialism have on American history?

3. What role did problems created by industrialism play in governmental regulation of the economy?

4. How did wealthy Americans deal with contradictions in American society produced by the concentration of wealth in the hands of a few while the masses remained poor? Does the same economic gap between rich and poor exist in the United States today? Why or why not?

THE SHERMAN ANTI-TRUST ACT OF 1890

Industrialization during the last half of the nineteenth century created the problem of trusts and monopolies. Big business faced cutthroat competition. They produced vast quantities of products and sold them quickly for small profits. To overcome the cutthroat competition, industrialists developed the pool, trust, and holding company. The purpose of these forms of business organizations was to eliminate or limit competition and thus raise profit margins. This was best done by getting rival businesses to cooperate or by driving competitors out of business. The first trust formed was Standard Oil in 1882. John D. Rockefeller's attorney, Samuel Dodd, thought of the idea. He created a board of trustees to control all companies Standard Oil had acquired, which allowed them to function as one company. Later, Rockefeller and Standard Oil created the Holding Company to serve the same purpose. Other corporations emulated Rockefeller, forming trusts of their own to restrain competition and raise prices.

By the mid 1880s the American public was fed up with monopolistic companies who drove up prices for products and services they produced. In 1888 both Democratic and Republican candidates for president promised to restrain the monopolies. This restraint occurred in 1890 when Congress passed the Sherman Anti-Trust Act by a vote of 51 to 1 in the

Senate and 242 to 0 in the House of Representatives. President Harrison signed the bill into law, and trusts and monopolies became illegal forms of business.

SECTION ONE:
Every contract, combination in the form of trust or otherwise, or conspiracy, in restraint of trade or commerce among the several States, or with foreign nations, is declared to be illegal. Every person who shall make any contract or engage in any combination or conspiracy hereby declared to be illegal shall be deemed guilty of a felony, and, on conviction thereof, shall be punished by fine not exceeding ten million dollars if a corporation, or, if any other person, three hundred and fifty thousand dollars, or by imprisonment not exceeding three years, or by both said punishments, in the discretion of the court.

SECTION TWO:
Every person who shall monopolize, or attempt to monopolize, or combine or conspire with any other person or persons, to monopolize any part of the trade or commerce among the several States, or with foreign nations, shall be deemed guilty of a felony, and, on conviction thereof, shall be punished by fine not exceeding ten million dollars if a corporation, or, if any other person, three hundred and fifty thousand dollars or by imprisonment not exceeding three years, or by both said punishments, in the discretion of the court.

HOW WELL DID YOU UNDERSTAND THIS SELECTION?

1. What was the penalty corporations faced for violating the Sherman Anti-Trust Act?

2. What penalties did individuals face for violating the Sherman Anti-Trust Act?

3. Does the Sherman Anti-Trust Act define what a monopoly is? If so, what is a monopoly?

4. What weaknesses can you find in the Sherman Anti-Trust Act?

5. Look at the Constitution in the appendix to your textbook? What part of the Constitution gives Congress the power to pass the Sherman Anti-Trust Act?

Andrew Carnegie, a poor immigrant from Scotland, became one of the world's wealthiest men. He made his vast fortune in the steel industry, which he dominated through vertical integration until he sold the Carnegie Steel Company to J. P. Morgan, a New York financier, for nearly half a billion dollars. Carnegie felt guilty about acquiring such a vast fortune, especially when he had been poor in his native land and because workers who produced his vast wealth lived little better than animals. To ease his conscious, Carnegie devised an idea called the gospel of wealth. Late in life, he gave away much of his fortune, especially to libraries and churches.

The problem of our age is the administration of wealth, so that the ties of brotherhood may still bind together the rich and poor in harmonious relationship. The conditions of human life have not only been changed, but revolutionized, within the past few hundred years. In former days there was little difference between the dwelling, dress, food, and environment of the chief and those of his retainers.... The contrast between the...millionaire and the... laborer...today measures the change which has come with civilization.... This change, however, is not to be deplored, but welcomed as highly beneficial....

There are but three modes in which surplus wealth can be disposed of. It can be left to the families of the descendents; or it can be bequeathed for public purposes; or finally it can be administered during life by its possessors.... Let us consider each of these modes. The first is the most injudicious. In monarchial countries, the estates and the greatest portion of the wealth are left to the first son, that the vanity of the parent may be gratified by the thought that his name and title are to descend to succeeding generations unimpaired. The condition of this class in Europe today teaches the futility of such hopes or ambitions. The successors have become impoverished through their follies or from the fall in the value of land.... Why should men leave great fortunes to their children? If this is done from affection, is it not misguided affection? Observation teaches that, generally speaking, it is not well for the children that they be so burdened. Neither is it well for the state....

As to the second mode, that of leaving at death for public uses, it may be said that this is only a means for the disposal of wealth, provided a man is content to wait until he is dead before it becomes of much good....

The growing disposition to tax more and more heavily large estates left at death is a cheering indication of the growth of a salutary change in public opinion.... Of all forms of taxation, this seems the wisest. Men who continue hoarding great sums all their lives, the proper use of which for public ends would work good to the community, should be made to feel that the community, in the form of the state, cannot thus be deprived of its proper share. By taxing estates heavily at death, the state marks its condemnation of the selfish millionaire's unworthy life.

Source: Andrew Carnegie, "Wealth," *North American Review*, 1889

HOW WELL DID YOU UNDERSTAND THIS SELECTION?

1. How does Carnegie feel about the economic gap between rich and poor?

2. What does he think the problem of his (the industrial) age was?

3. What does Carnegie think caused the great disparity of wealth?

4. How does Carnegie define wealth? How does he define competence?

5. How does Carnegie believe wealth should be disposed of?

6. Why does Carnegie want to heavily tax large estates left at death?

===

A SELECTION FROM THE CONSTITUTION OF THE KNIGHTS OF LABOR

American workers faced numerous problems created by the Industrial Revolution. These included: low wages, long hours, unsafe working conditions, no job security, no health insurance, and few fringe benefits like paid vacations and sick leave. Laborers attempted to solve these and other problems by forming unions. An early and important union was the Knights of Labor. Initially the Knights of Labor practiced secret rituals much like fraternal lodges did, but Terence V. Powderly, who assumed the organization's presidency in 1879, moved the Knights away from fraternalism to unionism. Under Powderly's leadership the Knights of Labor advocated an eight-hour work day, a graduated income tax, and abolition of child labor. Membership approached one million in the mid-1880s. The Knights of Labor Constitution defines many of the objectives of the organization. Unlike most unions active in the nineteenth century, the Knights of Labor organized on an industry-wide basis rather than by crafts and accepted both skilled and unskilled workers as well as women. Philosophically the Knights opposed strikes in favor of organized boycotts, mediation and arbitration, and political involvement. Ultimately Powderly wanted to create a political party that would represent labor. He hoped workers could improve their economic situation by electing candidates to governmental office who would support labor issues. Ironically, the downfall of the Knights of Labor came as a result of their involvement in a strike against the McCormick Reaper Company and the Haymarket Square incident it produced.

PREAMBLE

The recent alarming development and aggression of aggregated wealth, which, unless checked, will invariably lead to the pauperization and hopeless degradation of the toiling masses, render it imperative, if we desire to enjoy the blessings of life, that a check should be placed upon its power and upon unjust accumulation, and a system adopted which will secure to the laborer the fruits of his toil, and as this much-desired object can only be accomplished by the thorough unification of labor, and the united efforts of those who obey the divine injunction that "in the sweat of thy brow shalt thou eat bread," we have formed the Knights of Labor with a view of securing the organization and direction, by cooperative effort, of the power of the industrial classes; and we submit to the world the objects sought to be accomplished by our organization, calling upon all who believe in securing "the greatest good to the greatest number" to aid and assist us:

I. To bring within the folds of organization every department of productive industry, making knowledge a stand-point for action, and industrial and moral worth, not wealth, the true standard of individual and national greatness.

II. To secure to the toilers a proper share of the wealth that they create: more of the leisure that rightfully belongs to them, more societary advantages; more of the benefits, privileges, and emoluments of the world: in a word, all those rights and privileges necessary to make them capable of enjoying, appreciating, defending and perpetuating the blessings of good government.

III. To arrive at the true condition of the producing masses in their educational, moral, and financial condition, by demanding from the various governments the establishment of bureaus of Labor Statistics.

IV. The establishment of co-operative institutions, productive and distributive.

V. The reserving of the public lands—the heritage of the people—or the actual settler—not another acre for railroads or speculators.

VI. The abrogation of all laws that do not bear equally upon capital and labor, the removal of unjust technicalities, delays, and discriminations in the administration of justice, and the adopting of measures providing for the health and safety of those engaged in mining, manufacturing, or building pursuits.

VII. The enactment of laws to compel chartered corporations to pay their employes weekly, in full, for labor performed during the preceding week, in the lawful money of the country.

VIII. The enactment of laws giving mechanics and laborers a first lien on their work for their full wages.

IX. The abolishment of the contract system on national, State, and municipal work.

X. The substitution of arbitration for strikes, whenever and wherever employers and employees are willing to meet on equitable grounds.

XI. The prohibition of the employment of children in workshops, mines and factories before attaining their fourteenth year.

XII. To abolish the system of letting out by contract the labor of convicts in our prisons and reformatory institutions.

XIII. To secure for both sexes equal pay for equal work.

XIV. The reduction of the hours of labor to eight per day, so that the laborers may have more time for social enjoyment and intellectual improvement, and be enabled to reap the advantages conferred by the labor-saving machinery which their brains have created.

XV. To prevail upon governments to establish a purely national circulating medium, based upon the faith and resources of the nation, and issued directly to the people, without the intervention of any system of banking corporations, which money shall be a legal tender in payment of all debts…

Source: Terence V. Powderly, *Thirty Years of Labor*, 1899

HOW WELL DID YOU UNDERSTAND THIS SELECTION?

1. What is the primary objective of the Knights of Labor?

2. Why do the Knights of Labor want state governments to create Bureaus of Labor Statistics?

3. How do the Knights of Labor propose to solve problems between labor and management?

4. What are the Knights of Labor's views regarding female workers? Does this surprise you?

5. What were the Knights of Labor's ideas regarding money and banks?

6. What problems did workers have that the Knights of Labor tried to address?

EXCERPTS FROM JOHN MORRISON'S TESTIMONY BEFORE THE UNITED STATES SENATE

John Morrison was one of hundreds of workers who testified before the Senate Committee upon the Relations between Labor and Capital in 1884 and 1885. This committee, which was convened to investigate the cause of strikes, concluded that strikes resulted because industrialization caused the workers' status to decline. Morrison, at the time of his testimony, was a young machinist in New York City. His testimony supports the conclusions about strikes drawn by the committee.

Q: Is there any difference between the conditions under which machinery is made now and those that existed ten years ago?
A: A great deal of difference.
Q: State the differences as well as you can.
A: Well, the trade has been subdivided and those subdivisions have been again subdivided, so that a man never learns the machinist's trade now. Ten years ago he learned, not the whole of the trade, but a fair portion of it. Also, there is more machinery used in the business, which again makes machinery. In the case of making the sewing-machine, for instance, you find that the trade is so subdivided that a man is not considered a machinist at all. Hence it is merely laborers' work and it is laborers that work at that branch of our trade. The different branches of the trade are divided and subdivided so that one man may make just a particular part of a machine and may not know anything whatever about another part of the same machine. In that way machinery is produced a great deal cheaper than it used to be formerly, and in fact through this system of work, 100 men are able to do now what it took 300 or 400 men to do fifteen years ago. By the use of machinery and the subdivision of the trade they so simplify the work that it is made a great deal easier and put together a great deal faster. There is no system of apprenticeship, I may say, in the business. You simply go in and learn whatever branch you are put at, and you stay at that unless you are changed to another.
Q: Does a man learn his branch very rapidly?
A: Yes, sir, he can learn his portion of the business very rapidly. Of course he becomes very expert at it, doing that all the time and nothing else, and therefore he is able to do a great deal more work in that particular branch than if he were a general hand and expected to do everything in the business as it came along.
Q: Do you know from reading the papers or from your general knowledge of the business whether there are other places in other cities or other parts of the country that those men could have gone and got work?
A: I know from general reports of the condition of our trade that the same condition existed throughout the country generally.
Q: Then those men could not have bettered themselves by going to any other place, you think?
A: Not in a body.
Q: I am requested to ask you this question: dividing the public, as is commonly done, into the upper, middle, and

lower classes, to which class would you assign the average workingman of your trade at the time when you entered it, and to which class you would assign him now?

A: I now assign them to the lower class. At the time I entered the trade I should assign them as merely hanging on to the middle class, ready to drop out at any time.

Q: What is the character of the social intercourse of those workingmen? Answer first with reference to their intercourse with other people outside of their own trade—merchants, employers, and others.

A: Are you asking what sort of social intercourse exists between the machinists and the merchants? If you are, there is none whatever, or very little if any.

Q: What sort of social intercourse exists among the machinists themselves and their families, as to visiting, entertaining one another, and having little parties and other forms of sociability, those little things that go to make up the social pleasures of life?

A: In fact with the married folks that has died out—such things as birthday parties, picnics, and so on. The machinists today are on such small pay, and the cost of living is so high, that they have very little, if anything, to spend for recreation, and the machinist has to content himself with enjoying himself at home, either fighting with his wife or licking his children

Q: I hope that is not a common amusement in the trade. Was it so ten years ago?

A: It was not, from the fact that they then sought enjoyment in other places, and had a little more money to spend. But since they have had no organization worth speaking of, of course their pay has gone down. At that time they had a form of organization in some way or other which seemed to keep up the wages, and there was more life left in the machinist then, he had more ambition, he felt more like seeking enjoyment outside, and in reading and such things, but now it is changed to the opposite, the machinist has no such desires.

Q: What is the social air about the ordinary machinist's house? Are there evidences of happiness, and joy, and hilarity, or is the general atmosphere solemn, and somber, and gloomy?

A: To explain that fully, I would first of all state, that machinists have got to work ten hours a day in New York, and that they are compelled to work very hard. In fact the machinists of America are compelled to do about one-third more work than the machinists do in England in a day. Therefore, when they come home they are naturally played out from shoving the file, or using the hammer or the chisel, or whatever it may be, such long hours. They are pretty well played out when they come home, and the first thing they think of is having something to eat and sitting down, and resting, and then of striking a bed. Of course when a man is dragged out in that way he is naturally cranky, and he makes all around him cranky; so, instead of a pleasant house it is every day expecting to lose his job by competition from his fellow workman, there being so many out of employment, and no places for them, and his wages being pulled down through their competition, looking at all times to be thrown out of work in that way, and staring starvation in the face makes him feel sad, and the head of the house being sad, of course the whole family are the same, so the house looks like a dull prison instead of a home.

Q: Where do you work?

A: I would rather not have it in print. Perhaps I would have to go Monday morning if I did. We are so situated in the machinist's trade that we daren't let them know much about us. If they know that we open our mouths on the labor question, and try to form organizations, we are quietly told that "business is slack," and we have got to go.

Q: Do you know of anybody being discharged for making speeches on the labor question?

A: Yes, I do know of several. A little less than a year ago several members of the organization that I belong to were discharged because it was discovered that they were members of the organization.

Q: Do you say those men were members of the same organization that you belong to?

A: Yes sir; but not working in the same place where I work. And in fact many of my trade have been on the "black list," and have had to leave town to find work.

Q: Are the machinists here generally contented, or are they in a state of discontent and unrest?

A: There is mostly a general feeling of discontent, and you will find among the machinists the most radical workingmen, with the most revolutionary ideas. You will find that they don't so much give their thoughts simply to trades unions and other efforts of that kind, but they go far beyond that; they only look for relief through the ballot or through a revolution, a forcible revolution....

Q: You say they look for relief through a forcible revolution. In the alternative of a forcible revolution have they considered what form of government they would establish?

A: Yes; some of them have and some of them have not.

Q: What kind of government would they establish?

A: ...They want to form a government such as this was intended to be, a government "of the people, for the people, and by the people"—different entirely from the present form of government.

Source: Report of the Committee of the Senate upon the Relations between Labor and Capital, 48th Congress, 1885

HOW WELL DID YOU UNDERSTAND THIS SELECTION?

1. What does Morrison think has happened to the machinist's trade?

2. What does Morrison say has happened to machinists as a result of the Industrial Revolution? What is their economic status?

3. How does Morrison describe the life of workers?

4. What would likely happen if workers joined a union?

5. What is a black list?

6. How does Morrison say workers will seek relief?

The Spanish-American War generated much controversy within the United States. Many Americans opposed going to war with Spain to acquire colonies because they believed it violated one of America's founding principles, that of self-determination. Americans had maintained for years that they believed all people should have the right to determine their own government. After all, this is why Americans had fought England for independence during the American Revolution. An organization called the Anti-Imperialist League was organized. Grover Cleveland, who served two nonconsecutive terms as president from 1885 to 1889 and from 1893 to 1897, was a member of this group, as well as other notable Americans, such as the author Mark Twain, the Supreme Court Justice Morfield Story, and Speaker of the House of Representatives Thomas Reed, who resigned after serving forty years in Congress because he believed the acquisition of colonies soiled America. Former President Cleveland served as vice president of the Anti-Imperialist League and spoke out forcefully against imperialism as the following speech indicates.

When our Government entered upon a war for the professed purpose of aiding self-government and releasing from foreign rule a struggling people whose cries for liberty were heard at our very doors, it rallied to its enthusiastic support a nation of freemen, in whose hearts and minds there was deeply fixed by heredity and tradition the living belief that all just powers of government are derived from the consent of the governed.

It was the mockery of fate that led us to an unexpected and unforeseen incident in this conflict, and placed in the path of our Government, while professing national righteousness, representing an honest and liberty-loving people, and intent on a benevolent, self-sacrificing errand, the temptation of sordid aggrandizement and the false glitter of world-power.

No sincerely thoughtful American can recall what followed without amazement, nor without sadly realizing how the apathy of our people's trustfulness and their unreflecting acceptance of alluring representations can be played upon.

No greater national fall from grace was ever known than that of the Government of the United States, when in the midst of high design, while still speaking words of sympathy with the weak who struggled against the strong, and while still professing to exemplify before the world a great Republic's love for self-government and its impulse to stay the bloody hand of oppression and conquest, it embraced an opportunity offered by the exigencies of its beneficent undertaking, to possess itself of territory thousands of miles from our coast, and to conquer and govern, without pretense of their consent, millions of resisting people—a heterogeneous population largely mixed with elements hardly within the light of civilization, and all far from the prospect of assimilation with anything American.

.... Refusing to accept the shallow and discreditable pretense that our conquest in the Philippines has gone so far beyond recall or correction, we insist that a nation as well as an individual is never so magnanimous or great as when false steps are retraced and the path of honesty and virtue is regained.

The message of the Democracy to the American people should courageously enjoin that, in sincere and consistent compliance with the spirit and profession of our interference in behalf of Cuba's self-government, our beneficent designs toward her should also extend to the lands which, as an incident of such interference, have come under our control; that the people of the Philippine Islands should be aided in the establishment of a government of their own; and that when this is accomplished our interference in their domestic rule should cease.

Source: "Ex-President Grover Cleveland on the Philippine Problem," Boston: Anti-Imperialist League, 1904

HOW WELL DID YOU UNDERSTAND THIS SELECTION?

1. What does President Cleveland consider wrong about America's acquisition of colonies such as the Philippines?

2. What does he think the United States government should do regarding the Philippines?

3. Where does Cleveland think government is derived from?

4. Would Cleveland think America's acquisition of colonies was hypocritical? Why or why not?

THE WIZARD OF OZ: Industrial Themes in a Child's Story
By Doug Cantrell

*Practically everyone has either read the child's story, **The Wizard of Oz**, by L. Frank Baum or viewed the movie starring Judy Garland. On the surface, this tale of witches and wizards appears to be a simple child's story complete with magic, intrigue, and good triumphing over evil. Beneath the simple tale, however, lies political metaphor. While it might appear that **The Wizard of Oz** is a child's story, it is really a potent story about the industrial revolution and its impact on workers and farmers. Contained within the child's story are powerful images and symbols drawn from the presidential election of 1900 pitting Republican William McKinley against Democrat William Jennings Bryan, the former Populist. These symbols and images reflect many of the issues facing Americans that arose during the Industrial Revolution. The following pages will examine **The Wizard of Oz** from the perspective of the Industrial Revolution, beginning with its author L. Frank Baum.*

*Baum by profession was a journalist who experienced the Industrial Revolution first hand as a printer in the West and then a newspaper reporter in Chicago. As a printer in South Dakota, a state in which Populists were very active, Baum came to understand the problem farmers in the Great Plains states faced during the Industrial Revolution. He became aware of the importance farmers and Populists placed on inflation through their advocacy of the free coinage of silver. He also realized that the Industrial Revolution created a situation in which farmers saw their real incomes and social status decline because developments in agricultural technology enabled farmers to produce such a surplus that the market became glutted, driving down prices. It seemed as if the harder farmers worked the less compensation they received. As a printer, Baum experienced first hand the impact the Industrial Revolution had on skilled workers. Baum lost his printing business in South Dakota and had to move to Chicago and work for a big city newspaper (the equivalent of a blacksmith or tailor moving to the city to work in a factory). Like most skilled workers who were driven out of business by the factory, Baum's move to the city resulted in less income and a lowered social status. In the 1896 and 1900 presidential elections Baum actively supported the Populist/Democratic candidate, William Jennings Bryan. He wrote **The Wizard of Oz** in the context of the 1900 presidential election, incorporating themes from the Industrial Revolution and issues in the 1896 and 1900 elections. An analysis of the story will reflect those themes.*

The story begins in Kansas, a farming state whose residents had experienced a decline in income and social status as a result of the Industrial Revolution. Baum describes everything in Kansas as gray. The sky is gray, people are gray, animals are gray, the landscape is gray. This image of gray is a metaphor for the negative impact the Industrial

Revolution had on farmers in Kansas and elsewhere. Farmers have little to smile about. They are heavily in debt and are facing declining prices for farm produce as a result of the glut created by the use of industrial technology (machinery, fertilizer, hybrid seed, etc.) on the farm. Then, along comes a cyclone. The cyclone is symbolic of the presidential election of 1900. Baum believes that voters in the 1900 election will cleanse the political landscape much as a tornado cleanses the physical landscape. Everything will be swept clean in its path and Bryan's election to the presidency will represent a new beginning for Americans.

Dorothy, the central character in the story, and her little dog, Toto, hide in a farmhouse that is lifted high into the sky by the cyclone and deposited in a wonderful, magical land called Oz. There is much symbolism in this scene. Baum takes the name for his magical land, Oz, from the silver/gold issue so important to farmers and workers during the 1890s. Oz is the abbreviation for ounce and is taken from the formula Populists and workers urged the federal government to adopt to inflate the currency supply. They wanted sixteen ounces of silver to be equal to one ounce of gold. The fact that Oz is a magical land is also symbolic. Many farmers and workers believed that if the sixteen to one ratio was adopted and the nation got inflation many of their problems would magically disappear. Farmers would receive higher prices for their produce and could more easily pay debts with inflated currency while factory workers would see higher wages.

Dorothy's house had accidentally landed on a character called the Wicked Witch of the East, killing her. Dorothy emerges from the house and is greeted by small people called Munchkins who are dancing around the house expressing joy that Dorothy has killed the Wicked Witch of the East and hailing Dorothy as their liberator. Dorothy is taken aback. She quickly assures everyone that she did not mean to kill anyone, that it was an accident. The Wicked Witch of the East is symbolic for eastern capitalists, the so-called Robber Barons, the Rockefellers, the Carnegies, the Henry Fords, the corporations that oppressed workers and farmers. The witch's death represents what Baum believes will happen to the oppressors of workers and farmers when Bryan becomes president. He will crush them much as Dorothy's house crushed the Wicked Witch of the East. Munchkins, of course, are the common people who are oppressed by capitalism and conditions created by the Industrial Revolution.

Dorothy, after expressing remorse at the witch's death, becomes concerned about her family in Kansas. She asks the Munchkins if they can tell her how to return to Kansas. The Munchkins feel badly. They can't help their liberator. Suddenly, one of them has an idea. He tells Dorothy to see the Wizard. Dorothy is puzzled. She has never heard of the Wizard. The Munchkins explain that they have heard that a Wizard descended out of the clouds in Emerald City and that he is a good wizard who uses his magical powers to help common people. Dorothy agrees to see the Wizard but doesn't know how to get to Emerald City. The Munchkins tell her to take the yellow brick road. Dorothy, being a Midwestern farm girl, is bare footed (most rural residents did not wear shoes during warm months because leather was too expensive). The Munchkins tell her to take the shoes from the feet of the Wicked Witch of the East; after all, she is dead and will not need them. Dorothy takes the shoes from the witch's feet, which are made of silver (in the movie the slippers are ruby red because that color shows up better on the screen than does silver). She then proceeds to walk down the yellow brick road toward Emerald City wearing the silver slippers. There is a powerful metaphor here. Yellow is the color of gold. Dorothy wearing silver slippers walking down a golden road signifies the relationship between silver and gold so important to workers and farmers and the major issue in the 1896 and 1900 presidential elections.

After walking for a long time Dorothy and Toto stop to rest near a cornfield. As they are resting they hear a voice speaking to them. At first they can't figure out where the voice is coming from but finally determine it is that of the Scarecrow. The Scarecrow is in bad shape. He has had the straw that composed his body torn out by crows. Dorothy puts the straw back into the Scarecrow's body and he tells his tale. He says that the crows became so bold that they attacked him, the corn's guardian. After tearing out his stuffing, the crows stole the corn. The Scarecrow represents the American farmer and the fact that the stuffing is torn out of his body is symbolic of the negative impact the Industrial Revolution had on farmers. They were not in good shape. The crows are the factories that buy the farmer's produce—the canneries, the meat processors, and the tobacco companies. Farmers often believed that these companies stole from farmers by paying prices below what it cost to produce crops and livestock. The Scarecrow decides to go to Emerald City with Dorothy and Toto because he wants the Wizard to give him a brain. The journey to Emerald City represents the trek many farmers made to the city when their farms failed, as did the Scarecrows' when the crows stole his corn. Many farmers, like the Scarecrow, leave their farms, move to the city and become factory workers. The brain the Scarecrow wants is symbolic of prejudices rural people faced as a result of the Industrial Revolution. Farmers were often viewed as "hicks," "hayseeds," and "country bumpkins" who were not as smart or sophisticated as city residents. Before the Industrial Revolution almost everybody was a farmer and farmers were the backbone of American society; afterward, their social status had fallen.

Dorothy, Toto, and the Scarecrow proceed down the yellow brick road toward Emerald City. On the way they encounter the Tin Woodsman. Like the farmer, the Tin Woodsman is in a bad way. He is rusted over. Dorothy and the Scarecrow apply oil to the Tin Woodsman's joints, loosening the rust. He then tells them his story. He says that once he was human until the Wicked Witch of the East cast a spell on him that caused him to cut off an appendage every time he swung his ax. Fortunately, however, tinsmiths in Oz can replace human parts with metal. Like other scenes in the *Wizard of Oz*, there are powerful metaphors in this one. The Tin Woodsman is the American worker. Metal (the steel industry) represents the American Industrial Revolution. The rust is symbolic of the impact the Industrial Revolution had on workers, low wages, long hours, and horrible working conditions and depressions the United States experienced in 1873 and 1893. His metal body reflects the impact the Industrial Revolution had on workers. Once he had been human but factory work had dehumanized him. He was no longer a man but a machine. Severing limbs by swinging the ax reflects the high rate of accidents industrial workers experienced. The application of oil represents what Baum thinks will happen once Bryan becomes president; he will institute policies that will benefit the worker and break the hold industrial capitalism has on them. The Tin Woodsman decides to join Dorothy, Toto, and the Scarecrow on their journey to Emerald City. He wants a heart, again symbolic of the dehumanizing affect the Industrial Revolution had on workers. Getting a heart will make the worker human again.

The group set off down the yellow brick road toward Emerald City. Taken together, they represent the political coalition Baum thinks will be important to Bryan's election. Of course, the Scarecrow represents farmers and the Tin Woodsman represents workers. Dorothy and Toto are part of the coalition too. Dorothy represents a feminist and Toto is short for a teetotaler (someone who does not believe in consuming alcoholic beverages). Both the feminist movement and the prohibition movement were active in the United States around the turn of the twentieth century. Women reformers were campaigning for suffrage, more liberal divorce laws and birth control while prohibitionists wanted to make the country dry. Bryan himself advocated national prohibition and was a teetotaler. All these groups, farmers, workers, feminists, and prohibitionists must unite behind Bryan before he can win the presidency, or so Baum thinks.

While traveling down the yellow brick road toward Emerald City the group next encounters the Cowardly Lion. He roars but frightens nobody; he scratched the Tin Woodsman but dulled his claws on the tin man's body. The Cowardly Lion is William Jennings Bryan. The roar is symbolic of his oratorical abilities. Bryan was often called the "boy orator from the Platt." He had crisscrossed the country making speech after speech during the 1896 campaign while his opponent, McKinley, had stayed home. Bryan's speeches appeared to have little effect. They had not persuaded workers to vote for him. He had dulled his claws on their armor. The Cowardly Lion wants courage. This reflects Baum's belief that Bryan needs to be more courageous in persuading workers to vote for him. He needs to promise workers more in the 1900 campaign than he promised in 1896.

The political coalition continues down the yellow brick road until finally it reaches Emerald City. A gatekeeper meets Dorothy and her friends and makes them put on green goggles (glasses), which they are required to wear while in Emerald City. They are told that they must not take the goggles off. The goggles make everything appear to be a bright shiny green. Curious, Dorothy lifts one corner of the goggles and peeks at the city through the naked eye. What she sees is not a city that is bright and shiny but one that is a dull, dirty white. Emerald City, the capitol of Oz, represents Washington, D.C., America's political capitol, during the Gilded Age. Just as America on the surface during the Gilded Age appeared to be bright and shiny, if one takes off the glasses and looks beneath the surface, corruption will be found in the government. Industrialists often bribed government officials. Things, as Mark Twain pointed out when he coined the term Gilded Age, were not what they appeared to be.

When the group gets an audience with the Wizard he appears to be all powerful and promises Dorothy and her friends what each one wants if they will do something for him—kill the Wicked Witch of the West. The Wizard represents President McKinley. A political deal has been struck. To gain the support of feminist, workers, farmers and others in the upcoming election, McKinley has made numerous promises that he will have trouble keeping, typical behavior for a politician.

Dorothy and her entourage head west where they are told they will find the Wicked Witch of the West. The Wicked Witch of the West, like her sister in the east, is the capitalist who oppresses common people. Dorothy, Toto, the Scarecrow, the Tin Woodsman, and the Cowardly Lion encounter the Wicked Witch of the West through characters identified as Flying Monkeys. The Flying Monkeys and their king appear to be vicious creatures. They take Dorothy to the Wicked Witch of the West where she is imprisoned. One day, while taking a bath, Dorothy splashes water on the witch, which causes her to melt. The water is symbolic that the drought, which had hurt farmers in the west during the 1880s, finally came to an end in the 1890s. Dorothy has destroyed the Wicked Witch of the West, freeing the Flying Monkeys from her spell. Again, when Bryan wins the 1900 election, Baum thinks the power of the capitalist will be broken over workers and farmers. The Flying Monkeys represent the American Indian confined to western reservations. The Flying Monkeys turn out to be good people who have been oppressed just as Native Americans were oppressed in the West. Dorothy asks the Flying Monkeys to return with her to Emerald City but they reply that they can't because they are bound to the land. The Indian was confined to the reservation.

Dorothy and her friends return to Emerald City, seeking an audience with the Wizard. He cannot believe that the group has destroyed the Wicked Witch of the West. He thought that task was impossible to achieve. Baum is saying here that Bryan has overcome impossible obstacles to win the 1900 election, defeating McKinley, the Wizard. At first, the Wizard tries to avoid Dorothy, the Scarecrow, the Tin Woodsman, and the Cowardly Lion. When they force an audience with him, he then tries to avoid keeping the promise he made to each of them, typical behavior for politicians who promise voters many things they can't deliver. Toto doesn't like the Wizard and knocks down a screen in the throne room. Instead of concealing a powerful wizard, the screen hides a short bald headed man that Baum describes as a humbug. McKinley has no real power. He is a fake, a fraud, and a ventriloquist who makes people believe he is a powerful man. This reflects the view many Americans had that President McKinley had no real power but was controlled by his handlers, such as the industrialists Mark Hanna. The Wizard attempts to keep his promise to Dorothy and each of her friends. Even here, he is a fake. Instead of giving the Scarecrow a real brain he fills his head with needles which will prick the skin and make him believe he has a brain. The lion's courage is merely a dose of cod liver oil and the Tin Woodsman gets a paper heart rather than a real one. Since the Wizard had been a carnival barker in the United States who drew a crowd by ascending aloft in a hot air balloon he decides he wants to return home with Dorothy. He makes a balloon that he and Dorothy plan to use to transport them home. Unfortunately, the balloon gets loose from its moorings while Dorothy is hunting for Toto and the Wizard leaves without her. Before departing the Wizard made some changes. He makes the Scarecrow the ruler of Oz; thus the farmer is restored to his lofty position at the top of society before the Industrial Revolution knocked him from that perch. The Wizard's departure is symbolic of McKinley leaving power after having lost the 1900 election.

Since the Wizard has left without her, Dorothy appears to be stuck in Oz. She encounters Glinda, the Good Witch of the North. Glinda tells Dorothy that the silver slippers she is wearing have magical powers that can be used to transport her anywhere in the world. This reflects the magical power of silver to solve the problems of farmers and workers. They believed their problems would magically disappear if America's currency were inflated by use of silver. Dorothy clicks her heels together, says magical words and is transported back to Kansas. When she arrives, the sun is shining and things are looking up for farmers and workers. Bryan is president and the power of the robber barons and corporations they control is broken. A new day has dawned for workers and farmers.

HOW WELL DID YOU UNDERSTAND THIS SELECTION?

1. What figures do the characters in *The Wizard of Oz* represent?

2. What themes from the Industrial Revolution are present in this child's story?

3. Can you find symbolism, other than the themes discussed by Cantrell in the above essay, reflected in issues or events from the Industrial Revolution?

4. Do politicians behave much like the Wizard?

5. What is a political coalition? Has Baum correctly identified the coalition needed to sweep Bryan into the White House?

6. Do you think Baum was disappointed when Bryan did not defeat McKinley in the 1900 election? Why or why not?

FORCED LABOR IN WEST VIRGINIA
By Gino C. Speranza

*Gino C. Speranza was head of the Society for the Protection of Italian Immigrants in the United States. This organization existed to improve the lives of Italian immigrants in the United States. He wrote the following article for **The Outlook** after conducting an investigation of working conditions and debt peonage in West Virginia coal mining and lumber camps.*

It is a far cry from Harmon's Camp in the lonely mountains of Raleigh County, West Virginia to New York City, yet it speaks well for the unceasing vigilance of our militant philanthropy that a cry from that camp in the wilderness was heard and heeded. The adventures of the twenty-three Italian laborers who were sent to Raleigh County from New York reads like a page from the history of the Middle Ages, except that the splendid animal courage of those days is replaced here by the all-absorbing sordid interest of money-making.

In the early part of March, 1903, twenty-three Italians were shipped (I use the word advisedly) from New York by one of those numberless "bankers" who infest the Italian colony, to Beckley, West Virginia, to work on a railroad in process of building in the Piney Creek District. They were told, as is often done and as must be done to induce men to go to that region, that Beckley was a few hours from New York and the approximate cost of transportation would be eighty cents. When they arrived at Beckley, after a journey of nearly two days, hungry, bewildered, and conscious already that they had been betrayed, they were driven to Harmon's Camp, some four miles from town. Those who have not been to the West Virginian labor camps can hardly understand how lonely and isolated some of them are. Even though geographically near each other, they are completely shut in by high mountains, and the surrounding country is practically uninhabited. Conscious of having been sold by the agents in New York, the lonesomeness of the camp naturally increased the apprehension of the laborers. But they started in on the work of drilling and grading, even thought the work was not as it had been represented. Perhaps they worked because the presence of some armed guards and the sight of the contractor with a revolver ostentatiously stuck in his breast pocket was not reassuring. Moreover, to make matters worse, though they were at liberty to "buy anywhere," they had to buy from the camp commissary, no matter how extortionate the prices were, as the nearest store was miles away. The day came when such conditions grew unbearable and the men left; they were not paid, but it seemed better to lose money than to remain. The contractor, however, having advanced transportation, was not going to stand a loss if he could help it. It is true that the Governor of West Virginia, stirred by constant complaints of abuse, had urged the use of legal process in such cases rather than a recourse to force. However hampered legally the contractor might be, the storekeeper had a ready remedy under the "Boarding-House Law" of West Virginia, which gives the right of arrest for non-payment of board. It did not matter that it applied with doubtful propriety to shanty board in a camp, once an accommodating squire could be found to grant a warrant. And so the twenty-three "insurgents" were arrested and locked over night in the Grand Jury room at the County Court House at Beckley, on the charge of non-payment of board. The next morning enters the contractor; he is a private citizen, he in not an officer, he is not even a party of record to the proceedings. What right has he in that Grand Jury room used as a jail? And when the prisoners, in the actual custody of the law, refuse to go back to his camp, he and his henchman, in that room set apart for what has been called "the bulwark of Anglo-Saxon liberty," proceed to bind six of the prisoner with ropes. I cite from the sworn statement of one of the men, "He had tied my wrists and had thrown the rope around my neck, when I shouted to the storekeeper, who was present and spoke Italian, "Not this, not this!" "It is Holy Week and I know Christ's hands were tied, but there was no rope around his neck." Thereupon the contractor, convinced that the binding of the arms was sufficient bunched together six of the bound men and marched them out into the public street. There, before "the whole town," not excluding certain sworn officers of the law, seeing that the prisoners still refused to march back to camp, the contractor hitched the rope by which they were tied to a mule, urging it on. The squire who had issued the warrant of arrest fortunately appeared then and cut the men free. Praise be to him for this act! But why did he urge these men to go back, as he did, with that brute of a contractor, and why did he, instead of trying the prisoners then and there according to law, go back to camp with them and help to induce them to "work out" their "board" and transportation? Why did he not take action against the contractor caught *in flagrante?* Why was there no entry made in his official docket of the disposition of this case till months after? Why did not the Prosecuting Officer at Beckley, who knew of this barbarity, take any action until two months after the event, when a society six hundred miles away submitted to him evidence which he could have gathered fifty yards from his office; and even then why did he merely promise to submit "this small matter" to the next Grand Jury?

Of the twenty-two men who worked out their "debts," one escaped and cannot be traced; eleven walked practically all the way from Charleston, West Virginia, to Washington, District of Columbia; two I found in a Washington hospital; the others had money enough to return to New York.

I have given this case at length, not because it is an example of exceptional cruelty and lawlessness, but because it is an uncommonly well substantiated and corroborated case of the system of intimidation in force in some labor camps of West Virginia, ranging from the silent intimidation of armed guards to an active terrorism of blows and abuse, of which the general public knows nothing.

It was in the latter part of April, 1903, that I was sent by the Society for the Protection of Italian Immigrants of New York to investigate a large number of complaints of alleged maltreatment suffered by Italians in certain counties of West Virginia. That State is developing her splendid resources of coal and lumber, and this necessitates the building of railroads for the transportation of such products. The demand for labor is tremendous and the supply totally inadequate. If it is true that too many immigrants come to our shores, it hardly holds good for West Virginia. There capital is in danger of becoming paralyzed from lack of the labor supply. To supply the feverish demands, laborers of all conditions and classes have been literally dumped into that State by the brokers in human flesh in the cities—not only men unfit for the hard work required, but a lawless and criminal element as well. The problem for the contractor does not end with getting the men to West Virginia; an even harder task is to keep them there, for the isolation of the camps, the absence of human intercourse, and the hardships of life create a feeling of discontent among the laborers almost from the first day. It is not strange, under these circumstances, therefore, that contractors should resort to methods both to get and to keep laborers which are in defiance of law and repugnant to the moral sense. The temptation to illegitimate practices is further strengthened by the method employed of advancing transportation for the men. Thus, two hundred laborers at $10 each means an investment of $2,000; if the men become dissatisfied and leave, it means a clear loss to the contractor. Yet, however strong the temptation, it cannot justify acts of restraint which in practice amount to white slavery. The use of armed guards around the camps is notorious. Worse yet, the evidence seems to show that the men are charged for the expense of such unlawful surveillance.

Cases of brutality are frequent and inexcusable. One may find some palliation for the unlawful restraint exercised over men who wish to escape before they have "worked out" their transportation. But what can be said in extenuation of such acts of brutality as those of men felled with blows from iron bars or gun butts, or marched at the point of rifles and cursed and beaten if unable to keep up with the pace of the mounted overseers? I have before me the sworn declaration of one Girardi—a bright young Piedmontese, who had been employed by Boxley & Co. near Kayford. He was ordered to lift a heavy stone, and asked a negro co-laborer to help him. His was not, evidently, a permissible request, as his foreman, on hearing it, called him a vile name and thrust a revolver in his face. Thereupon Girardi lifted the stone, at the cost of a very bad rupture. That man to this day has had no redress.

"Tired of abuse," reads the sworn statement of another laborer, "we decided to escape from the camp; we had proceeded but a short distance when we were overtaken by several men armed with rifles and revolvers, who drove us back. One of the pursuing band took from me an iron rod which I held over my shoulder, over which I had slung my valise, and with it repeatedly struck several of my companions." Another, a splendid type of hardy Calabrian, described under oath the following picture: "My attention was drawn to the other side of the creek, where an Italian was shouting for help—appealing to us as fellow-countrymen to aid him. He had been felled by a blow of a heavy stick dealt him by one of the guards. Cervi, my friend, and I tried to cross over to help him, but were prevented by our boss, who drove us back at the point of a pistol; all I dared do was to shout to him not to resist or he would be killed, and to go back; the man who had struck him lifted him bodily by his coat and pushed him on, striking him every time he stumbled or fell from exhaustion."

These are a few of a number of well-substantiated cases. It will be hard for many of us to believe these facts; it will seem impossible that such barbarities should be allowed in a civilized community. Perhaps they would not be allowed if they were known. Publicity is the great hope for reform; a wide publicity that will, on the one hand, arouse public sentiment and react on the local authorities, and, on the other hand, that will further cut off the supply of laborers, thereby forcing the contractors to reform.

Little, if anything, can be hoped from the local officials. The Chief Executive of West Virginia admitted to me that it was practically impossible to obtain convictions through the local courts, and, however good his intentions, his powers seem very limited. In a recent letter the Governor of that State writes: "I am willing to do anything I can to bring about a better condition of affairs and to co-operate as I have the power in bringing to justice those guilty of the acts complained of, but you see my limitations. . . The executive in West Virginia has practically no power in controlling the administration of justice in our courts. . . .The legislature refused last winter to give me the necessary powers asked for in as grave a matter as lynching."

It is a reasonable presumption that contractors do not engage men with the express purpose of maltreating them, for it is a plain business principle that dissatisfied men make poor workers. I believe, therefore, that, with some few exceptions, these abuses are to a great extent due to that lack of mutual confidence and more especially of mutual understanding which is the basis of much of the unrest and spirit of reprisal in the labor situation. This lack of mutual understanding is especially evident in the relations between American employers and Italian laborers. It is not merely ignorance of the language, it is rather a lack of clear-sightedness and perception as regards what counts with these foreign laborers. Employers of Italian labor too often forget that their employees are proverbially sensitive, but are also susceptible to kind treatment. Courtesy and kindness will hold these men even in distant and isolated camps much better than curses and forcible threats. As a purely business proposition, the employment of a capable and honest interpreter or confidential secretary who knows both Italian and American ways, to whom laborers could go, would be a better and cheaper investment for contractors than the maintenance of armed guards or brutal foremen. As it is, not only in West Virginia but wherever Italian labor is employed the Italian is at the mercy of the middle-man, without any right of appeal. Whether it be the fraud of his own countryman, the banker-agent who sells his labor under false pretenses, or the extortion of his countryman, the camp storekeeper to whom the contractor lets the commissary privileges, whether it be the "rake-off" of the foreman or the peculations of the paymaster, whether it be the brutality of the boss or the unlawful order of the gang-foremen—no matter what the injustice may be, the laborer has no opportunity to appeal to his employer, either because the employer recognizes the decision of his middleman as final or because he will not "bother with details." While this system, popularly called the "pardone system," is tolerated by contractors, abuses will continue. Much, however, can be done to lessen its evils by institutions like the Society for the Protection of Italian Immigrants, a society administered by Americans, which aims to destroy the padrone system by competing with padrone, using legitimate methods in supplying laborers and safeguarding their rights.

The responsibility, in the last instance, however, rests on the employers. Their duty to the men should not cease with the payment of agreed wages; without the careful, businesslike, and humane supervision, workmen are very likely to be abused by the middlemen. Especially is this true of the foreign workman whose helplessness in the face of unlawful and brutal treatment such as that in West Virginia would almost justify an extra-judicial reprisal. Certainly it is of vital importance that these numberless foreign laborers who come to us should learn, as a first step towards assimilation, that Americanism means honesty, regard for law, fair play, and plain dealing.

Source: *The Outlook*, June 13, 1908

HOW WELL DID YOU UNDERSTAND THIS SELECTION?

1. Who is Gino Speranza?

2. What is labor peonage?

3. What does Speranza find in West Virginia?

4. How are immigrant workers treated in West Virginia if they don't pay transportation charges?

5. What is "on transportation"?

6. What is the padrone system?

7. What does Speranza think will solve the problem of labor peonage?

Booker T. Washington was an African-American leader who founded Tuskegee Institute in Alabama. A pioneer in education, he thought African Americans would best be served by obtaining a practical education in mechanical skills and agriculture. Washington was often accused of being an "Uncle Tom" because he was willing to accept racism and discrimination for slow economic gains for African Americans.

When a mere boy, I saw a young colored man, who had spent several years in school, sitting in a common cabin in the South, studying a French grammar. I noted the poverty, the untidiness, the want of system and thrift that existed about the cabin, notwithstanding his knowledge of French and other academic subjects. Another time, when riding on the outer edges of a town in the South, I heard the sound of a piano coming from a cabin of the same kind. Contriving some excuse, I entered, and began a conversation with the young colored woman who was playing, and who had recently returned from a boarding-school, where she had been studying instrumental music among other things. Despite the fact that her parents were living in a rented cabin, eating poorly cooked food, surrounded with poverty, and having almost none of the conveniences of life, she had persuaded them to rent a piano for four or five dollars per month. Many such instances as these, in connection with my own struggles, impressed upon me the importance of making a study of our needs as a race, and applying the remedy accordingly. Some one may be tempted to ask, Has not the negro boy or girl as good a right to study a French grammar and instrumental music as the white youth? I answer, Yes, but in the present condition of the negro race in this country there is need of something more. Perhaps I may be forgiven for the seeming egotism if I mention the expansion of my own life partly as an example of what I mean. My earliest recollection is of a small one-room log hut on a large slave plantation in Virginia. After the close of the war, while working in the coal-mines of West Virginia for the support of my mother, I heard in some accidental way of the Hampton Institute. When I learned that it was an institution where a black boy could study, could have a chance to work for his board, and at the same time be taught how to work and to realize the dignity of labor, I resolved to go there. Bidding my mother good-by, I started out one morning to find my way to Hampton, though I was almost penniless and had no definite idea where Hampton was. By walking, begging rides, and paying for a portion of the journey on the steam-cars, I finally succeeded in reaching the city of Richmond, Virginia. I was without money or friends. I slept under a sidewalk, and by working on a vessel next day I earned money to continue my way to the institute, where I arrived with a surplus of fifty cents. At Hampton I found the opportunity — in the way of buildings, teachers, and industries provided by the generous — to get training in the class-room and by practical touch with industrial life, to learn thrift, economy, and push. I was surrounded by an atmosphere of business, Christian influence, and a spirit of self-help that seemed to have awakened every faculty in me, and caused me for the first time to realize what it meant to be a man instead of a piece of property.

While there I resolved that when I had finished the course of training I would go into the far South, into the Black Belt of the South, and give my life to providing the same kind of opportunity for self-reliance and self-awakening that I had found provided for me at Hampton. My work began at Tuskegee, Alabama, in 1881, in a small shanty and church, with one teacher and thirty students, without a dollar's worth of property. The spirit of work and of industrial thrift, with aid from the State and generosity from the North, has enabled us to develop an institution of eight hundred students gathered from nineteen States, with seventy-nine instructors, fourteen hundred acres of land, and thirty buildings, including large and small; in all, property valued at $280,000. Twenty-five industries have been organized, and the whole work is carried on at an annual cost of about $80,000 in cash; two fifths of the annual expense so far has gone into permanent plant.

What is the object of all this outlay? First, it must be borne in mind that we have in the South a peculiar and unprecedented state of things. It is of the utmost importance that our energy be given to meeting conditions that exist right about us rather than conditions that existed centuries ago or that exist in countries a thousand miles away. What are the cardinal needs among the seven millions of colored people in the South, most of whom are to be found on the plantations? Roughly, these needs may be stated as food, clothing, shelter, education, proper habits, and a settlement of race relations. The seven millions of colored people of the South cannot be reached directly by any missionary agency, but they can be reached by sending out among them strong selected young men and women, with the proper training of head, hand, and heart, who will live among these masses and show them how to lift themselves up.

The problem that the Tuskegee Institute keeps before itself constantly is how to prepare these leaders. From the outset, in connection with religious and academic training, it has emphasized industrial or hand training as a means of finding the way out of present conditions. First, we have found the industrial teaching useful in giving the student a chance to work out a portion of his expenses while in school. Second, the school furnishes labor that has an economic value, and at the same time gives the student a chance to acquire knowledge and skill while performing the labor. Most of all, we find the industrial system valuable in teaching economy, thrift, and the dignity of labor, and in giving moral backbone to students. The fact that a student goes out into the world conscious of his power to build a house or a wagon, or to make a harness, gives him a certain confidence and moral independence that he would not possess without such training.

A more detailed example of our methods at Tuskegee may be of interest. For example, we cultivate by student labor six hundred and fifty acres of land. The object is not only to cultivate the land in a way to make it pay our boarding department, but at the same time to teach the students, in addition to the practical work, something of the chemistry of the soil, the best methods of drainage, dairying, the cultivation of fruit, the care of livestock and tools, and scores of other lessons needed by a people whose main dependence is on agriculture. Notwithstanding that eighty-five per cent of the colored people in the South live by agriculture in some form, aside from what has been done by Hampton, Tuskegee, and one or two other institutions practically nothing has been attempted in the direction of teaching them about the very industry from which the masses of our people must get their subsistence. Friends have recently provided means for the erection of a large new chapel at Tuskegee. Our students have made the bricks for this chapel. A large part of the timber is sawed by students at our own sawmill, the plans are drawn by our teacher of architecture and mechanical drawing, and students do the brick-masonry, plastering, painting, carpentry work, tinning, slating, and make most of the furniture. Practically, the whole chapel will be built and furnished by student labor; in the end the school will have the building for permanent use, and the students will have a knowledge of the trades employed in its construction. In this way all but three of the thirty buildings on the grounds have been erected. While the young men do the kinds of work I have mentioned, the young women to a large extent make, mend, and launder the clothing of the young men, and thus are taught important industries.

One of the objections sometimes urged against industrial education for the negro is that it aims merely to teach him to work on the same plan that he was made to follow when in slavery. This is far from being the object at Tuskegee. At the head of each of the twenty-five industrial departments we have an intelligent and competent instructor, just as we have in our history classes, so that the student is taught not only practical brick-masonry, for example, but also the underlying principles of that industry, the mathematics and the mechanical and architectural drawing. Or he is taught how to become master of the forces of nature so that, instead of cultivating corn in the old way, he can use a corn cultivator, that lays off the furrows, drops the corn into them, and covers it, and in this way he can do more work than three men by the old process of corn-planting; at the same time much of the toil is eliminated and labor is dignified. In a word, the constant aim is to show the student how to put brains into every process of labor; how to bring his knowledge of mathematics and the sciences into farming, carpentry, forging, foundry work; how to dispense as soon as possible with the old form of ante-bellum labor. In the erection of the chapel just referred to, instead of letting the money which was given us go into outside hands, we make it accomplish three objects: first, it provides the chapel; second, it gives the students a chance to get a practical knowledge of the trades connected with building; and third, it enables them to earn something toward the payment of board while receiving academic and industrial training.

Having been fortified at Tuskegee by education of mind, skill of hand, Christian character, ideas of thrift, economy, and push, and a spirit of independence, the student is sent out to become a centre of influence and light in show-ing the masses of our people in the Black Belt of the South how to lift themselves up. How can this be done? I give but one or two examples. Ten years ago a young colored man came to the institute from one of the large plantation districts; he studied in the class-room a portion of the time, and received practical and theoretical training on the farm the remainder of the time. Having finished his course at Tuskegee, he returned to his plantation home, which was in a county where the colored people outnumber the whites six to one, as is true of many of the counties in the Black Belt of the South. He found the negroes in debt. Ever since the war they had been mortgaging their crops for the food on which to live while the crops were growing. The majority of them were living from hand to mouth on rented land, in small, one-room log cabins, and attempting to pay a rate of interest on their advances that ranged from fifteen to forty per cent per annum. The school had been taught in a wreck of a log cabin, with no apparatus, and had never been in session longer than three months out of twelve. With as many as eight or ten persons of all ages and conditions and of both sexes huddled together in one cabin year after year, and with a minister whose only aim was to work upon the emotions of the people, one can imagine something of the moral and religious state of the community.

He took the three months' public school as a nucleus for his work. Then he organized the older people into a club, or conference, that held meetings every week. In these meetings he taught the people in a plain, simple manner how to save their money, how to farm in a better way, how to sacrifice, — to live on bread and potatoes, if need be, till they could get out of debt, and begin the buying of lands.

Soon a large proportion of the people were in condition to make contracts for the buying of homes (land is very cheap in the South), and to live without mortgaging their crops. Not only this: under the guidance and leadership of this teacher, the first year that he was among them they learned how, by contributions in money and labor, to build a neat, comfortable schoolhouse that replaced the wreck of a log cabin formerly used. The following year the weekly meetings were continued, and two months were added to the original three months of school. The next year two more months were added. The improvement has gone on, until now these people have every year an eight months' school.

I wish my readers could have the chance that I have had of going into this community. I wish they could look into the faces of the people and see them beaming with hope and delight. I wish they could see the two or three room cottages that have taken the place of the usual one-room cabin, the well-cultivated farms, and the religious life of the people that now means something more than the name. The teacher has a good cottage and a well-kept farm that serve as models. In a word, a complete revolution has been wrought in the industrial, educational, and religious life of this whole community by reason of the fact that they have had this leader, this guide and object-lesson, to show them how to take the money and effort that had hitherto been scattered to the wind in mortgages and high rents, in whiskey and gewgaws, and concentrate them in the direction of their own uplifting. One community on its feet presents an object-lesson for the adjoining communities, and soon improvements show themselves in other places.

Another student who received academic and industrial training at Tuskegee established himself, three years ago, as a blacksmith and wheelwright in a community, and, in addition to the influence of his successful business enterprise, he is fast making the same kind of changes in the life of the people about him that I have just recounted. It would be easy for me to fill many pages describing the influence of the Tuskegee graduates in every part of the South. We keep it constantly in the minds of our students and graduates that the industrial or material condition of the masses of our people must be improved, as well as the intellectual, before there can be any permanent change in their moral and religious life. We find it a pretty hard thing to make a good Christian of a hungry man. No matter how much our people "get happy" and "shout" in church, if they go home at night from church hungry, they are tempted to find something before morning. This is a principle of human nature, and is not confined to the negro.

The negro has within him immense power for self-uplifting, but for years it will be necessary to guide and stimulate him. The recognition of this power led us to organize, five years ago, what is now known as the Tuskegee Negro Conference, — a gathering that meets every February, and is composed of about eight hundred representative colored men and women from all sections of the Black Belt. They come in ox-carts, mule-carts, buggies, on muleback and horseback, on foot, by railroad: some traveling all night in order to be present. The matters considered at the conferences are those that the colored people have it within their own power to control: such as the evils of the mortgage system, the one-room cabin, buying on credit, the importance of owning a home and of putting money in the bank, how to build schoolhouses and prolong the school term, and how to improve their moral and religious condition.

As a single example of the results, one delegate reported that since the conferences were started five years ago eleven people in his neighborhood had bought homes, fourteen had got out of debt, and a number had stopped mortgaging their crops. Moreover, a schoolhouse had been built by the people themselves, and the school term had been extended from three to six months; and with a look of triumph he exclaimed, "We is done stopped libin' in de ashes!"

Besides this Negro Conference for the masses of the people, we now have a gathering at the same time known as the Workers' Conference, composed of the officers and instructors in the leading colored schools of the South. After listening to the story of the conditions and needs from the people themselves, the Workers' Conference finds much food for thought and discussion.

Nothing else so soon brings about right relations between the two races in the South as the industrial progress of the negro. Friction between the races will pass away in proportion as the black man, by reason of his skill, intelligence, and character, can produce something that the white man wants or respects in the commercial world. This is another reason why at Tuskegee we push the industrial training. We find that as every year we put into a Southern community colored men who can start a brick-yard, a sawmill, a tin-shop, or a printing-office, — men who produce something that makes the white man partly dependent upon the negro, instead of all the dependence being on the other side, — a change takes place in the relations of the races.

Let us go on for a few more years knitting our business and industrial relations into those of the white man, till a black man gets a mortgage on a white man's house that he can foreclose at will. The white man on whose house the mortgage rests will not try to prevent that negro from voting when he goes to the polls. It is through the dairy farm, the truck garden, the trades, and commercial life, largely, that the negro is to find his way to the enjoyment of all his rights. Whether he will or not, a white man respects a negro who owns a two-story brick house.

What is the permanent value of the Tuskegee system of training to the South in a broader sense? In connection with this, it is well to bear in mind that slavery taught the white man that labor with the hands was something fit for the negro only, and something for the white man to come into contact with just as little as possible. It is true that there was a large class of poor white people who labored with the hands, but they did it because they were not able to secure negroes to work for them; and these poor whites were constantly trying to imitate the slave-holding class in escaping labor, and they too regarded it as anything but elevating. The negro in turn looked down upon the poor whites with a certain contempt because they had to work. The negro, it is to be borne in mind, worked under constant protest, because he felt that his labor was being unjustly required, and he spent almost as much effort in planning how to escape work as in learning how to work. Labor with him was a badge of degradation. The white man was held up before him as the highest type of civilization, but the negro noted that this highest type of civilization himself did no labor; hence he argued that the less work he did, the more nearly he would be like a white man. Then, in addition to these influences, the slave system discouraged labor-saving machinery. To use labor-saving machinery intelligence was required, and intelligence and slavery were not on friendly terms; hence the negro always associated labor with toil, drudgery, something to be escaped. When the negro first became free, his idea of education was that it was something that would soon put him in the same position as regards work that his recent master had occupied. Out of these conditions grew the Southern habit of putting off till to-morrow and the day after the duty that should be done promptly to-day. The leaky house was not repaired while the sun shone, for then the rain did not come through. While the rain was falling, no one cared to expose himself to stop the leak. The plough, on the same principle, was left where the last furrow was run, to rot and rust in the field during the winter. There was no need to repair the wooden chimney that was exposed to the fire, because water could be thrown on it when it was on fire. There was no need to trouble about the payment of a debt to-day, for it could just as well be paid next week or next year. Besides these conditions, the whole South, at the close of the war, was without proper food, clothing, and shelter,— was in need of habits of thrift and economy and of something laid up for a rainy day.

This industrial training, emphasizing as it does the idea of economic production, is gradually bringing the South to the point where it is feeding itself. Before the war, and long after it, the South made what little profit was received from the cotton crop, and sent its earnings out of the South to purchase food supplies, — meat, bread, canned vegetables, and the like; but the improved methods of agriculture are fast changing this habit. With the newer methods of labor, which teach promptness and system, and emphasize the worth of the beautiful, — the moral value of the well-painted house, and the fence with every paling and nail in its place, — we are bringing to bear upon the South an influence that is making it a new country in industry, education, and religion.

Source: *Atlantic Monthly*, 1886

HOW WELL DID YOU UNDERSTAND THIS SELECTION?

1. What is the Tuskegee System?

2. What does Washington think is the solution to the problems African Americans face in the South?

3. What influence does Washington maintain Tuskegee Institute has had on the South?

4. What does Washington think is the key to improving race relations?

5. Why does Washington advocate industrial rather than academic training for African Americans?

6. How does Washington think Tuskegee Institute has changed southern attitudes about labor?

OF THE TRAINING OF BLACK MEN" By W.E.B. Du Bois

W.E.B. Du Bois was an African-American leader who often criticized Booker T. Washington, especially his views on race and education. Du Bois disagrees with Washington's idea that industrial training is the most appropriate education for African Americans. He thinks African Americans are suited for higher education, especially college.

From the shimmering swirl of waters where many, many thoughts ago the slave-ship first saw the square tower of Jamestown have flowed down to our day three streams of thinking: one from the larger world here and over-seas, saying, the multiplying of human wants in culture lands calls for the world-wide co-operation of men in satisfying them. Hence arises a new human unity, pulling the ends of earth nearer, and all men, black, yellow, and white. The larger humanity strives to feel in this contact of living nations and sleeping hordes a thrill of new life in the world, crying, If the contact of Life and Sleep be Death, shame on such Life. To be sure, behind this thought lurks the after-thought of force and dominion, — the making of brown men to delve when the temptation of beads and red calico cloys. The second thought streaming from the death-ship and the curving river is the thought of the older South: the sincere and passionate belief that somewhere between men and cattle God created a *tertium quid*, and called it a Negro, — a clownish, simple creature, at times even lovable within its limitations, but straitly foreordained to walk within the Veil. To be sure, behind the thought lurks the afterthought, — some of them with favoring chance might become men, but in sheer self-defense we dare not let them, and build about them walls so high, and hang between them and the light a veil so thick, that they shall not even think of breaking through. And last of all there trickles down that third and darker thought, the thought of the things themselves, the confused half-conscious mutter of men who are black and whitened, crying Liberty, Freedom, Opportunity — vouchsafe to us, O boastful World, the chance of living men! To be sure, behind the thought lurks the afterthought: suppose, after all, the World is right and we are less than men? Suppose this mad impulse within is all wrong, some mock mirage from the untrue?

So here we stand among thoughts of human unity, even through conquest and slavery; the inferiority of black men, even if forced by fraud; a shriek in the night for the freedom of men who themselves are not yet sure of their right to demand it. This is the tangle of thought and afterthought wherein we are called to solve the problem of training men for life. Behind all its curiousness, so attractive alike to sage and dilettante, lie its dim dangers, throwing across us shadows at once grotesque and awful. Plain it is to us that what the world seeks through desert and wild we have within our threshold; — a stalwart laboring force, suited to the semi-tropics; if, deaf to the voice of the Zeitgeist, we refuse to use and develop these men, we risk poverty and loss. If, on the other hand, seized by the brutal afterthought, we debauch the race thus caught in our talons, selfishly sucking their blood and brains in the future as in the past, what shall save us from national decadence? Only that saner selfishness which, education teaches men, can find the rights of all in the whirl of work.

Again, we may decry the color prejudice of the South, yet it remains a heavy fact. Such curious kinks of the human mind exist and must be reckoned with soberly. They cannot be laughed away, nor always successfully stormed at, nor easily abolished by act of legislature. And yet they cannot be encouraged by being let alone. They must be recognized as facts, but unpleasant facts; things that stand in the way of civilization and religion and common decency. They can be met in but one way: by the breadth and broadening of human reason, by catholicity of taste and culture. And so, too, the native ambition and aspiration of men, even though they be black, backward, and ungraceful, must not lightly be dealt with. To stimulate wildly weak and untrained minds is to play with mighty fires; to flout their striving idly is to welcome a harvest of brutish crime and shameless lethargy in our very laps. The guiding of thought and the deft coordination of deed is at once the path of honor and humanity.

And so, in this great question of reconciling three vast and partially contradictory streams of thought, the one panacea of Education leaps to the lips of all; such human training as will best use the labor of all men without enslaving or brutalizing; such training as will give us poise to encourage the prejudices that bulwark society, and stamp out those that in sheer barbarity deafen us to the wail of prisoned souls within the Veil, and the mounting fury of shackled men.

But when we have vaguely said Education will set this tangle straight, what have we uttered but a truism? Training for life teaches living; but what training for the profitable living together of black men and white? Two hundred years ago our task would have seemed easier. Then Dr. Johnson blandly assured us that education was needed solely for the embellishments of life, and was useless for ordinary vermin. Today we have climbed to heights where we would open at least the outer courts of knowledge to all, display its treasures to many, and select the few to whom its mystery of Truth is revealed, not wholly by truth or the accidents of the stock market, but at least in part according to deftness and aim, talent and character. This program, however, we are sorely puzzled in carrying out through that part of the land where the blight of slavery fell hardest, and where we are dealing with two backward peoples. To make here in human education that ever necessary combination of the permanent and the contingent — of the ideal and the practical in workable equilibrium — has been there, as it ever must be in every age and place, a matter of infinite experiment and frequent mistakes.

In rough approximation we may point out four varying decades of work in Southern education since the Civil War. From the close of the war until 1876 was the period of uncertain groping and temporary relief. There were army schools, mission schools, and schools of the Freedmen's Bureau in chaotic disarrangement, seeking system and cooperation. Then followed ten years of constructive definite effort toward the building of complete school systems in the South. Normal schools and colleges were founded for the freedmen, and teachers trained there to man the public schools. There was the inevitable tendency of war to underestimate the prejudice of the master and the ignorance of the slave, and all seemed clear sailing out of the wreckage of the storm. Meantime, starting in this decade yet especially developing from 1885 to 1895, began the industrial revolution of the South. The land saw glimpses of a new destiny and the stirring of new ideals. The educational system striving to complete itself saw new obstacles and a field of work ever broader and deeper. The Negro colleges, hurriedly founded, were inadequately equipped, illogically distributed, and of varying efficiency and grade; the normal and high schools were doing little more than common school work, and the common schools were training but a third of the children who ought to be in them, and training these too often poorly. At the same time the white South, by reason of its sudden conversion from the slavery ideal, by so much the more became set and strengthened in its racial prejudice, and crystallized it into harsh law and harsher custom; while the marvelous pushing forward of the poor white daily threatened to take even bread and butter from the mouths of the heavily handicapped sons of the freedmen. In the midst, then, of the larger problem of Negro education sprang up the more practical question of work, the inevitable economic quandary that faces a people in the transition from slavery to freedom, and especially those who make that change amid hate and prejudice, lawlessness and ruthless competition.

The industrial school springing to notice in this decade, but coming to full recognition in the decade beginning with 1895, was the proffered answer to this combined educational and economic crisis, and an answer of singular wisdom and timeliness. From the very first in nearly all the schools some attention had been given to training in handiwork, but now was this training first raised to a dignity that brought it in direct touch with the South's magnificent industrial development, and given an emphasis which reminded black folk that before the Temple of Knowledge swing the Gates of Toil.

Yet after all they are but gates, and when turning our eyes from the temporary and the contingent in the Negro problem to the broader question of the permanent uplifting and civilization of black men in America, we have a right to inquire, as this enthusiasm for material advancement mounts to its height, if after all the industrial school is the final and sufficient answer in the training of the Negro race; and to ask gently, but in all sincerity, the ever recurring query of the ages, Is not life more than meat, and the body more than raiment? And men ask this to-day all the more eagerly because of sinister signs in recent educational movements. The tendency is here born of slavery and quickened to renewed life by the crazy imperialism of the day, to regard human beings as among the material resources of a land to be trained with an eye single to future dividends. Race prejudices, which keep brown and black men in their "places," we are coming to regard as useful allies with such a theory, no matter how much they may dull the ambition and sicken the hearts of struggling human beings. And above all, we daily hear that an education that encourages aspiration, that sets the loftiest of ideals and seeks as an end culture and character than bread-winning, is the privilege of white men and the danger and delusion of black.

Especially has criticism been directed against the former educational efforts to aid the Negro. In the four periods I have mentioned, we find first boundless, planless enthusiasm and sacrifice; then the preparation of teachers for a vast public school system; then the launching and expansion of that school system amid increasing difficulties; and finally the training of workmen for the new and growing industries. This development has been sharply ridiculed as a logical anomaly and flat reversal of nature. Soothly we have been told that first industrial and manual training should have taught the Negro to work, then simple schools should have taught him to read and write, and finally, after years, high and normal schools could have completed the system, as intelligence and skill were demanded.

That a system logically so complete was historically impossible, it needs but a little thought to prove. Progress in human affairs is more often a pull than a push, surging forward of the exceptional man, and the lifting of his duller brethren slowly and painfully to his vantage ground. Thus it was no accident that gave birth to universities centuries before the common schools, that made fair Harvard the first flower of our wilderness. So in the South: the mass of the freedmen at the end of the war lacked the intelligence so necessary to modern workingmen. They must first have the common school to teach them to read, write, and cipher. The white teachers who flocked South went to establish such a common school system. They had no idea of founding colleges; they themselves at first would have laughed at the idea. But they faced, as all men since them have faced, that central paradox of the South, the social separation of the races. Then it was the sudden volcanic rupture of nearly all relations between black and white, in work and government and family life. Since then a new adjustment of relations in economic and political affairs has grown up, — an adjustment subtle and difficult to grasp, yet singularly ingenious, which leaves still that frightful chasm at the color line across which men pass at their peril. Thus, then and now, there stand in the South two separate worlds; and separate not simply in the higher realms of social intercourse, but also in church and school, on railway and street car, in hotels and theatres, in streets and city sections, in books and newspapers, in asylums and jails, in hospitals and graveyards. There is still enough of contact for large economic and group cooperation, but the separation is so thorough and deep, that it absolutely precludes for the present between the races anything like that sympathetic and effective group training and leadership of the one by the other, such as the American Negro and all backward peoples must have for effectual progress.

This the missionaries of '68 soon saw; and if effective industrial and trade schools were impractical before the establishment of a common school system, just as certainly no adequate common schools could be founded until there were teachers to teach them. Southern whites would not teach them; Northern whites in sufficient numbers could not be had. If the Negro was to learn, he must teach himself, and the most effective help that could be given him was the establishment of schools to train Negro teachers. This conclusion was slowly but surely reached by every student of the situation until simultaneously, in widely separated regions, without consultation or systematic plan, there arose a series of institutions designed to furnish teachers for the untaught. Above the sneers of critics at the obvious defects of this procedure must ever stand its one crushing rejoinder: in a single generation they put thirty thousand black teachers in the South; they wiped out the illiteracy of the majority of the black people of the land, and they made Tuskegee possible.

Such higher training schools tended naturally to deepen broader development: at first they were common and grammar schools, then some became high schools. And finally, by 1900, some thirty-four had one year or more of studies of college grade. This development was reached with different degrees of speed in different institutions: Hampton is still a high school, while Fisk University started her college in 1871, and Spelman Seminary about 1896. In all cases the aim was identical: to maintain the standards of the lower training by giving teachers and leaders the best practicable training; and above all to furnish the black world with adequate standards of human culture and lofty ideals of life. It was not enough that the teachers of teachers should be trained in technical normal methods; they must also, so far as possible, be broad-minded, cultured men and women, to scatter civilization among a people whose ignorance was not simply of letters, but of life itself.

It can thus be seen that the work of education in the South began with higher institutions of training, which threw off as their foliage common schools, and later industrial schools, and at the same time strove to shoot their roots ever deeper toward college and university training. That this was an inevitable and necessary development, sooner or later, goes without saying; but there has been, and still is, a question in many minds if the natural growth was not forced, and if the higher training was not either overdone or done with cheap and unsound methods. Among white Southerners this feeling is widespread and positive. A prominent Southern journal voiced this in a recent editorial: "The experiment that has been made to give the colored students classical training has not been satisfactory. Even though many were able to pursue the course, most of them did so in a parrot-like way, learning what was taught, but not seeming to appropriate the truth and import of their instruction, and graduating without sensible aim or valuable occupation for their future. The whole scheme has proved a waste of time, efforts, and the money of the state." While most far-minded men would recognize this as extreme and overdrawn, still without doubt many are asking, are there a sufficient number of Negroes ready for college training to warrant the undertaking? Are not too many students prematurely forced into this work? Does it not have the effect of dissatisfying the young Negro with his environment? And do these graduates succeed in real life? Such natural questions cannot be evaded, nor on the other hand must a nation naturally skeptical as to Negro ability assume an unfavorable answer without careful inquiry and patient openness to conviction. We must not forget that most Americans answer all queries regarding the Negro *a priori*, and that the least that human courtesy can do is to listen to evidence.

The advocates of the higher education of the Negro would be the last to deny the incompleteness and glaring defects of the present system: too many institutions have attempted to do college work, the work in some cases has not been thoroughly done, and quantity rather than quality has sometimes been sought. But all this can be said of higher education throughout the land: it is the almost inevitable incident of educational growth, and leaves the deeper question of the legitimate demand for the higher training of Negroes untouched. And this latter question can be settled in but one way — by a first-hand study of the facts. If we leave out of view all institutions which have not actually graduated students from a course higher than that of a New England high school, even though they be called colleges; if then we take the thirty-four remaining institutions, we may clear up many misapprehensions by asking searchingly, What kind of institutions are they, what do they teach, and what sort of men do they graduate?

From such schools about two thousand Negroes have gone forth with the bachelor's degree. The number in itself is enough to put at rest the argument that too large a proportion of Negroes are receiving higher training. If the ratio to population of all Negro students throughout the land, in both college and secondary training, be counted, Commissioner Harris assures us "it must be increased to five times its present average" to equal the average of the land.

Fifty years ago the ability of Negro students in any appreciable numbers to master a modern college course would have been difficult to prove. Today it is proved by the fact that four hundred Negroes, many of whom have been reported as brilliant students, have received the bachelor's degree from Harvard, Yale, Oberlin, and seventy other leading colleges. Here we have, then, nearly twenty-five hundred Negro graduates, of whom the crucial query must be made. How far did their training fit them for life? It is of course extremely difficult to collect satisfactory data on such a point, — difficult to reach the men, to get trustworthy testimony, and to gauge that testimony by any generally acceptable criterion of success. In 1900, the Conference at Atlanta University undertook to study these graduates, and published the results. First they sought to know what these graduates were doing, and succeeded in getting answers from nearly two thirds of the living. The direct testimony was in almost all cases corroborated by the reports of the colleges where they graduated, so that in the main the reports were worthy of credence. Fifty-three per cent of these graduates were teachers, — presidents of institutions, heads of normal schools, principals of city school systems, and the like. Seventeen per cent were clergymen; another seventeen per cent were in the professions, chiefly as physicians. Over six per cent were merchants, farmers, and artisans, and four per cent were in the government civil service. Granting even that a considerable proportion of the third unheard from are unsuccessful, this is a record of usefulness. Personally I know many hundreds of these graduates and have corresponded with more than a thousand; through others I have followed carefully the life-work of scores; I have taught some of them and some of the pupils whom they have taught, lived in homes which they have built, and looked at life through their eyes. Comparing them as a class with my fellow students in New England and in Europe, I cannot hesitate in saying that nowhere have I met men and women with a broader spirit of helpfulness, with deeper devotion to their life-work, or with more consecrated determination to succeed in the face of bitter difficulties than among Negro college-bred men.

Strange to relate! for this is certain, no secure civilization can be built in the South with the Negro as an ignorant, turbulent proletariat. Suppose we seek to remedy this by making them laborers and nothing more: they are not fools, they have tasted of the Tree of Life, and they will not cease to think, will not cease attempting to read the riddle of the world. By taking away their best equipped teachers and leaders, by slamming the door of opportunity in the faces of their bolder and brighter minds, will you make them satisfied with their lot? Or will you not rather transfer their leading from the hands of men taught to think to the hands of untrained demagogues? We ought not to forget that despite the pressure of poverty, and despite the active discouragement and even ridicule of friends, the demand for higher training steadily increases among Negro youth: there were, in the years from 1875 to 1880, twenty-two Negro graduates from Northern colleges; from 1885 to 1895 there were forty-three, and from 1895 to 1900, nearly 100 graduates. From Southern Negro colleges there were, in the same three periods, 143, 413, and over 500 graduates. Here, then, is the plain thirst for training; by refusing to give this Talented Tenth the key to knowledge can any sane man imagine that they will lightly lay aside their yearning and contentedly become hewers of wood and drawers of water?

The function of the Negro college then is clear: it must maintain the standards of popular education, it must seek the social regeneration of the Negro, and it must help in the solution of problems of race contact and cooperation. And finally, beyond all this, it must develop men. Above our modern socialism, and out of the worship of the mass, must persist and evolve that higher individualism which the centers of culture protect; there must come a loftier respect for the sovereign human soul that seeks to know itself and the world about it; that seeks a freedom for expansion and self-development; that will love and hate and labor in its own way, untrammeled alike by old and new. Such souls aforetime have inspired and guided worlds, and if we be not wholly bewitched by our Rhine-gold, they shall again.

Source: *Atlantic Monthly*, 1902

HOW WELL DID YOU UNDERSTAND THIS SELECTION?

1. What type of education does Du Bois advocate for African Americans?

2. Compare and contrast the ideas of Du Bois and Booker T. Washington regarding education for African Americans. How do the two men differ? Are there any similarities between them? Explain?

3. What does Du Bois think the ultimate value of college education will be for African Americans?

4. Is Du Bois an optimist or a pessimist?

5. What does Du Bois believe will be the consequence for American society if African Americans continue to be denied the right to a college education?

6. How does Du Bois respond to the white charge that African Americans are criminal?

7. How does Du Bois justify allowing African Americans to receive college education?

8. What are Du Bois' ideas on race relations? What does he think is necessary before improvements in race relations can occur?

SELF TEST

MULTIPLE CHOICE: Circle the correct response. The correct answers are given at the end.

1. Who was Andrew Carnegie?
   a. An important financier of the American Revolutionary War.
   b. One of the leaders of the oil refining industry.
   c. A wealthy steel magnet who used vertical integration to control all aspects of his business.
   d. A leader of the Progressive Movement who demanded that government place curbs on big business.

2. Which of the following industries can best be described as the engine that drove the American Industrial Revolution?
   a. Steel.
   b. Railroads.
   c. Oil.
   d. Coal.

3. Which of the following statements best describes the conditions of African Americans during the industrial era?
   a. Most lived in the North and had high paying jobs.
   b. In both the North and South blacks worked in the lowest paying jobs in the worst possible conditions.
   c. Most lived in the West where they worked as cowboys.
   d. Many were able to attend public universities in the South where upon graduation they found high paying jobs.

4. How did big business generally respond to Unions during the Industrial Era?
   a. By refusing to bargain with Unions.
   b. By signing Union contracts beneficial to workers.
   c. By forming company unions that workers could join.
   d. By raising wages to keep union out of factories and mines.

5. How much did immigrant workers earn, on average, during the last decades of the nineteenth century?
   a. $25,000 per year.
   b. $5,000 per year.
   c. $2,500 per year.
   d. $250 to $300 per year.

6. What Presidential candidate in the 1872 election is described as a spiritualist who advocated free love?
   a. Grover Cleveland.
   b. Elizabeth Cady Stanton.
   c. Victoria Woodhull.
   d. Horace Greeley.

7. Why did Congress enact the Sherman Anti-Trust Act?
   a. To encourage companies to become monopolies.
   b. Because monopolies were restricting competition.
   c. Because workers were being abused by large corporations.
   d. So that American companies could expand into overseas markets.

8. One result of American industrialism was:
   a. Safe working conditions in factories.
   b. The location of factories in rural areas.
   c. High wages for women and children.
   d. Explosive population growth in cities.

9. Why did the United States go to war with Spain in 1898?
   a. Because Spain was a barbaric nation.
   b. Because Spain destroyed the American battleship Maine.
   c. Because Spain refused to liberate Cuba.
   d. Because the United States wanted Spanish colonial possessions like Puerto Rico and the Philippines.

10. What did the theory of Social Darwinism hold?
   a. That government should develop affirmative action programs to help minorities.
   b. That an agricultural lifestyle was superior to an industrial lifestyle.
   c. That it was inevitable that a few exceptional people would rise to the top of society.
   d. That the American gene pool was being strengthened by immigration.

ANSWERS:
      1-c; 2-b; 3-b; 4-a; 5-d; 6-c; 7-b; 8-d; 9-d; 10-c

ESSAYS:

1. Discuss the impact the Industrial Revolution had on American politics and government. Pay attention to foreign policy and race relations.

2. Compare and contrast the impact the Industrial Revolution had on farmers and workers. How did both groups respond to industrialism? How successful were workers and farmers in solving problems both groups faced?

3. Should the government have done more to regulate industrialism? Why or why not?

4. Why did Andrew Carnegie and others adopt ideas like the Social Gospel and Social Darwinism? Do these ideas reflect elitism and racism? Why or why not?

OPTIONAL ACTIVITIES: (Use your knowledge **and** imagination.)

1. You are an immigrant in a West Virginia labor camp. Write a letter to a friend in your native country about your experiences in America.

2. You are Booker T. Washington. As president of Tuskegee Institute, you need to hire a new faculty member. Devise a set of interview questions to ask job applicants that reflect your views on African-American education.

3. Read other books in the Oz series written by L. Frank Baum. See if you can find symbolism from other historical periods and events (hint, one Oz book is about feminism).

WEB SITE LISTINGS:

Tsongas Industrial History Center
Educational programs about the American Industrial Revolution. http://www.uml.edu/tsongas/

The Blackstone Valley
The song "Blackstone Valley," written by Charlie Ball and performed by Plainfolk, tells the tale of the river that launched the American Industrial Revolution. http://www.plainfolk.com/BSV.html

Lowell Visitors Bureau
Visit website for historical information on such things as the beginnings of the Industrial Revolution in America. http://www.lowell.org/

Industrial Revolution
(Letsfindout.com) http://www.letsfindout.com/subjects/america/industri.html

Industrial Revolution
(Encyclopedia.com) http://www.encyclopedia.com/articles/06349.html

Carnegie, Andrew
(Encarta® Concise Encyclopedia Article)
http://encarta.msn.com/index/conciseindex/19/019E0000.htm?z=1&pg=2&br=1

Carnegie, Andrew
(Encyclopedia.com) http://www.encyclopedia.com/articles/02322.html

Ford, Henry
http://www.encyclopedia.com/search.asp?target=@DOCTITLE%20Ford%20%20Henry

The Magic of Oz
L. Frank Baum http://sailor.gutenberg.org/etext96/magoz10.txt

Lowell National Historical Park
The official expanded NPS website. Lowell National Historical Park preserves and interprets the history of the American Industrial Revolution in Lowell, MA. The park includes historic cotton textile mills, 5.6 miles of canals, operating gatehouses, and worker housing. http://www.nps.gov/lowe/home.htm

A Historical View of U.S. Immigration Policy
...the U.S. passed the **National Origins Act**. This **act**... www.missouri.edu/~socbrent/immigr.htm

Spotlight Biography: Labor Reformers
As the power and scale of American industry grew during the 19th century, working conditions for most Americans underwent radical change. Mechanized, large-scale factories staffed by unskilled laborers gradually came to replace specialized craftsmen and small workshops. Samuel Gompers, more than any other individual, helped to modernize the unions, organize them on a national scale, and open their doors to unskilled as well as skilled workers. http://educate.si.edu/spotlight/labor.html

United Mine Workers of America
(Encarta® Concise Encyclopedia Article)
http://encarta.msn.com/index/conciseindex/49/0494B000.htm?z=1&pg=2&br=1

The Homestead and Pullman Strikes

In light of the recent depression, the voters of 1896 were concerned with keeping money in their pockets. Within recent public memory lay two major events that led to this unease—the Homestead strike of 1892 and the Pullman Railroad strike of 1894. These two conflicts brought to the surface the deeper issues at work in an age of industrial progress. http://iberia.vassar.edu/1896/strikes.html

Haymarket Square

(Encyclopedia.com) http://www.encyclopedia.com/articles/05722.html

Haymarket Square Riot

(Encarta® Concise Encyclopedia Article)
http://www.encyclopedia.com/search.asp?target=@DOCTITLE%20Haymarket%20Square%20riot

Chapter Fourteen

THE TRANS-MISSOURI
WEST: The Last Frontier

Life west of the Mississippi River was vastly different for people living there than it was for people living east of the Mississippi River before the twentieth century. Native Americans were being forced onto reservations and conflict erupted when whites took Native American land by measures such as the Dawes Act. Native American leaders such as Red Cloud and W.C. Duncan protested before Congress and the American public but their words generally fell on deaf ears. After the Civil War thousands of farmers, miners, and outlaws went west seeking their fortune. These people did not care whether they took land from Native Americans; after all, they viewed Indians as standing in the way of progress. This migration was made possible in part by completion of the Transcontinental Railroad after the federal government offered huge subsidies to railroad companies willing to build this line. Life, for most, was difficult. Social mobility was no easier out West than it was back East. Individuals who came west with money had a much better chance of becoming wealthy than poor people. The West was, however, something of a melting pot as people from all over the world intermingled. Despite the multicultural nature of western society, ethnic minorities in western territories faced racism, prejudice, and discrimination. Congress passed the Chinese Exclusion Act to prevent more Chinese immigrants from settling in the West. Tejanos in Texas and other western states saw their land taken by white settlers. Conflict sometimes broke out between whites and Hispanics, between sheep ranchers and cattle barons, between miners and corporations, and between farmers and ranchers. During this time many myths about the West were created and passed down to future generations of Americans. The lonely cowboy, the gunfighter, the rancher, etc. are all images Americans living today think of when the West is mentioned. While the western myth has some validity, most of it is not true. Ironically, at the very time the western myth was being created, the West was ending. In 1880 the United States Census Bureau declared the frontier to be officially closed.

The Populist Party arose in the West and made a mark on the American political landscape. Its candidate, William Jennings Bryan, ran a spirited campaign in 1896 when he and western farmers indicted the Republicans for standing behind the gold standard. In many respects the 1896 election represents a clash between the old America, a land of farms, ranchers, and independent individuals, with the new America, a land of corporate monoliths, workers enslaved to the factory, and robber barons who made vast fortunes from the sweat of millions of ordinary laborers.

IDENTIFICATION: Briefly describe each term.

Chief Joseph

Buffalo Bill Cody

Blackfeet

Little Crow

Sioux

Quaker Policy

Heroes of Sand Creek

George Armstrong Custer

Crazy Horse

Sitting Bull

Geronimo

Wounded Knee

Ghost Dance

Dawes Act

Chinese Exclusion Act

Workingmen's Party

Santa Fe Ring

Texas Rangers

Exodusters

Buffalo Soldiers

Comstock Lode

Western Federation of Miners

Joseph McCoy

Johnson County War

Code of the West

Lincoln County War

O.K. Coral

Leland Stanford

Homestead Act of 1862

Defeated Legion

Morrill Act

Grange (Patrons of Husbandry)

Wabash Case

Interstate Commerce Commission

Populist Movement

William McKinley

William Jennings Bryan

Yellowstone National Park

Annie Oakley

Mark Twain

THINK ABOUT:

1. Describe Native American societies in the West. What importance did the buffalo play in these societies? What did the slaughter of the buffalo mean for Native Americans living in the West? What role did government policy play in the decline of Native American societies?

2. Describe your life as a Chinese immigrant? How do you feel about your treatment at the hands of the American government?

3. Examine the views of the Grangers, the Populist, and the Republicans. How were they different? How were they similar?

4. How did life in the West differ from life in the East?

5. Describe your life as a homesteader in the West. What process did you have to follow to acquire land?

THE HOMESTEAD ACT

Passage of the Homestead Act by Congress in 1862 created the first program for making public lands available to ordinary Americans. Thousands of Americans went west in search of new lands. By the time the Civil War had ended, about 15,000 homestead claims had been filed with the government. Thousands of additional claims were filed during the two decades following the war. Most people filing claims were poor farmers from the East and Midwest; city dwellers generally lacked the resources and knowledge to farm in the West. The Homestead Act was responsible for Native Americans losing most of their land from 1862 until 1890. Americans who homesteaded in western states usually faced countless hardships, ranging from periodic droughts to erosion and violence. Some preserved while others gave up and went back east.

An act to secure homesteads to actual settlers on the public domain.

Be it enacted, that any person who is the head of a family, or who has arrived at the age of twenty-one years, and is a citizen of the United States, or who shall have filed his declaration of intention to become such, as required by the naturalization laws of the United States, and who has never born arms against the United States Government or given aid and comfort to its enemies, shall, from and after the first of January, eighteen hundred and sixty-three, be entitled to enter one quarter-section or a less quantity of unappropriated public lands, upon which said person may have filed a pre-emption claim, or which may, at the time the application is made be subject to pre-emption at one dollar and twenty-five cents, or less, per acre; or eighty acres or less of such unappropriated lands, at two dollars and fifty cents per acre, to be located in a body, in conformity to the legal subdivisions of the public lands, and after the same shall have been surveyed; Provided, that any person owning or residing on land may, under the provisions of this act, enter other land lying contiguous to his or her said land, which shall not, with the land so already owned and occupied, exceed in the aggregate one hundred and sixty acres.

Section 2. That the person applying for the benefit of this act shall, upon application to the register of the land office in which he or she is about to make such entry, make affidavit before the said register or receiver that he or she is the head of a family, or is twenty-one or more years of age, or shall have performed service in the Army or Navy of the United States, and that he has never born arms against the Government of the United States or given aid and comfort to its enemies, and that such application is made for his or her exclusive use and benefit, and that said entry is made for the purpose of actual settlement and cultivation, and not, either directly or indirectly, for the use or benefit of any other person or persons whomsoever; and upon filing the said affidavit with the register or re-ceiver, and on payment of ten dollars, he or she shall thereupon be permitted to enter the quantity of land specified: Provided, however, that no certificate shall be given or patent issued therefore until the expiration of five years from the date of such entry; and if, at the expiration of such time, or at any time within two years thereafter, the person making such entry—or if he be dead, his widow; or in case of her death, his heirs or devisee; or in case of a widow making such entry, her heirs or devise, in case of her death—shall prove by two credible witnesses that he, she, or they have resided upon or cultivated the same for the term of five years immediately succeeding the time of filing the affidavit aforesaid, and shall make affidavit that no part of said land has been alienated, and that he has born true allegiance to the Government of the United States; then, in such case, he, she, or they, if at that time a citizen of the United States, shall be entitled to a patent, as in other cases provided for by law; And provided, further, that in case of the death of both father and mother, leaving an infant child or children under twenty-one years of age, the right and fee shall inure to the benefit of said infant child or children; and the executor, administrator, or guardian may, at any time within two years after the death of the surviving parent, and in accordance with the laws of the State in which such children for the time being have their domicile, sell said land for the benefit of said infants, but for no other purpose; and the purchaser shall acquire the absolute title by the purchase, and be entitled to a patent from the United States, on payment of the office fees and sum of money herein specified....

Source: U.S. Statutes at Large, Vol. 12

HOW WELL DID YOU UNDERSTAND THIS SELECTION?

1. Why did Congress enact the Homestead Act?

2. How much land could the head of a family acquire?

3. How much did the land cost the homesteader?

4. What effect did the Homestead Act have on settlement in the West? On Native Americans?

Perhaps the most important development in the history of the American West was construction of the transcontinental railroad. This railroad, which connected the East to the West, made it possible for western farmers and ranchers to get their crops and livestock to market. The transcontinental railroad would not likely have been built had the government not given tremendous subsidies to companies engaged in building the railway. The Pacific Railway Act, passed by Congress on July 1, 1862, made possible the construction of a railroad and telegraph line from the Missouri River to the Pacific Ocean.

Section 1. Be it enacted, That...five commissioners to be appointed by the Secretary of the Interior...are...erected into a body corporate...by the name of..."The Union Pacific Railroad Company"...and the...corporation is hereby authorized...to lay out, locate, construct, furnish, maintain and enjoy a continuous railroad and telegraph...from a point on the one hundredth meridian of longitude west from Greenwich, between the south margin of the valley of the Republican River and the north margin of the valley of the Platte River, to the western boundary of Nevada Territory, upon the route and terms hereinafter provided...

Section 2. That the right of way through...public lands be...granted to said company for the construction of said railroad and telegraph line; and the right...is hereby given to said company to take from the public lands adjacent to the line of said road, earth, stone, timber, and other materials for the construction thereof; said right of way is granted to said railroad to the extent of two hundred feet in width on each side of said railroad when it may pass over the public lands, including all necessary grounds, for stations, buildings, workshops, and depots, machine shops, switches, side tracks, turn tables, and water stations. The United States shall extinguish as rapidly as may be the Indian titles to all lands falling under the operation of this act...

Section 3. That there be...granted...for the purpose of aiding in the construction of...railroad and telegraph line, and to secure the safe and speedy transportation of mail, troops, munitions of war, and public stores thereon, every alternate section of public land, designated by odd numbers, to the amount of five alternate sections per mile on each side of said railroad, on the line thereof, and within the limits of ten miles on each side of...road... Provided That all mineral lands shall be excepted from the operation of act; but where the same shall contain timber, the timber thereon is...granted to said company...

Section 5. That for the purposes herein mentioned the Secretary of the Treasury shall...in accordance with the provisions of this act, issue to said company bonds of the United States of one thousand dollars each, payable in thirty years after date, paying six per centum per annum interest...to the amount of sixteen of said bonds per mile for each section of forty miles; and to secure the repayment to the United States...of the amount of said bonds...the issue of said bonds...shall ipso facto constitute a first mortgage on the whole line of the railroad and telegraph...

Section 9. That the Leavenworth, Pawnee and Western Railroad Company of Kansas are hereby authorized to construct a railroad and telegraph line...upon the same terms and conditions in all respects as are provided.... The Central Pacific Railroad Company of California is hereby authorized to construct a railroad and telegraph line from the Pacific coast...to the eastern boundaries of California, upon the same terms and conditions in all respects.

Section 10. ...And the Central Pacific Railroad Company of California after completing its road...is authorized to continue...construction...through the Territories of the United States to the Missouri River...upon the terms and conditions provided in this act...until said roads shall...connect...

Section 11. That for three hundred miles of said road most mountainous and difficult of construction, to wit: one hundred and fifty miles westerly from the eastern base of the Rocky Mountains, and one hundred and fifty miles eastwardly from the western base of the Sierra Nevada mountains...the bonds to be issued to aid in the construction thereof shall be treble the number per mile herein before provided...and between the sections last named of one hundred and fifty miles each, the bonds to be issued to aid in the constructions…shall be double the number per mile first mentioned…

Source: U.S. Statutes at Large, Vol. 12

HOW WELL DID YOU UNDERSTAND THIS SELECTION?

1. Why did Congress enact the Pacific Railway Act?

2. What incentives are railroads given to lay track across the West?

3. How did the government plan to finance the building of the transcontinental railroad?

4. What do you think would be the Populist Party's reaction to the fact that the government gave railroads so much western land? Why?

RED CLOUD SPEECH AT COOPER UNION, NEW YORK

Chief Red Cloud was one of the most important leaders of the Lakota Sioux. He was born in 1822 near the forks of the Platte River near what is now North Platte, Nebraska and died in 1909. Much of his early life was spent fighting whites and other Native American tribes in the West. His exploits as a warrior gave him enormous prominence within the Lakota nation. In 1866 Red Cloud led the Sioux in a war against the United States that represents the most successful conflict ever by a Native American tribe against the American government. The trouble began when the United States Army constructed forts along the Bozeman Trail in Wyoming to protect settlers and miners going to Montana and Colorado. Red Cloud attacked theses forts and defeated American forces, which caused the United States government in 1868 to sign the Fort Laramie Treaty, mandating that the United States would abandon its forts along the Bozeman Trail and guarantee the Lakota possession of the western half of South Dakota.

My brethren and my friends who are here before me this day. God Almighty has made us all, and He is here to bless what I have to say to you today. The Good Spirit made us both. He gave you lands and he gave us lands; he gave us these lands. You came in here, and we respected you as brothers. God Almighty made you but made you all white and clothed you. When he made us he made us with red skins and poor; now you have come.

When you first came we were very many, and you were few. Now you are many, and we are getting very few, and we are poor. You do not know who appears before you today to speak. I am a representative of the original American race, the first people of this continent. We are good and not bad. The reports that you hear concerning us are all on one side. We are always well disposed to them. You are here told that we are traitors and thieves, and it is not so. We have given you nearly all our lands, and if we had any more land to give we would be very glad to give it. We have nothing more. We are driven into a very little land, and we want you now, as our dear friends, to help us with the government of the United States.

The Great Father made us poor and ignorant—made you rich and wise and more skillful in these things that we know nothing about. The Great Father, the Good Father in heaven, made you all to eat tame food—made us to eat wild food—gives us the wild food. You ask anybody who has gone through our country to California; ask those who have settled there and in Utah, and you will find that we have treated them always well. You have children. We have children. You want to raise your children and make them happy and prosperous. We want to raise [ours] and make them happy and prosperous. We ask you to help us to do it.

At the mouth of the Horse Creek, in 1852, the Great Father made a treaty with us by which we agreed to let all that country open for fifty-five years for the transit of those who were going through. We kept this treaty. We never treated any man wrong. We never committed any murder or depredation until after the troops were sent into that country, and the troops killed our people and ill-treated them, and thus war and trouble arose, but before the troops were sent there we were quiet and peaceable, and there was no disturbance. Since that time there have been various goods sent from time to time to us, the only ones that ever reached us. After they reached us the government took them away. You, as good men, ought to help us to these goods.

Colonel Fitzpatrick of the government said we must all go to farm, and some of the people went to Fort Laramie and were badly treated. I only want to do that which is peaceful, and the Great Fathers know it, and also the Great Father who made us both. I came to Washington to see the Great Father in order to have peace and in order to have peace continue. That is all we want, and that is the reason why we are here now.

In 1868 men came out and brought papers. We are ignorant and do not read papers and they did not tell us right what was in these papers. We wanted them to take away their forts, leave our country, would not make war, and give our traders something. They said we had bound ourselves to trade on the Missouri, and we said, no, we did not want that. The interpreters deceived us. When I went to Washington I saw the Great Father. The Great Father showed me what the treaties were; he showed me all these points and showed me that the interpreters had deceived me and did not let me know what the right side of the treaty was. All I want is right and justice…. I represent the Sioux Nation, they will be governed by what I say and what I represent.

Look at me. I am poor and naked, but I am the chief of the Nation. We do not want riches, we do not ask for riches, but we want our children properly trained and brought up. We look to you for your sympathy. Our riches will … do us no good; we cannot take away into the other world anything we have—we want to have love and peace…. We would like to know why commissioners are sent out there to do nothing but rob [us] and get the riches of this world away from us?

I was brought up among the traders and those who came out there in those early times. I had a good time for they treated us nicely and well. They taught me how to wear clothes and use tobacco, and to use firearms and ammunition, and all went on very well until the Great Father sent out another kind of men—men who drank whisky. He sent out whisky men, men who drank and quarreled, men who were so bad that he could not keep them at home, and so he sent them out there.

I have sent a great many words to the Great Father, but I don't know that they ever reach the Great Father. They were drowned on the way, therefore I was a little offended with it. The words I told the Great Father lately would never come to him, so I thought I would come and tell you myself.

And I am going to leave you today, and I am going back to my home. I want to tell the people that we cannot trust his agents and superintendents. I don't want strange people that we know nothing about. I am very glad that you belong to us. I am very glad that we have come here and found you and that we can understand one another. I don't want any more such men sent out there, who are so poor that when they come out there their first thoughts are how they can fill their own pockets.

We want preserves in our reserves. We want honest men, and we want you to help to keep us in the lands that belong to us so that we may not be a prey to those who are viciously disposed. I am going back home. I am very glad that you have listened to me, and I wish you good-bye and give you an affectionate farewell.

Source: *The New York Times*, July 17, 1870

HOW WELL DID YOU UNDERSTAND THIS SELECTION?

1. How does Red Cloud describe Native Americans?

2. How does Red Cloud describe whites?

3. What similarities and differences does Red Cloud see in whites and Native Americans?

4. How does Red Cloud describe relations between Native Americans and the United States government?

5. Who is Red Cloud? What does he want? What is he doing?

THE DAWES ACT

The Dawes Act, passed by Congress in 1887 was designed to impose assimilation on all Native American tribes and enable land-hungry whites to take lands delegated to Indian peoples. By the 1880s most Native Americans were living on reservations. Many whites believed that the reservations were too large and wanted thousands of acres of land encompassed in these reservations taken away from Native Americans and given to white farmers. Congress, bowing to pressure from farmers and ranchers, passed the General Allotment Act (Dawes Act), which gave individual Indian families 160 acres of land. The hundreds of thousands of acres remaining were then sold at bargain prices to whites, many of whom were land speculators. Native Americans felt cheated again by the United States government. The land most were left with was not large enough to support a family. The Dawes Act is partly responsible for the poverty Native Americans living on reservations experienced during the nineteenth and twentieth centuries.

Be it enacted. That in all cases where any tribe or band of Indians has been, or shall hereafter be, located upon any reservation created for their use, either by treaty stipulation or by virtue of an act of Congress or executive order setting apart the same for their use, the President of the United States be, and he hereby is, authorized, whenever in his opinion any reservation or any part thereof of such Indians is advantageous for agriculture and grazing purposes to cause said reservation, or any part thereof, to be surveyed, or resurveyed if necessary, and to allot the lands in said reservation in severally to any Indian located thereon in quantities as follows: To each head of a family, one-quarter of a section; To each single person over eighteen years of age, one-eighth of a section; To each orphan child under eighteen years of age, one-eight of a section; and, To each other single person under eighteen years now living, or who may be born prior to the date of the order of the President directing an allotment of the lands embraced in any reservation, one-sixteenth of a section: ... .

That upon the approval of the allotments provided for in this act by the Secretary of the Interior, he shall ... declare that the United States does and will hold the land thus allotted, for the period of twenty-five years, in trust for the sole use and benefit of the Indian to whom such allotment shall have been made, ... and that at the expiration of said period the United States will convey the same by patent to said Indian, or his heirs as aforesaid, in fee, discharged of such trust and free of all charge or encumbrance whatsoever:...

That upon the completion of said allotments and the patenting of the lands to said allottees, each and every member of the respective bands or tribes of Indians to whom allotments have been made shall have the benefit of and be subject to the laws, both civil and criminal, of the State or Territory in which they may reside, ... And every Indian born within the territorial limits of the United States to whom allotments shall have been made under the provisions of this act or under any law or treaty, and every Indian born within the territorial limits of the United States who has voluntarily taken up, within said limits, his residence separate and apart from any tribe of Indians therein, and has adopted the habits of civilized life, is hereby declared to be a citizen of the United States, and is entitled to all the rights, privileges, and immunities of such citizens, whether said Indian has been or not, by birth or otherwise, a member of any tribe of Indians within the territorial limits of the United States without in any manner impairing or otherwise affecting the right of any such Indian to tribal or other property....

Source: United States Statutes at Large, Vol. 24

HOW WELL DID YOU UNDERSTAND THIS SELECTION?

1. What was the primary purpose of the Dawes Act?

2. How much land did Native Americans receive under the Dawes Act?

3. What effect do you think the Dawes Act had on Native Americans?

4. If you were a Native American, how would you have felt about the Dawes Act?

D. W. C. Duncan was a Cherokee Indian who testified before a United States Senate Committee in 1906 investigating the condition of Native Americans in the West. He testified against the General Allotment Act (the Dawes Act), which took land from Native Americans and allowed land speculators and white farmers to buy it at cheap prices from the government. His testimony provides a valuable record of the effect the Dawes Act had on Native Americans in the West. As his testimony makes clear, Native Americans were impoverished by this law.

Senators, just let me present to you a picture; I know this is a little digression, but let me present it. Suppose the Federal Government should send a survey company into the midst of some of your central counties of Kansas or Colorado or Connecticut and run off the surface of the earth into sections and quarter sections and quarter quarter sections and set apart to each one of the inhabitants of that county 60 acres, rescinding and annulling all title to every inch of the earth's surface which was not included in that 60 acres, would the State of Connecticut submit to it? Would Colorado submit to it? Would Kansas brook such an outrage? No! It would be ruin, immeasurable ruin—devastation. There is not an American citizen in any one of those states would submit to it, if it cost him every drop of his heart's blood. That, my Senators, permit me—I am honest, candid, and fraternal in my feelings—but let me ask a question? Who is that hastened on this terrible destruction upon these Cherokee people? Pardon me, it was the Federal Government. It is a fact; and, old as I am, I am not capable of indulging in euphemisms.

Before this allotment scheme was put in effect in the Cherokee Nation we were a prosperous people. We had farms. Every Indian in this nation that needed one and felt that he needed one had it. Orchards and gardens—everything that promoted the comforts of private life was ours, even as you—probably not so extensively—so far as we went, even as you in the States. The result has been, which I now want to illustrate, as I set out, by my own personal experience.

Under our old Cherokee regime I spent the early days of my life on the farm up here of 300 acres, and arranged to be comfortable in my old age, but the allotment scheme came along and struck me during the crop season while my corn was ripening in full ear. I was looking forward to the crop of corn hopefully for some comforts to be derived from it during the months of the winter. When I was assigned to that 60 acres, and I could take no more under the inexorable law of allotment enforced upon us Cherokees, I had to relinquish every inch of my premises outside of that little 60 acres. What is the result? There is a great scramble of persons to find land—the office was located here in our town— to file upon. Some of the friends in here, especially a white intermarried citizen, goes up and files upon a part of my farm—on a part of my growing crop, upon the crop upon which I had spent my labor and my money, and upon which I had based my hopes. I remonstrated with him. I said to him, "Sir, you don't want to treat me that way. We are neighbors and friends. You can't afford to take my property that way. Of course the Dawes Commission and the Curtis law will give you the land, although I have subdued it, and I have fenced it, and cultivated it. But for God's sake, my friend, don't take my crop." "Well," says he, "I had to surrender my crop to a fellow down here. He allotted on me, and I don't know why I should be any more lenient on you than others are on me. If you don't let that corn alone, I will go to the court and get an order." That was new to me, but when I came to examine the Curtis law, and investigated the orders and rules established by the Dawes Commission, I just folded my hands and said, "I give it up." Away went my crop, and if the same rule had been established in your counties in your State you would have lost your dwelling house, you would have lost your improvements. Now, that is what has been done to these Cherokees.

What a condition, I have 60 acres of land left me, the balance is all gone. I am an old man, not able to follow the plow as I used to when a boy. What am I going to do with it? For the last few years, since I have had my allotment, I have gone out there on that farm day after day I have used the ax, the hoe, the spade, the plow, hour for hour, until fatigue would throw me exhausted upon the ground. Next day I repeated the operation, and let me tell you, Senators, I have exerted all my ability, all industry, all my intelligence, if I have any, my will, my ambition, the love of my wife, all these agencies, I have employed to make my living out of that 60 acres, and God be my judge, I have not been able to do it. I am not able to do it. I can't do it. I have not been able to clear expenses. It will take every ear of the bounteous crop on that 60 acres, for this year is a pretty good crop year, it will take every bushel of it to satisfy the debts that I have incurred to eke out a living during the meager years just passed. And I am here today, a poor man upon the verge of starvation, my muscular energy gone. Hope gone I have nothing to charge my calamity to but the unwise legislation of Congress in reference to my Cherokee people.

I am in that fix. Senators, you will not forget now that when I use the word I, I mean the whole Cherokee people. I am in that fix. What am I to do? I have a piece of property that doesn't support me, and is not worth a cent to me under the same inexorable cruel provisions of the Curtis law that swept away our treaties, our system of nationality, our every existence, and wrested out of our possession our vast territory. The same provisions of that Curtis law that ought to have been satisfied with these achievements didn't stop there. The law goes on and that 60 acres of land, it says, shall not be worth one cent to me, although the Curtis law has given me 60 acres as the only inheritance I have in God's world, even that shall not be worth anything. Let me explain.

If you had a horse that you couldn't use, and some competent power ordained that that horse should have no value in any market on the face of the earth, and at the same time you should be compelled to keep that horse as long as he should live, or at least twenty-five years, at your expense, now, in the name of common sense, what would you do with that horse? He is not worth anything, his services are not worth anything to me, I can't ride him, I can't use him. There is no man in the world that will give me a cent for him, the law won't allow me to sell him. I would get rid of that horse somehow sure.

The point I am making here is applicable to every species of property, whether real or personal. Prevent the property from being purchasable in open market and you destroy it. Upon the same principle, my allotment up here is absolutely destroyed. What am I going to do with it? What can any Indian do with his allotment under similar circumstances?

Let me allude to myself again. It is not egotism I will tell you what I am going to do with my allotment. I sat down one day and wrote out my application for the removal of my restrictions. I went to work and pushed it through all the Federal machinery up to the Secretary of the Interior and back again, and a few days ago I was notified my restrictions were raised. Now for the next step. What am I going to do with that worthless piece of properly? I am going to hold it—how long I don't know—but I am going to wait until the white population becomes a little more multitudinous, when the price of real estate will rise. When I can get anything like an adequate value for my farm I am going to sell it. It is worthless to me.

The Government of the United States knows that these allotments of the Indians are not sufficient. Congress recognizes the fact forcibly, by implication, that these allotments are not sufficient. Why, one American citizen goes out on the western plain in North Dakota to make a home. What is the amount of land allotted to him? Isn't it 160 acres? Why, it is the general consensus all over the country that nothing less would be sufficient to support any family, and there are many years when you think, too, that 160 acres is not sufficient. Since this country has been split up, the Cherokee government abolished, and the allotments attained, immigration has come in from the surrounding States, consisting of persons of different kinds. I have tested them, and know what I am talking about, personally. Persons in pursuit of a sufficient quantity of land upon which to rear their families and take care of themselves, I have interrogated them time and again. I have said to them. "Look here, my friend, where are you going?" "To Indian Territory." "What for?" "To get a piece of land." "Did you have any land in Missouri or Kansas?" "Yes, sir; I had some up there, but it was too small and wasn't sufficient." "How much was it?" "Eighty or one hundred acres," as the case may be. "I have leased out my land up there to parties, and thought I would come down here and get a larger piece of ground." Well, now, that is the state of the case. I think, gentlemen, when you investigate the case fully you will find that these people have been put off with a piece of land that is absolutely inadequate for their needs.

Source: U.S. Senate Report 5013, 59th Congress, 2nd Session

HOW WELL DID YOU UNDERSTAND THIS SELECTION?

1. Who is Duncan? What is he reacting to?

2. How does Duncan describe Cherokee life before the Curtis Law took effect?

3. What happened to Duncan as a result of the Curtis Law?

4. What does Duncan want Congress to do?

REPORT ON WOUNDED KNEE MASSACRE, By Benjamin Harrison

Wounded Knee was the last battle fought between American forces and Native Americans in the West. On December 29, 1890, the Seventh Calvary (the unit massacred at Little Big Horn) of the United States Army and a group of Sioux Indians engaged in a skirmish that resulted in 64 casualties. In addition, 51 Indians, most of whom were women and children, were wounded. The battle was precipitated when the Sioux began to follow the prophet Wovoka and perform the Ghost Dance, which they believed would restore the tribe to its former glory. Settlers and Indian agents feared that this dancing might lead to renewed conflict and tried to suppress it. In the suppression the aging chief, Sitting Bull, was killed. The army feared that his death might cause an Indian uprising, and the Seventh Cavalry rounded up over three hundred Sioux who had left the reservation and camped at Wounded Knee, South Dakota. After the army had began the process of disarming the Sioux, one Indian, intentionally or unintentionally (the evidence is unclear) fired a hidden gun. The troops, fearing they were under attack, opened fire on the Sioux. Indians who had not yet been disarmed returned fire at the troops, killing 25 members of the Seventh Calvary. Bodies of the dead Sioux were buried in a mass grave and the wounded were carried to a local missionary church where they lay beneath a banner proclaiming "Peace on Earth; Good Will to Men." President Harrison addressed Congress about the Battle of Wounded Knee on December 9, 1891.

The outbreak among the Sioux which occurred in December last is as to its causes and incidents fully reported upon by the War Department and the Department of the Interior. That these Indians had some just complaints, especially in the matter of the reduction of the appropriation for rations and in the delays attending the enactment of laws to enable the Department to perform the engagements entered into with them, is probably true; but the Sioux tribes are naturally warlike and turbulent, and their warriors were excited by their medicine men and chiefs, who preached the coming of an Indian messiah who was to give them power to destroy their enemies. In view of the alarm that prevailed among the white settlers near the reservation and of the fatal consequences that would have resulted from an Indian incursion, I placed at the disposal of General Miles, commanding the Division of the Missouri, all such forces as we thought by him to be required. He is entitled to the credit of having given thorough protection to the settlers and of bringing the hostiles into subjection with the least possible loss of life. . . .

Since March 4, 1889, about 23,000,000 acres have been separated from Indian reservations and added to the public domain for the use of those who desired to secure free homes under our beneficent laws. It is difficult to estimate the increase of wealth which will result from the conversion of these waste lands into farms, but it is more difficult to estimate the betterment which will result to the families that have found renewed hope and courage in the ownership of a home and the assurance of a comfortable subsistence under free and healthful conditions. It is also gratifying to be able to feel, as we may, that this work has proceeded upon lines of justice toward the Indian, and that he may now, if he will, secure to himself the good influences of a settled habitation, the fruits of industry, and the security of citizenship.

Source: Third Annual Message to Congress, Dec. 9, 1891

HOW WELL DID YOU UNDERSTAND THIS SELECTION?

1. How does Harrison view the Sioux? Did Americans view all Native Americans in this light? Why or Why not?

2. What reason did the Sioux have for fighting American forces at Wounded Knee?

3. What does American policy attempt to force Native Americans to do?

BRYAN'S CROSS OF GOLD SPEECH

William Jennings Bryan was the Populist/Democratic candidate for president in 1896 and again in 1900. He was noted as a spectacular orator. In 1896 he criss-crossed the United States and made hundreds of speeches in attempt to convince voters to support him against William McKinley in the presidential election. He captured the Democratic presidential nomination in 1896 with his famous "Cross of Gold" speech in which he supported inflation of the American currency through the free coinage of silver. This position was important to Westerners, as most silver produced in the United States was mined in the West and farmers and ranchers living west of the Missouri River faced economic difficulties they believed inflation would solve. Bryan did not win the presidency, but the "Cross of Gold" speech is considered one of the best examples of political oratory in American political history.

Mr. Chairman and Gentlemen of the Convention I would be presumptuous, indeed, to present myself against the distinguished gentlemen to whom you have listened if this were a mere measuring of abilities, but this is not a contest between persons. The humblest citizen in all the land, when clad in the armor of a righteous cause, is stronger than all the hosts of error. I come to speak to you in defense of a cause as holy as the cause of liberty—the cause of humanity.

Never before in the history of this country has there been witnessed such a contest as that through which we have just passed. Never before in the history of American politics has a great issue been fought out as this issue has been, by the voters of a great party. With a zeal approaching the zeal which inspired the crusaders who followed Peter the hermit, our silver Democrats went forth from victory unto victory until they are now assembled, not to discuss, not to debate, but to enter up the judgment already rendered by the plain people of this country. In this contest brother has been arrayed against brother, father against son, the warmest ties of love, acquaintance and association have been disregarded, old leaders have been cast aside when they have refused to give expression to the sentiments of those whom they would lead, and new leaders have sprung up to give direction to the cause of truth. Thus has the contest been waged, and we have assembled here under as binding and solemn instructions as were ever imposed upon representatives of the people.

71

The gentleman who preceded me [Governor Russell, the former governor of MA.) spoke of the State of Massachusetts, let me assure him that not one present in all this convention entertains the least hostility to the people of the State of Massachusetts, but we stand here representing people who are the equals, before the law, of the greatest citizens in the State of Massachusetts. When you [the gold delegates] come before us and tell us that we are about to disturb your business interests, we reply that you have disturbed our business interests by your course.

We say to you that you have made the definition of a business man too limited in its application. The man who is employed for wages is as much a business man as his employer, the attorney in a country town is as much a business man as the corporation counsel in a great metropolis, the merchant at the cross-roads store is as much a business man as the merchant of New York, the farmer who goes forth in the morning and toils all day—who begins in the spring and toils all summer—and who by the application of brain and muscle to the natural resources of the country creates wealth, is as much a business man as the man who goes upon the board of trade and bets upon the price of grain, the miners who go down a thousand feet into the earth, or climb two thousand feet upon the cliffs, and bring forth from their hiding places the precious metals to be poured into the channels of trade are as much business men as the few financial magnates who, in a back room, corner the money of the world. We come to speak for this broader class of businessmen.

Ah, my friends, we say not one word against those who live upon the Atlantic coast, but the hardy pioneers who have braved all the dangers of the wilderness, who have made the desert to blossom as the rose—the pioneers away out there [in the West], who rear their children near to nature's heart, where they can mingle their voices with the voices of the birds—out there where they have erected schoolhouses for the education of their young, churches where they praise their Creator, and cemeteries where rest the ashes of their dead—these people, we say, are as deserving of the consideration of our party as any people in this country. It is for these that we speak. We do not come as aggressors. Our war is not a war of conquest, we are fighting in the defense of our homes, our families, and posterity. We have petitioned, and our petitions have been scorned, we have entreated, and our entreaties have been disregarded, we have begged, and they have mocked when our calamity came. We beg no longer, we entreat no more, we petition no more. We defy them.

The gentleman [Senator Vilas] from Wisconsin has said that he fears a Robespierre. My friends, in this land of the free you need not fear that a tyrant will spring up from among the people. What we need is an Andrew Jackson to stand, as Jackson stood, against the encroachments of organized wealth.

They tell us that this platform was made to catch votes. We reply to them that changing conditions make new issues, that the principles upon which democracy rests are as everlasting as the hills, but that they must be applied to new conditions as they arise. Conditions have arisen, and we are here to meet those conditions. They tell us that the income tax ought not to be brought in here, that it is a new idea. They criticize us for our criticism of the Supreme Court of the United States. My friends, we have not criticized, we have simply called attention to what you already know. If you want criticisms, read the dissenting opinions of the court. There you will find criticisms. They say that we passed an unconstitutional law, we deny it. The income tax law was not unconstitutional when it was passed, it was not unconstitutional when it went before the Supreme Court for the first time, it did not become unconstitutional until one of the judges changed his mind, and we cannot be expected to know when a judge will change his mind. The income tax is just. It simply intends to put the burdens of government justly upon the backs of the people. I am in favor of an income tax. When I find a man who is not willing to bear his share of the burdens of the government which protects him, I find a man who is unworthy to enjoy the blessings of a government like ours.

They say that we are opposing national bank currency, it is true. If you will read what Thomas Benton said, you will find he said that, in searching history, he could find but one parallel to Andrew Jackson, that was Cicero, who destroyed the conspiracy of Cataline and saved Rome. Benton said that Cicero only did for Rome what Jackson did for us when he destroyed the bank conspiracy and saved America. We say in our platform that we believe that the right to coin and issue money is a function of government. We believe it. We believe that it is a part of sovereignty, and can no more with safety be delegated to private individuals than we could afford to delegate to private individuals the power to make penal statutes or levy taxes. Mr. Jefferson, who was once regarded as good Democratic authority, seems to have differed in opinion from the gentleman who has addressed us on the part of the minority. Those who are opposed to this proposition tell us that the issue of paper money is a function of the bank, and that the Government ought to go out of the banking business. I stand with Jefferson rather than with them, and tell them, as he did, that the issue of money is a function of government, and that the banks ought to go out of the governing business.

They complain about the plank, which declares against life tenure in office. They have tried to strain it to mean that which it does not mean. What we oppose by that plank is the life tenure, which is being built up in Washington, and which excludes from participation in official benefits the humbler members of society.

Let me call your attention to two or three important things. The gentleman from New York says that he will propose an amendment to the platform providing that the proposed change in our monetary system shall not affect contracts already made. Let me remind you that there is no intention of affecting those contracts which according to present laws are made payable in gold, but if he means to say that we cannot change our monetary system without protecting those who have loaned money before the change was made, I desire to ask him where, in law or in morals, he can find justification for not protecting the debtors when the act of 1873 was passed, if he now insists that we must protect the creditors.

He says he will also propose an amendment, which will provide for the suspension of free coinage if we fail to maintain the parity within a year. We reply that when we advocate a policy which we believe will be successful, we are not compelled to raise a doubt as to our own sincerity by suggesting what we shall do if we fail. I ask him, if he would apply his logic to us, why he does not apply it to himself. He says he wants this country to try to secure an international agreement. Why does he not tell us what he is going to do if he fails to secure an international agreement? There is more reason for him to do that than there is for us to provide against the failure to maintain the parity. Our opponents have tried for twenty years to secure an international agreement, and those are waiting for it most patiently who do not want it at all.

And now, my friends, let me come to the paramount issue. If they ask us why it is that we say more on the money question than we say upon the tariff question, I reply that, if protection has slain its thousands, the gold standard has slain its tens of thousands. If they ask us why we do not embody in our platform all the things that we believe in, we reply that when we have restored the money of the Constitution all other necessary reforms will be possible, but that until this is done there is no other reform that can be accomplished.

Why is it that within three months such a change has come over the country? Three months ago, when it was confidently asserted that those who believe in the gold standard would frame our platform and nominate our candidates, even the advocates of the gold standard did not think that we could elect a president. And they had good reason for their doubt, because there is scarcely a state here today asking for the gold standard, which is not in the absolute control of the Republican Party. But note the change. Mr. McKinley was nominated at St. Louis upon a platform, which declared for the maintenance of the gold standard until it can be changed into bimetallism by international agreement. Mr. McKinley was the most popular man among the Republicans, and three months ago everybody in the Republican Party prophesied his election. How is it today? Why, the man who was once pleased to think that he looked like Napoleon—that man shudders today when he remembers that he was nominated on the anniversary of the battle of Waterloo. Not only that, but as he listens he can hear with ever-increasing distinctness the sound of the waves as they beat upon the lonely shores of St. Helena.

Why this change? Ah, my friends, is not the reason for the change evident to any one who will look at the matter? No private character, however pure, no personal popularity, however great, can protect from the avenging wrath of an indignant people a man who will declare that he is in favor of fastening the gold standard upon this country, or who is willing to surrender the right of self-government and place the legislative control of our affairs in the hands of foreign potentates and powers.

We go forth confident that we shall win. Why? Because upon the paramount issue of this campaign there is not a spot of ground upon which the enemy will dare to challenge battle. If they tell us that the gold standard is a good thing, we shall point to their platform and tell them that their platform pledges the party to get rid of the gold standard and substitute bimetallism. If the gold standard is a good thing, why try to get rid of it? I call your

73

attention to the fact that some of the very people who are in this convention today and who tell us that we ought to declare in favor of international bimetallism— thereby declaring that the gold standard is wrong and that the principle of bimetallism is better—these very people four months ago were open and avowed advocates of the gold standard, and were then telling us that we could not legislate two metals together, even with the aid of all the world. If the gold standard is a good thing, we ought to declare in favor of its retention and not in favor of abandoning it, and if the gold standard is a bad thing why should we wait until other nations are willing to help us to let go? Here is the line of battle, and we care not upon which issue they force the fight, we are prepared to meet them on either issue or on both. If they tell us that the gold standard is the standard of civilization, we reply to them that this, the most enlightened of all the nations of the earth, has never declared for a gold standard and that both the great parties this year are declaring against it. If the gold standard is the standard of civilization, why, my friends, should we not have it? If they come to meet us on that issue we can present the history of our nation. More than that, we can tell them that they will search the pages of history in vain to find a single instance where the common people of any land have ever declared themselves in favor of the gold standard. They can find where the holders of the fixed investments have declared for a gold standard, but not where the masses have.

Mr. Carlisle said in 1878 that this was a struggle between "the idle holders of idle capital" and "the struggling masses, who produce the wealth and pay the taxes of the country," and, my friends, the question we are to decide is upon which side will the Democratic party fight; upon the side of "the idle holders of idle capital" or upon the side of "the struggling masses?" That is the question, which the party must answer first, and then it must be answered by each individual hereafter. The sympathies of the Democratic Party, as shown by the platform, are on the side of the struggling masses who have ever been the foundation of the Democratic Party. There are two ideas of government. There are those who believe that, if you will only legislate to make the well to do prosperous, their prosperity will leak through on those below. The Democratic idea, however, has been that if you legislate to make the masses prosperous, their prosperity will find its way up through every class, which rests upon them.

You come to us and tell us that the great cities are in favor of the gold standard, we reply that the great cities rest upon our broad and fertile prairies. Burn down your cities and leave our farms, and your cities will spring up again as if by magic, but destroy our farms and the grass will grow in the streets of every city in the country.

My friends, we declare that this nation is able to legislate for its own people on every question, without waiting for the aid or consent of any other nation on earth, and upon that issue we expect to carry every State in the Union. I shall not slander the inhabitants of the fair State of Massachusetts nor the inhabitants of the State of New York by saying that, when they are confronted with the proposition, they will declare that this nation is not able to attend to its own business. It is the issue of 1776 over again. Our ancestors, when but three millions in number, had the courage to declare their political independence of every other nation, shall we, their descendants, when we have grown to seventy millions, declare that we are less independent than our forefathers? No, my friends, that will never be the verdict of our people. Therefore, we care not upon what lines the battle is fought. If they say bimetallism is good, but that we cannot have it until other nations help us, we reply that, instead of having a gold standard because England has, we will restore bimetallism, and then let England have bimetallism because the United States has it. If they dare to come out in the open field and defend the gold standard as a good thing, we will fight them to the uttermost.

Having behind us the producing masses of this nation and the world, supported by the commercial interests, the laboring interests, and the toilers everywhere, we will answer their demand for a gold standard by saying to them: You shall not press down upon the brow of labor this crown of thorns, you shall not crucify mankind upon a cross of gold.

Source: William Jennings Bryan, *The First Battle: A Story of the Campaign of 1896,* Chicago 1897

HOW WELL DID YOU UNDERSTAND THIS SELECTION?

1. Who was William Jennings Bryan? What does he advocate in the "Cross of Gold" speech?

2. Why was his message in the "Cross of Gold" speech so appealing to many Americans in 1896?

3. What is the gold standard? What is bimetallism?

4. What have critics said about Bryan's ideas? How does he answer the critics?

THE PAGE LAW

The Page Law, passed on March 3, 1875, was designed to prohibit immigration of Chinese women for the purpose of prostitution. This act was part of the racism present in the American West against Asian immigrants. While untrue, it was widely believed by Westerners in cities like San Francisco that Chinese "pimps" were importing Chinese women to supply prostitution services to Asian and American laborers.

Be it enacted by the Senate and House of Representatives of the United States of America in Congress-assembled,

That in determining whether the immigration of any subject of China, Japan, or any Oriental country, to the United States, is free and voluntary, as provided by section two thousand one hundred and sixty two of the Revised Code, title "Immigration," it shall be the duty of the consul-general or consul of the United States residing at the port from which it is proposed to convey such subjects, in any vessels enrolled or licensed in the United States, or any port within the same, before delivering to the masters of any such vessels the permit or certificate provided for in such section, in ascertain for a term of service within the United States, for lewd and immoral purposes; and if there be such contract or agreement, the said consul-general or consul shall not deliver the required permit or certificate....

SEC.3. That the importation into the United States of women for the purposes of prostitution is hereby forbidden; and all contracts and agreements in relation thereto, made in advance or in pursuance of illegal importation and purposes, are hereby declared void; and whoever shall knowingly and willfully hold, or attempt to hold, any woman to such purposes, in pursuance of such illegal importation and contract or agreement, shall be deemed guilty of a felony, and, on conviction thereof, shall be imprisoned not exceeding five years and pay a fine not exceeding five thousand dollars....

SEC.5. That it shall be unlawful for aliens of the following classes to immigrate into the United States, namely, persons who are undergoing sentence for conviction in their own country of felonious crimes other than political or growing out of or the result of such political offenses, and women "imported for the purposes of prostitution." Every vessel arriving in the United States may be inspected under the direction of the collector of the port at which it arrives, if he shall have reason to believe that such obnoxious persons are on board; and the officer making such inspection shall certify the result thereof to the master or other person in charge of such vessel, designating in such certificate are person or persons, if any there be, ascertained by him to be of either of the classes whose importation is hereby forbidden.....

Source: Proceedings of the Forty-third Congress, Second Session

HOW WELL DID YOU UNDERSTAND THIS SELECTION?

1. What does the Page Law do?

2. Why would the American government pass such a law?

3. How does the Page Law fit into the pattern of racism against Chinese immigrants in the United States?

CHINESE EXCLUSION ACT

Passage of the Chinese Exclusion Act represents the first real attempt by the United States government to close its doors to immigrants from any ethnic group. This law was enacted because a small but vocal minority of white Americans, primarily from the Western states, was racist. Westerners who wanted to prevent further immigration of Chinese to the United States were reacting to economic and labor problems that gripped the West during the 1870s and 1880s. White Americans in the West feared that Chinese laborers, who were highly sought after as miners and railroad workers, would take jobs from them. Chinese immigrants made easy scapegoats for western economic problems because, like Native Americans, they were different.

WHEREAS, in the opinion of the Government of the United States the coming of Chinese laborers to this country endangers the good order of certain localities within the territory thereof, Therefore, Be it enacted. That from and after the expiration of ninety days next after the passage of this act, and until the expiration often years next after the passage of this act, the coming of Chinese laborers to the Untied States be, suspended, and during such suspension it shall not be lawful for any Chinese laborer to come, or, having so come after the expiration of said ninety days, to remain within the United States.

SEC 2: That the master of any vessel who shall knowingly bring within the United States on such vessel, and land or permit to be landed, any Chinese laborer, from any foreign port or place, shall be deemed guilty of a misdemeanor, and on conviction thereof shall be punished by a fine of not more than five hundred dollars for each and every such Chinese laborer so brought, and may be also imprisoned for a term not exceeding one year.

SEC 3: That the two foregoing sections shall not apply to Chinese laborers who were in the United States on the seventeenth day of November, eighteen hundred and eighty, or who shall have come into the same before the expiration of ninety days next after the passage of this act,

SEC 6: That in order to the faithful execution of articles one and two of the treaty in this act before mentioned, every Chinese person other than a laborer who may be entitled by said treaty and this act to come within the United States, and who shall be about to come to the United States, shall be identified as so entitled by the Chinese Government in each case, such identity to be evidenced by a certificate issued under the authority of said government, which certificate shall be in the English language or (if not in the English language) accompanied by a translation into English, stating such right to come, and which certificate shall state the name, title, or official rank, if any, the age, height, and all physical peculiarities former and present occupation or profession and place of residence in China of the person to whom the certificate is issued and that such person is entitled conformably to the treaty in this act mentioned to come within the Untied States.

Source: United States Statutes at Large, Vol. 22

HOW WELL DID YOU UNDERSTAND THIS SELECTION?

1. What does the Chinese Exclusion Act do?

2. What penalties will be assessed against violators of the law?

3. What did non-laborers from China have to do to come to the United States?

4. Is the Chinese Exclusion Act racist? Why or why not?

REPUBLICAN PARTY PLATFORM

The 1896 presidential election was a pivotal one in American history. There was a clear difference between the parties and their stand on the issues. The Republican Party represented big business, imperialism, and the gold standard. The Republican candidate, William McKinley, ran a traditional campaign. Rather than crossing the country to ask for votes, he stayed at home in Ohio and let other Republicans, like Theodore Roosevelt, campaign for him. The issues he and his Republican campaigners stressed are summarized in the Republican Party Platform adopted at their St. Louis convention on June 16, 1896.

The Republicans of the United States, assembled by their representatives in National Convention, appealing for the popular and historical justification of their claims to the matchless achievements of thirty years of Republican rule, earnestly and confidently address themselves to the awakened intelligence, experience, and conscience of their countrymen in the following declaration of facts and principles:

For the first time since the Civil War the American people have witnessed the calamitous consequences of full and unrestricted Democratic control of the Government. It has been a record of unparalleled incapacity, dishonor and disaster. In administrative management it has ruthlessly sacrificed indispensable revenue, entailed an unceasing deficit, eked out ordinary current expenses with borrowed money, piled up the public debt by $262,000,000 in time of peace, forced an adverse balance of trade, kept a perpetual menace hanging over the redemption fund, pawned American credit to alien syndicates, and reversed all the measures and results of successful Republican rule. In the broad effect of its policy it has precipitated panic, blighted industry and trade with prolonged depression, closed factories, reduced work and wages, halted enterprise and crippled American production, while stimulating foreign production for the American market. Every consideration of public safety and individual interest demands that the Government shall be rescued from the hands of those who have shown themselves incapable of conducting it without disaster at home and dishonor abroad, and shall be restored to the party which for thirty years administered it with unequalled success and prosperity. And in this connection we heartily endorse the wisdom, patriotism and the success of the Administration of President Harrison.

Allegiance to Protection Renewed.
We renew and emphasize our allegiance to the policy of Protection as the bulwark of American industrial independence and the foundation of American development and prosperity. This true American policy taxes foreign products and encourages home industry; it puts the burden of revenue on foreign goods; it secures the American market for the American producer; it upholds the American standard of wages for the American workingman; it puts the factory by the side of the farm, and makes the American farmer less dependent on foreign demand and prices; it diffuses general thrift and founds the strength of all on the strength of each. In its reasonable application it is just, far and impartial, equally opposed to foreign control and domestic monopoly, to sectional discrimination and individual favoritism.

We denounce the present Democratic tariff as sectional, injurious to the public credit and destructive to business enterprise. We demand such an equitable tariff on foreign imports which come into competition with American products, as will not only furnish adequate revenue for the necessary expenses of the Government, but will protect American labor from degradation to the wage level of other lands. We are not pledged to any particular schedules. The question of rates is a practical question, to be governed by the conditions of the time and of production; the ruling and uncompromising principle is the protection and development of American labor and industry. The country demands a right settlement, and then it wants rest.

Reciprocity Demanded.
We believe the repeal of the reciprocity arrangements negotiated by the last Republican Administration was a national calamity, and we demand their renewal and extension on such terms as will equalize our trade with other nations, remove the restrictions which now obstruct the sale of American products in the ports of other countries, and secure enlarged markets for the products of our farms, forests and factories.

Protection and reciprocity are twin measures of Republican policy and go hand in hand. Democratic rule has recklessly struck down both, and both must be re-established. Protection for what we produce, free admission for the necessaries of life which we do not produce; reciprocal agreements of mutual interest which gain open markets for us in return for our open market to others. Protection builds up domestic industry and trade and secures our own market for ourselves; reciprocity builds up foreign trade and finds an outlet for our surplus.

We condemn the present Administration for not keeping faith with the sugar producers of this country; the Republican party favors such protection as will lead to the production on American soil of all the sugar which the American people use and for which they pay other countries more than $ 100,000,000 annually. To all our products--to those of the mine and the field, as well as those of the shop and the factory--to hemp, to wool, the product of the great industry of sheep husbandry, as well as to the finished woolens of the mill--we promise the most ample protection.

Merchant Marine.
We favor restoring the early American policy of discriminating duties for the upbuilding of our merchant marine and the protection of our shipping in the foreign carrying trade, so that American ships--the product of American

labor, employed in American shipyards, sailing under the Stars and Stripes, and manned, officered and owned by Americans--can regain the carrying of our foreign commerce.

The Currency Plank.
The Republican Party is unreservedly for sound money. It caused the enactment of the law providing for the resumption of specie payment in 1879; since then every dollar has been as good as gold.

We are unalterably opposed to every measure calculated to debase our currency or impair the credit of our country. We are, therefore, opposed to the free coinage of silver, except by international agreement with the leading commercial nations of the world, which we pledge ourselves to promote, and, until such agreement can be obtained, the existing gold standard must be preserved. All our silver and paper currency must be maintained at parity with gold, and we favor all measures designed to maintain inviolable the obligations of the United States and all our money, whether coin or paper, at the present standard, the standard of the most enlightened nations of the earth.

Justice to Veterans.
The veterans of the Union armies deserve and should receive fair treatment and generous recognition. Whenever practicable, they should be given the preference in the matter of employment, and they are entitled to the enactment of such laws as are best calculated to secure the fulfillment of the pledges made to them in the dark days of the country in peril. We denounce the practice in the Pension Bureau, so recklessly and unjustly carried on by the present administration, of reducing pensions and arbitrarily dropping names from the rolls, as deserving the severest condemnation of the American people.

Foreign Relations.
Our foreign policy should be at all times firm, vigorous and dignified, and all our interests in the Western hemisphere carefully watched and guarded. The Hawaiian Islands should be controlled by the United States, and no foreign Power should be permitted to interfere with them; the Nicaragua Canal should be built, owned, and operated by the United States, and, by the purchase of the Danish Islands, we should secure a seaport and much-needed naval station in the West Indies.

The massacres in Armenia have aroused the deep sympathy and just indignation of the American people, and we believe that the United States should exercise all the influence it can properly exert to bring these atrocities to an end. In Turkey, American residents have been exposed to the gravest dangers, and American property destroyed. There, and everywhere, American citizens and American property must be absolutely protected at all hazards and at any cost.

We reassert the Monroe Doctrine in its full extent, and we reaffirm the right of the United States to give the doctrine effect by responding to the appeals of any American State for friendly intervention in case of European encroachment. We have not interfered, and shall not interfere, with the existing possessions of any European Power in this hemisphere, but those possessions must not, on any pretext, be extended. We hopefully look forward to the eventual withdrawal of the European Powers from this hemisphere, and to the ultimate union of all the English-speaking part of the continent by the free consent of its inhabitants.

Suffering Cuba._
From the hour of achieving their own independence, the people of the United States have regarded with sympathy the struggles of other American peoples to free themselves from European domination. We watch with deep and abiding interest the heroic battle of the Cuban patriots against cruelty and oppression, and our best hopes go out for the full success of their determined contest for liberty. The Government of Spain, having lost control of Cuba, and being unable to protect the property or lives of resident American citizens, or to comply with its treaty obligations, we believe that the Government of the United States should actively use its influence and good offices to restore peace and give independence to the island.

The Navy.
The peace and security of the Republic, and the maintenance of its rightful influence among the nations of the earth, demand a naval power commensurate with its position and responsibility. We therefore favor the continued enlargement of the navy and a complete system of harbor and seacoast defenses.

Foreign Immigration.
For the protection of the equality of our American citizenship and of the wages of our workingmen against the fatal competition of low-priced labor, we demand that the immigration laws be thoroughly enforced and so extended as to exclude from entrance to the United States those who can neither read nor write.

Civil Service.
The Civil Service law was placed on the statute book by the Republican Party, which has always sustained it, and we renew our repeated declarations that it shall be thoroughly and honestly enforced and extended wherever practicable.

Free Ballot.
We demand that every citizen of the United States shall be allowed to cast one free and unrestricted ballot, and that such ballot shall be counted and returned as cast.

Lynchings.
We proclaim our unqualified condemnation of the uncivilized and barbarous practices well known as lynching and killing of human beings, suspected or charged with crime, without process of law.

National Arbitration.
We favor the creation of a National Board of Arbitration to settle and adjust differences which may arise between employers and employed engaged in inter-State commerce.

Homesteads.
We believe in an immediate return to the free homestead policy of the Republican party, and urge the passage by Congress of the satisfactory free homestead measure which has already passed the House and is now pending in the Senate.

Territories.
We favor the admission of the remaining Territories at the earliest practicable date, having due regard to the interests of the people of the Territories and of the United States. All the Federal officers appointed for the Territories should be selected from bona fide residents thereof, and the right of self-government should be accorded as far as practicable.

We believe the citizens of Alaska should have representation in the Congress of the United States, to the end that needful legislation may be intelligently enacted.

Temperance and the Rights of Women.
We sympathize with all wise and legitimate efforts to lessen and prevent the evils of intemperance and promote morality.

The Republican Party is mindful of the rights and interests of women. Protection of American industries includes equal opportunities, equal pay for equal work, and protection to the home. We favor the admission of women to wider spheres of usefulness, and welcome their co-operation in rescuing the country from Democratic and Populistic mismanagement and misrule.

Such are the principles and policies of the Republican Party. By these principles we will abide, and these policies we will put into execution. We ask for them the considerate judgment of the American people. Confident alike in the history of our great party and in the justice of our cause, we present our platform and our candidates in the full assurance that the election will bring victory to the Republican party and prosperity to the people of the United States.

Source: Proceedings of the Republican National Convention, 1896

HOW WELL DID YOU UNDERSTAND THIS SELECTION?

1. How does the Republican Party Platform criticize the Democratic-controlled government?

2. Identify the various planks within the Republican Party Platform.

3. Does the Republican Party Platform favor business? Why or why not?

4. Does the Republican Party favor giving women the right to vote? Why or why not? What is the Republican stand on the women's rights movement?

5. Discuss Republican views on foreign policy.

The Populist or People's Party was one of the most successful third parties in American history. It elected candidates to many positions in the 1880s and 1890s, including the United States Congress, state governors, and state legislatures. In 1892 and 1896 the Populist Party ran candidates for president. Most supporters of the Populist Party came from the South and West because those states were largely agricultural, and the Populist Party was clearly the party of farmers. The Populist Party largely disappeared after the 1896 election because the Democratic Party "stole" its issues and presidential candidate (William Jennings Bryan) in that year. Even though the People's Party disappeared, most issues it advocated later became law. These issues are summarized in the Populist Platform adopted at its convention in St. Louis on July 24, 1896.

The People's party, assembled in National Convention, reaffirms its allegiance to the principles declared by the founders of the Republic, and also to the fundamental principles of just government as enunciated in the platform of the party in 1892. We recognize that, through the connivance of the present and preceding. Administrations, the country has reached a crisis in its national life as predicted in our declaration four years ago, and that prompt and patriotic action is the supreme duty of the hour. We realize that, while we have political independence, our financial and industrial independence is yet to be attained by restoring to our country the constitutional control and exercise of the functions necessary to a people's government, which functions have been basely surrendered by our public servant to corporate monopolies. The influence of European money changers has been more potent in shaping legislation than the voice of the American people. Executive power and patronage have been used to corrupt our Legislatures and defeat the will of the people, and plutocracy has thereby been enthroned upon the ruins of Democracy. To restore the Government intended by the fathers and for the welfare and prosperity of this and future generations, we demand the establishment of an economic and financial system, which shall make us masters of our own affairs and independent of European control by the adoption of the following:

Declaration of Principles.

FIRST. We demand a national money, safe and sound, issued by the General Government only, without the intervention of banks of issue, to be a full legal tender for all debts, public and private, a just, equitable, and efficient means of distribution direct to the people and through the lawful disbursements of the Government.

SECOND. We demand the free and unrestricted coinage of silver and gold at the present ratio of 16 to 1, without waiting for the consent of foreign nations.

THIRD. We demand the volume of circulating medium be speedily increased to an amount sufficient to meet the demands of the business and population and to restore the just level of prices of labor and production.

FOURTH. We denounce the sale of bonds and the increase of the public interest-bearing debt made by the present Administration as unnecessary and without authority of law, and demand that no more bonds be issued except by specific act of Congress.

FIFTH. We demand such legislation as will prevent the demonetization of the lawful money of the United States by private contract.

SIXTH. We demand that the Government, in payment of its obligations, shall use its option as to the kind of lawful money in which they are to be paid, and we denounce the present and preceding Administrations for surrendering this option to the holders of Government obligations.

SEVENTH. We demand a graduated income tax to the end that aggregated wealth shall bear its just proportion of taxation, and we regard the recent decision of the Supreme Court relative to the Income Tax law as a misinterpretation of the Constitution and an invasion of the rightful powers of Congress over the subject of taxation.

EIGHTH. We demand that postal savings banks be established by the Government for the safe deposit of the savings of the people and to facilitate exchange.

Transportation.

FIRST. Transportation being a means of exchange and a public necessity, the Government should own and operate the railroads in the interest of the people and on a non-partisan basis, to the end that all may be accorded the same treatment in transportation and that the tyranny and political power now exercised by the great railroad corporations, which result in the impairment if not the destruction of the political rights and personal liberties of the citizen, may be destroyed. Such ownership is to be accomplished gradually, in a manner consistent with sound public policy.

SECOND. The interest of the United States in the public highways built with public moneys and the proceeds of extensive grants of land to the Pacific Railroads should never be alienated, mortgaged, or sold, but guarded and protected for the general welfare as provided by the laws organizing such railroads. The foreclosure of existing liens of the United States on these roads should at once follow default in the payment thereof by the debtor companies, and at the foreclosure sales of said roads the Government shall purchase the same if it becomes necessary to protect its interests therein, or if they can be purchased at a reasonable price, and the Government shall operate said railroads as public highways for the benefit of the whole people and not in the interest of the few under suitable provisions for protection of life and property, giving to all transportation interests equal privileges and equal rates for fares and freights.

THIRD. We denounce the present infamous schemes for refunding these debts, and demand that the laws now applicable thereto be executed and administered according to their interest and spirit.

Telegraph.

The telegraph, like the Post-office system, being a necessity for the transmission of news, should be owned and operated by the Government in the interest of the people.

Land.

FIRST. True policy demands that the National and State legislation shall be such as will ultimately enable every prudent and industrious citizen to secure a home, and, therefore, the land should not be monopolized for speculative purposes. All lands now held by railroads and other corporations in excess of their actual needs, should by lawful means be reclaimed by the Government and held for natural settlers only, and private land monopoly as well as alien ownership should be prohibited.

SECOND. We condemn the frauds by which the land grant Pacific Railroad Companies have, through the connivance of the Interior Department, robbed multitudes of actual bona fide settlers of their homes and miners of their claims, and we demand legislation by Congress which will enforce the exception of mineral land from such grants after as well as before the patent.

THIRD. We demand that bona fide settlers on all public lands be granted free homes, as provided in the National Homestead law, and that no exception be made in the case of Indian reservations when opened for settlement, and that all lands not now patented come under this demand.

Direct Legislation.

We favor a system of direct legislation, through the initiative and referendum, under proper constitutional safeguards.

General Propositions.

FIRST. We demand the election of President, Vice-President, and United States Senators by a direct vote of the people.

SECOND. We tender to the patriotic people of the country our deepest sympathies in their heroic struggle for political freedom and independence, and we believe the time has come when the United States, the great Republic of the world, should recognize that Cuba is and of right ought to be a free and independent State.

THIRD. We favor home rule in the Territories and the District of Columbia, and the early admission of the Territories as States.

FOURTH. All public salaries should be made to correspond to the price of labor and its products.

FIFTH. In times of great industrial depression idle labor should be employed on public works as far as practicable.

SIXTH. The arbitrary course of the courts in assuming to imprison citizens for indirect contempt, and ruling them by injunction, should be prevented by proper legislation.

SEVENTH. We favor just pensions for our disabled Union soldiers.

EIGHTH. Believing that the elective franchise and an untrammeled ballot are essential to government of, for, and by the people, the People's party condemn the wholesale system of disfranchisement adopted in some of the States as unrepublican and undemocratic, and we declare it to be the duty of the several State Legislatures to take such action as will secure a full, free and fair ballot and honest count.

NINTH. While the foregoing propositions constitute the platform upon which our party stands, and for the vindication of which its organization will be maintained, we recognize that the real and pressing issue of the pending campaign, upon which the present election will turn, is the financial question, and upon this great and specific issue between the parties we cordially invite the aid and co-operation of all organizations and citizens agreeing with us upon this vital question.

Source: Proceedings of People's Party (Populist) Convention, 1896

HOW WELL DID YOU UNDERSTAND THIS SELECTION?

1. What does the Populist Party appear to be reacting against?

2. Identify the various planks in the Populist Party Platform.

3. Contrast Populist views with those of Republicans in the 1896 election.

4. What is the most significant issue in the Populist Party Platform?

SELF TEST:

MULTIPLE CHOICE: Circle the correct response. The correct answers are given at the end.

1. How much land did the Dawes Act provide for each head of a Native American family?
   a. Three acres.
   b. 140 acres.
   c. 160
   d. one-quarter section (60 acres).

2. What does William Jennings Bryan advocated in the "Cross of Gold" speech?
   a. A strict gold standard.
   b. A currency that is deflated.
   c. Government policies that will help corporations but discriminate against agriculture.
   d. Inflation through the coinage of silver.

3. The final battle between whites and Native Americans in the West was
   a. Wounded Knee.
   b. Little Big Horn
   c. Custer's Last Stand
   d. Sand's Creek.

4. What was the most significant factor in the destruction of the Plains Tribes?
   a. Introduction of the horse.
   b. Destruction of the Buffalo.
   c. The demise of Salmon populations in the Pacific Northwest.
   d. The coming of the Railroad into western territories.

5. Why did the United States want to limit Chinese immigration to the United States?
   a. Because of racist views in the United States.
   b. Because China was traditionally an enemy of the United States.
   c. Because there was not enough work for Chinese laborers to do in the United States.
   d. Because Chinese immigrants were put on the welfare rolls in higher numbers than were other immigrant groups.

6. What was the African-American settlement in northwestern Kansas called?
   a. Exoduster.
   b. Deadeye Dick.
   c. Isom Dart.
   d. Nicodemus.

7. Which of the following did William McKinley and the Republican Party favor in the 1896 election?
   a. The free coinage of silver to create inflation.
   b. Giving 18 year old citizens the right to vote in national elections.
   c. Making Hawaii an independent nation.
   d. Tariffs, big business, and the gold standard.

8. Which of the following was not part of the Populist Party Platform in 1896?
   a. Direct election of United States Senators.
   b. A graduated income tax.
   c. A strict gold standard.
   d. The free coinage of silver.

9. The first great economic boom in the Far West occurred in which of the following industries?
   a. Petroleum.
   b. Farming.
   c. Cattle ranching.
   d. Mining.

10. What was perhaps the worst problem women who lived in the Great Plains faced?
    a. Loneliness and isolation.
    b. Hard labor.
    c. Indian attacks.
    d. Few men to serve as mates.

ANSWERS: 1-c; 2-d; 3-a; 4-b; 5-a; 6-d; 7-d; 8-c; 9-d; 10-a

ESSAYS:

1. There are many myths prevalent in American society about the West. Identify some of these myths and examine their validity.

2. Compare and contrast the views of the Populist Party with those of the Republican Party in the 1896 election.

3. Discuss the mistreatment of Native Americans. How could this mistreatment have been avoided?

4. Examine the racism present in the United States against minority ethnic groups. Why were Americans so racist? How can racism be overcome?

5. Examine the effect the Homestead Act had on the West. What happened to most of the land that was filed on? How was the act abused?

OPTIONAL ACTIVITIES: (Use your knowledge **and** imagination.)

1. You are a Native American confined to a reservation in the West. Keep a diary for the semester in which you compare and contrast your life before and after life on the reservation.

2. You are a member of a United States Senate Committee investigating conditions and events that led to the massacre at Wounded Knee. Write a report that summarizes the findings of your committee.

3. You have just been nominated by the Populist Party to run for Congress in a district from South Dakota in 1896. Write and deliver a campaign speech to your class that reflects your views on the issues dominant in American politics in 1896.

WEB SITE LISTINGS:

Populist Party
> http://www.encyclopedia.com/search.asp?target=@DOCTITLE%20Populist%20party
> (Encyclopedia.com)
> http://www.encyclopedia.com/searchpool.asp?target=@DOCTITLE%20Populist%20party

CyberSoup's Wild West
> Colorful educational site covering Western legends and Native Americans. http://www.thewildwest.org/

Bryan, William Jennings
> Essays and speeches about imperialism (1898-1913) by one of the most influential leaders of the Democratic Party during the late 19th and early 20th centuries. http://www.boondocksnet.com/ail/bryan.html

Bryan, William Jennings
> (Encarta® Concise Encyclopedia Article)
> http://encarta.msn.com/index/conciseindex/0C/00C50000.htm?z=1&pg=2&br=1

Biography of Jesse James
> In-depth article about the legendary outlaw and gunman
> http://www.crimelibrary.com/americana/jesse/index.htm

Angel Island Immigration Station
> Historical information about Angel Island State Park in California, site of the Immigration Station, a National Historic Landmark, which played a role in the Chinese Exclusion Act of 1882.
> http://www.angelisland.org/immigr02.html

Women of the West Museum
> An educational organization that traces and interprets the history, contributions, and roles of women of all cultures—past, present, and future in the American West. http://www.wowmuseum.org/

American West Heritage Center
> dedicated to honoring, celebrating, and re-creating the heritage and culture of the American West from the period of 1820 to 1920 http://www.americanwestcenter.org/

Legends of the American West - Wyatt Earp & the Gunfighters
> Reviews on Legends of the American West - Wyatt Earp & the Gunfighters written by consumers at Epinions.com. http://www.epinions.com/mvie_mu-1037468

Ghost Town Museum
> A complete and authentic old western town built from the very buildings abandoned after the Pikes Peak Region's gold mining era and straight out of the days of America's frontier.
> http://www.ghosttownmuseum.com/

Buffalo Soldiers and Indian Wars
> Sixteen photographs of Buffalo Soldiers, 14 of their legendary Native American foes, two mini-videos and 24 story/page links are displayed. Buffalo Soldier battles, skirmishes and background events are given. http://www.buffalosoldier.net

The Buffalo Soldiers on the Western Frontier
> History of the 9th and 10th Cavalry
> http://www.imh.org/imh/buf/buftoc.html

Chapter Fifteen

THE IMPERIAL REPUBLIC

Toward the latter decades of the nineteenth century several different forces of imperialism converged within the United States and the result was a drastic change in foreign policy from isolation to an active involvement in world affairs. Industrialists demanded overseas markets in which to sell their products. Churches wanted colonies controlled by the United States so that their missionaries could spread Christianity to nonbelievers. Social Darwinists believed that Americans were racially superior to Africans and Asians and had a duty to "civilize" their little brown brothers. Super patriots favored conquest because they thought war for the acquisition of overseas colonies would strengthen America economically and militarily and enable the nation to take its rightful place among the great colonial powers of Europe. Pessimists looked with fondness back to the Civil War and favored colonial acquisition because they believed America had lost its way due to the materialistic society created by the Industrial Revolution and thought war would reawaken the American spirit, putting the country back on the right track. Others were concerned with the closing of the frontier and supported imperialism as a safety value to relieve pressure on the United States after western land was no longer available.

After these forces converged in the 1890s the United States became imperialistic, and the government actively pursued colonies and a larger role within the world. American imperialism was initiated in 1898 when war broke out with Spain over Cuba. The United States ironically began this war by demanding Spain free its Cuban colony after Spain instituted policies distasteful to Americans to defeat a revolution by Cubans to free the island from Spanish control. Following the war, which concluded after only a few weeks of fighting, the United States acquired Guam, the Philippines, and Puerto Rico from Spain. In that same year, the Congress annexed Hawaii, and for the first time in its history, the United States had colonies to rule.

America's acquisition of colonies produced much initial opposition within the United States. Members of the Anti-Imperial League included prominent individuals such as the author Mark Twain, Speaker of the House of Representatives Thomas Reed (who resigned in protest), Supreme Court Justice Morfield Storey, industrialist Andrew Carnegie, American Federation of Labor head Samuel Gompers, and former Populist Presidential candidate William Jennings Bryan. They, along with others, spoke out against colonial acquisition, arguing that America was violating self-determination, one of its founding principles. America, they said, should promote self-determination and allow all peoples to choose their own government rather than imposing a government on hapless people. The Senate largely ignored Anti-Imperialists arguments and ratified the Treaty of 1898, making the United States an imperial power.

Imperialism and the Spanish-American War marked a significant transformation in American History. After 1898 the United States played an active role throughout the world, sending troops to help European nations crush the Boxer Rebellion in China, intervening militarily numerous times throughout Latin America, crushing a rebellion in the Philippines against American rule, and promulgating policies such as the Open Door in China designed to give America access to markets throughout the world.

Theodore Roosevelt, who became President after William McKinley's assassination in 1901, was a staunch proponent of imperialism. Roosevelt was particularly interested in extending American influence throughout the Caribbean and Latin America. He sent American troops into several Western Hemisphere nations, including the

Dominican Republic. There he seized the custom houses and collected taxes to repay debts the Dominican Republic owed European powers. As a result of the Dominican intervention, Roosevelt issued the Roosevelt Corollary to the Monroe Doctrine that made American intervention into nations of the Western Hemisphere easier. Roosevelt also engineered a revolution that broke Panama away from Columbia so that the United States could construct the Panama Canal linking the Atlantic and Pacific Oceans. This shortcut between the oceans made America's ability to control its Pacific colonies easier.

William Howard Taft, Roosevelt's successor as president, continued America's imperialistic policies. Taft devised what historians call "Dollar Diplomacy," which used American diplomatic influence and the threat of military intervention to promote American economic growth.

Imperialism that began with the Spanish-American War created much animosity against and hatred for Americans around the world. Foreign people grew to distrust Americans due to policies that promoted American interests at the expense of foreign interests. This hatred of Americans carries over into the modern era. Perhaps the ultimate result of imperialism was American entrance into World War I in 1917. For the first time in history, Americans got involved in a conflict on the European continent.

IDENTIFICATION: Briefly describe each item.

Imperialism

Alfred Thayer Mahan

William McKinley

James G. Blair

Hawaii

Grover Cleveland

Queen Liliuokalani

John Hay

Open Door Policy

Boxer Rebellion

Jingoists

Valeriano Wyler

William Randolph Hearst

Joseph Pulitzer

Yellow Journalism

deLome Letter

U.S.S. Maine

George Dewey

Roosevelt Corollary to the Monroe Doctrine

Rough Riders

Mark Twain

Anti-Imperial League

Dollar Diplomacy

William Howard Taft

Treaty of Paris of 1898

Emilio Aguinaldo

Teller Amendment

Panama Canal

Filipino-American War

Spanish-American War

Spheres of Influence

Russo-Japanese War

Great White Fleet

Josiah Strong

THINK ABOUT:

1. How might American history been different had the United States not have become imperialistic? Would most twentieth century wars have occurred? Why or why not?

2. What lasting impact has imperialism left on the United States? Are other nation's reservations about the U. S. justified? Why or why not?

3. Was imperialism merely a continuation of American expansion that began with the settlement of Jamestown in 1607? Why or why not? Support your answer with historical facts and other evidence.

JOSIAH STRONG ON ANGLO-SAXON PREDOMINANCE, 1891

One root of American imperialism in the 1890s was religious missionary activity. Protestant churches and ministers generally supported the acquisition of overseas colonies because they wanted fertile grounds to spread their brand of Christianity to "nonbelievers." Not only did Protestant missionaries believe that they could convert "heatherns" to Christianity but that they could also spread American civilization around the world, uplifting uncivilized people in the process. Josiah Strong, a member of the Evangelical Alliance for the United States, merged Social Darwinistic ideas of white racial superiority with ideas of the Christian mission to spread the "Good News" around the world in the following selection.

It is not necessary to argue to those for whom I write that the two great needs of mankind, that all men may be lifted up into the light of the highest Christian civilization, are, first, a pure, spiritual Christianity, and second, civil liberty. Without controversy, these are the forces which, in the past, have contributed most to the elevation of the human race, and they must continue to be, in the future, the most efficient ministers to its progress. It follows, then, that the Anglo-Saxon, as the great representative of these two ideas, the despositary of these two greatest blessings, sustains peculiar relations to the world's future, is divinely commissioned to be, in a peculiar sense, his brother's keeper. Add to this the fact of his rapidly increasing strength in modem times, and we have well-nigh a demonstration of his destiny. In 1700 this race numbered less than 6,000,000 souls. In 1800, Anglo-Saxons (I use the term somewhat broadly to include all English speaking peoples) had increased to about 20,500,000, and now, in 1890, they number more than 120,000,000, having multiplied almost six-fold in ninety years. At the end of the reign of Charles 11, the English colonists in America numbered 200,000. During these two hundred years, our population has increased two hundred and fifty-fold. And the expansion of this race has been no less remarkable than its multiplication. In one century the United States has increased its territory ten-fold, while the enormous acquisition of foreign territory by Great Britain-and chiefly within the last hundred years-is wholly unparalleled in history. This mighty Anglo-Saxon race, though comprising only one-thirteenth part of mankind, now rules more than one-third of the earth's surface, and more than one-fourth of its people. And if this race, while growing from 6,000,000 to 120,000,000, thus gained possession of a third portion of the earth, is it to be supposed that when it numbers 1,000,000,000, it will lose the disposition, or lack the power to extend its sway? ...

America is to have the great preponderance of numbers and of wealth, and by the logic of events will follow the scepter of controlling influence. This will be but the consummation of a movement as old as civilization—a result to which men have looked forward for centuries. John Adams records that nothing was "more ancient in his memory than the observation that arts, sciences and empire had traveled westward; and in conversation it was always added that their next leap would be over the Atlantic into America." He recalled a couplet that had been inscribed or rather drilled, into a rock on the shore of Monument Bay in our old colony of Plymouth:

The Eastern nations sink, their glory ends,
And empire rises where the sun descends. . .

Mr. Darwin is not only disposed to see, in the superior vigor of our people, an illustration of his favorite theory of natural selection, but even intimates that the world's history thus far has been simply preparatory for our future, and tributary to it. He says: "There is apparently much truth in the belief that the wonderful progress of the United States, as well as the character of the people, are the results of natural selection; for the more energetic, restless, and courageous men from all parts of Europe have emigrated during the last ten or twelve generations to that great country, and have there succeeded best. Looking at the distant future, I do not think that the Rev. Mr. Zincke takes an exaggerated view when he says: 'All other series of events-as that which resulted in the culture of mind in Greece, and that which resulted in the Empire of Rome-only appear to have purpose and value when viewed in connection with, or rather as subsidiary to, the great stream of Anglo-Saxon emigration to the West.'"
There is abundant reason to believe that the Anglo-Saxon race is to be, is, indeed, already becoming, more effective here than in the mother country. The marked superiority of this race is due, in large measure, to its highly mixed origin. Says Rawlinson: "It is a general rule, now almost universally admitted by ethnologists, that the mixed races of mankind are superior to the pure ones"; and adds: "Even the Jews, who are so often cited as an example of a race at once pure and strong, may, with more reason, be adduced on the opposite side of the argument." The ancient Egyptians, the Greeks, and the Romans, were all mixed races. Among modem races, the most conspicuous example is afforded by the AngloSaxons.... There is here a new commingling of races; and, while the largest injections of foreign blood are substantially the same elements that constituted the original Anglo-Saxon admixture, so that we may infer the general type will be preserved, there are strains of other bloods being added, which, if Mr. Emerson's remark is true, that "the best nations are those most widely related," may be expected to improve the stock, and aid it to a higher destiny. If the dangers of immigration, which have been pointed out, can be successfully met for the next few years, until it has passed its climax, it may be expected to add value to the amalgam which will constitute the new Anglo-Saxon race of the New World. Concerning our future, Herbert Spencer says: "One great result is, I think, tolerably clear. From biological truths it is to be inferred that the eventual mixture of the allied varieties of the Aryan race, forming the population, will produce a more powerful type of man than has hitherto existed, and a type of man more plastic, more adaptable, more capable of undergoing the modifications needful for complete social life. I think, whatever difficulties they may have to surmount, and whatever tribulations they may have to pass through, the Americans may reasonably look forward to a time when they will have produced a civilization grander than any the world has known."

It may be easily shown, and is of no small significance, that the two great ideas of which the Anglo-Saxon is the exponent are having a fuller development in the United States than in Great Britain. There the union of Church and State tends strongly to paralyze some of the members of the body of Christ. Here there is no such influence to destroy spiritual life and power. Here, also, has been evolved the form of government consistent with the largest possible civil liberty. Furthermore, it is significant that the marked characteristics of this race are being here emphasized most. Among the most striking features of the Anglo-Saxon is his money-making powera power of increasing importance in the widening commerce of the world's future. We have seen . . . that, although England is by far the richest nation of Europe, we have already outstripped her in the race after wealth, and we have only begun the development of our vast resources.

Again, another marked characteristic of the Anglo-Saxon is what may be called an instinct or genius for colonizing. His unequaled energy, his indomitable perseverance, and his personal independence, made him a pioneer. He excels all others in pushing his way into new countries. It was those in whom this tendency was strongest that came to America, and this inherited tendency has been further developed by the westward sweep of successive generations across the continent. So noticeable has this characteristic become that English visitors remark it. Charles Dickens once said that the typical American would hesitate to enter heaven unless assured that he could go farther west.

Again, nothing more manifestly distinguishes the Anglo-Saxon than his intense and persistent energy, and he is developing in the United States an energy which, in eager activity and effectiveness, is peculiarly American.

This is due partly to the fact that Americans are much better fed than Europeans, and partly to the undeveloped resources of a new country, but more largely to our climate, which acts as a constant stimulus. Ten years after the landing of the Pilgrims, the Rev. Francis Higginson, a good observer, wrote: "A sup of New England air is better than a whole flagon of English ale." Thus early had the stimulating effect of our climate been noted. Moreover, our social institutions are stimulating. In Europe the various ranks of society are, like the strata of the earth, fixed and fossilized. There can be no great change without a terrible upheaval, a social earthquake. Here society is like the waters of the sea, mobile; as General Garfield said, and so signally illustrated in his own experience, that which is at the bottom today may one day flash on the crest of the highest wave. Every one is free to become whatever he can make of himself; free to transform himself from a rail splitter or a tanner or a canal-boy, into the nation's President. Our aristocracy, unlike that of Europe, is open to all comers. Wealth, position, influence, are prizes offered for energy; and every farmer's boy, every apprentice and clerk, every friendless and penniless immigrant, is free to enter the lists. Thus many causes co-operate to produce here the most forceful and tremendous energy in the world.

What is the significance of such facts? These tendencies infold the future; they are the mighty alphabet with which God writes his prophecies. May we not, by a careful laying together of the letters, spell out something of his meaning? It seems to me that God, with infinite wisdom and skill, is training the Anglo-Saxon race for an hour sure to come in the world's future. Heretofore there has always been in the history of the world a comparatively unoccupied land westward, into which the crowded countries of the East have poured their surplus populations. But the widening waves of migration, which millenniums ago rolled east and west from the valley of the Euphrates, meet to-day on our Pacific coast. There are no more new worlds. The unoccupied arable lands of the earth are limited, and will soon be taken. The time is coming when the pressure of population on the means of subsistence will be felt here as it is now felt in Europe and Asia. Then will the world enter upon a new stage of its history-the *final competition of races, for which the Anglo-Saxon is being schooled.* Long before the thousand millions are here, the mighty *centrifugal* tendency, inherent in this stock and strengthened in the United States, will assert itself. Then this race of unequaled energy, with all the majesty of numbers and the might of wealth behind it-the representative, let us hope, of the largest liberty, the purest Christianity, the highest civilization-having developed peculiarly aggressive traits calculated to impress its institutions upon mankind, will spread itself over the earth. If I read not amiss, this powerful race will move down upon Mexico, down upon Central and South America, out upon the islands of the sea, over upon Africa and beyond. And can any one doubt that the results of this competition of races will be the "survival of the fittest?" "Any people," says Dr. Bushnell, "that is physiologically advanced in culture, though it be only in a degree beyond another which is mingled with it on strictly equal terms, is sure to live down and finally live out its inferior. Nothing can save the inferior race but a ready and pliant assimilation. Whether the feebler and more abject races are going to be regenerated and raised up, is already, very much of a question. What if it should be God's plan to people the world with better and finer material?"

HOW WELL DID YOU UNDERSTAND THIS SELECTION?

1. How does Strong think colonization will help people who are colonized?

2. Discuss the principles of Social Darwinism found in this selection.

3. What is the link between religion, Social Darwinism, and colonialism?

4. How does Strong see the future? Who will dominate the future and why will their dominance be possible?

Transcript of the de Lôme letter, 1898: intercepted by Cuban rebels and published by William Randolph Hearst in the New York _Journal_, 9 February 1898

---

*Although the primary cause of the Spanish-American War was American Imperialism, interception of a letter written by Dupuy deLome, Spain's Ambassador to the United States by Cuban rebels in February 1898 contributed to American animosity toward Spain. This letter, which was stolen from the Cuban postal service, was published in the **New York Journal** by William Randolph Hearst on February 9, 1898. DeLome's assertion that President McKinley was a weak leader inflamed the American population, especially proponents of imperialism. They immediately demanded war with Spain and used deLome's criticism of McKinley to fan anti-Spanish sentiment within the United States.*

His Excellency
Don José Canalejas.

My distinguished and dear friend:
    You have no reason to ask my excuses for not having written to me, I ought also to have written to you but I have put off doing so because overwhelmed with work and nous sommes quittes.
    The situation here remains the same. Everything depends on the political and military outcome in Cuba. The prologue of all this, in this second stage (phase) of the war, will end the day when the colonial cabinet shall be appointed and we shall be relieved in the eyes of this country of a part of the responsibility for what is happening in Cuba while the Cubans, whom these people think so immaculate, will have to assume it.
    Until then, nothing can be clearly seen, and I regard it as a waste of time and progress, by a wrong road, to be sending emissaries to the rebel camp, or to negotiate with the autonomists who have as yet no legal standing, or to try to ascertain the intentions and plans of this government. The (Cuban) refugees will keep on returning one by one and as they do so will make their way into the sheep-fold, while the leaders in the field will gradually come back. Neither the one nor the other class had the courage to leave in a body and they will not be brave enough to return in a body.
    The Message has been a disillusionment to the insurgents who expected something different; but I regard it as bad (for us).

Besides the ingrained and inevitable bluntness (grosería) with which is repeated all that the press and public opinion in Spain have said about Weyler, it once more shows what McKinley is, weak and a bidder for the admiration of the crowd besides being a would-be politician (politicastro) who tries to leave a door open behind himself while keeping on good terms with the jingoes of his party.

Nevertheless, whether the practical results of it (the Message) are to be injurious and adverse depends only upon ourselves.

I am entirely of your opinions; without a military end of the matter nothing will be accomplished in Cuba, and without a military and political settlement there will always be the danger of encouragement being give to the insurgents, buy a part of the public opinion if not by the government.

I do not think sufficient attention has been paid to the part England is playing.

Nearly all the newspaper rabble that swarms in your hotels are Englishmen, and while writing for the Journal they are also correspondents of the most influential journals and reviews of London. It has been so ever since this thing began.

As I look at it, England's only object is that the Americans should amuse themselves with us and leave her alone, and if there should be a war, that would the better stave off the conflict which she dreads but which will never come about.

It would be very advantageous to take up, even if only for effect, the question of commercial relations and to have a man of some prominence sent hither, in order that I may make use of him here to carry on a propaganda among the seantors and others in opposition to the Junta and to try to win over the refugees.

So, Amblard is coming. I think he devotes himself too much to petty politics, and we have got to do something very big or we shall fail.

Adela returns your greeting, and we all trust that next year you may be a messenger of peace and take it as a Christmas gift to poor Spain.

Ever your attached friend and servant,
ENRIQUE DUPUY de LÔME.

Source: National Archives & Record Administration

HOW WELL DID YOU UNDERSTAND THIS SELECTION?

1. How did deLome see President McKinley? Based on what you know about the Spanish-American War, were his views accurate? Why or why not?

2. What was deLome's analysis of the Cuban situation?

3. Was deLome's criticism of President McKinley grounds for war? Why or why not?

4. What does deLome think Spain should do regarding Cuba?

In April 1898 Congress passed a joint resolution allowing President McKinley to wage war against Spain to free Cuba. Because Anti-imperialists were suspicious that the declaration of war was a pretext for the United States to grab Cuba and other Spanish colonial possessions, Senator Harry Teller in an attempt to satiate Anti-imperialists included a statement in the joint resolution stating that the United States had no interest in acquiring Cuba as a colony. The Teller Amendment, eased fears among some Americans heading into the conflict about imperialism. The ink was hardly dry on the Teller Amendment, however, until the United States acquired the Philippines and other Spanish colonies.

Joint resolution for the recognition of the independence of the people of Cuba, demanding that the government of Spain relinquish its authority and government in the Island of Cuba, and to withdraw its land and naval forces from Cuba and Cuban waters, and directing the President of the United States to use the land and naval forces of the United States to carry these resolutions into effect.

Whereas the abhorrent conditions which have existed for more than three years in the Island of Cuba, so near our own borders, have shocked the moral sense of the people of the United States, have been a disgrace to Christian civilization, culminating, as they have, in the destruction of a United States battle ship, with two hundred and sixty-six of its officers and crew, while on a friendly visit in the harbor of Havana, and can not longer be endured, as has been set forth by the President of the United States in his message to Congress of April eleventh. eighteen hundred and ninety-eight, upon which the action of Congress was invited:

Therefore,

Resolved, First. That the people of the Island of Cuba are, of right ought to be, free and independent.

Second. That it is the duty of the United States to demand, and the Government of the United States does hereby demand, that the Government of Spain at once relinquish its authority and government in the Island of Cuba and withdraw its land and naval forces from Cuba and Cuban waters.

Third. That the President of the United States be, and he hereby is, directed and empowered to use the entire land and naval forces of the United States, and to call into the actual service of the United States the militia of the several States, to such extent as may be necessary to carry these resolutions into effect.

Fourth. That the United States hereby disclaims any disposition or intention to exercise sovereignty, jurisdiction, or control over said Island except for the pacification thereof, and asserts its determination, when that is accomplished, to leave the government and control of the Island to its people.

HOW WELL DID YOU UNDERSTAND THIS SELECTION?

1. According to the joint resolution, why exactly is Congress authorizing war with Spain?

2. What does the American government demand Spain do?

3. Did the United States honor the Teller Amendment? Why or why not?

4. How would Anti-imperialists react to the Teller Amendment? To the acquisition of the Philippines and other Spanish colonial territory? Was their reaction justified? Why or why not?

After hostilities ceased in the Spanish-American War, American and Spanish negotiators reached agreement in Paris on December 10, 1898 that officially ended the war. This Treaty of Paris, as the agreement was called, freed Cuba and transferred Spain's colonial possessions, including Guam, Puerto Rico, and the Philippine Islands, to the United States. Americans now had colonies to rule and an empire to control. War between the United States and Filipino rebels soon broke out after the U.S. refused to grant independence to the Philippines and significant opposition to ratification of the Treaty of 1898 from Anti-imperialists surfaced within the United States.

Article I.

Spain relinquishes all claim of sovereignty over and title to Cuba. And as the island is, upon its evacuation by Spain, to be occupied by the United States, the United States will, so long as such occupation shall last, assume and discharge the obligations that may under international law result from the fact of its occupation, for the protection of life and property.

Article II.

Spain cedes to the United States the island of Porto Rico and other islands now under Spanish sovereignty in the West Indies, and the island of Guam in the Marianas or Ladrones.

Article III.

Spain cedes to the United States the archipelago known as the Philippine Islands, and comprehending the islands lying within the following line:

A line running from west to east along or near the twentieth parallel of north latitude, and through the middle of the navigable channel of Bachi, from the one hundred and eighteenth (118th) to the one hundred and twenty-seventh (127th) degree meridian of longitude east of Greenwich, thence along the one hundred and twenty seventh (127th) degree meridian of longitude east of Greenwich to the parallel of four degrees and forty five minutes (4 [degree symbol] 45']) north latitude, thence along the parallel of four degrees and forty five minutes (4 [degree symbol] 45') north latitude to its intersection with the meridian of longitude one hundred and nineteen degrees and thirty five minutes (119 [degree symbol] 35') east of Greenwich, thence along the meridian of longitude one hundred and nineteen degrees and thirty five minutes (119 [degree symbol] 35') east of Greenwich to the parallel of latitude seven degrees and forty minutes (7 [degree symbol] 40') north, thence along the parallel of latitude of seven degrees and forty minutes (7 [degree symbol] 40') north to its intersection with the one hundred and sixteenth (116th) degree meridian of longitude east of Greenwich, thence by a direct line to the intersection of the tenth (10th) degree parallel of north latitude with the one hundred and eighteenth (118th) degree meridian of longitude east of Greenwich, and thence along the one hundred and eighteenth (118th) degree meridian of longitude east of Greenwich to the point of beginning. The United States will pay to Spain the sum of twenty million dollars ($20,000,000) within three months after the exchange of the ratifications of the present treaty.

Article IV.

The United States will, for the term of ten years from the date of the exchange of the ratifications of the present treaty, admit Spanish ships and merchandise to the ports of the Philippine Islands on the same terms as ships and merchandise of the United States.

Article V.

The United States will, upon the signature of the present treaty, send back to Spain, at its own cost, the Spanish soldiers taken as prisoners of war on the capture of Manila by the American forces. The arms of the soldiers in question shall be restored to them.

Spain will, upon the exchange of the ratifications of the present treaty, proceed to evacuate the Philippines, as well as the island of Guam, on terms similar to those agreed upon by the Commissioners appointed to arrange for the evacuation of Porto Rico and other islands in the West Indies, under the Protocol of August 12, 1898, which is to continue in force till its provisions are completely executed.

The time within which the evacuation of the Philippine Islands and Guam shall be completed shall be fixed by the two Governments. Stands of colors, uncaptured war vessels, small arms, guns of all calibres, with their carriages and accessories, powder, ammunition, livestock, and materials and supplies of all kinds, belonging to the land and naval forces of Spain in the Philippines and Guam, remain the property of Spain. Pieces of heavy ordnance, exclusive of field artillery, in the fortifications and coast defences, shall remain in their emplacements for the term of six months, to be reckoned from the exchange of ratifications of the treaty; and the United States may, in the meantime, purchase such material from Spain, if a satisfactory agreement between the two Governments on the subject shall be reached.

Article VI.

Spain will, upon the signature of the present treaty, release all prisoners of war, and all persons detained or imprisoned for political offences, in connection with the insurrections in Cuba and the Philippines and the war with the United States.

Reciprocally, the United States will release all persons made prisoners of war by the American forces, and will undertake to obtain the release of all Spanish prisoners in the hands of the insurgents in Cuba and the Philippines.

The Government of the United States will at its own cost return to Spain and the Government of Spain will at its own cost return to the United States, Cuba, Porto Rico, and the Philippines, according to the situation of their respective homes, prisoners released or caused to be released by them, respectively, under this article.

Article VII.

The United States and Spain mutually relinquish all claims for indemnity, national and individual, of every kind, of either Government, or of its citizens or subjects, against the other Government, that may have arisen since the beginning of the late insurrection in Cuba and prior to the exchange of ratifications of the present treaty, including all claims for indemnity for the cost of the war.

The United States will adjudicate and settle the claims of its citizens against Spain relinquished in this article.

Article VIII.

In conformity with the provisions of Articles I, II, and III of this treaty, Spain relinquishes in Cuba, and cedes in Porto Rico and other islands in the West Indies, in the island of Guam, and in the Philippine Archipelago, all the buildings, wharves, barracks, forts, structures, public highways and other immovable property which, in conformity with law, belong to the public domain, and as such belong to the Crown of Spain.

And it is hereby declared that the relinquishment or cession, as the case may be, to which the preceding paragraph refers, can not in any respect impair the property or rights which by law belong to the peaceful possession of property of all kinds, of provinces, municipalities, public or private establishments, ecclesiastical or civic bodies, or any other associations having legal capacity to acquire and possess property in the aforesaid territories renounced or ceded, or of private individuals, of whatsoever nationality such individuals may be.

The aforesaid relinquishment or cession, as the case may be, includes all documents exclusively referring to the sovereignty relinquished or ceded that may exist in the archives of the Peninsula. Where any document in such archives only in part relates to said sovereignty, a copy of such part will be furnished whenever it shall be requested. Like rules shall be reciprocally observed in favor of Spain in respect of documents in the archives of the islands above referred to.

In the aforesaid relinquishment or cession, as the case may be, are also included such rights as the Crown of Spain and its authorities possess in respect of the official archives and records, executive as well as judicial, in the islands above referred to, which relate to said islands or the rights and property of their inhabitants. Such archives and records shall be carefully preserved, and private persons shall without distinction have the right to require, in accordance with law, authenticated copies of the contracts, wills and other instruments forming part of notorial protocols or files, or which may be contained in the executive or judicial archives, be the latter in Spain or in the islands aforesaid.

Article IX.

Spanish subjects, natives of the Peninsula, residing in the territory over which Spain by the present treaty relinquishes or cedes her sovereignty, may remain in such territory or may remove therefrom, retaining in either event all their rights of property, including the right to sell or dispose of such property or of its proceeds; and they shall also have the right to carry on their industry, commerce and professions, being subject in respect thereof to such laws as are applicable to other foreigners. In case they remain in the territory they may preserve their allegiance to the Crown of Spain by making, before a court of record, within a year from the date of the exchange of ratifications of this treaty, a declaration of their decision to preserve such allegiance; in default of which declaration they shall be held to have renounced it and to have adopted the nationality of the territory in which they may reside.

The civil rights and political status of the native inhabitants of the territories hereby ceded to the United States shall be determined by the Congress.

Article X.

The inhabitants of the territories over which Spain relinquishes or cedes her sovereignty shall be secured in the free exercise of their religion.

Article XI.

The Spaniards residing in the territories over which Spain by this treaty cedes or relinquishes her sovereignty shall be subject in matters civil as well as criminal to the jurisdiction of the courts of the country wherein they reside, pursuant to the ordinary laws governing the same; and they shall have the right to appear before such courts, and to pursue the same course as citizens of the country to which the courts belong.

Article XII.

Judicial proceedings pending at the time of the exchange of ratifications of this treaty in the territories over which Spain relinquishes or cedes her sovereignty shall be determined according to the following rules:

1. Judgments rendered either in civil suits between private individuals, or in criminal matters, before the date mentioned, and with respect to which there is no recourse or right of review under the Spanish law, shall be deemed to be final, and shall be executed in due form by competent authority in the territory within which such judgments should be carried out.

2. Civil suits between private individuals which may on the date mentioned be undetermined shall be prosecuted to judgment before the court in which they may then be pending or in the court that may be substituted therefor.

3. Criminal actions pending on the date mentioned before the Supreme Court of Spain against citizens of the territory which by this treaty ceases to be Spanish shall continue under its jurisdiction until final judgment; but, such judgment having been rendered, the execution thereof shall be committed to the competent authority of the place in which the case arose.

Article XIII.

The rights of property secured by copyrights and patents acquired by Spaniards in the Island of Cuba and in Porto Rico, the Philippines and other ceded territories, at the time of the exchange of the ratifications of this treaty, shall continue to be respected. Spanish scientific, literary and artistic works, not subversive of public order in the territories in question, shall continue to be admitted free of duty into such territories, for the period of ten years, to be reckoned from the date of the exchange of the ratifications of this treaty.

Article XIV.

Spain will have the power to establish consular officers in the ports and places of the territories, the sovereignty over which has been either relinquished or ceded by the present treaty.

HOW WELL DID YOU UNDERSTAND THIS SELECTION?

1. Summarize the major provisions of the treaty?

2. Did the treaty justify Anti-imperialists concern about American entrance into the Spanish-American War? Why or why not?

3. What territories did Spain cede to the United States? Was the United States justified in taking these territories? Why or why not?

4. After reading the Treaty of Paris of 1898, why did the United States go to war with Spain? Fully explain your answer.

5. What changes did the Treaty of Paris of 1898 bring in American history?

Although Congress pledged in the Teller Amendment that the United States was declaring war on Spain to liberate Cuba and that Cubans should be free to establish their own government, the actual government for Cuba was established under American military occupation of the island. In 1901 Senator Orville Platt attached an amendment to a military appropriations bill that gave the United States a significant degree of control over the Cuban government. This control remained in effect until 1934.

Whereas the Congress of the United States of America, by an Act approved March 2, 1901, provided as follows:

Provided further, That in fulfillment of the declaration contained in the joint resolution approved April twentieth, eighteen hundred and ninety-eight, entitled "For the recognition of the independence of the people of Cuba, demanding that the Government of Spain relinquish its authority and government in the island of Cuba, and withdraw its land and naval forces from Cuba and Cuban waters, and directing the President of the United States to use the land and naval forces of the United States to carry these resolutions into effect," the President is hereby authorized to "leave the government and control of the island of Cuba to its people" so soon as a government shall have been established in said island under a constitution which, either as a part thereof or in an ordinance appended thereto, shall define the future relations of the United States with Cuba, substantially as follows:

"I.-That the government of Cuba shall never enter into any treaty or other compact with any foreign power or powers which will impair or tend to impair the independence of Cuba, nor in any manner authorize or permit any foreign power or powers to obtain by colonization or for military or naval purposes or otherwise, lodgement in or control over any portion of said island."

"II. That said government shall not assume or contract any public debt, to pay the interest upon which, and to make reasonable sinking fund provision for the ultimate discharge of which, the ordinary revenues of the island, after defraying the current expenses of government shall be inadequate."

"III. That the government of Cuba consents that the United States may exercise the right to intervene for the preservation of Cuban independence, the maintenance of a government adequate for the protection of life, property, and individual liberty, and for discharging the obligations with respect to Cuba imposed by the treaty of Paris on the United States, now to be assumed and undertaken by the government of Cuba."

"IV. That all Acts of the United States in Cuba during its military occupancy thereof are ratified and validated, and all lawful rights acquired thereunder shall be maintained and protected."

"V. That the government of Cuba will execute, and as far as necessary extend, the plans already devised or other plans to be mutually agreed upon, for the sanitation of the cities of the island, to the end that a recurrence of epidemic and infectious diseases may be prevented, thereby assuring protection to the people and commerce of Cuba, as well as to the commerce of the southern ports of the United States and the people residing therein."

"VI. That the Isle of Pines shall be omitted from the proposed constitutional boundaries of Cuba, the title thereto being left to future adjustment by treaty."

"VII. That to enable the United States to maintain the independence of Cuba, and to protect the people thereof, as well as for its own defense, the government of Cuba will sell or lease to the United States lands necessary for coaling or naval stations at certain specified points to be agreed upon with the President of the United States."

"VIII. That by way of further assurance the government of Cuba will embody the foregoing provisions in a permanent treaty with the United States."

Source: United States Government Printing Office, Washington D. C.

HOW WELL DID YOU UNDERSTAND THIS SELECTION?

1. Some historians maintain that the Platt Amendment repudiated the Teller Amendment. Is this assessment accurate? Why or why not?

2. Discuss the controls placed on the Cuban government in the Platt Amendment.

3. Why did the American government want to place restrictions on Cuba's government? Were these restrictions justified? Why or why not?

ANTI-IMPERIALEST LEAGUE PLATFORM

Not all Americans supported the acquisition of colonies. They were incensed when the Treaty of Paris of 1898 gave Spain's colonial possessions to the United States and worked to defeat ratification in the Senate. Leading opposition to ratification of the treaty was the Anti-imperial League whose members included author Mark Twain, Supreme Court Justice Morfield Storey, former President Grover Cleveland, and House of Representative Speaker Thomas Reed. The Anti-imperial League articulated its opposition to American colonial expansion in the following platform.

We hold that the policy known as imperialism is hostile to liberty and tends toward militarism, an evil from which it has been our glory to be free. We regret that it has become necessary in the land of Washington and Lincoln *to* reaffirm that all men, of whatever race or color, are entitled to life, liberty and the pursuit of happiness. We maintain that governments derive their just powers from the consent of the governed. We insist that the subjugation of any people is "criminal aggression" and open disloyalty to the distinctive principles of our Government.

We earnestly condemn the policy of the present National Administration in the Philippines. It seeks to extinguish the spirit of 1776 in those islands. We deplore the sacrifice of our soldiers and sailors, whose bravery deserves admiration even in an unjust war. We denounce the slaughter of the Filipinos as a needless horror. We protest against the extension of American sovereignty by Spanish methods.

We demand the immediate cessation of the war against liberty, begun by Spain and continued by us. We urge that Congress be promptly convened to announce to the Filipinos our purpose to concede to them the independence for which they have so long fought and which of right is theirs.

The United States have always protested against the doctrine of international law which permits the subjugation of the weak by the strong. A self-governing state cannot accept sovereignty over an unwilling people. The United States cannot act upon the ancient heresy that might makes right.

Imperialists assume that with the destruction of self-government in the Philippines by American hands, all opposition here will cease. This is a grievous error. Much as we abhor the war of "criminal aggression" in the Philippines, greatly as we regret that the blood of the Filipinos is on American hands, we more deeply resent the betrayal of American institutions at home. The real firing line is not in the suburbs of Manila. The foe is of our own household. The attempt of 1861 was to divide the country. That of 1899 is to destroy its fundamental principles and noblest ideals.

Whether the ruthless slaughter of the Filipinos shall end next month or next year is but an incident in a contest that must go on until the Declaration of Independence and the Constitution of the United States are rescued from the hands of their betrayers. Those who dispute about standards of value while the foundation of the Republic is undermined will be listened to as little as those who would wrangle about the small economies of the household while the house is on fire. The training of a great people for a century, the aspiration for liberty of a vast immigration are forces that will hurl aside those who in the delirium of conquest seek to destroy the character of our institutions.

We deny that the obligation of all citizens to support their Government in times of grave National peril applies to the present situation. If an Administration may with impunity ignore the issues upon which it was chosen, deliberately create a condition of war anywhere on the face of the globe, debauch the civil service for spoils to promote the adventure, organize a truth-suppressing censorship and demand of all citizens a suspension of judgment and their unanimous support while it chooses to continue the fighting, representative government itself is imperiled.

We propose to contribute to the defeat of any person or party that stands for the forcible subjugation of any people. We shall oppose for reelection all who in the White House or in Congress betray American liberty in pursuit of un-American ends. We still hope that both of our great political parties will support and defend the Declaration of Independence in the closing campaign of the century.

We hold, with Abraham Lincoln, that "no man is good enough to govern another man without that other's consent. When the white man governs himself, that is self-government, but when he governs himself and also governs another man, that is more than self-government-that is despotism." "Our reliance is in the love of liberty which God has planted in us. Our defense is in the spirit which prizes liberty as the heritage of all men in all lands. Those who deny freedom to others deserve it not for themselves, and under a just God cannot long retain it."

We cordially invite the cooperation of all men and women who remain loyal to the Declaration of Independence and the Constitution of the United States.

HOW WELL DID YOU UNDERSTAND THIS SELECTION?

1. Why, basically, did Anti-imperialists object to America's acquisition of colonies?

2. How did the platform of the Anti-imperial League appeal to American traditions?

3. How did Anti-imperialists think imperialism violated the principle of self-determination?

4. What impact did the Anti-imperial League fear colonialism might have on the United States?

THE OPEN DOOR POLICY

After ratification of the Treaty of Paris of 1898 the United States became openly imperialistic. Americans demanded open access to newly emerging markets in Asia and elsewhere in the world. The American Secretary of State under President McKinley, John Hay, became particularly concerned about gaining access to China's markets for the United States. Preventing American access to Chinese markets was the division of China into "Spheres of Influence" by other countries. Secretary Hay sent a diplomatic message to Germany and other European nations on September 6, 1899 demanding that they open the door to China for the United States. The Open Door policy established by this note became a part of American foreign policy.

At the time when the Government of the United States was informed by that of Germany that it had leased from His Majesty the Emperor of China the port of Kiao-chao and the adjacent territory in the province of Shantung, assurances were given to the ambassador of the United States at Berlin by the Imperial German minister for foreign affairs that the rights and privileges insured by treaties with China to citizens of the United States would not thereby suffer or be in anywise impaired within the area over which Germany had thus obtained control.

More recently, however, the British Government recognized by a formal agreement with Germany the exclusive right of the latter country to enjoy in said leased area and the contiguous "sphere of influence or interest" certain privileges, more especially those relating to railroads and mining enterprises; but as the exact nature and extent of the rights thus recognized have not been clearly defined, it is possible that serious conflicts of interest may at any time arise not only between British and German subjects within said area, but that the interests of our citizens may also be jeopardized thereby.

Earnestly desirous to remove any cause of irritation and to insure at the same time to the commerce of all nations in China the undoubted benefits which should accrue from a formal recognition by the various powers claiming "spheres of interest" that they shall enjoy perfect equality of treatment for their commerce and navigation within such "spheres," the Government of the United States would be pleased to see His German Majesty's Government give formal assurances, and lend its cooperation in securing like assurances from the other interested powers, that each, within its respective sphere of whatever influence—

First. Will in no way interfere with any treaty port or any vested interest within any so-called "sphere of interest" or leased territory it may have in China.

Second. That the Chinese treaty tariff of the time being shall apply to all merchandise landed or shipped to all such ports as are within said "sphere of interest" (unless they be "free ports"), no matter to what nationality it may belong, and that duties so leviable shall be collected by the Chinese Government.

Third. That it will levy no higher harbor dues on vessels of another nationality frequenting any port in such "sphere" than shall be levied on vessels of its own nationality, and no higher railroad charges over lines built, controlled, or operated within its "sphere" on merchandise belonging to citizens or subjects of other nationalities transported through such "sphere" than shall be levied on similar merchandise belonging to its own nationals transported over equal distances.

The liberal policy pursued by His Imperial German Majesty in declaring Kiao-chao a free port and in aiding the Chinese Government in the establishment there of a custom-house are so clearly in line with the proposition which this Government is anxious to see recognized that it entertains the strongest hope that Germany will give its acceptance and hearty support.

The recent ukase of His Majesty the Emperor of Russia declaring the port of Ta-lien-wan open during the whole of the lease under which it is held from China to the merchant ships of all nations, coupled with the categorical assurances made to this Government by His Imperial Majesty's representative at this capital at the time and since repeated to me by the present Russian ambassador, seem to insure the support of the Emperor to the proposed measure. Our ambassador at the Court of St. Petersburg has in consequence been instructed to submit it to the Russian Government and to request their early consideration of it. A copy of my instruction on the subject to Mr. Tower is herewith inclosed for your confidential information.

The commercial interests of Great Britain and Japan will be so clearly served by the desired declaration of intentions, and the views of the Governments of these countries as to the desirability of the adoption of measures insuring the benefits of equality of treatment of all foreign trade throughout China are so similar to those entertained by the United States, that their acceptance of the propositions herein outlined and their cooperation in advocating their adoption by the other powers can be confidently expected. I inclose herewith copy of the instruction which I have sent to Mr. Choate on the subject.

In view of the present favorable conditions, you are instructed to submit the above considerations to His Imperial German Majesty's Minister for Foreign Affairs, and to request his early consideration of the subject.

Copy of this instruction is sent to our ambassadors at London and at St. Petersburg for their information.
Source: United States Department of State, Papers Relating to Foreign Affairs

HOW WELL DID YOU UNDERSTAND THIS SELECTION?

1. What does Secretary Hay want Germany and other nations to do in regards to China?

2. What motivated Secretary Hay to send the Hay Note to Germany?

3. Why did the policy established in the Hay Note come to be called the Open Door Policy?

4. Is the Open Door Policy another example of American imperialism? Why or why not?

U.S./PANAMA CONVENTION ON THE CANAL ZONE

The United States, long before the Civil War, had been interested in building a canal connecting the Atlantic and Pacific Oceans in Central America. After the Spanish-American War America imperialistic interest in building the canal heightened. In 1903 President Theodore Roosevelt engineered a revolution that broke Panama away from Columbia and dispatched Secretary of State John Hay to negotiate an agreement allowing the United States to construct the canal through Panama's territory. On November 18, 1903, Hay and Panama's representative Philippines Bunau-Varilla inked an agreement giving the United States land on which to construct the Panama Canal. The text of this agreement follows.

Article I

The United States guarantees and will maintain the independence of the Republic of Panama.

Article II

The Republic of Panama grants to the United States in perpetuity, the use, occupation and control of a zone of land and land under water for the construction, maintenance, operation, sanitation and protection of said Canal of the width of ten miles extending to the distance of five miles on each side of the center line of the route of the Canal to be constructed; the said zone beginning in the Caribbean Sea three marine miles from mean low water mark and extending to and across the Isthmus of Panama into the Pacific Ocean to a distance of three marine miles from mean low water mark with the proviso that the cities of Panama and Colon and the harbors adjacent to said cities, which are included within the boundaries of the zone above described, shall not be included within this grant. The Republic of Panama further grants to the United States in perpetuity, the use, occupation and control of any other lands and waters outside of the zone above described which may be necessary and convenient for the construction, maintenance, operation, sanitation and protection of the said Canal or of any auxiliary canals or other works necessary and convenient for the construction, maintenance, operation, sanitation and protection of the said enterprise.

The Republic of Panama further grants in like manner to the United States in perpetuity, all islands within the limits of the zone above described and in addition thereto, the group of small islands in the Bay of Panama, named Perico, Naos, Culebra and Flamenco.

Article III

The Republic of Panama grants to the United States all the rights, power and authority within the zone mentioned and described in Article II of this agreement, and within the limits of all auxiliary lands and waters mentioned and described in said Article II which the United States would possess and exercise, if it were the sovereign of the territory within which said lands and waters are located to the entire exclusion of the exercise by the Republic of Panama of any such sovereign rights, power or authority.

Article IV

As rights subsidiary to the above grants the Republic of Panama grants in perpetuity, to the United States the right to use the rivers, streams, lakes and other bodies of water within its limits for navigation, the supply of water or waterpower or other purposes, so far as the use of said rivers, streams, lakes and bodies of water and the waters thereof may be necessary and convenient for the construction, maintenance, operation, sanitation and protection of the said Canal.

Article V

The Republic of Panama grants to the United States in perpetuity, a monopoly for the construction, maintenance and operation of any system of communication by means of canal or railroad across its territory between the Caribbean Sea and the Pacific Ocean.

Article VI

The grants herein contained shall in no manner invalidate the titles or rights of private land holders or owners of private property in the said zone or in or to any of the lands or waters granted to the United States by the provisions of any Article of this treaty, nor shall they interfere with the rights of way over the public roads passing through the said zone or over any of the said lands or waters unless said rights of way or private rights shall conflict with rights herein granted to the United States in which case the rights of the United States shall be superior. All damages caused to the owners of private lands or private property of any kind by reason of the grants contained in this treaty or by reason of the operations of the United States, its agents or employees, or by reason of the construction, maintenance, operation, sanitation and protection of the said Canal or of the works of sanitation and protection herein provided for, shall be appraised and settled by a joint Commission appointed by the Governments of the United States and the Republic of Panama, whose decisions as to such damages shall be final and whose awards as to such damages shall be paid solely by the United States. No part of the work on said Canal or the Panama railroad or on any auxiliary works relating thereto and authorized by the terms of this treaty shall be prevented, delayed or impeded by or pending such proceedings to ascertain such damages. The appraisal of said private lands and private property and the assessment of damages to them shall be based upon their value before the date of this convention.

Article VII

The Republic of Panama grants to the United States within the limits of the cities of Panama and Colon and their adjacent harbors and within the territory adjacent thereto the right to acquire by purchase or by the exercise of the right of eminent domain, any lands, buildings, water rights or other properties necessary and convenient for the construction, maintenance, operation and protection of the Canal and of any works of sanitation, such as the collection and disposition of sewage and the distribution of water in the said cities of Panama and Colon, which, in the discretion of the United States may be necessary and convenient for the construction, maintenance, operation, sanitation and protection of the said Canal and railroad. All such works of sanitation, collection and disposition of sewage and distribution of water in the cities of Panama and Colon shall be made at the expense of the United States, and the Government of the United States, its agents or nominees shall be authorized to impose and collect water rates and sewage rates which shall be sufficient to provide for the payment of interest and the amortization of the principal of the cost of said works within a period of fifty years and upon the expiration of said term of fifty years the system of sewers and water works shall revert to and become the properties of the cities of Panama and Colon respectively, and the use of the water shall be free to the inhabitants of Panama and Colon, except to the extent that water rates may be necessary for the operation and maintenance of said system of sewers and water.

The Republic of Panama agrees that the cities of Panama and Colon shall comply in perpetuity, with the sanitary ordinances whether of a preventive or curative character prescribed by the United States and in case the Government of Panama is unable or fails in its duty to enforce this compliance by the cities of Panama and Colon with the sanitary ordinances of the United States the Republic of Panama grants to the United States the right and authority to enforce the same.

The same right and authority are granted to the United States for the maintenance of public order in the cities of Panama and Colon and the territories and harbors adjacent thereto in case the Republic of Panama should not be, in the judgment of the United States, able to maintain such order.

Article VIII

The Republic of Panama grants to the United States all rights which it now has or hereafter may acquire to the property of the New Panama Canal Company and the Panama Railroad Company as a result of the transfer of sovereignty from the Republic of Columbia to the Republic of Panama over the Isthmus of Panama and authorizes the New Panama Canal Company to sell and transfer to the United States its rights, privileges, properties and concessions as well as the Panama Railroad and all the shares or part of the shares of that company; but the public lands situated outside of the zone described in Article II of this treaty now included in the concessions of both said enterprises and not required in the construction or operation of the Canal shall revert to the Republic of Panama except any property now owned by or in the possession of said companies within Panama or Colon or the ports or terminals thereof.

Article IX

The United States agrees that the ports at either entrance of the Canal and the waters thereof, and the Republic of Panama agrees that the towns of Panama and Colon shall be free for all time so that there shall not be imposed or collected custom house tolls, tonnage, anchorage, lighthouse, wharf, pilot, or quarantine dues or any other charges or taxes of any kind upon any vessel using or passing through the Canal or belonging to or employed by the United States, directly or indirectly, in connection with the construction, maintenance, operation, sanitation and protection of the main Canal, or auxiliary works, or upon the cargo, officers, crew, or passengers of any such vessels, except such tolls and charges as may be imposed by the United States for the use of the Canal and other works, and except tolls and charges imposed by the Republic of Panama upon merchandise destined to be introduced for the consumption of the rest of the Republic of Panama, and upon vessels touching at the ports of Colon and Panama and which do not cross the Canal.

The Government of the Republic of Panama shall have the right to establish in such ports and in the towns of Panama and Colon such houses and guards as it may deem necessary to collect duties on importations destined to other portions of Panama and to prevent contraband trade. The United States shall have the right to make use of the towns and harbors of Panama and Colon as places of anchorage, and for making repairs, for loading, unloading, depositing, or transshipping cargoes either in transit or destined for the service of the Canal and for other works pertaining to the Canal.

Article X

The Republic of Panama agrees that there shall not be imposed any taxes, national, municipal, departmental, or of any other class, upon the Canal, the railways and auxiliary works, tugs and other vessels employed in the service of the Canal, store houses, work shops, offices, quarters for laborers, factories of all kinds, warehouses, wharves, machinery and other works, property, and effects appertaining to the Canal or railroad and auxiliary works, or their officers or employees, situated within the cities of Panama and Colon, and that there shall not be imposed contributions or charges of a personal character of any kind upon officers, employees, laborers, and other individuals in the service of the Canal and railroad and auxiliary works.

Article XI

The United States agrees that the official dispatches of the Government of the Republic of Panama shall be transmitted over any telegraph and telephone lines established for canal purposes and used for public and private business at rates not higher than those required from officials in the service of the United States.

Article XII

The Government of the Republic of Panama shall permit the immigration and free access to the lands and work-shops of the Canal and its auxiliary works of all employees and workmen of whatever nationality under contract to work upon or seeking employment upon or in any wise connected with the said Canal and its auxiliary works, with their respective families, and all such persons shall be free and exempt from the military service of the Republic of Panama.

Article XIII

The United States may import at any time into the said zone and auxiliary lands, free of custom duties, imposts, taxes, or other charges, and without any restrictions, any and all vessels, dredges, engines, cars, machinery, tools, explosives, materials, supplies, and other articles necessary and convenient in the construction, maintenance, operation, sanitation and protection of the Canal and auxiliary works, and all provisions, medicines, clothing, supplies, and other things necessary and convenient for the officers, employees, workmen and laborers in the service and employ of the United States and for their families. If any such articles are disposed of for use outside of the zone and auxiliary lands granted to the United States and within the territory of the Republic, they shall be subject to the same import or other duties as like articles imported under the laws of the Republic of Panama.

Article XIV

As the price or compensation for the rights, powers and privileges granted in this convention by the Republic of Panama to the United States, the Government of the United States agrees to pay to the Republic of Panama the sum of ten million dollars ($10,000,000) in gold coin of the United States on the exchange of the ratification of this convention and also an annual payment during the life of this convention of two hundred and fifty thousand dollars ($250,000) in like gold coin, beginning nine years after the date aforesaid.

The provisions of this Article shall be in addition to all other benefits assured to the Republic of Panama under this convention.

But no delay or difference of opinion under this Article or any other provisions of this treaty shall affect or interrupt the full operation and effect of this convention in all other respects.

Article XV

The joint commission referred to in Article VI shall be established as follows:

The President of the United States shall nominate two persons and the President of the Republic of Panama shall nominate two persons and they shall proceed to a decision; but in case of disagreement of the Commission (by reason of their being equally divided in conclusion), an umpire shall be appointed by the two Governments who shall render the decision. In the event of the death, absence, or incapacity of a Commissioner or Umpire, or of his omitting, declining or ceasing to act, his place shall be filled by the appointment of another person in the manner above indicated. All decisions by a majority of the Commission or by the umpire shall be final.

Article XVI

The two Governments shall make adequate provision by future agreement for the pursuit, capture, imprisonment, detention and delivery within said zone and auxiliary lands to the authorities of the Republic of Panama of persons charged with the commitment of crimes, felonies, or misdemeanors without said zone and for the pursuit, capture, imprisonment, detention and delivery without said zone to the authorities of the United States of persons charged with the commitment of crimes, felonies and misdemeanors within said zone and auxiliary lands.

Article XVII

The Republic of Panama grants to the United States the use of all the ports of the Republic open to commerce as places of refuge for any vessels employed in the Canal enterprise, and for all vessels passing or bound to pass through the Canal which may be in distress and be driven to seek refuge in said ports. Such vessels shall be exempt from anchorage and tonnage dues on the part of the Republic of Panama.

Article XVIII

The Canal, when constructed, and the entrances thereto shall be neutral in perpetuity, and shall be opened upon the terms provided for by Section I of Article three of, and in conformity with all the stipulations of, the treaty entered into by the Governments of the United States and Great Britain on November 18, 1901.

Article XIX

The Government of the Republic of Panama shall have the right to transport over the Canal, its vessels and its troops and munitions of war in such vessels at all times without paying charges of any kind. The exemption is to be extended to the auxiliary railway for the transportation of persons in the service of the Republic of Panama, or of the police force charged with the preservation of public order outside of said zone, as well as to their baggage, munitions of war and supplies.

Article XX

If by virtue of any existing treaty in relation to the territory of the Isthmus of Panama, whereof the obligations shall descend or be assumed by the Republic of Panama, there may be any privilege or concession in favor of the Government or the citizens and subjects of a third power relative to an interoceanic means of communication which in any of its terms may be incompatible with the terms of the present convention, the Republic of Panama agrees to cancel or modify such treaty in due form, for which purpose it shall give to the said third power the requisite notification within the term of four months from the date of the present convention, and in case the existing treaty contains no clause permitting its modifications or annulment, the Republic of Panama agrees to procure its modification or annulment in such form that there shall not exist any conflict with the stipulations of the present convention.

Article XXI

The rights and privileges granted by the Republic of Panama to the United States in the preceding Articles are understood to be free of all anterior debts, liens, trusts, or liabilities, or concessions or privileges to other Governments, corporations, syndicates or individuals, and consequently, if there should arise any claims on account of the present concessions and privileges or otherwise, the claimants shall resort to the Government of the Republic of Panama, and no to the United States for any indemnity or compromise which may be required.

Article XXII

The Republic of Panama renounces and grants to the United States, the participation to which it might be entitled in the future earnings of the Canal under Article XV of the concessionary contract with Lucien N. B. Wyse, now owned by the New Panama Canal Company and any all other rights or claims of a pecuniary nature arising under or relating to said concession, or arising under or relating to the concessions to the Panama Railroad Company or any extension or modification thereof; and it likewise renounces, confirms and grants to the United States, now and hereafter, all the rights and property reserved in the said concessions which otherwise would belong to Panama at or before the expiration of the terms of ninety - nine years of the concessions granted to or held by the above mentioned party and companies, and all right, title and interest which it now has or may hereafter have, in and to the lands canal, works, property and rights held by the said companies under said concessions or otherwise, and acquired or to be acquired by the United States from or through the New Panama Canal Company, including any property and rights which might or may in the future either by lapse of time, forfeiture or otherwise, revert to the Republic of Panama under any contracts or concessions, with said Wyse, the Universal Panama Canal Company, the Panama Railroad Company and the New Panama Canal Company.

The aforesaid rights and property shall be and are free and released from any present or reversionary interest in or claims of Panama and the title of the United States thereto upon consummation of the contemplated purchase by the United States from the New Panama Canal Company, shall be absolute, so far as concerns the Republic of Panama, excepting always the rights of the Republic specifically secured under this treaty.

Article XXIII

If it should become necessary at any time to employ armed forces for the safety or protection of the Canal, or of the ships that make use of the same, or the railways and auxiliary works, the United States shall have the right, at all times and in its discretion, to use its police and its land and naval forces or to establish fortifications for these purposes.

Article XXIV

No change either in the Government or in the laws and treaties of the Republic of Panama shall, without the consent of the United States, affect any right of the United States under the present convention, or under any treaty stipulation between the two countries that now exists or may hereafter exist touching the subject matter of this convention.

If the Republic of Panama shall hereafter enter as a constituent into any other Government or into any union or confederation of states, so as to merge her sovereignty or independence in such Government, union or confederation, the rights of the United States under this convention shall not be in any respect lessened or impaired.

Article XXV

For the better performance of the engagements of this convention and to the end of the efficient protection of the Canal and the preservation of its neutrality, the Government of the Republic of Panama will sell or lease to the United States lands adequate and necessary for the naval or coaling stations on the Pacific coast and on the western Caribbean coast of the Republic at certain points to be agreed upon with the President of the United States.

Article XXVI

This convention when signed by the Plenipotentiaries of the Contracting Parties shall be ratified by the respective Governments and the ratifications shall be exchanged at Washington at the earliest date possible.

HOW WELL DID YOU UNDERSTAND THIS SELECTION?

1. What are the major provisions of this convention?

2. Did the agreement benefit Panama? Why or why not?

3. Was construction of the Panama Canal part of American Imperialism? Why or why not?

4. Who seemed to benefit most from this convention, the U.S. or Panama? Why?

ROOSEVELT COROLLARY TO THE MONROE DOCTRINE

Theodore Roosevelt was a staunch proponent of imperialism. He believed that the United States should be the dominant power in the Western Hemisphere and was unwilling to tolerate foreign intervention. After sending troops to seize custom houses in the Dominican Republic and collect taxes to repay European debts to stave off foreign intervention in the Caribbean, President Roosevelt issued a significant foreign policy statement in his 1904 State of the Union address to Congress stating how the United States would enforce the Monroe Doctrine issued in 1823 to prevent European intervention into Western Hemisphere nations. Roosevelt's statement became known as the Roosevelt Corollary to the Monroe Doctrine. Excerpts from Roosevelt's address to Congress are included below.

… The steady aim of this Nation, as of all enlightened nations, should be to strive to bring ever nearer the day when there shall prevail throughout the world the peace of justice. There are kinds of peace which are highly undesirable, which are in the long run as destructive as any war. Tyrants and oppressors have many times made a wilderness and called it peace. Many times peoples who were slothful or timid or shortsighted, who had been enervated by ease or by luxury, or misled by false teachings, have shrunk in unmanly fashion from doing duty that was stern and that needed self-sacrifice, and have sought to hide from their own minds their shortcomings, their ignoble motives, by calling them love of peace. The peace of tyrannous terror, the peace of craven weakness, the peace of injustice, all these should be shunned as we shun unrighteous war. The goal to set before us as a nation, the goal which should be set before all mankind, is the attainment of the peace of justice, of the peace which comes when each nation is not merely safe-guarded in its own rights, but scrupulously recognizes and performs its duty toward others. Generally peace tells for righteousness; but if there is conflict between the two, then our fealty is due first to the cause of righteousness. Unrighteous wars are common, and unrighteous peace is rare; but both should be shunned. The right of freedom and the responsibility for the exercise of that right can not be divorced. One of our great poets has well and finely said that freedom is not a gift that tarries long in the hands of cowards. Neither does it tarry long in the hands of those too slothful, too dishonest, or too unintelligent to exercise it. The eternal vigilance which is the price of liberty must be exercised, sometimes to guard against outside foes; although of course far more often to guard against our own selfish or thoughtless shortcomings....

... It is not true that the United States feels any land hunger or entertains any projects as regards the other nations of the Western Hemisphere save such as are for their welfare. All that this country desires is to see the neighboring countries stable, orderly, and prosperous. Any country whose people conduct themselves well can count upon our hearty friendship. If a nation shows that it knows how to act with reasonable efficiency and decency in social and political matters, if it keeps order and pays its obligations, it need fear no interference from the United States. Chronic wrongdoing, or an impotence which results in a general loosening of the ties of civilized society, may in America, as elsewhere, ultimately require intervention by some civilized nation, and in the Western Hemisphere the adherence of the United States to the Monroe Doctrine may force the United States, however reluctantly, in flagrant cases of such wrongdoing or impotence, to the exercise of an international police power. If every country washed by the Caribbean Sea would show the progress in stable and just civilization which with the aid of the Platt Amendment Cuba has shown since our troops left the island, and which so many of the republics in both Americas are constantly and brilliantly showing, all question of interference by this Nation with their affairs would be at an end. Our interests and those of our southern neighbors are in reality identical. They have great natural riches, and if within their borders the reign of law and justice obtains, prosperity is sure to come to them. While they thus obey the primary laws of civilized society they may rest assured that they will be treated by us in a spirit of cordial and helpful sympathy. We would interfere with them only in the last resort, and then only if it became evident that their inability or unwillingness to do justice at home and abroad had violated the rights of the United States or had invited foreign aggression to the detriment of the entire body of American nations. It is a mere truism to say that every nation, whether in America or anywhere else, which desires to maintain its freedom, its independence, must ultimately realize that the right of such independence can not be separated from the responsibility of making good use of it.

In asserting the Monroe Doctrine, in taking such steps as we have taken in regard to Cuba, Venezuela, and Panama, and in endeavoring to circumscribe the theater of war in the Far East, and to secure the open door in China, we have acted in our own interest as well as in the interest of humanity at large. There are, however, cases in which, while our own interests are not greatly involved, strong appeal is made to our sympathies. Ordinarily it is very much wiser and more useful for us to concern ourselves with striving for our own moral and material betterment here at home than to concern ourselves with trying to better the condition of things in other nations. We have plenty of sins of our own to war against, and under ordinary circumstances we can do more for the general uplifting of humanity by striving with heart and soul to put a stop to civic corruption, to brutal lawlessness and violent race prejudices here at home than by passing resolutions and wrongdoing elsewhere. Nevertheless there are occasional crimes committed on so vast a scale and of such peculiar horror as to make us doubt whether it is not our manifest duty to endeavor at least to show our disapproval of the deed and our sympathy with those who have suffered by it. The cases must be extreme in which such a course is justifiable. There must be no effort made to remove the mote from our brother's eye if we refuse to remove the beam from our own. But in extreme cases action may be justifiable and proper. What form the action shall take must depend upon the circumstances of the case; that is, upon the degree of the atrocity and upon our power to remedy it. The cases in which we could interfere by force of arms as we interfered to put a stop to intolerable conditions in Cuba are necessarily very few. Yet it is not to be expected that a people like ours, which in spite of certain very obvious shortcomings, nevertheless as a whole shows by its consistent practice its belief in the principles of civil and religious liberty and of orderly freedom, a people among whom even the worst crime, like the crime of lynching, is never more than sporadic, so that individuals and not classes are molested in their fundamental rights—it is inevitable that such a nation should desire eagerly to give expression to its horror on an

113

occasion like that of the massacre of the Jews in Kishenef, or when it witnesses such systematic and long-extended cruelty and oppression as the cruelty and oppression of which the Armenians have been the victims, and which have won for them the indignant pity of the civilized world....

HOW WELL DID YOU UNDERSTAND THIS SELECTION?

1. What does the Roosevelt Corollary to the Monroe Doctrine essentially do?

2. What does Roosevelt mean when he uses the phrases "the peace of justice?"

3. Is the Roosevelt Corollary another part of American imperialism? Why or why not?

4. What did Roosevelt want other nations to do? If other nations did not abide by the Monroe Doctrine how would the U.S. react?

5. How does Roosevelt justify America's stance regarding the Western Hemisphere?

DOLLAR DIPLOMACY: WILLIAM HOWARD TAFT'S FOREIGN POLICY

William Howard Taft succeeded Theodore Roosevelt as president in 1904. Like Roosevelt, Taft was a proponent of imperialism. Along with Philander Knox, his Secretary of State, Taft pursued a brand of imperialism that promoted American commercial interests. The president's critics mockingly called Taft's policy Dollar Diplomacy. In the following selection Taft explains Dollar Diplomacy.

The foreign relations of the United States actually and potentially affect the state of the Union to a degree not widely realized and hardly surpassed by any other factor in the welfare of the whole nation. The position of the United States in the moral, intellectual, and material relations of the family of nations should be a matter of vital interest to every patriotic citizen. The national prosperity and power impose upon us duties which we cannot shirk if we are to be true to our ideals. The tremendous growth of the export trade of the United States has already made that trade a very real factor in the industrial and commercial prosperity of the country. With the development of our industries, the foreign commerce of the United States must rapidly become a still more essential factor in its economic welfare.

Whether we have a farseeing and wise diplomacy and are not recklessly plunged into unnecessary wars, and whether our foreign policies are based upon an intelligent grasp of present-day world conditions and a clear view of the potentialities of the future, or are governed by a temporary and timid expediency or by narrow views befitting an infant nation, are questions in the alternative consideration of which must convince any thoughtful citizen that no department of national polity offers greater opportunity for promoting the interests of the whole people on the one hand, or greater chance on the other of permanent national injury, than that which deals with the foreign relations of the United States.

The fundamental foreign policies of the United States should be raised high above the conflict of partisanship and wholly dissociated from differences as to domestic policy. In its foreign affairs the United States should present to the world a united front. The intellectual, financial, and industrial interests of the country and the publicist, the wage earner, the farmer, and citizen of whatever occupation must cooperate in a spirit of high patriotism to promote that national solidarity which is indispensable to national efficiency and to the attainment of national ideals. . . .

The diplomacy of the present administration has sought to respond to modern ideas of commercial intercourse. This policy has been characterized as substituting dollars for bullets. It is one that appeals alike to idealistic humanitarian sentiments, to the dictates of sound policy and strategy, and to legitimate commercial aims. It is an effort frankly directed to the increase of American trade upon the axiomatic principle that the government of the United States shall extend all proper support to every legitimate and beneficial American enterprise abroad.

How great have been the results of this diplomacy, coupled with the maximum and minimum provision of the Tariff Law, will be seen by some consideration of the wonderful increase in the export trade of the United States. Because modern diplomacy is commercial, there has been a disposition in some quarters to attribute to it none but materialistic aims. How strikingly erroneous is such an impression may be seen from a study of the results by which the diplomacy of the United States can be judged.

In the field of work toward the ideals of peace, this government negotiated, but to my regret was unable to consummate, two arbitration treaties which set the highest mark of the aspiration of nations toward the substitution of arbitration and reason for war in the settlement of international disputes. Through the efforts of American diplomacy, several wars have been prevented or ended. I refer to the successful tripartite mediation of the Argentine Republic, Brazil, and the United States between Peru and Ecuador; the bringing of the boundary dispute between Panama and Costa Rica to peaceful arbitration; the staying of warlike preparations when Haiti and the Dominican Republic were on the verge of hostilities; the stopping of a war in Nicaragua; the halting of internecine strife in Honduras.

The government of the United States was thanked for its influence toward the restoration of amicable relations between the Argentine Republic and Bolivia. The diplomacy of the United States is active in seeking to assuage the remaining ill feeling between this country and the Republic of Colombia. In the recent civil war in China, the United

States successfully joined the other interested powers in urging an early cessation of hostilities. An agreement has been reached between the governments of Chile and Peru whereby the celebrated Tacna-Arica dispute, which has so long embittered international relations on the west coast of South America, has at last been adjusted. Simultaneously came the news that the boundary dispute between Peru and Ecuador had entered upon a stage of amicable settlement.

The position of the United States in reference to the Tacna-Arica dispute between Chile and Peru has been one of nonintervention, but one of friendly influence and pacific counsel throughout the period during which the dispute in question has been the subject of interchange of views between this government and the two governments immediately concerned. In the general easing of international tension on the west coast of South America, the tripartite mediation, to which I have referred, has been a most potent and beneficent factor.

In China the policy of encouraging financial investment to enable that country to help itself has had the result of giving new life and practical application to the open door policy. The consistent purpose of the present administration has been to encourage the use of American capital in the development of China by the promotion of those essential reforms to which China is pledged by treaties with the United States and other powers. The hypothecation to foreign bankers in connection with certain industrial enterprises, such as the Hukuang railways, of the national revenues upon which these reforms depended, led the Department of State, early in the administration, to demand for American citizens participation in such enterprises, in order that the United States might have equal rights and an equal voice in all questions pertaining to the disposition of the public revenues concerned.

The same policy of promoting international accord among the powers having similar treaty rights as ourselves in the matters of reform, which could not be put into practical effect without the common consent

of all, was likewise adopted in the case of the loan desired by China for the reform of its currency. The principle of international cooperation in matters of common interest upon which our policy had already been based in all of the above instances has admittedly been a great factor in that concert of the powers which has been so happily conspicuous during the perilous period of transition through which the great Chinese nation has been passing.

In Central America the aim has been to help such countries as Nicaragua and Honduras to help themselves. They are the immediate beneficiaries. The national benefit to the United States is twofold. First, it is obvious that the Monroe Doctrine is more vital in the neighborhood of the Panama Canal and the zone of the Caribbean than anywhere else. There, too, the maintenance of that doctrine falls most heavily upon the United States. It is therefore essential that the countries within that sphere shall be removed from the jeopardy involved by heavy foreign debt and chaotic national finances and from the ever present danger of international complications due to disorder at home. Hence, the United States has been glad to encourage and support American bankers who were willing to lend a helping hand to the financial rehabilitation of such countries because this financial rehabilitation and the protection of their customhouses from being the prey of would-be dictators would remove at one stroke the menace of foreign creditors and the menace of revolutionary disorder.

The second advantage to the United States is one affecting chiefly all the Southern and Gulf ports and the business and industry of the South. The republics of Central America and the Caribbean possess great natural wealth. They need only a measure of stability and the means of financial regeneration to enter upon an era of peace and prosperity, bringing profit and happiness to themselves and at the same time creating conditions sure to lead to a flourishing interchange of trade with this country.

I wish to call your especial attention to the recent occurrences in Nicaragua, for I believe the terrible events recorded there during the revolution of the past summer - the useless loss of life, the devastation of property, the bombardment of defenseless cities, the killing and wounding of women and children, the torturing of noncombatants, to exact contributions, and the suffering of thousands of human beings - might have been averted had the Department of State, through approval of the loan convention by the Senate, been permitted to carry out its now well-developed policy of encouraging the extending of financial aid to weak Central American states, with the primary objects of avoiding just such revolutions by assisting those republics to rehabilitate their finances, to establish their currency on a stable basis, to remove the customhouses from the danger of revolutions by arranging for their secure administration, and to establish reliable banks.

During this last revolution in Nicaragua, the government of that republic having admitted its inability to protect American life and property against acts of sheer lawlessness on the part of the malcontents, and having requested this government to assume that office, it became necessary to land over 2,000 Marines and Bluejackets in Nicaragua. Owing to their presence the constituted government of Nicaragua was free to devote its attention wholly to its internal troubles, and was thus enabled to stamp out the rebellion in a short space of time. When the Red Cross supplies sent to Granada had been exhausted, 8,000 persons having been given food in one day upon the arrival of the American forces, our men supplied other unfortunate, needy Nicaraguans from their own haversacks.

I wish to congratulate the officers and men of the United States Navy and Marine Corps who took part in reestablishing order in Nicaragua upon their splendid conduct, and to record with sorrow the death of seven American Marines and Bluejackets. Since the reestablishment of peace and order, elections have been held amid conditions of quiet and tranquility. Nearly all the American Marines have now been withdrawn. The country should soon be on the road to recovery. The only apparent danger now threatening Nicaragua arises from the shortage of funds. Although American bankers have already rendered assistance, they may naturally be loath to advance a loan adequate to set the country upon its feet without the support of some such convention as that of June 1911, upon which the Senate has not yet acted. . . .

It is not possible to make to the Congress a communication upon the present foreign relations of the United States so detailed as to convey an adequate impression of the enormous increase in the importance and activities of those relations. If this government is really to preserve to the American people that free opportunity in foreign markets which will soon be indispensable to our prosperity, even greater efforts must be made. Otherwise the American merchant, manufacturer, and exporter will find many a field in which American trade should logically predominate preempted through the more energetic efforts of other governments and other commercial nations.

There are many ways in which, through hearty cooperation, the legislative and executive branches of this government can do much. The absolute essential is the spirit of united effort and singleness of purpose. I will allude only to a very few specific examples of action which ought then to result.

America cannot take its proper place in the most important fields for its commercial activity and enterprise unless we have a Merchant Marine. American commerce and enterprise cannot be effectively fostered in those fields unless we have good American banks in the countries referred to. We need American newspapers in those countries and proper means for public information about them.

We need to assume the permanency of a trained foreign service. We need legislation enabling the members of the foreign service to be systematically brought in direct contact with the industrial, manufacturing, and exporting interests of this country in order that American businessmen may enter the foreign field with a clear perception of the exact conditions to be dealt with and the officers themselves may prosecute their work with a clear idea of what American industrial and manufacturing interests require.

Congress should fully realize the conditions which obtain in the world as we find ourselves at the threshold of our middle age as a nation. We have emerged full grown as a peer in the great concourse of nations. We have passed through various formative periods. We have been self-centered in the struggle to develop our domestic resources and deal with our domestic questions. The nation is now too mature to continue in its foreign relations those temporary expedients natural to a people to whom domestic affairs are the sole concern.

In the past, our diplomacy has often consisted, in normal times, in a mere assertion of the right to international existence. We are now in a larger relation with broader rights of our own and obligations to others than ourselves. A number of great guiding principles were laid down early in the history of this government. The recent task of our diplomacy has been to adjust those principles to the conditions of today, to develop their corollaries, to find practical applications of the old principles expanded to meet new situations. Thus are being evolved bases upon which can rest the superstructure of policies which must grow with the destined progress of this nation.

The successful conduct of our foreign relations demands a broad and a modern view. We cannot meet new questions nor build for the future if we confine ourselves to outworn dogmas of the past and to the perspective appropriate at our emergence from colonial times and conditions. The opening of the Panama Canal will mark a new era in our international life and create new and worldwide conditions which, with their vast correlations and consequences, will obtain for hundreds of years to come. We must not wait for events to overtake us unawares. With continuity of purpose we must deal with the problems of our external relations by a diplomacy modern, resourceful, magnanimous, and fittingly expressive of the high ideals of a great nation.

HOW WELL DID YOU UNDERSTAND THIS SELECTION?

1. What are the main tenants of Taft's Dollar Diplomacy?

2. How does Taft see trade, diplomacy, and American national interest as related?

3. Do you agree with Dollar Diplomacy? Why or why not?

4. Is Taft's Dollar Diplomacy part of American imperialism? Why or why not?

5. What is the relationship between Roosevelt's Big Stick policy and Dollar Diplomacy? How do these policies differ?

SELF TEST:

MULTIPLE CHOICE: Circle the correct response. The correct answers are given at the end.

1. Which one of the following did not contribute to American imperialism?
    a. Social Darwinism
    b. Business wanting to establish new markets
    c. Religious missionary activity
    d. The Civil War

2. _____ wrote the Influence of Sea Power on History that promoted imperialism.
    a. Theodore Roosevelt
    b. Fredrick Jackson Turner
    c. Alfred Thayer Mahan
    d. Fredrick Douglass

3. The Spanish minister who criticized President McKinley in a letter intercepted by Cuban rebels was
   a. Dupuy de Lome
   b. Felipe Valdaz
   c. Hermano de Soto
   d. Jorge Martinez

4. Which one of the following territories was not acquired from Spain as a result of the Spanish-American War?
   a. Guam
   b. Hawaii
   c. Puerto Rico
   d. The Philippine Islands

5. _____ was the diplomatic agreement that officially ended the Spanish-American War and gave the United States overseas colonies.
   a. The Open Door Treaty
   b. The Hay-Pauncefote Treaty
   c. The Treaty of Paris 1898
   d. The Panama Canal Treaty

6. What did the Teller Amendment state?
   a. That the U.S. wanted to acquire Cuba as a colony.
   b. That the U.S. had no desire to assert control over Cuba.
   c. That the U.S. was entering the Spanish-America War to acquire overseas colonies.
   d. That the U.S. was going to annex Hawaii.

7. Why did Anti-imperialists object to American acquisition of overseas colonies?
   a. They thought territorial acquisition violated the founding principle of self-determination.
   b. They believed that American business would face a serious decline if the U.S. acquired colonies.
   c. They wanted to send American missionaries to "freely" convert heathens to Christianity.
   d. They believed the U.S. budget deficit could not support territorial acquisition.

8. Which one of the following was not an Anti-imperialist?
   a. Mark Twain
   b. Thomas Reed
   c. Morfield Storey
   d. Theodore Roosevelt

9. Theodore Roosevelt's policy promoting American imperialism is called
   a. Dollar Diplomacy
   b. The Square Deal
   c. The Big Stick Policy
   d. Jingoist Diplomacy

10. William Howard Taft's policy that promoted American economies interests was called
   a. The Big Stick
   b. Dollar Diplomacy
   c. Imperial Capitalism
   d. Industrial Imperialism

Answers: 1-d; 2-c; 3-a; 4-b; 5-c; 6-b; 7-a; 8-d; 9-c; 10-b

Essays:

1. Why did the U.S. become imperialistic?

2. 1898 is often said to mark a turning point in American History. Explain why this year marked a significant change for the United States.

3. Compare and contrast the foreign policy of Theodore Roosevelt and William Howard Taft.

4. Discuss the impact, both positive and negative, that imperialism had on the United States.

Optional Activities:

1. Pretend that you are an Anti-Imperialist. Write a letter to President McKinley urging a reconsideration of the declaration of war on Spain.

2. Your class is the United States Senate. Stage a debate over ratification of the Treaty of Paris of 1898.

3. Conduct research on Social Darwinism. What were its main tenants? Who was responsible for its development? What impact has the theory had on American development? Do Americans still believe in Social Darwinism?

WEB SITE LISTINGS:

Spanish American War
> http://www.loc.gov/rr/hispanic/1898/

Several interesting images from the Spanish-American War are found at this Smithsonian Institute site:
> http://americanhistory.si.edu/militaryhistory/printable/section.asp?id=7

Companion site to PBS documentary *Crucible of Empire: The Spanish-American War*
> http://www.pbs.org/crucible/

This Library of Congress site provides information about and access to the role of motion pictures in the first war they impacted. Click on various links and presentations at this site for information about various aspects of the war.
> http://memory.loc.gov/ammem/sawhtml/sawhome.html

Historic Maps of the Philippines
> http://www.loc.gov/rr/hispanic/1898/mapphil.html

Treaties & Proclamations Texts and Other Documents
> http://www.msc.edu.ph/centennial/philam-documents.html
> http://www.yale.edu/lawweb/avalon/19th.htm
> http://www.mtholyoke.edu/acad/intrel/to1914.htm
> http://www.fordham.edu/halsall/mod/modsbook34.html#American%20Imperialism

U.S. Navy site on the war
> http://www.history.navy.mil/photos/events/spanam/eve-pge.htm

New York Public Library online exhibition "A War in Perspective 1898-1998"
> http://www.nypl.org/research/chss/epo/spanexhib/

University of Virginia site on yellow fever research conducted in the context of American occupation of Cuba by a commission headed by Walter Reed.
> http://www.healthsystem.virginia.edu/internet/library/historical/medical_history/yellow_fever/index.c

Chapter Sixteen

PROGRESSIVISM

Periodically, forces of reform arise within the United States. These include the American Revolutionary War and the Constitution, the Jeffersonian Revolution, Jacksonian Democracy, the Civil War and Reconstruction, the agrarian Populist Revolt of the 1890s, the New Deal of the 1930s, and the Great Society of the 1960s. Progressivism was such a period of reform that broke out nationally around 1900 and lasted until about 1920. Progressivism, however, was different from previous reform movements in that it was urban based rather than rural based. In general, Progressivism, which drew upon the Populist Revolt of the preceding decade, was a reaction to the evils and problems created by the Industrial Revolution. Progressive reformers realized that robber barons such as John D. Rockerfeller, Andrew Carnegie, J. P. Morgan, and others had become so wealthy that only government could curb their power. Thus, reformers like Robert LaFollette, Theodore Roosevelt, Ida Tarbell, Jane Addams, and others favored the use of governmental power at all levels—municipal, county, state, and national—to curb the child labor, corporate and political corruption, horrible working conditions, poor sanitation in the meat processing industry, poverty, poor housing, and other problems the industrialization brought to America.

Although Progressive reformers were primarily white, middle class, educated, and Protestant, the movement to a limited degree cut across socio-economic and class lines and party lines. Occasionally, the poor became active in the Progressive movement, working alongside their rich and middle-class brothers and sisters, especially in settlements houses like Hull House operated by Jane Addams in Chicago. Certainly, Progressives resided within both the Democratic and Republican Parties and Progressives could be found in practically every racial and ethnic group, including white, African American, Old Immigrants from Northern and Western European countries and New Immigrants from Southern and Eastern European nations. Mostly, however, Progressive reformers felt sorry for the less fortunate and wanted to rid society of the excesses created by industrial capitalism. They wanted to Americanize the millions of new immigrants who had come to America from southern and eastern European countries and prevent others from coming. Progressives also exhibited racism when it came to African Americans. Ridding society of racial injustice was not an item on the Progressive agenda.

Progressives certainly were not radicals in that they wanted to abolish capitalism in favor of socialism. Nor were Progressives anti-business. In fact, many reforms pushed by Progressives, including industrial accident insurance and the Meat Inspection Acts and the Pure Food and Drug Acts, actually helped business by leveling the playing field for all companies in the industry. Progressives were motivated by different concerns, including moral outrage, humanitarianism, idealism, fear, anxiety, self-interest, concern about societal changes, economic self preservation, political interests, and a desire to preserve their class status in society. Progressive goals and objectives were often contradictory and conservative in nature. Some Progressive reformers, for example, supported legislation to control the poor and working class but at the same time advocated social justice measures that would improve the lives of poor workers. Other Progressives supported immigration restriction, prohibition of alcohol, and laws to sterilize the poor to prevent them from having children.

Three groups of people were extremely important to the Progressive reform movement—Muckrakers, women reformers, and politicians. Muckrakers, named by President Theodore Roosevelt who said they raked around in the muck and exposed the sleazy side of American life, were investigative journalists employed by newspapers and magazines read by the middle class. Muckrakers primarily identified the myriad problems that existed in America as a result of industrial development and demanded that something be done to solve them. The thousands of Americans who read muckraking accounts of wealthy industrialists who lived in palatial mansions practically within site of the tenement houses their workers, who were paid wages of a few cents per hour, resided in, or stories about child labor, or corporate greed, or the thousands of other problems and inequities created by corporate America became outraged and demanded governmental action to deal with these issues. Women reformers, like Jane Addams and others, were crucial to Progressive reform because they organized ordinary Americans to demand intervention from the various governmental units throughout the United States. Much of their work was done through an institution known as the settlement house. After visiting a settlement house in England, Addams established America's first such institution, Hull House, in Chicago. An entire generation of women reformers trained at Hull House in social work and fanned out across America, establishing settlement houses and schools in many localities and using them to organize people for reform. Some elected officials listened to the demand for reform and were willing to enact legislation and issue executive orders to deal with many of America's problems. In fact, Robert LaFollette is often called the father of the Progressive Movement as he was perhaps the first politician as mayor of Milwaukee to use the power of government to curb corporate abuses. He later held office in state government and was elected to the United States Senate, bringing Progressive reform with him to all levels of government. Three American presidents—Theodore Roosevelt, William Howard Taft, and Woodrow Wilson—were Progressives. Each used the power of the federal government to curb the abuses of the Industrial Revolution. Roosevelt, the first Progressive president, used the Sherman Antitrust Act to break up monopolistic corporations, enacted the Pure Food and Drug Act, and two Meat Inspection Acts, placed thousands of acres of land under conservation, and did a host of other things to solve America's problems. Taft and Wilson continued Roosevelt's Progressive reforms, putting even more land under conservation, enacting more laws to regulate business, and breaking more trusts.

Progressivism began to end after 1916 due in part to the outbreak of World War I and because Americans had become tired of crusades to bring about reform. Even though few new Progressive laws were enacted after 1916, Progressivism has never completely ended. Many laws enacted by Progressive politicians, such as the Clayton Antitrust Act, the Federal Reserve Act, and compulsory education laws enacted to overcome the Supreme Court's declaration of the National Child Labor Act as unconstitutional are still important to Americans.

IDENTIFICATION: Briefly describe each item.

Muckrakers

Henry Demarest Lloyd

Jacob Riis

Lincoln Steffens

Ida Tarbell

Upton Sinclair

Ida Wells Barnett

Women's Christian Temperance Union

Social Gospel

Jane Addams

Hull House

Florence Kelley

Carrie Chapman Catt

National American Woman Suffrage Association [NAWSA]

Alice Paul

Muller v Oregon

Theodore Roosevelt

Hepburn Act

Pure Food and Drug Act

Meat Inspection Act

William Howard Taft

Progressive or Bull Moose Party

Woodrow Wilson

Underwood Tariff

Sixteenth Amendment

Seventeenth Amendment

Federal Reserve Act

Federal Trade Commission Act

Clayton Antitrust Act

Eighteenth Amendment

Nineteenth Amendment

THINK ABOUT:

1. What problems did the American Industrial Revolution create?

2. How did Americans in general react to the millions of New Immigrants who migrated to the United States in search of a better life? Could American industrialization have proceeded without the New Immigrants? Why or why not?

3. What positive and negative changes did America's rapid industrialization cause?

4. How did Progressive Reforms change American society? How did Progressive reforms change the American government?

5. Did the Progressive Movement ever really end? Why or why not?

At the urging of Woodrow Wilson, Congress enacted the Clayton Antitrust Act in 1914 to control huge corporations and provide protection for the American public against monopolistic companies. Specifically, the Clayton Act gave the government stronger teeth to go after violators of the nation's antitrust laws. In 1890 Congress passed the Sherman Antitrust Act, which represented America's first real effort to curb monopolies that arose from the Industrial Revolution. While the Sherman Act declared that trusts and monopolies were illegal business organizations, it did not define exactly what a monopoly or trust was. Every time the federal government filed an antitrust suit against a company alleging monopolistic practices, the company's defense was generally that the Sherman Act was vague and that the actions of the company in that particular incident did not constitute a violation of the law. The Clayton Antitrust Act was designed to supplement the Sherman Antitrust Act by specifically identifying business practices that would be considered monopolistic, thus making it easier for the federal government to prosecute monopolistic corporations. Because the Clayton Antitrust Act is a lengthy document, only selected sections have been included.

Section 13: Discrimination in Prices, Services, or Facilities

It shall be unlawful for any person engaged in commerce, in the course of such commerce, either directly or indirectly, to discriminate in price between different purchasers of commodities of like grade and quality, where either or any of the purchases involved in such discrimination are in commerce, where such commodities are sold for use, consumption, or resale within the United States or any Territory thereof or the District of Columbia or any insular possession or other place under the jurisdiction of the United States, and where the effect of such discrimination may be substantially to lessen competition or tend to create a monopoly in any line of commerce, or to injure, destroy, or prevent competition with any person who either grants or knowingly receives the benefit of such discrimination, or with customers of either of them: Provided, That nothing herein contained shall prevent differentials which make only due allowance for differences in the cost of manufacture, sale, or delivery resulting from the differing methods or quantities in which such commodities are to such purchasers sold or delivered: Provided, however, That the Federal Trade Commission may, after due investigation and hearing to all interested parties, fix and establish quantity limits, and revise the same as it finds necessary, as to particular commodities or classes of commodities, where it finds that available purchasers in greater quantities are so few as to render differentials on account thereof unjustly discriminatory or promotive of monopoly in any line of commerce; and the foregoing shall then not be construed to permit differentials based on differences in quantities greater than those so fixed and established: And provided further, That nothing herein contained shall prevent persons engaged in selling goods, wares, or merchandise in commerce from selecting their own customers in bona fide transactions and not in restraint of trade: And provided further, That nothing herein contained shall prevent price changes from time to time where in response to changing conditions affecting the market for or the marketability of the goods concerned, such as but not limited to actual or imminent deterioration of perishable goods, obsolescence of seasonal goods, distress sales under court process, or sales in good faith in discontinuance of business in the goods concerned.

It shall be unlawful for any person engaged in commerce, in the course of such commerce, to pay or grant, or to receive or accept, anything of value as a commission, brokerage, or other compensation, or any allowance or discount in lieu thereof, except for services rendered in connection with the sale or purchase of goods, wares, or merchandise, either to the other party to such transaction or to an agent, representative, or other intermediary therein where such intermediary is acting in fact for or in behalf, or is subject to the direct or indirect control, of any party to such transaction other than the person by whom such compensation is so granted or paid.

It shall be unlawful for any person engaged in commerce to pay or contact for the payment of anything of value to or for the benefit of a customer of such person in the course of such commerce as compensation or in consideration for any services or facilities furnished by or through such customer in connection with the processing, handling, sale, or offering for sale of any products or commodities manufactured, sold, or offered for sale by such person, unless

125

such payment or consideration is available on proportionally equal terms to all other customers competing in the distribution of such products or commodities.

It shall be unlawful for any person to discriminate in favor of one purchaser against another purchaser or purchasers of a commodity bought for resale, with or without processing, by contracting to furnish or furnishing, or by contributing to the furnishing of, any services or facilities connected with the processing, handling, sale, or offering for sale of such commodity so purchased upon terms not accorded to all purchasers on proportionally equal terms.

It shall be unlawful for any person engaged in commerce, in the course of such commerce, knowingly to induce or receive a discrimination in price which is prohibited by this section.

It shall be unlawful for any person engaged in commerce, in the course of such commerce, to be a party to, or assist in, any transaction of sale, or contract to sell, which discriminates to his knowledge against competitors of the purchaser, in that, any discount, rebate, allowance, or advertising service charge is granted to the purchaser over and above any discount, rebate, allowance, or advertising service charge available at the time of such transaction to said competitors in respect of a sale of goods of like grade, quality, and quantity; to sell, or contract to sell, goods in any part of the United States at prices lower than those exacted by said person elsewhere in the United States for the purpose of destroying competition, or eliminating a competitor in such part of the United States; or, to sell, or contract to sell, goods at unreasonably low prices for the purpose of destroying competition or eliminating a competitor.

Any person violating any of the provisions of this section shall, upon conviction thereof, be fined not more than $5,000 or imprisoned not more than one year, or both.

It shall be unlawful for any person engaged in commerce, in the course of such commerce, to lease or make a sale or contract for sale of goods, wares, merchandise, machinery, supplies, or other commodities, whether patented or unpatented, for use, consumption, or resale within the United States or any Territory thereof or the District of Columbia or any insular possession or other place under the jurisdiction of the United States, or fix a price charged therefor, or discount from, or rebate upon, such price, on the condition, agreement, or understanding that the lessee or purchaser thereof shall not use or deal in the goods, wares, merchandise, machinery, supplies, or other commodities of a competitor or competitors of the lessor or seller, where the effect of such lease, sale, or contract for sale or such condition, agreement, or understanding may be to substantially lessen competition or tend to create a monopoly in any line of commerce.

> No person engaged in commerce or in any activity affecting commerce shall acquire, directly or indirectly, the whole or any part of the stock or other share capital and no person subject to the jurisdiction of the Federal Trade Commission shall acquire the whole or any part of the assets of another person engaged also in commerce or in any activity affecting commerce, where in any line of commerce or in any activity affecting commerce in any section of the country, the effect of such acquisition may be substantially to lessen competition, or to tend to create a monopoly.

No person shall acquire, directly or indirectly, the whole or any part of the stock or other share capital and no person subject to the jurisdiction of the Federal Trade Commission shall acquire the whole or any part of the assets of one or more persons engaged in commerce or in any activity affecting commerce, where in any line of commerce or in any activity affecting commerce in any section of the country, the effect of such acquisition, of such stocks or assets, or of the use of such stock by the voting or granting of proxies or otherwise, may be substantially to lessen competition, or to tend to create a monopoly.

HOW WELL DID YOU UNDERSTAND THIS SECTION?

1. Based on your reading of the Clayton Antitrust Act, describe what a trust actually is?

2. What specific business practices does the Clayton Antitrust Act make illegal?

3. What does the Clayton Antitrust Act say about stock acquisition?

KEATING OWEN CHILD LABOR ACT, 1916

Progressives were immensely concerned about child welfare. Part of their concern stemmed from the fact that thousands of children younger than ten years of age worked in America's factories and coal mines. A crusade to outlaw child labor had been under way for years. By 1916 practically every state except North Carolina had already abolished child labor. In that year, President Wilson, at the behest of Progressive Reformers signed the Keating Owen Child Labor Act of 1916, which prohibited most children from working. For a short time it seemed that the tireless efforts of reformers, social workers and unions had been successful. Unfortunately, two years later, a conservative Supreme Court declared the Keating Owen Child Labor Act to be unconstitutional. Progressives were back to square one. Plucky Progressive reformers, however, were not so easily defeated. If they could not prohibit child labor by passing a national law, they would prohibit it by enacting compulsory education laws in states that generally required children to remain in school until they reached the age of 16. Progressives reasoned that if children were required to be in school by the law they could not work. School districts were authorized to appoint truant officers who could file charges against and arrest parents who did not send children to school on a regular basis.

AN ACT To prevent interstate commerce in the products of child labor, and for other purposes. Be it enacted by the Senate and House of Representatives of the United States of America in Congress assembled, That no producer, manufacturer, or dealer shall ship or deliver for shipment in interstate or foreign commerce, any article or commodity the product of any mine or quarry situated in the United States, in which within thirty days prior to the time of the removal of such product therefrom children under the age of sixteen years have been employed or permitted to work, or any article or commodity the product of any mill, cannery, workshop, factory, or manufacturing establishment, situated in the United States, in which within thirty days prior to the removal of such product therefrom children under the age of fourteen years have been employed or permitted to work, or children between the ages of fourteen years and sixteen years have been employed or permitted to work more than eight hours in any day, or more than six days in any week, or after the hour of seven o'clock postmeridian, or before the hour of six o'clock antemeridian: Provided, That a prosecution and conviction of a defendant for the shipment or delivery for shipment of any article or commodity under the conditions herein prohibited shall be a bar to any further prosecution against the same defendant for shipments or deliveries for shipment of any such article or commodity before the beginning of said prosecution.

SEC. 2. That the Attorney General, the Secretary of Commerce and the Secretary of Labor shall constitute a board to make and publish from time to time uniform rules and regulations for carrying out the provisions of this Act.

SEC. 3. That for the purpose of securing proper enforcement of this Act the Secretary of Labor, or any person duly authorized by him, shall have authority to enter and inspect at any time mines quarries, mills, canneries, workshops, factories, manufacturing establishments, and other places in which goods are produced or held for interstate commerce; and the Secretary of Labor shall have authority to employ such assistance for the purposes of this Act as may from time to time be authorized by appropriation or other law.

SEC. 4. That it shall be the duty of each district attorney to whom the Secretary of Labor shall report any violation of this Act, or to whom any State factory or mining or quarry inspector, commissioner of labor, State medical inspector or school-attendance officer, or any other person shall present satisfactory evidence of any such violation to cause appropriate proceedings to be commenced and prosecuted in the proper courts of the United States without delay for the enforcement of the penalties in such cases herein provided: Provided, That nothing in this Act shall be construed to apply to bona fide boys' and girls' canning clubs recognized by the Agricultural Department of the several States and of the United States.

SEC. 5. That any person who violates any of the provisions of section one of this Act, or who refuses or obstructs entry or inspection authorized by section three of this Act, shall for each offense prior to the first conviction of such person under the provisions of this Act, be punished by a fine of not more than $200, and shall for each offense subsequent to such conviction be punished by a fine of not more than $1,000, nor less than $100, or by imprisonment for not more than three months, or by both such fine and imprisonment, in the discretion of the court: Provided, That no dealer shall be prosecuted under the provisions of this Act for a shipment, delivery for shipment, or transportation who establishes a guaranty issued by the person by whom the goods shipped or delivered for shipment or transportation were manufactured or produced, resident in the United States, to the effect that such goods were produced or manufactured in a mine or quarry in which within thirty days prior to their removal therefrom no children under the age of sixteen years were employed or permitted to work, or in a mill, cannery, workshop, factory, or manufacturing establishment in which within thirty days prior to the removal of such goods therefrom no children under the ages of fourteen years were employed or permitted to work, nor children between the ages of fourteen years and sixteen years employed or permitted to work more than eight hours in any day or more than six days in any week or after the hour of seven o'clock postmeridian o before the hour of six o'clock antemeridian; and in such event, if the guaranty contains any false statement or a material fact the guarantor shall be amenable to prosecution and to the fine or imprisonment provided by this section for violation of the provisions of this Act. Said guaranty, to afford the protection above provided, shall contain the name and address of the person giving the same: And provided further, That no producer, manufacturer, or dealer shall be prosecuted under this Act for the shipment, delivery for shipment, or transportation of a product of any mine, quarry, mill, cannery, workshop, factory, or manufacturing establishment, if the only employment therein within thirty days prior to the removal of such product there from, of a child under the age of sixteen years has been that of a child as to whom the producer, or manufacturer has in; good faith procured, at the time of employing such child, and has since in good faith relied upon and kept on file a certificate, issued in such form, under such conditions, any by such persons as may be prescribed by the board, showing the child to be of such an age that the shipment, delivery for shipment, or transportation was not prohibited by this Act. Any person who knowingly makes a false statement or presents false evidence in or in relation to any such certificate or application therefor shall be amenable to prosecution and to the fine or imprisonment provided by this section for violations of this Act. In any State designated by the board, an employment certificate or other similar paper as to the age of the child, issued under the laws of that State and not inconsistent with the provisions of this Act, shall have the same force and effect as a certificate herein provided for.

SEC. 6. That the word person as used in this Act shall be construed to include any individual or corporation or the members of any partnership or other unincorporated association. The term ship or deliver for shipment in interstate or foreign commerce as used in this Act means to transport or to ship or deliver for shipment from any State or Territory or the District of Columbia to or through any other State or Territory or the District of Columbia or to any foreign country; and in the case of a dealer means only to transport or to ship or deliver for shipment from the State, Territory or district of manufacture or production.

SEC. 7. That this Act shall take effect from and after one year from the date of its passage. Approved, September 1, 1916.

Source: US Department of Labor

HOW WELL DID YOU UNDERSTAND THIS SELECTION?

1. Upon what legal/constitutional basis did the Keating Owen Child Labor Act seek to end child labor?

2. What penalties were prescribed for violation of the Keating Owen Child Labor Act?

HOW THE OTHER HALF LIVES: Studies Among the Tenements of New York, By Jacob Riis, 1890

---

*Jacob Riis, a Danish immigrant, worked as a police reporter in New York City. His work, coupled with an interest in photography, led him to record images of life in New York's slums. In 1890 he published **How the Other Half Lives** to document life in New York City slums that made use of the many photographs Riis had taken of people, buildings, and life in New York. Progressives used **How the Other Half Lives** to call attention to the deplorable living conditions in New York and bring about reforms by Progressives for the immigrant and working class people living in inner city ghettos.*

Introduction

Long ago it was said that "one half of the world does not know how the other half lives." That was true then. It did not know because it did not care. The half that was on top cared little for the struggles, and less for the fate of those who were underneath, so long as it was able to hold them there and keep its own seat. There came a time when the discomfort and crowding below were so great, and the consequent upheavals so violent, that it was no longer an easy thing to do, and then the upper half fell to inquiring what was the matter. Information on the subject has been accumulating rapidly since, and the whole world has had its hands full answering for its old ignorance.

In New York, the youngest of the world's great cities, that time came later than elsewhere, because the crowding had not been so great. There were those who believed it would never come; but their hopes were vain. Greed and reckless selfishness wrought like results here as in cities of older lands....

...To-day three-fourths of its [New York's—Ed.] people live in the tenements, and the nineteenth century drift of the population to the cities is sending ever-increasing multitudes to crowd them. The fifteen thousand tenant-houses that were the despair of the sanitarian in the past generation have swelled into thirty-seven thousand, and more than twelve hundred thousand persons call them home...We know now that there is no way out; that the "system" that was the evil offspring of public neglect and private greed has come to stay, a storm-centre forever of our civilization....

...If it shall appear that the sufferings and sins of the "other half," and the evil they breed, are but as a just punishment upon the community that gave it no other choice, it will be because that is the truth....in the tenements all the influences make for evil; because they are the hot-beds of the epidemics that carry death to rich and poor alike; that throw off a scum of forty thousand human wrecks to the asylums and workhouses year by year; that turned out in the last eight years a round half million beggars to prey upon our charities; that maintain a standing army of ten thousand tramps with all that that implies; because, above all, they touch the family life with deadly moral contagion. This is their worst crime, inseparable from the system.

Chapter 3: The Mixed Crowd

The Italian scavenger of our time is fast graduating into exclusive control of the corner fruit-stands, while his black-eyed boy monopolizes the boot-blacking industry in which a few years ago he was an intruder. The Irish hod-carrier in the second generation has become a brick-layer, if not the Alderman of his ward, while the Chinese coolie is in almost exclusive possession of the laundry business. The reason is obvious. The poorest immigrant comes here with the purpose and ambition to better himself and, given half a chance, might be reasonably expected to make the most of it. To the false plea that he prefers the squalid homes in which his kind are housed there could be no better answer. The truth is, his half chance has too long been wanting, and for the bad result he has been unjustly blamed....

The Irishman is the true cosmopolitan immigrant. All-pervading, he shares his lodging with perfect impartiality with the Italian, the Greek, and the "Dutchman," yielding only to sheer force of numbers, and objects equally to them all. A map of the city, colored to designate nationalities, would show more stripes than on the skin of a zebra, and more colors than a rainbow.

Hardly less aggressive than the Italian, the Russian and Polish Jew, having overrun the district between Rivington and Division Streets, east of the Bowery, to the point of suffocation, is filling the tenements of the old Seventh Ward to the river front, and disputing with the Italian every foot of available space in the back alleys of Mulberry Street. The two races, differing hopelessly in much, have this in common: they carry their slums with them wherever they go, if allowed to do it. Little Italy already rivals its parent, the "Bend," in foulness. Other nationalities that begin at the bottom make a fresh start when crowded up the ladder. Happily both are manageable, the one by rabbinical, the other by the civil law. Between the dull gray of the Jew, his favorite color, and the Italian red, would be seen squeezed in on the map a sharp streak of yellow, marking the narrow boundaries of Chinatown. Dovetailed in with the German population, the poor but thrifty Bohemian might be picked out by the sombre hue of his life as of his philosophy, struggling against heavy odds in the big human bee-hives of the East Side...The Bohemian is the only foreigner with any considerable representation in the city who counts no wealthy man of his race, none who has not to work hard for a living, or has got beyond the reach of the tenement.

Down near the Battery the West Side emerald would be soiled by a dirty stain, spreading rapidly like a splash of ink on a sheet of blotting paper, headquarters of the Arab tribe, that in a single year has swelled from the original dozen to the twelve hundred, intent, every mother's son, on trade and barter. Dots and dashes of color here and there would show where the Finnish sailors worship their djumala (God), the Greek pedlars the ancient name of their race, and the Swiss the goddess of thrift. And so on to the end of the long register, all toiling together in the galling fetters of the tenement. Were the question raised who makes the most of life thus mortgaged, who resists most stubbornly its levelling tendency—knows how to drag even the barracks upward a part of the ways at least toward the ideal plane of the home—the palm must be unhesitatingly awarded the Teuton. The Italian and the poor Jew rise only by compulsion. The Chinaman does not rise at all; here, as at home, he simply remains stationary. The Irishman's genius runs to public affairs rather than domestic life; wherever he is mustered in force the saloon is the gorgeous centre of political activity. The German struggles vainly to learn his trick; his Teutonic wit is too heavy, and the political ladder he raises from his saloon usually too short or too clumsy to reach the desired goal. The best part of his life is lived at home, and he makes himself a home independent of his surroundings, giving the lie to the saying, unhappily become a maxim of social truth, that pauperism and drunkenness naturally grow in the tenements. He makes the most of his tenement, and it should be added that whenever and as soon as he can save up money enough, he gets out and never crosses the threshold of one again.

Chapter V: The Italian in New York

.....The Italian comes in at the bottom, and in the generation that came over the sea he stays there. In the slums he is welcomed as a tenant who "makes less trouble" than the contentious Irishman or the order-loving German, that is to say: is content to live in a pig-sty and submits to robbery at the hands of the rent-collector without murmur. Yet this very tractability makes of him in good hands, when firmly and intelligently managed, a really desirable tenant. But it is not his good fortune often to fall in with other hospitality upon his coming than that which brought him here for its own profit, and has no idea of letting go its grip upon him as long as there is a cent to be made out of him....His ignorance and unconquerable suspicion of strangers dig the pit into which he falls. He not only knows no word of English, but he does not know enough to learn. Rarely only can he write his own language. Unlike the German, who begins learning English the day he lands as a matter of duty, or the Polish Jew, who takes it up as soon as he is able as an investment, the Italian learns slowly, if at all....

Did the Italian always adapt himself as readily to the operation of the civil law as to the manipulation of political "pull" on occasion, he would save himself a good deal of unnecessary trouble. Ordinarily he is easily enough governed by authority—always excepting Sunday, when he settles down to a game of cards and lets loose all his bad passions. Like the Chinese, the Italian is a born gambler. His soul is in the game the moment the cards are on the table, and very frequently his knife is in it too before the game is ended.....

With all his conspicuous faults, the swarthy Italian immigrant has his redeeming traits. He is as honest as he is hot-headed. There are no Italian burglars in the Rogues' Gallery; the ex-brigand toils peacefully with pickaxe and shovel on American ground....The women are faithful wives and devoted mothers....The Italian is gay, lighthearted and, if his fur is not stroked the wrong way, inoffensive as a child. His worst offence is that he keeps the stale-beer dives.....

Chapter IX: Chinatown

Between the tabernacles of Jewry and the shrines of the Bend, Joss has cheekily planted his pagan worship of idols, chief among which are the celestial worshipper's own gain and lusts. Whatever may be said about the Chinaman being a thousand years behind the age on his own shores, here he is distinctly abreast of it in his successful scheming to "make it pay." It is doubtful if there is anything he does not turn to a paying account, from his religion down, or up, as one prefers. At the risk of distressing some well-meaning, but, I fear, too trustful people, I state it in advance as my opinion, based on the steady observation of years, that all attempts to make an effective Christian of John Chinaman will remain abortive in this generation; of the next I have, if anything, less hope. Ages of senseless idolatry, a mere grub-worship, have left him without the essential qualities for appreciating the gentle teachings of a faith whose motive and unselfish spirit are alike beyond his grasp. He lacks the handle of a strong faith in something, anything, however wrong, to catch him by. There is nothing strong about him, except his passions when aroused. I am convinced that he adopts Christianity, when he adopts it at all, as he puts on American clothes, with what the politicians would call an ulterior motive, some sort of gain in the near prospect—washing, a Christian wife perhaps, anything he happens to rate for the moment above his cherished pigtail. It may be that I judge him too harshly. Exceptions may be found. Indeed, for the credit of the race, I hope there are such. But I am bound to say my hope is not backed by lively faith.

Chapter X: Jewtown

The tenements grow taller, and the gaps in their ranks close up rapidly as we cross the Bowery and, leaving Chinatown and the Italians behind, invade the Hebrew quarter....No need of asking here where we are. The jargon of the street, the signs of the sidewalk, the manner and the dress of the people, their unmistakable physiognomy, betray their race at every step. Men with queer skull-caps, elbow the ugliest and the handsomest women in the land....

Thrift is the watchword of Jewtown, as of its people the world over. It is at once its strength and its fatal weakness, its cardinal virtue and its foul disgrace. Become an over-mastering passion with these people who come here in droves from Eastern Europe to escape persecution, from which freedom could be bought only with gold, it has enslaved them in bondage worse than that from which they fled. Money is their God. Life itself is of little value compared with even the leanest bank account. In no other spot does life wear so intensely bald and materialistic an aspect as in Ludlow Street. Over and over again I have met with instances of these Polish or Russian Jews deliberately starving themselves to the point of physical exhaustion, while working night and day at a tremendous pressure to save a little money....

Source: Jacob Riis, *How the Other Half Lives*, Charles Scribner's, New York, 1890

HOW WELL DID YOU UNDERSTAND THIS SELECTION?

1. Upon what does Riis blame the problems New York is experiencing on?

2. How does Riis describe the different immigrant groups living in New York? How does his description reflect the ethnic and racial stereotypes of Progressives and others living during his day?

3. Would Riis be considered an optimist or a pessimist? Support your choice with evidence from the text.

Calls for a new banking system arose from several liberal groups prior to the Progressive Era. The Populist, for example, inserted a provision in their 1896 and 1900 presidential election platforms calling for nationalization of banks. Farmers, workers, and others were dissatisfied with American banks because interest rates varied greatly from bank to bank and because banks often would not readily loan individuals from the lower and middle classes money when needed. Bankers were also dissatisfied with the banking system because the American economy due to the expansion created by the Industrial Revolution had simply outgrown the banking system which had arisen to meet the needs of a smaller, agrarian country. President Woodrow Wilson, upon taking office, appointed Louis Brandeis to write legislation that would reform the banking industry by addressing the concerns of farmers, bankers and others. The result was the Federal Reserve Act of 1913. This act divided the nation into various banking districts, each with a Federal Reserve Bank within it. Each of the Regional Reserve Districts would be controlled by a board of directors chosen from participating banks within that region. Overseeing the overall system, however, would be the Federal Reserve Board whose membership could not be comprised of an active banker. The Federal Reserve Act gave the federal government some control over America's banking system, especially with its power to set interest rates. The Federal Reserve Act, which has been amended numerous times, is still in effect and the banking system it established in 1913 generally still works well.

Section 2—Federal Reserve Districts

Part 1. Establishment of Reserve Cities and Districts

As soon as practicable, the Secretary of the Treasury, the Secretary of Agriculture and the Comptroller of the Currency, acting as "The Reserve Bank Organization Committee," shall designate not less than eight nor more than twelve cities to be known as Federal reserve cities, and shall divide the continental United States, excluding Alaska, into districts, each district to contain only one of such Federal reserve cities. The determination of said organization committee shall not be subject to review except by the Board of Governors of the Federal Reserve System when organized: *Provided,* That the districts shall be apportioned with due regard to the convenience and customary course of business and shall not necessarily be coterminous with any State or States. The districts thus created may be readjusted and new districts may from time to time be created by the Board of Governors of the Federal Reserve System, not to exceed twelve in all. Such districts shall be known as Federal reserve districts and may be designated by number. When the State of Alaska or Hawaii is hereafter admitted to the Union the Federal Reserve districts shall be readjusted by the Board of Governors of the Federal Reserve System in such manner as to include such State. Every national bank in any State shall, upon commencing business or within ninety days after admission into the Union of the State in which it is located, become a member bank of the Federal Reserve System by subscribing and paying for stock in the Federal Reserve bank of its district in accordance with the provisions of this Act and shall thereupon be an insured bank under the Federal Deposit Insurance Act, and failure to do so shall subject such bank to the penalty provided by the sixth paragraph of this section.

Section 2A—Monetary Policy Objectives

The Board of Governors of the Federal Reserve System and the Federal Open Market Committee shall maintain long run growth of the monetary and credit aggregates commensurate with the economy's long run potential to increase production, so as to promote effectively the goals of maximum employment, stable prices, and moderate long-term interest rates.

Part 1. Composition of Board Members

The Board of Governors of the Federal Reserve System (hereinafter referred to as the "Board") shall be composed of seven members, to be appointed by the President, by and with the advice and consent of the Senate, after the date of enactment of the Banking Act of 1935, for terms of fourteen years except as hereinafter provided, but each appointive member of the Federal Reserve Board in office on such date shall continue to serve as a member of the Board until February 1, 1936, and the Secretary of the Treasury and the Comptroller of the Currency shall continue to serve as members of the Board until February 1, 1936. In selecting the members of the Board, not more than one of whom shall be selected from any one Federal Reserve district, the President shall have due regard to a fair representation of the financial, agricultural, industrial, and commercial interests, and geographical divisions of the country. The members of the Board shall devote their entire time to the business of the Board and shall each receive an annual salary of $15,000, payable monthly, together with actual necessary traveling expenses.

Part 2. Members Ineligible to Serve Member Banks: Terms of Office; Chairman and Vice Chairman

The members of the Board shall be ineligible during the time they are in office and for two years thereafter to hold any office, position, or employment in any member bank, except that this restriction shall not apply to a member who has served the full term for which he was appointed. Upon the expiration of the term of any appointive member of the Federal Reserve Board in office on the date of enactment of the Banking Act of 1935, the President shall fix the term of the successor to such member at not to exceed fourteen years, as designated by the President at the time of nomination, but in such manner as to provide for the expiration of the term of not more than one member in any two-year period, and thereafter each member shall hold office for a term of fourteen years from the expiration of the term of his predecessor, unless sooner removed for cause by the President. Of the persons thus appointed, one shall be designated by the President, by and with the advice and consent of the Senate, to serve as Chairman of the Board for a term of four years, and one shall be designated by the President, by and with the consent of the Senate, to serve as Vice Chairman of the Board for a term of four years. The chairman of the Board, subject to its supervision, shall be its active executive officer. Each member of the Board shall within fifteen days after notice of appointment make and subscribe to the oath of office. Upon the expiration of their terms of office, members of the Board shall continue to serve until their successors are appointed and have qualified. Any person appointed as a member of the Board after the date of enactment of the Banking Act of 1935 shall not be eligible for reappointment as such member after he shall have served a full term of fourteen years.

Part 4. Principal Offices; Expenses; Deposit of Funds; Members Not to Be Officers or Stockholders of Banks.

The principal offices of the Board shall be in the District of Columbia. At meetings of the Board the chairman shall preside, and, in his absence, the vice chairman shall preside. In the absence of the chairman and the vice chairman, the board shall elect a member to act as chairman pro tempore. The Board shall determine and prescribe the manner in which its obligations shall be incurred and its disbursements and expenses allowed and paid, and may leave on deposit in the Federal Reserve banks the proceeds of assessments levied upon them to defray its estimated expenses and the salaries of its members and employees, whose employment, compensation, leave, and expenses shall be governed solely by the provisions of this Act, specific amendments thereof, and rules and regulations of the Board not inconsistent therewith; and funds derived from such assessments shall not be construed to be Government funds or appropriated moneys. No member of the Board of Governors of the Federal Reserve System shall be an officer or director of any bank, banking institution, trust company, or Federal Reserve bank or hold stock in any bank, banking institution, or trust company; and before entering upon his duties as a member of the Board of Governors of the Federal Reserve System he shall certify under oath that he has complied with this requirement, and such certification shall be filed with the secretary of the Board. Whenever a vacancy shall occur, other than by expiration of term, among the six members of the Board of Governors of the Federal Reserve System appointed by the President as above provided, a succcessor shall be appointed by the President, by and with the advice and consent of the Senate, to fill such vacancy, and when appointed he shall hold office for the unexpired term of his predecessor.

Part 8. Issuance of National Currency and Federal Reserve Notes

Section three hundred and twenty-four of the Revised Statutes of the United States shall be amended so as to read as follows:

Sec. 324. There shall be in the Department of the Treasury a bureau charged with the execution of all laws passed by Congress relating to the issue and regulation of national currency secured by United States bonds, and under the general supervision of the Board of Governors of the Federal Reserve System, of all Federal Reserve notes, except for the cancellation and destruction, and accounting with respect to such cancellation and destruction, of Federal Reserve notes unfit for circulation, the chief officer of which bureau shall be called the Comptroller of the Currency and shall perform his duties under the general directions of the Secretary of the Treasury. The Comptroller of the Currency shall have the same authority over matters within the jurisdiction of the Comptroller as the Director of the Office of Thrift Supervision has over matters within the Director's jurisdiction under section 3(b)(3) of the Home Owners' Loan Act. The Secretary of the Treasury may not delay or prevent the issuance of any rule or the promulgation of any regulation by the Comptroller of the Currency.

Source: Board of Governors of the Federal Reserve System

HOW WELL DID YOU UNDERSTAND THIS SELECTION?

1. What is the principle job of the Federal Reserve?

2. How is the Federal Reserve System organized?

3. Who is eligible to serve on the Federal Reserve Board of Governors? How does an individual become a member of the Federal Reserve Board of Governors?

MONROE TROTTER PROTESTS PRESIDENT WILSON'S SEGREGATION OF FEDERAL EMPLOYEES

Democrat Thomas Woodrow Wilson, the last of the eight presidents elected from Virginia, like Republicans Theodore Roosevelt and William Howard Taft before him, believed in using the power of the federal government to curb the excesses of the Industrial Revolution and heal the ills in American society. Like many whites of his day, however, Wilson was not inclined to help African Americans overcome the segregation they faced in everyday life. All southern states had enacted Jim Crow laws that legally required blacks and whites to remain separated from each other. Whites and blacks could not live in the same neighborhoods, attend the same schools, dine at the same restaurants, drink from the same water fountains, use the same restrooms, or ride in the same railroad coaches. Even though he had lived in New Jersey, Wilson, who was raised in Virginia, brought with him traditional southern attitudes toward race when he came to Washington as president. He openly allowed departments of the federal government to be segregated on the basis of race. As might be expected, black leaders, including civil rights activists and journalist Monroe Trotter, were upset. In November 1913 Trotter and several other black leaders met with President Wilson to call his attention to the segregation of restroom and dining facilities. At that meeting Wilson denied that he knew about the discrimination and doubted Trotter's assertion that it in fact existed. Wilson did, however, promise to investigate the matter. After a year passed and the discrimination continued in the federal government, Trotter and black leaders again met with President Wilson. The following is an account of that meeting.

Mr. Monroe Trotter: Mr. President, we are here to renew our protest against the segregation of colored employees in the departments of our National Government. We [had] appealed to you to undo this race segregation in accord with your duty as President and with your pre-election pledges to colored American voters. We stated that such segregation was a public humiliation and degradation, and entirely unmerited and far-reaching in its injurious effects….

President Woodrow Wilson. The white people of the country, as well as I, wish to see the colored people progress, and admire the progress they have already made, and want to see them continue along independent lines. There is, however, a great prejudice against colored people….It will take one hundred years to eradicate this prejudice, and we must deal with it as practical men. Segregation is not humiliating but a benefit, and ought to be so regarded by you gentlemen. If your organization goes out and tells the colored people of the country that it is a humiliation, they will so regard it, but if you do not tell them so, and regard it as a benefit, they will regard it the same. The only harm that will come will be if you cause them to think it is a humiliation.

Mr. Monroe Trotter. It is not in accord with the known facts to claim that the segregation was started because of race friction of white and colored [federal] clerks. The indisputable facts of the situation will not permit of the claim that the segregation is due to the friction. It is untenable, in view of the established facts, to maintain that the segregation is simply to avoid race friction, for the simple reason that for fifty years white and colored clerks have been working together in peace and harmony and friendliness, doing so even through two [President Grover Cleveland] Democratic administrations. Soon after your inauguration began, segregation was drastically introduced in the Treasury and postal departments by your appointees.

President Woodrow Wilson. If this organization is ever to have another hearing before me it must have another spokesman. Your manner offends me….Your tone, with its background of passion.

Mr. Monroe Trotter. But I have no passion in me, Mr. President, you are entirely mistaken; you misinterpret my earnestness for passion.

Source: *The Crisis*, 9 (January 1915): 119-120, W.E.B. Du Bois, ed.

HOW WELL DID YOU UNDERSTAND THIS SELECTION?

1. Why do you think Wilson doubted that segregation existed in the federal government?

2. How did Wilson regard segregation?

3. Why do you think Trotter offended Wilson?

"OF OUR SPIRITUAL STRIVINGS," *The Souls of Black Folk,* By W.E.B. Du Bois, 1903

W.E.B. Du Bois, a historian and sociologist educated at Harvard, was one of the best known African-American scholars of his generation. In fact, his work is still highly valued and praised by modern scholars. In addition to his debate with Booker T. Washington over the proper place of blacks in American society, Du Bois was concerned about fostering understanding and acceptance between blacks and whites by allowing whites to look into the souls of blacks and to teach blacks more about their distinct history, culture, and spirituality. "Of Our Spiritual Strivings" is an attempt by Du Bois to do these things. Unfortunately, Du Bois writings fell largely on deaf ears during the Progressive era as most whites during this time perceived black to be racially inferior.

Between me and the other world there is ever an unasked question: unasked by some through feelings of delicacy; by others through the difficulty of rightly framing it. All, nevertheless, flutter round it. They approach me in a half-hesitant sort of way, eye me curiously or compassionately, and then, instead of saying directly, How does it feel to be a problem? they say, I know an excellent colored man in my town; or, I fought at Mechanicsville; or, Do not these Southern outrages make your blood boil? At these I smile, or am interested, or reduce the boiling to a simmer, as the occasion may require. To the real question, How does it feel to be a problem? I answer seldom a word.

And yet, being a problem is a strange experience, - peculiar even for one who has never been anything else, save perhaps in babyhood and in Europe. It is in the early days of rollicking boyhood that the revelation first bursts upon one, all in a day, as it were. I remember well when the shadow swept across me. I was a little thing, away up in the hills of New England, where the dark Housatonic winds between Hoosac and Taghkanic to the sea. In a wee wooden schoolhouse, something put it into the boys' and girls' heads to buy gorgeous visiting-cards—ten cents a package—and exchange. The exchange was merry, till one girl, a tall newcomer, refused my card,—refused it peremptorily, with a glance. Then it dawned upon me with a certain suddenness that I was different from the others; or like, mayhap, in heart and life and longing, but shut out from their world by a vast veil. I had thereafter no desire to tear down that veil, to creep through; I held all beyond it in common contempt, and lived above it in a region of blue sky and great wandering shadows. That sky was bluest when I could beat my mates at examination-time, or beat them at a foot-race, or even beat their stringy heads. Alas, with the years all this fine contempt began to fade; for the worlds I longed for, and all their dazzling opportunities, were theirs, not mine. But they should not keep these prizes, I said; some, all, I would wrest from them. Just how I would do it I could never decide: by reading law, by healing the sick, by telling the wonderful tales that swam in my head,—some way. With other black boys the strife was not so fiercely sunny: their youth shrunk into tasteless sycophancy, or into silent hatred of the pale world about them and mocking distrust of everything white; or wasted itself in a bitter cry, Why did God make me an outcast and a stranger in mine own house? The shades of the prison-house closed round about us all: walls strait and stubborn to the whitest, but relentlessly narrow, tall, and unscalable to sons of night who must plod darkly on in resignation, or beat unavailing palms against the stone, or steadily, half hopelessly, watch the streak of blue above.

After the Egyptian and Indian, the Greek and Roman, the Teuton and Mongolian, the Negro is a sort of seventh son, born with a veil, and gifted with second-sight in this American world,—a world which yields him no true self-consciousness, but only lets him see himself through the revelation of the other world. It is a peculiar sensation, this double-consciousness, this sense of always looking at one's self through the eyes of others, of measuring one's soul by the tape of a world that looks on in amused contempt and pity. One ever feels his twoness,—an American, a Negro; two souls, two thoughts, two unreconciled strivings; two warring ideals in one dark body, whose dogged strength alone keeps it from being torn asunder.

The history of the American Negro is the history of this strife,—this longing to attain self-conscious manhood, to merge his double self into a better and truer self. In this merging he wishes neither of the older selves to be lost. He would not Africanize America, for America has too much to teach the world and Africa. He would not bleach his Negro soul in a flood of white Americanism, for he knows that Negro blood has a message for the world. He simply wishes to make it possible for a man to be both a Negro and an American, without being cursed and spit upon by his fellows, without having the doors of Opportunity closed roughly in his face.

This, then, is the end of his striving: to be a co-worker in the kingdom of culture, to escape both death and isolation, to husband and use his best powers and his latent genius. These powers of body and mind have in the past been strangely wasted, dispersed, or forgotten. The shadow of a mighty Negro past flits through the tale of Ethiopia the Shadowy and of Egypt the Sphinx. Throughout history, the powers of single black men flash here and there like falling stars, and die sometimes before the world has rightly gauged their brightness. Here in America, in the few days since Emancipation, the black man's turning hither and thither in hesitant and doubtful striving has often made his very strength to lose effectiveness, to seem like absence of power, like weakness. And yet it is not weakness,—it is the contradiction of double aims. The double-aimed struggle of the black artisan—on the one hand to escape white contempt for a nation of mere hewers of wood and drawers of water, and on the other hand to plough and nail and dig for a poverty-stricken horde—could only result in making him a poor craftsman, for he had but half a heart in either cause. By the poverty and ignorance of his people, the Negro minister or doctor was tempted toward quackery and demagogy; and by the criticism of the other world, toward ideals that made him ashamed of his lowly tasks. The would-be black *savant* was confronted by the paradox that the knowledge his people needed was a twice-told tale to his white neighbors, while the knowledge which would teach the white world was Greek to his own flesh and blood. The innate love of harmony and beauty that set the ruder souls of his people a-dancing and a-singing raised but confusion and doubt in the soul of the black artist; for the beauty revealed to him was the soul-beauty of a race his larger audience despised, and he could not articulate the message of another people. This waste of double aims, this seeking to satisfy two unreconciled ideals, has wrought sad havoc with the courage and faith and deeds of ten thousand thousand people, - has sent them often wooing false gods and invoking false means of salvation, and at times has even seemed about to make them ashamed of themselves.

Away back in the days of bondage they thought to see in one divine event the end of all doubt and disappointment; few men ever worshipped Freedom with half such unquestioning faith as did the American Negro for two centuries. To him, so far as he thought and dreamed, slavery was indeed the sum of all villainies, the cause of all sorrow, the root of all prejudice; Emancipation was the key to a promised land of sweeter beauty than ever stretched before the eyes of wearied Israelites. In song and exhortation swelled one refrain—Liberty; in his tears and curses the God he implored had Freedom in his right hand. At last it came,—suddenly, fearfully, like a dream. With one wild carnival of blood and passion came the message in his own plaintive cadences:

"Shout, O children!
Shout, you're free!
For God has bought your liberty!"

Years have passed away since then,—ten, twenty, forty; forty years of national life, forty years of renewal and development, and yet the swarthy spectre sits in its accustomed seat at the Nation's feast. In vain do we cry to this our vastest social problem:—

"Take any shape but that, and my firm nerves
  Shall never tremble!"

The Nation has not yet found peace from its sins; the freedman has not yet found in freedom his promised land. Whatever of good may have come in these years of change, the shadow of a deep disappointment rests upon the Negro people,—a disappointment all the more bitter because the unattained ideal was unbounded save by the simple ignorance of a lowly people....

Up the new path the advance guard toiled, slowly, heavily, doggedly; only those who have watched and guided the faltering feet, the misty minds, the dull understandings, of the dark pupils of these schools know how faithfully, how piteously, this people strove to learn. It was weary work....To the tired climbers, the horizon was ever dark, the mists were often cold, the Canaan was always dim and far away. If however, the vistas disclosed as yet no goal, no resting-place, little but flattery and criticism, the journey at least gave leisure for reflection and self-examination; it changed the child of Emancipation to the youth with dawning self-consciousness, self-realization, self-respect. In those sombre forests of his striving his own soul rose before him, and he saw himself,—darkly as through a veil; and yet he saw in himself some faint revelation of his power, of his mission. He began to have a dim feeling that, to attain his place in the world, he must be himself, and not another. For the first time he sought to analyze the burden he bore upon his back, that dead-weight of social degradation partially masked behind a half-named Negro problem. He felt his poverty; without a cent, without a home, without land, tools, or savings, he had entered into competition with rich, landed, skilled neighbors. To be a poor man is hard, but to be a poor race in a land of dollars is the very bottom of hardships. He felt the weight of his ignorance,—not simply of letters, but of life, of business, of the humanities; the accumulated sloth and shirking and awkwardness of decades and centuries shackled his hands and feet. Nor was his burden all poverty and ignorance. The red stain of bastardy, which two centuries of systematic legal defilement of Negro women had stamped upon his race, meant not only the loss of ancient African chastity, but also the hereditary weight of a mass of corruption from white adulterers, threatening almost the obliteration of the Negro home.

A people thus handicapped ought not to be asked to race with the world, but rather allowed to give all its time and thought to its own social problems. But alas! while sociologists gleefully count his bastards and his prostitutes, the very soul of the toiling, sweating black man is darkened by the shadow of a vast despair. Men call the shadow prejudice, and learnedly explain it as the natural defence of culture against barbarism, learning against ignorance, purity against crime, the "higher" against the "lower" races. To which the Negro cries Amen! and swears that to so much of this strange prejudice as is founded on just homage to civilization, culture, righteousness, and progress, he humbly bows and meekly does obeisance. But before that nameless prejudice that leaps beyond all this he stands helpless, dismayed, and well-nigh speechless; before that personal disrespect and mockery, the ridicule and systematic humiliation, the distortion of fact and wanton license of fancy, the cynical ignoring of the better and the boisterous welcoming of the worse, the all-pervading desire to inculcate disdain for everything black, from Toussaint to the devil, - before this there rises a sickening despair that would disarm and discourage any nation save that black host to whom "discouragement" is an unwritten word.

But the facing of so vast a prejudice could not but bring the inevitable self-questioning, self-disparagement, and lowering of ideals which ever accompany repression and breed in an atmosphere of contempt and hate. Whisperings and portents came borne upon the four winds: Lo! we are diseased and dying, cried the dark hosts; we cannot write, our voting is vain; what need of education, since we must always cook and serve? And the Nation echoed and enforced this self-criticism, saying: Be content to be servants, and nothing more; what need of higher culture for half-men? Away with the black man's ballot, by force or fraud,—and behold the suicide of a race! Nevertheless, out of the evil came something of good,—the more careful adjustment of education to real life, the clearer perception of the Negroes' social responsibilities, and the sobering realization of the meaning of progress.

So dawned the time of *Sturm und Drang*: storm and stress to-day rocks our little boat on the mad waters of the worldsea; there is within and without the sound of conflict, the burning of body and rending of soul; inspiration strives with doubt, and faith with vain questionings. The bright ideals of the past,—physical freedom, political power, the training of brains and the training of hands, - all these in turn have waxed and waned, until even the last grows dim and overcast. Are they all wrong,—all false? No, not that, but each alone was over-simple and incomplete,—the dreams of a credulous race-childhood, or the fond imaginings of the other world which does not know and does not want to know our power. To be really true, all these ideals must be melted and welded into one. The training of the schools we need to-day more than ever,—the training of deft hands, quick eyes and ears, and above all the broader, deeper, higher culture of gifted minds and pure hearts. The power of the ballot we need in sheer self-defence,—else

139

what shall save us from a second slavery? Freedom, too, the long-sought, we still seek,—the freedom of life and limb, the freedom to work and think, the freedom to love and aspire. Work, culture, liberty,—all these we need, not singly but together, not successively but together, each growing and aiding each, and all striving toward that vaster ideal that swims before the Negro people, the ideal of human brotherhood, gained through the unifying ideal of Race; the ideal of fostering and developing the traits and talents of the Negro, not in opposition to or contempt for other races, but rather in large conformity to the greater ideals of the American Republic in order that some day on American soil two world-races may give each to each those characteristics both so sadly lack. We the darker ones come even now not altogether empty-handed: there are to-day no truer exponents of the pure human spirit of the Declaration of Independence than the American Negroes; there is no true American music but the wild sweet melodies of the Negro slave; the American fairy tales and folk-lore are Indian and African; and, all in all, we black men seem the sole oasis of simple faith and reverence in a dusty desert of dollars and smartness. Will America be poorer if she replace her brutal dyspeptic blundering with light-hearted but determined Negro humility? or her coarse and cruel wit with loving jovial good-humor? or her vulgar music with the soul of the Sorrow Songs?

Merely a concrete test of the underlying principles of the great republic is the Negro Problem, and the spiritual striving of the freedmen's sons is the travail of souls whose burden is almost beyond the measure of their strength, but who bear it in the name of an historic race, in the name of this land of their fathers' fathers, and in the name of human opportunity.

Source: W.E.B. Du Bois, *The Souls of Black Folk*, A.C. McClurg, Chicago, 1903

HOW WELL DID YOU UNDERSTAND THIS SELECTION?

1. How does Du Bois describe Black feelings?

2. When Du Bois uses the word "veil," what does he mean? Why does he argue that both whites and blacks must see through the veil?

3. Why does Du Bois say it is impossible for a person to be both an African American and American at the same time? Can a black person be black and an American today?

4. Is Du Bois optimistic or pessimistic? Why?

5. Discuss the idea that whites are less than fully human because they denied rights to blacks? Do you agree or disagree with this idea?

One of the worst fires in American history killed 146 workers on March 25, 1911, at the Triangle Shirtwaist Company in New York City. Most of the dead were young Italian and Jewish immigrant women. The deaths occurred largely because factory owners and managers had locked outside doors to the factory through which the workers likely could have escaped. Locking factory doors was a common practice during the early years of the Twentieth Century to make sure workers remained on the job until dismissed by factory supervisors. The Triangle Shirtwaist factory had only one fire escape. Some of the deaths occurred not because of burns or smoke inhalation but because the fire escape collapsed when so many workers used it in a panicked attempt to escape. Other deaths occurred due to the faulty or inadequate New York fire department equipment. Ladders, for example, were not long enough to reach many workers trapped on the building's top floors. Some of these workers tried to escape by jumping into fire safety nets but the nets broke when the weight of bodies hit the nets. A grisly scene gripped New York's Lower East Side as broken, torn, and mangled bodies of these immigrant women were piled high on the pavement in front of the Triangle Shirtwaist Company building. This event had a tremendous impact on safety regulations for American factories. Progressive reformers demanded that new regulations be enacted to prevent such future disasters from happening, and state legislatures began to enact more stringent safety laws. Rose Schneiderman, a Polish immigrant, a Jew, and a union organizer, spoke at a memorial honoring the victims of the Triangle Fire at the Metropolitan Opera House on April 2, 1911.

I would be traitor to these poor burned bodies if I came here to talk good fellowship. We have tried you good people of the public, and we have found you wanting. The old Inquisition had its rack and its thumbscrews and its instruments of torture with iron teeth. We know what these things are today: the iron teeth are our necessities, the thumbscrews are the high-powered and swift machinery close to which we must work, and the rack is here in the firetrap structures that will destroy us the minute they catch on fire.

This is not the first time girls have been burned alive in the city. Every week I must learn of the untimely death of one of my sister workers. Every year thousands of us are maimed. The life of men and women is so cheap and property is so sacred. There are so many of us for one job it matters little if 146 of us are burned to death.

We have tried, you citizens; we are trying you now, and you have a couple of dollars for the sorrowing mothers and daughters and sisters by way of a charity gift. But every time the workers come out in the only way they know to protest against conditions which are unbearable, the strong hand of the law is allowed to press down heavily upon us.

Public officials have only words of warning to us—warning that we must be intensely orderly and must be intensely peaceable, and they have the workhouse just back of all their warnings. The strong hand of the law beats us back, when we rise, into the conditions that make life bearable.

I can't talk fellowship to you who are gathered here. Too much blood has been spilled. I know from my experience it is up to the working people to save themselves. The only way they can save themselves is by a strong working-class movement.

Source: *The Survey*, April 8, 1911

HOW WELL DID YOU UNDERSTAND THIS SELECTION?

1. What solution does Schneiderman advocate to solve problems such as deaths from fires and other work place tragedies?

2. Why does Schneiderman say she can't talk good fellowship to her audience? So you agree or disagree with her views?

3. What is Schneiderman's overall attitude toward workers at the time she speaks? Have things improved for workers? Why or why not?

Jane Addams, the founder of the settlement house movement in the United States, did much to push Progressive reform. In addition to helping immigrants and poor people at Hull House, the settlement house she established in Chicago, Addams and others became concerned with problems such as alcoholism, crime disease, and prostitution that seemed to be getting worse in America's growing cities as a result of industrialization. Addams in particular was concerned with prostitution and the "white slave trade." She wrote a book, published in 1911, entitled A New Conscience and An Ancient Evil, *that addressed the above problems in American cities and called upon the federal and state governments to enact measures to solve the various problems urban people faced. Addams was in particular a strong advocate of laws to raise wages, shorten work hours, and improve the everyday living conditions that impoverished immigrants and other working women faced every day. She felt that government action was the only thing that could force greedy factory owners to pay working women a wage that would enable them to find economic fulfillment and meaning in life. The following is a selection from* A New Conscience and an Ancient Evil.

Chapter III: Amelioration of Economic Conditions

....It is as yet difficult to distinguish between the results of long hours and the results of overstrain. Certainly the constant sense of haste is one of the most nerve-racking and exhausting tests to which the human system can be subjected. Those girls in the sewing industry whose mothers thread needles for them far into the night that they may sew without a moment's interruption during the next day; those girls who insert eyelets into shoes, for which they are paid two cents a case, each case containing twenty-four pairs of shoes, are striking victims of the over-speeding which is so characteristic of our entire factory system....

Yet factory girls who are subjected to this overstrain and overtime often find their greatest discouragement in the fact that after all their efforts they earn too little to support themselves. One girl said that she had first yielded to temptation when she had become utterly discouraged because she had tried in vain for seven months to save enough money for a pair of shoes. She habitually spent two dollars a week for her room, three dollars for her board, and sixty cents a week for carfare, and she had found the forty cents remaining from her weekly wage of six dollars inadequate to do more than re-sole her old shoes twice. When the shoes became too worn to endure a third soling and she possessed but ninety cents towards a new pair, she gave up her struggle; to use her own contemptuous phrase, she "sold out for a pair of shoes."

Usually the phrases are less graphic but after all they contain the same dreary meaning: "Couldn't make both ends meet," "I had always been used to having nice things," "Couldn't make enough money to live on," "I got sick and ran behind," "Needed more money," "Impossible to feed and clothe myself," "Out of work, hadn't been able to save." Of course a girl in such a strait does not go out deliberately to find illicit methods of earning money, she simply yields in a moment of utter weariness and discouragement to the temptations she has been able to withstand up to that moment. The long hours, the lack of comforts, the low pay, the absence of recreation, the sense of "good times" all about her which she cannot share, the conviction that she is rapidly losing health and charm, rouse the molten forces within her. A swelling tide of self-pity suddenly storms the banks which have hitherto held her and finally overcomes her instincts for decency and righteousness, as well as the habit of clean living, established by generations of her forebears.

The aphorism that "morals fluctuate with trade" was long considered cynical, but it has been demonstrated in Berlin, in London, in Japan, as well as in several American cities, that there is a distinct increase in the number of registered prostitutes during periods of financial depression and even during the dull season of leading industries. Out of my own experience I am ready to assert that very often all that is necessary to effectively help the girl who is on the edge of wrong-doing is to lend her money for her board until she finds work, provide the necessary clothing for which she is in such desperate need, persuade her relatives that she should have more money for her own expenditures, or find her another place at higher wages. Upon such simple economic needs does the tried virtue of a good girl sometimes depend....

Another experience during which a girl faces a peculiar danger is when she has lost one "job" and is looking for another. Naturally she loses her place in the slack season and pursues her search at the very moment when positions are hardest to find, and her unemployment is therefore most prolonged. Perhaps nothing in our social order is so unorganized and inchoate as our method, or rather lack of method, of placing young people in industry. This is obvious from the point of view of their first positions when they leave school at the unstable age of fourteen, often as high as ten a year, then they are dismissed or change voluntarily through sheer restlessness....

Difficult as is the position of the girl out of work when her family is exigent and uncomprehending, she has incomparably more protection than the girl who is living in the city without home ties. Such girls form sixteen per cent of the working women of Chicago. With absolutely every penny of their meagre wages consumed in their inadequate living, they are totally unable to save money. That loneliness and detachment which the city tends to breed in its inhabitants is easily intensified in such a girl into isolation and a desolating feeling of belonging nowhere. As youth resents the sense of the enormity of the universe in relation to the insignificance of the individual life, and youth, with that intense self-consciousness which makes each young person the very centre of all emotional experience, broods over this as no older person can possibly do. At such moments of black oppression, the instinctive fear of solitude, will send a lonely girl restlessly to walk the streets even when she is "too tired to stand," and when her desire for companionship in itself constitutes a grave danger. Such a girl living in a rented room is usually without any place in which to properly receive callers....Many girls quite innocently permit young men to call upon them in their bedrooms, pitifully disguised as "sitting-rooms," but the danger is obvious, and the standards of the girl gradually become lowered.

Certainly during the trying times when a girl is out of work she should have much more intelligent help than is at present extended to her; she should be able to avail herself of the state employment agencies much more than is now possible, and the work of the newly established vocational bureaus should be enormously extended.

When once we are in earnest about the abolition of the social evil, society will find that it must study industry from the point of view of the producer in a sense which has never been done before. Such a study with reference to industrial legislation will ally itself on one hand with the trades-union movement, which insists upon a living wage and shorter hours for the workers, and also upon an opportunity for self-direction, and on the other hand with the efficiency movement, which would refrain from over-fatiguing an operator as it would from over-speeding a machine....

As working women enter fresh fields of labor which ever open up anew as the old fields are submerged behind them, society must endeavor to speedily protect them by an amelioration of the economic conditions which are now so unnecessarily harsh and dangerous to health and morals. The world-wide movement for establishing governmental control of industrial conditions is especially concerned for working women....

Although amelioration comes about so slowly that many young girls are sacrificed each year under conditions which could so easily and reasonably be changed, nevertheless it is apparently better to overcome the dangers in this new and freer life, which modern industry has opened to women, than it is to attempt to retreat into the domestic industry of the past; for all statistics of prostitution give the largest number of recruits for this life as coming from domestic service and the second largest number from girls who live at home with no definite occupation whatever. Therefore, although in the economic aspect of the social evil more than in any other, do we find ground for despair, at the same time we discern, as nowhere else, the young girl's stubborn power of resistance. Nevertheless, the most superficial survey of her surroundings shows the necessity for ameliorating, as rapidly as possible, the harsh economic conditions which now environ her.

That steadily increasing function of the state by which it seeks to protect its workers from their own weakness and degradation, and insists that the livelihood of the manual laborer shall not be beaten down below the level of efficient citizenship, assumes new forms almost daily. From the human as well as the economic standpoint there is an obligation resting upon the state to discover how many victims of the white slave traffic are the result of social neglect, remedial incapacity, and the lack of industrial safeguards, and how far discontinuous employment and non-employment are factors in the breeding of discouragement and despair.

Is it because our modern industrialism is so new that we have been slow to connect it with the poverty and vice all about us? The socialists talk constantly of the relation of economic law to destitution and point out the connection between industrial maladjustment and individual wrong-doing, but certainly the study of social conditions, the obligation to eradicate vice, cannot belong to one political party or to one economic school. It must be recognized as a solemn obligation of existing governments, and society must realize that economic conditions can only be made more righteous and more human by the unceasing devotion of generations of men.

Source: Jane Addams, *A New Conscience and an Ancient Evil*, Macmillan, New York, 1911

HOW WELL DID YOU UNDERSTAND THIS SELECTION?

1. What does Addams blame for causing young women to become prostitutes? Do you agree or disagree with her views? Why or why not?

2. What does Addams see as the solution to the problem?

3. Are the views of Addams applicable in today's society? Why or why not?

SENATORS VS. WORKING WOMEN: A Reply to New York Senators on Delicacy and Charm of Women, By Rose Schneiderman, 1912

Rose Schneiderman, like Jane Addams, wanted to improve the wages paid to women who worked and to lower the hours they labored in factories and in other locations. Schneiderman also supported ratification of the Nineteenth Amendment, giving women the right to vote in all local, state, and national elections. The following selection is a response Schneiderman made to speeches by New York representatives at a meeting of women workers at Cooper Union on April 22, 1912.

Rose Schneiderman, Cap Maker, answers the New York Senator who says:

> "Get women into the arena of politics with its alliances and distressing contests—the delicacy is gone, the charm is gone, and you emasculize women."

Fellow-workers, it already has been whispered to you that there is a possibility that our New York Senators don't know what they are talking about. I am here to voice the same sentiment. It seems to me that if our Senators really represented the people of New York State, they ought to know the conditions under which the majority of the people live. Perhaps, working women are not regarded as women, because it seems to me, when they talk all this trash of theirs about finer qualities and "man's admiration and devotion to the sex"—"Cornelia's Jewels" "Preserving Motherhood"—"Woman's duty to minister to man in the home"—"The delicacy and charm of women being gone," they cannot mean the working women. We have 800,000 women in New York State who go out into the industrial world, not through any choice of their own, but because necessity forces them out to earn their daily bread.

I am inclined to think if we were sent home now we would not go home.

We want to work, that is the thing. We are not afraid of work, and we are not ashamed to work, but we do decline to be driven; we want to work like human beings; we want to work for the welfare of the community and not for the welfare of a few....

We have women working in the foundries, stripped to the waist, if you please, because of the heat. *Yet the Senator says nothing about these women losing their charm.* They have got to retain their charm and delicacy and work in foundries. Of course, you know the reason they are employed in foundries is that they are cheaper and work longer hours than men.

144

Women in the laundries, for instance, stand for 13 or 14 hours in the terrible steam and heat with their hands in hot starch. Surely these women won't lose any more of their beauty and charm by putting a ballot in a ballot box once a year than they are likely to lose standing in foundries or laundries all year round.

There is no harder contest than the contest for bread, let me tell you that. Women have got to meet it and in a good many instances they contest for the job with their brother workman. When the woman is preferred, it is because of her weakness, because she is frail, because she will sell her labor for less money than man will sell his.

When our Senators acknowledge that our political life has *alliances and distressing contests* which would take the charm away from women if she got into them, let me reassure the gentlemen that women's great charm has always been that when she found things going she has set to work to make them go right. Do our Senators fear that when women get the vote they will demand clean polling places, etc.? It seems to me that this rather gives them away....

What about the delicacy and charm of women who have to live with men in the condition of a good many male voters on election day? Perhaps the Senators would like them to keep that condition all year round; they would not demand much of their political bosses and he could be sure that they would cast their votes for the man who gave them the most booze....

We hear our anti-suffragettes saying, "Why, when you get the vote it will hinder you from doing welfare work, doing uplift work." Who are they going to uplift? Is it you and I they want to uplift? I think if they would lift themselves off our shoulders they would be doing a better bit of useful work. I think you know by now that if the workers got what they earn there would be no need of uplift work and welfare work or anything of that kind.

We want to tell our Senators that the working women of our State demand the votes as an economic necessity. We need it because we are workers and because the workers are the ones that have to carry civilization on their backs.

What does all this talk about becoming mannish signify? I wonder if it will add to my height when I get the vote. I might work for it all the harder if it did. It is too ridiculous, this talk of becoming less womanly, just as if a woman could be anything else except a woman.

This vote that she is going to cast is going to work this marvellous change in her all of a sudden. Just by beginning to think of how the laws are made and using such intelligence as she has to put good men in office with her vote she will be made over into a creature without delicacy or charm...

I honestly believe that it is fear of the enfranchisement of working-women that prompts the Senators to oppose us. They do not want the working-women enfranchised because politicians know that a woman who works will use her ballot intelligently; she will make the politicians do things which he may not find so profitable; therefore, they come out with all these subterfuges....

Source: *Senators vs. Working Women, Miss Rose Scheiderman, CapMaker replies to New York Senator on Delicacy and Charm of Women*, Wage Earners' Suffrage League: New York, 1912
online at: www.binghamton.edu/womhist/law/doc19.htm

HOW WELL DID YOU UNDERSTAND THIS SELECTION?

1. How does Schneiderman respond to the argument that giving women the right to vote would destroy their femininity and domesticity?

2. What is the real reason Schneiderman believes New York's senators oppose woman suffrage for? Are her views correct? Why or why not?

3. How does Schneiderman attack the anti-suffragettes argument?

*Upton Sinclair was perhaps the best-known muckraker of them all. His novel, **The Jungle**, intended to promote socialism, had the effect of causing the federal government to pass legislation to regulate the meat processing industry. Sinclair actually visited with workers in meat processing facilities in Chicago in order to write **The Jungle**. His account of the filth and vermin that meat processors sold to the public turned American stomachs and ignited a debate within Congress and the American public about the need for governmental oversight of the meat processors. Of course, the meat packers lost business as the public became acutely aware of the bad meat that unscrupulous meat processing companies was selling. The decline in sales cause several owners of meat processing plants to request that the federal government regulate the industry so that the public would know that meat purchased at lunch counters and grocery stores was good and of course, owners would benefit from an increase in sales. The result was passage of the Meat Inspection Act of 1907, which gave governmental inspectors authority to ensure that meat processing facilities followed sanitary rules when producing their product. A selection from Sinclair's **The Jungle** follows.*

With one member trimming beef in a cannery, and another working in a sausage factory, the family had a firsthand knowledge of the great majority of Packingtown swindles. For it was the custom, as they found, whenever meat was so spoiled that it could not be used for anything else, either to can it or else to chop it up into sausage. With what had been told them by Jonas, who had worked in the pickle rooms, they could now study the whole of the spoiled- meat industry on the inside, and read a new and grim meaning into that old Packingtown jest—thai they use everything of the pig except the squeal.

Jonas had told them how the meat that was taken out of pickle would often be found sour, and how they would rub it up with soda to take away the smell, and sell it to be eaten on free-lunch counters; also of all the miracles of chemistry which they performed, giving to any sort of meat, fresh or salted, whole or chopped, any color and any flavor and any odor they chose. In the pickling of hams they had an ingenious apparatus, by which they saved time and increased the capacity of the plant—a machine consisting of a hollow needle attached to a pump; by plunging this needle into the meat and working with his foot a man could fill a ham with pickle in a few seconds. And yet, in spite of this, there would be hams found spoiled, some of them with an odor so bad that a man could hardly bear to be in the room with them. To pump into these the packers had a second and much stronger pickle which destroyed the odor—a process known to the workers as "giving them thirty per cent." Also, after the hams had been smoked, there would be found some that had gone to the bad. Formerly these had been sold as "Number Three Grade," but later on some ingenious person had hit upon a new device, and now they would extract the bone, about which the bad part generally lay, and insert in the hole a white-hot iron. After this invention there was no longer Number One, Two, and Three Grade—there was only Number One Grade. The packers were always originating such schemes—they had what they called "boneless hams," which were all the odds and ends of pork stuffed into casings, and "California hams" which were the shoulders, with big knuckle joints, and nearly all the meat cut out: and fancy "skinned hams," which were made of the oldest hogs, whose skins were so heavy and coarse that no one would buy them—that is until they had been cooked and chopped fine and labelled "head cheese"!

It was only when the whole ham was spoiled that it came into the department of Elzbieta. Cut up by the two-thousand-revolutions-a-minute flyers, and mixed with half a ton of other meat, no odor that ever was in a ham could make any difference. There was never the least attention paid to what was cut up for sausage; there would come all the way back from Europe old sausage that had been rejected, and that was mouldy and white—it would be dosed with borax and glycerine, and dumped into the hoppers, and made over again for home consumption. There would be meat that had tumbled out on the floor, in the dirt and sawdust, where the workers had tramped and spit uncounted billions of consumption germs. There would be meat stored in great piles in rooms; and the water from leaky roofs would drip over it, and thousands of rats would race about on it. It was too dark in these storage places to see well, but a man could run his hand over these piles of meat and sweep off handfuls of the dried dung of rats. These rats were nuisances, and the packers would put poisoned bread out for them, they would die, and then rats, bread, and meat would go into the hoppers together. This is no fairy story and no joke; the meat would be shovelled into carts, and the man who did the shovelling would not trouble to lift out a rat even when he saw one—there were things that went into the sausage in comparison with which a poisoned rat was a tidbit.

Source: Upton Sinclair, *The Jungle*, Doubleday, Page & Company: New York, 1906

HOW WELL DID YOU UNDERSTAND THIS SELECTION?

1. How do you think a member of the American public who read this passage might react? How would you react if this situation existed today?

2. Why do you think meat processing facilities produced their product in such an unsanitary manner?

3. What is wrong with what the meat processors were doing?

NATIONAL AMERICAN WOMAN SUFFRAGE ASSOCIATION SPEECH, Remarks on Emotionalism in Politics, by Anna Howard Shaw, 1913

Women throughout the United States had struggled to gain the vote almost since the beginning of the American Republic when Abigail Adams asked husband John to remember the women at the Constitutional Convention in 1787. Eventually, a few states, such as Utah, gave women the right to vote in state and local elections. Many American women, however, wanted legal rights equal to men, which included the right to vote in all elections. Women eventually formed an organization, the National American Woman Suffrage Association (NAWSA), that worked for several decades to bring about suffrage for women. Anna Howard Shaw, a medical doctor and Protestant preacher, served as president of NAWSA from 1904 to 1915. As NAWSA president, she was at the forefront of the women's suffrage movement. The following is a speech she made to delegates at the NAWSA Convention in 1913.

By some objectors women are supposed to be unfit to vote because they are hysterical and emotional, and of course men would not like to have emotion enter into a political campaign. They want to cut out all emotion and so they would like to cut us out. I had heard so much about our emotionalism that I went to the last Democratic National Convention, held at Baltimore, to observe the calm repose of male politicians. I saw some men take a picture of one gentleman whom they wanted elected, and it was so big they had to walk sidewise as they carried it forward; they were followed by hundreds of other men screaming and yelling, shouting and singing the "Houn' Dawg;" then, when there was a lull, another set of men would start forward under another man's picture, not to be outdone by the "Houn' Dawg" melody, whooping and howling still louder. I saw men jump up on the seats and throw their hats in the air and shout: "What's the matter with Champ Clark?" Then when those hats came down, other men would kick them back in the air, shouting at the top of their voices: "He's all right!!" Then I heard others howling for "Underwood Underwood, first, last and all the time!!" No hysteria about it—just patriotic loyalty, splendid manly devotion to principle. And so they went on and on until 5 o'clock in the morning—the whole night long. I saw men jump up on their seats and jump down again and run around in a ring. I saw two men turn towards another man to hug him both at once, and they split his coat up the middle of his back and sent him spinning around like a wheel. All this with the perfect poise of the legal male mind in politics!

I have been to many women's conventions in my day, but I never saw a woman leap up on a chair and take off her bonnet and toss it up in the air and shout: "What's the matter with" some-body. I never saw a woman knock another woman's bonnet off her head as she screamed: "She's all right!" I never heard a body of women whooping and yelling for five minutes when somebody's name was mentioned in the convention. But we are willing to admit that we are emotional. I have actually seen women stand up and wave their handkerchiefs. I have even seen them take hold of hands and sing "Blest be the tie that binds." Nobody denies that women are excitable. Still, when I hear how emotional and how excitable we are, I cannot help seeing in my mind's eye the fine repose and dignity of this Baltimore and other political conventions I have attended!

Source: *History of Woman Suffrage*, Susan B. Anthony, ed., vol. 5, Fowler & Wells, New York, 1922

HOW WELL DID YOU UNDERSTAND THIS SECTION?

1. How does Shaw counter the argument of those opposed to giving women the right to vote because women were supposedly too emotional to be involved in politics?

2. How does Shaw's speech support the effort to give women the right to vote? Can you think of any way that Shaw's speech might hurt the effort to give women the right?

SELF TEST

MULTIPLE CHOICE: Circle the correct response. The correct answers are given at the end.

1. Progressives believed:
    a. the unequal distribution of wealth in America was beneficial
    b. government was becoming more democratic
    c. poverty in America needed to be addressed
    d. economic consolidation benefited workers and consumers

2. Muckraking refers to:
    a. digging up of dirt by farmers to promote higher crop yields
    b. investigative journalism that exposed societal ills
    c. the practice of employing child laborers
    d. a business practice used to drive out competitors

3. The primary objective of settlement houses was:
    a. to offer an alternative to the courts in settling labor disputes
    b. to provide halfway houses to victims of alcoholism
    c. to aid poverty-stricken slum dwellers by providing a nurturing environment
    d. to demonstrate alternative means of constructing high-density housing

4. Progressivism championed all of the following *except*:
    a. extension of the right to vote to eighteen-year-olds
    b. reliance upon a commission of administrators to run cities
    c. government regulation of big business
    d. the redistribution of wealth in America

5. The amendment to the U.S. Constitution that gave women the vote was:
    a. the Seventeenth Amendment
    b. the Eighteenth Amendment
    c. the Nineteenth Amendment
    d. the Twentieth Amendment

6. Each of the following were major concerns of Progressive reformers *except* :
    a. safety in the workplace
    b. long hours of factory work by women and children
    c. high rates of crime, prostitution, and disease
    d. discrimination suffered by African Americans

7. The progressive who first carried progressive reform to the federal level was:
    a. William McKinley
    b. Theodore Roosevelt
    c. William Taft
    d. Woodrow Wilson

8. In the election of 1912, all of the following events took place *except*:
    a. a third-party candidate garnered a sizable portion of the popular vote
    b. a split occurred in the Republican ranks
    c. a Democrat was elected president
    d. the election marked the end of the Progressive era

9. Progressive era foreign policy was marked by:
   a. a reluctance to extend America's involvement beyond her domestic borders
   b. the conviction that American interests did not extend into the Caribbean
   c. a "gentleman's agreement" barring Latin American workers from the U.S.
   d. an effort to link the Atlantic and Pacific Oceans by constructing a canal

10. Progressive era reforms that have become entrenched aspects of American government and American life include all of the following *except* the:
    a. Federal Reserve system
    b. Eighteenth Amendment
    c. Federal Trade Commission
    d. Sixteenth Amendment

Answers: 1-c; 2-b; 3-c; 4-a; 5-c; 6-d; 7-b; 8-d; 9-d; 10-b

ESSAYS:

1. Rejecting the Social Darwinists' claim that poverty was the product of character, Progressives asserted poverty was a product of environment. It would no longer be absurd, then, to attempt to make the world over. Explain, citing specific historical examples of the Progressive conviction that social engineering would lead to social progress.

2. What were Progressivism's strengths and weaknesses? Consider the effectiveness of government regulation of large corporations, of efforts to redistribute wealth and power, of reforms directed at improving working and living conditions, as well as the overall quality of life in urban America.

3. Ethnocentrism is the belief in the superiority of one's own group. It results when one group uses its values, beliefs, and attitudes as the standard to judge another group or groups. Cite specific examples of ethnocentrism displayed by Progressives.

OPTIONAL ACTIVITIES: (Use your knowledge **and** imagination.)

1. Presentism is the practice of taking the values of one historical era and using them to evaluate another period of history. Are we guilty of presentism and therefore unfair when we label many Progressive reformers prejudiced?

2. In your estimation, what were Progressivism's greatest accomplishments and failures?

3. Find an article in a current newspaper or periodical that is an example of present-day muckraking. What evil, injustice, or corruption does it expose?

WEB SITE LISTINGS:

Cartoons of the Gilded Age and Progressive Era
http://www.history.ohio-state.edu/projects/
uscartoons/GAPECartoons.htm

On the Lower East Side: Observations of Life in Lower Manhattan at the Turn of the Century
http://tenant.net:80/Community/LES/contents.html

Immigration History Research Center
http://www1.umn.edu/ihrc

The Triangle Shirtwaist Factory Fire
http://www.ilr.cornell.edu/trianglefire

The Gilded Age and Progressive Era
http://www.uccs.edu/~history/index/shgape.html

Online Texts of the Gilded Age and Progressive Era
http://www.library.csi.cuny.edu/dept/history/lavender/gilded.html

Walter Rauschenbusch: The Social Gospel
http://www.fordham.edu/halsall/mod/rausch-socialgospel.html

Woman Suffrage and the Nineteenth Amendment
http://www.nara.gov/education/teaching/woman/home.html

Margaret Sanger Papers Project
http://www.nyu.edu/projects/sanger

Votes for Women
http://henry.huntington.org/vfw/main.html

Chapter Seventeen

THE "GREAT" WAR:
World War I

American and world history forever changed on a fateful day in June 1914 when the assassination of Austro-Hungarian Archduke Franz Ferdinand by Gavrilo Princip, a Serbian nationalist, ignited World War I. The assassination called into play a complicated alliance system formed as a result of nationalistic and imperialistic rivalries among Germany, Austro-Hungary, Russia, England, France, Italy, and other European nations. Once national armies were mobilized after Ferdinand's assassination, it became impossible to demobilize due to fear of an attack during the demobilization process, and Europe became engulfed in the first major conflict that lasted for more than four years, resulted in millions of casualties, and saw nations around the world dragged into the conflagration.

When the war first erupted among the Triple Alliance (Germany Austro-Hungary, Italy) and the Triple Entente (England, France, and Russia), President Woodrow Wilson pledged to keep the United States out of the conflict and proclaimed American neutrality. Neutrality, however, did not last. The United States was dragged into the war during its latter stages due to Germany's use of unrestricted submarine warfare and interception of the Zimmerman Telegram in which Germany promised Mexico American territory in return for Mexico attacking the United States if America entered World War I on the side of the Triple Entente.

Americans generally were shocked when the war broke out. Most accepted the idea of "History as Progress," believing that science and technology had given humans the ability to solve problems in a rational, humane way without resorting to war. Proponents of this held that advanced nations within the western world were civilized enough that intricate diplomacy would create a balance of power system sufficient to ensure peace and prosperity for all nations. The idea of "History of Progress" was itself a war casualty. Weapons produced by science and technology, including the machine gun, poison gas, tanks, submarines, airplanes, and an array of large guns capable of launching projectiles long distances, were employed by armies on both sides to kill millions. The use of these and other weapons caused American and European intellectuals to question the idea that western civilization was advancing through scientific and technological progress. In fact, several intellectuals concluded that eventually science and technology likely would give humans the ability to destroy civilization and all life on earth.

As the war progressed, American neutrality waned. From the beginning, American policy favored the Triple Entente. A shared democracy, religion, language, history, ethnic background, and economy tilted American neutrality in favor of England. President Wilson, who personally favored England due to his background as a political science professor who admired English democracy, allowed American banks to loan Triple Entente nations money to finance the war and allowed American companies to extend credit to Entente nations that was used to buy weapons and other war materials. Germany and other Triple Alliance nations resented the bias within America's supposed policy of neutrality. Consequently, tensions between Germany and the United States remained high until America entered the conflict in 1917.

Adding to tensions between Germany and the United States was disruption of American trade with England. Germany declared waters around the British Isles a war zone, which meant that Americans travelling on passenger ships bound for England and American merchant ships trading with England were subject to attack. Wilson demanded that Germany respect America's rights as a neutral nation, allow American ships safe passage through waters surrounding England, and refrain from attacking passenger ships carrying Americans. After the British luxury liners *Lusitiania* and *Arabic* were sunk by German submarines in 1915, resulting in the deaths of American passengers, Wilson threatened war with Germany unless the attacks stopped. In the Sussex Pledge Germany agreed to restrict the use of unrestricted submarine warfare, which satisfied Wilson and delayed America's entry into the conflict.

Wilson, however, felt that the United States had little choice but to enter the First World War after Germany revoked the Sussex Pledge in February 1917 and again began using submarines to attack passenger and neutral merchant ships in waters surrounding England. On April 2, 1917, Wilson, concerned about German attacks on neutral ships and information contained in the Zimmerman Telegram, addressed Congress asking for a declaration of war against Germany. Wilson told Congress that the United States needed to enter the conflict to make the world safe for democracy. Congress, despite objections from a few antiwar members, compiled with the president's request and America officially entered World War I.

America's contribution to the English and French victory was immense. American soldiers, along with vast quantities of war materials, proved invaluable in ending the conflict. American troops were particularly valuable in offsetting large numbers of German troops moved to the Western Front after Russia dropped out of the war due to the Bolshevik Revolution. The presence of American troops enabled the stalemate along the Western Front to continue and Germany sued for peace. On November 11, 1918, the war ended when both sides signed an armistice ending combat.

After the war ended, representatives of the victorious nations met at Versailles, near Paris, to hammer out a treaty officially ending the war. Wilson personally led the American delegation and brought with him the Fourteen Points, a plan of peace that included establishment of the League of Nations, an international agency to prevent future wars through collective security. Many of Wilson's Fourteen Points were rejected by English and French leaders at Versailles and the treaty that emerged from the conference is generally viewed as a failure that led to the outbreak of the Second World War because of its harsh treatment of Germany.

Once negotiations were concluded, Wilson faced a tough fight within the United States Senate over ratification of the Treaty of Versailles. Republicans generally opposed the treaty because Wilson broke the spirit of bipartisan cooperation that existed in Congress during World War I when he did not include prominent Republicans in the delegation he led to Paris to negotiate the treaty. Wilson launched a national campaign to pressure Senators to accept the Versailles Treaty and overcome Republican objections to collective security and the League of Nations. Unfortunately, Wilson suffered a debilitating stroke on a trip to promote the treaty. Without pressure from the president, the Senate rejected the agreement.

American participation in World War I also brought significant change within the United States. Congress granted Wilson tremendous power, which he used to mobilize both the economy and society for war. Governmental control over the American economy increased greatly. Approximately five hundred new federal agencies were created to oversee wartime production as free enterprise capitalism was replaced by centralized planning. Anti-trust laws were suspended by governmental administrators, collective bargaining agreements were imposed on defense industries, and companies doing business with the federal government were subject to excess profits provisions in contracts.

World War I created tremendous economic opportunity for women and minorities who filled jobs vacated by men sent overseas to fight. About nine million women were employed by factories making war materials and countless others aided the nation's war effort as nurses, YMCA volunteers, and Signal Corps workers. African Americans and other ethnic minorities also found economic opportunity during the war. About 400,000 blacks migrated into northern factories. The movement of blacks to the North during World War I represents the first significant migration of blacks from the South and gave rise to riots and racism as the ethnic composition of northern communities changed. Hundreds of thousands of black males joined the military in a vain attempt to escape poverty, racism, discrimination, and segregation.

The American government employed propaganda to promote public support for the war. A Committee on Public Information was established to control American public opinion. Its use of patriotic propaganda created a violent backlash against immigrants and their descendants from Germany and Central European nations now considered enemies of the United States. Civil liberties of many American residents were ignored as the government opened concentration camps in which "enemy" aliens from Germany and Austro-Hungarian provinces were interred along with American citizens who opposed the war for religious or other reasons.

World War I also brought positive change to the United States. Women reformers persuaded President Wilson to support the Nineteenth Amendment that granted women the right to vote as a wartime necessity. Congress and the states agreed and women, after more than a century of struggle, received the franchise.

Once the war ended, Americans faced a difficult struggle returning to a normal life. Governmental control over the economy had to be relaxed, civilian production had to resume, and thousands of soldiers returning from European battlefields had to be absorbed into the labor force. Violence and racial riots often disrupted northern cities when returning white soldiers discovered blacks living in northern communities and working in factory jobs previously held by whites. In the South the Ku Klux Klan was revived and a campaign of intimidation, lynching, and terror was used to control the black population. Labor unrest, marked by strikes for higher wages, flared up across the nation as workers facing inflation demanded more pay for their labor. When management refused to increase wages, violence often ensued. The press blamed the labor unrest on Bolshevik activity, which resulted in a fear of Communism and further violations of American Civil Liberties after World War I ended.

IDENTIFICATION: Briefly describe each term.

Triple Alliance

Triple Entente

Unrestricted Submarine Warfare

Lusitania

Sussex Pledge

Zimmerman Note

Treaty of Versailles

War Industries Board

Gavrilo Princip

Machine Gun

Committee on Public Information

Propaganda

Espionage and Sedition Acts

National War Labor Board

Food Administration

American Expeditionary Force

Fourteen Points

Selective Service Act

Policy of Neutrality

War Reparations

War Guilt Clause

Eugene Debs

Nineteenth Amendment

League of Nations

Article X

A. Mitchell Palmer

Schenck v. United States

THINK ABOUT:

1. Why did the United States get involved in World War I? Could America have stayed out of the conflict? Why or why not?

2. What changes did American involvement in World War I bring about in the economy and society? Were these changes beneficial? Why or why not?

3. How did wartime propaganda affect civil liberties?

4. What affect did World War I have on racism and prejudice within the United States?

PRESIDENT WOODROW WILSON'S WAR MESSAGE TO THE U. S. CONGRESS, April 2, 1917

President Wilson called Congress into special session in early April 1917 to request a declaration of war on Germany. Wilson was particularly upset that the German government was again using submarines to sink passenger and neutral merchant ships in waters surrounding the British Isles. Congress complied with Wilson's request by voting on April 6, 1917 to declare war against Germany.

Gentlemen of the Congress:

I have called the Congress into extraordinary session because there are serious, very serious, choices of policy to be made, and made immediately, which it was neither right nor constitutionally permissible that I should assume the responsibility of making.

On the 3d of February last I officially laid before you the extraordinary announcement of the Imperial German Government that on and after the 1st day of February it was its purpose to put aside all restraints of law or of humanity and use its submarines to sink every vessel that sought to approach either the ports of Great Britain and Ireland or the western coasts of Europe or any of the ports controlled by the enemies of Germany within the Mediterranean. That had seemed to be the object of the German submarine warfare earlier in the war, but since April of last year the Imperial Government had somewhat restrained the commanders of its undersea craft in conformity with its promise then given to us that passenger boats should not be sunk and that due warning would be given to all other vessels which its submarines might seek to destroy, when no resistance was offered or escape attempted, and care taken that their crews were given at least a fair chance to save their lives in their open boats. The precautions taken were meagre and haphazard enough, as was proved in distressing instance after instance in the progress of the cruel and unmanly business, but a certain degree of restraint was observed The new policy has swept every restriction aside. Vessels of every kind, whatever their flag, their character, their cargo, their destination, their errand, have been ruthlessly sent to the bottom without warning and without thought of help or mercy for those on board, the vessels of friendly neutrals along with those of belligerents. Even hospital ships and ships carrying relief to the sorely bereaved and stricken people of Belgium, though the latter were provided with safe-conduct through the proscribed areas by the German Government itself and were distinguished by unmistakable marks of identity, have been sunk with the same reckless lack of compassion or of principle.

I was for a little while unable to believe that such things would in fact be done by any government that had hitherto subscribed to the humane practices of civilized nations. International law had its origin in the attempt to set up some law which would be respected and observed upon the seas, where no nation had right of dominion and where lay the free highways of the world. By painful stage after stage has that law been built up, with meagre enough results, indeed, after all was accomplished that could be accomplished, but always with a clear view, at least, of what the heart and conscience of mankind demanded. This minimum of right the German Government has swept aside under the plea of retaliation and necessity and because it had no weapons which it could use at sea except these which it is impossible to employ as it is employing them without throwing to the winds all scruples of humanity or of respect for the understandings that were supposed to underlie the intercourse of the world. I am not now thinking of the loss of property involved, immense and serious as that is, but only of the wanton and wholesale destruction of the lives of noncombatants, men, women, and children, engaged in pursuits which have always, even in the darkest periods of modern history, been deemed innocent and legitimate. Property can be paid for; the lives of peaceful and innocent people can not be. The present German submarine warfare against commerce is a warfare against mankind.

It is a war against all nations. American ships have been sunk, American lives taken, in ways which it has stirred us very deeply to learn of, but the ships and people of other neutral and friendly nations have been sunk and over-whelmed in the waters in the same way. There has been no discrimination. The challenge is to all mankind. Each nation must decide for itself how it will meet it. The choice we make for ourselves must be made with a moderation of counsel and a temperateness of judgment befitting our character and our motives as a nation. We must put excited feeling away. Our motive will not be revenge or the victorious assertion of the physical might of the nation, but only the vindication of right, of human right, of which we are only a single champion....

With a profound sense of the solemn and even tragical character of the step I am taking and of the grave respon-sibilities which it involves, but in unhesitating obedience to what I deem my constitutional duty, I advise that the Congress declare the recent course of the Imperial German Government to be in fact nothing less than war against the Government and people of the United States; that it formally accept the status of belligerent which has thus been thrust upon it, and that it take immediate steps not only to put the country in a more thorough state of defense but also to exert all its power and employ all its resources to bring the Government of the German Empire to terms and end the war....

While we do these things, these deeply momentous things, let us be very clear, and make very clear to all the world what our motives and our objects are....Our object....is to vindicate the principles of peace and justice in the life of the world as against selfish and autocratic power and to set up amongst the really free and self-governed peoples of the world such a concert of purpose and of action as will henceforth ensure the observance of those principles. Neutrality is no longer feasible or desirable where the peace of the world is involved and the freedom of its peoples, and the menace to that peace and freedom lies in the existence of autocratic governments backed by organized force which is controlled wholly by their will, not by the will of their people. We have seen the last of neutrality in such circumstances. We are at the beginning of an age in which it will be insisted that the same standards of conduct and of responsibility for wrong done shall be observed among nations and their governments that are observed among the individual citizens of civilized states....

We are accepting this challenge of hostile purpose because we know that in such a government, following such methods, we can never have a friend; and that in the presence of its organized power, always lying in wait to accom-plish we know not what purpose, there can be no assured security for the democratic governments of the world. We are now about to accept gage of battle with this natural foe to liberty and shall, if necessary, spend the whole force of the nation to check and nullify its pretensions and its power. We are glad, now that we see the facts with no veil of false pretense about them, to fight thus for the ultimate peace of the world and for the liberation of its peoples, the German peoples included: for the rights of nations great and small and the privilege of men everywhere to choose their way of life and of obedience. The world must be made safe for democracy. Its peace must be planted upon the tested foundations of political liberty. We have no selfish ends to serve. We desire no conquest, no dominion. We seek no indemnities for ourselves, no material compensation for the sacrifices we shall freely make. We are but one of the champions of the rights of mankind. We shall be satisfied when those rights have been made as secure as the faith and the freedom of nations can make them.

Just because we fight without rancor and without selfish object, seeking nothing for ourselves but what we shall wish to share with all free peoples, we shall, I feel confident, conduct our operations as belligerents without passion and ourselves observe with proud punctilio the principles of right and of fair play we profess to be fighting for....

It is a distressing and oppressive duty, gentlemen of the Congress, which I have performed in thus addressing you. There are, it may be, many months of fiery trial and sacrifice ahead of us. It is a fearful thing to lead this great peaceful people into war, into the most terrible and disastrous of all wars, civilization itself seeming to be in the bal-ance. But the right is more precious than peace, and we shall fight for the things which we have always carried nearest our hearts,—for democracy, for the right of those who submit to authority to have a voice in their own governments, for the rights and liberties of small nations, for a universal dominion of right by such a concert of free peoples as shall bring peace and safety to all nations and make the world itself at last free. To such a task we can dedicate our lives and our fortunes, everything that we are and everything that we have, with the pride of those who know that the day has come when America is privileged to spend her blood and her might for the principles that gave her birth and happiness and the peace which she has treasured. God helping her, she can do no other.

Source: 65th Congress, 1st Session Senate Document No. 5, Serial No. 7264, Washington, D.C., 1917

HOW WELL DID YOU UNDERSTAND THIS SELECTION?

1. What appears to be Wilson's major gripe with Germany?

2. What reasons does Wilson cite for declaring war on Germany?

3. In the larger scheme of things, why does Wilson think it necessary for the U.S. to enter World War I on the side of England?

4. How does Wilson portray the German government? Is this view accurate? Why or why not?

AT THE FRENCH FRONT, By Alan Seeger, May 22, 1915

Young, idealistic Americans like Alan Seeger left home to fight for England and France after World War I began in 1914. These young men apparently believed they could find glory and honor in war. What they soon realized is that war was not what they imagined. Seeger joined the French Foreign Legion in 1914 and was killed at the Battle of Somme. He becomes a member of the "Lost Poets," writes who died in World War I. His writings provide a realistic picture of what life was like for front line soldiers. A complete book of Seeger's poetry was published after his death.

TO THE "NEW YORK SUN" AT THE FRENCH FRONT, May 22, 1915.

Night of violent attacks. All yesterday we listened to the hum of aeroplanes overhead and watched them cruising about amid their little satellites of shrapnel puffs as the vertical batteries bombarded them. About an hour after nightfall the firing began on a sector a few miles to our right, at first the abrupt fusillade, then the rumble of grenades, then the cannon entered into the medley, and the rattle of rifle and machine gun was completely drowned in the steady thunder of high explosives. At regular intervals a terrific explosion as a heavy piece bombarded a village behind our lines to embarrass re-enforcements coming up....

Today was the sixth and last at second line *petit poste*. Fine weather, warm and sunny. Some of the men, careless after a week without bombardment were up on top of the turf-covered bombproof playing cards. Suddenly the distant boom of a cannon, and then, half a second later—whang! A shrapnel had burst twenty yards away in the branches of the grove that screened us from the enemy.

The sudden stampede into the dugout, then a heart-rending cry, and the frantic voices: "Pick up-! pick up-!" Two men go out, braving the momentary recurrence of the danger with that unassuming courage which is a matter of course in the trenches. They bring in the poor comrade, cruelly, mortally wounded. Another, less badly, has had his shoulder torn. We wait till the next shell bursts immediately overhead with a deafening crash. A man has been waiting for it, crouching in the doorway like a sprinter waiting for the signal. By the time the third shell comes he is far away in his race for the litter-bearers half a mile back. Until they arrive we who are not necessary to tend the wounded sit with downcast eyes and shaken nerves, trying not to look or listen, while six other shells in regular succession burst outside, the fragments pattering on the roof of the dugout and the acrid smell of the powder drifting inside.

This is the most distressing thing about the kind of warfare we are up against here. Never a sight of the enemy, and them some fine day when a man is almost tempted to forget that he is on the front—when he is reading cards or writing home that he is in the best of health—bang! And he is carried off or mangled by a cannon fired five kilometers away. It is not glorious. The gunner has not the satisfaction of knowing that he has hit, nor the wounded at least of hitting back. You cannot understand how after months of this one longs for the day when this miserable trench warfare will cease and when in the *elan* of open action he can return blow for blow.

How is it that the enemy know so well our positions, for we are well hidden and they probably see no more of us than we of them? One principal way was explained to me by a friend who had visited the aviation fields a few days ago. While we take pains to keep concealed from the enemy's lines opposite, the aeroplanes are so much a matter of course that one scarcely takes the trouble to look up when the hum of a motor is heard, much less of ducking underground.

But here is a very real danger. It is not so much from the bombs that occasionally drop on the lines and on the villages in the rear, but the observer up there with a camera of powerful telescopic lens is photographing all the time the country underneath. The film is developed that night and the prints scrutinized under a microscope. Details show up in this way that would escape the naked eye. It is thus that batteries and camps, posts and all kinds of military works are located.

In billets again. Was out on guard early this morning. Suppressed excitement in the little village as the streets begin to fill with officers and soldiers. Then a friend passes. "*Eh bien! On y met,*" he calls out.......means that we are going to clear out. The rumor is soon confirmed. Yes, after just seven months in this more or less tranquil sector we are actually going to get the change we have all been longing for, and on twelve hours notice too. We leave tonight. Where? Nobody knows; but nobody doubts that it is to be into the thick of it.

I should like to give you some impressions of the state of mind before going into action, but unfortunately there is no time. The sacks must be made right away. Let me only say that I am heartily glad, and this feeling is increased when the news comes that poor little ——, who was wounded the other day, has died in hospital. Poor boy! It was the best thing for him.

It is good to get away from the constant danger here of dying thus ingloriously. If it must be, let it come in the heat of action. Why flinch? It is by far the noblest form in which death can come. It is in a sense almost a privilege to be allowed to meet it in this way. The cause is worth fighting for. If one goes it is in company with the elite of the world. *Ave atque vale!* If I write again it will no doubt be to tell you of wonderful things.

We are all in fine form, fit and eager for the assault. I think it will come soon. *Le jour de gloire est arrive!*

From: Letters and Diary of Alan Seeger, Charles Scribner's Sons, NY: 1917
Source- ukans.edu lib website: www.ukans.edu/~libsite/wwi-www/Seeger/Alan1.htm

HOW WELL DID YOU UNDERSTAND THIS SELECTION?

1. How does Seeger describe war?

2. Does Seeger think he has found glory in battle? Why or why not?

3. What does Seeger hope will change about the way World War I is being fought?

4. Is Seeger's attitude about the war optimistic or pessimistic? Explain.

5. How is World War I different from previous wars?

6. How does Seeger feel about leaving the trenches?

7. Were Seeger's views on war typical of the average soldier in World War I? Why or why not?

8. How does Seeger describe existence in the trenches? Is his description accurate? Why or why not?

*THE BACKWASH OF WAR: The Human Wreckage of the Battlefield as Witnessed
by an American Hospital Nurse, 1916, By Ellen N. LaMott*

American women, like their male counterparts, volunteered to help the English and French armies during the First World War. Many of these women, like Ellen LaMott, served as nurses. In that capacity they witnessed firsthand the horrors of war. LaMott, who served as a nurse in a French field hospital in Belgium, published in 1916 **The Backlash of War**, *an account of her war experiences. Her account of the horrors of war was so graphic and realistic that publishers refused to reprint her work until 1934.*

Pour la Patrie [For the fatherland]

THIS is how it was. It is pretty much always like this in a field hospital. Just ambulances rolling in, and dirty, dying men, and the guns off there in the distance! Very monotonous, and the same, day after day, till one gets so tired and bored. Big things may be going on over there, on the other side of the captive balloons that we can see from a distance, but we are always here, on this side of them, and here, on this side of them, it is always the same. The weariness of it—the sameness of it! The same ambulances, and dirty men, and groans, or silence. The same hot operating rooms, the same beds, always full, in the wards. This is war. But it goes on and on, over and over, day after day, till it seems like life. Life in peace time. It might be life in a big city hospital, so alike is the routine. Only the city hospitals are bigger, and better equipped, and the ambulances are smarter, and the patients don't always come in ambulances—they walk in sometimes, or come in street cars, or in limousines, and they are of both sexes, men and women, and have ever so many things the matter with them—the hospitals of peace time are not nearly so stupid, so monotonous, as the hospitals of war. Bah! War's humane compared to peace! More spectacular, I grant you, more acute,—that's what interests us,—but for the sheer agony of life—oh, peace is way ahead!

War is so clean. Peace is so dirty. There are so many foul diseases in peace times. They drag on over so many years, too. No, war's clean! I'd rather see a man die in prime of life, in war time, than see him doddering along in peace time, broken hearted, broken spirited, life broken, and very weary, having suffered many things,—to die at last, at a good, ripe age! How they have suffered, those who drive up to our city hospitals in limousines, in peacetime. What's been saved them, those who die young, and clean and swiftly, here behind the guns. In the long run it dots up just the same. Only war's spectacular, that's all.

Well, he came in like the rest, only older than most of them. A shock of iron-gray hair, a mane of it, above heavy, black brows, and the brows were contracted in pain. Shot, as usual, in the abdomen. He spent three hours on the table after admission—the operating table—and when he came over to the ward, they said, not a dog's chance for him. No more had he. When he came out of ether, he said he didn't want to die. He said he wanted to live. Very much. He said he wanted to see his wife again and his children. Over and over he insisted on this, insisted on getting well. He caught hold of the doctor's hand and said he must get well, that the doctor must get him well. Then the doctor drew away his slim fingers from the rough, imploring grasp, and told him to be good and patient.

"Be good! Be patient!" said the doctor, and that was all he could say, for he was honest. What else could he say, knowing that there were eighteen little holes, cut by the bullet, leaking poison into that gashed, distended abdomen? When these little holes, that the doctor could not stop, had leaked enough poison into his system, he would die. Not today, no, but day after tomorrow. Three days more.

So all that first day, the man talked of getting well. He was insistent on that. He was confident. Next day, the second of the three days the doctor gave him, very much pain laid hold of him. His black brows bent with pain and he grew puzzled. How could one live with such pain as that? That afternoon, about five o'clock, came the General. The one who decorates the men. He had no sword, just a riding whip, so he tossed the whip on the bed, for you can't do an accolade with anything but a sword. Just the *Médaille Militaire*. Not the other one. But the *Médaille Militaire* carries a pension of a hundred francs a year, so that's something. So the General said, very briefly: "In the name of the Republic of France, I confer upon you the *Médaille Militaire*." Then he bent over and kissed the man on his forehead, pinned the medal to the bedspread, and departed.

There you are! Just a brief little ceremony, and perfunctory. We all got that impression. The General has decorated so many dying men. And this one seemed so nearly dead. He seemed half-conscious. Yet the General might have put a little more feeling into it, not made it quite so perfunctory. Yet he's done this thing so many, many times before. It's all right, he does it differently when there are people about, but this time there was no one present—just the doctor, the dying man, and me. And so we four knew what it meant—just a widow's pension. Therefore there wasn't any reason for the accolade, for the sonorous, ringing phrases of a dress parade—We all knew what it meant. So did the man. When he got the medal, he knew too. He knew there wasn't any hope. I held the medal before him, after the General had gone, in its red plush case. It looked cheap, somehow. The exchange didn't seem even. He pushed it aside with a contemptuous hand sweep, a disgusted shrug.

"I've seen these things before!" he exclaimed. We all had seen them too. We all knew about them too, he and the doctor, and the General and I. He knew and understood, most of all. And his tone was bitter.

After that, he knew the doctor couldn't save him, and that he could not see his wife and children again. Where upon he became angry with the treatment, and protested against it. The piqûres [injections] hurt—they hurt very much, and he did not want them. Moreover, they did no good, for his pain was now very intense, and he tossed and tossed to get away from it. So the third day dawned, and he was alive, and dying, and knew that he was dying. Which is unusual and disconcerting. He turned over and over, and black fluid vomited from his mouth into the white enamel basin. From time to time, the orderly emptied the basin, but always there was more, and always he choked and gasped and knit his brows in pain. Once his face broke up as a child's breaks up when it cries. So he cried in pain and loneliness and resentment. He struggled hard to hold on. He wanted very much to live, but he could not do it. He said, "Je ne tiens plus."

Which was true. He couldn't hold on. The pain was too great. He clenched his hands and writhed, and cried out for mercy. But what mercy had we? We gave him morphia, but it did not help. So he continued to cry to us for mercy, he cried to us and to God. Between us, we let him suffer eight hours more like that, us and God.

Then I called the priest. We have three priests on the ward, as orderlies, and I got one of them to give him the Sacrament. I thought it would quiet him. We could not help him with drugs, and he had not got it quite in his head that he must die, and when he said, "I am dying," he expected to be contradicted. So I asked Capolarde to give him the Sacrament, and he said yes, and put a red screen around the bed, to screen him from the ward. Then Capolarde turned to me and asked me to leave. It was summer time. The window at the head of the bed was open, the hay outside was new cut and piled into little haycocks. Over in the distance the guns rolled. As I turned to go, I saw Capolarde holding a tray of Holy Oils in one hand, while with the other he emptied the basin containing black vomitus out the window.

No, it did not bring him comfort, or resignation. He fought against it. He wanted to live, and he resented Death, very bitterly. Down at my end of the ward—it was a silent, summer afternoon—I heard them very clearly. I heard the low words from behind the screen.

"Dites: Dieu je vous donne ma vie librement pour ma patrie" (God, I give you my life freely for my country). The priests usually say that to them, for death has more dignity that way. It is not in the ritual, but it makes a soldier's death more noble. So I suppose Capolarde said it. I could only judge by the response. I could hear the heavy, labored breath, the choking, wailing cry.

"Oui! Oui!" Gasped out at intervals. "Ah mon Dieu! Oui!"

Again the mumbling, guiding whisper.

"Oui—oui!" came sobbing, gasping, in response.

So I heard the whispers, the priest's whispers, and the stentorous choke, the feeble, wailing, rebellious wailing in response. He was being forced into it. Forced into acceptance. Beaten into submission, beaten into resignation.

"Oui—oui!" came the protesting moans. "Ah, oui!"

It must be dawning upon him now. Capolarde is making him see.

"Oui! Oui!" The choking sobs reach me. "Ah, mon Dieu, oui!" Then very deep, panting, crying breaths: "Dieu je vous donne ma vie librement pour ma patrie!"

"Librement! Librement! Au, oui! Oui!" He was beaten at last. The choking, dying, bewildered man had said the noble words.

"God, I give you my life freely for my country!"

After which came a volley of low toned Latin phrases, rattling in the stillness like the popping of a mitrailleuse [machine-gun].

Two hours later he was still alive, restless, but no longer resentful. "It is difficult to go," he murmured, and then: "Tonight, I shall sleep well." A long pause followed, and he opened his eyes.

162

"Without doubt, the next world is more chic than this," he remarked smiling, and then: "I was mobilized against my inclination. Now I have won the *Médaille Militaire*. My Captain won it for me. He made me brave. He had a revolver in his hand."

Source: Ellen N. La Motte, *The Backwash of War,* G.P. Putnam's Sons, New York, 1916

HOW WELL DID YOU UNDERSTAND THIS SELECTION?

1. How does LaMott describe war? Is her portrayal realistic? Why or why not?

2. Why would American publishers refuse to issue reprints of LaMott's work?

3. How does LaMott view suffering?

4. Why does LaMott include the passage about military decorations in the selection?

SECRET INFORMATION CONCERNING BLACK AMERICAN TROOPS,
French Military Mission, Stationed with the American Army, August 7, 1918

Idealistic young African Americans joined the army in World War I to express their patriotism and in hopes of overcoming the racism present in their everyday life. Sadly, the racism, prejudice and discrimination blacks faced were also present in the armed forces. W.E.B. DuBois, a black civil rights leader and editor of the NAACP journal, **The Crisis,** *published in 1919 a series of articles documenting the prejudice, racism, and discrimination black soldiers faced during World War I. The article reprinted below was part of this series. It clearly shows the attitude toward blacks held by officials in both the Wilson administration and the military. These officials generally feared that blacks who fought for their country might not be willing to resume their subservient role to whites in American society once World War I ended. Most blacks who were part of the American Expeditionary Force sent to France were used in noncombat positions due to racist attitudes prevalent at that time. Whites simply feared that arming black troops might threaten Jim Crow within the United States and requested that French officials issue instructions to French officers commanding black American troops about how these troops should be treated. DuBois printed a copy of these instructions in* **The Crisis.**

1.   It is important for French officers who have been called upon to exercise command over black American troops, or to live in close contact with them, to have an exact idea of the position occupied by Negroes in the United States. The information set forth in the following communication ought to be given to these officers and it is to their interest to have these matters known and widely disseminated.   It will devolve likewise on the French Military Authorities, through the medium of the Civil Authorities, to give information on this subject to the French population residing in the cantonments occupied by American colored troops.

2.   The American attitude upon the Negro question may seem a matter for discussion to many French minds. But we French are not in our province if we undertake to discuss what some call "prejudice." American opinion is unanimous on the "color question" and does not admit of any discussion.

The increasing number of Negroes in the United States (about 15,000,000) would create for the white race in the Republic a menace of degeneracy were it not that an impassable gulf has been made between them.

As this danger does not exist for the French race, the French public has become accustomed to treating the Negro with familiarity and indulgence. This indulgence and this familiarity are matters of grievous concern to the Americans. They consider them an affront to their national policy. They arc afraid that contact with the French will inspire in black Americans aspirations which to them [the whites] appear intolerable. It is of the utmost importance that every effort be made to avoid profoundly estranging American opinion.

Although a citizen of the United States, the black man is regarded by the white American as an inferior being with whom relations of business or service only are possible. The black is constantly being censured for his want of intelligence and discretion, his lack of civic and professional conscience and for his tendency toward undue familiarity.

The vices of the Negro are a constant menace to the American who has to repress them sternly. For instance, the black American troops in France have, by themselves, given rise to as many complaints for attempted rape as all the rest of the army.   And yet the [black American] soldiers sent to us have been the choicest with respect to physique and morals, for the number disqualified at the time of mobilization was enormous.

CONCLUSION

1.   We must prevent the rise of any pronounced degree of intimacy between French officers and black officers. We may be courteous and amiable with these last, but we cannot deal with them on the same plane as with the white American officers without deeply wounding the latter. We must not eat with them, must not shake hands or seek to talk or meet with them outside of the requirements of military service.

2.   We must not commend too highly the black American troops, particularly in the presence of [white] Americans. It is all right to recognize their good qualities and their services, but only in moderate terms, strictly in keeping with the truth.

3.   Make a point of keeping the native cantonment population from "spoiling" the Negroes. [White] Americans become greatly incensed at any public expression of intimacy between white women with black men. They have recently uttered violent protests against a picture in the "Vie Parisienne" entitled "The Child of the Desert" which shows a [white] woman in a "cabinet particulier" with a Negro. Familiarity on the part of white women with black men is furthermore a source of profound regret to our experienced colonials who see in it an over-weening menace to the prestige of the white race.

Military authority cannot intervene directly in this question, but it can through the civil authorities exercise some influence on the population.

(Signed) LINARD.

Source: "Documents of the War," *The Crisis*, (May, 1919) vol.18: 1, pp. 16-18, W.E.B. Du Bois, ed

HOW WELL DID YOU UNDERSTAND THIS SELECTION?

1. Why did American officials issue orders to French officers regarding the treatment of black troops?

2. What is the American attitude toward black soldiers?

3. If black troops were treated equal to white troops by French officers, what danger might this pose to the United States?

4. How did Americans justify discriminatory treatment against blacks?

5. The French Ministry of War later ordered all copies of these instructions destroyed. Why would the French government issue orders to destroy this directive?

6. How might allowing blacks to serve in armed combat affect Jim Crow in the South?

7. Is the attitude toward blacks expressed in these instructions the general attitude of most Americans living during World War I? Why or why not?

Governmental power expanded greatly during the First World War. Numerous laws were enacted to give the federal government control over society and the economy. The American government regulated things that previously had been solely controlled by the private sector in an effort to mobilize the American population and their productive capacities to win the war. In the fall of 1917 Congress passed the Lever Act, granting the chief executive authority to regulate the nation's food and fuel supplies. President Wilson, to carry out the mandate given him by the Lever Act, created the United States Food Administration. Herbert Hoover was chosen to head this new government agency. He quickly realized the value of advertising and ordered the Food Administration to create an advertising campaign urging Americans to plant vegetable gardens to grow food in support of the war effort and to avoid wasting food.

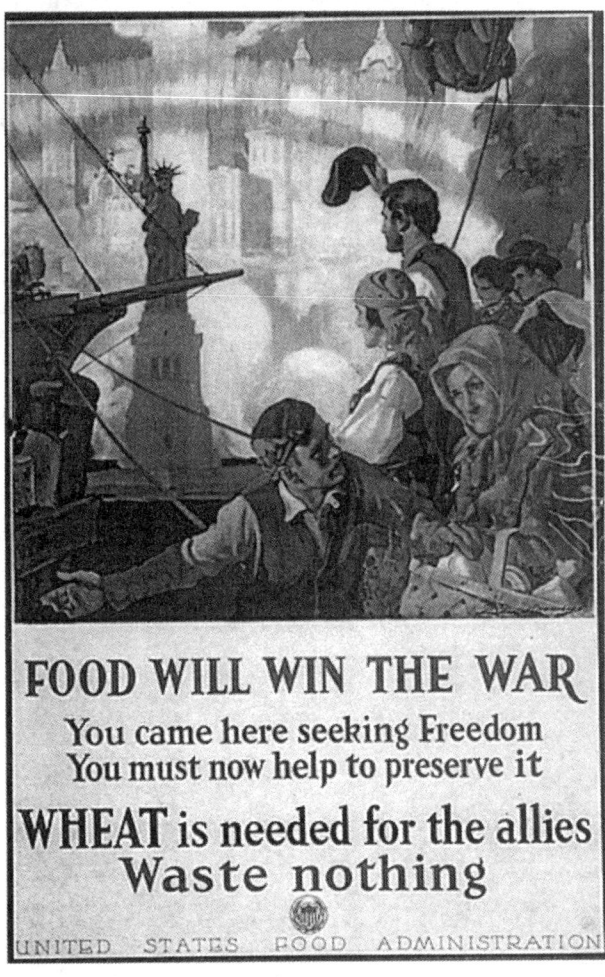

HOW WELL DID YOU UNDERSTAND THIS SELECTION?

1. What emotions within the public do the posters tap into?

2. Are these posters propaganda? Why or why not?

3. Was the government's advertising campaign effective? Why or why not?

4. Identify particular items in each poster aimed at eliciting an emotional response from the American public.

*Once the United States entered World War I, government officials became fearful of individuals who held antiwar views and began to persecute these people under the Espionage Act Congress passed in 1917. Prosecutors particularly targeted writers and other intellectuals who used their First Amendment freedom of speech and the press to oppose America's entry into the First World War. In 1917 a number of writers and artists who published antiwar articles and cartoons in **The Masses,** a socialist periodical, were indicted and tried for conduct detrimental to the war effort. The following cartoon published in the August 1917 issue of **The Masses** was introduced as evidence against the artists at their trial because government prosecutors considered it extremely harmful to America's war effort. H. J. Glintenkamp, the artist who drew the cartoon, left the country rather than face trial on what he believed were bogus charges. The authors and artists were tried twice but were not convicted due to a hung jury both times. After the war ended the government elected not to try the individuals a third time. Clearly, the U.S. government recognized the power of images to shape public sentiment both for and against the war.*

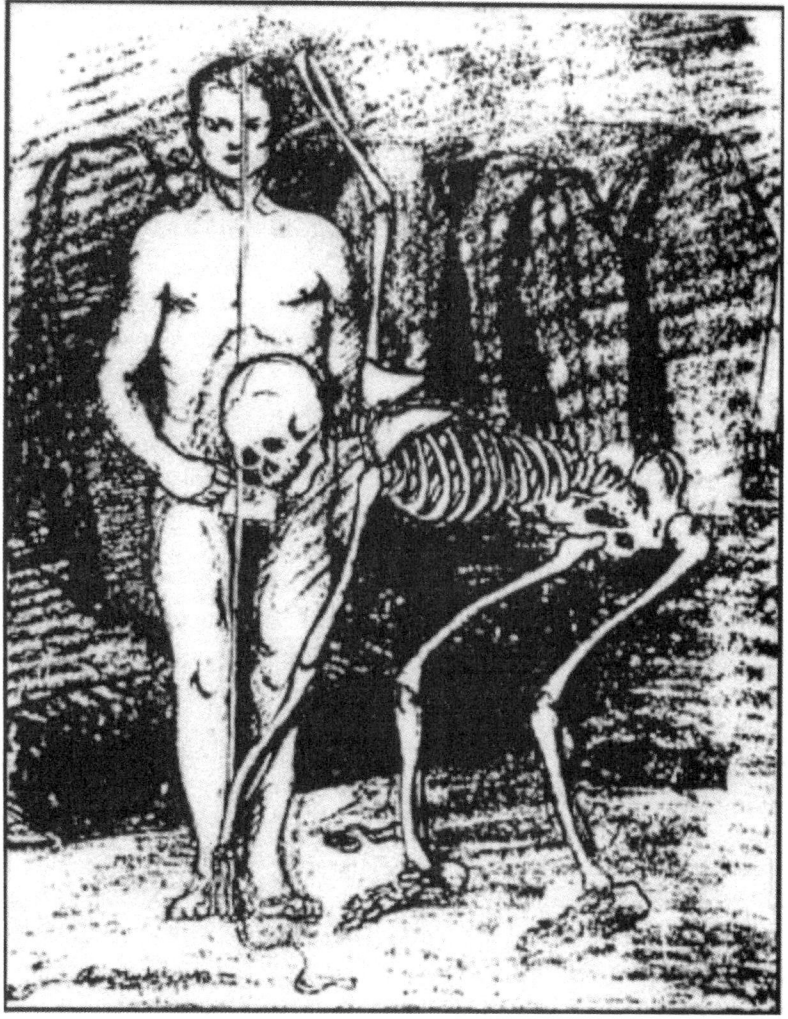

Source: *The Masses,* New York, August, 1917

HOW WELL DID YOU UNDERSTAND THIS SELECTION?

1. What message does this cartoon convey?

2. How would the American public have viewed this cartoon?

3. Why did the artists call the cartoon "Conscription?"

4. Did the artist have the right to publish this cartoon? Why or why not?

Although President Wilson told Americans World War I was fought "to make the world safe for democracy," the American government often ignored and openly violated the democratic principles upon which the republic was founded. Congress enacted two laws, the Espionage Act of 1917 and the Sedition Act of 1918, that loosely defined treason and allowed the Wilson administration to arrest over 2,000 American citizens who actually did little but verbally oppose the draft and America's participation in World War I. Eugene Debs, a labor leader, and Charles Schenck, the Socialist Party's general secretary, were jailed under these laws. Debs protested against what many felt was an unjust conviction by running as a socialist candidate for president while incarcerated in prison and Schenck appealed his conviction for violating the Espionage Act to the U.S. Supreme Court. Justice Oliver Wendell Holmes wrote the unanimous opinion of the court affirming the judgment.

MR. JUSTICE HOLMES delivered the opinion of the Court:
This is an indictment in three counts. The first charges a conspiracy to violate the Espionage Act of June 15, 1917, by causing and attempting to cause insubordination, in the military and naval forces of the United States, and to obstruct the recruiting and enlistment service of the United States, when the United States was at war with the German Empire, to-wit, that the defendants wilfully conspired to have printed and circulated to men who had been called and accepted for military service under the Act of May 18, 1917, a document set forth and alleged to be calculated to cause such insubordination and obstruction. The count alleges overt acts in pursuance of the conspiracy, ending in the distribution of the document set forth. The second count alleges a conspiracy to commit an offense against the United States, to-wit, to use the mails for the transmission of . . . the above mentioned document.... The third count charges an unlawful use of the mails for the transmission of the same matter and otherwise as above. The defendants were found guilty on all the counts. They set up the First Amendment to the Constitution forbidding Congress to make any law abridging the freedom of speech, or of the press, and bringing the case here on that ground have argued some other points also of which we must dispose.... The document in question upon its first printed side recited the first section of the Thirteenth Amendment, said that the idea embodied in it was violated by the Conscription Act and that a conscript is little better than a convict. In impassioned language it intimated that conscription was despotism in its worst form and a monstrous wrong against humanity in the interest of Wall Street's chosen few. It said "Do not submit to intimidation," but in form at least confined itself to peaceful measures such as a petition for the repeal of the act. The other and later printed side of the sheet was headed "Assert Your Rights." . . . it denied the power to send our citizens away to foreign shores to shoot up the people of other lands, and added that words could not express the condemnation such coldblooded ruthlessness deserves, &c., &c., winding up "You must do your share to maintain, support and uphold the rights of the people of this country." Of course the document would not have been sent unless it had been intended to have some effect, and we do not see what effect it could be expected to have upon persons subject to the draft except to influence them to obstruct the carrying of it out. The defendants do not deny that the jury might find against them on this point. But it is said, suppose that that was the tendency of this circular, it is protected by the First Amendment to the Constitution....We admit that in many

places and in ordinary times the defendants in saying all that was said in the circular would have been within their constitutional rights. But the character of every act depends upon the circumstances in which it is done. The most stringent protection of free speech would not protect a man in falsely shouting fire in a theatre and causing a panic. It does not even protect a man from an injunction against uttering words that may have all the effect of force. The question in every case is whether the words used are used in such circumstances and are of such a nature as to create clear and present danger that they will bring about the substantive evils that Congress has a right to prevent. It is a question of proximity and degree. When a nation is at war many things that might be said in time of peace are such a hindrance to its effort that their utterance will not be endured so long as men fight and that no Court could regard them as protected by any constitutional right. It seems to be admitted that if an actual obstruction of the recruiting service were proved, liability for words that produced that effect might be enforced. The statute of 1917 in section …4 punishes conspiracies to obstruct as well as actual obstruction. If the act, (speaking, or circulating a paper), its tendency and the intent with which it is done are the same, we perceive no ground for saying that success alone warrants making the act a crime....

Judgments affirmed.

Source: www.thisnation.com/library/schenck.html

HOW WELL DID YOU UNDERSTAND THIS SELECTION?

1. What did Schenck base appeal of his conviction on?

2. What factors did the court consider when making its decision?

3. Was Schenck fairly or unfairly convicted? Why or why not?

4. Under what circumstances does the court allow suppression of free speech?

Governmental control of the media, coupled with a propaganda campaign, stirred patriotic emotions in Americans that sometimes went to the extreme. Mobs of "patriotic" Americans ferreted out and punished without trial or evidence individuals suspected of disloyalty. Many innocent people were beaten and sometimes killed because some super patriot believed they were spies or because they did not join those who condemned disloyalty. One such individual was Robert Prager, a German immigrant coal miner, lynched by a mob of super patriots, near Collinsville, Illinois. Eleven people in the mob that hanged Prager were arrested and tried for the crime but a jury acquitted them. Afterwards, the prosecuting attorney remarked the acquittal was "an approval of mob law."

The St. Louis Globe-Democrat (April 5, 1918)

GERMAN ENEMY OF U.S. HANGED BY MOB
ST. LOUIS COLLINSVILLE MAN KILLED FOR ABUSING WILSON

Robert P. Prager Taken from Jail and Strung Up to Tree by 300 Men and Boys After Officers are Overpowered

Robert P. Prager, 45 years old, of Collinsville, Ill., a coalminer, charged with making disloyal utterances against the United States and President Wilson, was hanged to a tree on Mauer Heights, one mile west of Collinsville on the St. Louis road, by a mob of 300 men and boys after he had twice escaped mob violence, at 12:15 o'clock this morning. Collinsville is ten miles northeast of East St. Louis. Prager was taken from the Collinsville Jail by the mob, which battered down the doors. The prisoner was found hidden under a pile of rubbish in the basement of the Jail, where he had been placed by the police when they had learned that the mob was on the way to the Jail. The police were overpowered, there being only four on the night force, and the prisoner was carried down the street, the mob cheering and waving flags. The police were not allowed to follow the mob by a guard which had been placed over them. When led to the tree upon which he was hanged Prager was asked if he had anything to say. "Yes," he replied in broken English. "I would like to pray." He then fell to his knees, clasped his hands to his breast and prayed for three minutes in German. Without another word the noose was placed about his neck and the body pulled 10 feet into the air by a hundred or more hands which grasped the rope. Before praying, Prager wrote a letter to his parents, Mr. and Mrs. Carl Henry Prager, Preston, Germany. It follows: "Dear Parents - I must this day, the 5th of April, 1918, die. Please pray for me, my dear parents. This is my last letter. Your dear son. ROBERT PAUL PRAGER." Prager was an enemy alien and registered in East St. Louis.

Prager Attended Socialist Meeting Short Time Before He was Lynched

After the mob had returned to Collinsville, several residents at Collinsville who had heard of the hanging went to the scene. Two unidentified persons were found guarding the body. They would let no one approach and warned whoever came close that they would meet the same fate if they attempted to cut down the body. The mob took their prisoner from the jail about 10 o'clock last night. Prager earlier in the evening had attended a Socialist meeting in Maryville, where it is alleged he made a speech in which he uttered remarks which were termed disloyal. After word had been passed around Maryville, a mob collected there and started a search for the miner. Prager had been informed about that the mob was after him and he escaped to Collinsville. They told of the remarks of Prager and finally a mob of 300 was assembled. Prager was found on the street in front of his home, 208 Vandalia Avenue. He was marched to the main street, where his shoes were removed and a large American flag was wrapped about his body. Prager was made to kiss the flag many times and march up and down the street waving two small flags which he carried in his hands. For fear that violence would result from the mob, the police took Prager from them and placed him in jail.

Mayor Induces Mob to Go Home, but It Reassembles Later

Mayor J. H. Siegel pleaded with the mob and asked them to go to their homes. He had previously closed all the saloons. "We do not want a stigma marking Collinsville," said Mayor Siegel, "and I implore you to go to your homes and discontinue this demonstration." The mob disbanded and the mayor, thinking that everything had quieted down, went to his home. But a short time later the mob again formed and stormed the jail, taking the prisoner from the police. This is the first killing for disloyalty in the United States, although many persons have been mobbed and tarred and feathered. Prager begged for mercy. He said that he was a loyal citizen, and in a signed statement, which he had previously made to the police, he said that his heart and soul were for the United States. He admitted being a native of Germany. He said that he had applied for naturalization papers and that his second papers were waiting for him. Prager had been in Maryville looking for work. He was a coal miner. He found he could not obtain employment because the union had rejected his application. On March 22, four men, including a Polish Catholic priest, were tarred and feathered at Christopher, Ill., a mining town eighty miles from St. Louis. Previous to that time two other men were tarred and feathered in the same mining district. For the past three months many loyalty demonstrations have occurred in an effort to drive disloyal persons from Southern Illinois.

Edwardsville Intelligencer (June 8, 1918)

JURY FINDS PRAGER DEFENDANTS NOT GUILTY AND OTHERS ARE FREE

Edwardsville—Eleven residents of Collinsville walked from the court house Saturday afternoon, exonerated for the death of Robert P. Prager, German alien enemy, who was lynched in that city during the early morning hours of April 5. On the second ballot and with deliberations of only a few minutes the jury reached its verdict.... On the first vote the jurors stood 11 to 1 for acquittal, the discussions, it is understood, lasted but a few minutes and then the second vote was taken. It found the defendants not guilty..... The court room was filled with spectators when the defendants were taken back to the court room Saturday afternoon to hear their fate. A few minutes later the court was ready to receive the jury and the twelve men filed into the court room and took their places in the jury box....There was wild applauding and cheers from most everyone present. Relatives, friends and acquaintances rushed toward the bar to shake hands with the defendants. In a few minutes the crowd was quieted and the jury was discharged by Judge Bernreuter. Afterwards the defendants shook hands with the members of the jury.

There was a peculiar coincidence at the trial Saturday. The Jackie Band was in Edwardsville for a patriotic demonstration. When a shower of rain came up the musicians were sent to the court house where it had been arranged to give a program. At 2:40 o'clock Judge Bernreuter ordered a recess after the completion of arguments and before reading the instructions. Then word was sent that the band might play until court re-convened. The first number of all concerts is the Star Spangled Banner and it was played Saturday. The strains from the Jackie Band caused tears to flow down the cheeks of Riegel [a defendant-Ed.]. He was still crying when he returned to the court room. As the jury came in with its verdict the band was at the head of a procession of draft boys and in passing the court house played "Over There." The acquittal of most of the prisoners was no great surprise to most of those who heard the evidence. After returning the verdict, several of the jurors told reporters that the state had failed to connect up the charges and remove the reasonable doubts, even to those charged with being most prominently connected with the death....

State's Attorney Streuber made the following statement today: "Since the trial of the eleven defendants charged with the murder of Robert Paul Prager, there have been intimations and expressions that the acquittal of the defendants was, in substance, an approval of mob law. With this view I do not concur...."

Sources: *The St. Louis Globe-Democrat*, April 5, 1918; *Edwardsville Intelligencer*, June 8, 1918

HOW WELL DID YOU UNDERSTAND THIS SELECTION?

1. What had Prager allegedly done to inflame the mob against him?

2. What role might governmental propaganda have played in the lynching?

3. Was Streuber's assessment that the lynching represented "an approval of mob law" accurate? Why or why not?

4. Why did the jury acquit the people charged with lynching Prager?

5. Is vigilante justice an oxymoron? Why or why not?

PETITION FROM THE WOMEN VOTERS ANTI-SUFFRAGE PARTY, 1917

American women finally got the right to vote after World War I due to ratification of the Nineteenth Amendment in 1919. Supporters of women's suffrage pointed out the hypocrisy in the argument that World War I was fought to defend democracy throughout the world when slightly more than half the adult population in the United States was denied the franchise. Women also had worked hard to ensure an American victory during the war. Their work in wartime industries had proven invaluable to American success on European battlefields, and many argued that giving women the vote would be a fitting reward for their contributions to the war effort. Congress agreed and sent the Nineteenth Amendment to the states who ratified it in 1920. Opponents of women's suffrage fought hard against the Nineteenth Amendment as demonstrated by the following anti-suffrage petition sent to Congress in 1917.

PETITION
From the Women Voters Anti-suffrage Party of New York
TO THE
United States Senate

Whereas, This country is now engaged in the greatest war in history, and

Whereas, The advocates of the Federal Amendment, though urging it as a war measure, through their president, Mrs. Catt, that its passage "means a simultaneous campaign in 48 States. It demands organization in every precinct; activity, agitation, education in every corner. Nothing less than this nation-wide vigilant, unceasing campaign will win the ratification," therefore be it

Resolved, That our country, in this hour of peril should be spared the harassing of its public men and the distracting of its people from work for the war, and further

Resolved, That the United States Senate be respectfully urged to pass no measure involving such a radical change in our government while the attention of the patriotic portion of the people is concentrated on the all-important task of winning the war, and during the absence of over a million men abroad.

[Signatures]

Source: National Archives and Records Administration, Woman Suffrage and the Nineteenth Amendment, Primary Documents. website: http://www.nara.gov/education/teaching/woman/ww1pet.html

HOW WELL DID YOU UNDERSTAND THIS SELECTION?

1. What arguments did the anti-suffrage party make in the petition sent to Congress?

2. Was the position of the anti-suffrage party correct? Why or why not?

3. Was the argument of Carrie Chapman Catt, president of the National American Women Suffrage Association, linking suffrage to democracy valid? Why or why not?

THE NEGRO IN CHICAGO: A Study of Race Relations and a Race Riot, 1922

Shortly after the conclusion of the First World War a series of race riots rocked the United States. Washington, D.C., Knoxville, TN, Charleston, S.C., Omaha, Nebraska, Chicago, IL, and other cities saw riots erupt after white soldiers returned from Europe and encountered difficulty finding employment. Many returning soldiers blamed blacks for taking their jobs. World War I opened employment opportunities for blacks who migrated from the South in record numbers. Jobs that had been filled exclusively by whites before World War I were afterward open to blacks. As the black population of northern cities swelled, society changed as well. Black soldiers had received equal treatment from European whites during the war and were not as willing to endure racial discrimination and prejudice upon their return from Europe. Tension created by lack of employment, the changing population of northern cities, and the transformation from a wartime to a peacetime economy caused a week-long race riot in Chicago during the hot summer of 1919. Thirty-eight people were killed during this riot and over 500 received serious injuries. The Illinois governor appointed a biracial commission to investigate the riots. The following article, published in 1922, is a summary of the commission's findings.

Background

In July, 1919, a race riot involving whites and Negroes occurred in Chicago. For some time thoughtful citizens, white and Negro, had sensed increased tension, but having no local precedent of riot and wholesale bloodshed, had neither prepared themselves for it nor taken steps to prevent it. The collecting of arms by members of both races was known to the authorities, and it was evident that this was in preparation for aggression as well as for self-defense.

Several minor clashes preceded the riot. On July 3, 1917, a white saloon-keeper who, according to the coroner's physician, died of heart trouble, was incorrectly reported in the press to have been killed by a Negro. That evening a party of young white men riding in an automobile fired upon a group of Negroes at Fifty-third and Federal Streets. In July and August of the same year recruits from the Great Lakes Naval Training Station clashed frequently with Negroes, each side accusing the other of being the aggressor.

Gangs of white "toughs," made up largely of the membership of so-called "athletic clubs"....were a constant menace to Negroes who traversed sections of the territory going to and returning from work. The activities of these gangs and "athletic clubs" became bolder in the spring of 1919, and on the night of June 21, five weeks before the riot, two wanton murders of Negroes occurred, those of Sanford Harris and Joseph Robinson. Harris, returning to his home....about 11:30 at night, passed a group of young white men. They threatened him and he ran. He had gone but a short distance when one of the group shot him. He died soon afterward. Policemen who came on the scene made no arrests, even when the assailant was pointed out by a white woman witness of the murder. On the same evening Robinson, a Negro laborer....was attacked while returning from work by a gang of white "roughs".... apparently without provocation, and stabbed to death.

Negroes were greatly incensed over these murders, but their leaders, joined by many friendly whites, tried to allay their fears and counseled patience.

After the killing of Harris and Robinson notices were conspicuously posted on the South Side that an effort would be made to "get all the niggers on July 4th." The notices called for help from sympathizers. Negroes in turn whispered around the warning to prepare for a riot; and they did prepare....

Aside from general lawlessness and disastrous riots that preceded the riot here discussed, there were other factors which may be mentioned briefly here. In Chicago considerable unrest had been occasioned in industry by increasing competition between white and Negro laborers following a sudden increase in the Negro population due to the migration of Negroes from the South. This increase developed a housing crisis. The Negroes overran the hitherto recognized area of Negro residence, and when they took houses in adjoining neighborhoods, friction ensued. In the two years just preceding the riot, twenty-seven Negro dwellings were wrecked by bombs thrown by unidentified persons.

Story of the Riot

Sunday afternoon, July 27, 1919, hundreds of white and Negro bathers crowded the lake-front beaches at Twenty-sixth and Twenty-ninth Streets. This is the eastern boundary of the thickest Negro residence area. At Twenty-sixth Street Negroes were in great majority; at Twenty-ninth Street there were more whites. An imaginary line in the water separating the two beaches had been generally observed by the two races. Under the prevailing relations, aided by wild rumors and reports, this line served virtually as a challenge to either side to cross. Four Negroes who attempted to enter the water from the "white" side were driven away by the whites. They returned with more Negroes, and then there followed a series of attacks with stones, first one side gaining the advantage, then the other.

Eugene Williams, a Negro boy of seventeen, entered the water from the side used by Negroes and drifted across the line supported by a railroad tie. He was observed by the crowd on the beach and promptly became a target for stones. He suddenly released the tie, and went down and was drowned. Guilt was immediately placed on Stauber, a young white man, by Negro witnesses who declared that he threw the fatal stone.

White and Negro dived for the boy without result. Negroes demanded that the policeman arrest Stauber. He refused, and at this crucial moment arrested a Negro on a white man's complaint. Negroes then attacked the officer. These two facts, the drowning and the refusal of the policeman to arrest Stauber, together marked the beginning of the riot.

Two hours after the drowning, a Negro, James Crawford, fired into a group of officers summoned by the policeman at the beach and was killed by a Negro policeman. Reports and rumors circulated rapidly, and new crowds began to gather. Five white men were injured in clashes near the beach. As darkness came Negroes in white districts to the west suffered severely. Between 9:00PM and 3:00AM twenty-seven Negroes were beaten, seven stabbed, and four shot. Monday morning was quite, and Negroes went to work as usual.

Returning from work in the afternoon many Negroes were attacked by white ruffians. Street-car routes, especially at transfer points, were the centers of lawlessness. Trolleys were pulled from the wires, and Negro passengers were dragged into the street, beaten, stabbed, and shot. The police were powerless to cope with these numerous assaults. During Monday, four Negro men and one white assailant were killed, and thirty Negroes were severely beaten in street-car clashes. Four white men were killed, six stabbed, five shot, and nine severely beaten. It was rumored that the white occupants of the Angelus Building....had shot a Negro. Negroes gathered about the building. The white tenants sought police protection, and one hundred policemen, mounted and on foot responded. In a clash with the mob the police killed four Negroes and injured many.

Raids into the Negro residence area then began. Automobiles sped through the streets, the occupants shooting at random. Negroes retaliated by "sniping" from ambush. At midnight, surface and elevated car service was discontinued because of a strike for wage increases, and thousands of employees were cut off from work.

174

On Tuesday, July 29, Negro men enroute on foot to their jobs through hostile territory were killed. White soldiers and sailors in uniform, aided by civilians, raided the "Loop" business section, killing two Negroes and beating and robbing several others. Negroes living among white neighbors in Englewood, far to the south, were driven from their homes, their household goods were stolen, and their houses were burned or wrecked. On the West Side an Italian mob, excited by a false rumor that an Italian girl had been shot by a Negro, killed Joseph Lovings, a Negro.

Wednesday night at 10:30 Mayor Thompson yielded to pressure and asked the help of three regiments of militia which had been stationed in nearby armories during the most severe rioting, awaiting the call. They immediately took up positions throughout the South Side. A rainfall Wednesday night and Thursday kept many people in their homes, and by Friday the rioting had abated. On Saturday incendiary fires burned forty-nine houses in the immigrant neighborhood west of the Stock Yards. Nine hundred and forty-eight people, mostly Lithuanians, were made homeless, and the property loss was about $250,000. Responsibility for the fires was never fixed.

The total casualties of this reign of terror were thirty-eight deaths—fifteen white, twenty-three Negro—and 537 people injured. Forty-one per cent of the reported clashes occurred in the white neighborhood....and 34 per cent in the "Black Belt"....Others were scattered....

Source: *The Negro in Chicago; A Study of Race Relations and a Race Riot,* Chicago Commission on Race Relations: Chicago, 1922

HOW WELL DID YOU UNDERSTAND THIS SELECTION?

1. What does the commission say caused the riot?

2. What role did white toughs and athletic clubs play in causing the riot?

3. What brought an end to the riot?

4. Did racial segregation play a role in causing the riots? Why or why not?

*On the eleventh hour of the eleventh day of the eleventh month of 1918, an armistice was signed that officially ended hostilities in World War I. Americans celebrated victory and eagerly awaited a formal peace agreement with Germany and the defeated Central Powers. The following cartoon appeared in the **Chicago Tribune** on November 14, 1918. Its title, "The New Menace," raised concerns about the coming peace. The victory might not have been as glorious or as complete as celebrating Americans thought.*

THE NEW MENACE

Source: *Chicago Tribune*, November, 14, 1918

HOW WELL DID YOU UNDERSTAND THIS SELECTION?

1. What message is the cartoon trying to convey?

2. What, exactly, does the cartoonist think is the new menace? What do each of the three figures represent? Did history prove that the cartoonist's concerns were valid?

SELF TEST

MULTIPLE CHOICE: Circle the correct response. The correct answers are given at the end.

1. The German monarch at the onset of World War I was
   a. Franz-Josef II.
   b. Franz Ferdinand.
   c. Kaiser Wilhelm II.
   d. Czar Nicholas II.

2. World War I was touched off by the assassination of
   a. Franz-Josef II.
   b. Franz Ferdinand.
   c. Kaiser Wilhelm II.
   d. Czar Nicholas II.

3. When the First World War began, President Wilson
   a. Declared American neutrality.
   b. Immediately declared war against Germany and the Triple Alliance.
   c. Entered the war on the side of the Central Powers.
   d. Supported Germany and Austro-Hungary.

4. In his war message to Congress President Wilson presented American entrance into World War I as
   a. Necessary to prevent England from losing the conflict.
   b. Necessary to ensure that the United States could exert more influence in the world after the war ended.
   c. Necessary to prevent Communism from spreading from Russia to the entire world.
   d. Necessary to protect and preserve democracy in the world.

5. What principle did the Supreme Court establish in *Schenck v. U.S.*?
   a. That the government could limit profits of private companies during war.
   b. That the government could limit freedom of speech to protect American interest during war.
   c. That labor unions could not strike during a national emergency.
   d. That the government's authority to regulate interstate commerce is limited by the Constitution.

6. In American society, World War I
   a. Caused Americans to become more liberal politically.
   b. Shrunk economic opportunities for blacks.
   c. Cost women the right to vote.
   d. Inflamed racial tensions and prejudice.

7. Which of the following did not happen during World War I?
   a. Passage of the Equal Rights Amendment.
   b. Jobs opened for women and ethnic minorities in industries traditionally dominated by white males.
   c. Racial tensions and prejudice against ethnic minorities heightened.
   d. President Wilson openly sided with the Triple Alliance when war broke out in Europe.

8. Which of the following did the government not do during World War I?
   a. Attempt to mobilize and control public opinion.
   b. Imprison Americans under the Espionage Act.
   c. Enact the Sedition Act.
   d. Nationalize all private property and businesses.

9. Which of the following statements is not accurate?
   a. The American government engaged in economic planning.
   b. The American economy experienced economic recession.
   c. The economy experienced inflation.
   d. The government nationalized the nation's railroads.

10. How did the American government finance World War I?
    a. By borrowing money.
    b. By increasing taxes on the wealthy.
    c. By printing new paper money.
    d. By nationalizing the railroads.

Answers: 1-c; 2-b; 3-a; 4-d; 5-b; 6-d; 7-a; 8-d; 9-b; 10-a

ESSAYS:

1. Discuss the impact World War I had on the United States.

2. Discuss the inherent contradictions in the idea that America entered World War I to make the world safe for democracy in light of restrictions placed on democracy within the United States.

3. Why did the U.S. Senate refuse to ratify the Treaty of Versailles?

4. Could the United States have stayed out of World War I? Why or why not?

OPTIONAL ACTIVITIES: (Use your knowledge **and** imagination.)

1. Your class members represent different nations and interests at the Versailles Peace Conference. Meet together and attempt to write a treaty to end World War I.

2. You are a member of the biracial commission investigating the Chicago race riot. Write a report detailing your findings.

WEB SITE LISTINGS:

Trenches on the Web
   http://www.worldwar1.com

The Soldier's Experience in World War I
   http://www.people.virginia.edu/~egl2r/wwi.html

The Great War Society
   http://www.mcs.net/~mikei/tgws

The First World War
   http://www.spartacus.schoolnet.co.uk/FWW.htm

The World War I Document Archive and Primary Documents Archive
   http://www.lib.byu.edu/~rdh/wwi
   http://www.ukans.edu/~kansite/ww_one

Posters from the Food Administration During World War I
   http://www.nara.gov/education/cc/foodww1.html

The Lost Poets of World War I
   http://www.emory.edu/ENGLISH/LostPoets

Chapter Eighteen

THE ROARING TWENTIES

Americans often romanticize the 1920s. Images associated in the popular imagination with the 1920s include Jazz music, the Charleston, Henry Ford's model T, radio, talking motion pictures, electricity, and economic prosperity. What Americans forget, however, is that the 1920s were born out of World War I. Things were not always as rosy as optimists remember them. The nation was rocked by a series of strikes in northern cities, and farmers lost over a billion dollars at the beginning of the decade. Wages were generally low, work was hard, and job security non-existent. The stock market enjoyed a tremendous run in the middle years of the decade but crashed spectacularly in 1929, bankrupting thousands and signaling the onset of the Great Depression.

Economic problems and a desire by Americans to return to a normal life following World War I gave rise to a conservative, fundamentalistic, intolerant society. Religious extremists preached against sin, Satan, and Demon Rum. Throughout the 1920s Americans could not legally purchase alcohol for consumption. Religious zealots successfully brought about national prohibition and America officially remained dry the entire decade. Liquor, however, was available during the 1920s. Bootleggers sold distilled spirits illegally across the nation and the tremendous demand for alcohol gave rise to organized crime in the United States. Al Capone in Chicago and the Purple Gang in Detroit controlled alcohol distribution in their cities and along with criminals in other cities reaped millions from the sale of alcohol. Christian fundamentalists also attacked science, especially Darwin's Theory of Evolution and tried to ban its teaching in public schools. The attack on evolution resulted in the Scopes Trial in Dayton, TN during the Summer of 1925. This trial, which was the media sensation of its day, attracted prominent lawyers Clarence Darrow and William Jennings Bryan and was followed on the radio and in the print media by millions of Americans. Dislocation and economic troubles also gave rise to the First American Red Scare, rebirth of the Ku Klux Klan, and passage of the National Origins Act to restrict immigration from southern and eastern European countries. Proponents of immigration restriction, religious fundamentalists, members of the Ku Klux Klan, and those who fermented the Red Scare all believed that American life was threatened and that they had to save the country from ruin.

Others, however, had a different view and embraced the changes that occurred in American society during the 1920s. Modern women, for example, enjoyed the freedom they gained and did not want to return to a time when women were considered subservient to fathers and husbands. The new woman enjoyed the abandonment of traditional roles and mode of dress, embracing the new sexuality and the freedom to wear short skirts, bobbed hair, smoke cigarettes, and engage in petting. Blacks also, especially those who had served in the Great War and experienced equal treatment by white Europeans, wanted change in a racially stratified society in which they were subservient to whites. Black unwillingness to accept traditional social roles following World War I caused the Ku Klux Klan, a terrorist organization reborn at Stone Mountain, Georgia in 1915, to move out of its traditional home in the South

179

to northern states, such as Indiana. There the Klan broadened its bigotry, opposing not only blacks but Catholics, Jews, immigrants, and any other group conservatives perceived as a threat to the traditional American way of life.

Economic change also engulfed America in the 1920s. The economic prosperity enjoyed by some Americans was dependant on increased productivity. Technology was largely responsible for the increase in productivity. The use of assembly lines, electricity, and modern managerial techniques propelled production in American factories to unheard of levels. Americans seemingly became enthralled with business and generally viewed capitalism and business in messianic terms, accepting the view that "what is good for GM is good for America." Consequently, the American government, firmly controlled by the Republican Party, promoted laissez-faire capitalism. Central to the new productive economy of the 1920s was the automobile. Demand for automobiles gave rise to satellite industries and created employment for Americans in steel mills, tire factories, and glass plants.

The 1920s also was a decade of mass consumption. For the first time, Americans could buy on credit. The Federal Reserve Board kept interest rates low throughout the decade and banks eagerly loaned Americans funds to purchase consumer goods. Thousands of automobiles, appliances, homes, radios, and jewelry were purchased on the installment plan under which the purchaser could pay a little down and a little each week until the item and finance charges were fully paid. Someone who wanted a new Ford, for example, could pay $5.00 down and $5.00 per month until the car was paid for.

Facilitating the demand for consumer products was advertising. Businesses used advertising to create demand for their products. Slick ads on radio and in newspapers and magazines convinced Americans that they could not live without this new gadget promoted by the commercial. Advertisers also used sex and self-image to convince individuals to purchase products. Cars, jewelry, and clothing became status symbols, and Americans were convinced that living a full life required these products.

Intellectuals, however, saw through the hype of advertising. Writers, poets, and other intellectuals reacted against the mass consumerism of the 1920s. Known as the Lost Generation, writers like F. Scott Fitzgerald and Ernest Hemmingway, questioned the materialism and conformity of the 1920s. The intellectual disillusionment of the 1920s produced a flowering of American literature. New York's Harlem community attracted a large number of black writers, artists, and other intellectuals.

Even though Americans romanticized the twenties, the period was actually a decade of discord. Not every American shared in the consumer society and economic prosperity and old values were cast aside amid much strife and controversy. A new America did, however, begin to take shape in the 1920s. For the first time, America became an urban nation as the 1920 census showed that more Americans lived in towns and cities than in the countryside.

IDENTIFICATION: Briefly describe each term.

John Scopes

William Jennings Bryan

Clarence Darrow

Eighteenth Amendment

Al Capone

Warren G. Harding

Calvin Coolidge

Herbert Hoover

Scopes Trial

Ku Klux Klan

National Origins Act

Birth of a Nation

Sacco and Vanzetti

Teapot Dome Scandal

Washington Naval Conference

Kellogg-Briand Pact

Installment Plan

Aimee Semple McPherson

Henry Ford

A Philip Randolph

Marcus Garvey

Harlem Renaissance

Flapper

Margaret Sanger

United Negro Improvement Association

Prohibition

Volstead Act

Red Scare

THINK ABOUT:

1. Some historians believe that modern America began to take shape during the 1920s. Do you agree or disagree with this assessment? Why or why not?

2. Why was the 1920s marked by so much conflict and tension?

3. Describe the most significant cultural and social changes that occurred in the U.S. during the 1920s.

THE RISING TIDE OF COLOR AGAINST WHITE WORLD SUPREMACY,
By Lothrop Stoddard, 1920

Racism and prejudice had been part of American culture since the first settlements were established along the eastern seaboard of North America. No decade exhibited a higher level of racial tensions than did the 1920s. Jim Crow segregation was at its height in southern states, the Ku Klux Klan had moved into northern states, and efforts to restrict immigration from southern and eastern European nations were successful with passage of the National Origins Act. Underpinning the racist society that existed in the United States was the pseudo-science of eugenics. Proponents of eugenics wanted to breed humans selectively to improve the human race and society. Of course, eugenics stressed the superiority of the Anglo-Saxon people and taught that blacks, along with Asians and southern and eastern Europeans, were inferior. Eugenic ideas gained popularity in the United States during the 1920s when white Americans became concerned about the movement of southern blacks into northern cities and the large numbers of new immigrants from Italy, Russia, Poland, Hungary, and other regions in southern and eastern Europe that migrated to northern urban areas. Proponents of eugenics tapped into American concerns about immigration and black migration by promoting a program of immigration restriction, a racially stratified society, and legally mandated sterilization for select individuals and groups. Lothrop Stoddard, a leading spokesperson of the eugenic movement, sets forth in the following selection, the movement's main tenents.

....since the various human stocks differ widely in genetic worth, nothing should be more carefully studied than the relative values of the different strains in a population, and nothing should be more rigidly scrutinized than new strains seeking to add themselves to a population, because such new strains may hold simply incalculable potentialities for good or for evil. The potential reproductive powers of any stock are almost unlimited. Therefore the introduction of even a small group of prolific and adaptable but racially undesirable aliens may result in their subsequent prodigious multiplication, thereby either replacing better native stocks or degrading these by the injection of inferior blood.

The admission of aliens should, indeed, be regarded just as solemnly as the begetting of children, for the racial effect is essentially the same. There is no more damning indictment of our lopsided, materialistic civilization than the way in which, throughout the nineteenth century, immigration was almost universally regarded, not from the racial, but from the material point of view, the immigrant being viewed not as a creator of race-values but as a mere vocal tool for the production of material wealth.

Immigration is thus, from the racial standpoint, a form of procreation, and like the more immediate form of procreation it may be either the greatest blessing or the greatest curse. Human history is largely the story of migrations, making now for good and now for ill. Migration peopled Europe with superior white stocks displacing ape-like aborigines, and settled North America with Nordics instead of nomad redskins. But migration also bastardized the Roman world with Levantine mongrels, drowned the West Indies under a black tide, and is filling our own land with the sweepings of the European east and south.

Migration, like other natural movements, is of itself a blind force. It is man's divine privilege as well as duty, having been vouchsafed knowledge of the laws of life, to direct these blind forces, rejecting the bad and selecting the good for the evolution of higher and nobler destinies....

Probably few persons fully appreciate what magnificent racial treasures America possessed at the beginning of the nineteenth century. The colonial stock was perhaps the finest that nature had evolved since the classic Greeks. It was the very pick of the Nordics of the British Isles and adjacent regions of the European continent—picked at a time when those countries were more Nordic than now, since the industrial revolution had not yet begun and the consequent resurgence of the Mediterranean and Alpine elements had not taken place.

The immigrants of colonial times were largely exiles for conscience's sake, while the very process of migration was so difficult and hazardous that only persons of courage, initiative, and strong will-power would voluntarily face the long voyage overseas to a life of struggle in an untamed wilderness haunted by ferocious savages.

Thus the entire process of colonial settlement was one continuous, drastic cycle of eugenic selection. Only the racially fit ordinarily came, while the few unfit who did come were mostly weeded out by the exacting requirements of early American life.

The eugenic results were magnificent. As Madison Grant well says: "Nature had vouchsafed to the Americans of a century ago the greatest opportunity in recorded history to produce in the isolation of a continent a powerful and racially homogeneous people, and had provided for the experiment a pure race of one of the most gifted and vigorous stocks on earth, a stock free from the diseases, physical and moral, which have again and again sapped the vigor of the older lands. Our grandfathers threw away this opportunity in the blissful ignorance of national childhood and inexperience." (Madison Grant, *The Passing of the Great Race*....) The number of great names which America produced at the beginning of its national life shows the high level of ability possessed by this relatively small people (only about 3,000,000 whites in 1790). With our hundred-odd millions we have no such output of genius to-day.

The opening decades of the nineteenth century seemed to portend for America the most glorious of futures. For nearly seventy years after the Revolution, immigration was small, and during that long period of ethnic isolation the colonial stock, unperturbed by alien influences, adjusted its cultural differences and began to display the traits of a genuine new type, harmonious in basic homogeneity and incalculably rich in racial promise. The general level of ability continued high and the output of talent remained extraordinarily large. Perhaps the best feature of the nascent "native American" race was its strong idealism....It was a wonderful time and it was only the dawn!

But the full day of that wondrous dawning never came. In the late forties of the nineteenth century the first waves of the modern immigrant tide began breaking on our shores, and the tide swelled to a veritable deluge which never slackened till temporarily restrained by the late war. This immigration, to be sure, first came mainly from northern Europe, was thus largely composed of kindred stocks, and contributed many valuable elements. Only during the last thirty years have we been deluged by the truly alien hordes of the European east and south. But, even at its best, the immigrant tide could not measure up to the colonial stock which it displaced, not reinforced, while latterly it became a menace to the very existence of our race, ideals, and institutions. All our slowly acquired balance—physical, mental, and spiritual—has been upset, and we to-day flounder in a veritable Serbonian bog, painfully trying to regain the solid ground on which our grandsires confidently stood....

The perturbing influence of recent immigration must vex American life for many decades. Even if laws are passed tomorrow so drastic as to shut out permanently the influx of undesirable elements, it will yet take several generations before the combined action of assimilation and elimination shall have restabilized our population and evolved a new type-norm approaching in fixity that which was on the point of crystallizing three-quarters of a century ago....

Thus, under even the most favorable circumstances, we are in for generations of racial readjustment—an immense travail, essentially needless, since the final product will probably not measure up to the colonial standard. We will probably never (unless we adopt positive eugenic measures) be the race we might have been if America had been reserved for the descendants of the picked Nordics of colonial times.

But that is no reason for folding our hands in despairing inaction. On the contrary, we should be up and doing, for though some of our race-heritage has been lost, more yet remains. We can still be a very great people—if we will it so. Heaven be praised, the colonial stock was immensely prolific before the alien tide wrought its sterilizing havoc. Even to-day nearly one-half of our population is of the old blood, while many millions of the immigrant stock are sound in quality and assimilable in kind. Only the immigrant tide must at all costs be stopped and America given a chance to stabilize her ethnic being. It is the old story of the sibylline books. Some, to be sure, are ashes of the dead past; all the more should we conserve the precious volumes which remain.

One fact should be clearly understood: If America is not true to her own race-soul, she will inevitably lose it, and the brightest star that has appeared since Hellas will fall like a meteor from the human sky, its brilliant radiance fading into the night. "We Americans," says Madison Grant, "must realize that the altruistic ideals which have controlled our social development during the past century and the maudlin sentimentalism that has made America 'an asylum for the oppressed,' are sweeping the nation toward a racial abyss. If the melting-pot is allowed to boil without control and we continue to follow our national motto and deliberately blind ourselves to 'all distinctions of race, creed, or color,' the type of native American of colonial descent will become as extinct as the Athenian of the age of Pericles and the Viking of the days of Rollo."....

And let us not lay any sacrificial unction to our souls. If we cheat our country and the world of the splendid promise of American life, we shall have no one to blame but ourselves, and we shall deserve, not pity, but contempt.....

Source: Lothrop Stoddard, *The Rising Tide of Color Against White World Supremacy*, Scribner, New York, 1920

HOW WELL DID YOU UNDERSTAND THIS SELECTION?

1. Identify the main argument or thesis present in Stoddard's article.

2. What impact does Stoddard believe immigration will have on American civilization?

3. Were the views expressed by Stoddard generally held by most Americans during the 1920s? Why or why not?

4. Are Stoddard's arguments about the need to restrict immigration valid? Why or why not?

5. What difference does Stoddard see in immigration during the colonial period and the new immigration (from 1880-1920)?

Immigration restriction was on the minds of many Americans during the 1920s. Racists and religious bigots favored passage of the National Origins Act that restricted immigration from southern and eastern European nations. Migrants from these regions of Europe, in addition to speaking a language other than English, dressing as they dressed in the old country, and practicing native customs, were overwhelmingly Catholic and Jewish. American Protestants felt threatened by the settlement of a large number of Catholics and Jews in industrial cities. When the 1921 National Origins Act did not sufficiently restrict the number of immigrants allowed into the United States from southern and Eastern Europe, the act was revised in 1924 to make it more restrictive. David Walsh, a Democratic Senator from Massachusetts, spoke against revision of the National Origins Act in a 1924 speech before the Senate. An excerpt from his speech follows.

Mr. President, the proposal to make the census of 1890, instead of that of 1910, the basis for the quota hereafter to be admitted, as advocated by many, is objectionable on many grounds.

A few facts regarding the population census of 1890, as compared with the census of 1910, give practical assurance that a great American principle would be violated by the change proposed.

Two per cent of the alien inhabitants in 1890 would total about 160,000, whereas the same percentage in 1910 would number about 238,000. This represents a material reduction in the number of aliens to be admitted and indicates a tendency to further restrict the number of admissible immigrants.

The most important aspect of this question, however, is that such a change would inject into the law a very apparent discrimination against immigrants of certain nationalities. The census of 1890 shows that a large majority of our alien inhabitants were then natives of northern and western Europe, while the census of 1910 shows more nearly equal proportions from southern and eastern Europe. In 1890 about 87 per cent of our alien population were people from northern and western Europe, as compared with 56 per cent in 1910. Who can say that it would be fair to abandon a basis of calculation that is very close to an equal division between the races of northern and western Europe and the races of southern and eastern Europe and adopt a basis that will give the peoples of northern and western Europe 87 per cent of our immigration during the coming years?

Since we have said to the people of all nations, "We are going to admit only a certain percentage of your future immigrants," can we go further and add that to certain nationalities we shall extend preference? That is what the suggestion of the 1890 census basis means. It simply amounts to reducing and practically eliminating all emigration from southern and eastern Europe.

Whatever may be the surface reason for the change in date, it must be insisted that the true reason is social discrimination. An attempt is being made to slip by this proposal, which is aimed clearly and mercilessly at the Slav, the Latin, and the Jew, under the harmless guise of a change in the date of the census....

Mr. President, what is the real driving force behind the movement of basing the quota on the census of 1890? The peoples of the world will attribute it to our belief that the "Nordic" is a superior race. The world will assume that our Government considers the Italians, Greeks, Jews, Poles, and the Slavs inferior to the Nordics, congenitally as well as culturally. It is a dangerous assumption. Millions of people here in America will resent this slur upon their racial character....

What are the nationalities whose coming to America is chiefly curtailed by this arbitrary resort to the 1890 census? The Greeks, to whom civilization owes so much in the fields of literature, science, art, and government. The Italians, who from the day of early Roman history have contributed immensely to civilization along the lines of government, literature, art, music, and navigation, including the gift of the discoverer of America. The liberty-loving Poles, whose sacrifices and struggles for freedom have arrested the admiration of mankind and who saved all Europe from the Turks at Vienna scarcely two centuries ago, and who were once in the van of culture. The Jews, who contributed to the world literature, religion, standards of righteous conduct that can not be overvalued....

Have we learned nothing from the earlier generations' mistaken notions about the Dutch, the French, the Irish, the Germans, and the Scandinavians, now an essential element in our assumed racial superiority? They were condemned and criticized by the earlier settlers, just as we are now undertaking to condemn the races from southern Europe. Have we forgotten that at the time of the Revolution one-fifth of the population of America could not speak the English language? Have we forgotten that more than one-half of the population of America at the time of the Revolution was not Anglo-Saxon?

Factors of all sorts enter into play in determining race values, and often an alien most desirable from one point of view is least so from another. But is not the whole concept in variance with fundamental American principles and policies?....

Attempt to grade our aliens! Which race is to be rated "100 per cent American"? It is a shortsighted view which measures the desirability or undesirability of any group of aliens only by the rapidity or tardiness with which they forget their past spiritual connections and allow themselves to be rapidly molded into an undeterminate type which is vaguely termed a "100 percent American." . . .

"Keep America American." Yes; but do not keep out of America through discriminatory immigration laws any lover of liberty, whatever his accident of birth may be, if he is willing to live in America, accept its ideals, and die, if necessary, for the preservation of American institutions....

Source: Congressional Record, 68th Cong., Ist Sess., pp. 6355ff.

HOW WELL DID YOU UNDERSTAND THIS SELECTION?

1. How would revision of the National Origins Act restrict immigration from southern and Eastern Europe?

2. What is Walsh's view regarding immigration restriction?

3. How does Walsh respond to bigots and others who argue in favor of immigration restriction for reasons of race?

4. How does Walsh view American history and American society

"THE KLAN'S FIGHT FOR AMERICANISM," by Hiram W. Evans, 1926

On Stone Mountain, Georgia in 1915 the Ku Klux Klan was reborn. Afterwards, the racist and terrorist group portrayed itself as the protector of old stock American values and the traditional way of life. In the 1920s the Klan moved out of its traditional home in the South and into northern cities where it targeted not only blacks but Catholics, Jews, and immigrants. The Klan broadened bigotry appealed particularly to discontented workers who believed immigrants and blacks took jobs from "native Americans" and restricted wages and to Protestants disturbed by the migration of Catholic and Jewish immigrants to the United States. The Klan, which proclaimed that it was the protector of American morality, had a membership of three to four million in the 1920s before the rape of a young woman by a high ranking Klan official in Indiana exposed the organization's bigotry. Afterwards, membership in the Klan declined. Hiram Evans, the Klan's Imperial Wizard, outlined the group's achievements and objectives in the selection that appears below.

The greatest achievement so far has been to formulate, focus, and gain recognition for an idea—the idea of preserving and developing America first and chiefly for the benefit of the children of the pioneers who made America....we have won the leadership in the movement for Americanism. Except for a few lonesome voices, almost drowned by the claim of the alien and the alien-minded "Liberal," the Klan alone faces the invader....

Other achievements of these ten years have been the education of the millions of our own membership in citizenship, the suppression of much lawlessness and increase of good government wherever we have become strong, the restriction of immigration, and the defeat of the Catholic attempt to seize the Democratic party. All these we have helped; and all are important.

The outstanding proof of both our influence and our service, however, has been in creating, outside our ranks as well as in them, not merely the growing concentration on the problem of Americanism, but also a growing sentiment against radicalism, cosmopolitanism, and alienism of all kinds....We have enlisted our racial instincts for the work of preserving and developing our American traditions and customs....

The Klan....has now come to speak for the great mass of Americans of the old pioneer stock. We believe that it does fairly and faithfully represent them, and our proof lies in their support. To understand the Klan, then, it is necessary to understand the character and present mind of the mass of old-stock Americans. The mass, it must be remembered, as distinguished from the intellectually mongrelized "Liberals."

These are....a blend of various peoples of the so-called Nordic race, the race which, with all its faults, has given the world almost the whole of modern civilization. The Klan does not try to represent any people but these.

There is no need to recount the virtues of the American pioneers; but it is too often forgotten that in the pioneer period a selective process of intense rigor went on. From the first only hardy, adventurous and strong men and women dared the pioneer dangers; from among these all but the best died swiftly, so that the new Nordic blend which became the American race was bred up to a point probably the highest in history. This remarkable race character, along with the new-won continent and the new-created nation, made the inheritance of the old-stock Americans the richest ever given to a generation of men.

In spite of it, however, these Nordic Americans for the last generation have found themselves increasingly uncomfortable, and finally deeply distressed. There appeared first confusion in thought and opinion, a groping and hesitancy about national affairs and private life alike, in sharp contrast to the clear, straightforward purposes of our earlier years. There was futility in religion, too, which was in many ways even more distressing. Presently we began to find that we were dealing with strange ideas; policies that always sounded well, but somehow always made us still more uncomfortable.

Finally came the moral breakdown that has been going on for two decades. One by one all our traditional moral standards went by the boards, or were so disregarded that they ceased to be binding. The sacredness of our Sabbath, of our homes, of chastity, and finally even of our right to teach our own children in our own schools fundamental facts and truths were torn away from us. Those who maintained the old standards did so only in the face of constant ridicule.

Along with this went economic distress. The assurance for the future of our children dwindled. We found our great cities and the control of much of our industry and commerce taken over by strangers, who stacked the cards of success and prosperity against us. Shortly they came to dominate our government....Every kind of inhabitant except the Americans gathered in groups which operated as units in politics, under orders of corrupt, self-seeking and un-American leaders, who both by purchase and threat enforced their demands on politicians. Thus it came about that the interests of Americans were always the last to be considered by either national or city governments, and that the native Americans were constantly discriminated against, in business, in legislation and in administrative government.

So the Nordic American today is a stranger in large parts of the land his fathers gave him....

All this has been true for you years, but it was the World War that gave us our first hint of the real cause of our troubles, and began to crystallize our ideas. The war revealed that millions whom we had allowed to share our heritage and prosperity, and whom we had assumed had become part of us, were in fact not wholly so. They had other loyalties....the excitement caused by the discovery of disloyalty subsided rapidly after the war ended. But it was not forgotten by the Nordic Americans. They had been awakened and alarmed; they began to suspect that the hyphenism which had been shown was only a part of what existed; their quiet was not that of renewed sleep, but of strong men waiting very watchfully....

They decided that even the crossing of salt-water did not dim a single spot on a leopard; that an alien usually remains an alien no matter what is done to him, what veneer of education he gets, what oaths he takes, nor what public attitudes he adopts. They decided that the melting pot was a ghastly failure, and remembered that the very name was coined by a member of one of the races—the Jews—that most determinedly refuses to melt....They decided that in character, instincts, thought, and purposes—in his whole soul—an alien remains fixedly alien to American and all it means......

They learned, though more slowly, that alien ideas are just as dangerous to us as the alien themselves, no matter how plausible such ideas may sound....

One more point about the present attitudes of the old stock American: he has revived and increased his distrust of the Roman Catholic Church....The fact is, of course, that our quarrel with the Catholics is not religious but political....

The real indictment against the Roman Church is that it is fundamentally and irredeemably, in its leadership, in politics, in thought, and largely in membership, actually and actively alien, un-American and usually anti-American. The old stock Americans, with the exception of the few such of Catholic faith—who are in a class by themselves, standing tragically torn between their faith and their racial and national patriotism—see in the Roman Church today the chief leader of alienism, and the most dangerous alien power with a foothold inside our boundaries....

Thus the Klan goes back to the American racial instincts, and to the common sense which is their first product, as the basis of its beliefs and methods. The fundamentals of our thought are convictions, not mere opinions. We are pleased that modern research is finding scientific backing for these convictions....

There are three of these great racial instincts, vital elements in both the historic and the present attempts to build an America which shall fulfill the aspirations and justify the heroism of the men who made the nation. These are the instincts of loyalty to the white race, to the traditions of America, and to the spirit of Protestantism, which has been an essential part of Americanism ever since the days of Roanoke and Plymouth Rock. They are condensed into the Klan slogan: "Native, white, Protestant supremacy."......

The Negro the Klan considers a special duty and the problem of the white American. He is among us through no wish of his; we owe it to him and to ourselves to give him full protection and opportunity. But his limitations are evident; we will not permit him to gain sufficient power to control our civilization. Neither will we delude him with promises of social equality which we know can never be realized. The Klan looks forward to the day when the Negro problem will have been solved on some much saner basis than miscegenation, and when every State will enforce laws making any sex relations between a white and a colored person a crime......

The Jew is a more complex problem. His abilities are great, he contributes much to any country where he lives. This is particularly true of the Western Jew, those of the stocks we have known so long. Their separation from us is more religious than racial. When freed from persecution these Jews have shown a tendency to disintegrate and amalgamate. We may hope that shortly, in the free atmosphere of America, Jews of this class will cease to be a problem. Quite different are the Eastern Jews of recent immigration, the Jews known as the Askhenasim. It is interesting to note that anthropologists now tell us that these are not true Jews, but only Judaized Mongols—Chazars. These, unlike the true Hebrew, show a divergence from the American type so great that there seems little hope of their assimilation.

The most menacing and most difficult problem facing America today is this of the permanently unassimilable alien.....This is a problem which must shortly engage the best American minds. We can neither expel, exterminate nor enslave these low-standard aliens, yet their continued presence on the present basis means our doom. Those who know the American character know that if the problem is not soon solved by wisdom, it will be solved by one of those cataclysmic outbursts which have so often disgraced—and saved!—the race. Our attempt to find a sane solution is one of the best justifications of the Klan's existence.....

The Klan today, because of the position it has come to fill, is by far the strongest movement recorded for the defense and fulfillment of Americanism. It has a membership of millions, the support of millions more. If there be any truth in the statement that the voice of the people is the voice of God, we hold a Divine commission....

Originally published in: North American Review, CCXXII (March 1926).
[Online Source]: American Radicalism Digital Collection; Michigan State Univ
www.lib.msu.edu/spc/digital/radicalism/hs2330.k63e.htm

189

HOW WELL DID YOU UNDERSTAND THIS SELECTION?

1. How does Evans see America?

2. How does Evans see immigrants?

3. What does Evans think is the problem with the Roman Catholic Church?

4. What does Evans say was important about the First World War?

5. How does the Klan view Blacks?

6. What threat does Evans think immigrants, Jews, Catholics, and blacks pose to white Americans?

7. What does Evans see as the chief problem facing America?

8. Do you agree with the views of Evans and the Klan? Why or why not?

"BIG IDEAS FROM BIG BUSINESS" by Edward Earle Purinton, 1921

The 1920s is generally viewed as a decade of business supremacy. "The business of America is business" as one commentator put it. Most Americans held a favorable view of business, which had cooperated with government to win World War I. Business and the wealth it created became the new messiah in the 1920s. Business owners and successful entrepreneurs became models of American morality and virtue after advertisers linked Christianity and business during the 1920s. In the following selection Edward Earle Purinton attempts to link religion, virtue, and morality to business.

Among the nations of the earth today America stands for one idea: Business. National opprobrium? National opportunity. For in this fact lies, potentially, the salvation of the world.

Thru business, properly conceived, managed and conducted, the human race is finally to be redeemed. How and why a man works foretells what he will do, think, have, give and be. And real salvation is in doing, thinking, having, giving and being—not in sermonizing and theorizing. I shall base the facts of this article on the personal tours and minute examinations I have recently made of twelve of the world's largest business plants: U.S. Steel Corporation, International Harvester Company, Swift & Company, E. I. du Pont de Nemours & Company, National City Bank, National Cash Register Company, Western Electric Company, Sears, Roebuck & Company, H. J. Heinz Company, Peabody Coal Company, Statler Hotels, Wanamaker Stores.

These organizations are typical, foremost representatives of the commercial group of interests loosely termed "Big Business." A close view of these corporations would reveal to any trained, unprejudiced observer a new conception of modern business activities. Let me draw a few general conclusions regarding the best type of business house and business man.

What is the finest game? Business. The soundest science? Business. The truest art? Business. The fullest education? Business. The fairest opportunity? Business. The cleanest philanthropy? Business. The sanest religion? Business.

You may not agree. That is because you judge business by the crude, mean, stupid, false imitation of business that happens to be located near you.

The finest game is business. The rewards are for everybody, and all can win. There are no favorites-Providence always crowns the career of the man who is worthy. And in this game there is no "luck"—you have the fun of taking chances but the sobriety of guaranteeing certainties. The speed and size of your winnings are for you alone to determine; you needn't wait for the other fellow in the game—it is always your move. And your slogan is not "Down the Other Fellow!" but rather "Beat Your Own Record!" or "Do It Better Today!" or "Make Every job a Masterpiece!" The great sportsmen of the world are the great business men.

The soundest science is business. All investigation is reduced to action, and by action proved or disproved. The idealistic motive animates the materialistic method. Hearts as well as minds are open to the truth. Capital is furnished for the researches of "pure science"; yet pure science is not regarded pure until practical. Competent scientists are suitably rewarded—as they are not in the scientific schools.

The truest art is business. The art is so fine, so exquisite, that you do not think of it as art. Language, color, form, line, music, drama, discovery, adventure—all the components of art must be used in business to make it of superior character.

The fullest education is business. A proper blend of study, work and life is essential to advancement. The whole man is educated. Human nature itself is the open book that all business men study; and the mastery of a page of this educates you more than the memorizing of a dusty tome from a library shelf. In the school of business, moreover, you teach yourself and learn most from your own mistakes. What you learn here you live out, the only real test.

The fairest opportunity is business. You can find more, better, quicker chances to get ahead in a large business house than anywhere else on earth. The biographies of champion business men show how they climbed, and how you can climb. Recognition of better work, of keener and quicker thought, of deeper and finer feeling, is gladly offered by the men higher up, with early promotion the rule for the man who justifies it. There is, and can be, no such thing as buried talent in a modern business organization.

The cleanest philanthropy is business. By "clean" philanthropy I mean that devoid of graft, inefficiency and professionalism, also of condolence, hysterics and paternalism. Nearly everything that goes by the name of Charity was born a triplet, the other two members of the trio being Frailty and Cruelty. Not so in the welfare departments of leading corporations. Savings and loan funds; pension and insurance provisions; health precautions, instructions and safeguards; medical attention and hospital care; libraries, lectures and classes; musical, athletic and social features of all kinds; recreational facilities and financial opportunities—these types of "charitable institutions" for employees add to the worker's self-respect, self-knowledge and self-improvement, by making him an active partner in the welfare program, a producer of benefits for his employer and associates quite as much as a recipient of bounty from the company. I wish every "charity" organization would send its officials to school to the heads of the welfare departments of the big corporations; the charity would mostly be transformed into capability, and the minimum of irreducible charity left would not be called by that name.

The sanest religion is business. Any relationship that forces a man to follow the Golden Rule rightfully belongs amid the ceremonials of the church. A great business enterprise includes and presupposes this relationship. I have seen more Christianity to the square inch as a regular part of the office equipment of famous corporation presidents than may ordinarily be found on Sunday in a verbalized but not vitalized church congregation. A man is not wholly religious until he is better on weekdays than he is on Sunday. The only ripened fruits of creeds are deeds. You can fool your preacher with a sickly sprout or a wormy semblance of character, but you can't your employer. I would make every business house a consultation bureau for the guidance of the church whose members were employees of the house.

I am aware that some of the preceding statements will be challenged by many readers. I should not myself had made them, or believed them, twenty years ago, when I was a pitiful specimen of a callow youth and cocksure professional man combined. A thorough knowledge of business has implanted a deep respect for business and real business men.

The future work of the business man is to teach the teacher, preach to the preacher, admonish the parent, advise the doctor, justify the lawyer, superintend the statesman, fructify the farmer, stabilize the banker, harness the dreamer, and reform the reformer.

Source: Edward Earle Purinton, "Big Ideas from Big Business, *The Independent,* (April 16, 1921)

HOW WELL DID YOU UNDERSTAND THIS SELECTION?

1. How does Purinton see business?

2. Is Purinton's portrayal of business accurate? Why or why not?

3. How does Purinton deal with critics of his view?

4. What distinction does Purinton make between business in its pure and crude forms? Why does he need to make this distinction?

5. Do you agree with the claim that business will not bury talent? Why or why not?

Recession gripped the American economy at the beginning of the 1920s. Lagging sales created economic hardship for many companies and their owners. Listerine was one such company. This modern day mouthwash was sold as an antiseptic after its invention by J. W. Lambert, a St. Louis druggist in the 1880s. When sales of the product declined during the 1920s recession, the company hired advertising companies to market the product. Advertising and company executives decided to sell Listerine as a cure for bad breath and devised the medical term "halitosis" to discreetly promote the product. Reproduced below is a Listerine advertisement that appeared in 1923 promoting Listerine as a treatment for halitosis.

In his discreet way he told her

IT had never occurred to her before. But in his discreet, professional way he was able to tell her. And she was sensible enough to be grateful instead of resentful.

In fact, the suggestion he made came to mean a great deal to her.

It brought her greater poise—that feeling of self-assurance that adds to a woman's charm—and, moreover, a new sense of daintiness that she had never been quite so sure of in the past.

. . . .

Many people suffer in the same way. Halitosis (the scientific term for unpleasant breath) creeps upon you unawares. Usually you are not able to detect it yourself. And, naturally enough, even your best friends will not tell you.

Fortunately, however, halitosis is usually due to some local condition— often food fermentation in the mouth; something you have eaten; too much smoking. And it may be corrected by the systematic use of Listerine as a mouth wash and gargle.

Dentists know that this well-known antiseptic they have used for half a century, possesses these remarkable properties as a breath deodorant.

Your druggist will supply you. He sells lots of Listerine. It has dozens of other uses as a safe antiseptic. It is particularly valuable, too, at this time of year in combating sore throat. Read the circular that comes with each bottle.—*Lambert Pharmacal Company, Saint Louis, U. S. A.*

For HALITOSIS use LISTERINE

Source: *The Literary Digest*, November 17, 1923 Used with the permission of Warner-Lambert Company

HOW WELL DID YOU UNDERSTAND THIS SELECTION?

1. How does the ad convince consumers to buy Listerine?

2. To whom is this ad aimed? Support your answer with evidence from the ad itself.

3. Do you think the ad was effective? Why or why not?

4. Does the ad contain gender and sexual stereotyping? Explain.

"PETTING AND THE CAMPUS," Eleanor Rowland Wembridge, 1925

One issue that produced tension within the United States during the 1920s was the changing role of women in American society. Many women no longer were willing to remain subservient to men. These women, often called Flappers, became more liberal and exercised a greater degree of freedom than did their mothers and grandmothers. Flappers and other young women changed their appearance and behavior, wearing makeup, cutting and curling their hair, donning short skirts and low cut blouses, smoking cigarettes, and drinking alcoholic beverages. Particularly upsetting to conservative Americans was the new found sexual freedom some women began to enjoy. Older generations of Americans saw behavior such as "petting and kissing in public" as examples of a spreading sexual immorality.

...Last summer I was at a student conference of young women comprised of about eight hundred college girls from the middle western states. The subject of petting was very much on their minds, both as to what attitude they should take toward it with the younger girls (being upperclassmen themselves), and also how much renunciation of this pleasurable pastime was required of them. If I recall correctly, two entire mornings were devoted to discussing the matter, two evenings, and another overflow meeting.

So far as I could judge from their discussion groups, the girls did not advise younger classmen not to pet-they merely advised them to be moderate about it, not lose their heads, not go too far—in fact the same line of conduct which is advised for moderate drinking. Learn temperance in petting, not abstinence. . . .

Just what does petting consist in? What ages take it most seriously? Is it a factor in every party? Do "nice" girls do it, as well as those who are not so "nice"? Are they "stringing" their elders, by exaggerating the prevalence of petting, or is there more of it than they admit? . . .

One fact is evident, that whether or not they pet, they hesitate to have anyone believe that they do not. It is distinctly the mores of the time to be considered as ardently sought after, and as not too priggish to respond. As one girl said—"I don't particularly care to be kissed by some of the fellows I know, but I'd let them do it any time rather than think I wouldn't dare. As a matter of fact, there are lots of fellows I don't kiss. It's the very young kids that never miss a chance."

That petting should lead to actual illicit relations between the petters was not advised nor countenanced among the girls with whom I discussed it. They drew the line quite sharply. That it often did so lead, they admitted, but they were not ready to allow that there were any more of such affairs than there had always been. School and college scandals, with their sudden departures and hasty marriages, have always existed to some extent, and they still do. But only accurate statistics, hard to arrive at, can prove whether or not the sex carelessness of the present day extends to an increase of sex immorality, or whether since so many more people go to college, there is an actual decrease in the amount of it, in proportion to the number of students. The girls seemed to feel that those who went too far were more fools than knaves, and that in most cases they married. They thought that hasty and secret marriages, of which most of them could report several, were foolish, but after all about as likely to turn out well as any others. Their attitude toward such contingencies was disapproval, but it was expressed with a slightly amused shrug, a shrug which one can imagine might have sat well on the shoulders of Voltaire. In fact the writer was torn, in her efforts to sum up their attitude, between classifying them as eighteenth century realists and as Greek nymphs existing before the dawn of history!

I sat with one pleasant college Amazon, a total stranger, beside a fountain in the park, while she asked if I saw any harm in her kissing a young man whom she liked, but whom she did not want to marry. "It's terribly exciting. We get such a thrill. I think it is natural to want nice men to kiss you, so why not do what is natural?" There was no embarrassment in her manner. Her eyes and her conscience were equally untroubled. I felt as if a girl from the Parthenon frieze had stepped down to ask if she might not sport in the glade with a handsome faun. Why not indeed? Only an equally direct forcing of twentieth century science on primitive simplicity could bring us even to the same level in our conversation, and at that, the stigma of impropriety seemed to fall on me, rather than on her. It was hard to tell whether her infantilism were real, or half-consciously assumed in order to have a child's license and excuse to do as she pleased. I am inclined to think that both with her and with many others, it is assumed. One girl said, "When I have had a few nights without dates I nearly go crazy. I tell my mother she must expect me to go out on a fearful necking party." In different parts of the country, petting and necking have opposite meanings. One locality calls necking (I quote their definition) "petting only from the neck up." Petting involves anything else you please. Another section reverses the distinction, and the girl in question was from the latter area. In what manner she announces to her mother her plans to neck, and in what manner her mother accepts the announcement, I cannot be sure.

But I imagine that the assumed childish attitude of the daughter is reflected by her mother, who longs to have her daughter popular, and get her full share of masculine attention. And if the daughter takes for granted that what her mother does not know will not hurt her, so does her mother's habit of blind and deaf supervision indicate that she too does not want to know any more than she has to. The college student is no longer preeminently from a selected class. One has only to look at the names and family status in the college registers to see that. If petting is felt to be poor taste in some families, there are many more families of poor taste than there used to be, whose children go to college. Their daughters are pretty and their sons have money to spend, and they seem prodigies of learning and accomplishment, especially to their unlettered mothers, who glow with pride over their popularity. The pleasant side of the picture is that anybody's daughter may go to college and pass on her own merits. The less agreeable side is that more refined, but timid and less numerous stocks feel obliged to model their social behavior on the crude amorousness and doubtful pleasantries which prevail at peasant parties. If anyone charges the daughters with being vulgar, the chances are that the mothers, though more shy, are essentially just as vulgar. The mothers have no accomplishments in which the daughters cannot surpass them, or no alternate social grace or cultivated recreation to suggest, if petting is denied them. Indeed the daughters are really at war with their mothers in point of view, I do not believe. On the contrary, thousands of mothers live all their emotional life in the gaiety of their daughters—having nothing else to live it in, and they suffer quite as deeply as their daughters if maternal strictness threatens to make wallflowers of them. Do not listen to what their mothers *say*, but *watch* them, if you want to know how they feel about their daughter's petting! Their protests are about as genuine, as the daughter's, "Aren't you terrible?" when a young man starts to pet.

The sex manners of the large majority of uncultivated and uncritical people have become the manners for all, because they have prospered, they are getting educated, and there are so many of them. They are not squeamish, and they have never been. But their children can set a social standard as the parents could not. The prudent lawyer's child has no idea of letting the gay daughter of the broad-joking workman get the dates away from her. If petting is the weapon Miss Workman uses, then petting it must be, and in nine cases out of ten, not only Mrs. Workman, but also Mrs. Lawyer agree not to see too much. At heart both women are alike. Neither one can bear to see her daughter take a back seat in the struggle for popularity, and neither woman has any other ambition for her daughter but a successful husband. If by any chance, petting led *away* from popularity and possible husbands instead of to them, the mothers would be whole-heartedly against it, and if they were—petting, as a recognized recreation, would stop.

Source: *Survey*, LIV, (July 1, 1925)

HOW WELL DID YOU UNDERSTAND THIS SELECTION?

1. How do college girls generally see petting?

2. Does the selection present the view of older Americans regarding petting? If so, how?

3. Who does Wembridge blame for the widespread petting on campuses? Is her assessment correct? Why or why not?

4. What does Wembridge think the ultimate goal of petting is? Do you agree? Why or why not?

5. What does the author think would stop campus petting?

6. Does class play a role in petting? Explain?

Birth control was another contentious issue that produced tension in the 1920s. Margaret Sanger, a nurse, devoted her life to legalizing birth control. In 1914 she was charged with violating obscenity laws when she informed women how to avoid pregnancy. In 1916 Sanger opened America's first birth control clinic in Brooklyn, New York. There she taught women how to avoid pregnancy through use of contraceptives. After the clinic was raided and Sanger arrested, she formed the American Birth Control League to make it easier for women to get information on birth control.

....By birth control, I mean a voluntary, conscious control of the birth rate by means that prevent conception—scientific means that prevent conception. I don't mean birth control by abstinence or by continence or anything except the thing that agrees with most of us, and as we will develop later on, most of us are glad that there are means of science at the present time that are not injurious, not harmful, and all conception can be avoided.

Now let us look upon life as it really is, and we see society today is divided distinctly into two groups: those who use the means of birth control and those who do not.

On the one side we find those who do use means in controlling birth. What have they? They are the people who bring to birth few children. They are the people who have all the happiness, who have the wealth and the leisure for culture and mental and spiritual development. They are people who rear their children to manhood and womanhood and who fill the universities and the colleges with their progeny. Nature has seemed to be very kind to that group of people....

On the other hand we have the group who have large families and have for generations perpetuated large families, and I know from my work among them that the great percentage of these people that are brought into the world in poverty and misery have been unwanted. I know that most of these women are just as desirous to have means to control birth as the women of wealth. I know she tries desperately to obtain the information, not for selfish purposes, but for her own benefit and for that of her children. In this group, what do we have? We have poverty, misery, disease, overcrowding, congestion, child labor, infant mortality, maternal mortality, all the evils which today are grouped in the crowd where there are large families of unwanted and undesired children.

Take the first one and let us see how these mothers feel. I claim that a woman, whether she is rich or poor, has a right to be a mother or not when she feels herself fit to be so. She has just as much right not to be a mother as she has to be a mother. It is just as right and as moral for people to talk of small families and to demand them as to want large families. It is just as moral.

If we let, as we are supposed to do, Nature take her course, we know that any woman from the age of puberty until the age of the period of menopause could have anywhere from 15 to 20 children in her lifetime, and it will only take one relationship between man and woman to give her one a year, to give her that large family. Let us not forget that.

Are we today, as women who wish to develop, who wish to advance in life, are we willing to spend all of our time through those years of development in bringing forth children that the world does not appreciate? Certainly, anyone who looks into that will find that there is very little place in the world for children. And besides, if a woman does spend all her time in child-bearing, do you know that, even with healthy women, one out of ten who have children as often as Nature sends them, dies from child bearing? One out of every ten women who lets Nature take her course and has from 12 to 16 children dies from child bearing. Furthermore, there are many cases where it is absolutely indispensable for a woman's health, for her life, in fact, to have means to control birth. There are cases.... of syphilis, cases of tuberculosis; do you realize that out of every seven women who have tuberculosis today four of them die, not from tuberculosis, my friends, but from pregnancy. They die because they have not that knowledge of birth control, because physicians and all the others who should be disseminating information and safeguarding these women's lives are not giving them the fundamental things to cure their disease, but allowing them to become pregnant. They keep them in ignorance of this particular knowledge that should assist them in recovering their health. Not only tuberculosis, but there are other diseases that are inimical to woman's health and happiness. Heart disease is another thing that pregnancy absolutely stimulates and it means a woman's death....

The only weapon that women have, and the most uncivilized weapon that they must use, if they will not submit to having children every year and a half, is abortion. We know how detrimental abortion is to the physical side as well as to the psychic side of woman's life. Yet there are in this nation, because of these generalities and opinions that are here before us, and that are stopping the tide of progress, more than one million women who have abortions performed on them each year.

What does this mean? It is a very bad sign when women indulge in it, and it means they are absolutely determined that they cannot continue bringing children into the world that they cannot clothe, feed, and shelter. It is a woman's instinct, and she knows herself when she should and should not give birth to children, and it is much more natural to trust this instinct and to let her be the judge than it is to let her judge herself by some unknown God. I claim it is a woman's duty and right to have for herself the power to say when she shall and shall not have children.

We know that the death rate, maternal death rate, has not been falling in the United States of America, although the death rate from diseases has been falling. That shows woman is given little consideration in scientific and medical lines. But then woman will never get her own freedom until she fights for it, and she has to fight hard to hold and keep it. We know too that when the children that come to these mothers against their will and against their desires, are born into the world, we have the appalling number of 300,000 if you please, and it is safe to say, as anyone knows who has gone among these mothers and these children—it is safe to say that the great percentage of these children that are born have been unwanted. The mother knows that the child should not come to birth, when the five or six or seven that she has have not enough to eat. That takes common sense and every working woman has that common sense.

We have these 300,000 babies, this oppression of little coffins, and we shake our heads sadly and say something must be done to reduce the number; but nevertheless we go right on allowing 600,000 parents to remain in ignorance of how to prevent 300,000 more babies coming to birth the next year only to die from poverty and sickness.

We speak of the rights of the unborn. I say that it is time to speak of those who are already born. I also say and know that the infant death rate is affected tremendously by those who arrive last. The first child that comes—the first or second or third child which arrives in a family, has a far better chance than those that arrive later.

We know that out of a thousand children born 200 of them die when they are either the second or third child. When the seventh arrives there are 300 that die out of that thousand, and by the time that the twelfth child arrives, 600 of this thousand pass away, and so we can see that the man or woman who brings to birth two or three children has a far better chance of bringing them to maturity than if they continued to have nine or ten or twelve children.

Those are facts. They are not generalities or opinions. The United States Government stands behind these facts....

Haldeman-Julius, Girard, Kansas, c. 1921
Source: electronic text, in Radicalism Collection, Birth Control Movement, www.msu.edu/spc/digital/radicalism/hq766.s281921.htm

HOW WELL DID YOU UNDERSTAND THIS SELECTION?

1. Does Sanger view birth control as a right? Explain.

2. What role does Sanger see class playing in birth control?

3. What benefits does Sanger think will accrue to American society if birth control becomes legal?

4. How will birth control help women? Explain.

5. What effect does Sanger think birth control will have on abortions? Explain.

6. What reasons does Sanger offer for legalizing birth control?

Sinclair Lewis, the first American to win the Nobel Prize for Literature, was part of a group of writers known as the Lost Generation. In works such as **Babbitt***, Lewis criticizes the shallow materialistic culture the Industrial Revolution created. Nothing matters within the society George Babbitt inhabits other than appearance and material possessions.*

The Towers of Zenith aspired above the morning mist; austere towers of steel and cement and limestone, sturdy as cliffs and delicate as silver rods. They were neither citadels nor churches, but frankly and beautifully office-buildings.....

In one of the skyscrapers the wires of the Associated Press were closing down....The dawn mist spun away. Cues of men with lunch boxes clumped toward the immensity of new factories, sheets of glass and hollow tile, glittering shops where five thousand men worked beneath one roof, pouring out the honest wares that would be sold up the Euphrates and across the veldt. The whistles rolled out in greeting a chorus cheerful as the April dawn; the song of labor in a city built—it seemed—for giants.

There was nothing of the giant in the aspect of the man who was beginning to awaken on the sleeping-porch of a Dutch Colonial house in that residential district of Zenith known as Floral Heights.

His name was George F. Babbitt. He was forty-six years old now, in April, 1920, and he made nothing in particular, neither butter nor shoes nor poetry, but he was nimble in the calling of selling houses for more than people could afford to pay....

Rumble and bang of the milk-truck.

Babbitt moaned, turned over, struggled back toward his dream....

He escaped from reality till the alarm-clock rang, at seven-twenty.

It was the best of nationally advertised and quantitatively produced alarm-clocks, with all modern attachments, including cathedral chime, intermittent alarm, and a phosphorescent dial. Babbitt was proud of being awakened by such a rich device. Socially it was almost as creditable as buying expensive cord tires.

He sulkily admitted now that there was no more escape, but he lay and detested the grind of the real-estate business, and disliked his family, and disliked himself for disliking them....

From the bedroom beside the sleeping-porch, his wife's detestably cheerful "Time to get up, Georgie boy," and the itchy sound, the brisk and scratchy sound, of combing hairs out of a stiff brush....

He creaked to his feet....he looked blurrily out at the yard. It delighted him, as always; it was the neat yard of a successful business man of Zenith, that is, it was perfection, and made him also perfect. He regarded the corrugated iron garage. For the three-hundred-and-sixty-fifth time in a year he reflected,

"No class to that tin shack. Have to build me a frame garage. But by golly it's the only thing on the place that isn't up-to-date!" While he stared he thought of a community garage for his acreage development, Glen Oriole. He stopped puffing and jiggling. His arms were akimbo. His petulant, sleep-swollen face was set in harder lines. He suddenly seemed capable, an official, a man to contrive, to direct, to get things done.

On the vigor of his idea he was carried down the hard, clean, unused-looking hall into the bathroom.

Though the house was not large it had, like all houses on Floral Heights, an altogether royal bathroom of porcelain and glazed tile and metal sleek as silver. The towel-rack was a rod of clear glass set in nickel. The tub was long enough for a Prussian Guard, and above the set bowl was a sensational exhibit of tooth-brush holder, shaving-brush holder, soap-dish, sponge-dish, and medicine cabinet, so glittering and so ingenious that they resembled an electrical instrument-board. But the Babbitt whose god was Modern Appliances was not pleased. The air of the bathroom was thick with the smell of a heathen toothpaste....He finished his shaving......When he was done, his round face smooth and steamy and his eyes stinging from soapy water, he reached for a towel. The family towels were wet, he found, as he blindly snatched them......Then George F. Babbitt did a dismaying thing. He wiped his face on the guest-towel! It was a pansy-embroidered trifle which always hung there to indicate that the Babbitts were in the best Floral Heights society. No one had ever used it. No guest had ever dared to. Guests secretively took a corner of the nearest regular towel.....

Myra Babbitt—Mrs. George F. Babbitt—was definitely mature...........She had become so dully habituated to married life that in her full matronliness she was as sexless as an anemic nun. She was a good woman, a kind woman, a diligent woman, but no one, save perhaps Tinka her ten-year-old, was at all interested in her or entirely aware that she was alive...

He was fairly amiable in the conference on the brown suit.

"What do you think, Myra?.......How about it? Shall I wear the brown suit another day?"

"Well, it looks awfully nice on you."

"I know, but gosh, it needs pressing."

"That's so. Perhaps it does."

"It certainly could stand being pressed, all right."

"Yes, perhaps it wouldn't hurt it to be pressed."

"But gee, the coat doesn't need pressing. No sense in having the whole darn suit pressed, when the coat doesn't need it."

That's so."..............

"Well, why don't you put on the dark gray suit to-day, and stop in at the tailor and leave the brown trousers?".......

He was able to get through the other crises of dressing with comparative resoluteness and calm.

His first adornment was the sleeveless dimity B.V.D. undershirt.....His second embellishment was combing and slicking back his hair.....But most wonder-working of all was the donning of his spectacles.

There is character in spectacles—the pretentious tortoise-shell, the meek pince-nez of the school teacher, the twisted silver-framed glasses of the old villager. Babbitt's spectacles had huge, circular, frameless lenses of the very best glass; the ear-pieces were thin bars of gold. In them he was the modern business man; one who gave orders to clerks and drove a car and played occasional golf and was scholarly in regard to Salesmanship. His head suddenly appeared not babyish but weighty, and you noted his heavy, blunt nose, his straight mouth and thick, long upper lip, his chin over-fleshy but strong; with respect you beheld him put on the rest of his uniform as a Solid Citizen...............

A sensational event was changing from the brown suit to the gray the contents of his pockets. He was earnest about these objects. They were of eternal importance, like baseball or the Republican Party. They included a fountain pen and silver pencil (always lacking a supply of new leads) which belonged in the righthand upper vest pocket. Without them he would have felt naked. On his watch-chain were a gold pen-knife, silver cigar-cutter, seven keys (the use of two of which he had forgotten), and incidentally a good watch. Depending from the chain was a large, yellowish elk's-tooth-proclamation of his membership in the Benevolent and Protective Order of Elks. Most significant of all was his loose-leaf pocket note-book, that modern and efficient note-book which contained the addresses of people whom he had forgotten, prudent memoranda of postal money-orders which had reached their destinations months ago, stamps which had lost their mucilage, clippings of verses by T. Cholmondeley Frink and of the newspaper editorials from which Babbitt got his opinions and his polysyllables, notes to be sure and do things which he did not intend to do...........

Last, he stuck in his lapel the Boosters' Club button. With the conciseness of great art the button displayed two words: "Boosters-Pep!" It made Babbitt feel loyal and important. It associated him with Good Fellows, with men who were nice and human, and in important business circles. It was his V.C., his Legion of Honor ribbon, his Phi Beta Kappa key......

Before he followed his wife, Babbitt stood at the western-most window of their room. This residential settlement, Floral Heights, was on a rise; and though the center of the city was three miles away—Zenith had between three and four hundred thousand inhabitants now—he could see the top of the Second National Tower, an Indiana limestone building of thirty-five stories.

Its shining walls rose against April sky to a simple cornice like a streak of white fire. Integrity was in the tower, and decision. It bore its strength lightly as a tall soldier. As Babbitt stared, the nervousness was soothed from his face, his slack chin lifted in reverence. All he articulated was "That's one lovely sight!" but he was inspired by the rhythm of the city; his love of it renewed. He beheld the tower as a temple-spire of the religion of business, a faith passionate, exalted, surpassing common men; and as he clumped down to breakfast he whistled the ballad "Oh, by gee, by gosh, by jingo" as though it were a hymn melancholy and noble.

Source: Sinclair Lewis, *Babbitt*, Harcourt Brace: New York, 1922

HOW WELL DID YOU UNDERSTAND THIS SELECTION?

1. What kind of man is George F. Babbitt? Explain.

2. How is Mrs. Babbitt described?

3. Is George Babbitt happy? Explain.

4. What does Babbitt value?

5. What is significant about the use of "Zenith" as the name for the city Babbitt lives in?

6. Does the name "Floral Heights" signify anything of importance? Explain.

7. How would you describe Babbitt's life?

8. Are the majority of Americans today like George Babbitt? Explain.

Harlem, New York was the site of a flourishing African-American literary, artistic, and social movement in the 1920s called the Harlem Renaissance. Blacks from the South and other parts of the nation and world migrated to Harlem to participate in this flowering of African-American culture. An important figure in the Harlem Renaissance was Langston Hughes. His essay, "The Negro Artists and the Racial Mountain," analyzed problems black artists had and concluded that they should not emulate white artists. Instead, Hughes suggested that African Americans should produce work that was different from standardized white work and that emphasized the artist's unique culture and experiences. Hughes put his advice into practice as the following selection from his poetry illustrates.

The Negro Speaks Of Rivers

I've known rivers;
I've known rivers ancient as the world and older than the
    flow of human blood in human veins.

My soul has grown deep like the rivers.

I bathed in the Euphrates when dawns were young.
I built my hut near the Congo and it lulled me to sleep.
I looked upon the Nile and raised the pyramids above it.
I heard the singing of the Mississippi when Abe Lincoln
    went down to New Orleans, and I've seen its muddy
    bosom turn all golden in the sunset.

I've known rivers;
Ancient, dusky rivers.

My soul has grown deep like the rivers.

Source: *The Crisis*, June, 1921 (vol. 22), W.E.B. DuBois, ed.

HOW WELL DID YOU UNDERSTAND THIS SELECTION?

1. What is the central meaning of the poem?

2. Why does Hughes talk about rivers throughout the world?

3. What is the meaning of "My soul has grown deep like the rivers"?

*Marcus Garvey gained international attention during the 1920s for advocating black racial pride and black nationalism and rejecting ideas of black leaders such as Booker T. Washington and W.E.B. DuBois that African Americans should try to fit into white American society with the hope of ultimately achieving integration and full racial equality. Garvey, a Jamaican native, moved to Harlem, New York in 1916 and began to call for racial separation. He worked through the Universal Negro Improvement Association to promote a "Back to Africa Movement" in which American blacks would establish colonies they controlled on the African continent. Garvey founded and edited a black newspaper, **The Negro World,** to promote his Back to Africa Movement. Eventually, Garvey was imprisoned for mail fraud and deported to Jamaica. The two selections below provide insight into Garvey's views on blacks and race.*

MARCUS GARVEY, Editorial, 1925

Fellow Men of the Negro Race, Greeting:

The time has come for the Negro to forget and cast behind him his hero worship and adoration of other races, and to start out immediately, to create and emulate heroes of his own.

We must canonize our own saints, create our own martyrs, and elevate to positions of fame and honor black men and women who have made their distinct contributions to our racial history. Sojourner Truth is worthy of the place of sainthood alongside of Joan of Arc; Crispus Attucks and George William Gordon are entitled to the halo of martyrdom with no less glory than that of the martyrs of any other race. Toussaint L'Ouverture's brilliancy as a soldier and statesman outshone that of a Cromwell, Napoleon and Washington; hence, he is entitled to the highest place as a hero among men. Africa has produced countless numbers of men and women, in war and in peace, whose lustre and bravery outshine that of any other people. Then why not see good and perfection in ourselves?

We must inspire a literature and promulgate a doctrine of our own without any apologies to the powers that be. The right is ours and God's. Let contrary sentiment and cross opinions go to the winds. Opposition to race independence is the weapon of the enemy to defeat the hopes of an unfortunate people. We are entitled to our own opinions and not obligated to or bound by the opinions of others....

The world today is indebted to us for the benefits of civilization. They stole our arts and sciences from Africa. Then why should we be ashamed of ourselves?....

As the Jew is held together by his religion, the white races by the assumption and the unwritten law of superiority, and the Mongolian by the precious tie of blood, so likewise the African must be united in one grand racial hierarchy. Our union must know no clime, boundary, or nationality. Like the great Church of Rome, Negroes the world over must practice one faith, that of Confidence in themselves, with One God! One Aim! One Destiny! Let no religious scruples, no political machination divide us, but let us hold together under all climes and in every country, making among ourselves a Racial Empire upon which "the sun shall never set."....

Source: Editorial, *Negro World*, June 6, 1925

Marcus Garvey, An Appeal to the Soul of White America: The Solution to the
Problem of Competition Between Two Opposite Races: Negro Leader Appeals to the
Conscience of White Race to Save His Own, 1923

Surely, the soul of liberal, philanthropic, liberty-loving white America is not dead....

It is to that feeling that I appeal at this time for four hundred million Negroes of the world, and fifteen million of America in particular.

There is no real white man in America, who does not desire a solution of the Negro problem. Each thoughtful citizen has probably his own idea of how the vexed question of the races should be settled. To some the Negro could be gotten rid of by wholesale butchery, by lynching, economic starvation, by a return to slavery and legalized oppression; while others would have the problem solved by seeing the race all herded together and kept somewhere among themselves, but a few—those in whom they have an interest should be allowed to live around as the wards of a mistaken philanthropy; yet, none so generous as to desire to see the Negro elevated to a standard of real progress, and prosperity, welded into a homogeneous whole, creating of themselves a mighty nation with proper systems of government, civilization, and culture, to mark them admissible to the fraternities of nations and races without any disadvantage....

Let white and black stop deceiving themselves. Let the white race stop thinking that all black men are dogs and not be considered as human beings. Let foolish Negro agitators and so-called reformers, encouraged by deceptive and unthinking white associates, stop preaching and advocating the doctrine of "social equality," meaning thereby the social intermingling of both races, intermarriages, and general social co-relationship....

There is but one solution, and that is to provide an outlet for Negro energy, ambition, and passion, away from the attraction of white opportunity and surround the race with opportunities of its own. If this is not done, and if the foundation for same is not laid now, then the consequences will be sorrowful for the weaker race, and be disgraceful to white ideals of justice, and shocking to white civilization.

The Negro must have a country, and a nation of his own....We have found a place, it is Africa and as black men for three centuries have helped white men build America, surely generous and grateful white men and women will help black men build Africa.

And why shouldn't Africa and America travel down the ages as protectors of human rights and guardians of democracy? Why shouldn't black men help white men secure and establish universal peace? We can only have peace when we are just to all mankind; and for that peace, and for the reign of universal love I now appeal to the soul of white America. Let the Negroes have a Government of their own account proving to the world that they are capable of evolving a civilization of their own....

I appeal to the considerate and thoughtful conscience of white America not to condemn the cry of the Universal Negro Improvement Association for a nation in Africa for Negroes, but to give us a chance to explain ourselves to the world. White America is too big and when informed and touched, too liberal to turn down the cry of the awakened Negro for "a place in the sun."

Source: *Philosophy and Opinions of Marcus Garvey*, Amy Jacques-Garvey, ed., The Universal Publishing House, New York, 1923-1925

HOW WELL DID YOU UNDERSTAND THIS SELECTION?

1. What does Garvey say blacks should do?

2. How does Garvey see white/black relations? Was his view accurate during the 1920s? Why or why not?

3. How would blacks and whites in the United States have reacted to the Back to Africa Movement?

MULTIPLE CHOICE: Circle the correct response. The correct answers are given at the end.

1. The Red Scare is best described by which of the following
   a. A fear of business supremacy.
   b. A fear of communism and radicalism.
   c. Rejection of organized religion.
   d. A celebration of things American.

2. Artists, writers, and intellectuals disillusioned with the materialism of the 1920s were called
   a. Red Americans
   b. Anti-materialistic poets
   c. The Complete Socialists
   d. The Lost Generation

3. Which of the following is not true about the Ku Klux Klan of the 1920s?
   a. The organization remained confined to the South.
   b. It broadened its bigotry to include not only blacks but Catholics, Jews, and immigrants.
   c. It was brought down by the rape of a white woman by a Klan leader.
   d. Its membership numbered over two million.

4. Which of the following was not elected President during the decade of the 1920s?
   a. Warren G. Harding.
   b. Calvin Coolidge.
   c. Herbert Hoover.
   d. Franklin Roosevelt.

5. What did the National Origins Act do?
   a. Allow unlimited immigration from southern and western Europe.
   b. Restrict immigration from northern and western European countries more than from southern and eastern European countries.
   c. Restrict immigration from southern and eastern European countries.
   d. Allow more immigration from Latin American countries.

6. Women in the 1920s who wore short skirts, bobbed hair, smoked cigarettes, and drank alcohol were called
   a. Flappers
   b. Wipers
   c. Genomes
   d. Rascals

7. The Scopes Trial was held because
   a. A public school teacher allowed students to openly violate prohibition laws in Tennessee.
   b. A public school teacher taught Darwin's Theory of Evolution in his classroom.
   c. A county judge executive posted the Ten Commandments in a Tennessee courthouse.
   d. A public school teacher displayed the Ten Commandments in his classroom.

8. National prohibition was made possible by
   a. Governmental regulation of the liquor industry.
   b. Congressional rejection of the Volstead Act.
   c. Ratification of the Eighteenth Amendment.
   d. The election of Warren G. Harding, a religious fundamentalist, president in 1920.

9. A scandal that rocked the Harding Administration when government oil reserves were leased to private companies was
   a. the Sinclair Scandal.
   b. the Lay Low Scandal.
   c. the Petroleum Pit Scandal.
   d. the Teapot Dome Scandal.

10. The stock market crash
   a. Signaled the beginning of the Great Depression.
   b. Had little impact on the American economy.
   c. Enabled ordinary American workers to invest in stock.
   d. Increased American confidence in the government's ability to protect the public from unscrupulous bankers.

Answers: 1-b; 2-d; 3-a; 4-d; 5-c; 6-a; 7-b; 8-c; 9-d; 10-a

ESSAYS:

1. Discuss the differences between rural and urban Americans during the 1920s.

2. Do you agree with the statement that the 1920s was a decade of "conservatism, fundamentalism, and intolerance?" Why or why not? Use historical evidence to support your answer.

3. Write an essay that explains how economic weakness coupled with governmental policies caused the Great Depression.

4. Compare and contrast the views of Marcus Garvey with those of W. E. B. DuBois and Booker T. Washington.

OPTIONAL ACTIVITIES: (Use your knowledge **and** imagination.)

1. You are a young woman from a rural farm state who moves to Chicago after graduating from high school to find a job. Write a letter to your family describing your new life in the big city.

2. Read a literary work of a member of the Lost Generation. Describe the author's depiction of American materialism.

3. You are a member of a fundamentalist Protestant Church. Write a letter to the local newspaper discussing problems you see in American society.

WEB SITE LISTINGS:

Woman Suffrage and the Nineteenth Amendment
http://www.nara.gov/education/teaching/woman/home.html

The Volstead Act and Related Prohibition Documents
http://www.nara.gov/education/cc/prohib.html

The Red Scare
http://newman.baruch.cuny.edu/digital/redscare

Prosperity and Thrift: The Coolidge Era and the Consumer Economy, 1921-1929.
http://memory.loc.gov/ammem/coolhtml/coolhome.html

The 1920s
http://www.louisville.edu/~kprayb01/1920s.html

F. Scott Fitzgerald
http://www.sc.edu/fitzgerald/index.html

Ku Klux Klan
http://www.lib.msu.edu/coll/main/spec_col/radicalism/klan.htm

The Scopes Trial
http://www.law.umkc.edu/faculty/projects/ftrials/scopes/scopes.htm

Harlem Renaissance: New York in the Twenties
http://www.humanitieswest.org/Harlem.html

Marcus Garvey and the Universal Negro Improvement Association
http://www.isop.ucla.edu/mgpp

Chapter Nineteen

THE DEPRESSION

Black Thursday, October 24, 1929 saw the stock market crash. Thousands of investors tried to sell but it was difficult to find buyers. Financiers raised enough money to buy millions of dollars worth of stocks to stem the downturn. For a few days this seemed to work but the bottom dropped out of the market on Black Tuesday, October 29, wiping out $30 billion in stock values and signaling the beginning of the Great Depression. Fundamental weaknesses in the economy of the 1920s produced the crash and the ensuing depression. Farmers, textile workers, and coal miners were depressed even in the prosperous twenties. Wages of workers were far less than needed to consume what the economy produced. The Mellon Tax Plan favored the rich who used their income to finance luxurious living and speculation. American workers became more productive, which created a need for increasing consumption, but greedy business owners refused to increase wages that would have enabled employees to buy more products. When demand for consumer goods fell in 1929, factories laid off workers. The layoffs caused a further decline in consumer purchases, which produced more layoffs. The nation found itself in a vicious cycle of declining consumption and joblessness that seemed to have no end. About one year after the Great Depression began four million Americans (9 percent of the work force) had lost their jobs. Two years later twenty-one million (one quarter of the work force) were unemployed. Perhaps another 25 to 30 percent were under employed, working only one or two days per week. The unemployment and under employment produced hunger and homelessness. Thousands of Americans were evicted from their residences and lived outside in tents and cardboard boxes, which they called Hoover Homes in honor of President Herbert Hoover, blamed by many for causing the Great Depression. Others roamed the streets and rode the rails as Hobos, looking for work. Hunger was widespread. Countless Americans stood in soup lines operated by churches and other charities in cities waiting for food. These lines sometimes stretched several blocks in length. By 1933, over nine thousand banks had failed as a result of the banking crisis that gripped the nation. Panicked depositors tried to withdraw their money before the bank closed its doors. Millions of Americans lost their life savings when the bank they had trusted did not have enough cash to cover deposits.

The Great Depression did more than create unemployment, poverty, hunger, homelessness, and bankruptcy. It deprived Americans of the belief that they were somehow special in the world. People lost faith in the idea of history as progress. No longer did they believe that history inevitably moved forward in an unending line of progress. It also changed American government and its relationship to the larger society. The executive branch was strengthened, and the government began to regulate the economy much more heavily than ever before.

Most of the changes in government came with Franklin Delano Roosevelt's New Deal. Its goals were three fold—relief, reform, and recovery. Numerous government programs, such as the National Bank Holiday and the Works Progress Administration (WPA), were initiated to ease the suffering of Americans. Some, like the Federal Deposit Insurance Corporation, sought to bring fundamental reform to the economy to prevent future depressions while others, like the National Industrial Recovery Act, attempted to restore the economy to it pre-depression status. The New Deal caused much debate within American society about government involvement in shaping social and economic policy and represented the single largest legislative program in American history up to that time. The New Deal did not end the Great Depression, but it forever changed America.

IDENTIFICATION: Briefly describe each item.

Bonus Army

Herbert Hoover

FDIC

New Deal

Franklin D. Roosevelt

Stock Market Crash

Okies

CIO

A. Philip Randolph

Cesar Chavez

RFC

Frances Perkins

Bank Holiday

Brain Trust

The Hundred Days

Homeowners Loan Corporation

TVA

AAA

National Industrial Recovery Act

NRA

FERA

PWA

CWA

CCC

Harry Hopkins

Harold Ickes

Securities and Exchange Commission

Francis Townsend

Charles Coughlin

Huey Long

Share the Wealth Plan

Scottsboro case

Social Security Act

Schecter v. United States

<u>National Labor Relations Act</u>

<u>Emergency Relief Appropriations Act</u>

<u>Alf Landon</u>

<u>Court Packing Plan</u>

<u>National Housing Act</u>

THINK ABOUT:

1. How did the Great Depression change the outlook of Americans about the future? How do views of people who survived the Great Depression compare with views of contemporary Americans?

2. What caused the Great Depression? Could an event similar to the Great Depression happen again? Why or why not?

3. How did the Great Depression change the nature of the American government and economy?

4. How did critics of the New Deal attack the program? Do politicians today use these same tactics to sway public opinion in their favor?

FRANKLIN D. ROOSEVELT'S FIRST INAUGURAL ADDRESS

Franklin Delano Roosevelt was elected president in 1932. When he took office in March 1933, the nation was at its lowest point in the Great Depression. The government faced problems with unemployment, hunger, and homelessness. Capitalism, the economic system that had sustained Americans for decades, was near collapse. Roosevelt perceived that his primary job was restoring confidence in the American people that things would get better. He used his first inaugural address to do just that. Speaking over the radio to countless millions of Americans he uttered the famous phrase "the only thing we have to fear is fear itself...." He also used this speech to outline his plans for bringing the country out of the Great Depression.

I am certain that my fellow Americans expect that on my induction into the Presidency I will address them with a candor and a decision which the present situation of our nation impels. This is preeminently the time to speak the truth, the whole truth, frankly and boldly nor need we shrink from honestly facing conditions in our country today. This great Nation will endure as it has endured, will revive and will prosper. So, first of all, let me assert my firm belief that the only thing we have to fear is fear itself-nameless, unreasoning, unjustified terror which paralyzes needed efforts to convert retreat into advance. In every dark hour of our national life a leadership of frankness and vigor has met with that understanding and support of the people themselves, which is essential to victory. I am convinced that you will again give that support to leadership in these critical days.

212

In such a spirit on my part and on yours we face our common difficulties. They concern, thank God, only material things. Values have shrunken to fantastic levels, taxes have risen, our ability to pay has fallen, government of all kinds is faced by serious curtailment of income, the means of exchange are frozen in the currents of trade, the withered leaves of industrial enterprise lie on every side, farmers find no markets for their produce, the savings of many years in thousands of families are gone.

More important, a host of unemployed citizens face the grim problem of existence, and an equally great number toil with little return. Only a foolish optimist can deny the dark realities of the moment.

Yet our distress comes from no failure of substance. We are stricken by no plague of locusts. Compared with the perils which our forefathers conquered because they believed and were not afraid, we have still much to be thankful for. Nature still offers her bounty and human efforts have multiplied it. Plenty is at our doorstep, but a generous use of it languishes in the very sight of the supply. Primarily this is because the rulers of the exchange of mankind's goods have failed, through their own stubbornness and their own incompetence, have admitted their failure, and abdicated. Practices of the unscrupulous money changers stand indicted in the court of public opinion, rejected by the hearts and minds of men.

True they have tried, but their efforts have been cast in the pattern of an outworn tradition. Faced by failure of credit they have proposed only the lending of more money. Stripped of the lure of profit by which to induce our people to follow their false leadership, they have resorted to exhortations, pleading tearfully for restored confidence. They know only the rules of a generation of self-seekers. They have no vision, and when there is no vision the people perish.

The money changers have fled from their high seats in the temple of our civilization. We may now restore that temple to the ancient truths. The measure of the restoration lies in the extent to which we apply social values more noble than mere monetary profit.

Happiness lies not in the mere possession of money, it lies in the joy of achievement, in the thrill of creative effort. The joy and moral stimulation of work no longer must be forgotten in the mad chase of evanescent profits. These dark days will be worth all they cost us if they teach us that our true destiny is not to be ministered unto but to minister to ourselves and to our fellow men.

Recognition of the falsity of material wealth as the standard of success goes hand in hand with the abandonment of the false belief that public office and high political position are to be valued only by the standards of pride of place and personal profit, and there must be an end to a conduct in banking and in business which too often has given to a sacred trust the likeness of callous and selfish wrongdoing. Small wonder that confidence languishes, for it thrives only on honesty, on honor, on the sacredness of obligations, on faithful protection, on unselfish performance, without them it cannot live.

Restoration calls, however, not for changes in ethics alone. This Nation asks for action, and action now.

Our greatest primary task is to put people to work. This is no unsolvable problem if we face it wisely and courageously. It can be accomplished in part by direct recruiting by the Government itself, treating the task as we would treat the emergency of a war, but at the same time, through this employment, accomplishing greatly needed projects to stimulate and reorganize the use of our natural resources.

Hand in hand with this we must frankly recognize the overbalance of population in our industrial centers and, by engaging on a national scale in a redistribution, endeavor to provide a better use of the land for those best fitted for the land. The task can be helped by definite efforts to raise the values of agricultural products and with this the power to purchase the output of our cities. It can be helped by preventing realistically the tragedy of the growing loss through foreclosure of our small homes and our farms. It can be helped by insistence that the Federal, State, and local governments act forthwith on the demand that their cost be drastically reduced. It can be helped by the unifying of relief activities which today are often scattered, uneconomical, and unequal. It can be helped by national planning for and supervision of all forms of transportation and of communications and other utilities which have a definitely public character. There are many ways in which it can be helped, but it can never be helped merely by talking about it. We must act and act quickly.

Finally, in our progress toward a resumption of work we require two safeguards against a return of the evils of the old order, there must be a strict supervision of all banking and credits and investments, there must be an end to speculation with other people's money, and there must be provision for an adequate but sound currency.

There are the lines of attack I shall presently urge upon a new Congress in special session detailed measures for their fulfillment, and I shall seek the immediate assistance of the several States.

Through this program of action we address ourselves to putting our own national house in order and making income balance outgo. Our international trade relations, though vastly important, are in point of time and necessity secondary to the establishment of a sound national economy. I favor as a practical policy the putting of first things first. I shall spare no effort to restore world trade by international economic readjustment, but the emergency at home cannot wait on that accomplishment.

The basic thought that guides these specific means of national recovery is not narrowly nationalistic. It is the insistence, as a first consideration, upon the interdependence of the various elements in all parts of the United States-a recognition of the old and permanently important manifestation of the American spirit of the pioneer. It is the way to recovery. It is the immediate way. It is the strongest assurance that the recovery will endure.

In the field of world policy I would dedicate this nation to the policy of the good neighbor-the neighbor who resolutely respects himself and, because he does so, respects the rights of others-the neighbor who respects his obligations and respects the sanctity of his agreements in and with a world of neighbors.

If I read the temper of our people correctly, we now realize as we have never realized before our interdependence on each other, that we can not merely take but we must give as well, that if we are to go forward, we must move as a trained and loyal army willing to sacrifice for the good of a common discipline, because without such discipline no progress is made, no leadership becomes effective. We are, I know, ready and willing to submit our lives and property to such discipline, because it makes possible a leadership which aims at a larger good. This I propose to offer, pledging that the larger purposes will bind upon us all as a sacred obligation with a unity of duty hitherto evoked only in time of armed strife.

With this pledge taken, I assume unhesitatingly the leadership of this great army of our people dedicated to a disciplined attack upon our common problems.

Action in this image and to this end is feasible under the form of government which we have inherited from our ancestors. Our Constitution is so simple and practical that it is possible always to meet extraordinary needs by changes in emphasis and arrangement without loss of essential form. That is why our constitutional system has proved itself the most superbly enduring political mechanism the modern world has produced. It has met every stress of vast expansion of territory, of foreign wars, of bitter internal strife, of world relations.

It is to be hoped that the normal balance of executive and legislative authority may be wholly adequate to meet the unprecedented task before us. But it may be that an unprecedented demand and need for undelayed action may call for temporary departure from that normal balance of public procedure.

I am prepared under my constitutional duty to recommend the measures that a stricken nation in the midst of a stricken world may require. These measures, or such other measures as the Congress may build out of its experience and wisdom, I shall seek, within my constitutional authority, to bring to speedy adoption.

But in the event that the Congress shall fail to take one of these two courses, and in the event that the national emergency is still critical, I shall not evade the clear course of duty that will then confront me. I shall ask the Congress for the one remaining instrument to meet the crisis-broad executive power to wage a war against the emergency, as great as the power that would be given to me if we were in fact invaded by a foreign foe. For the trust reposed in me I will return the courage and the devotion that befit the time I can do no less. We face the arduous days that lie before us in the warm courage of the national unity, with the clear consciousness of seeking old and precious moral values, with the clean satisfaction that comes from the stern performance of duty by old and young alike. We aim at the assurance of a rounded and permanent national life. We do not distrust the fixture of essential democracy. The people of the United States have not failed. In their need they have registered a mandate that they want direct, vigorous action. They have asked for discipline and direction under leadership. They have made me the present instrument of their wishes. In the spirit of the gift I take it. In this dedication of a nation we humbly ask the blessing of God. May he protect each and every one of us. May he guide me in the days to come.

Source: Public Papers and Address of Franklin D. Roosevelt

HOW WELL DID YOU UNDERSTAND THIS SELECTION?

1. How does Roosevelt describe the condition America is in?

2. What does Roosevelt say he will do to end the Great Depression?

3. Does Roosevelt's speech give hope to the millions of Americans listening on the radio? Why or Why not?

4. What does Roosevelt ask ordinary Americans to do?

5. Does Roosevelt's speech give any hint of the changing relationship between American government and the economy? Why or why not? Support your answer with evidence from the speech.

FRANKLIN D. ROOSEVELT'S SECOND INAUGURAL ADDRESS

Roosevelt's second inaugural was on January 20, 1937, the first presidential inauguration to occur in January. States had amended the Constitution (Twentieth Amendment) to move the president's inauguration from March back to January so that the time in which a president was a lame duck would be lessened. Roosevelt, having been elected by a wide margin over his Republican opponent, Alf Landon, in November 1936, outlined plans in his Second Inaugural Address to continue programs of the New Deal Americans apparently liked.

When four years ago we met to inaugurate a President, the Republic, single-minded in anxiety, stood in spirit here. We dedicated ourselves to the fulfillment of a vision-to speed the time when there would be for all the people that security and peace essential to the pursuit of happiness. We of the Republic pledged ourselves to drive from the temple of our ancient faith those who had profaned it, to end by action, tireless and unafraid, the stagnation and despair of that day. We did those first things first.

Our covenant with ourselves did not stop there. Instinctively we recognized a deeper need—the need to find through government the instrument of our united purpose to solve for the individual the ever-rising problems of a complex civilization. Repeated attempts at their solution without the aid of government had left us baffled and bewildered. For, without that aid, we had been unable to create those moral controls over the services of science

215

which are necessary to make science a useful servant instead of a ruthless master of mankind. To do this we knew that we must find practical controls over blind economic forces and blindly selfish men.

We of the Republic sensed the truth that democratic government has innate capacity to protect its people against disasters once considered inevitable, to solve problems once considered unsolvable. We would not admit that we could not find a way to master economic epidemics just as, after centuries of fatalistic suffering we had found a way to master epidemics of disease. We refused to leave the problems of our common welfare to be solved by the winds of chance and the hurricanes of disaster.

In this we Americans were discovering no wholly new truth, we were writing a new chapter in our book of self-government.

This year marks the one hundred and fiftieth anniversary of the Constitutional Convention which made us a nation. At that convention our forefathers found the way out of the chaos which followed the Revolutionary War, they created a strong government with powers of united action sufficient then and now to solve problems utterly beyond individual or local solution. A century and a half ago they established the Federal Government in order to promote the general welfare and secure the blessings of liberty to the American people.

Today we invoke those same powers of government to achieve the same objectives.

Four years of new experience have not belied our historic instinct. They hold out the clear hope that government within communities, government within the separate States, and government of the United States can do the things the times require, without yielding its democracy. Our tasks in the last four years did not force democracy to take a holiday.

Nearly all of us recognize that as intricacies of human relationships increase, so power to govern them also must increase—power to stop evil, power to do good. The essential democracy of our Nation and the safety of our people depend not upon the absence of power, but upon lodging it with those whom the people can change or continue at stated intervals through an honest and free system of elections. The Constitution of 1787 did not make our democracy impotent.

In fact, in these last four years, we have made the exercise of all power more democratic, for we have begun to bring private autocratic powers into their proper subordination to the public's government. The legend that they were invincible—above and beyond the processes of a democracy—has been shattered. They have been challenged and beaten.

Our progress out of the depression is obvious But that is not all that you and I mean by the new order of things. Our pledge was not merely to do a patchwork job with secondhand materials. By using the new materials of social justice we have undertaken to erect on the old foundations a more enduring structure for the better use of future generations.

In that purpose we have been helped by achievements of mind and spirit. Old truths have been relearned, untruths have been unlearned. We have always known that heedless self-interest was bad morals; we know now that it is bad economics. Out of the collapse of a prosperity whose builders boasted their practicality has come the conviction that in the long run economic morality pays. We are beginning to wipe out the line that divides the practical from the ideal, and in so doing we are fashioning an instrument of unimagined power for the establishment of a morally better world.

This new understanding undermines the old admiration of worldly success as such. We are beginning to abandon our tolerance of the abuse of power by those who betray for profit the elementary decencies of life.

In this process evil things formerly accepted will not be so easily condoned. Hardheadedness will not so easily excuse hardheartedness. We are moving toward an era of good feeling. But we realize that there can be no era of good feeling save among men of good will.

For these reasons I am justified in believing that the greatest change we have witnessed has been the change in the moral climate of America.

Among men of good will, science and democracy together offer an ever-richer life and ever-larger satisfaction to the individual. With this change in our moral climate and our rediscovered ability to improve our economic order, we have set our feet upon the road of enduring progress.

Shall we pause now and turn our back upon the road that lies ahead? Shall we call this the promised land? Or, shall we continue on our way? For each age is a dream that is dying, or one that is coming to birth.

Many voices are heard as we face a great decision. Comfort says, tarry a while. Opportunism says, this is a good spot. Timidity asks, how difficult is the road ahead?

True, we have come far from the days of stagnation and despair. Vitality has been preserved. Courage and confidence have been restored. Mental and moral horizons have been extended.

But our present gains were won under the pressure of more than ordinary circumstances. Advance became imperative under the goad of fear and suffering. The times were on the side of progress.

To hold to progress today, however, is more difficult. Dulled conscience, irresponsibility, and ruthless self-interest already reappear Such symptoms of prosperity may become portents of disaster. Prosperity already tests the persistence of our progressive purpose.

Let us ask again, have we reached the goal of our vision of that fourth day of March, 1937? Have we found our happy valley?

I see a great nation, upon a great continent, blessed with a great wealth of natural resources. Its hundred and thirty million people are at peace among themselves, they are making their country a good neighbor among the nations. I see a United States which can demonstrate that, under democratic methods of government, national wealth can be translated into a spreading volume of human comforts hitherto unknown, and the lowest standard of living can be raised far above the level of mere subsistence.

But here is the challenge to our democracy. In this nation I see tens of millions of its citizens—a substantial part of its whole population—who at this very moment are denied the greater part of what the very lowest standards of today call the necessities of life.

I see millions of families trying to live on incomes so meager that the pall of family disaster hangs over them day by day.

I see millions whose daily lives in city and on farm continue under conditions labeled indecent by a so-called polite society half a century ago.

I see millions denied education, recreation, and the opportunity to better their lot and the lot of their children.

I see millions lacking the means to buy the products of farm and factory and by their poverty denying work and productiveness to many other millions.

I see one-third of a nation ill-housed, ill-clad, ill-nourished.

It is not in despair that I paint you that picture. I paint it for you in hope—because the nation, seeing and understanding the injustice in it, proposes to paint it out. We are determined to make every American citizen the subject of his country's interest and concern, and we will never regard any faithful law-abiding group within our borders as superfluous. The test of our progress is not whether we add more to the abundance of those who have much, it is whether we provide enough for those who have too little.

If I know aught of the spirit and purpose of our Nation, we will not listen to comfort, opportunism, and timidity. We will carry on.

Overwhelmingly, we of the Republic are men and women of good will, men and women who have more than warm hearts of dedication, men and women who have cool heads and willing hands of practical purpose as well. They will insist that every agency of popular government use effective instruments to carry out their will. Government is competent when all who compose it work as trustees for the whole people. It can make constant progress when it keeps abreast of all the facts. It can obtain justified support and legitimate criticism when the people receive true information of all that government does.

If I know aught of the will of our people, they will demand that these conditions of effective government shall be created and maintained. They will demand a nation uncorrupted by cancers of injustice and, therefore, strong among the nations in its example of the will to peace.

Today we reconsecrate our country to long-cherished ideals in a suddenly changed civilization. In every land there are always at work forces that drive men apart and forces that draw men together. In our personal ambitions we are individualists. But in our seeking for economic and political progress as a nation, we all go up, or else we all go down, as one people.

To maintain a democracy of effort requires a vast amount of patience in dealing with differing methods, a vast amount of humility. But out of the confusion of many voices rises an understanding of dominant public need. Then political leadership can voice common ideals, and aid in their realization.

In taking again the oath of office as President of the United States, I assume the solemn obligation of leading the American people forward along the road over which they have chosen to advance.

While this duty rests upon me I shall do my utmost to speak their purpose and to do their will, seeking Divine guidance to help us each and every one to give light to them that sit in darkness and to guide our feet into the way of peace.

Source: Public Papers and Address of Franklin D. Roosevelt

HOW WELL DID YOU UNDERSTAND THIS SELECTION?

1. Compare Roosevelt's first inaugural address with his second. How are they different? How are they similar?

2. Does Roosevelt think his New Deal has been successful? Why or why not?

3. How does Roosevelt refer to America's past to refute charges that his New Deal destroyed democracy?

4. What does Roosevelt say the greatest change in America has been? Explain what he means.

5. Does Roosevelt outline what he will do over the next four years? Explain.

SHARE OUR WEALTH PLAN By Huey Long

Huey Long was a prominent politician in Louisiana. He represented Louisiana as both governor and United States Senator. At first, he supported Roosevelt's New Deal but eventually decided it was too conservative. Long decided to challenge Roosevelt for the Democratic presidential nomination in 1936. He campaigned largely on a program he devised called the Share Our Wealth Plan. This plan was designed to appeal to people unemployed, hungry, and homeless from the Great Depression. Like Roosevelt, Long was a master of radio and exploited its political possibilities. He most likely would have run for president had an assassins' bullet not have taken his life before the election was underway. The following is Long's Share Our Wealth Plan.

Here is the whole sum and substance of the Share Our Wealth movement:

1. Every family to be furnished by the government a homestead allowance, free of debt, of not less than one-third the average family wealth of the country, which means, at the lowest that every family shall have the reasonable comforts of life up to a value of from $5,000 to $6,000: No person to have a fortune of more than

100 to 300 times the average family fortune, which means that the limit to fortune is between $1,500.000 and 5,000,000, with annual capital levy taxes imposed on all above $1,000,000.

2. The yearly income of every family shall be not less than one-third of the average family income, which means that, according to the estimates of the statisticians of the U. S. Government and Wall Street, no family's annual income would be less than from $2,000 to $2,500.

3. No yearly income shall be allowed to any person larger than from 100 to 300 times the size of the average family income, which means that no person would be allowed to earn in any year more than $600,000 to $1,800,000, all to be subject to present income tax laws.

4. To limit or regulate the hours of work to such an extent as to prevent over-production; the most modern and efficient machinery would be encouraged so that as much would be produced as possible so as to satisfy all demands of the people, but also to allow the maximum time to the workers for recreation, convenience, education, and luxuries of life.

5. An old age pension to the persons over 60.

6. To balance agricultural production with what can be consumed according to the laws of God, which includes the preserving and storing of surplus commodities to be paid for and held by the Government for emergencies when such are needed. Please bear in mind, however, that when the people of America have had money to buy things they needed, we have never had a surplus of any commodity. This plan of God does not call for destroying any of the things raised to eat or wear, nor does it countenance whole destruction of hogs, cattle or milk.

7. To pay the veterans of our wars what we owe them and to care for their disabled.

8. Education and training for all children to be equal in opportunity in all schools, colleges, universities and other institutions for training in the professions and vocations of life; to be regulated on the capacity of children to learn, and not on the ability of parents to pay the costs. Training for life's work to be as much universal and thorough for all walks in life as has been the training in the arts of killing.

9. The raising of revenues and taxes for the support of this program to come from the reduction of swollen fortunes from the top, as well as for the support of public works.

10. Give employment whenever there may be any slackening necessary in private enterprise.

Source: Congressional Record, 73rd Congress, 2nd Session, 1934

HOW WELL DID YOU UNDERSTAND THIS SELECTION?

1. Summarize the Share Our Wealth Plan. What kind of income and housing did it promise Americans?

2. How did Long propose to finance the Share Our Wealth Plan?

3. What limits did Long place on income?

4. Could the Share Our Wealth Plan have worked? Why or Why not?

5. What weaknesses can you find in the Share Our Wealth Plan? Explain.

NATIONAL LABOR RELATIONS ACT

Roosevelt's New Deal struck a tremendous blow for organized labor in 1935 with passage of the National Labor Relations Act. This statute gave workers the right to join a labor union and gave the union the right to engage in collective bargaining for its members. With passage of the National Labor Relations Act, Congress also created the National Labor Relations Board to oversee union elections and contract negotiations. Workers now had the right to choose whether they wanted to join a union. Employers were forbidden from denying employees this right. The National Labor Relations Board was also empowered to investigate allegations of unfair labor practices by employers, employees, and unions. If unfair labor practices were proven, the National Labor Relations Board had the right to stop them and provide redress for all grievances. The National Labor Relations Act was one of the most popular New Deal laws and cemented the relationship between Roosevelt's Democratic Party and organized labor.

FINDINGS AND POLICY

SECTION I The denial by employers of the right of employees to organize and the refusal by employers to accept the procedure of collective bargaining lead to strikes and other forms of industrial strife or unrest, which have the intent or the necessary effect of burdening or obstructing commerce by (a) impairing the efficiency, safety, or operation of the instrumentalities of commerce, (b) occurring in the current of commerce, (c) materially affecting, restraining, or controlling the flow of raw materials or manufactured or processed goods from or into the channels of commerce, or the prices of such materials or goods in commerce, or (d) using diminution of employment and wages in such volume as substantially to impair or disrupt the market for goods flowing from or into the channels of commerce. The inequality of bargaining power between employees who do not possess full freedom of association or actual liberty of contract, and employers who are organized in the corporate or other forms of ownership association substantially burdens and affects the flow of commerce, and tends to aggravate recurrent business depressions, by depressing wage rates and the purchasing power of wage earners in industry and by preventing the stabilization of competitive wage rates and working conditions within and between industries. Experience has proved that protection by law of the right of employees to organize and bargain collectively safeguards commerce from injury, impairment, or interruption, and promotes the flow of commerce by removing certain recognized sources of industrial strife and unrest, by encouraging practices fundamental to the friendly adjustment of industrial disputes arising out of differences as to wages, hours, or other working conditions, and by restoring equality of bargaining power between employers and employees. It is hereby declared to be the policy of the United States to eliminate the causes of certain substantial obstructions to the free flow of commerce and to mitigate and eliminate these obstructions when they have occurred by encouraging the practice and procedure of collective bargaining and by protecting the exercise by workers of full freedom of association, self-organization, and designation of representatives of their own choosing, for the purpose of negotiating the terms and conditions of their employment or other mutual aid or protection.

NATIONAL LABOR RELATIONS BOARD

SEC 3 (a) There is hereby created a board, to be known as the National Labor Relations Board, which shall be composed of three members, who shall be appointed by the President, by and with the advice and consent of the Senate. One of the original members shall be appointed for a term of one year, one for a term of three years, and one for a term of five years, but their successors shall be appointed for terms of five years each, except that any individual chosen to fill a vacancy shall be appointed only for the unexpired term of the member whom he shall succeed. The President shall designate one member to serve as chairman of the Board. Any member of the Board may be removed by the President, upon notice and hearing, for neglect of duty or malfeasance in office, but for no other cause.

RIGHTS OF EMPLOYEES

SEC 7 Employees shall have the right of self organization, to form, join, or assist labor organizations, to bargain collectively through representatives of their own choosing, and to engage in concerted activities, for the purpose of collective bargaining or other mutual aid or protection.

SEC 8 It shall be an unfair labor practice for an employer (1) To interfere with, restrain, or coerce employees in the exercise of the rights guaranteed in section 7 (2) To dominate or interfere with the formation or administration of any labor organization or contribute financial or other support to it. Provided, that subject to rules and regulations made and published by the Board pursuant to section 6 (a), an employer shall not be prohibited from permitting employees to confer with him during working hours without loss of time or pay. (3) By discrimination in regard to hire or tenure of employment or any term or condition of employment to encourage or discourage membership in any labor organization provided, that nothing in this Act, or in the National Industrial Recovery Act, as amended from time to time, or in any code or agreement approved or prescribed thereunder, or in any other statute of the United States, shall preclude an employer from making an agreement with a labor organization (not established, maintained or assisted by any action defined in this Act as an unfair labor practice) to require as a condition of employment membership therein, if such labor organization is the representative of the employees as provided in section 9 (a), in the appropriate collective bargaining unit covered by such agreement when made (4) To discharge or otherwise discriminate against an employee because he has filed charges or given testimony under this Act (5) To refuse to bargain collectively with the representatives of his employees....

Source: U.S. Statutes at Large, Vol. XLIX

HOW WELL DID YOU UNDERSTAND THIS SELECTION?

1. What problems led to passage of the National Labor Relations Act?

2. What rights does the National Labor Relations Act guarantee workers? Employers? Unions?

3. How are labor disputes to be resolved?

OKIES: TESTIMONY OF CAREY MCWILLIAMS IN CONGRESS

Okie was the term given to migrant farmers who moved to California from Oklahoma and other areas in the Midwest and Southwest during the 1930s. It was generally considered to be a derogatory term. Countless thousands of these migrants, victimized by the Dust Bowl and the Great Depression, drove rickety old jalopies along Route 66 to California in search of a better life. They had heard that work was available in California. Once there, however, most faced poor living conditions and limited opportunities for employment or land ownership. Some found seasonal work on vegetable and fruit farms. Like people across the nation, they settled in cardboard and tent colonies. Carey McWilliams, a journalist, visited and wrote about living conditions in migrant communities. He provided the following testimony to a committee in the House of Representatives investigating the problems Okies faced in California.

The most characteristic of all housing in California in which migrants reside at the moment is the shacktown or cheap subdivision. Most of these settlements have come into existence since 1933 and the pattern which obtains is somewhat similar throughout the State. Finding it impossible to rent housing in incorporated communities on their meager incomes, migrants have created a market for a very cheap type of subdivision of which the following may be taken as being representative. In Monterey County, according to a report of Dr. D. M. Bissell, county health officer, under date of November 28, 1939, there are approximately three well established migrant settlements. One of these, the development around the environs of Salinas, is perhaps the oldest migrant settlement of its type in California. In connection with this development I quote a paragraph of the report of Dr. Bissell: "This area is composed of all manners and forms of housing without a public sewer system. Roughly 10,000 persons are renting or have established homes there. A chief element in this area is that of refugees from the Dust Bowl who inhabit a part of Alisal called Little Oklahoma. Work in lettuce harvesting and packing and sugar beet processing have attracted these people who, seeking homes in Salinas without success because they aren't available, have resorted to makeshift adobes outside the city limits. Complicating the picture is the impermeable substrata which makes septic tanks with leaching fields impractical. Sewer wells have resulted with the corresponding danger to adjacent water wells and to the water wells serving the Salinas public. Certain districts, for example, the Airport Tract and parts of Alisal have grown into communities with quite satisfactory housing but others as exemplified by the Graves district are characterized by shacks and lean-tos which are unfit for human habitation. Typical of the shacktown problem are two such areas near the city limits of Sacramento, one on the eastside of B Street, extending from Twelfth Street to the Sacramento city dump and incinerator; and the other so-called Hoovertown, adjacent to the Sacramento River and the city filtration plant. In these two areas there were on September 17, 1939, approximately 650 inhabitants living in structures that, with scarcely a single exception, were rated by the inspectors of this division as unfit for human occupancy. The majority of the inhabitants were white Americans, with the exception of 50 or 60 Mexican families, a few single Mexican men, and a sprinkling of Negroes. For the most part they are seasonally employed in the canneries, the fruit ranches, and the hop fields of Sacramento County. Most of the occupants are at one time or another upon relief, and there are a large number of occupants in these shacktowns from the Dust Bowl area." Describing the housing, an inspector of this division reports: The dwellings are built of brush, rags, sacks, boxboard, odd bits of tin and galvanized iron, pieces of canvas and whatever other material was at hand at the time of construction. Wood floors, where they exist, are placed directly upon the ground, which because of the location of the camps with respect to the Sacramento River, is damp most of the time. To quote again from the report: entire families, men, women, and children, are crowded into hovels, cooking and eating in the same room. The majority of the shacks have no sinks or cesspools for the disposal of kitchen drainage, and this, together with garbage and other refuse, is thrown on the surface of the ground. Because of the high-water table, cesspools, where they exist, do not function properly; there is a large overflow of drainage and sewage to the surface of the ground. Many filthy shack latrines are located within a few feet of living quarters. Rents for the houses in these shacktowns range from $3 to $20 a month. In one instance a landlord rents ground space for $1.50 to $5 a month, on which tenants are permitted to erect their own dugouts. The Hooverville section is composed primarily of tents and trailers, there being approximately 125 tent structures in this area on September 17, 1939. Both areas are located in unincorporated territory. They are not subject at the present time to any State or county building regulation. In Hooverville, at the date of the inspection, many families were found that did not have even a semblance of tents or shelters. They were cooking and sleeping on the ground in the open and one water tap at an adjoining industrial plant was found to be the source of the domestic water supply for the camp....

Source: U.S. Congress, House Select Committee to Investigate the Interstate Migration of Destitute Citizens, Hearings, 76th Cong., 3rd Sess., 1941.

HOW WELL DID YOU UNDERSTAND THIS SELECTION?

1. Describe the living conditions of migrant workers. How do they compare to living conditions elsewhere in the nation during the Great Depression?

2. What problems do migrant workers face in California? Are they similar to problems faced by other workers across the nation?

3. If you were a New Dealer, how would you solve the problems of migrant workers?

President Roosevelt was a master at radio. He had a well modulated voice that reassured the American public during the Great Depression. Roosevelt made use of his ability to communicate by radio through what he called "fireside chats." Periodically, he addressed the public in an informal setting, outlining accomplishments of the New Deal and informing Americans about future programs. One such fireside chat was delivered on June 28, 1934. Not only did Roosevelt talk about what the New Deal had done but he seemed to foreshadow Social Security, a program he later enacted.

It has been several months since I have talked with you concerning the problems of government. Since January, those of us in whom you have vested responsibility have been engaged in the fulfillment of plans and policies which had been widely discussed in previous months. It seems to us our duty not only to make the right path clear but also to tread that path.

As we review the achievement of the session of the Seventy-third Congress, it is made increasingly clear that its task was essentially that of completing and fortifying the work it had begun in March, 1933. That was no easy task, but the congress was equal to it. It has been well said that while there were a few exceptions, this Congress displayed a greater freedom from mere partisanship than any other peace-time Congress since the Administration of President Washington himself. The session was distinguished by the extent and variety of legislation enacted and by the intelligence and good will of debate upon these measures.

I mention only a few of the major enactments. It provided for the readjustment of the debt burden through the corporate and municipal bankruptcy acts and the farm relief act. It lent a hand to industry by encouraging loans to solvent industries unable to secure adequate help from banking institutions. It strengthened the integrity of finance through the regulation of securities exchanges. It provided a rational method of increasing our volume of foreign trade through reciprocal trading agreements. It strengthened our naval forces to conform with the intentions and permission of existing treaty rights. It made further advances toward peace in industry through the labor adjustment. It supplemented our agricultural policy through measures widely demanded by farmers themselves and intended to avert price destroying surpluses. It strengthened the hand of the Federal Government in its attempts to suppress gangster crime. It took definite steps toward a national housing program through an act which I signed today designed to encourage private capital in the rebuilding of the homes of the Nation. It created a permanent Federal body for the just regulation of all forms of communication, including the telephone, the telegraph and the radio. Finally, and I believe most important, it reorganized, simplified and made more fair and just our monetary system, setting up standards and policies adequate to meet the necessities of modern economic life, doing justive to both gold and silver as the metal bases behind the currency of the United States. In the consistent development of our previous efforts toward the saving and safeguarding of our national life, I have continued to recognize three related steps. The first was relief, because the primary concern of any Government dominated by the humane ideals of democracy is the simple principle that in a land of vast resources no one should be permitted to starve. Relief was and continues to be our first consideration. It calls for large expenditures and will continue in modified form to do so for a long time to come. We may as well recognize that fact. It comes from the paralysis that arose as the aftereffect of that unfortunate decade characterized by a mad chase for unearned riches and an unwillingness of leaders in almost every walk of life to look beyond their own schemes and speculations. In our administration of relief we follow two principles: First, that direct giving shall, whenever possible, be supplemented by provision for useful and remunerative work and, second, that where families in their existing surroundings will in all human probability never find an opportunity for full self-maintenance, happiness and enjoyment, we will try to give them a new chance in new surroundings.

The second step was recovery, and it is sufficient for me to ask each and every one of you to compare the situation in agriculture and in industry today with what it was fifteen months ago.

At the same time we have recognized the necessity of reform and reconstruction-reform because much of our trouble today and in the past few years has been due to a lack of understanding of the elementary principles of justice and fairness by those in whom leadership in business and finance was placed-reconstruction because new conditions in our economic life as well as old but neglected conditions had to be corrected. Substantial gains well known to all of you have justified our course. I could cite statistics to you as unanswerable measures of our national progress-statistics to show the gain in the average weekly pay envelope of workers in the great majority of industries-statistics to show hundreds of thousands reemployed in private industries and other hundreds of thousands given new employment through the expansion of direct and indirect government assistance of many kinds, although, of course, there are those exceptions in professional pursuits whose economic improvement, of necessity, will be delayed. I also could cite statistics to show the great rise in the value of farm products-statistics to prove the demand for consumers' goods, ranging all the way from food and clothing to automobiles and of late to prove the rise in the demand for durable goods-statistics to cover the great increase in bank deposits and to show the scores of thousands of homes and of farms which have been saved from foreclosure.

But the simplest way for each of you to judge recovery lies in the plain facts of your own individual situation. Are you better off than you were last year? Are you debts less burdensome? Is your bank account more secure? Are your working conditions better? Is your faith in your own individual future more firmly grounded?

Also, let me put to you another simple question: Have you as an individual paid too high a price for these gains? Plausible self-seekers and theoretical die-hards will tell you of the loss if individual of liberty. Answer this question also out of the fact of your own life. Have you lost any of your rights or liberty or constitutional freedom of action and choice? Turn to the Bill of rights of the Constitution, which I have solemnly sworn to maintain and under which your freedom rests secure. Read each provision of that Bill of rights and ask yourself whether you personally have suffered the impairment of a single jot of these great assurances. I have no question in my mind as to what your answer will be. The record is written in the experiences of your own personal lives.

In other words, it is not the overwhelming majority of the farmers or manufacturers or workers who deny the substantial gains of the past year. The most vociferous of the doubting Thomases may be divided roughly into two groups: First, those who seek special political privilege and, second, those who seek special financial privilege. About a year ago I used as an illustration the 90% of the cotton manufacturers of the United States who wanted to do the right thing by their employees and by the public but were prevented from doing so by the 10% who undercut them by unfair practices and un-American standards. It is well for us to remember that humanity is a long way from being perfect and that a selfish minority in every walk of life-farming, business, finance and even Government service itself-will always continue to think of themselves first and their fellow-being second.

In the working out of a great national program which seeks the primary good of the greater number, it is true that the toes of some people are being stepped on are going to be stepped on. But these toes belong to the comparative few who seek to retain or to gain position or riches or both by some short cut which is harmful to the greater good. In the execution of the powers conferred on it by Congress, the Administration needs and will tirelessly seek the best ability that the country affords. Public service offers better rewards in the opportunity for service than ever before in our history-not great salaries, but enough to live on. In the building of this service there are coming to us men and women with ability and courage from every part of the Union. The days of the seeking of mere party advantage through the misuse of public power are drawing to a close. We are increasingly demanding and getting devotion to the public service on the part of every member of the Administration, high and low.

The program of the past year is definitely in operation and that operation month by month is being made to fit into the web of old and new conditions. This process of evolution is well illustrated by the constant changes in detailed and organization and method going on in the National Recovery Administration. With every passing month we are making strides in the orderly handling of the relationship between employees and employers. Conditions differ, of course, in almost every part of the country and in almost every industry. Temporary methods of adjustment are being replaced by more permanent machinery and, I am glad to say, by a growing recognition on the part of employers and employees of the desirability of maintaining fair relationships all around.

So also, while almost everybody has recognized the tremendous strides in the elimination of child labor, in the payment of not less than fair minimum wages and in the shortening of hours, we are still feeling our way in solving problems which relate to self-government in industry, especially where such self-government tends to eliminate the fair operation of competition.

In this same process of evolution we are keeping before us the objectives of protecting on the one hand industry against chiselers within its own ranks, and on the other hand the consumer through the maintenance of reasonable competition for the prevention of the unfair sky-rocketing of retail prices. But in addition to this our immediate task, we must still look to the larger future. I have pointed out to the Congress that we are seeking to find the way once more to well-known, long-established but to some degree forgotten ideals and values. We seek the security of the men, women and children of the Nation. That security involves added means of providing better homes for the people of the Nation. That is the first principle of our future program.

The second is to plan the use of land and water resources of this country to the end that the means of livelihood of our citizens may be more adequate to meet their daily needs. And, finally, the third principle is to use the agencies of government to assist in the establishment of means to provide sound and adequate protection against the vicissitudes of modern life-in other words, social insurance.

Later in the year I hope to talk with you more fully about these plans. A few timid people, who fear progress, will try to give you new and strange names for what we are doing. Sometimes they will call it "Fascism," sometimes "Communism," sometimes "Regimentation," sometimes "Socialism." But in so doing, they are trying to make very complex and theoretical something that is really very simple and very practical. I believe in practical explanations and in practical policies. I believe that what we are doing today is a necessary fulfillment of what Americans have always been doing-a fulfillment of old and tested American ideals.

Let me give you a simple illustration: While I am away from Washington this summer, a long needed renovation of and addition to our White House office building is to be started. The architects have planned a few new rooms built into the present all too small one-story structure. We are going to include in this addition and in this renovation modern electric wiring and modern plumbing and modern means of keeping the offices cool in the hot Washington summers. But the structural lines of the old Executive Office Building will remain. The artistic lines of the White House buildings were the creation of master builders when our Republic was young. The simplicity and the strength of the structure remain in the face of every modern test. But within this magnificent pattern, the necessities of modern government business require constant reorganization and rebuilding. If I were to listen to the arguments of some prophets of calamity who are talking these days, I should hesitate to make these alterations. I should fear that while I am away for a few weeks the architects might build some strange new Gothic tower or a factory building or perhaps a replica of the Kremlin or of the Potsdam Palace. But I have no such fears. The architects and builders are men of common sense and of artistic American tastes. They know that the principles of harmony and of necessity itself require that the building of the new structure shall blend with the essential lines of the old. It is this combination of the old and the new that marks orderly peaceful progress-not only in building buildings but in building government itself. Our new structure is part of and a fulfillment of the old.

All that we do seeks to fulfill the historic traditions of the American people. Other nations may sacrifice democracy for the transitory stimulation of old and discredited autocracies. We are restoring confidence and well-being under the rule of the people themselves. We remain, as John Marshall said a century ago, "emphatically and truly, a government of the people." Our government "in form and in substance ... emanates from them. Its powers are granted by them, and are to be exercised directly on them, and for their benefits." Before I close, I want to tell you of the interest and pleasure with which I look forward to the trip on which I hope to start in a few days. It is a good thing for everyone who can possibly do so to get away at least once a year for a change of scene. I do not want to get into the position of not being able to see the forest because of the thickness of the trees.

I hope to visit our fellow Americans in Puerto Rico, in the Virgin Islands, in the Canal Zone and in Hawaii. And, incidentally, it will give me an opportunity to exchange a friendly word of greeting to the Presidents of our sister Republics: Haiti, Columbia and Panama.

After four weeks on board ship, I plan to land in our Pacific northwest, and then will come the best part of the whole trip, for I am hoping to inspect a number of our new great national projects on the Columbia, Missouri and Mississippi Rivers, to see some of our national parks and, incidentally, to learn much of the actual conditions during the trip across the continent back to Washington.

While I was in France during the War our boys used to call the United States "God's country." Let us make it and keep it "God's country."

Source: Social Security Administration Web Site http://www.ssa.gov/history/history6.html

HOW WELL DID YOU UNDERSTAND THIS SELECTION?

1. What does Roosevelt say the Seventy-third Congress accomplished?

2. What three principles of the New Deal does Roosevelt identify? Explain what each means.

3. How does Roosevelt refute the charge that the New Deal has destroyed American liberty?

4. Does Roosevelt identify what future course the New Deal will take? If so, what is he planning to do?

5. What does Roosevelt compare the New Deal to? Why does he do this?

REPUBLICAN PARTY PLATFORM, ELECTION OF 1936

Not everyone agreed with the New Deal. People seemed either to love or hate Roosevelt and the New Deal. Republicans believed the New Deal had destroyed individual liberty in the United States. The 1936 election was viewed as a popular referendum on the New Deal. The Republican Party nominated Alf Landon to oppose Roosevelt. The platform Landon and Republicans ran on in 1936 discusses the conservative complaints about the New Deal. The election was marked by bitter, personal attacks on Roosevelt and negative campaigning, which did not work. Roosevelt and the Democratic Party won landslides. Republicans were thoroughly trounced. The outcome of this election is viewed as a strong endorsement of the New Deal by the American public.

America is in peril. The welfare of American men and women and the future of our youth are at stake. We dedicate ourselves to the preservation of their political liberty, their individual opportunity and their character as free citizens, which today for the first time are threatened by Government itself.

For three long years the New Deal Administration has dishonored American traditions and flagrantly betrayed the pledges upon which the Democratic Party sought and received public support.

The powers of Congress have been usurped by the President.

The integrity and authority of the Supreme Court have been flouted.

The rights and liberties of American citizens have been violated.

Regulated monopoly has displaced free enterprise.

The New Deal Administration constantly seeks to usurp the rights reserved to the States and to the people.

It has insisted on the passage of laws contrary to the Constitution.

It has intimidated witnesses and interfered with the right of petition.

It has dishonored our country by repudiating its most sacred obligations.

It has been guilty of frightful waste and extravagance, using public funds for partisan political purposes.

It has promoted investigations to harass and intimidate American citizens, at the same time denying investigations into its own improper expenditures.

It has created a vast multitude of new offices, filled them with its favorites, set up a centralized bureaucracy, and sent out swarms of inspectors to harass our people.

It has bred fear and hesitation in commerce and industry, thus discouraging new enterprises, preventing employment and prolonging the depression.

It secretly has made tariff agreements with our foreign competitors, flooding our markets with foreign commodities.

It has coerced and intimidated voters by withholding relief from those opposing its tyrannical policies.

It has destroyed the morale of many of our people and made them dependent upon Government.

Appeals to passion and class prejudice have replaced reason and tolerance.

To a free people these actions are insufferable. This campaign cannot be waged on the traditional differences between the Republican and Democratic parties. The responsibility of this election transcends all previous political divisions. We invite all Americans, irrespective of party, to join us in defense of American institutions.

CONSTITUTIONAL GOVERNMENT AND FREE ENTERPRISE

WE PLEDGE OURSELVES:

1. To maintain the American system of constitutional and local self government, and to resist all attempts to impair the authority of the Supreme Court of the United States, the final protector of the rights of our citizens against the arbitrary encroachments of the legislative and executive branches of Government. There can be no individual liberty without an independent judiciary.

2. To preserve the American system of free enterprise, private competition, and equality of opportunity, and to seek its constant betterment in the interests of all.

REEMPLOYMENT

The only permanent solution of the unemployment problem is the absorption of the unemployed by industry and agriculture. To that end, we advocate:

Removal of restrictions on production.

Abandonment of all New Deal policies that raise production costs, increase the cost of living, and thereby restrict buying, reduce volume and prevent reemployment.

Encouragement instead of hindrance to legitimate business.

Withdrawal of Government from competition with private payrolls.

Elimination of unnecessary and hampering regulations.

Adoption of such policies as will furnish a chance for individual enterprise, industrial expansion, and the restoration of jobs.

RELIEF

The necessities of life must be provided for the needy, and hope must be restored pending recovery. The administration of relief is a major failure of the New Deal. It has been faithless to those who most deserve our sympathy. To end confusion, partisanship, waste and incompetence,

WE PLEDGE:

1. The return of responsibility for relief administration to non-political local agencies familiar with community problems.

2. Federal grants-in-aid to the States and Territories while the need exists, upon compliance with these conditions: (a) a fair proportion of the total relief burden to be provided from the revenues of States and local governments; (b) all

engaged in relief administration to be selected on the basis of merit and fitness; (c) adequate provisions to be made for the encouragement of those persons who are trying to become self-supporting.

3. Undertaking of Federal public works only on their merits and separate from the administration of relief.

4. A prompt determination of the facts concerning relief and unemployment.

SECURITY

Real security will be possible only when our productive capacity is sufficient to furnish a decent standard of living for all American families and to provide a surplus for future needs and contingencies. For the attainment of that ultimate objective, we look to the energy, self-reliance and character of our people, and to our system of free enterprise.

Society has an obligation to promote the security of the people, by affording some measure of protection against involuntary unemployment and dependency in old age. The New Deal policies, while purporting to provide social security, have, in fact, endangered it....

We propose to encourage adoption by the States and Territories of honest and practical measures for meeting the problems of unemployment insurance.

The unemployment insurance and old age annuity sections of the present Social Security Act are unworkable and deny benefits to about two-thirds of our adult population, including professional men and women and all those engaged in agriculture and domestic service, and the self employed, while imposing heavy tax burdens upon al. The so-called reserve fund estimated at forty-seven billion dollars for old age insurance is not reserve at all, because the fund will contain nothing but the Government's promise to pay, while the taxes collected in the guise of premiums will be wasted by the Government in reckless and extravagant political schemes.

LABOR

The welfare of labor rests upon increased production and the prevention of exploitation. We pledge ourselves to:

Protect the right of labor to organize and to bargain collectively though representatives of its own choosing without interference from any source.

Prevent governmental job holders from exercising autocratic power over labor.

Support the adoption of State laws and interstate compacts to abolish sweatshops and child labor, and to protect women and children with respect to maximum hours, minimum wages and working conditions. We believe that this can be done within the Constitution as it now stands.

AGRICULTURE

The farm problem is an economic and social, not a partisan problem....

Our paramount object is to protect and foster the family type of farm, traditional in American life, and to promote policies which will bring about an adjustment of agriculture to meet the needs of domestic and foreign markets. As an emergency measure, during the agricultural depression, Federal benefit payments or grants-in-aid when administered within the means of the Federal Government are consistent with a balanced budged.

WE PROPOSE:

1. To facilitate economical production and increased consumption on a basis of abundance instead of scarcity.

2. A national land-use program, including the acquisition of abandoned and non-productive farm lands by voluntary sale or lease, subject to approval of the legislative and executive branches of the States concerned, and the devotion of such land to appropriate public use, such as watershed protection and flood prevention, reforestation, recreation, and conservation of wild life.

3. That an agricultural policy be pursued for the protection and restoration of the land resources designed to bring about such a balance between soil-building and soil-depleting crops as will permanently insure productivity, with reasonable benefits to cooperating farmers on family-type farms, but so regulated as to eliminate the New Deal's destructive policy toward the dairy and live-stock industries.

4. To extent experimental aid to farmers developing new crops....

REGULATION OF BUSINESS

We recognize the existence of a field within which governmental regulation is desirable and salutary. The authority to regulate should be vested in an independent tribunal acting under clear and specific laws establishing definite standards. Their determinations on law and facts should be subject to review by the Courts. We favor Federal regulation, within the Constitution, of the marketing of securities to protect investors. We also favor Federal regulation of the interstate activities of public utilities....

GOVERNMENT FINANCE

The New Deal Administration has been characterized by shameful waste and general financial irresponsibility. It has piled deficit upon deficit. It threatens national bankruptcy and the destruction through inflation of insurance policies and savings bank deposits.

WE PLEDGE OURSELVES TO:

Stop the folly of uncontrolled spending.
   Balance the budget-not by increasing taxes but by cutting expenditures, drastically and immediately.
   Revise the Federal tax system and coordinate it with State and local tax systems.
   Use the taxing power for raising revenue and not for punitive or political purposes.

MONEY AND BANKING

We advocate a sound currency to be preserved at all hazards. The first requisite to a sound and stable currency is a balanced budget.
   We oppose further devaluation of the dollar.
   We will restore to the Congress the authority lodged with it by the Constitution to coin money and regulate the value thereof by repealing all the laws delegating this authority to the Executive.
   We will cooperate with other countries toward stabilization of currencies as soon as we can do so with due regard for our national interests and as soon as other nations have sufficient stability to justify such action.

CONCLUSION

We assume the obligations and duties imposed upon Government by modern conditions. We affirm our unalterable conviction that, in the future as in the past, the fate of the nation will depend, not so much on the wisdom and power of Government, as on the character and virtue, self-reliance, industry and thrift of the people and on their willingness to meet the responsibilities essential to the preservation of a free society.
   Finally, as our party affirmed in its first Platform in 1856: "Believing that the spirit of our institutions as well as the Constitution of our country guarantees liberty of conscience and equality of rights among our citizens, we oppose all legislation tending to impair them," and "we invite the affiliation and cooperation of the men of all parties, however differing from us in other respects, in support of the principles herein declared."
   The acceptance of the nomination tendered by this Convention carries with it, as a matter of private honor and public faith, an undertaking by each candidate to be true to the principles and program herein set forth.

Source: Proceedings, 21st Republican National Convention

HOW WELL DID YOU UNDERSTAND THIS SELECTION?

1. Why do Republicans disagree with the New Deal?

2. How do Republicans attack the New Deal?

3. What do Republicans propose to replace the New Deal with?

4. Identify the major planks of the Republican Party Platform of 1936.

5. Has the New Deal changed the Republican position on any issues since the 1920s? If so, explain.

6. What do Republicans propose to do regarding labor? Agriculture? Relief? Old age security? Regulation of business? Government finances? Currency?

FOLK SONGS FROM THE GREAT DEPRESSION

Poor people affected by the Great Depression often sang songs that reflected the suffering they had to endure. There were literally thousands of these songs that were heard at work, in Hoovervilles, on the road, and on radio. Most of these songs have no known author but were passed down from person to person. Others have their origins in ballads and legends American immigrants brought with them from Ireland, England, Germany, Italy, and other countries. The following songs were collected during the Great Depression by government workers and housed in the Library of Congress.

EVERY MAN A KING

Huey Long, the dominant politician in Louisiana who served as governor and United States Senator, like Franklin D. Roosevelt, was a master at radio. He understood the political uses of radio and employed it to advance his Share Our Wealth Plan. In 1935 he hired Castro Carrazo, the band director at Louisiana State University, to write a song depicting ideas found in the Share Our Wealth Plan. When Long was contemplating a run for the presidency in 1936, he declared that "Every Man a King" would be his campaign slogan and song. He even had it recorded on a national news reel by Ina Ray Hutton and her All Girl Orchestra.

Why weep or slumber America

Land of brave and true
With castles and clothing and food
for all
All belongs to you
Ev'ry man a King, ev'ry man a King
For you can be a millionaire
But there's something belonging to others
There's enough for all people to share
When its sunny June and December too
or in the Winter time or Spring
There'll be peace without end
Ev'ry neighbor a friend
With ev'ry man a King.

SOME MORE GREENBACK DOLLAR
(Unknown Author)

I don't want your little rag houses
I don't want your navy beans
All I want is a greenback dollar
For to buy some gasoline.

The scenery here is getting rusty
I'll go further up the line
Where the fields are green and purty
It will satisfy my mind.

We don't want to be a burden
On the people of this land
We just want to earn our money
And you people know we can.

So goodby my friends and neighbors
We are on the tramp
Many thanks to all officials
Of this migratory camp.

SUNNY CAL
(Unknown Author)

You all have heard the story
Of old Sunny Cal
The place where it never rains
They say it don't know how.

They say, Come on, you Okies,
Work is easy found
Bring along your cotton pack
You can pick the whole year round.

Get your money every night
Spread your blanket on the ground

It is always bright and warm
You can sleer right on the ground.

But listen to me Okies
I came out here one day
Spent all my money getting here
Now I can't get away.

THREE CROWS
(Unknown Author)

There were three crows that sat on a tree
They were as black as could be.

Said one crow unto his mate
What shall we do for meat to eat?

There is a horse in yonder field
Was by some cruel butcher slain.

We'll sit upon him in the sun
And pick his eyes out one by one.

Source: Library of Congress

HOW WELL DID YOU UNDERSTAND THIS SELECTION?

1. Why did Huey Long have "Every Man a King" written? What idea is he trying to convey with the song?

2. Who might have been the composer of "Some More Greenback Dollar" and "Sunny Cal"? What ideas do these songs reflect?

3. What problem from the Great Depression does the "Three Crows" address?

4. Do these songs have any common thread that connects them? If so, explain what it is.

The Federal Writers Project of the Works Progress Administration of the New Deal put unemployed writers to work doing various things. They wrote community histories, individual histories, and documented conditions during the Great Depression. Overall, the Federal Writers Project collected information that spans the years 1889 to 1942. The manuscripts below are part of a larger project entitled The American Memory Collection, which was itself part of the Folklore Project of the Federal Writers Project of the WPA. Both provide information on life for poor people during the Great Depression.

BEGGING
by Anne Winn Stevens

BEGGING REDUCED TO A SYSTEM

Four Garrett children, the oldest a girl of fifteen, huddled at the door of the principle's office in the public school. When asked why they had been absent from school for five weeks, the children could give no intelligible answer. The idea uppermost in their minds was that their mother had told them to ask for free lunches. They were scantily clad for a November day. Their clothers were clean, but they seemed to hae on little underclothing and to possess neither coats nor sweaters. Their shoes were full of holes. The group was obviously under-nourished, thin, pasty of complexion, anemic. One of the teachers said, "They look just like poor little rats."

The principle reached for the telephone. He called the State Aid worker assigned to the school. "Mrs. Holt look up the Garrett children; you know the address," he said. "Find out whay they have been absent from school for five weeks, and why they wish to be put on the free lunch list. They are always asking for something."

A few minutes later the worker parked her car near a large, yellow house on a sparsely settled street inhabited mostly by negroes. A muddy road led to it. On its door, a fly-specked, weather beaten, yellow card, hanging aslant, announced, "Quarantine, Measles." The small boy who stuck his head out at Mrs. Holt's knock was thickly broken out with a rash.

After a few minutes, Mrs. Garrett came out and stood with her visitor on the windy porch. She was a thin woman, about thirty-five years old, with a pasty complexion, and projecting teeth. Her hair was much too yellow-drug store gold. Although the morning was raw and cold she wore a thin, sleeveless summer dress and no wrap.

"Yes, I live here," she said, hugging herself to keep warm; "me and my husband and our six children live in three rooms, upstairs."

The Henson's, who are her parents, ant their youngest daughter and orphaned grandchildren occupy the lower floor.

She explained the children's absences. No they have had measles long ago; it was the children under school age who had it now. "My husband had been out of work for nine weeks," she declared. "When we was asked to leve the cabin whar we wuz living;" pointing to a tiny, log house in a hollow across the street, "we tuk the children and went to my brother's at Emma looking for work." That was five weeks ago.

"No'm, we didn't find no work. But my husband and me tuck in washin'. He'd go out and get the clothes, help me do them. Then he got back on WPA and we come back to Asheville." She explained that her husband had been on the WPA for some time. The project on which he was working "run out," as she put it. So he had been suspended until work could be found for him elsewhere.

"He has always been a hard worker," she maintained. He had worked in the mills. He had been a clerk in a grocery store at $12 a week. He had been a truck driver for the city, and for various transfer companies. Before the depression, he had made $20 a week.

"We lived real well then," she said. "But there wasn't as many of us."

But for the past few years he had worked mainly as an unskilled laborer on the WPA.

234

"He goes back to work tomorrow," she said. "After he gets his first pay check, we can get along. But we haven't had anything in the house to eat for a week now but two messes of flour and a peck of meal. The children has nothin' for breakfast but a biscuit or a slice of corn bread. They come home after school begging for food. But I can't give them but two meals a day. That's why I want to get free lunches."

So the family was given commodities by the welfare department; beans, flour, and dried milk. The school agreed to give them lunches, and a member of the parent-teacher association offered to find clothers and shoes for them.

Several weeks later, Mrs. Garrett, head tied up in a white cloth, was found trying to divert a fretful two-year old. The room was clean, but rather bare, with shappby linoleum on the floor. The bed was without sheets or pillow cases. But the mattress was covered by an unbleached coverslip. The blankets were clean, but mostly cotton.

"That's my baby," she said, indicating the two-year old. "He shore has had a hard time." She enumerted the illnesses of his two short years; diptheria, pneumonia, measles, and now an abscess in his ear. He had a bad cikd also, and a sore on his upper lip, which his mother wiped every now and then with a not-too-clean cotton cloth. Like the other children, he had too waxen a look.

"The doctor says as how he should have orange juice every day, and tomatoes and onions mashed with potatoes, but I don't have no money to buy them things for him. I ain't nothing to give him but cereal." However, she admitted some one was sending him milk every day. But she didn't know who.

She was still feeding the older children on biscuits, cornbread and now "white beans," but not bread and beans at the same meal. Christmas had been a great help to the family. "Nine dollars a week for eight people," she maintained nevertheless, "doesn't go far, after rent and coal has been paid for."

But they had "gotten" a bag of coal from a dealer, whose trucks her husband loaded on his way from work. Still, "It was mostly dust," she complained. "When it was poured into the stove it flew all over the room, until we was all sneezing."

The Christmas basket from a civic organization had helped. But again she said, "How long could five dollars worth of groceries last for eight people?"

However, she had profited by various Christman charities.

"I stood in line before Pender's Shoe Store two or three hours Christman morning. You know he allus gives away shoes on Christmas. I got three good pair for the children. And I got two of the boys into the dinner given by the Y.M.C.A. While I was waiting for them I went by the doctor's office and asked the nurse for a sample bottle of cod-liver oil for the baby. She gives me three bottles of it." she narrated.

It is easy to see where the Garrett children get their habit of always asking for something. As far as charitable organizations are concerned, their mother knows all the answers.

She enumerated her further needs. "You know," she said plaintively, "I ain't got but one sheet, no pillow cases, and only one towel, and I asked the Red Cross, and the welfare department both, for some. It looks like someone might give me a few towels; they are so cheap!"

Finally she admitted that she was seven months advanced in pregnancy, and as yet had no layette. "The Red Cross," she declared, "used to give lovely ones, all put up in a nice basket. "But," in an aggrieved tone, "they told me as how they didn't have any more."

But Mrs. Garrett, who says she completed only the third grade in school, and never learned "to figger," has found a neighbor who is quite sympathetic. "Mrs. Garrett, my husband has a good steady job," said the neighbor, "I guess I'm just plum licky; so I'll find you some of my baby's things that he don't need, or has outgrowed."

However, there is a shoemaker in the neighborhood who is wondering: "Where do you suppose Garrett got those six new shirts he sold me last week?" Can it be that the Garretts are making money off charitable organizations, or off sympathetic individuals?

When Mr. Garrett came in, he was asked about his WPA job, his wages, and his situation in general.

"I used to be a foreman, but now I'm just doing common labor, getting a little over $18 every pay period, whenever the weather is good enough to put in full time. Weather like this-we'll lose some time this month. That ain't much for eight people to live on, is it? A little over $9 a week. They used to give us Government food, but they won't give us anything now. One fellow down there is the cause of it all. When they get it in for you, there ain't nothing you can do. Who'd you say you was with?"

"The Federal Writer's Project."

"Well, the WPA and the welfare department ought to be cleaned up. You can't get a thing now. My wife is going to have another baby soon, and I can't get any clothers for it, or anything. They won't do a thing. They've just got it in for me, that's all. Why right over on the next street is a WPA foreman who gets Government food every week-and clothes-and he only has four children. They won't give me a thing. Tht boy there, now, has got a sore throat, and I can't get a thing for him."

"Don't the chidren get medical attention from the city authoritities, or the county?"

"No. They won't do nothing for anybody that ain't on relief. I have to just get whatever doctor I can."

"How is the house rented?"

"I rent the house for $15 a month, and the people downstirs pay $7.50 for their half."

"Do they pay regularly?"

"Yes; but they are going to move out next week, and I reckon we'll hae to move, too-then. The Wood Reality Company has got this house, and they're awful strict."

"Couldn't you rent the downstairs part to someone else?"

"Naw."

But Mrs. Garret, in the kitchen, at the same moment said, "Sure; there's somebody by here almost every day wants to rent a place." Mr. Garrett ignored this.

"They's only one bathroom in this house, and it's up here. I don't want strangers running in and out of my bathrom. They ain't no locks on none of the doors, either."

Indeed, ther are neither locks nor knobs, but each door has a string by which it is pulled open, or shut. However the radio, which was turned off to facilitate the conversation, is the very latest in design, and quite new. It came from one of the large mail-order houses that now maintain retail stores in principal cities, and it has the automatic features characteristic of the modern sets. The furniture, too, is of recent design, and not very old, but there is not much of it. Chairs are scarce, and there is no rug on the floor.

"Is your furniture paid for?"

"No, it ain't. They'll be taking that back, next."

"What will you do then?"

"Well, I don't know. Maybe I can get some more, somewhere."

"On credit?"

"Sure. I can't pay for no furniture."

"Do you buy other things on credit, too-that radio, for example?"

"Of course, I had to make a down payment on that, same as furniture, but you can't hardly get nop credit any-where else."

It was apparent from further conversation that he must have sought credit everywhere, practically, and, failing to obtain credit, asked for gifts, although he would not acknowledge this. All efforts to draw him out further were in vain. He would not admit receiving gifts, money, or help from private individuals or organization. He always returned to the complaint that the public agencies seemed to have it in for him, and would not give him anything, would not help him; while others, already more fortunate, were getting free food, clothes, medicine, etc. He said it was not easy, on his wages, to keep the electric power turned on, but they had oil lamps to use whenever the power was off. However, he missed the radio during those times.

AFTERNOON IN A PUSHCART PEDDLERS' COLONY
by Frank Byrd

It was snowing and, shortly after noontime, the snow changed to sleet and beat a tattoo against the rocks and board shacks that had been carelessly thrown together on the west bank of the Harlem. It was windy too and the cold blasts that came in from the river sent the men shivering for cover behind their shacks where some of them had built huge bonfires to ward off the icy chills that swept down from the hills above.

Some of them, unable to stand it any linger, went below into the crudely furnished cabins that were located in the holds of some old abandoned barges that lay half in, half our of the water. But the men did not seem to mind. Even the rotting barges afforded them some kind of shelter. It was certainly better than nothing, not to mention the fact that it was their home; address, the foot of 133rd Street at Park Avenue on the west bank of the Harlem River; depression residence of a little band of part-time pushcart peddlers whose cooperative colony is one of the most unique in the history of New York City.

These men earn their living by cruising the streets long before daylight, collecting old automobile parts, pasteboard, paper, rags, rubber, magazines, brass, iron, steel, old clother or anything they can find that is saleable as junk. They wheel their little pushcarts around exploring cellars, garbage cans and refuse heaps. When they have a load, they turn their footsteps in the direction of the American Junk Dealers, Inc., whose site of wholesale and retail operations is locted directly opposite the pushcart colony at 134th Street and Park Avenue. Of the fifty odd colonists, many are ex-carpenters, painters, brick-masons, auto-mechanics, upholsters, plumbers and even an artist or two.

Most of the things the men collect they sell, but once in a while they run across something useful to themselves, like auto parts, pieces of wire, or any electrical equipment, especially in view of the fact that there are two or three electrical engineers in the group.

Joe Elder, a tall, serious minded Negro, was the founder of the group that is officially known as the National Negro Civil Association. Under his supervision, electrically inclined members of the group set up a complete power plant that supplied all the barges and shacks with electric light. It was constructed with an old automobile engine and an electrical generator brought from the City of New York.

For a long time it worked perfectly. After awhile, when a city inspector came around, he condemned it and the shacks were temporarily without light. It was just as well, perhaps, since part of the colony was forced to vacate the site in order to make room for a mooring spot for a coal company that rented a section of the waterfront.

A rather modern and up-to-date community hall remains on the site, however. One section of it is known as the gymnasium and many pieces of apparatus are to be found there. There are also original oil paintings in the other sections known as the library and recreation room. Here, one is amazed (to say the least) by the comfortable divans, lounges, bookshelves and, of all things, a drinking fountain. The water is purchased from the City and pumped directly to the hall and barges by a homemade, electrically motored pump. In the recreation room there are also three pianos. On cold nights when the men want companionship and relaxation, they bring the women there and dance to the accompaniment of typical Harlem jazz...jazz that is also supplied by fellow colonists....

After being introduced to some of the boys, we went down into Oliver's barage. It was shaky, weather-beaten and sprawling, like the other half-dozen that surrounded it. Inside, he had set up an old iron range and attached a pipe to it that carried the smoke out and above the upper deck. On top of the iron grating that had been laid across the open hole on the back of the stove were some spare-ribs that had been generously seasoned with salt, pepper, sage and hot-sauce. Later I discovered a faint flavor of mace in them. The smell and pungency os spices filled the low ceilinged room with an appetizing aroma. The faces of the men were alight and hopeful with anticipation.

There was no real cause for worry, however, since Oliver had more than enough for everybody. Soon he began passing out tin plates for everyone. It makes my mouth water just to think of it. When we had gobbled up everything in sight, all of us sat back in restful contemplation puffing on our freshly lighted cigarettes. Afterwards there was conversation, things the men elected to talk about of their own accord.

"You know one thing," Oliver began, "ain't nothin' like a man being his own boss. Now take today, here we is wit' plenty to eat, ha'f a jug of co'n between us and nairy a woman to fuss aroun' wantin' to wash up dishes or mess aroun' befo' duh grub gits a chance to settle good."

"Dat sho is right," Evans Drake agreed. He was Oliver's helper when there were trucks to be repaired. "A 'oman ain't good fuh nuthin' but one thing."

The conversation drifted along until I was finally able to ease in a query or two. "Boys," I ventured, "how is it that none of you ever got on Home Relief? You can get a little grub out of it, at least, and that would take a little of the load off you, wouldn't it?"

At this they all rose up in unanimous protest.

"Lis'en," one of them said, "befo' I'd take Home Relief I'd go out in duh street an' hit some bastard oveh de haid an' take myse'f some'n'. I know one uv duh boys who tried to git it an' one of dem uppity little college boys ovah der talked tuh him lak he was some damn jailbird or some'n'. If it had been me, I'd a busted hell outn' him an' walked outa duh place. What duh hell do we wants wid relief anynow? We is all able-bodied mens an' can take it. We can make our own livin's."

This, apparently, was the attitude of every man there. They seemed to take fierce pride in the fact that every member of Joe Elder's National Negro Civil Association (it used to be called the National Negro Boat Terminal) was entirely self-supporting. They even had their own unemployment insurance fund that provided an income for any member of the group who was ill and unable to work. Each week the men give a small part of their earnings toward this common fund and automatically agree to allow a certain amount to any temporarily incapacitated member. In addition to that, they divide among themselves their ill brother's work and provide a day and night attendant near his shack if his illness is at all serious.

After chatting awhile longer with them, I finally decided to leave.

"Well boys," I said getting up, "I guess I'll have to be shoving off. Thanks, a lot, for the ribs. See you again sometime."

Before leaving, however, I gave them a couple of packs of cigarettes I had on me in part payment for my dinner.

"O. K." they said. "Come ovah ag'in some time. Some Sat'd'y. Maybe we'll have a few broads (women) and a little co'n."

"Thanks."

Outside the snow and sleet had turned to rain and the snow that had been feathery and white was running down the river bank in brown rivulets of slush and mud. It was a little warmer but the damp air still had a penetrating sharpness to it. I shuddered, wrapped my muffler a little tighter and turned my coat collar up about my ears.

There was wind in the rain, and behind me lay the jagged outline of the ramshackle dwelling. I hated to think of what it would be like, living in them when there was a scarcity of wood or when the fires went out.

Source: Library of Congress Web Page http://rs6.loc.gov/wpaintro/wpahome.html

HOW WELL DID YOU UNDERSTAND THIS SELECTION?

1. Compare life in urban and rural America during the Great Depression. How is it similar? How is it different?

2. Compare the attitudes of the characters in "Beggin" with those in the Harlem pushcart colony? How are they similar? How are they different?

3. Do you think the experiences of the Garrett family are typical of people in the rural South during the Great Depression? Why or why not?

4. Are the experiences of urban dwellers similar to those detailed in "Afternoon in a Pushcart Peddlers' Colony"? Why or why not?

5. How did the Garrett family survive?

6. How did push cart people suvive?

<hr>
<hr>

THE TOWNSEND PLAN

<hr>
<hr>

Dr. Charles Townsend was a critic of the New Deal. He believed Roosevelt's program did not do enough to address the problems of old age and unemployment. He devised a plan to provide every elderly American with a pension upon retirement contingent upon their spending the money within thirty days. Townsend believed that the retirement of elderly citizens would make room for younger people in the workforce and the pension they received would stimulate the economy through consumer spending, thus creating full employment. Most historians believe Townsend's criticism of the New Deal played a role in the creation of Social Security.

THE TOWNSEND PLAN IN BRIEF

Have the National Government enact legislation to the effect that all citizens of the United States-man or woman-over the age of 60 years may retire on a pension of $200 per month on the following conditions:

1. That they engage in no further labor, business or profession for gain.
2. That their past life is free from habitual criminality.
3. That they take oath to, and actually do spend, within the confines of the United States, the entire amount of their pension within thirty days after receiving same.

Have the National Government create the revolving fund by levying a general sales tax; have the rate just high enough to produce the amount necessary to keep the Old Age Revolving Pensions Fund adequate to pay the monthly pensions.

Have the act so drawn that such sales tax can only be used for the Old Age Revolving Pensions Fund.

ANALYSIS OF THE TOWNSEND PLAN

Insurance statistics show that only 8% of people reaching that age have achieved financial success to such a degree that they may live comfortably thereafter without depending upon further earnings. Eighty-five percent of the 92% of all people sixty years of age and over are still employed or are endeavoring in some manner to earn all or a part of their livelihood and the remainder are dependent upon public or private charity for their keep. Those of the 85% who are still earning are capable of producing only enough to partially pay for their living. A very small percentage actually earn enough for their total needs and but vary few earn any surplus for their declining years.

Approximately 8,000,000 people will be eligible to apply for the pension. Economists estimate that each person spending $200.00 per month creates a job for one additional worker. The retirement of all citizens of 60 years and over from all productive industry and gainful occupation, will thereby create jobs for 8,000,000 workers which will solve our national labor problem.

RETIREMENT ON A MONTHLY PENSION OF $200

The spending of $200 per month is for a constructive purpose. First, to place an adequate amount of buying power in the hands of these citizens which will permit them to satisfy their wants that have been so restricted for the past four years. Second, to create such a demand for new goods of all descriptions that all manufacturing plants in the country will be called upon to start their wheels of production at full speed and provide jobs for all workers.

This money made suddenly available to the channels of trade will immediately start a tremendous flood of buying, since the country has been on short commodity rations for the past four years, and since all sections of the country will be affected alike (the old are everywhere) and the poorest sections will at once become important buying centers.

All factories and avenues of production may be expected to start producing at full capacity and all workers called into activity at high wages, since there will be infinitely more jobs available and many less workers to fill the jobs, the old folks having retired from competition for places as producers.

HOW WILL THIS MONEY BE SPENT

It will go into the regular channels of trade for food, clothing, homes, rent, furniture, automobiles-all manner and description of things dear to the human heart. It will go for travel, the pleasure of riding hobbies, theatre tickets, professional and servant employment and the thousand and one things which modern man demands.

HOW WILL THIS EFFECT THE OWNERS OF PROPERTY OR BUSINESS

Those of 60 years and over owning income property, whose income is greater than the pension, would not need or possibly care to apply for this pension, as it is not designed to be compulsory. Those whose income is less than the pension, undoubtedly would dispose of their interests in income investment to younger people and receive the pension for their declining years. Thus performing the two-fold function that the plan provides, that of relieving industry of their productiveness and increasing industry through their consumption of goods and farm products.

Establishment of homes by those now living with relatives or in institutions, either through ownership or rental, or the holding of homes, now occupied, are encouraged under this plan. Each new home established simply means greater consumption of goods and use of labor.

This plan will effect a marked reduction in the tax burden which they are now compelled to carry and make more secure the profits that should accrue from business and property investment, since it will be less expensive to collect and spend two billions of money monthly than it is to maintain the monthly present-day costs of organized charity in its multiple forms, plus much of the cost of crime and disease due to overcrowding and undernourishment. It will add immensely to the volume of business done and thereby make possible profits in greater amount without increasing the cost of goods.

PENSIONERS TO RETIRE WITHOUT FURTHER GAIN FROM LABOR OR PROFESSION

This is an important feature of the plan since the idea is to create jobs for the young and able, eliminating competition for such jobs and positions on the part of elderly people.

Consumption of the products of farm and factory is the vital problem now facing our nation. The success of this plan is based entirely on the creation of jobs of production and by retiring all those pensioned, with adequate spending power, that they may consume for all their needs in comforts, necessities and pleasure.

RECORDS FREE FROM CRIME

This clause is designed to have a strong effect in restraining the young and impatient from taking the short cut of criminal activity to obtain money. They will hesitate to jeopardize their future welfare for the sake of getting money now by criminal activities.

The desire to honestly earn is uppermost in the minds of American people. The records of our law enforcement departments show that crime is largely the result of lack of opportunity to provide necessities of life through the sale of labor. Provide these opportunities for our younger generations and the crime problem will be greatly lessened.

SAVING FOR OLD AGE

We have been taught in the past that saving was essential in planning for security in old age. But recent experience has taught us that no one has yet been able to devise a sure method of saving. Statistical records show that ninety-two percent of all people reaching the age of sixty-five have, in spite of their best efforts, been unable to save enough to guard them from the humiliation of accepting charity in some form, either from relatives or from the state. Experience proves that no form of investment is infallible that human mind can devise which is based upon the small group or individual financing. The Townsend plan proposes that all who serve society to the best of their ability in whatever capacity shall not be denied that security in their declining years to which their services in active years have entitled them.

COSTS OF MAINTAINING THE HUGH REVOLVING FUND

The unthinking see a great increase in the cost of living due to the necessity for the retailer to raise his prices to meet the government tax for maintaining the pension roll. He fails to take into consideration the fact that the elimination of poor houses, organized state and county relief agencies, public and private pension systems, community chests, etc., are not costing the country the many millions of dollars per month that the Townsend plan would eliminate. And, too, would not the cost of crime and insane asylums be greatly reduced after the public became assured of the permanency of our prosperity? Further, the tremendous increase in the volume of retail business which this hugh revolving fund would insure makes certain that bigger profits would be possible to the retailer through his old rates than ever before and make unnecessary the advance in prices on any articles except those classed as luxuries. Estimated from the sources available a tax of 10% will be ample to raise this fund and the tax can be materially lowered as the volume of trade increases. Competition will still continue to operate and the profit hog will still find competitors who will hold him to a fair price rate. It is the logical foundation for our worthy President's NRA-National Recovery Act.

No one will object to paying the slight advance in price for commodities for the purpose of re-establishing prosperity and, in so doing, making it possible for the elderly people to retire and live comfortably the remainder of their days, since everyone in making his purchases will be providing for his own security when he reaches the age of sixty.

SALES TAX TO BE USED EXCLUSIVELY FOR THE PENSIONS

It is the intent of the plan to apply the sales tax solely to the one purpose of maintaining the pensions roll until such time as the public becomes fully assured of the beneficent and fair system of taxation for all that can be devised. Every individual who enjoys the benefits of the numerous social agencies maintained for his benefit, such as schools, police protection, sanitation, public health supervision and the thousand and one functions of government, should be compelled to carry his share of the costs just in proportion to his ability to do so; that is, in proportion to his ability to spend money. This compels the child to become a taxpayer at an early age and accustoms him to the idea that he must do his share throughout his life.

NO CHANGE IN FORM OF GOVERNMENT

This plan of Old Age Revolving Pensions interferes in no way with our present form of government, profit system of business or change of specie in our economic setup. It is a simple American plan dedicated to the cause of prosperity and the abolition of poverty. It retains the rights of freedom of speech and of press and of religious belief and insures us the right to perpetuate and make glorious the liberty we so cherish and enjoy.

THE MEANING OF SECURITY TO HUMANITY

Here lies the true value in the Townsend Plan. Humanity will be forever relieved from the fear of destitution and want. The seeming need for sharp practices and greedy accumulation will disappear. Benevolence and kindly consideration for others will displace suspicion and avarice, brotherly love and tolerance will blossom into full flower and the genial sun of human happiness will dissipate the dark clouds of distrust and gloom and despair

---

CARTOONS THAT APPEARED IN THE TOWNSEND WEEKLY ON MAY 25, 1940

This cartoon, from the Townsend Plan's "Weekly" newspaper, expresses the group's continuing dissatisfaction with the Social Security program. In their view, the Social Security Act was an obstacle to passage of their own plan.

This cartoon, from the Townsend Plan's "Weekly" newspaper, expresses the group's main objection to Social Security—that it was not generous enough in the benefits it offered. The Townsend Plan promised every senior citizen $200 per month, regardless of past earnings. Under the social insurance program of the Social Security Act a worker whose earnings averaged $100 month for 40 years would collect a Social Security retirement benefit of only $35 month. This gave the Townsend Plan an immediate appeal, which is reflected in the cartoon. (Keep in mind, however, that economists estimated it would require one-half of the nation's total income to fund the level of benefits promised by Townsend!)

Source: Web Pages of Social Security Administration
http://www.ssa.gov/history/townbrief.html (http://www.ssa.gov/history/towns46.html)

HOW WELL DID YOU UNDERSTAND THIS SELECTION?

1. What are Dr. Townsend's objectives?

2. How does he propose to fund his pensions?

3. What effect does Dr. Townsend think his plan will have on crime?

4. Why does Dr. Townsend want to require elderly citizens to spend their pension within thirty days?

5. What problems do you find with the Townsend Plan?

SELF TEST

MULTIPLE CHOICE: Circle the correct response. The correct answers are given at the end.

1. Roosevelt's plan to combat the Great Depression was called:
    a. The New Frontier.
    b. The Great Society.
    c. The New Freedom.
    d. The New Deal.

2. Huey Long's plan to have the government guarantee every American a basic income and ownership of property was called:
    a. The Townsend Plan.
    b. Share the Wealth Plan.
    c. The Income/Property Plan.
    d. Social Security.

3. The National Labor Relations Act provided:
    a. A minimum wage.
    b. That the government would enforce collective bargaining rights.
    c. The Open Shop.
    d. Time and a half.

4. People from the Midwest and Southwest who came to California in search of economic opportunity during the Great Depression were called:
    a. Texarkanas.
    b. Okies.
    c. Forty-niners.
    d. Middies.

5. What did Dr. Charles Townsend advocate?
    a. A return to pure capitalism.
    b. An end to the New Deal.
    c. Prenatal care for pregnant women.
    d. A retirement pension for elderly Americans.

6. How did Townsend propose to pay for his plan?
    a. By taxing the wealthy.
    b. By imposing a sales tax.
    c. By redistributing the nation's wealth.
    d. By printing paper money not backed by gold.

7. Which of the following statements best describes President Hoover's attitude about the Great Depression?
    a. Government should not help with relief and suffering.
    b. Government should establish social programs to provide jobs for unemployed Americans.
    c. Congress should issue food stamps to help those who can't help themselves.
    d. Congress should tax the wealthy to pay for social programs to combat the Great Depression.

8. What effect did Eleanor Roosevelt have on the position of First Lady?
   a. She had little effect.
   b. She continued the tradition of past First Ladies, making no changes.
   c. She broke with tradition and exerted a strong influence on the President and the nation.
   d. She made the position of First Lady one that stressed traditional feminine values of home and husband.

9. What did the Agricultural Adjustment Act do?
   a. Provide loans to farmers to prevent mortgage foreclosures.
   b. Gave cash allotments to farmers who cut production of tobacco, wheat, corn, cotton, hogs, rice and dairy products.
   c. Gave farmers the right to sell their products directly to food processors and raised incomes by cutting out the middleman.
   d. Forced landowners to rent to tenant farmers.

10. Who was the Republican candidate Franklin Roosevelt defeated in the 1936 election?
   a. Huey Long.
   b. Charles Townsend.
   c. Herbert Hoover.
   d. Alf Landon.

ANSWERS: 1-d; 2-b; 3-b; 4-b; 5-d; 6-a; 7-a; 8-c; 9-b; 10-d

ESSAYS:

1. How did the Great Depression and New Deal shape modern America?

2. Did Roosevelt and the New Deal save capitalism? Support your answer with historical evidence.

3. Compare and contrast the approach critics of the New Deal used to oppose Roosevelt's plan.

OPTIONAL ACTIVITIES: (Use your knowledge **and** imagination.)

1. Imagine that you are an Okie. Compose several entries in your journal in which you describe the difficulties you face as a result of the Great Depression.

2. Interview someone in the United States who lived through the Great Depression. How do his/her experiences compare with what you have learned in your history class.

3. Search newspapers during the Great Depression for political cartoons. Use them to show the view Americans had of the New Deal.

WEB SITE LISTINGS:

Federal Writer's Project Collection.
   A collection of the Library of Congress 2,900 life history manuscripts from the Folklore Project of the Federal Writer's Project, 1936-1940. http://memory.loc.gov/ammem/wpaintro/wpahome.html
Dear Mrs. Roosevelt.
   Information and statistics about the Great Depression. This site contains letters from children written to Eleanor Roosevelt and her responses. http://newdeal.feri.org/eleanor/index.htm

Federal Theatre Project Collection.
This site contains original documents for the WPA Federal Theatre Project, an effort by the WPA to produce theater events. http://memory.loc.gov/ammem/fedtp/wpa.html

Songs of the Great Depression.
Lyrics to popular Derpession era songs, including "We're in the Money" and "Brother, Can You Spare a Dime?" are found at this site. http://www.library.csi.cuny.edu/dept/history/lavender/cherries.html

Documenting America.
Images from the Farm Security Administration taken by government photographers. http://rs6.loc.gov/ammem/fsowhome.html

WebQuest 1930s.
Offers access to sites related to 1930s history and society. Features links to biographies, timelines, and events of the Great Depression. http://www.nde.state.ne.us/SS/1930.html

New Deal Network
New Deal Network is a database of photographs, political cartoons, and texts (speeches, letters, and other historic documents) from the New Deal period. newdeal.feri.org

Great Depression & New Deal
Provides links to various sources on the Great Depression and the New Deal americanhistory.about.com/cs/greatdepression

Great Depression of the 1930's History Guide
Covers a variety of topics, including a Great Depression of the 1930's History Guide with top history re sources, timelines, FDR, Hoover and more! history.searchbeat.com/greatdepression.htm

New Deal/WPA Art Project
Provides a look at the WPA Art Project. www.wpamurals.com

Franklin D. Roosevelt Library & Museum Photos of FDR
Offers photographs of FDR and other people important in the New Deal. www.fdrlibrary.marist.edu/gdphotos.html

Depression and New Deal
Provedes access to photographs of the Great Depression and New Deal housed by the Library of Congress. homepages.ius.edu/Special/OralHistory/GreatDepression2.htm

Picturing the Century : The Great Depression and the New Deal
An exhibition of 20th century photographs from the holdings of the National Archives and Records Administration. www.archives.gov/exhibit_hall/picturing_the_century/galleries/greatdep...

Labor Unions During the Great Depression and New Deal
The Library of Congress home Overview Documents relating to labor unions and strikes during the Great Depression. lcweb2.loc.gov/ammem/ndlpedu/features/timeline/depwwii/unions/unions.h...

Photographs of the Great Depression
A large compilation of photos from the Great Depression, including photos of dust storms, farm foreclosures, migrant workers, women and children, unemployed, and breadlines and soup kitchens, Unemployed Workers Marching in New Jersey, etc. history1900s.about.com/library/photos/blyindexdepression.htm

Chapter Twenty

THE "GOOD" WAR:
World War II

The Japanese attack on Pearl Harbor thrust the United States directly into war following the most devastating economic depression the country had faced. Unlike previous wars America had fought, practically the entire population supported entrance into World War II. The totalitarian governments of Germany, Japan, and Italy were viewed as dangerous to world peace, prosperity, and order. When the conflict broke out between Germany, France, and England in 1939 President Franklin D. Roosevelt was determined that the United States would be prepared for a conflict he thought the country could not avoid. Roosevelt also openly supported England because he feared the growing power of Nazi Germany. Following his election to an unprecedented third term in 1940, Roosevelt secured from Congress passage of the Lend Lease Act that allowed the United States to supply England with ships, planes, tanks, and other weapons for use against Germany. These and other American supplies were vital to the English victory over Germany in the Battle of Britain, which ensured that England would not be invaded and would survive until the United States officially entered the conflict.

For the first time in history the United States had to fight two wars simultaneously—one against the Japanese in the Pacific and another against Germany and Italy in Europe. Roosevelt and England's new Prime Minister Winston Churchill, even before America's entry into World War II, had decided to focus most of their war effort in Europe because they viewed Germany as a much greater threat than Japan. Thus, in the early years of the conflict the United States fought a holding war against Japan in the Pacific. After softening up Nazi forces by delivering blows to the "soft underbelly" in Italy and the Balkans, Roosevelt and Churchill decided to deliver a knock-out blow to German forces in western Europe. On June 6, 1944, General Dwight David Eisenhower authorized the D-Day invasion. American, British, and Canadian troops stormed the beaches at Normandy, France in the largest amphibious military operation in world history and began driving Nazi forces from France.

Following the surrender of Nazi Germany in May 1945, the United States and England turned their full military might on Japan. General Douglas MacArthur initiated a strategy known as island-hopping that isolated and drove Japanese forces from the numerous islands they occupied. The war against Japan was won in August 1945 after President Harry Truman (Roosevelt died in April 1945) authorized use of atomic bombs on the Japanese cities of Hiroshima and Nagasaki. Shortly after use of the bomb on Nagasaki, Japan surrendered and the Second World War officially ended.

World War II changed American history forever. The Allied victory was largely made possible by America's industrial might. Millions of Americans served directly in the military or worked in war industries. Mobilization of America's factories for war ended the Great Depression as jobs became plentiful. Countless thousands of women entered the workforce reserved for males. The tremendous demand for products by the military created a severe shortage of consumer goods within the United States. Roosevelt and the government dealt with the shortages by instituting massive recycling programs and issuing ration coupons allowing Americans to purchase limited quantities of scarce goods.

President Roosevelt was instrumented in creating the United Nations, a new international agency that replaced the League of Nations and that was designed to keep world peace. The U.N. would be caught up in the Cold War between the United States and the Soviet Union that followed World War II. These two superpowers dominated the world for the next half century and the United States found it impossible to return to its tradition of isolation from world affairs that had largely been the norm prior to the outbreak of World War II.

IDENTIFICATION: Briefly describe each term.

Adolf Hitler

Axis Alliance

Munich Conference

Neville Chamberlain

Appeasement

Winston Churchill

Franklin D. Roosevelt

Josef Stalin

Harry Truman

Blitzkrieg

Lend Lease

Douglas MacArthur

Dwight David Eisenhower

Pearl Harbor

Manhattan Project

Holocaust

Tuskegee Airman

D-Day

Island Hopping

Soft Underbelly

Hiroshima

Nagasaki

WAC

WAVE

WASP

War Production Board

Office of War Information

Rosie the Riveter

Yalta Conference

Potsdam Conference

V-E Day

V-J Day

Neutrality Acts

Nazi-Soviet Pact

Detroit Riot of 1943

"Zoot suit" Riots

Koregmatsu v. United States

THINK ABOUT:

1. Could German, Italian, and Japanese aggression have been halted during the 1930s? Why or why not?

2. Could a change in America's policy of isolation during the 1930s have prevented World War II? Explain?

3. Was use of the atomic bombs on Hiroshima and Nagasaki necessary to end the war in the Pacific? Why or why not?

4. Were democratic nations in Europe and North America powerless to stop the Holocaust? Explain?

5. Discuss the violation of civil liberties in the United States during World War II.

ROOSEVELT'S NEW INTERNATIONALISM

For most of its history, the United States had generally been isolated from international affairs and events. With the exception of imperialism and participation in World War I, American leaders generally followed George Washington's advice in his Farewell Address to remain aloof from entangling European Alliances and the wars they produced. This situation changed as a result of Nazi aggression throughout Europe that engulfed the continent in the Second World War. Franklin Roosevelt, in his "Four Freedoms" speech in January 1941 and in the Atlantic Charter agreement with England in August 1941 concluded that the United States could no longer remain isolated in a world threatened by totalitarianism. FDR understood that totalitarian aggression directly threatened the United States in a global world and that as the world's bastion of democracy, the U.S. had a moral duty to oppose totalitarianism in all its forms.

Roosevelt's "Four Freedoms" Speech, January 6, 1941

...Every realist knows that the democratic way of life is at this moment being directly assailed in every part of the world-assailed either by arms, or by secret spreading of poisonous propaganda by those who seek to destroy unity and promote discord in nations still at peace. During sixteen months this assault has blotted out the whole pattern of democratic life in an appalling number of independent nations, great and small. The assailants are still on the march, threatening other nations, great and small ....

As men do not live by bread alone, they do not fight by armaments alone. Those who man our defenses, and those behind them who build our defenses, must have the stamina and courage which come from an unshakable belief in the manner of life which they are defending. The mighty action which they are calling for cannot be based on a disregard of all things worth fighting for.

The Nation takes great satisfaction and much strength from the things which have been done to make its people conscious of their individual stake in the preservation of democratic life in America. Those things have toughened the fibre of our people, have renewed their faith and strengthened their devotion to the institutions we make ready to protect. Certainly this is no time to stop thinking about the social and economic problems which are the root cause of the social revolution which is today a supreme fact in the world.

There is nothing mysterious about the foundations of a healthy and strong democracy. The basic things expected by our people of their political and economic system are simple. They are: equality of opportunity for youth and for others: jobs for those who can work; security for those who need it; the ending of special privilege for the few, the preservation of civil liberties for all; the enjoyment of the fruits of scientific progress in a wider and constantly rising standard of living.

These are the simple and basic things that must never be lost sight of in the turmoil and unbelievable complexity of our modern world. The inner and abiding strength of our economic and political systems is dependent upon the degree to which they fulfill these expectations.

Many subjects connected with our social economy call for immediate improvement. As examples: We should bring more citizens under the coverage of old age pensions and unemployment insurance. We should widen the opportunities for adequate medical care. We should plan a better system by which persons deserving or needing gainful employment may obtain it.

I have called for personal sacrifice. I am assured of the willingness of almost all Americans to respond to that call ....

In the future days, which we seek to make secure, we look forward to a world founded upon four essential human freedoms.

The first is freedom of speech and expression-everywhere in the world.

The second is freedom of every person to worship God in his own way—everywhere in the world.

The third is freedom from want-which, translated into world terms, means economic understandings which will secure to every nation a healthy peace time life for its inhabitants—everywhere in the world.

The fourth is freedom from fear-which, translated into world terms, means a worldwide reduction of armaments to such a point and in such a thorough fashion that no nation will be in a position to commit an act of physical aggression against any neighbor-anywhere in the world.

That is no vision of a distant millennium. It is a definite basis for a kind of world attainable in our own time and generation. That kind of world is the very antithesis of the so-called new order of tyranny which the dictators seek to create with the crash of a bomb.

To that new order we oppose the greater conception—the moral order. A good society is able to face schemes of world domination and foreign revolutions alike without fear.

Since the beginning of our American history we have been engaged in change in a perpetual peaceful revolution-a revolution which goes on steadily, quietly adjusting itself to changing conditions-without the concentration camp or the quicklime in the ditch. The world order which we seek is the cooperation of free countries, working together in a friendly, civilized society.

This nation has placed its destiny in the hands and heads and hearts of its millions of free men and women; and its faith in freedom under the guidance of God. Freedom means the supremacy of human rights everywhere. Our support goes to those who struggle to gain those rights or keep them. Our strength is in our unity of purpose.

To that high concept there can be no end save victory.

Source: Franklin D. Roosevelt, Annual Message to Congress, January 6, 1941. Quoted from *The Public Papers of F. D. Roosevelt*, vol. 9, p. 663. Washington, D.C.: United States Government Printing Office.

The Atlantic Charter, August 14, 1941

The President of the United States of America and the Prime Minister, Mr. Churchill, representing His Majesty's Government in the United Kingdom, being met together, deem it right to make known certain common principles in the national policies of their respective countries on which they base their hopes for a better future for the world.

First, their countries seek no agrandizement, territorial or other;

Second, they desire to see no territorial changes that do not accord with the freely expressed wishes of the peoples concerned;

Third, they respect the right of all peoples to choose the form of government under which they will live; and they wish to see sovereign rights and self government restored to those who have been forcibly deprived of them;

Fourth, they will endeavor, with due respect for their existing obligations, to further the enjoyment by all States, great or small, victor or vanquished, of access, on equal terms, to the trade and to the raw materials of the world which are needed for their economic prosperity;

Fifth, they desire to bring about the fullest collaboration between all nations in the economic field with the object of securing, for all, improved labor standards, economic advancement and social security;

Sixth, after the final destruction of the Nazi tyranny, they hope to see established a peace which will afford to all nations the means of dwelling in safety within their own boundaries, and which will afford assurance that all the men in all the lands may live out their lives in freedom from fear and want;

Seventh, such a peace should enable all men to traverse the high seas and oceans without hindrance:

Eighth, they believe that all of the nations of the world, for realistic as well as spiritual reasons must come to the abandonment of the use of force. Since no future peace can be maintained if land, sea or air armaments continue to be employed by nations which threaten, or may threaten, aggression outside of their frontiers, they believe, pending the establishment of a wider and permanent system of general security, that the disarmament of such nations is essential. They will likewise aid and encourage all other practicable measures which will lighten for peace-loving peoples the crushing burden of armaments.

Franklin D. Roosevelt
Winston S. Churchill

Source: *The Public Papers of F. D. Roosevelt*, vol. 10, p. 314. Washington, D.C.: United States Government Printing Office.

HOW WELL DID YOU UNDERSTAND THIS SELECTION?

1. What are the Four Freedoms Roosevelt highlights?

2. Compare and contrast ideas in the Four Freedoms speech with those in the Atlantic Charter.

3. How did Americans in 1941 receive ideas expressed in the Four Freedoms speech and in the Atlantic Charter?

4. What did FDR think was necessary for democracy to survive?

December 7, 1941 was, according to Franklin Roosevelt, "a date which will live in infamy." On that day the Empire of Japan carried out an attack on Pearl Harbor, an American naval base in the Hawaiian Islands. This attack, which contrary to popular perception was neither a surprise nor unprovoked, thrust the United States into World War II. President Roosevelt addressed Congress to secure a declaration of war against Japan. Shortly thereafter, Germany, invoking a previous treaty with Japan, declared war on the United States.

Address to Congress (1941)
Franklin D. Roosevelt

Yesterday, December 7, 1941—a date which will live in infamy—the United States of America was suddenly and deliberately attacked by naval and air forces of the Empire of Japan.

The United States was at peace with that nation and, at the solicitation of Japan, was still in conversation with its Government and its Emperor looking toward the maintenance of peace in the Pacific. Indeed, one hour after Japanese air squadrons had commenced bombing in Oahu, the Japanese Ambassador to the United States and his colleague delivered to the Secretary of State a formal reply to a recent American message. While this reply stated that it seemed useless to continue the existing diplomatic negotiations, it contained no threat or hint of war or armed attack.

It will be recorded that the distance of Hawaii from Japan makes it obvious that the attack was deliberately planned many days or even weeks ago. During the intervening time the Japanese Government has deliberately sought to deceive the United States by false statements and expressions of hope for continued peace.

The attack yesterday on the Hawaiian Islands has caused severe damage to American naval and military forces. Very many American lives have been lost. In addition American ships have been reported torpedoed on the high seas between San Francisco and Honolulu.

Yesterday the Japanese Government also launched an attack against Malaya. Last night Japanese forces attacked Hong Kong. Last night Japanese forces attacked Guam. Last night Japanese force's attacked the Philippine Islands. Last night the Japanese attacked Wake Island. This morning the Japanese attacked Midway Island.

Japan has, therefore, undertaken a surprise offensive extending throughout the Pacific area. The facts of yesterday speak for themselves. The people of the United States have already formed their opinions and well understand the implications to the very life and safety of our nation.

As Commander-in-Chief of the Army and Navy, I have directed that all measures be taken for our defense.

Always will we remember the character of the onslaught against us.

No matter how long it may take us to overcome this premeditated invasion, the American people in their righteous might will win through to absolute victory

I believe I interpret the will of the Congress and of the people when I assert that we will not only defend ourselves to the uttermost but will make very certain that this form of treachery shall never endanger us again.

Hostilities exist. There is no blinking at the fact that our people, our territory and our interests are in grave danger.

With confidence in our armed forces—with the unbounded determination of our people—we will gain the inevitable triumph-so help us God.

I ask that the Congress declare that since the unprovoked and dastardly attack by Japan on Sunday, December seventh, a state of war has existed between the United States and the Japanese Empire.

Source: The *New York Times*, December 9, 1941

HOW WELL DID YOU UNDERSTAND THIS SELECTION?

1. How does Roosevelt justify a declaration of war against Japan?

2. What is the meaning of the phrase "a date which will live in infamy."?

3. How do you think the American public reacted to Roosevelt's speech?

4. How does Roosevelt portray the Japanese attack on Pearl Harbor? Are his views accurate? Why or why not?

INTERNMENT OF JAPANESE AMERICANS

The Japanese attack on Pearl Harbor alarmed most Americans. They were particularly concerned about the large number of Americans whose ancestry was Japanese living along the west coast. Racism and prejudice caused Americans to believe that Japanese Americans would aid Japanese forces if they decided to invade California or another western coastal state. Western residents became fanatical, and Franklin Roosevelt reluctantly signed an executive order allowing the government to forcefully relocate Japanese Americans living in the west to concentration camps. Conditions in the camps were crowded and less than desirable, but the United Supreme Court upheld the legality of Roosevelt's Action in 1944.

Conditions in the Camps (1942-1945)

A visiting reporter from The San Francisco Chronicle described quarters at Tule Lake:

Room size—about 15 by 25, considered too big for two reporters.
Condition—dirty.
Contents—two Army cots, each with two Army blankets, one pillow, some sheets and pillow cases (these came as a courtesy from the management), and a coal-burning stove (no coal). There were no dishes, rugs, curtains, or housekeeping equipment of any kind. (We had in addition one sawhorse and three pieces of wood, which the management did not explain.)

The furnishings at other camps were similar. At Minidoka, arriving evacuees found two stacked canvas cots, a pot-bellied stove and a light bulb hanging from the ceiling; at Topaz, cots, two blankets, a pot-bellied stove and some cotton mattresses. Rooms had no running water, which had to be carried from community facilities. Running back and forth from the laundry room to rinse and launder soiled diapers was a particular inconvenience ....

Others, however, found not even the minimal comforts that had been planned for them. An unrealistic schedule combined with wartime shortages of labor and materials meant that the WRA (Wartime Relocation Administration) had difficulty meeting its construction schedule. In most cases, the barracks" were completed, but at some centers evacuees lived without electric light, adequate toilets or laundry facilities ....

Mess Halls planned for about 300 people had to handle 600 or 900 for short periods. Three months after the project opened, Manzanar still lacked equipment for 16 of 36 messhalls. At Gila:

There were 7,700 people crowded into space designed for 5,000. They were housed in messhalls, recreation halls, and even latrines. As many as 25 persons lived in a space intended for four.

As at the assembly centers, one result was that evacuees were often denied privacy in even the most intimate aspects of their lives .... Even when families had separate quarters, the partitions between rooms failed to give much privacy. Gladys Bell described the situation at Topaz:

[T]he evacuees . . . had only one room, unless there were around ten in the family. Their rooms had a pot-bellied stove, a single electric light hanging from the ceiling, an Army cot for each person and a blanket for the bed. Each barrack had six rooms with only three flues. This meant that a hole had to be cut through the wall of one room for the stovepipe to join the chimney of the next room. The hole was large so that the wall would not burn. As a result, everything said and some things whispered were easily heard by people living in the next room. Sometimes the family would be a couple with four children living next to an older couple, perhaps of a different religion, older ideas and with a difference in all ways of life—such as music.

Despite these wretched conditions the evacuees again began to rebuild their lives. Several evacuees recall "foraging for bits of wallboard and wood" and dodging guards to get materials from the scrap lumber piles to build shelves and furniture .... Eventually, rooms were partitioned and shelves, tables, chairs and other furniture appeared. Paint and cloth for curtains and spreads came from mail order houses at evacuee expense. Flowers bloomed and rock gardens emerged; trees and shrubs were planted. Many evacuees grew victory gardens. One described the change:

[W]hen we entered camp, it was a barren desert. When we left camp, it was a garden that had been built up without tools, it was green around the camp with vegetation, flowers, and also with artificial lakes, and that's how we left it.

The success of evacuees' efforts to improve their surroundings, however, was always tempered by the harsh climate. In the western camps, particularly Heart Mountain, Poston, Topaz and Minidoka, dust was a principal problem. Monica Sone described her first day at Minidoka:

[W]e were given a rousing welcome by a dust storm....We felt as if we were standing in a gigantic sand-mixing machine as the sixty mile gale lifted the loose earth up into the sky, obliterating everything. Sand filled our mouths and nostrils and stung our faces and hands like a thousand darting needles. Henry and Father pushed on ahead while Mother, Sumi and I followed, hanging onto their jackets, banging suitcases into each other. At last we staggered into our room, gasping and blinded. We sat on our suitcases to rest, peeling off our jackets and scarves. The window panels rattled madly, and the dust poured through the cracks like smoke. Now and then when the wind subsided, I saw other evacuees, hanging on to their suitcases, heads bent against the stinging dust. The wind whipped their scarves and towels from their heads and zipped them out of sight.

In desert camps, the evacuees met severe extremes of temperature as well. In winter it reached 35 degrees below zero and summers brought temperature as high as 115°. Because the desert did not cool off at night, evacuees would splash water on their cots to be cool enough to sleep. Rattlesnakes and desert wildlife added danger to discomfort.

The Arkansas camps had equally unpleasant weather. Winters were cold and snowy while summers were unbearably hot and humid, heavy with chiggers and clouds of mosquitos ....

Source: Commission on Wartime Relocation and Internment of Civilians, *Personal Justice Denied* (Washington, D.C. Government Printing Office, 1984), pp. 159-161.

Korematsu v. U.S.: The Majority Opinion

The petitioner, an American citizen of Japanese descent, was convicted in a federal district court for remaining in San Leandro, California, a "Military Area," contrary to Civil Exclusion Order No. 34, of the Commanding General of the Western Command, U.S. Army, which directed that after May 9, 1942, all persons of Japanese ancestry should be excluded from that area....

It should be noted, to begin with, that all legal restrictions which curtail the civil rights of a single racial group are immediately suspect. That is not to say that all such restrictions are unconstitutional. It is to say that courts must subject them to the most rigid scrutiny. Pressing public necessity may sometimes justify the existence of such restrictions; racial antagonism never can.

....Regardless of the true nature of the assembly and relocation centers—and we deem it unjustifiable to call them concentration camps with all the ugly connotations that term implies—we are dealing specifically with nothing but an exclusion order. To cast this case into outlines of racial prejudice, without reference to the real military dangers which were presented, merely confuses the issue.

Korematsu was not excluded from the Military Area be cause of hostility to him or his race. He was excluded because we are at war with the Japanese Empire, because the properly constituted military authorities feared an invasion of our West Coast . . . the military authorities considered that the need for action was great and time was short. We cannot—by availing ourselves of the calm perspective of hindsight—now say that at that time these actions were unjustified.

Dissent by Justice Frank Murphy

This exclusion of "all persons of Japanese ancestry, both alien and nonalien," from the Pacific Coast area on a plea of military necessity in the absence of martial law ought not to be approved. Such exclusion goes over "the very brink of constitutional power" and falls into the ugly abyss of racism . . . .

No adequate reason is given for the failure to treat these Japanese Americans on an individual basis by holding investigations and hearings to separate the loyal from the disloyal, as was done in the case of persons of German and Italian ancestry . . . .

Moreover, there was no adequate proof that the Federal Bureau of Investigation and the military and naval intelligence services did not have the espionage and sabotage situation well- in hand during this long period. Nor is there any denial of the fact that not one person of Japanese ancestry was accused or convicted of espionage or sabotage after Pearl Harbor- while they were still free . . . . It seems incredible that under these circumstances it would have been impossible to hold loyalty hearings for the mere 112,000 persons involved-or at least for the 70,000 American citizens especially when a large part of this number- represented children and elderly men and women. .

I dissent, therefore, from this legalization of racism . . . . All residents of this nation are kin is some way by blood or culture to a foreign land. Yet they are primarily and necessarily a part of the new and distinct civilization of the United States. They must accordingly be treated at all times as the heirs of the American experiment and as entitled to all the rights and freedoms guaranteed by the Constitution.

Source: U. S. Supreme Court, *Korematsu v. U. S.* (1944)

HOW WELL DID YOU UNDERSTAND THIS SELECTION?

1. Describe conditions in the concentration camps.

2. What rational did the Supreme Court use to justify internment of Japanese-Americans in the camps?

3. Why did Justice Murphy dissent?

4. Was the American government justified in putting Japanese Americans in the concentration camps? Why or why not?

"A LOYAL NEGRO SOLDIER"

Despite facing racism and prejudice, African American soldiers served bravely in World War II. More than one million blacks were drafted or enlisted in the armed forces between 1941 and 1945. In all branches of the military, African Americans served in segregated units. Most found the segregation hypocritical because government propaganda during World War II proclaimed that the United States was fighting against Fascism to protect individual liberty, freedom, self-determination, and democracy. Black leaders attempted to show Americans the contradiction between racism and prejudice at home and the fight for liberty, equality, and democracy in Europe. The letter written by an unknown black soldier below deals with the issue of racism and democracy.

November 5, 1943

Truman K Gibson, Jr.
Civilian Aide to the Secretary of War
Washington, D.C.

Dear Mr. Gibson:

And I fight—for Democracy?
Upon reading the title of this article the average reader would assume that I am a member of the armed forces in the U.S.A. In your assumption, reader, you are definitely correct. I was selected by the President and citizens, to

fight for a "non-existing Democracy." I am one soldier who waited to be drafted. I didn't volunteer out. I am learning to fight to protect whatever cause for which the Allies are fighting. I am forced to learn to be ready to kill or be killed-for "Democracy." When fighting time arrives I will fight for it.

I learned early in life that for the Negro there is no Democracy. Of course I know the principles set forth in the Amendments and the Bill of Rights. I learned that I knew nothing of the operation of a true democratic form of government. I found that a Negro in civilian life has [a] very tough time with segregation in public places and discrimination in industry. I knew this and I thought that white people would react differently toward a colored soldier.

I had heard and read of the cruel treatment given colored soldiers and somehow, even among existing conditions of civilian life, I couldn't understand how white people could be so down on one who wears the uniform of the fighting forces of their country. From civilian life I was drafted and now I prepare to fight for the continuation of discriminatory practices against me and my people.

I have long known that the fighting forces are composed of two divisions. Namely, a white division composed of Germans, Jews, Italians, Dutch and all white people of the remaining countries (The question is: Are they loyal?). A Negro division composed of American Negroes and all dark skin people. The American Negro has fought in every war since the Revolutionary War. There can be no question as to his loyalty. He is put into a division composed of the members of his race not because of his educational qualities, his fighting abilities or his inability to live with others, but he's put into a separate division because of the color of his skin.

This is serious since the Negroes are trained to a large extent in Southern States whose white civilians are more drastic in showing their dislike than in Northern white people.

I prayed that I'd be sent to a camp in my home state or that I'd be sent to some camp in a Northern State. My prayers weren't answered and I find myself at this outpost of civilization. I never wanted to be within twenty hundred miles of Alexandria, Louisiana. I am here and I can do nothing to improve my condition. Nevertheless, I prepare to fight for a country where I am denied the rights of being a full-fledged citizen.

A few weeks after my arrival at this camp, I went to a post exchange on my regimental area. I knew that each area has an exchange but I thought that I could make my purchase at any of them. Upon entering I could feel the place grow cold. All conversation ceased. It was then that I noticed that all the soldiers and the saleswomen were white. Not to be outdone I approached the counter and was told (even before asking for the article) that, "Negroes are not served here. This post exchange is for white soldiers. You have one near your regiment. Buy what you want there."

My answer to these abrupt and rudely made statements was in the form of a question—"I thought that post exchanges are for soldiers regardless of color, am I right?"

I left this post exchange and returned to my regimental area. I know that these saleswomen knew not the way of a true democracy.

As long as I am a soldier I fight for a mock Democracy. I was called to report to the camp hospital for an eye examination last week. I was surprised to find the waiting room full of Negro and white soldiers who were sharing the same seats and reading the same newspapers. I was shocked. I didn't believe that the camp hospital could be so free from segregation while the camp itself was built on prejudice.

My second surprise came when registering. Each person filled out a blank and all blanks were placed in the same basket in order of the entrance regardless of the race of the entree. I was just beginning to feel proud of the hospital when a list of names were called off and my name was last on the list. I found myself in line of sixteen (16) men, seven of whom were white. The white men gradually fell out of line and the Negroes found themselves continually waiting . . . waiting for the white soldiers to finish their examinations.

It wouldn't have been noticed had not the sergeant in charge been contented to carry only those white soldiers in the line, but he proceeded to bring more from the waiting room. When I could stand this no longer I protested.

Result: We were immediately examined and allowed to return to our regimental area. I was asked a few days later, "Don't you want to fight for the U.S.A. and its policies?"

I am a soldier; I made no answer, but deep down inside I knew when I faced America's enemies I will fight for the protection of my loved ones at home.

Listen, Negro America, I am writing this article believing that it will act as a stimulant. You need awakening. Many of you have come to realize that your race is fighting on the battlefields of the world, but do you know why they fight? I can answer this question.

259

The right on the battlefield is for your existence, not for Democracy. It is upon you that each soldier depends. In my fight my thoughts will invariably return to you who can fight for Democracy. You must do this for the soldiers because Democracy will be, and Democracy must, must be won at home—not on battlefields but through your bringing pressure to bear on Congress.

A Loyal Negro Soldier

HOW WELL DID YOU UNDERSTAND THIS SELECTION?

1. How does the letter's author describe the situation in the military? In American society?

2. What part of the country was the soldier from? Why did he not want to be sent to a southern base?

3. What is the soldier's view about democracy in the U.S.?

4. What does the soldier say he will fight for? Why does he question the loyalty of white soldiers?

"Rosie the Riveter" symbolized working women during World War II. The Federal Government actively recruited American women for factory work because so many males were serving in the armed forces and because it realized that without women workers factories could not produce enough to enable the United States to defeat Germany, Japan, and Italy. The number of women in the American workforce more than doubled during the Second World War. In general, American society accepted working women but assumed that once the war ended these women would voluntarily give up their jobs and return to life as housewives. The selection below is from the diary of a female welder in a shipyard about her wartime experience.

Sunday

I am back from my first day on the Ways [staging on which ships are built], and I feel as if I had seen some giant phenomenon. It's incredible! It's inhuman! It's horrible! And it's marvelous! I don't believe a blitz could be noisier—I didn't dream that there could be so much noise, anywhere. My ears are still ringing like high-tension wires, and my head buzzes. When you first see it, when you look down Way after Way, when you see the thousands each going about his own business and seeming to know what to do, you're so bewildered you can't see anything or make sense out of it.

First came the bus ride to the Yard. Crowded as usual. I was intrigued by knowing that this time I was going to Mart's Marsh. The name has always fascinated me. I gather that it refers to bottom or marshy land once owned by a family named Mart. From the [welding] school our road led along the water where I could see several of the ships already launched and now lying at the outfitting dock to receive the finishing touches. It was easy to spot the various stages of completion; each ship gets moved up one when a new ship arrives for outfitting.

When the bus came to a stop, I followed the crowd across a pontoon bridge between rails at which stood guards checking for badges. The far side of the bridge brought us to the part of the Yard where the prefabricated parts are stored, right in the open, pile upon pile. I saw a huge building marked "Assembly Shop," another "Marine Shop," and still another "Pipe Assembly." There were lots of little houses marked with numbers. Most of them seemed to be in the sixties. And I was looking for check-in station No. 1.

I hunted and hunted without success, and finally asked someone where "new hires" check in. He immediately directed me. I showed my badge, told my number, and was given another badge to be picked up and turned in daily as we did at school. It was marked "New Hire." About then who should come along but Red-headed Marie and the Big Swede! We went together to the Welders' Office where our off days were assigned to us. I was given "C" day and told that it was the only day available. This means that I get Tuesday off this week, Wednesday next, and so on. The Big Swede said she had to have "D" day to get a ride to work and to have the same day as her husband. Although "C" day was "the only one available," strangely enough she was given "D" day. One has to learn to insist on what one wants even when told it is impossible.

The Big Swede is a real pal. She had not forgotten the patch for my overall trouser leg. She had cut a piece from an old pair of her husband's, scrubbed it to get the oil out, and brought it to me with a needle stuck in the center and a coil of black thread ready for action. "Here," she said, "I knew you wouldn't have things handy in a hotel room. Now you mend that hole before you catch your foot in it and fall." . . .

Today my book on welding came from the Washington office. I read that a welder's qualifications are "physical fitness which insures a reasonable degree of endurance during a full day of work; steady nerves and considerable muscular strength." For a shipyard welder I'd amend that to read: "An unreasonable degree of endurance during a full day of strain, plus muscular strength, plus no nerves." If you haven't the muscular strength before you start, you will have it afterward. If you haven't the nerves before, you may have them afterward, though I doubt it. By tomorrow I shall be "reasonably" acclimated, but tonight I quite frankly "ain't."

I, who hate heights, climbed stair after stair after stair till I thought I must be close to the sun. I stopped on the top deck. I, who hate confined spaces, went through narrow corridors, stumbling my way over rubbercoats leads—dozens of them, scores of them, even hundreds of them. I went into a room about four feet by ten where two ship-fitters, a shipfitter's helper, a chipper, and I all worked. I welded in the poop deck lying on the floor while another welder spattered sparks from the ceiling and chippers like giant woodpeckers shattered our eardrums. I, who've taken welding, and have sat at a bench welding flat and vertical plates, was told to weld braces along a baseboard below a door opening. On these a heavy steel door was braced while it was hung to a fine degree of accuracy. I welded more braces along the side, and along the top. I did overhead welding, horizontal, flat, vertical. I welded around curved hinges which were placed so close to the side wall that I had to bend my rod in a curve to get it in. I made some good welds and some frightful ones. But now a door in the poop deck of an oil tanker is hanging, four feet by six of solid steel, by my welds. Pretty exciting!

The men in the poop deck were nice to me. The shipfitter was toothless. The grinder had palsy, I guess, for his hands shook pitifully and yet he managed to handle that thirty-pound grinder. The welder was doing "pickup" work, which meant touching up spots that had been missed. An inspector came through and marked places to chip, and the ship's superintendent stopped and woke the shipfitter's helper....

As a result of all this, I feel very strongly that we'd go to the Yard better prepared if in the school we did more welding in varied positions. Even a fillet weld of two plates could be placed on the floor, and one could get down and do it there and so learn something of what will later be required in the Yard. I don't see why, too, the butterflies, the clips, and even the bolts couldn't be welded at various angles in school. We could practice some   one-handed welding instead of always using two hands while sitting at a bench with plates conveniently placed. There are times when you have to use one hand to cling to a ladder or a beam while you weld with the other. I notice that the most experienced welders I have watched seldom use two hands. One large, fine-looking woman (Norwegian, I think) who has been there three months told me: "They don't teach us enough at school. Why don't they let us weld there the same things we'll do here?" I countered with, "Oh, they do teach a lot or we'd be no good here at all; but what you say would certainly help." I think she "has something," however. We do need more experience in setting our machines and recognizing when they are too hot or too cold. Struggling with an inaccurate setting and the wrong amount of heat makes a harder day than doing a lot of actual work. Yet it's hardly the fault of the training that we lack adequate experience. More and more I marvel at training that in eight days can give enough to make us worth anything on the job. And we are worth something. We're building ships.

Source: *Augusta Clawson,* Diary of a Woman Welder, 1945

HOW WELL DID YOU UNDERSTAND THIS SELECTION?

1. How does the welder describe her first day on the job?

2. What changes does she suggest to make the job easier?

3. Did she grow during the first day on the job?

4. What skills and qualifications are needed for the welder's job?

5. How do other workers treat her?

IWO JIMA

Edgar L. Jones, *Atlantic Monthly*, February 1945

The Pacific Theater of Operations posed a difficult challenge for American soldiers. The South Pacific contained numerous islands Japanese forces had captured. General Douglas MacArthur, the supreme American commander in the Pacific, devised an island-hopping strategy in which American forces would invade and capture strategically located islands rather than invading every island occupied by Japanese soldiers. One island American troops landed on and where they encountered fierce fighting was Iwo Jima. On February 23, 1945, four days after landing on the island a group of American soldiers were photographed raising the flag on Mt. Suribachi. Edward Jones wrote a brief account of the fighting on Iwo Jima for the Atlantic Monthly.

I went in with a large group of Fourth Division Marines.... The Japanese were lobbing shells into supply dumps, ammunition depots, communication centers, and every other place where they saw men or machinery concentrated. No man on the beach felt secure. The Americans held about one square mile of low ground at that point, most of which I toured. Everywhere men were struggling: to keep landing craft from submerging, to dig roads in the deep sand, to push mired trucks onto solid ground, to haul equipment to sheltered locations, and to fight nature for the chance to get on with the battle. And all the time the Japanese shells whined down and tore into sand and flesh with indiscriminate fury.

No one who was at Iwo can analyze the battle objectively. The carnage was so horrifying that the blood and agony of the struggle saturated one's mind, dismally coloring all thought. Iwo was unlike any war I had ever seen. It was a fight to the finish, with no man asking for quarter until he was dead. Of the nearly 20,000 American casualties, approximately two thirds were wounded, but all except a few score of the 20,000 Japanese died where they fell. There is such a thing as dying decently, but not on Iwo. I do not believe anything practical can be achieved by describing men blown apart. Veterans of two and three years of war in the Pacific were sickened. An estimated 26,000 men died in eight square miles of fighting. There were 3,000 dead and wounded American and Japanese soldiers for every square mile.

I returned to Iwo on D Day (a standard military term, not referring to events in Europe) plus six, seven and eight. By that time the Marines had captured territory where Japanese had lain dead in the hot sun for more than a week. I crawled into pillboxes burned out by flamethrowers, and into deep caves where the Japanese had been burning their own dead to conceal the extent of their losses. I was torturing myself to look at the results of war, because I think it is essential for civilians occasionally to hold their noses and see what is going on.

The sight on Iwo which I could not force myself to see again was the section of the beach allotted for an American cemetery.... On the afternoon I walked by, there was half an acre of dead Marines stretched out so close together that they blanketed the beach for two hundred yards. The stench was overpowering.... The smell of one's countrymen rotting in the sun is a lasting impression.

Source: "To the Finish; A Letter from Iwo Jima," *The Atlantic Monthly*, 1945

HOW WELL DID YOU UNDERSTAND THIS SELECTION?

1. How does Jones describe the battle?

2. What does Jones' description of Iwo Jima say about the idea of "glory on the battlefield?"

3. How would you have reacted had you been at Iwo Jima?

4. Why did the Japanese burn bodies of dead soldiers?

5. How many soldiers died on Iwo Jima?

U.S. GOVERNMENT ACQUIESCENCE IN THE MURDER OF JEWS

Adolf Hitler devised a "final solution" for what he saw as the Jewish problem in Europe. His plan was to exterminate the Jewish race in concentration labor camps and in gas ovens. Overall, Hitler and Nazi officials killed about six million Jews. Other countries, including the United States, failed to stop the extermination once evidence of it surfaced. In January 1944 Henry Morgenthau, Secretary of the Treasury wrote a memorandum to President Roosevelt stating that the American State Department could have prevented much of the Holocaust had it acted sooner. An excerpt of this memorandum, entitled "Report to the Secretary of the Acquiescence of This Government in the Murder of Jews," is printed below.

One of the greatest crimes in history, the slaughter of the Jewish people in Europe, is continuing unabated.

This Government has for a long time maintained that its policy is to work out programs to save those Jews of Europe who could be saved.

I am convinced on the basis of the information which is available to me that certain officials in our State Department, which is charged with carrying out this policy, have been guilty not only of gross procrastination and willful failure to act, but even of willful attempts to prevent action from being taken to rescue Jews from Hitler.

I fully recognize the graveness of this statement and I make it only after having most carefully weighed the shocking facts which have come to my attention during the last several months.

Unless remedial steps of a drastic nature are taken, and taken immediately, I am certain that no effective action will be taken by this Government to prevent the complete extermination of the Jews in German controlled Europe, and that this Government will have to share for all time responsibility for this extermination.

The tragic history of this Government's handling of this matter reveals that certain State Department officials are guilty of the following:

(1) They have not only failed to use the *Governmental machinery* at their disposal to rescue Jews from Hitler, but have even gone so far as to use this Government machinery to prevent the rescue of these Jews.

(2) They have not only failed to cooperate with *private organizations* in the efforts of these organizations to work out individual programs of their own, but have taken steps designed to prevent these programs from being put into effect.

(3) They not only have failed to facilitate the obtaining of information concerning Hitler's plans to exterminate the Jews of Europe but in their official capacity have gone so far as to surreptitiously attempt to stop the obtaining of information concerning the murder of the Jewish population of Europe.

(4) They have tried to cover up their guilt by:
    (a) concealment and misrepresentation;
    (b) the giving of false and misleading explanations for their failures to act and their attempts to prevent
        action; and
    (c) the issuance of false and misleading statements concerning the "action" which they have taken to date.

Source: *Diaries of Henry Morgenthau Jr.*—available at Franklin D. Roosevelt Library, Hyde Park, N.Y.

HOW WELL DID YOU UNDERSTAND THIS SELECTION?

1. What does Morgenthau allege in this document?

2. Do you think Morgenthau's allegations are valid? Explain.

3. What did Morgenthau hope to accomplish with this memo? Was he successful? Why or why not?

4. Could the American government had done anything to prevent or lessen the Holocaust's severity? If so, what? If not, why not?

5. Why do you think Morgenthau wrote this memorandum?

Franklin Delano Roosevelt was unquestionably one of the greatest presidents in American history. He successfully guided the nation through two great crises—the Great Depression and the Second World War. He was the only president who served more than two terms. News of his sudden death just weeks before Nazi Germany was defeated shocked Americans. Merriman Smith, a United Press reporter allowed on the funeral train that carried the fallen leader's body back to Washington, D.C. and Hyde Park, New York after his death at Warm Spring, Georgia on April 121, 1945, wrote a moving account describing the reaction of Americans to the death of their beloved chief.

EN ROUTE TO WASHINGTON

Franklin Delano Roosevelt was borne across the hushed Southern countryside today on the long, last journey to the White House and Hyde Park. The eleven-coach funeral train made a slow trip northward from Warm Springs, Ga., where he died Thursday afternoon...

The funeral procession from the "Little White House," where the President died, was a pageant of grief. Mr. Roosevelt made his last trip through the grounds he loved so well in a black hearse. An Army honor guard of 2,000 troops marched before it, kicking up red clay dust on the winding country road to the village. Behind the hearse rode Mrs. Roosevelt, sitting stiffly upright. Fala, the President's Scottie, sat quietly at her feet, as if aware that something was wrong. At the end of the thirty-five minute procession from the cottage to the terminal, Mrs. Roosevelt's eyes were misty. She was fighting hard to retain composure.

...The patients [of the Warm Springs Foundation] with whom the President shared such a deep bond were not forgotten. It was Mr. Roosevelt's custom, when he ended each Warm Springs visit, to give a brief call and wave of the hand to those gathered before the foundation's main dormitory. Today, the hearse came to a full stop before the crowded porch. In mute grief, the patients watched. Two hours before the faint beat of drums signaled its approach, some had hobbled out to wait. Some were wheeled out. To them, the President was a magnificent inspiration.

A thirteen-year-old, Jay Fribourg, said: "I loved him so much." He clenched his teeth as he held back the tears. Chief Petty Officer Graham Jackson, a Georgia Negro, a favorite of Mr. Roosevelt, stepped out from the circle with the accordion which he had played often for the President. As the procession approached he began the plaintive strains of "Going Home." Then he played "Nearer My God to Thee." There was scarcely a dry eye.

...Farther down the road, troops--overseas veterans-wept openly as [the hearse] passed. When it reached the tiny station, the troops moved into company front and presented arms. The townspeople bared their heads and watched the funeral party board the train. They stood silently as the train gathered speed and rumbled northward. Then it rounded a bend, and all that could be seen was a thin trail of black smoke. Still they stood, with the scorching sun beating down on the row of modest stores that lined the street. Then, finally, they began to leave.

Source: *New York Herald Tribune,* April 14, 1945

HOW WELL DID YOU UNDERSTAND THIS SELECTION?

1. How did Americans generally react to Roosevelt's death?

2. Why do you think Roosevelt's death produced so much grief?

3. Did Roosevelt's death make him larger than life? Explain?

DROPPING THE ATOMIC BOMB

Following Roosevelt's death in April 1945, Vice President Harry Truman was sworn in as the nation's leader. Like most Vice Presidents, Truman was largely kept in the dark regarding the war effort. Nevertheless, he soon faced the decision of whether to use the atom bomb, a new weapon of mass destruction developed in secret by the Manhattan Project. Truman consulted with the joint chief of staff and his cabinet before deciding to end World War II by bombing Hiroshima and Nagasaki, two cities on the Japanese mainland. Truman's decision to unlease nuclear destruction on Japan was controversial. Nevertheless, use of the atomic bombs ended the war.

Harry S Truman (from his *Memoirs*).
My own knowledge of these developments had come about only after I became President, when Secretary Stimson had given me the full story. He had told me at that time that the project was nearing completion and that a bomb could be expected within another four months. It was at his suggestion, too, that I had then set up a committee of top men and had asked them to study with great care the implications the new weapon might have for us...

[Here Truman identifies the eight-man Interim Committee, composed of leading figures in government, business, and education, and reports that the Interim Committee's recommendations were brought to him by Stimson on June 1, 1945.]

It was their recommendation that the bomb be used against the enemy as soon as it could be done. They recommended further that it should be used without specific warning and against a target that would clearly show its devastating strength. I had realized, of course, that an atomic bomb explosion would inflict damage and casualties beyond imagination. On the other hand, the scientific advisers of the committee reported, "We can propose no technical demonstration likely to bring an end to the war; we see no acceptable alternative to direct military use." It was their conclusion that no technical demonstration they might propose, such as over a deserted island, would be likely to bring the war to an end. It had to be used against an enemy target.

The final decision of where and when to use the atomic bomb was up to me. Let there be no mistake about it. I regarded the bomb as a military weapon and never had any doubt that it should be used. The top military advisers to the President recommended its use, and when I talked to Churchill he unhesitatingly told me that he favored the use of the atomic bomb if it might aid to end the war.

In deciding to use this bomb I wanted to make sure that it would be used as a weapon of war in the manner prescribed by the laws of war. That meant that I wanted it dropped on a military target. I had told Stimson that the bomb should be dropped as nearly as possible upon a war production center of prime military importance....

Source: Harry S. Truman, *Memoirs: Year of Decisions* (New York, 1955), pp. 10-11

HOW WELL DID YOU UNDERSTAND THIS SELECTION?

1. How did Truman learn about development of the atomic bomb?

2. What factors did Truman consider when making the decision to use the atomic bomb against Japan?

3. Was Truman justified in using the bomb? Why or why not?

4. Could Truman have ended the war without use of the bomb? Why or why not?

SELF TEST

MULTIPLE CHOICE: Circle the correct response. The correct answers are given at the end.

1. The English and French response to Nazi Aggression at the Munich Conference is generally referred to by which of the following terms?
   a. Appeasement
   b. Rapproachment
   c. War-mongering
   d. Brinkmanship

2. At the Munich Conference, what territory did Hitler receive?
   a. Eastern Poland
   b. Western Russia
   c. Rumania
   d. The Sudentenland of Czechoslovakia

3. What event officially got the United States involved in World War II?
   a. The Nazi-Soviet Pact
   b. Japan's attack on Pearl Harbor
   c. The Lend Lease Policy
   d. The Axis Agreement

4. Which of the following statements is accurate about African American soldiers during the Second World War?
   a. They served in integrated units.
   b. They received treatment equal to that of white soldiers.
   c. They served in segregated units and faced prejudice and discrimination.
   d. They were accorded civil rights for the first time in American History.

5. Which of the following ethnic groups were placed in concentration camps by the American government during World War II?
   a. African Americans
   b. Italian Americans
   c. German Americans
   d. Japanese Americans

6. Which of the following statements about women is accurate during World War II?
   a. Women generally refused to help the war effort by working outside the home.
   b. Large numbers of women found employment in factories and other places of work outside the home to aid the war effort.
   c. Factory owners generally refused to hire female workers to replace males serving in the armed forces during World War II.
   d. American society generally refused to permit women to work outside the home during World War II.

7. Which of the following did not result from World War II?
   a. Establishment of the United Nations.
   b. The power of the Federal Government increased.
   c. Racial segregation ended in the United States.
   d. Economic growth and the end of the Great Depression.

8. Which Japanese cities were destroyed by atomic bombs in August 1945?
   a. Hiroshima and Nagasaki.
   b. Tokyo and Edo
   c. Nuguskry and Shanghai
   d. Hong Kong and Tokyo

9. The Nazi extermination of Jews during World War II was called
   a. The Final Pogrom
   b. The Holocaust
   c. The Nazi Plan
   d. Hitler's Dream

10. Prior to American entry into World War II, Franklin Roosevelt
    a. Generally supported the British with policies such as Lend Lease.
    b. Generally remained neutral.
    c. Often developed policies to support Germany.
    d. Told the American public that the U.S. could certainly avoid the war.

ANSWERS: 1-a; 2-d; 3-b; 4-c; 5-d; 6-b; 7-c; 8-a; 9-b; 10-a

ESSAYS:

1. Discuss the changes World War II brought to the United States in both foreign policy and domestic affairs.

2. Could World War II have been prevented? Why or why not?

3. Discuss the Nazi policy of exterminating Jews and other European minorities such as Gypsies and Homosexuals. How many people died as a result of this policy? Could England, the United States, and other nations have prevented the slaughter of Jews and other minorities in Nazi extermination camps? Explain.

OPTIONAL ACTIVITIES : (Use your knowledge **and** imagination when appropriate.)

1. Have a class debate on whether it was necessary for the United States to use atomic bombs against Japan.

2. Pretend that you are a female factory worker during World War II. Write a letter to a family member about your work experiences.

3. Write a letter to your hometown newspaper discussing the differences in treatment of black and white soldiers.

WEB SITE LISTINGS:

Oral history
   http://www.tankbooks.com/dayone.htm
Battles and American Experiences
   http://www.historyplace.com/worldwar2
   http://www.historyplace.com/worldwar2/pacificwar/index.html
   http://www.thehistorynet.com/WorldWarII
   http://www.thehistorynet.com/WorldWarII/THNarchives/eyewitnessaccounts (Bataan Death March)
The National Archives site includes Advertisements, Posters, Speeches
   http://www.nara.gov/education/teaching/fdr/infamy.html
   http://www.nara.gov/powers/stampem.html
   http://www.nara.gov/exhall/powers/powers.html
   http://www.nara.gov/exhall/powers/manguns.html
   http://www.nara.gov/people/people/html
   http://www.nara.gov/people/newroles.html
   http://www.nara.gov/originals/fdr.html
Afroam.org includes sections on Tuskegee Airmen & other black units
   http://www.afroam.org/history/history.html
Pictures of Women At War
   http://lcweb.loc.gov/exhibits/wcf/wcf0001.html
   http://www.u.arizona.edu/~kari/rosie.htm
   http://www.nara.gov/exhall/powers/women.html
   http://userpages.aug.com/captbarb/
Japanese American Internment
   http://www.geocities.com/Athens/8420/main.html

Chapter Twenty-one

THE COLD WAR:
The Truman-Eisenhower Years

Harry Truman entered the presidency with little knowledge about the presidency or experience as chief executive following Franklin Roosevelt's death in April 1945. Like most vice presidents that preceded him, Truman had largely been kept in the dark about American policy and relations with other nations. Nevertheless, he had to lead the United States into the post war world. The biggest challenge Truman and the United States faced was the antagonistic relationship that developed with the Soviet Union. Joseph Stalin, the Soviet leader, viewed with suspicion American intentions following World War II, and Truman believed that the Soviet Union planned to spread its Communist ideology around the world. Acting on the advice of George Kennan and other close associates, Truman adopted the policy of Containment designed to ensure that Communism did not spread beyond the Soviet Union and countries of Eastern Europe controlled by the Soviet Union after the defeat of Nazi forces in that part of the world. Although Dwight D. Eisenhower, the World War II general who succeeded Truman as president, criticized Containment during the 1952 campaign against Adali E. Stevenson, his Democratic opponent, once he became president, the popular "Ike" adopted Containment and geared his foreign policy to preventing the spread of Communism outside the Soviet Union and Eastern Europe.

The American attempt at containing Communism alienated the Soviet Union and brought about a period historians call the Cold War. During the Truman and Eisenhower administrations the United States and the Soviet Union were hostile toward each other but rarely confronted each other directly on the battlefield because leaders of both nations realized that since both possessed nuclear weapons the next world war likely would end in nuclear annihilation.

Most historians date the Cold War's beginning to the refusal of the Soviet Union to give up control of territory in Eastern Europe their forces had driven Nazi occupiers out of at the end of World War II. Three times in the last two centuries Russia had been invaded by France and Germany through Eastern Europe. Stalin likely refused to cede control of Eastern Europe because he wanted to establish a buffer zone to prevent a future invasion of Soviet Russia. England and the United States, however, did not understand the realities of Russian history. They demanded that free elections be held in all countries occupied by Nazi forces after World War II as Roosevelt and Churchill had promised in the Atlantic Charter and as Stalin had seemingly agreed to at Yalta in February 1945.

After it became clear that Stalin was not going to permit the establishment of democratically elected governments in Eastern Europe, Truman and American officials became convinced that the Soviet Union's real objective was to expand Communist influence outside Eastern Europe. In 1947 Kennan convinced Truman to adopt policies designed to prevent Soviet expansion. When Greece and Turkey appeared to be threatened by Communism, Truman developed the Truman Doctrine in which he stated that the United States would aid free nations threatened by an internal or external Communist takeover. The United States began sending millions of dollars to Greece and Turkey for use in rebuilding economies devastated by World War II. Both countries staved off the threat of Communism and became staunch American allies. Due to the success of aid to Greece and Turkey, Truman in 1947 devised the Marshall Plan, which sent billions of American dollars to rebuild the economies of Western European countries and prevent the spread of Communism into that region of Europe. When aid was offered to the Soviet Union and Communist Eastern Europe, Stalin took offense and created a crisis by denying American access to the city of West Berlin, a city controlled by the United States, England, and France that was located in Communist East Germany. Rather than risking World War III, Truman initiated an airlift that supplied residents of West Berlin with necessities in 1948 and 1949. After the Berlin Blockade ended in 1949 Truman successfully established NATO (the North Atlantic Treaty Organization) that put Western European nations under the American nuclear umbrella to protect them from Soviet expansion. Stalin retaliated the next year (1950) by creating the Warsaw Pact to protect Eastern Europe from American attempts to overthrow Communist governments established there.

Europe was not the only region of the world threatened by Communism. Asia and the Middle East were areas of concern for both Truman and Eisenhower. In 1949 Communist Mao Zedong overthrew the nationalist government of Chiang Kai-shek and aligned China with the Soviet Union, marking the first failure for Containment. Truman and Eisenhower both faced problems on the Korean Peninsulas. In June 1950 Communist North Korea launched a surprise invasion of South Korea in an attempt to unify Korea under a Communist dictatorship. Truman responded by having the United Nations declare the Korean Conflict a peacekeeping operation to militarily drive the Communist invaders out of South Korea. Eventually, the conflict broadened when Communist China sent troops to aid North Korea. Eisenhower ended the Korean Conflict in 1953 with acceptance of a cease fire agreement that returned the borders of North and South Korea to their prewar location.

Following the creation of Israel in the late 1940s, turmoil engulfed the Middle East. Arab nations generally regarded the new Jewish state as an illegal American creation. In the context of the Cold War the Soviet Union aided Arab nations in the various wars fought with Israel. Eisenhower and the United States were particularly concerned after Egypt nationalized the Suez Canal due to the withdrawal of the United States from the Aswan Dam project in an attempt to punish Egyptian leader Gamel Nasser for accepting Soviet aid. Nationalization of the Suez Canal began the Suez War in 1956. This conflict, which began to expand, threatened world peace and security until Eisenhower and the new Soviet leader, Nikita Khruschev, pressured Israel and Arab nations to stop the conflict.

Eisenhower also faced difficulty in the Western Hemisphere after the Central Intelligence Agency, which Eisenhower allowed to overthrow governments in foreign countries, tried to oust the government of Fidel Castro in Cuba. Castro, realizing the peril his regime faced, aligned Cuba with the Soviet Union during the Cold War. Communism, under Eisenhower had spread to the Caribbean. Although the Cold War continued after Eisenhower left office, its parameters had been set by 1961.

IDENTIFICATION: Briefly describe each term.

The Cold War

Yalta Agreement

Truman Doctrine

Marshall Plan

Berlin Blockade and Airlift

Containment

George Kennan

George Marshall

NATO

Warsaw Pact

The Suez War

United Nations

Iron Curtain

Korean Conflict

Nasser

Douglas MacArthur

John Foster Dulles

Dean Acheson

Eisenhower Doctrine

Fidel Castro

CIA

The Military-Industrial Complex

Brinkmanship

Chiang Kai-shek

Mao Zedong

Ho Chi minh

Peoples Republic of China

East Germany

Geneva Accords

Hungarian Crisis

Nagy

Indochina

National Security Act

38th parallel

Domino Theory

THINK ABOUT:

1. Discuss the origins of the Cold War. Could the conflict have been prevented? Explain.

2. How successful was Containment? Explain.

3. Who caused the Cold War, the Soviet Union or the United States? Support your answer with historical evidence.

4. Discuss the most important events in the Cold War during the Truman and Eisenhower administrations.

5. Why is the conflict between the United States and the Soviet Union called the Cold War? Was it actually a war? Explain.

"THE SINEWS OF PEACE" OR THE IRON CURTAIN SPEECH BY WINSTON CHURCHILL

Winston Churchill, the hero who led England to victory over Nazi Germany in World War II, was between terms as Great Britain's Prime Minister when he delivered his famous Sinews of Peace (better known as the Iron Curtain speech on March 5, 1946 at Westminster College in Fulton, Missouri). Excerpts from the speech are reproduced below:

The Sinews of Peace, March 5, 1946, Westminster College, Fulton, Missouri

...The United States stands at this time at the pinnacle of world power. It is a solemn moment for the American Democracy. For with primacy in power is also joined an awe-inspiring accountability to the future. If you look around you, you must feel not only the sense of duty done but also you must feel anxiety lest you fall below the level of achievement. Opportunity is here now, clear and shining for both our countries. To reject it or ignore it or fritter it away will bring upon us all the long reproaches of the after-time. It is necessary that constancy of mind, persistency of purpose, and the grand simplicity of decision shall guide and rule the conduct of the English-speaking peoples in peace as they did in war. We must, and I believe we shall, prove ourselves equal to this severe requirement...

...To give security to these countless homes, they must be shielded from the two giant marauders, war and tyranny. We all know the frightful disturbances in which the ordinary family is plunged when the curse of war swoops down upon the bread-winner and those for whom he works and contrives. The awful ruin of Europe, with all its vanished glories, and of large parts of Asia glares us in the eyes. When the designs of wicked men or the aggressive urge of

275

mighty States dissolve over large areas the frame of civilized society, humble folk are confronted with difficulties with which they cannot cope. For them all is distorted, all is broken, even ground to pulp.

When I stand here this quiet afternoon I shudder to visualize what is actually happening to million now and what is going to happen in this period when famine stalks the earth. None can compute what has been called "the unestimated sum of human pain." Our supreme task and duty is to guard the homes of the common people from the horrors and miseries of another war. We all are agreed on that...

...Now I come to the second danger of these two marauders which threatens the cottage, the home, and the ordinary people—namely, tyranny. We cannot be blind to the fact that the liberties enjoyed by individual citizens throughout the British Empire are not valid in a considerable number of countries, some of which are very powerful. In these States control is enforced upon the common people by various kinds of all-embracing police governments. The power of the State is exercised without restraint, either by dictators or by compact oligarchies operating through a privileged party and a political police. It is not our duty at this time when difficulties are so numerous to interfere forcibly in the internal affairs of countries which we have not conquered in war. But we must never cease to proclaim in fearless tones the great principles of freedom and the rights of man which are the joint inheritance of the English-speaking world and which through Magna Carta, the Bill of Rights, the Habeas Corpus, trial by jury, and the English common law find their most famous expression in the American Declaration of Independence.

All this means that the people of any country have the right, and should have the power by constitutional action, by free unfettered elections, with secret ballot, to choose or change the character or form of government under which they dwell; that freedom of speech and thought should reign; that courts of justice, independent of the executive, unbiased by any party, should administer laws which have received the broad assent of large majorities or are consecrated by time and custom. Here are the title deeds of freedom which should lie in every cottage home. Here is the message of the British and American peoples to mankind. Let us preach what we practice—let us practice—what we preach...

...A shadow has fallen upon the scenes so lately lighted by the Allied victory. Nobody knows what Soviet Russia and its Communist international organization intends to do in the immediate future, or what are the limits, if any, to their expansive and proselytizing tendencies. I have a strong admiration and regard for the valiant Russian people and for my wartime comrade, Marshal Stalin. There is deep sympathy and goodwill in Britain—and I doubt not here also—towards the peoples of all the Russias and a resolve to persevere through many differences and rebuffs in establishing lasting friendships. We understand the Russian need to be secure on her western frontiers by the removal of all possibility of German aggression. We welcome Russia to her rightful place among the leading nations of the world. We welcome her flag upon the seas. Above all, we welcome constant, frequent and growing contacts between the Russian people and our own people on both sides of the Atlantic. It is my duty, however, for I am sure you would wish me to state the facts as I see them to you, to place before you certain facts about the present position in Europe.

From Stettin in the Baltic to Trieste in the Adriatic, an iron curtain has descended across the Continent. Behind that line lie all the capitals of the ancient states of Central and Eastern Europe. Warsaw, Berlin, Prague, Vienna, Budapest, Belgrade, Bucharest, and Sofia, all these famous cities and the populations around them lie in what I must call the Soviet sphere, and all are subject in one form or another, not only to Soviet influence but to a very high, and, in many cases, increasing measure of control from Moscow. Athens, alone—Greece with its immortal glories—is free to decide its future at an election under British, American and French observation. The Russian-dominated Polish Government has been encouraged to make enormous and wrongful inroads upon Germany, and mass expulsions of millions of Germans on a scale grievous and undreamed-of are now taking place. The Communist parties, which were very small in all these Eastern States of Europe, have been raised to pre-eminence and power far beyond their numbers and are seeking everywhere to obtain totalitarian control. Police governments are prevailing in nearly every case, and so far, except in Czechoslovakia, there is no true democracy. Turkey and Persia are both profoundly alarmed and disturbed at the claims which are being made upon them and at the pressure being exerted by the Moscow Government. An attempt is being made by the Russians in Berlin to build up a quasi-Communist party in their zone of Occupied Germany by showing special favors to groups of left-wing German leaders. At the end of the fighting last June, the American and British Armies withdrew westwards, in accordance with an earlier agreement, to a depth at some points of 150 miles upon a front of nearly four hundred miles, in order to allow our Russian allies to occupy this vast expanse of territory which the Western Democracies had conquered.

If now the Soviet Government tries, by separate action, to build up a pro-Communist Germany in their areas, this will cause new serious difficulties in the British and American zones, and will give the defeated Germans the power of putting themselves up to auction between the Soviets and the Western Democracies. Whatever conclusions may be drawn from these facts—and facts they are—this is certainly not the Liberated Europe we fought to build up. Nor is it one which contains the essentials of permanent peace.

The safety of the world requires a new unity in Europe, from which no nation should be permanently outcast. It is from the quarrels of the strong parent races in Europe that the world wars we have witnessed, or which occurred in former times, have sprung. Twice in our own lifetime we have seen the United States, against their wishes and their traditions, against arguments, the force of which it is impossible not to comprehend, drawn by irresistible forces, into these wars in time to secure the victory of the good cause, but only after frightful slaughter and devastation had occurred. Twice the United States has had to send several millions of its young men across the Atlantic to find the war; but now war can find any nation wherever it may dwell between dusk and dawn. Surely we should work with conscious purpose for a grand pacification of Europe, within the structure of the United Nations and in accordance with its Charter. That I feel is an open cause of policy of very great importance.

In front of the iron curtain which lies across Europe are other causes for anxiety. In Italy the Communist Party is seriously hampered by having to support the Communist-trained Marshal Tito's claims to former Italian territory at the head of the Adriatic. Nevertheless the future of Italy hangs in the balance. Again one cannot imagine a regenerated Europe without a strong France. All my public life I have worked for a strong France and I never lost faith in her destiny, even in the darkest hours. I will not lose faith now. However, in a great number of countries, far from the Russian frontiers and throughout the world, Communist fifth columns are established and work in complete unity and absolute obedience to the United States where Communism is in its infancy, the Communist parties or fifth columns constitute a growing challenge and peril to Christian civilization. These are somber facts for anyone to have to recite on the morrow of a victory gained by so much splendid comradeship in arms and in the cause of freedom and democracy; but we should be most unwise not to face them squarely while time remains…

…On the other hand I repulse the idea that a new war is inevitable; still more that it is imminent. It is because I am sure that our fortunes are still in our own hands and that we hold the power to save the future, that I feel the duty to speak out now that I have the occasion and the opportunity to do so. I do not believe that Soviet Russia desires war. What they desire is the fruits of war and the indefinite expansion of their power and doctrines. But what we have to consider here today while time remains, is the permanent prevention of war and the establishment of conditions of freedom and democracy as rapidly as possible in all countries. Our difficulties and dangers will not be removed by closing our eyes to them. They will not be removed by mere waiting to see what happens; nor will they be removed by a policy of appeasement. What is needed is a settlement, and the longer this is delayed, the more difficult it will be and the greater our dangers will become.

From what I have seen of our Russian friends and Allies during the war, I am convinced that there is nothing they admire so much as strength, and there is nothing for which they have less respect than for weakness, especially military weakness. For that reason the old doctrine of a balance of power is unsound. We cannot afford, if we can help it, to work on narrow margins, offering temptations to a trial of strength. If the Western Democracies stand together in strict adherence to the principles of the United Nations Charter, their influence for furthering those principles will be immense and no one is likely to be allowed to slip away then indeed catastrophe may overwhelm us all.

Last time I saw it all coming and cried aloud to my own fellow-countrymen and to the world, but no one paid any attention. Up till the year 1933 or even 1935, Germany might have been saved from the awful fate which has overtaken her and we might all have been spared the miseries Hitler let loose upon mankind. There never was a war in all history easier to prevent by timely action than the one which has just desolated such great areas of the globe. It could have been prevented in my belief without the firing of a single shot, and Germany might be powerful, prosperous and honored today; but no one would listen and one by one we were all sucked into the awful whirlpool. We surely must not let that happen again. This can only be achieved by reaching now, in 1946, a good understanding on all points with Russia under the general authority of the United Nations Organization and by the maintenance of that good understanding through many peaceful years, by the world instrument, supported by the whole strength of the English-speaking world and all its connections. There is the solution which I respectfully offer to you in this Address to which I have given the title "The Sinews of Peace…"

HOW WELL DID YOU UNDERSTAND THIS SELECTION?

1. Why did Churchill call the speech the Sinews of Peace?

2. What "giant marauders" does Churchill say the world must be protected from?

3. In what context does Churchill use the phrase "iron curtain"? What is the meaning of the term?

4. Is Churchill optimistic or pessimistic in the speech? Explain.

5. What does Churchill think the U.S. and Great Britain should do or not do?

===

THE TRUMAN DOCTRINE

===

In 1946 and 1947 Communist insurgents attempted to take control of governments in Greece and Turkey. After looking at the situation in both countries, President Truman and his foreign policy advisors decided that the United States could not allow Communism to spread outside the Soviet Union and Eastern Europe. Compounding the problem was that the economies of both Greece and Turkey had been wrecked by World War II and that the Communist insurgents were promising to improve the economies in both countries and provide jobs for the large number of unemployed Greeks and Turks. In this context, Truman and his advisors decided to adopt and apply Containment to stave off Communism in Greece and Turkey. On March 12, 1947, President Truman ask Congress for permission to intervene in Greece and elsewhere to prevent the spread of Communism. American intervention in Greece and Turkey was primarily economic. Millions of dollars in foreign aid was sent to rebuild the economics of both countries.

March 12, 1947
Washington, D.C.

PRESIDENT HARRY TRUMAN

The peoples of a number of countries of the world have recently had totalitarian regimes forced upon them against their will. The Government of the United States has made frequent protests against coercion and intimidation in violation of the Yalta agreement, in Poland, Rumania, and Bulgaria. I must also state that in a number of other countries there have been similar developments.

At the present moment in world history nearly every nation must choose between alternative ways of life. The choice is too often not a free one.

One way of life is based upon the will of the majority, is distinguished by free institutions, representative government, free elections, guarantees of individual liberty, freedom of speech and religion, and freedom from political oppression.

The second way of life is based on upon the will of a minority forcibly imposed upon the majority. It relies upon terror and oppression, a controlled press and radio, fixed elections, and the suppression of personal freedom.

I believe that it must be the policy of the United States to support free peoples who are resisting attempted subjugation by armed minorities or by outside pressure.

I believe that we must assist free peoples to work out their own destinies in their own way.

I believe that our help should be primarily through economic stability and orderly political processes.

The world is not static, and the *status quo* is not sacred. But we cannot allow changes in the *status quo* in violation of the Charter of the United Nations by such methods as coercion, or by such subterfuges as political infiltration. In helping free and independent nations to maintain their freedom, the United States will be giving effect to the principles of the Charter of the United Nations.

It is necessary only to glance at a map to realize that the survival and integrity of the Greek nation are of grace importance in a much wider situation. If Greece should fall under the control of an armed minority, the effect upon its neighbor, Turkey, would be immediate and serious. Confusion and disorder might be well spread throughout the entire Middle East.

Moreover, the disappearance of Greece as an independent state would have a profound effect upon those countries in Europe whose peoples are struggling against great difficulties to maintain their freedoms and their independence while they repair the damages of war.

It would be an unspeakable tragedy if these countries, which have struggled so long against overwhelming odds, should lose that victory for which they sacrificed so much. Collapse of free institutions and loss of independence would be disastrous not only for them but for the world. Discouragement and possibly failure would quickly be the lot of neighboring peoples striving to maintain their freedom and independence…

We must take immediate and resolute action.

I therefore ask the Congress to provide authority for assistance to Greece and Turkey in the amount of $400,000,000 for the period ending June 30, 1948. In requesting these funds, I have taken into consideration the maximum amount of relief assistance which would be furnished to Greece out of the $350,000,000 which I recently requested that the Congress authorize for the prevention of starvation and suffering in countries devastated by the war.

In addition to funds, I ask the Congress to authorize the detail of American civilian and military personnel to Greece and Turkey, at the request of those countries, to assist in the tasks of reconstruction, and for the purpose of supervising the use of such financial and material assistance as may be furnished. I recommend that authority also be provided for the instruction and training of selected Greek and Turkish personnel.

Source: Harry S. Truman Speech 3/12/47

Public Papers of the Presidents, Harry S. Truman, 1947 (Washington: Government Printing Office, 1963) 176-180

HOW WELL DID YOU UNDERSTAND THIS SELECTION?

1. What did the U.S. fear would happen if Communists got power in Greece?

2. Identify the basic tenents of the Truman Doctrine.

3. What basically does Truman propose to do?

<hr>

GEORGE MARSHALL'S STATEMENT ON CHINESE COMMUNISM, 1947

<hr>

General George Marshall, chairman of the Joint Chiefs of Staff during the Truman administration, issued a statement on the difficulties the United States faced in establishing peace in China between the Nationalist government of Chiang Kai-shek and Communist insurgents led by Mao Zedong.

Statement by General Marshall, January 7, 1947

In this intricate and confused situation, I shall merely endeavor here to touch on some of the more important considerations—as they appeared to me—during my connection with the negotiations to bring about peace in China and a stable democratic form of government.

In the first place, the greatest obstacle to peace has been the complete, almost overwhelming suspicion with which the Chinese Communist Party and the Kuomintang regard each other.

On the one hand, the leaders of the Government are strongly opposed to a communistic form of government. On the other, the Communists frankly state that they are Marxists and intend to work toward establishing a communistic form of government of the American or British type....

I think the most important factors involved in the recent break-down of negotiations are these: On the side of the National Government, which is in effect the Kuomintang, there is a dominant group of reactionaries who have been opposed, in my opinion, to almost every effort I have made to influence the formation of a genuine coalition government...This group includes military as well as political leaders.

On the side of the Chinese Communist Party there are, I believe, liberals as well as radicals, though this view is vigorously opposed by many who believe that the Chinese Communist Party discipline is too rigidly enforced to admit of such differences of viewpoint. Nevertheless, it has appeared to me that there is a definite liberal group among the Communists, especially of young men who have turned to the Communists in disgust at the corruption evident in the local governments--men who would put the interest of the Chinese people above ruthless measures to establish a Communist ideology in the immediate future. The dyed-in-the-wool Communists do not hesitate at the most drastic measures to gain their end...They completely distrust the leaders of the Kuomintang and appear convinced that every Government proposal is designed to crush the Chinese Communist Party. I must say that the quite evidently inspired mob actions of last February and March, some within a few blocks of where I was then engaged in completing negotiations, gave the Communists good excuse for such suspicions...

Sincere efforts to achieve settlement have been frustrated time and again by extremist elements of both sides. The arguments reached by the Political Consultative Conference a year ago were a liberal and forward-looking charter which then offered China a basis for peace and construction. However, irreconcilable groups within the Kuomintang, interested in the preservation of their own feudal control of China, evidently had no real intention of implementing them...

Between this dominant reactionary group in the Government and the irreconcilable Communists who, I must state, did not so appear last February, lies the problem of how peace and well-being are to be brought to the long-suffering and presently inarticulate mass of the people of China. The reactionaries in the Government have evidently counted on substantial American support regardless of their actions. The Communists by their unwillingness to compromise in the national interest arc evidently counting on an economic collapse to bring about the fall of the Government, accelerated by extensive guerilla action against the long lines of rail communications--regardless of the cost in suffering to the Chinese people.

The salvation of the situation, as I see it, would be the assumption of leadership by the liberals in the Government and in the minority parties, a splendid group of men, but who as yet lack the political power to exercise a controlling influence. Successful action on their part under the leadership of Generalissimo Chiang Kai-shek would, I believe, lead to unity through good government...

I have spoken very frankly because in no other way can I hope to bring the people of the United States to even a partial understanding of this complex problem. I have expressed all these views privately in the course of negotiations; they are well known, I think, to most of the individuals concerned. I express them now publicly, as it is my duty, to present my estimate of the situation and its possibilities to the American people who have a deep interest in the development of conditions in the Far East promising an enduring peace in the Pacific.

HOW WELL DID YOU UNDERSTAND THIS SELECTION?

1. What does Marshall see as the main obstacle to peace in China?

2. What does Marshall think is the key to establishing peace in China?

3. Based on what you know about China, was Marshall's assessment of the situation correct? Explain.

Like Germany, the Korean Peninsula was divided into two nations at the end of World War II. South Korea was controlled by a government allied with the United States and North Korea was governed by a Communist dictatorship aligned with the Soviet Union. In June 1950 North Korean forces launched a surprise invasion of South Korea. Most Americans, including President Truman, believed the Soviet Union had ordered the invasion. In an address to the American public, Truman justified military intervention to repel the Communist invaders from South Korea.

June 27, 1950
Washington, D.C.

PRESIDENT HARRY S. TRUMAN

At noon today I sent a message on the Congress about the situation in Korea. I want to talk to you tonight about that situation, and about what it means to the security of the United States and to our hopes for peace in the world.

Korea is a small country, thousands of miles away, from what is happening there is important to every American.

On Sunday, June 25th, Communist forces attacked the Republic of Korea.

This attack has made it clear, beyond all doubt, that the international Communist movement is willing to use armed invasion to conquer independent nations. An act of aggressions such as this creates a very real danger to the security of all free nations.

The attack upon Korea was an outright breach of the peace and a violation of the Charter of the United Nations. By their actions in Korea, Communist leaders have demonstrated their contempt for the basic moral principles on which the United Nations is founded. This is a direct challenge to the efforts of the free nations to build the kind of world in which men can live in freedom and peace.

This challenge has been presented squarely. We must meet it squarely...

Under the flag of the United Nations a unified command has been established for all forces of the members of the United Nations fighting in Korea. Gen. Douglas MacArthur is the commander of this combined force.

The prompt action of the United Nations to put down lawless aggression, and the prompt response to this action by free peoples all over the world, will stand as a landmark in mankind's long search for a rule of law among nations.

Only a few countries have failed to endorse the efforts of the United Nations to stop the fighting in Korea. The most important of these is the Soviet Union. The Soviet Union has boycotted the meetings of the United Nations Security Council. It has refused to support the actions of the United Nations with respect to Korea. The United States requested the Soviet Government, 2 days after the fighting stated, to use it influence with the North Koreans to have them withdraw. The Soviet Government refused.

The Soviet Government has said many times that it wants peace in the world, but its attitude toward this act of aggression against the Republic of Korea is in direct contradiction of its statements.

For our part, we shall continue to support the United Nations action to restore peace in the world.

Furthermore, the fact that Communist forces have invaded Korea is a warning that there may be similar acts of aggression in other parts of the world. The free nations must be on their guard, more than ever before, against this kind of sneak attack...

When we have worked out with other free countries an increased program for our common defense, I shall recommend to the congress that additional funds be provided for this purpose. This is of great importance. The free nations face a worldwide threat. It must be met with a worldwide defense. The United States and other free nations can multiply their strength by joining with one another in a common effort to provide this defense. This is our best hope for peace.

The things we need to do to build up our military defense will require considerable adjustment in our domestic economy. We have a tremendously rich and productive economy, and it is expanding every year.

Our job now is to divert to defense purposes more of that tremendous productive capacity-more steel, more aluminum, more of a good many things.

In the message which I sent to the Congress today, I described the economic measures which are required at this time.

First, we need laws which will insure prompt and adequate supplies for military and essential civilian use. I have therefore recommended that the Congress give the Government power to guide the flow of materials into essential uses, to restrict their use for nonessential purposes, and to prevent the accumulation of unnecessary inventories.

Second, we must adopt measures to prevent inflation and to keep out Government in a sound financial condition. One of the major causes of inflation is the excessive use of credit. I have recommended that the Congress authorize the Government to set limits on installment buying and to curb speculation in agricultural commodities. In the housing field, where government credit is an important factor, I have already directed that credit be applied, and I have recommended that the Congress authorize further controls.

As an additional safeguard against inflation, and to help finance our defense needs, it will be necessary to make substantial increases in taxes. This is a contribution to our national security that every one of us should stand ready to make. As soon as a balanced and fair tax program can be worked out, I shall lay it before the Congress. This tax program will have as a major aim the elimination of profiteering.

Third, we should increase the production of goods needed for national defense. We must plan to enlarge our defense production, not just for the immediate future, but for the next several years. This will be primarily a task for our businessmen and workers. However, to help obtain the necessary increases, the Government should be authorized to provide certain types of financial assistance to private industry to increase defense production.

We have the sources to meet our needs. Far more important, the American people are unified in their belief in democratic freedom. We are united in detesting Communist slavery.

We know that the cost of freedom is high. But we are determined to preserve our freedom—no matter what the cost.

Our country stands before the world as an example of how free men, under God, can build a community of neighbors, working together for the good of all.

This is the goal we seek not only for ourselves, but for all people. We believe that freedom and peace are essential if men are to live as our Creator intended us to live. It is this faith that has guided us in the past, and it is this faith that will fortify us in the stern days ahead.

From public Papers of the Presidents of the United States: Harry S. Truman
(Government Office, Washington, D.C., 1961 – 1966), 1950: 537 – 540

HOW WELL DID YOU UNDERSTAND THIS SELECTION?

1. Why does President Truman say the U.S. should intervene in Korea?

2. How was the United Nations involved? Explain.

3. What did President Truman propose to do within the U.S. to fight the war? Why did he place so much emphasis on internal economic issues?

4. What was Truman's attitude toward the response of the Soviet Union?

*Space exploration became part of the Cold War as the United States and the Soviet Union both raced to see which nation could be the first to launch a vehicle into orbit around the earth. Americans reacted with shock and dismay when the Soviet Union launched **Sputnik** into orbit on October 4, 1957. They, along with President Eisenhower, could not believe the Soviet Union, a nation most considered technologically inferior to the United States, had actually beaten the United States into space. Eisenhower and his advisors, fearing the Soviets might use space-based weapons to gain an advantage over the U.S. in the Cold War, discussed the situation on October 8, 1957. The memorandum below is a record of that meeting.*

Memorandum of Conference with the President
October 8, 1957, 8:30 AM

S E C R E T

Declassified: 11-17-76

Others Present: Secretary Quarles
Dr. Waterman
Mr. Hagen
Mr. Holaday
Governor Adams
General Persons
Mr. Hagerty
Governor Pyle
Mr. Harlow
General Cutler
General Goodpaster

Secretary Quarles began by reviewing a memorandum prepared in Defense of the President on the subject of the earth satellite (dated October 7, 1957). He left a copy with the President. He reported that the Soviet launching on October 4th had apparently been highly successful.

The President asked Secretary Quarles about the report that had come to his attention to the effect that Redstone could have been used and could have placed a satellite in orbit many months ago. The Science Advisory Committee had felt, however, that it was better to have the earth satellite proceed separately from military development. One reason was to stress the peaceful character of the effort, and a second was to avoid the inclusion of materiel, to which foreign scientists might be given access, which is used in our own military rockets. He said that the Army feels it could erect a satellite four months prior to the estimated date for the Vanguard. The President said that when this information reaches Congress, they are bound to ask why this action was not taken. He recalled, however, that timing was never given too much importance in our own program, which was tied to the IGY and confirmed that, in order for all scientists to be able to look at the instrument, it had to be kept away from military secrets. Secretary Quarles pointed out that the Army plan would require some modification of the instrumentation in the missile.

He went on to add that the Russians have in fact done us a good turn, unintentionally, in establishing the concept of freedom of international space —this seems to be generally accepted as orbital space, in which the missile is making an inoffensive passage.

The President asked what kind of information could be conveyed by the signals reaching us from the Russian satellite. Secretary Quarles said the soviets say that it is simply a pulse to permit location of the missile through the radar direction finders. Following the meeting, Dr. Waterman indicated that there is some kind of modulation on the signals, which may mean that some coding is being done, although it might conceivably be accidental.

The President asked the group to look ahead five years, and asked about a reconnaissance vehicle. Secretary Quarles said the Air Force has a research program in this area and gave a general description of the project.

Governor Adams recalled that Dr. Pusey had said that we had never thought of this as a crash program, as the Russians apparently did. We were working simply to develop and transmit scientific knowledge. The President thought that to make a sudden shift in our approach now would be to belie the attitude we have had all along. Secretary Quarles said that such a shift would create service tensions in the Pentagon. Mr. Holaday said he planned to study with the Army the back up of the Navy program with the Redstone, adapting it to the instrumentation.

There was some discussion concerning the Soviet request as to whether we would like to put instruments of ours aboard one of their satellites. He said our instruments would be ready for this. Several present pointed out that our instruments contain parts which, if made available to the Russians, would give them substantial technological information.

A. J. Goodpaster
Brigadier General, USA

Source: Memorandum of Conference with President Eisenhower on October 8, 1957, Dwight D. Eisenhower Library, Abilene, Kansas

HOW WELL DID YOU UNDERSTAND THIS SELECTION?

1. Why did the Soviets beat Americans into space, according to the memo? Could the U.S. have launched a satellite earlier? If so, why did the launch not occur?

2. Why would the Soviet Union offer to allow the U.S. to put instruments on board Sputnik? Do you think the U.S. would accept this offer? Explain.

3. What do Eisenhower's advisors suggest the U.S. do?

In 1953 the National Security Council submitted a report to President Eisenhower suggesting psychological methods the United States could employ during the Cold War. This report, dated June 29, 1953, was classified top secret when originally written but declassified after the Cold War ended. It basically states that President Eisenhower accepted recommendations of the Psychological Strategy Board and directed all executive branch departments and agencies to implement the suggestions.

June 29, 1953   TOP SECRET SECURITY INFORMATION

NOTE BY THE ACTING EXECUTVE SECRETARY
to the
NATIONAL SECURITY COUNCIL
on
UNITED STATES OBJECTIVES AND ACTIONS TO EXPLOIT
THE UNREST IN THE SATELLITE STATES

References: A.   NSC action Nos. 817 and 820
            B.   Memo for NSC form Executive Secretary Subject, "United States Policies and Actions to Exploit
                 The Unrest in the Satellite States," dated June 24, 1953
            C.   NSC 143/2

The National Security Council, the Secretary of the Treasury and the Director, Bureau of the Budget, at the 151st Council meeting on June 25, 1953, approved the recommendations of the Psychological Strategy Board contained in the enclosure to the reference memorandum of June 24 subject to: (a) more emphasis being placed on passive resistance in implementing paragraph 2-(a), and (b) revision of paragraph 3-(b) to read: "Consider advocacy of (1) free elections in the satellites and association with the Western European community, with emphasis on economic cooperation and rehabilitation, and (2) subsequent withdrawal of all foreign troops from Germany, Austria and the satellites" (NSC Action No. 826).

The President on June 26, 1953, approved the recommendations of the Psychological Strategy Board, as amended and approved by the Council, and directs their implementation by all appropriate executive departments and agencies of the U.S. Government under the coordination of the Psychological Strategy Board. The President directs, as recommended by the Council, that more emphasis be place upon passive resistance in implementing paragraph 2-a. The report of the Psychological Strategy Board, as amended by the Council and approved by the President, is enclosed herewith.

Special security precautions are requested in the handling of the enclosure.

S. EVERETT GLEASON
Acting Executive Secretary

cc: The Secretary of the Treasury
      The Chairman, Joint Chiefs of Staff
      The Director of Central Intelligence

NSC 158
June 29, 1953   TOP SECRET SECURITY INFORMATION
Report by
THE NATIONAL SECURITY COUNCIL
on
INTERIM UNITED STATES OBJECTIVES AND ACTIONS
TO EXPLOIT THE UNREST IN THE SATELLITE STATES

1. Psychological Objectives
    a. To nourish resistance to communist oppression throughout satellite Europe,
    short of mass rebellion in areas under Soviet military control, and without compromising its spontaneous nature.

b. To undermine satellite puppet authority.

c. To exploit satellite unrest as demonstrable proof that the Soviet Empire is beginning to crumble.

d. To convince the free world, particularly Western Europe, that love of liberty and hatred of alien oppression are stronger behind the Iron Curtain than it has been dared to believe and that resistance to totalitarianism is less hopeless than has been imagined.

2. Courses of Action-Phase I (Requiring less than 60 days to initiate)

a. In East Germany and other satellite areas, where feasible, covertly stimulate acts and attitudes of resistance short of mass rebellion aimed at putting pressure on communist authority for specific reforms, discrediting such authority and provoking open Soviet intervention.

b. Establish, where feasible, secure resistance nuclei capable of further large-scale expansion.

c. Intensify defection programs, aimed at satellite police leaders and military personnel (especially pilots) and Soviet Military personnel.

d. Stimulate free world governmental, religious, and trade union activities capable of psychological effect behind the Iron Curtain, such as:

(1) International campaign to honor martyrs of the East German revolt.

HOW WELL DID YOU UNDERSTAND THIS SELECTION?

1. What recommendations did the Psychological Strategy Board make?

2. What is the ultimate goal of the U.S.?

3. What strategy is the U.S. going to use?

4. Do you think this is a good plan? Why or why not?

In 1948 President Truman initiated an airlift to defeat an attempt by the Soviet Union to starve the population of West Berlin into submission to Communism. Toward the end of his administration, President Eisenhower feared that the Soviet Union would again attempt to deny the United States access to West Berlin. A top secret report recently declassified outlines a possible American response if the United States faced another Berlin Blockade.

TOP SECRET
April 22, 1959

AN ANALYSIS OF THE POLITICAL AND MILITARY
IMPLICATIONS OF ALTERNATIVE USES OF FORCE
TO MAINTAIN ACCESS TO BERLIN

SUMMARY AND CONCLUSIONS

This paper deals with an alternative with respect to the use of force at some stage after military access to Berlin has been unacceptably interfered with. It does not discuss the criterion of unacceptability.

A.   A Substantial Effort to Reopen Ground Access by Local Action

1.   Force Required: Up to a reinforced division with tactical air support as required, composed of US-UK-French contingents.

2.   Method of Employment: The Allied force would remain on the autobahn and not fire unless fired upon. If fired upon, it would deploy and seek to overcome such resistance as feasible without use of nuclear weapons. If faced with insuperable resistance, the Allied force would seek to remain in the Soviet Zone during UN or other emergency consideration of the crisis.

3.   Bloc Reaction: If passive obstruction failed, the USSR would probably use its own and GDR territory.

4.   Free World Reaction: There would be considerable though varying public disapproval in the non-Communist world generally, stemming primarily from fear of war. NATO public reaction would be mixed and would depend largely on how far the issue at stake appeared to be survival of a free Berlin, rather than the technicality of GDR supervision of access. NATO governments probably would approve, but most neutralists would be opposed. The UN would probably call for a compromise solution.

5.   Conclusion: We would probably no*t be able to reopen and maintain ground access with the forces committed, in the face of the estimated Bloc reaction.*

HOW WELL DID YOU UNDERSTAND THIS SELECTION?

1.   What does the paper state the U.S. should do?

2.   What would likely be the result if the U.S. used force to gain access to West Berlin?

3.   Could this lead to thermonuclear war? Why or why not?

After serving two terms as president, the popular Dwight D. "Ike" Eisenhower left office. On January 7, 1961, he addressed the American public on national radio and television. In this speech Ike warned Americans about the dangers posed by the military-industrial complex.

January 18, 1961, Washington, D.C.
PRESIDENT DWIGHT D. EISENHOWER

A vital element in keeping the peace is our military establishment. Ours arms must be mighty, ready for instant action, so that no potential aggressor may be tempted to risk his own destruction.

Our military organization today bears little relation to that known by any of my predecessors in peacetime or indeed by the fighting men of World War II or Korea.

Until the latest of our world conflicts, the United States had no armaments industry. American makers of plowshares could, with time and as required, make swords as well. But now we can no longer risk emergency improvisation of national defense; we have been compelled to create a permanent armaments industry of vast proportions. Added to this, three and a half million men and women are directly engaged in the defense establishment. We annually spend on military security more than the net income of all United States corporations.

This conjunction of an immense military establishment and a large arms industry is new in the American experience. The total influence-economic, political, even spiritual-is felt in every city, every statehouse, every office of the federal government. We recognize the imperative need for this development. Yet we must not fail to comprehend its grave implications. Our toil, resources, and livelihood are all involved; so is the very structure of our society.

In the councils of government, we must guard against the acquisition of unwarranted influence, whether sought or unsought, by the military-industrial complex. The potential for the disastrous rise of misplaced power exists and will persist.

We must never let the weight of this combination endanger our liberties or democratic processes. We should take nothing for granted. Only an alert and knowledgeable citizenry can compel the proper meshing of the huge industrial and military machinery of defense with our peaceful methods and goals, so that security and liberty may prosper together.

Akin to, and largely responsible for the sweeping changes in our industrial-military posture, has been the technological revolution during recent decades.

In this revolution, research has become central; it also becomes more formalized, complex, and costly. A steadily increasing share is conducted for, by, or at the direction of, the federal government....

The prospect of domination of the nation's scholars by federal employment, project allocations, and the power of money is ever present-and is gravely to be regarded.

Yet, in holding scientific research and discovery in respect, as we should, we must also be alert to the equal and opposite danger that public policy could itself become the captive of a scientific-technological elite.

It is the task of statesmanship to mold, to balance, and to integrate these and other forces, new and old, within the principles of our democratic system-ever aiming toward the supreme goals of our free society.

Another factor in maintaining balance involves the element of time. As we peer into society's future, we - you and I, and our government – must avoid the impulse to live only for today, plundering, for our own ease and convenience, the precious resources of tomorrow. We cannot mortgage the material assets of our grandchildren without risking the loss also of their political and spiritual heritage. We want democracy to survive for all generations to come, not to become the insolvent phantom of tomorrow.

Down the long lane of the history yet to written America knows that this world of ours, ever growing smaller, must avoid becoming a community of dreadful fear and hate, and be, instead, a proud confederation of mutual trust and respect.

Such a confederation must be one of equals. The weakest must come to the conference table with the same confidence as do we, protected as we are by our moral, economic, and military strength. That table, through scarred by many past frustrations, cannot be abandoned for the certain agony of the battlefield.

Disarmament, with mutual honor and confidence, is a continuing imperative. Together we must learn how to compose differences, not with arms, but with intellect and decent purpose. Because this need is so sharp and apparent I confess that I lay down my official responsibilities in this field with a definite sense of disappointment. As one who witnessed the honor and the lingering sadness of war – as one who knows that another war could destroy this civilization which has been so slowly and painfully built over thousands of years – I wish I could say tonight that a lasting peace is in sight.

Happily, I can say that war has been avoided. Steady progress toward our ultimate goal has been made. But, so much remains to be done. As a private citizen, I shall never cease to do with little I can to help the world advance along that road....

HOW WELL DID YOU UNDERSTAND THIS SELECTION?

1. What does Eisenhower mean by the military-industrial complex?

2. What dangers does Eisenhower see in regards to the military-industrial complex?

3. Why do you think Eisenhower chose to speak about the military-industrial complex in his farewell address?

4. Have Eisenhower's fears been realized? Explain.

SELF TEST

MULTIPLE CHOICE: Circle the correct response. The correct answers are given at the end.

1. Which American president adopted the policy of Containment?
   a. Eisenhower.
   b. Truman.
   c. Franklin Roosevelt.
   d. Kennedy.

2. What was the purpose of Containment?
   a. To prevent the spread of Communism outside the Soviet Union and Eastern Europe.
   b. To contain the military might of other nations.
   c. To prevent increased global warming.
   d. To stop Islamic militarism from destroying Israel in the Middle East.

3. Which American general did President Truman fire for insubordination?
   a. Eisenhower.
   b. Patton.
   c. Marshall.
   d. MacArthur.

4. How did President Truman respond to the Berlin Blockade?
   a. By airlifting supplies to West Berlin.
   b. By using military force to open the road to Berlin.
   c. By launching an air strike against East Germany.
   d. By threatening to attack the Soviet Union with nuclear weapons.

5. The Nationalist leader of China was
   a. Mao Zedong.
   b. Chiang Kuk Woh.
   c. Chiang Kai-shek.
   d. Ho Chi Minh.

6. The military alliance between the United States and Western European nations is called
   a. The Warsaw Pact.
   b. NATO.
   c. SEATO.
   d. The Marshall Plan.

7. The first satellite launched into orbit around the earth was
   a. Lenordo.
   b. Apollo I.
   c. Sputnik.
   d. Challenger.

8. Which Cuban leader did the American CIA plot to overthrow?
   a. Juan Valdez.
   b. Ho Chi Minh.
   c. Fidel Castro.
   d. Jose Pasten.

9. The Middle Eastern conflict that erupted when Egypt nationalized the Suez Canal was
   a. The Suez War.
   b. The Six Days War.
   c. The Golan Heights War.
   d. Armageddon.

10. What did the Truman Doctrine state?
    a. That the U.S. was not concerned about Communism.
    b. That the U.S. would support the United Nations.
    c. That the U.S. would intervene in North Korea to overthrow the Communist regime.
    d. That the U.S. would aid free peoples if their freedom was threatened internally or externally.

ANSWERS: 1-b; 2-a; 3-d; 4-a; 5-c; 6-b; 7-c; 8-c; 9-a; 10-d

ESSAYS:

1. Explain why the Cold War originated?

2. Was the United States or the Soviet Union more responsible for the Cold War? Use historical evidence to support your answer.

3. Discuss the major developments in the Cold War during the Truman and Eisenhower administrations.

OPTIONAL ACTIVITIES: (Use your knowledge and imagination when appropriate.)

1. Choose members from your class to represent President Truman's cabinet. Have them debate the merits and problems with the policy of Containment.

2. Pretend that you are Dwight D. Eisenhower running for president in 1952. Write a campaign stump speech in which you discuss your views on Containment.

3. Choose two members of your class to be Nikita Khruschev and President Eisenhower at a Summit Meeting between the U.S. and U.S.S.R. Have them discuss the major issues confronting the U.S. and the Soviet Union during the Cold War.

WEB SITE LISTINGS:

Containment/War
"The Cold War," CNN series
    http://www.cnn.com/coldwar

"Documents Relating to American Foreign Policy: The Cold War," Vincent Ferraro, Mount Holyoke College
    http://www.mtholyoke.edu/acad/intrel/coldwar.htm

Smithsonian Institution's Soviet Archives Exhibition
    http://www.ibiblio.org/expo/soviet.exhibit/coldwar.html

"Senator Joseph McCarthy," Webcorp Multimedia
    http://webcorp.com/mccarthy/
"Cold War International History Project, Virtual Archive" Woodrow Wilson International Center for Scholars
    http://wwics.si.edu/index.cfm?topic_id=1409&fuseaction=library.Collection

The National Security Archive, George Washington University
    http://www.gwu.edu/~nsarchiv/

Korean War Project
    http://www.koreanwar.org/index1.html

Avalon Project: Yale's Archive for Documents in Law, History, and Diplomacy
    The Cold War: http://www.yale.edu/lawweb/avalon/coldwar.htm

"Truman Doctrine Collection," Harry S. Truman Library & Museum
    http://www.trumanlibrary.org/whistlestop/study_collections/doctrine/large/doctrine.htm

Middle Class Life
Kingwood College Library
   http://kclibrary.nhmccd.edu/decade50.html

"United States Culture and Society in the 1950s," Jessamyn Neuhaus
   http://home.earthlink.net/~neuhausj/1950s/

"The Literature & Culture of the American 1950s," Alan Filreis, University of Pennsylvania
   http://www.english.upenn.edu/~afilreis/50s/home.html

Civil Rights
"The History of Jim Crow,"
   http://www.jimcrowhistory.org/history/transition.htm

"In Pursuit of Freedom & Equality: Brown v. Board of Education of Topeka," Washburn University School of Law,
   http://brownvboard.org/

"Landmark Supreme Court Cases: Brown v. Board of Education," Street Law & the Supreme Court Historical Society
   http://www.landmarkcases.org/brown/

"Little Rock Central High, 40th Anniversary,"
   http://www.centralhigh57.org/

"The Rosa Parks Portal,"
   http://e-portals.org/Parks/

"The Murder of Emmett Till," PBS
   http://www.pbs.org/wgbh/amex/till/filmmore/

"The Martin Luther King, Jr. Papers Project," Stanford University
   http://www.stanford.edu/group/King/

Chapter Twenty-two

AMERICAN CULTURE
FROM 1945 TO 1960

Victory over the Nazis ushered in a period historian Robert Toohey calls the Age of Americana. American culture and ideas spread throughout the world via the medium of television. Presidents Truman and Eisenhower, despite bumps in the road, generally presided over a prosperous, peaceful nation that experienced some of the most profound social change in history. African American men and women who had served bravely in the armed forces during the Second World War were not willing to tolerate racism, prejudice, and discrimination after they returned home from the war. They and thousands of others participated in the Civil Rights Movement that began when Rosa Parks refused to relinquish her seat on a Montgomery, Alabama bus to a white passenger. Black and white protestors participated in marches, demonstrations, sit-ins, and other activities that eventually ended Jim Crow segregation. Other groups, including women, homosexuals, Latinos, and Asians also demanded equal treatment within the American legal and cultural system.

American women in particular experienced many positive changes from 1945 to 1960. The 1950 saw the number of women who worked outside the home increase. Driving female employment to some degree was consumerism. Families increasingly needed two incomes to purchase the dazzling array of consumer goods available after World War II. Despite working outside the home, American women faced social pressures to marry, bear children, and keep a good house for their husbands and children. Most women married around the age of 20 and bore on average about three or four children. The high number of marriages and children produced in them ushered in the period historians call the Baby Boom from 1946 to 1964. Many women, however, did not find fulfillment in marriage and family. Educated women often felt their intellectual abilities were wasted in marriage and wanted more. Even though a double standard regarding sexuality existed in American culture, research indicated that about one-fourth of married women engaged in extramarital affairs during the 1950s.

Television, which became a primary mode of entertainment and communication during the 1950s, greatly shaped American culture. The number of households with television receivers increased dramatically; by 1955 about two-thirds of all families owned a television and the number of broadcast stations expanded nationwide. Commercial interests realized the advantages of promoting products on television and spent billions of dollars on advertising. Scores of television shows were produced. They ranged from westerns and drama to talk and variety. Television actors and actresses became national and even international stars.

Television also increased the popularity of college and professional sports. Baseball, boxing, wrestling, football, basketball, tennis, golf, automobile racing, and other sports became popular viewing alternatives for the millions of Americans with television sets in their homes. Athletes like Mickey Mantle, Jackie Robinson, Rocky Marciano, Joe

DiMaggio, Wilt Chamberlain, and Bill Russell became heroes to many Americans. Professional football was particularly suited for television. The fast pace of the game kept Americans glued to their television on Sunday afternoons during the latter years of the 1950s when over a third of all television viewers watched National Football League games.

American musical tastes also changed during the Truman and Eisenhower administrations. Rock 'n' Roll became popular with younger Americans and represented a blending of various musical styles present within the United States. Memphis, Tennessee record producer Sam Phillips, owner of Sun Recording Studio, signed to contracts musicians that dominated American music for years to come. Phillips' most important find was Elvis Presley. No performer was as popular as Presley during the 1950s. He became America's first rock 'n' roll superstar. Older generations did not embrace Presley and rock 'n' roll as readily as did young people. Parents of teenagers were concerned that rock music would cause their sons and daughters to become sexually active before marriage. White racists also rejected rock 'n' roll because of its African roots, seeing performances by rock musicians as degrading to the white race and undermining the morals of American youth.

American life was transformed in major ways during the 1950s by construction of the interstate highway system. President Eisenhower, impressed by the German autobahn during World War II, wanted the United States to build a system of super roads that would link together every part of the country. In 1956 Eisenhower's desire was fulfilled when Congress enacted the Interstate Highway Act authorizing construction of a series of four, six, and eight lane roads throughout the United States. American life quickly changed as people preferred driving their privately owned automobiles to far destinations rather than taking public transportation. Automobile sales soared and the American economy boomed as a result. Thousands of new businesses, including service stations, fast food restaurants, and motels, opened to cater to the millions of automobile drivers and passengers traversing America's interstates.

The increase in automobile travel, unfortunately, harmed public transportation. Railroad passenger service seriously declined and disappeared in many communities. Trolley lines in many cities saw a decline in riders and automobile manufacturing companies such as General Motors purchased numerous urban trolley and light rail companies to eliminate competition for the cars, busses, and trucks they built. Although automobile travel gave Americans a sense of freedom and independence, it increased pollution, urban congestion, and dependence on foreign oil, which eventually created a tremendous trade deficit for the United States.

American reliance on the automobile also prompted a mass exodus from downtown to suburbia. Millions of Americans purchased houses in suburbs such as Levittown, New York to escape the congestion of urban centers. Cars and good roads made possible a daily commute to work in downtown factories and offices. Businesses, realizing the profits possible in suburbia, began opening locations close to their customers. The exodus of people and businesses from downtown centers caused massive urban deterioration as once thriving neighborhoods became slums after people and businesses fled to the suburbs.

IDENTIFICATION: Briefly describe each term.

Interstate Highway Act

Elvis Presley

Rock 'n' Roll

Walter-McCarran

Harry Truman

Dwight David Eisenhower

President's Committee on Civil Rights

Executive Order 9981

Martin Luther King, Jr.

Herman Marion Sweatt

Smith vs. Allwright

Brown vs. Board of Education of Topeka, (KS), et.al.

The Uptown Klan (White Citizens Council)

Emmett Till

Rosa Parks

Orval Faubus

Earl Warren

Bracero Program

League of United Latin American Citizens

Mendez v. Westminister School District

Dr. Hector Garcia

Baby Boom

Betty Friedan

Petting

Alfred Kinsey

Hugh Hefner

Joseph McCarthy

Gay Scare

Mattachine Society

Edward Sagarin

Interstate Highway Act

Levittown

Rod Serling

The "idiot box"

Jackie Robinson

Beatniks

William Burroughs

Jack Kerovac

Bebop

Comic Book Wars

William M. Gaines

Dr. Fredrick Werthem

Comic Code Authority

Sam Phillips

Rocket 88

Alan Nadel

THINK ABOUT:

1. Describe the changes and challenges American culture faced from 1945 to 1960.

2. Discuss the difficulties minorities experienced in the United States after World War II. Describe improvements brought about the Civil Rights, Gay Rights, and women's movement.

3. Describe changes in music and culture from 1945 to 1960.

HUAC VS. HOLLYWOOD

During the Truman and Eisenhower administrations the United States experienced a second Red Scare. Government officials, such as Congressman Richard Nixon and Senator Joseph McCarthy, accused numerous Americans of being Communists without any real evidence to support their allegations. Actors and actress working in the television and movie industries were favorite targets of the Red Baiters. In 1946 the House Un-American Activities Committee, popularly called HUAC, began hearings to investigate Communism within the entertainment industry. Anybody suspected of harboring Communist sympathizers could be forced to testify before HUAC. Actors, actresses, directors, writers, or anyone who refused to cooperate were subject to fines, imprisonment, and blacklisting, making it nearly impossible for them to find employment within the industry. Reproduced below is the transcript of John Howard Lawson, a Hollywood screenwriter, testifying before HUAC.

October 27, 1947
House of Representatives, Washington, D.C.
John Howard Lawson, Hollywood screenwriter, testifying before HUAC

John Howard Lawson, Screenwriter
Mr. Stripling, the first witness.

MR. CRUM. Mr. Chairman————
MR. STRIPLING.   Mr. John Howard Lawson.
MR. CRUM.   Mr. Chairman————
THE CHAIRMAN.   I am sorry————
MR. CRUM. May I request the right of cross-examination? I ask you to bring back and   permit us to cross-examination the witness, Adolph Menjou, Fred Niblo, John Charles Moffitt, Richard Macauley, Rupert Hughes, Sam Wood, Ayn Rand, James McGuinness————
THE CHAIRMAN. The request————
MR. CRUM. Howard Rushmore————

(The chairman pounding gavel.)

MR. CRUM. Morrie Ryskind, Oliver Carlson———

THE CHAIRMAN. That request is denied.

MR. CRUM. In order to show that these witnesses lied.

THE CHAIRMAN. That request is denied. Mr. Stripling, the first witness.

MR. STRIPLING. John Howard Lawson.

(John Howard Lawson, accompanied by Robert W. Kenny and Barley Crum takes places at witness table.)

THE CHAIRMAN. Stand and please raise your right hand. Do you solemnly swear the testimony you are about to give is the truth, the whole truth, and nothing but the truth, so help you God?

MR. LAWSON. I do.

THE CHAIRMAN. Sit down, please.

MR. LAWSON. Mr. Chairman, I have a statement here which I wish to make———

THE CHAIRMAN. Well, all right; let me see your statement.

(Statement handed to the chairman)

MR. STRIPLING. Do you have a copy of that?

MR. CRUM. We can get you copies.

THE CHAIRMAN. I don't care to read any more of the statement. The statement will not be read. I read the first line.

MR. LAWSON. You have spent 1 week vilifying me before the American public———

THE CHAIRMAN. Just a minute———

MR. LAWSON. And you refuse to allow me to make a statement on my rights as an American citizen.

THE CHAIRMAN. I refuse you to make the statement, because of the first sentence in your statement. That statement is not pertinent to the inquiry.

Now this is a congressional committee—a congressional committee set up by law. We must have orderly procedure, and we are going to have orderly procedure.

Mr. Stripling, identify the witness.

MR. LAWSON. The rights of American citizens are important in this room here, and I intend to stand up for those rights, Congressman Thomas.

MR. STRIPLING. Mr. Lawson, will you state your full name, please!

MR. LAWSON. I wish to protest against the unwillingness of this committee to read a statement, when you permitted Mr. Warner, Mr. Mayer, and others to read statements in this room.

My name is John Howard Lawson.

MR. STRIPLING. What is your present address?

MR. LAWSON. 9354 Burnett Avenue, San Fernando, Calif.

MR. STRIPLING. When and where were you born?

MR. LAWSON. New York City.

MR. STRIPLING. What year?

MR. LAWSON. 1894.

MR. STRIPLING. Give us a exact date.

MR. LAWSON. September 25.

MR. STRIPLING. Mr. Lawson, you are here in response to a subpoena which was served upon you on September 19, 1947; is that true?

MR. LAWSON. That is correct....

MR. STRIPLING. What is your occupation, Mr. Lawson?

MR. LAWSON. I am a writer.

MR. STRIPLING. How long have you been a writer?

MR. LAWSON. All my life-at least 35 years-all my adult life.

MR. STRIPLING. Are you a member of the Screen Writers Guild?

MR. LAWSON. The raising of any question here in regard to membership, political beliefs, or affiliation—

MR. STRIPLING. Mr. Chairman—

MR. LAWSON. Is absolutely beyond the powers of this committee.

MR. STRIPLING. Mr. Chairman———

MR. LAWSON. But——-

(The chairman pounding gavel)

MR. LAWSON. It is a matter of public record that I am a member of the Screen Writers Guild.

MR. STRIPLING. I ask——-

[Applause.]

THE CHAIRMAN. I want to caution the people in the audience: You are the guests of this committee and you will have to maintain order at all times. I do not care for any applause or any demonstrations of one kind or another.

MR. STRIPLING. Now, Mr. Chairman, I am also going to request that you instruct the witness to be responsive to the questions.

THE CHAIRMAN. I think the witness will be more responsive to the questions.

MR. LAWSON. Mr. Chairman, you permitted——-

THE CHAIRMAN (pounding gavel). Never mind——-

MR. LAWSON (continuing). Witnesses in this room to make answers of three or five hundred words to questions here.

THE CHAIRMAN. Mr. Lawson, you will please be responsive to these questions and not continue to try to disrupt these hearings.

MR. LAWSON. I am not on trial here, Mr. Chairman. This committee is on trial here before the American people. Let us get that straight.

THE CHAIRMAN. We don't want you to be on trial.

MR. STRIPLING. Have you ever held any office in the guild?

MR. LAWSON. The question of whether I have held office is also a question which is beyond the purview of this committee.

(The chairman pounding gavel.)

MR. LAWSON. It is an invasion of the right of association under the Bill of Rights of this country.

THE CHAIRMAN. Please be responsive to the question.

MR. LAWSON. It is also a matter——-

(The chairman pounding gavel.)

MR. LAWSON. Of public record——-

THE CHAIRMAN. You asked to be heard. Through your attorney, you asked to be heard, and we want you to be heard. And if you don't care to be heard, then we will excuse you and we will put the record in without your answers.

MR. LAWSON. I wish to frame my own answers to your questions, Mr. Chairman, and I intend to do so.

THE CHAIRMAN. And you will be responsive to the questions or you will be excused from the witness stand.

MR. LAWSON. I will frame my own answers, Mr. Chairman.

THE CHAIRMAN. Go ahead, Mr. Stripling.

MR. LAWSON. Correct.

MR. STRIPLING. You have probably written others; have you not, Mr. Lawson?

MR. LAWSON. Many others. You have missed a lot of them.

MR. STRIPLING. You don't care to furnish them to the committee, do you?

MR. LAWSON. Not in the least interested.

MR. STRIPLING. Mr. Lawson, are you now, or have you ever been a member of the Communist Party of the United States?

MR. LAWSON. In framing my answer to that question I must emphasize the points that I have raised before. The question of communism is in no way related to this inquiry, which is an attempt to get control of the screen and to invade the basic rights of American citizens in all fields.

MR. MCDOWELL. Now I must object——-

MR. STRIPLING. Mr. Chairman——-

(The chairman pounding gavel.)

MR. LAWSON (continuing). Which has been historically denied to any committee of this sort, to invade the rights and privileges and immunity of American citizens, whether they be Protestant, Methodist, Jewish, or Catholic, whether they be Republican or Democrats or anything else.

THE CHAIRMAN (pounding gavel). Mr. Lawson just quiet down again.

Mr. Lawson, the most pertinent question that we can ask is whether or not you have ever been a member of a Communist Party. Now, do you care to answer that question?

MR. LAWSON. You are using the old technique, which was used in Hitler Germany in order to create a scare here——-

THE CHAIRMAN (pounding gavel). Oh——-

MR. LAWSON. In order to create an entirely false atmosphere in which this hearing is conducted——-

(The chairman pounding gavel.)

MR. LAWSON. In order that you can smear the motion-picture industry, and you can proceed to the press, to any form of communication in this country.

THE CHAIRMAN. You have learned——-

MR. LAWSON. The Bill of Rights was established precisely to prevent the operation of any committee which could invade the basic rights of Americans.

Now, if you want to know——-

MR. STRIPLING. Mr. Chairman, the witness is not answering the question.

MR. LAWSON. If you want to know——-

(The chairman pounding gavel.)

THE CHAIRMAN. Mr. Lawson——-

MR. LAWSON. You permit me and my attorneys to bring in here the witnesses that testified last week and you permit us to cross-examine these witnesses, and will show up the whole tissue of lie——-

THE CHAIRMAN (pounding gavel). We are going to get the answer to that question if we have to stay here for a week.

Are you a member of the Communist Party, or have you ever been a member of the Communist Party?

MR. LAWSON. It is unfortunate and tragic that I have to teach this committee the basic principles of American——-

THE CHAIRMAN (pounding gavel). That is not the question. That is not the question. The question is: Have you ever been a member of the Communist Party?

MR. LAWSON. I am framing my answer in the only way in which any American citizen can frame his answer to a question which absolutely invades his rights.

THE CHAIRMAN. Then you refuse to answer that question; is that correct?

MR. LAWSON. I have told you that I will offer my beliefs, affiliations, and everything else to the American public, and they will know where I stand.

THE CHAIRMAN (pounding gavel). Excuse the witness——-

MR. LAWSON. As they do from what I have written.

THE CHAIRMAN (pounding gavel). Stand away from the stand——-

MR. LAWSON. I have written Americanism for many years, and I shall continue to fight for the Bill of Rights, which you are trying to destroy.

THE CHAIRMAN. Officers, take this man away from the stand——-

THE CHAIRMAN (pounding gavel). There will be no demonstrations. No demonstrations, for or against. Everyone will please be seated...

Source: House of Representatives, Committee on Un-American Activities, October 20 – 30, 1947
(Washington: Government Printing Office, 1947) 289 -295

HOW WELL DID YOU UNDERSTAND THIS SELECTION?

1. How was the witness treated? Explain.

2. What does Lawson accuse HUAC of doing? Is he correct? Why or why not?

3. Why did Lawson refuse to answer the question about whether he was a member of the Communist Party?

BROWN V. TOPEKA, BOARD OF EDUCATION

The United States Supreme Court on May 17, 1954 overturned its 1896 decision in **Plessy v. Ferguson** *that allowed separate but equal schools for blacks and whites. In* **Brown v. the Board of Education of Topeka, Kansas** *the court under direction of Chief Justice Earl Warren declared segregated schools illegal. This decision represented a tremendous victory for the National Association for the Advancement of Colored People, which for two decades had worked to overturn the separate but equal doctrine established by* **Plessy v. Ferguson.**

We come then to the question presented: Does segregation of children in public schools solely on the basis of race, even though the physical facilities and other "tangible" factors may be equal, deprive the children of the minority group of equal educational opportunities? We believe that it does...

To separate them from others of similar age and qualifications solely because of their race generates a feeling of inferiority as to their status in the community that may affect their hearts and minds in a way unlikely to ever be undone. The effect of this separation on their educational opportunities as well as stated by a finding in the Kansas case by a court which nevertheless felt compelled to rule against the Negro plaintiffs:

> *Segregation of white and colored children in public schools has a detrimental effect upon the colored children. The impact is greater when it has the sanction of the law, therefore, has a tendency to retard the educational and mental development of Negro children and to deprive them of some of the benefits they would receive in a racially integrated school system.*

Whatever may have been the extent of psychological knowledge at the time of *Plessy v. Ferguson* contrary to this finding is rejected.

We conclude that in the field of public education the doctrine of "separate but equal" has no place. Separate educational facilities are inherently unequal. Therefore, we hold that the plaintiffs and others similarly situated for whom the action have been brought are, by reason of the segregation complained of, deprived of the equal protection of the laws guaranteed by the Fourteenth Amendment. This disposition makes unnecessary any discussion whether such segregation also violates the Due Process Clause of the Fourteenth Amendment.

Because these are class actions, because of the wide applicability of this decision, and because of the great variety of local conditions, the formulation of decrees in these cases presents problems of considerable complexity. On reargument, the consideration of appropriate relief was necessarily subordinated to the primary question – the constitutionality of segregation in public education. We have now announced that such segregation is a denial of the equal protection of the laws.

Source: *Brown v. Board of Education, Topeka,* United States Reports, 347 U.S. 483 [1954]

HOW WELL DID YOU UNDERSTAND THIS SELECTION?

1. What, basically, did the Warren Court rule in *Brown v. the Board of Education of Topeka, Kansas?*

2. What was likely to be the reaction of whites in states that had segregated schools? How would blacks likely have reacted?

3. What rationale did the Court use in overturning *Plessy v. Ferguson?*

PRESIDENT EISENHOWER ENFORCES THE *BROWN* DECISION IN LITTLE ROCK, 1957

President Eisenhower, seeking votes for the Republican Party in the traditional Democratic South, did not want to force integration of public schools as ordered by the Supreme Court in the **Brown** *decision for fear of alienating white voters. Faced with world condemnation after Arkansas governor Orval Faubus used the National Guard to prevent integration of Central High School in Little Rock, Eisenhower put partisan politics aside and dispatched federal troops to escort nine black students safely to the school's campus, protecting them from a mob of angry whites trying to prevent school desegregation. On September 25, 1957, President Eisenhower addressed the nation in a televised speech explaining why he used the military to enforce court ordered desegregation in Arkansas.*

September 25, 1957,
PRESIDENT DWIGHT D. EISENHOWER

My Fellow Citizens.... I must speak to you about the serious situation that had arisen in Little Rock...In that city, under the leadership of demagogic extremists, disorderly mobs have deliberately prevented the carrying out of proper orders from a federal court. Local authorities have not eliminated that violent opposition and, under the law, I yesterday issued a proclamation calling upon the mob to disperse.

This morning the mob again gathered in front of the Central High School of Little Rock, obviously for the purpose of again preventing the carrying out of the court's order relating to the admissions of Negro children to that school.

Whenever normal agencies prove inadequate to the task and it becomes necessary for the executive branch of the federal government to use its powers and authority to uphold federal courts, the President's responsibility is inescapable.

In accordance with that responsibility, I have today issued and Executive Order directing the use of troops under federal authority to aid in the execution of federal law at Little Rock, Arkansas. This became necessary when my Proclamation of yesterday was not observed, and the obstruction of justice still continues.....

A foundation of our American way of life is our national respect of law.

In the South, as elsewhere, citizens are keenly aware of the tremendous disservice that has been don't to the people of Arkansas in the eyes of the nation, and that has been done to the nation in the eyes of the world.

At a time when we face grave situations abroad because of the hatred that communism bears toward a system of government based on human rights, it would be difficult to exaggerate the harm that is being done to the prestige and influence, and indeed to the safety, of our nation and the world.

Our enemies are gloating over this incident and using it everywhere to misrepresent our whole nation. We are portrayed as a violator of those standards of conduct which the peoples of the world united to proclaim in the Charter of the United Nations. There they affirmed "faith in fundamental human rights" and "in the dignity and worth of the human person" and they did so "without distinction as to race, sex, language or religion."

And so, with deep confidence, I call upon the citizens of the State of Arkansas to assist in bringing to an immediate end all interference with the law and its processes. If resistance to the federal court orders ceases at once, the further presence of federal troops will be unnecessary and the City of Little Rock will return to its normal habits of peace and order and a blot upon the fair name and high honor of our nation in the world will be removed.

Thus will be restored the image of America and of all its parts as one nation, indivisible, with liberty and justice for all.

HOW WELL DID YOU UNDERSTAND THIS SELECTION?

1. How did Eisenhower justify the use of federal troops to integrate Central High in Little Rock?

2. Did the Cold War and international relations play a role in Eisenhower's decision? Explain.

3. What does the speech convey about Eisenhower's views on school desegregation? On civil rights for blacks? On the rule of law?

HOMOSEXUALS IN GOVERNMENT, 1950

Some observers have described the American government and people as paranoid following World War II. Massive fear gripped Americans in the early years of the Cold War period. Most feared nuclear annihilation at the hands of the Soviet Union. Many believed that the United States was threatened by a Communist conspiracy to gain control of the government by planting individuals throughout the bureaucracy. This paranoia within American society sparked fears of gay Americans. Wisconsin Senator Joseph McCarthy, who had gained fame and popularity by leading the crusade against Communism, linked homosexuals to Communism, stating that gay Americans were part of a conspiracy to destroy the American family, masculinity, and the military so that the Soviet Union could more easily take over the government. Heterosexuals claimed that homosexual government workers created a security risk for the United States because the gay lifestyle rendered them susceptible to blackmail by Soviet Agents. Republican members of Congress charged that the Truman administration was completely infiltrated by gays and demanded that all homosexuals employed by the Federal Government be immediately dismissed. As a result, thousands of federal workers suspected of being homosexual were fired. Congress, beginning in 1950, held hearings on the subject of American homosexuality and on the dangers gays posed to the United States. The selection that follows is a transcript of a hearing on homosexuality from the 81st Congress.

HOMOSEXUALS IN GOVERNMENT, 1950
Congressional Record, Volume 96, Part 4
81st Congress 2nd Session, March 29—April 24, 1950

pages 4527-4528

ON THE FLOOR OF THE HOUSE OF REPRESENTATIVES:

Mr. Miller of Nebraska. Mr. Chairman, I realize that I am discussing a very delicate subject I cannot lay the bones bare like I could before medical colleagues. I would like to strip the fetid, stinking flesh off this skeleton of homosexuality and tell my colleagues of the House some of the facts of nature. I cannot expose all the putrid facts as it would offend the sensibilities of some of you. It will be necessary to skirt some of the edges, and I use certain Latin terms to describe some of these individuals. Make no mistake several thousand, according to police records, are now employed by the Federal Government.

I offer this amendment to the Vorys amendment in good faith. Recently the spotlight of publicity has been focused not only upon the State Department but upon the Department of Commerce because of homosexuals being employed in these and other departments of Government. Recently Mr. Peurifoy, of the State Department, said he had allowed 91 individuals in the State Department to resign because they were homosexuals. Now they are like birds of a feather, they flock together. Where did they go?

You must know what a homosexual is. It is amazing that in the Capital City of Washington we are plagued with such a large group of those individuals. Washington attracts many lovely folks. The sex crimes in the city are many.

In the Eightieth Congress I was the author of the sex pervert bill that passed this Congress and is now a law in the District of Colombia. It can confine some of these people in St. Elizabeths Hospital for treatment. They are sex perverts. Some of them are more to be pitied than condemned, because in many it is a pathological condition, very much like the kleptomaniac who must go out and steal, he has that urge; or like the pyromaniac, who goes to bed and wakes up in the middle of the night with an urge to go out and set a fire. He does that. Some of these homosexuals are in that class. Remember there were 91 of them dismissed in the State Department. That is a small percentage of those employed in Government. We learned 2 years ago that there were around 4,000 homosexuals in the District. The Police Department the other day said there were between five and six thousand in Washington who are active and that 75 percent were in Government employment. There are places in Washington where they gather for the purpose of sex orgies, where they worship at the cesspool and flesh pots of iniquity. There is a restaurant downtown where you will find male prostitutes. They solicit business for other male customers. They are pimps and undesirable characters. You will find odd words in the vocabulary of the homosexual. There are many types such as the necrophilia, fettichism, pygmalionism, fellatios, cunnilinguist, sodomatic, pederasty, saphism, sadism, and masochist. Indeed, there are many methods of practices among the homosexuals. You will find those people using the words as, "He is a fish. He is a bull-dicker. He is mamma and he is papa, and punk, and pimp." Yes; in one of our prominent restaurants rug parties and sex orgies go on. Some of those people have been in the State Department, and I understand some of them are now in the other departments. The 91 who were permitted to resign have gone some place, and, like birds of a feather, they flock together. Those people like to be known to each other. They have signs used on streetcars and in public places to call attention to others of like mind. Their rug and fairy parties are elaborate.

So I offer this amendment, and when the time comes for voting upon it, I hope that no one will object. I sometimes wonder how many of these homosexuals have had a part in shaping our foreign policy. How many have been in sensitive positions and subject to blackmail. It is a known fact that homosexuality goes back to the Orientals, long before the time of Confucius; that the Russians are strong believers in homosexuality, and that those same people are able to get into the State Department and get somebody in their embrace, and once they are in their embrace, fearing blackmail, will make them go to any extent. Perhaps if all the facts were known these same homosexuals have been used by the Communists.

I realize that there is some physical danger to anyone exposing all of the details and nastiness of homosexuality, because some of these people are dangerous. They will go to any limit. These homosexuals have strong emotions. They are not to be trusted and when blackmail threatens they are a dangerous group.

The Army at one time gave these individuals a dishonorable discharge and later changed the type of discharge. They are not knowingly kept in Army service. They should not be employed in Government. I trust both sides of the aisle will support the amendment.

Pages 5401-5402

Mr. DONDERO. Was there any evidence or testimony before the gentleman's committee with respect to the number of people who were separated from the service in the Department of State who had later acquired positions in other departments of Government? I refer to those whose employment was considered a security risk. Was anything said before your committee on that subject?

Mr. CLEVENGER. I will say to the gentleman, I brought that question up a year ago, as to whether the other departments would be alerted so that they might not hire these—we can name them now—these homosexuals. Until the Assistant Secretary of State, Mr. Peurifoy, made that word public over in the other body, we had insufficient information so far as the committee was concerned and could not tell you. In reply to my question we were informed they were not, and unofficially we were told, or at least I was told, that they have been employed in other sections of the Government, at least most of them were.

Mr. DONDERO. The reason I asked the question is that I made inquiry by letter to find out where these people went and whether they are now employed by our Government and I have not yet received a reply giving me any information on the subject.

Mr. CLEVENGER. If the gentleman will look at the report he will find some information on that subject. I am going to address myself now to conditions we have discovered in the Department of Commerce. When I asked the security officer if he would flag them, he said he would. I told him I was very much afraid he could not, because of an Executive order which was issued restricting the information being given on these people. The air is full of stories. The press is full of stories. I am not passing on that. In discussing the constitutionality of the so-called loyalty program, John Edgar Hoover, Director of the FBI, had occasion to cite a decision of the circuit court of appeals rendered on August 11, 1949, involving the Joint Anti-Fascist Committee. A portion of that decision is worthy of repetition here:

> Contrary to the contentions of the committee, nothing in the Hatch Act or the loyalty program deprives the committee or its members of any property rights. Freedom of speech and assembly is denied no one. Freedom of though and belief is not impaired. Anyone is free to join the committee and give it his support and encouragement. Everyone has the constitutional right to do these things, but no one has a constitutional right to be a Government employee.

For emphasis permit me to repeat the last phrase, "but no one has a constitutional right to be a Government employee."

It seems to me that the crux of our entire security program lies in that phrase. It is indeed a privilege and certainly not a right to work for the Government and it is time we cleared the air on the misconceptions of a good many well-intentioned people who have been misled by the propaganda of the Communist and the fellow traveler into the belief that the burden of "proof of qualification" lies on the employer in this case, the Government, rather than on the employee. Nothing could be further from the truth. The Government has the right, nay the obligation, to set up standards for performance of duty not only for prospective employees but for those already on the rolls. This sacred obligation to the taxpayer implies the summary removal of any employee who does not measure up to these standards, the avails and crocodile tears of the fuzzy-minded to the contrary notwithstanding. It is tragically true that our present administration has been sadly lacking in the courage or capacity necessary to carry out these obligations but this does not excuse, or in no way alter or mitigate these obligations.

We have heard a great deal in recent weeks concerning the security risks within the Department of State and I would like to say that while I am not familiar with the charges being bandied about I think the basic issue has been somewhat obscured in the unfortunate partisanship that has developed in this inquiry that is of prime importance to every American, Republican, or Democrat.

The sob sisters and thumb-sucking liberals are crying for proof of disloyalty in the form of overt acts, on any security risks who are being removed from the Government rolls, but shed no tears for the lives lost as a result of the activities of the Hiss', Coplon's, and the Wadleigh's, all of whom would or did pass the loyalty standards with flying colors.

307

I wish the American people would keep in mind the fact that a security risk does not have to be a member of the Communist Party or even of a Communist-front organization. It is not only conceivable but highly probable that many security risks are loyal Americans; however, there is something in their background that represents a potential possibility that they might succumb to conflicting emotions to the detriment of the national security. Perhaps they have relatives behind the iron curtain and thus would be subject to pressure. Perhaps they are addicted to an over-indulgence in alcohol or maybe they are just plain garrulous. The most flagrant example is the homosexual who is subject to the most effective blackmail. It is an established fact that Russia makes a practice of keeping a list of sex perverts in enemy countries and the core of Hitler's espionage was based on the intimidation of these unfortunate people.

Despite this fact however, the Under Secretary of State recently testified that 91 sex perverts had been located and fired from the Department of State. For this the Department must be commended. But have they gone far enough? Newspaper accounts quote Senate testimony indicating there are 400 more in the State Department and 4,000 in Government? Where are they? Who hired them? Do we have a cell of these perverts hiding around Government? Why are they not ferreted out and dismissed? Does the Department of State have access to information in the files of the Washington Police Department? Are we to assume that the State Department has a monopoly on this problem? What are the other Departments of Government doing about this?

For years we had a public prejudice against mentioning in public such loath some diseases as gonorrhea and cancer. In effecting cures for these maladies the medical people recognized the first step was in public education. These matters were brought before the public and frankly discussed and it was not until then the progress was really made. It is time to bring this homosexual problem into the open and recognize the problem for what it is.

The Commerce Department hearings are somewhat enlightening in regard to the entire security problem and I would suggest that interested Members read them in detail beginning on page 2260.

Here we find that the Commerce Department has not located any homosexuals in their organization. Are we to believe that in the face of the testimony of the District of Columbia police that 75 percent of the 4,000 perverts in the District of Columbia are employed by the Government, that the Department of Commerce has none?

What is wrong with this loyalty program that does not uncover these matters, and when it does, adopts an attitude of looking for proof of disloyalty in the form of overt acts rather than elements of security risk? Is it not possible for the Government to refuse employment on the grounds of lack of qualifications where risk is apparent? This is not necessarily an indictment or conviction; it is merely the exercise of caution for the common welfare.

HOW WELL DID YOU UNDERSTAND THIS SELECTION?

1. What is Congressman Miller's view regarding gays? Explain.

2. What words and phrases does Miller use to describe gays?

3. What danger does Miller and other congressmen think homosexuals pose to the United States? Explain.

4. What does Mr. Dondero and Mr. Clevenger maintain happened to the gay employees who were allowed to resign from the State Department?

President Truman, despite being raised in a racist society and uttering racial slurs in private conversation, signed Executive Order 9981 on July 26, 1948. This order righted a wrong and created an integrated military.

EXECUTIVE ORDER 9981

Established the President's Committee on Equality of Treatment and Opportunity in the Armed Forces.
WHEREAS it is essential that there be maintained in the armed services of the United States the highest standards of democracy, with equality of treatment and opportunity for all those who serve in our country's defense:
NOW THEREFORE, by virtue of the authority vested in me as President of the United States, by the Constitution and the statutes of the United States, and as Commander in Chief of the armed services, it is hereby ordered as follows:

1. It is hereby declared to be the policy of the President that there shall be equality of treatment and opportunity for all persons in the armed services without regard to race, color, religion or national origin. This policy shall be put into effect as rapidly as possible, having due regard to the time required to effectuate any necessary changes without impairing efficiency or morale.

2. There shall be created in the National Military Establishment an advisory committee to be known as the President's Committee on Equality of Treatment and Opportunity in the Armed Services, which shall be composed of seven members to be designated by the President.

3. The Committee is authorized on behalf of the President to examine the rules, procedures and practices of the Armed Services in order to determine in what respect such rules, procedures and practices may be altered or improved with a view to carrying out the policy of this order. The Committee shall confer and advise the Secretary of Defense, the Secretary of the Army, the Secretary of the Navy, and the Secretary of the Air Force, and shall make such recommendations to the President and to said Secretaries as in the judgment of the Committee will effectuate the policy hereof.

4. All executive departments and agencies of the Federal Government are authorized and directed to cooperate with the Committee in its work, and to furnish the Committee such information or the services of such persons as the Committee may require in the performance of its duties.

5. When requested by the Committee to do so, persons in the armed services or in any of the executive departments and agencies of the Federal Government shall testify before the Committee and shall make available for use of the Committee such documents and other information as the Committee may require.

6. The Committee shall continue to exist until such time as the President shall terminate its existence by Executive order.

Harry Truman, The White House, July 26, 1948.

HOW WELL DID YOU UNDERSTAND THIS SELECTION?

1. What did Executive Order 9981 do?

2. Why do you think President Truman issued Executive Order 9981?

3. How did Executive Order 9981 change the military?

The Hispanic population, especially in the western states, increased dramatically during the period following World War II. Like African Americans, Hispanic veterans faced racism, prejudice, and discrimination upon their return home from the war, and, like blacks, they were unwilling to tolerate the situation. Seeing assimilation into American society as beneficial economically, Hispanics demanded equal access to public education and an end to segregated schools. In 1946, the **United States District Court in Mendez v. Westminister School District** *ruled that California's system in which Hispanic children were forced to attend segregated schools violated the United States Constitution. The Ninth Circuit Court of Appeals later affirmed this decision, and as a result, California had to dismantle its segregated school system.*

Mendez v. Westminister School Dist. of Orange County
64 F.Supp. 544 (D.C. CAL. 1946)

McCORMICK, District Judge.

Gonzalo Mendez, William Guzman, Frank Palomino, Thomas Estrada and Lorenzo Ramirez, as citizens of the United States, and on behalf of their minor children, and as they allege in the petition, on behalf of 'some 5000' persons similarly affected, all of Mexicans or Latin descent, have filed a class suit pursuant to Rule 23 of Federal Rules of Civil Procedure. 28 U.S.C.A. following section 723c, against the Westminister, Garden Grove and El Modeno School Districts, and the Santa Ana City Schools, all of Orange County, California, and the respective trustees and superintendents of said school districts.

The complaint, grounded upon the Fourteenth Amendment to the Constitution of the United States and Subdivision 14 of Section 24 of the Judicial Code, Title 28, Section 41, subdivision 14, U.S.C.A., alleges a concerted policy and design of class discrimination against 'persons of Mexican or Latin descent or extraction' of elementary school age by the defendant school agencies in the conduct and operation of public schools of said districts, resulting in the denial of the equal protection of the laws to such class of persons among which are the petitioning school children.

Specifically, plaintiffs allege:

'That for several years last past respondents have and do now in furtherance and in execution of their common plan, design and purpose within their respective Systems and Districts, have by their regulation, custom and usage and in execution thereof adopted and declared: That all children or persons of Mexican or Latin descent or extraction, though Citizens of the United States of America, shall be, have been and are now excluded from attending, using, enjoying and receiving the benefits of the education, health and recreation facilities of certain schools within their respective Districts and Systems but that said children are now and have been segregated and required to and must attend and use certain schools in said Districts and Systems reserved for and attended solely and exclusively by children and persons of Mexican and Latin descent, while such other schools are maintained attended and used exclusively by and for persons and children purportedly known as White or Anglo-Saxon children.

'That in execution of said rules and regulations, each, every and all the foregoing children are compelled and required to and must attend and use the schools in said respective Districts reserved for and attended solely and exclusively by children of Mexican and Latin descent and are forbidden, barred and excluded from attending any other school in said District and System solely for the reason that said children or child are Mexican or Latin descent.'

The petitioners demand that the alleged rules, regulations, customs, and usages be adjudged void and unconstitutional and that an injunction issue restraining further application by defendant school authorities of such rules, regulations, customs, and usages.

It is conceded by all parties that there is no question of race discrimination in this action. It is, however, admitted that segregation per se is practiced in the above-mentioned school districts as the Spanish-speaking children enter school life and as they advance through the grades in the respective school districts. It is also admitted by the defendants that the petitioning children are qualified to attend the public schools in the respective districts of their residences.

In the Westminister, Garden Grove and El Modeno school districts the respective boards of trustees had taken official action, declaring that there be no segregation of pupils on a racial basis but that non-English-speaking children (which group, excepting as to a small number of pupils, was made up entirely of children of Mexican ancestry or descent), be required to attend schools designated by the boards separate and apart from English-speaking pupils; that such group should attend such schools until they had acquired some proficiency in the English language.

The petitioners contend that such official action evinces a covert attempt by the school authorities in such school districts to produce an arbitrary discrimination against school children of Mexican extraction or descent and that such illegal result has been established in such school districts respectively. The school authorities of the City of Santa Ana have not memorialized any such official action, but petitioners assert that the same custom and usage exists in the schools of the City of Santa Ana under the authority of appropriate school agencies of such city.

The concrete acts complained of are those of the various school district officials in directing which schools in the petitioning children and others of the same class or group must attend. The segregation exists in the elementary schools to and including the sixth grade in two of the defendant districts, and in the two other defendant districts through the eighth grade. The record before us shows without conflict that the technical facilities and physical conveniences offered in the schools housing entirely the segregated pupils, the efficiency of the teachers therein and the curricula are identical and in some respects superior to those in the other schools in the respective districts.

The ultimate question for decision may be thus stated: Does such official action of defendant district school agencies and the usages and practices pursued by the respective school authorities as shown by the evidence operate to deny or deprive the so-called non-English-speaking school children of Mexican ancestry or descent within such school districts of the equal protection of the laws?

The defendants at the outset challenge the jurisdiction of this court under the record as it exists at this time. We have already denied the defendant's motion to dismiss the action upon the 'face' of the complaint. No reason has been shown which warrants reconsideration of such decision.

While education is a State matter, it is not so absolutely or exclusively. *Cumming v. Board of Education of Richmond County*, 175 U.S. 528, 20 S.Ct. 197, 201, 44 L.Ed. 262. In the Cumming decision the Supreme Court said: 'That education of the people in schools maintained by state taxation is a matter belonging to the respective states, and any interference on the part of Federal authority with the management of such schools cannot be justified except in the case of a clear and unmistakable disregard of rights secured by the supreme law of the land.' See, also, *Gong Lum v. Rice*, 275 U.S. 78, 48 S.Ct. 91, 72 L.Ed. 172; *Wong Him v. Callahan, C.C.*, 119 F. 381; *Ward v. Flood*, 48 Cal. 36, 17 Am. Rep. 405; *Piper et al. v. Big Pine School District*, 193 Cal. 664, 226 P. 926.

Obviously, then, a violation by a State of a personal right or privilege protected by the Fourteenth Amendment in the exercise of the State's duty to provide for the education of its citizens and inhabitants would justify the Federal Court to intervene. State of Missouri ex rel. *Gaines v. Canada*, 305 U.S. 337, 59 S.Ct. 232, 83 L.Ed. 208. The complaint before us in this action, having alleged an invasion by the common school authorities of the defendant districts of the equal opportunity of pupils to acquire knowledge, confers jurisdiction on this court if the actions complained of are deemed those of the State. *Hamilton v. Regents of University of California*, 293 U.S. 245, 55 S.Ct. 197, 79 L.Ed. 343; cf. *Meyer v. Nebraska*, 262 U.S. 390, 43 S.Ct. 625, 67 L.Ed. 1042, 29 A.L.R. 1446. Are the actions of public school authorities of a rural or city school in the State of California, as alleged and established in this case, to be considered actions of the State within the meaning of the Fourteenth Amendment so as to confer jurisdiction on this court to hear and decide this case under the authority of Section 24, Subdivision 14 of the Judicial Code, supra? We think they are.

In the public school system of the State of California the various local school districts enjoy a considerable degree of autonomy. Fundamentally, however, the people of the State have made the public school system a matter of the State supervision. Such system is not committed to the exclusive control of local governments. Article IX, Constitution of California, *Butterworth v. Boyd*, 12 Cal.2d 140, 82 P.2d 434, 126 A.L.R. 838. It is a matter of general concern, and not a municipal affair. *Esberg v. Badaracco*, 202 Cal. 110, 259 P. 730; *Becker v. Council of City of Albany*, 47 Cal. App.2d 702, 118 P.2d 924.

The Education Code of California provides for the requirements of teachers' qualifications, the admission and exclusion of pupils, the courses of study and the enforcement of them, the duties of superintendents of schools and of the school trustees of elementary schools in the State of California. The appropriate agencies of the State of California allocate to counties all the State school money exclusively for the payment of teachers' salaries in the public schools and such funds are apportioned to the respective school districts within the counties. While, as previously observed, local school boards and trustees are vested by State legislation with considerable latitude in the administration of their districts, nevertheless, despite the decentralization of the educational system in California, the rules of the local school district are required to follow the general pattern laid down by the legislature, and their practices must be consistent with law and with the rules prescribed by the State Board of Education. See Section 2204, Education Code of California.

When the basis and composition of the public school system is considered, there can be no doubt of the oneness of the system in the State of California, or of the restricted powers of the elementary school authorities in the political subdivisions of the State. See *Kennedy v. Miller*, 97 Cal. 429, 32 P. 558; *Bruch v. Colombet*, 104 Cal. 347, 38 P. 45; *Ward v. San Diego School District*, 203 Cal. 712, 265 P. 821.

In the *Hamilton v. Regents of University of California*, supra, and *West Virginia State Board of Education v. Barnette*, 319 U.S. 624, 63 S.Ct. 1178, 87 L.Ed. 1628, 147 A.L.R._674, the acts of university regents and of a board of education were held acts of the State. In the recent Barnette decision the court stated: 'The Fourteenth Amendment, as now applied to the States, protects the citizen against the State itself and all of its creatures—Boards of Education not excepted.' Although these cases dealt with State rather than local Boards, both are agencies and parts of the State educational system, as is indicated by the Supreme Court in the Barnette case, wherein it stated: 'Such Boards are numerous and their territorial jurisdiction often small. But small and local authority may feel less sense of responsibility to the Constitution, and agencies of publicity may be less vigilant in calling to account.' Upon an appraisal of the factual situation before this court as illumined by the laws of the State of California relating to the public school system, it is clear that the respondents should be classified as representatives of the State to such an extent and in such a sense that the great restraints of the Constitution set limits to their action. *Screws v. United States*, 325 U.S. 91, 65 S.Ct. 1051; *Smith v. Allwright*, 321 U.S. 649, 64 S.Ct. 757, 88 L.Ed. 987, 151 A.L.R. 1110; *Hague v. Committee for Industrial Organization*, 307 U.S. 496, 59 S.Ct. 954, 83 L.Ed. 1423; *Home Tel. & Tel. Co. v. Los Angeles* 227 U.S. 278, 33 S.Ct. 312, 57 L.Ed. 510.

We therefore turn to consider whether under the record before us the school boards and administrative authorities in the respective defendant districts have by their segregation policies and practices transgressed applicable law and Constitutional safeguards and limitations and thus have invaded the personal right which every public school pupil has to the equal protection provision of the Fourteenth Amendment to obtain the means of education.

We think the pattern of public education promulgated in the Constitution of California and effectuated by provisions of the Education Code of State prohibits segregation of the pupils of Mexican ancestry in the elementary schools from the rest of the school children.

Section 1 of Article IX of the Constitution of California directs the legislature to 'encourage by all suitable means the promotion of intellectual, scientific, moral, and agricultural improvement of the people. Pursuant to this basic directive by the people of the State many laws stem authorizing special instruction in the public schools for handicapped children. See Division 8 of the Education Code. Such legislation, however, is general in its aspects. It includes all those who fall within the described classification requiring the special consideration provided by the statutes regardless of their ancestry or extraction. The common segregation attitudes and practices of the school authorities in the defendant school districts in Orange County pertain solely to children of Mexican ancestry and parentage. They are singled out as a class for segregation. Not only is such method of public school administration contrary to the general requirements of the school laws of the State, but we think it indicates an official school policy that the educational advantages to their commingling with other pupils is regarded as being so important to the school system of the State that it is provided for even regardless of the citizenship of the parents. We perceive in the laws regulating to the public educational system in the State of California a clear purpose to avoid and forbid distinctions among pupils based upon race or ancestry except in specific situations not pertinent to this action. Distinctions of that kind have recently been declared by the highest judicial authority of the United States 'by their very nature odious to a free people whose institutions are founded upon the doctrine of equality.' They are said to be 'utterly inconsistent with American traditions and ideals.' *Kiyoshi Hirabayashi v. United States*, 320 U.S. 81, 63 S.Ct. 1375, 1385, 87 L.Ed. 1774.

Our conclusions in this action, however, do not rest solely upon what we conceive to be the utter irreconcilability of the segregation practices in the defendant school districts with the public educational system authorized and sanctioned by the laws of the State of California. We think such practices clearly and unmistakably disregard rights secured by the supreme law of the land. *Cumming v. Board of Education of Richmond County*, supra.

'The equal protection of the laws' pertaining to the public school system in California is not provided by furnishing in separate schools the same technical facilities, text books and courses of instruction to children of Mexican ancestry that are available to the other public school children regardless of their ancestry. A paramount requisite in the American system of public education is social equality. It must be open to all children by unified school association regardless of lineage.

We think that under the record before us the only tenable ground upon which segregation practices in the defendant school districts can be defended lies in the English language deficiencies of some of the children of Mexican ancestry as they enter elementary public school life as beginners. But even such situations do not justify the general and continuous segregation in separate schools of the children of Mexican ancestry from the rest of the elementary school population as has been shown to be the practice in the defendant school districts—in all of them to the sixth grade, and in two of them through the eighth grade.

The evidence clearly shows that Spanish-speaking children are retarded in learning English by lack of exposure to its use because of segregation, and that commingling of the entire student body instills and develops a common cultural attitude among the school children which is imperative for the perpetuation of American institutions and ideals. It is also established by the record that the methods of segregation prevalent in the defendant school districts foster antagonisms in the children and suggest inferiority among them where none exists. One of the flagrant examples of the discriminatory results of segregation in two of the schools involved in this case is shown by the record. In the district under consideration there are two schools, the Lincoln and the Roosevelt, located approximately 120 yards apart on the same school grounds, hours of opening and closing, as well as recess periods, are not uniform. No credible language test is given to the children of Mexican ancestry upon entering the first grade in Lincoln School. This school has an enrollment of 249 so-called Spanish-speaking pupils, and no so-called English-speaking pupils; while the Roosevelt, (the other) school, has 83 so-called English-speaking pupils and 25 so-called Spanish-speaking pupils. Standardized tests as to mental ability are given to the respective classes in the two schools and the same curricula are pursued in both schools and, of course, in the English language as required by State law, Section 8251, Education Code. In the last school year the students in the seventh grade of the Lincoln were superior scholarly to the same grade in the Roosevelt School and to any group in the seventh grade in either of the schools in the past. It further appears that not only did the class as a group have such mental superiority but that certain pupils in the group were also outstanding in the class itself. Notwithstanding this showing, the pupils of such excellence were kept in the Lincoln School. It is true that there is no evidence in the record before us that shows that any of the members of this exemplary class requested transfer to the other so-called intermingled school, but the record does show without contradiction that another class had protested against the segregation policies and practices in the schools of this El Modeno district without avail. While the pattern or ideal of segregating the school children of Mexican ancestry from the rest of the school attendance permeates and is practiced in all of the four defendant districts, there are procedural deviations among the school administrative agencies in effectuating the general plan.

In Garden Grove Elementary School District the segregation extends only through the fifth grade. Beyond, all pupils in such district, regardless of their ancestry or linguistic proficiency, are housed, instructed and associate in the same school facility. This arrangement conclusively refutes the reasonableness or advisability of any segregation of children of Mexican ancestry beyond the fifth grade in any of the defendant school districts in view of the standardized and uniform curricular requirements in the elementary schools of Orange County.

But the admitted practice and long established custom in this school district whereby all elementary public school children of Mexican descent are required to attend one specified school (the Hoover) until they attain the sixth grade, while all other pupils of the same grade are permitted to and do attend two other elementary schools of this district, notwithstanding that some of such pupils live within the Hoover School division of the district, clearly establishes an unfair and arbitrary class distinction in the system of public education operative in the Garden Grove Elementary School District.

The long-standing discriminatory custom prevalent in this district is aggravated by the fact shown by the record that although there are approximately 25 children of Mexican descent living in the vicinity of the Lincoln School, none of them attend that school, but all are peremptorily assigned by the school authorities to the Hoover School, although evidence shows that there are no school zones territorially established in the district. The record before us shows a paradoxical situation concerning the segregation attitude of the school authorities in the Westminister School District. There are two elementary schools in this undivided area. Instruction is given pupils in each school from kindergarten to the eighth grade, inclusive. Westminister School has 642 pupils, of which 628 are so-called

313

English-speaking children, and 14 so-called Spanish-speaking pupils. The Hoover School is attended solely by 152 children of Mexican descent. Segregation of these from the rest of the school population precipitated such vigorous discriminatory results of segregation, resolved to unite the two schools and thus abolish the objectionable practices which had been operative in the schools of the district for a considerable period. A bond issue was submitted to the electors to raise funds to defray the cost of contemplated expenditures in the school consolidation. The bonds were not voted and the record before us in this action reflects no execution or carrying out of the official action of the board of trustees taken on or about the 16th of January, 1944. It thus appears that there has been no abolishment of the traditional segregation practices in this district pertaining to pupils of Mexican ancestry through the gamut of elementary school life. We have adverted to the unfair consequences of such practices in the similarly situated El Modeno School District.

Before considering the specific factual situation in the Santa Ana City Schools it should be noted that the omnibus segregation of children of Mexican ancestry from the rest of the student body in the elementary grades in the schools involved in this case because of language handicaps is not warranted by the record before us. The tests applied to the beginners are shown to have been generally hasty, superficial and not reliable. In some instances separate classification was determined largely by the Latinized or Mexican name of the child. Such methods of evaluating language knowledge are illusory and are not conductive to the inculcation and enjoyment of civil rights which are of primary importance in the public school system of education in the United States.

It has been held that public school authorities may differentiate in the exercise of their reasonable discretion as to the pedagogical methods of instruction to be pursued with different pupils. And foreign language handicaps may be to such a degree in the pupils in elementary schools as to require special treatment in separate allocations, however, can be lawfully made only after credible examination by the appropriate school authority of each child whose capacity to learn is under consideration and the determination of such segregation must be based wholly upon indiscriminate foreign language impediments in the individual child, regardless of his ethnic traits or ancestry.

The defendant Santa Ana School District maintains fourteen elementary schools which furnish instruction from kindergarten to the sixth grade, inclusive. About the year 1920 the Board of Education, available at such schools, divided the district into fourteen zones and assigned to the school established in each zone all pupils residing within such zone. There is no evidence that any discriminatory or other objectionable motive or purpose actuated the School Board in locating or defining such zones. Subsequently the influx of people of Mexican ancestry in large numbers and their voluntary settlement in certain of the fourteen zones resulted in three of the zones becoming occupied almost entirely by such group of people.

Two zones, that in which the Fremont School is located, and another contiguous area in which the Franklin School is situated, present the only flagrant discriminatory situation shown by the evidence in this case in the Santa Ana City Schools. The Fremont School has 325 so-called Spanish-speaking pupils and no so-called English-speaking pupils. The Franklin School has 237 pupils of which 161 are so-called English-speaking children, 76 so-called Spanish-speaking children.

The evidence shows that approximately 26 pupils of Mexican descent who reside within the Fremont zone are permitted by the School Board to attend the Franklin School because their families had always gone there. It also appears that there are approximately 35 other pupils not of Mexican descent who live within the Fremont zone who are not required to attend the Fremont School but who are also permitted by the Board of Education to attend the Franklin School.

Sometime in the fall of the year 1944 there arose dissatisfaction by the parents of some of the so-called Spanish-speaking pupils in the Fremont School zone who were not granted the privilege that approximately 26 children also of Mexican descent, enjoyed in attending the Franklin School. Protest was made en masse by such dissatisfied group of parents, which resulted in the Board of Education directing its secretary to send a letter to the parents of all of the so-called Spanish-speaking pupils living in the Fremont zone and attending the Franklin School that beginning September, 1945, the permit to attend Franklin School would be withdrawn and the children would be required to attend the school of the zone in which they were living, viz., the Fremont School.

There could have been no arbitrary discrimination claimed by plaintiffs by the action of the school authorities if the same official course had been applied to the 35 other so-called English-speaking pupils exactly situated as were the approximate 26 children of Mexican lineage, but the record is clear that the requirement of the Board of Education was intended for and directed exclusively to the specified pupils of Mexican ancestry and if carried out becomes operative solely against such group of children.

It should be stated in fairness to the Superintendent of the Santa Ana City Schools that he testified he would recommend to the Board of Education that the children of those who protested the action requiring transfer from the Franklin School be allowed to remain there because of long attendance and family tradition. However, there was no official recantation shown of the action of the Board of Education reflected by the letters of the Secretary and sent only to the parents of the children of Mexican ancestry.

The natural operation and effect of the Board's official action manifests a clear purpose to arbitrarily discriminate against the pupils of Mexican ancestry and to deny to them the equal protection of the laws. The court may not exercise legislative or administrative functions in this case to save such discriminatory act from inoperativeness. *Cf. Yu Cong Eng v. Trinidad*, 271 U.S. 500, 46 S.Ct. 70 L.Ed.1059. there are other discriminatory customs, shown and extraction, but we deem it unnecessary to discuss them in this memorandum.

We conclude by holding that the allegations of the complaint (petition) have been established sufficiently to justify injunctive relief against all defendants, restraining further discriminatory practices against the pupils of Mexican descent in the public schools of defendant school districts. See *Morris v. Williams*, 8 Cir., 149 F.2d. 703.

Findings of fact, conclusions of law, and decree of injunction are accordingly ordered pursuant to Rule 52, F.R.C.P. Attorney for plaintiffs will within ten days from date hereof prepare and present same under local Rule 7 of this court.

HOW WELL DID YOU UNDERSTAND THIS SELECTION?

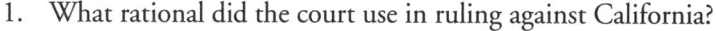

1. What rational did the court use in ruling against California?

2. What affect did the judge say segregation had on Hispanic children?

Periodically, Congress passed legislation restricting immigration into the United States. In 1952 the 82nd Congress enacted the Immigration and Nationality Act, better known as the McCarren-Walter Act. This legislation excluded certain immigrants from migrating to the United States following World War II. Rather than exclude immigrants solely based on a racial quota as the National Origins Act of 1921 did, the McCarran-Walter Act denied entrance into the United States to anyone who was immoral, a criminal, diseased, or who held radical political views. Communists in particular were targeted as a result of the Cold War and Red Scare. The act intended to accept immigrants perceived as beneficial to the American society and economy and who were thought to be willing and able to assimilate into the American culture. President Truman vetoed the bill because he believed it discriminated against immigrants from certain nations while favoring those from other nations but proponents of the bill mustered enough votes in Congress to override the veto. Selected excerpts from the act are reproduced below.

1950s: McCarren-Walter Act, 1952
United States Statutes at Large, 1952, Vol. 66, 82nd Cong., p. 163-282

AN ACT
To revise the laws relating to immigration, naturalization, and nationality; and for other purposes.
Be it enacted by the Senate and House of Representatives of the United States of America in Congress assembled, that this Act, divided into titles, chapters, and sections according to the following table of contents, may be cited as the "Immigration and Nationality Act."

TITLE II-IMMIGRATION
Chapter 1-Quota System
Numerical Limitations; Annual Quota Based upon National Origin; Minimum Quotas Sec.201.

(a) The annual quota of any quota area shall be one-sixth of 1 per centum of the number of inhabitants in the continental United States in 1920, which number, except for the purpose of computing quotas for quota areas within the Asia-Pacific triangle, shall be the same number heretofore determined under the provisions of section 11 of the Immigration Act of 1924, attributable by national origin to such quota area: Provided, that the quota existing for Chinese persons prior to the date of enactment of this Act shall be continued, and, except as otherwise provided in section 202 (e), the minimum quota area shall be one hundred.
(b) The determination of the annual quota of any quota area shall be made by the Secretary of State, the Secretary of Commerce, and the Attorney General, jointly. Such officials shall, jointly, report to the President the quota of each quota area, and the President shall proclaim and make known the quotas so reported. Such determination and report shall be made and such proclamation shall be issued as soon as practicable after the date of enactment of this Act. Quotas proclaimed therein shall take effect on the first day of the fiscal year, or the next fiscal half year, next following the expiration of six months after the date of the proclamation, and until such date the existing quotas proclaimed under the Immigration Act of 1924 shall remain in effect. After the making of a proclamation under the subsection the quotas proclaimed therein shall continue with the same effect as if specifically stated herein and shall be final and conclusive for every purpose, except (1) insofar as it is made to appear to the satisfaction of such officials and proclaimed by the President, that an error of fact has occurred in such determination or in such proclamation, or (2) in the case provided for in section 202 (e).
(c) There shall be issued to quota immigrants chargeable to any quota (1) no more immigrant visas in any fiscal year than the quota for such year, and (2) in any calendar month of any fiscal year, no more immigrant visas than 10 per centum of the quota for such year, except that during the last two months of any fiscal year immigrant visas may be issued without regard to the 10 per centum limitation contained herein.
(d) Nothing in this Act shall prevent the issuance (without increasing the total number of quota immigrant visas which may be issued) of an immigrant visa to an immigrant as a quota immigrant even though he is a nonquota immigrant.

(e) The quota numbers available under the annual quotas of each quota area proclaimed under this Act shall be reduced by the number of quota numbers which have been ordered to be deducted from the annual quotas authorized prior to the effective date of the annual quotas proclaimed under this Act under-

(1) section 19 (c) of the Immigration Act of 1917, as amended;

(2) the Displaced Persons Act of 1948, as amended; and

(3) any other Act of Congress enacted prior to the effective date of the quotas proclaimed under this Act.

Determination of Quota to which an immigrant is chargeable Sec. 202.

(a) Each independent country, self-governing dominion, mandated territory, and territory under the international trusteeship system of the United Nations, other than the United States and its outlying possessions by the Secretary of State. All other inhabited lands shall be attributed to a quota area specified by the Secretary of State. For the purposes of this Act, the annual quota to which an immigrant is chargeable shall be determined by birth within a quota area, except that-

(1) An alien child, when accompanied by his alien parent or parents may be charged to the quota of the accompanying parent of either accompanying parent is such parent has received or would be qualified for an immigrant visa, if necessary to prevent the separation of the child from the accompanying parent or parents, and if the quota to which such parent has been or would be chargeable is not exhausted for that fiscal year;

(2) If an alien is chargeable to a different quota form that of his accompanying spouse, the quota to which such alien is chargeable may, if necessary to prevent the separation of husband and wife, be determined by the quota of the accompanying spouse, if such spouse has received or would be qualified for an immigrant visa and if the quota to which such spouse had been or would be chargeable is not exhausted for that fiscal year;

(3) An alien born in the United States shall be considered as having been born in the country of which he is a citizen or subject, or if he is not a citizen or subject of any country then in the last foreign country in which he had his residence as determined by the consular officer;

(4) An alien born within any quota area in which neither of his parents was born and in which neither of his parents had a residence at the time of such alien's birth may be charged to the quota area of either parent;

(5) Notwithstanding the provisions of paragraphs (2), (3), and (4) of this subsection, any alien who is attributable by as much as one-half of his ancestry to a people or peoples indigenous to the Asia-Pacific triangle defined in subsection

(b) of this section, unless such alien is entitled to a nonquota immigrant status under paragraph (27) (A), (27) (B), (27) (D), (27) (E), (27) (F), (27) (G) of section 101, (a) shall be chargeable to a quota as specified accompanying or following to join him, shall be classified under section 101 (a) (27) (C), if accompanying or following to join him, shall be classified under section 101 (a) (27) (C), notwithstanding the provisions of subsection (b) of this section.

General Classes of Aliens Ineligible to Receive Visas and Excluded from Admission Sec. 212.

(a) Except as otherwise provided in this Act, the following classes of aliens shall be ineligible to receive visas and shall be excluded from admission into the United States:

(1) Aliens who are feeble-minded;

(2) Aliens who are insane;

(3) Aliens who have had one or more attacks of insanity;

(4) Aliens afflicted with psychopathic personality, epilepsy, or a mental defect;

(5) Aliens who are narcotic drug addicts or chronic alcoholics;

(6) Aliens who are afflicted with tuberculosis in any form, or with leprosy, or any dangerous contagious disease;

(7) Aliens not comprehended within any of the foregoing classes who are certified by the examining surgeon as having a physical defect, disease, or disability, when determined by the consular or immigration officer to be of such a nature that it may affect the ability of the alien to earn a living, unless the alien affirmatively establishes that he will not have to earn a living;

(8) Aliens who are paupers, professional beggars, or vagrants;

(9) Aliens who have been convicted of a crime involving moral turpitude (other than a purely political offense), or aliens who admit having committed such a crime, or aliens who admit committing acts which constitute the essential elements of such a crime; except that aliens who have committed only one such crime while under the age of

eighteen years may be granted a visa and admitted if the crime was committed more than five years prior to the date of the application for a visa or other documentation, and more than five years prior to date of application for admission to the United States, unless the crime resulted confinement in a prison or correctional institution, in which case such alien must have been released from such confinement more than five years prior to the date of the application for a visa or other documentation, and for admission, to the United States;

(10) Aliens who have been convicted of two or more offenses (other than purely political offenses), regardless of whether the conviction was in a single trial or whether the offenses arose from a single scheme of misconduct and regardless of whether the offenses involved moral turpitude, for which the aggregate sentences to confinement actually imposed were five years or more;

(11) Aliens who are polygamists or who practice polygamy or advocate the practice of polygamy;

(12) Aliens who are prostitutes or who have engaged in prostitution, or aliens coming to the United States solely, principally, or incidentally to engage in prostitution; aliens who directly or indirectly procure or attempt to procure, or who have procured or attempted to procure or to import, prostitutes or persons for the purpose of prostitution or for any other immoral purpose; and aliens who are or have been supported by, or receive or have received, in whole or in part, the proceeds of prostitution or aliens coming to the United States to engage in any other unlawful commercialized vice, whether or not related to prostitution;

(13) Aliens coming to the United States to engage in any immoral sexual act;

(14) Aliens seeking to enter the United States for the purpose of performing skilled or unskilled labor, if the Secretary of Labor has determined and certified to the Secretary of State and to the Attorney General that (A) sufficient workers in the United States who are able, willing, and qualified are available at the time (of application for a visa and for admission to the United States) and place (to which the alien is destined) to perform such skilled or unskilled labor, or (B) the employment of such aliens will adversely affect the wages and working conditions of the workers in the United States similarly employed. The exclusion of aliens under this paragraph shall apply only to the following classes: (i) those aliens described in the nonpreference category of section 203 (a) (4), (ii) those aliens described in section 101 (a) (27) (C), (27) (D), or (27) (E) (other than the parents, spouses, or children of United States citizens or of aliens lawfully admitted to the United State for permanent residence), unless their services are determined by the Attorney General to be needed urgently in the United States because of the high education, technical training, specialized experience, or exceptional ability of such immigrants and to be substantially beneficial prospectively to the national economy, cultural interest or welfare of the United States;

(15) Aliens who, in the opinion of the consular officer at the time of application for a visa, or in the opinion of the Attorney General at the time of application for admission, are likely at any time to become public charges;

(16) Aliens who have been excluded from admission and deported and who again seek admission within one year from the date of such deportation, unless prior to their reembarkation at a place outside the United States or their attempt to be admitted from foreign contiguous territory the Attorney General has consented to their reapplying for admission;

(17) Aliens who have been arrested and deported, or who have fallen into distress and have been removed pursuant to this or any prior act, or who have been removed as alien enemies, or who have been removed at Government expense in lieu of deportation pursuant to section 242 (b), unless prior to their embarkation or reembarkation at a place outside the United States or their attempt to be admitted from foreign contiguous territory the Attorney General has consented to their applying or reapplying for admission;

(18) Aliens who are stowaways;

(19) Any alien who seeks to procure, or has sought to procure, or has procured a visa or other documentation, or seeks to enter the United States, by fraud, or by willfully misrepresenting a material fact;

(20) Except as otherwise specifically provided in this Act, any immigrant who at the time of application for admission is not in possession of a valid unexpired immigrant visa, reentry permit, border crossing identification card, or other valid entry document required by this Act, and a valid unexpired passport, or other suitable travel document, or document of identity and nationality, if such document Certificate of Nationality to Be Issued by the Secretary of State for a Person not a Naturalized Citizen of the United States for Use in Proceedings of a Foreign State.

HOW WELL DID YOU UNDERSTAND THIS SELECTION?

1. Describe how the McCarren-Walter Act restricted immigration. What groups were favored? What groups faced the most restrictions?

2. Why do you think Congress enacted this law in 1952? Explain.

3. What groups of immigrants were completely denied entrance to the United States?

4. Evaluate the immigration policy of the McCarren-Walter Act in light of the American Dream. What does the Act communicate about the promise of America to foreigners? Explain?

Nothing changed American culture as much as perhaps the automobile. After Henry Ford began mass production of cars most Americans purchased one. By about 1925 on average there was one automobile on the road per American family. President Eisenhower irrevocably committed the country to transportation by automobile in 1956 when he signed into law the Federal-Aid Highway Act authorizing construction of a series of multilane interstate highways that eventually connected every region of the United States to every other region. Major arteries of the interstate highway system ran north to south and east to west. Eisenhower's highway system was the largest construction project in American history.

AN ACT

To amend and supplement the Federal-Aid Road Act approved July 11, 1916, to authorize appropriations for continuing the construction of highways; to amend the Internal Revenue Code of 1954 to provide additional revenue from the taxes on motor fuel, tires, and trucks and buses; and for other purposes.
Be it enacted by the Senate and House of Representatives of the United States of America in Congress assembled,

TITLE I—FEDERAL-AID HIGHWAY ACT OF 1956

SEC. 101. SHORT TITLE FOR TITLE I.
This title may be cited as the "Federal-Aid Highway Act of 1956".

SEC. 102. FEDERAL-AID HIGHWAYS.
(a) (1) AUTHORIZATION OF APPROPRIATIONS.—For the purpose of carrying out the provisions of the Federal-Aid Road Act approved July 11, 1916 (39 Stat. 355), and all Acts amendatory thereof and supplementary thereto, there is hereby authorized to be appropriated for the fiscal year ending June 30, 1957, $125,000,000 in addition to any sums heretofore authorized for such fiscal year; the sum of $850,000,000 for the fiscal year ending June 30, 1958; and the sum of $875,000,000 for the fiscal year ending June 30, 1959. The sums herein authorized for each fiscal year shall be available for expenditure as follows:
    (A) 45 per centum for projects on the Federal-aid primary high- way system.
    (B) 30 per centum for projects on the Federal-aid secondary high- way system.
    (C) 25 per centum for projects on extensions of these systems within urban areas.
    (2) APPORTIONMENTS.—The sums authorized by this section shall be apportioned among the several States in the manner now provided by law and in accordance with the formulas set forth in section 4 of the Federal-Aid Highway Act of 1944; approved December 20, 1944 (58 Stat. 838) : Provided, That the additional amount herein authorized for the fiscal year ending June 30, 1957, shall be apportioned immediately upon enactment of this Act.
(b) AVAILABILITY FOR EXPENDITURE.—Any sums apportioned to any State under this section shall be available for expenditure in that State for two years after the close of the fiscal year for which such sums are authorized, and any amounts so apportioned remaining unexpended at the end of such period shall lapse: Provided, That such funds shall be deemed to have been expended if a sum equal to the total of the sums herein and heretofore apportioned to the State is covered by formal agreements with the Secretary of Commerce for construction, reconstruction, or improvement of specific projects as provided in this title and prior Acts: Provided further, That in the case of those sums heretofore, herein, or hereafter apportioned to any State for projects on the Federal-aid secondary highway system, the Secretary of Commerce may, upon the request of any State, discharge his responsibility relative to the plans, specifications, estimates, surveys, contract awards, design, inspection, and construction of such secondary road projects by his receiving and approving a certified statement by the State highway department setting forth that the plans, design, and construction for such projects are in accord with the standards and procedures of such State applicable...

SEC. 108. NATIONAL SYSTEM OF INTERSTATE AND DEFENSE HIGHWAYS.

(a) INTERSTATE SYSTEM.—It is hereby declared to be essential to the national interest to provide for the early completion of the "National System of Interstate Highways", as authorized and designated in accordance with section 7 of the Federal-Aid Highway Act of 1944 (58 Stat. 838). It is the intent of the Congress that the Interstate System be completed as nearly as practicable over a thirteen-year period and that the entire System in all the States be brought to simultaneous completion. Because of its primary importance to the national defense, the name of such system is hereby changed to the "National System of Interstate and Defense Highways". Such National System of Interstate and Defense Highways is hereinafter in this Act referred to as the "Interstate System".

(b) AUTHORIZATION OF APPROPRIATIONS.—For the purpose of expediting the construction, reconstruction, or improvement, inclusive of necessary bridges and tunnels, of the interstate System, including extensions thereof through urban areas, designated in accordance with the provisions of section 7 of the Federal-Aid Highway Act of 1944 (58 Stat. 838), there is hereby authorized to be appropriated the additional sum of $1,000,000,000 for, the fiscal year ending June 30, 1957 , which sum shall be in addition to the authorization heretofore made for that year, the additional sum of $1,700,000,000 for the fiscal year ending June 30, 1958, the additional sum of $2,000,000,000 for the fiscal year ending June 30, 1959, the additional sum of $2,200,000,000 for the fiscal year ending June 30, 1960, the additional sum of $2,200,000,000 for the fiscal year ending June 30, 1961, the additional sum of $2,200,000,000 for the fiscal year ending June 30, 1962, the additional sum of $2,200,000,000 for the fiscal year ending June 30, 1963, the additional sum of $2,200,000,000 for the fiscal year ending June 30, 1964, the additional sum of $2,200,000,000 for the fiscal year ending June 30, 1965, the additional sum of $2,200,000,000 for the fiscal year ending June 30, 1966, the additional sum of $2,200,000,000 for the fiscal year ending June 30, 1967, the additional sum of $1,500,000,000 for the fiscal year ending June 30, 1968, and the additional sum of $1,025,000,000 for the fiscal year ending .June 30, 1969...

HOW WELL DID YOU UNDERSTAND THIS SELECTION?

1. Why did Eisenhower and Congress enact this legislation?

2. How much money did the bill initially appropriate?

3. How long was construction authorized?

In 1954 Dr. Frederic Werthem published a psychological study of the effect comic books had on young people. His book, **The Seduction of the Innocent: The Influence of Comic Books on Today's Youth**, *charged that comic books like Batman were filled with subliminal messages promoting homosexuality among their youthful readers. Dr. Werthem also alleged that popular comic books advocated violence, contributed to juvenile crime, encouraged antisocial behavior, and led to early sexual activity among teenaged readers. Publications of T***he Seduction of the Innocent*** led to political pressure to regulate the comic book industry. The United States Senate appointed a committee to investigate the industry. After publisher William Gaines infuriated Congress and the American public with his testimony before the committee, the comic book industry, fearing public scrutiny and a decline in sales, formed the Comic Magazine Association of America. This trade industry group then created the Comic Code Authority, which evaluated every issue of a comic book and either gave or withheld its seal of approval. Comic books found in bad taste would be denied the Comic Code Authority seal. The selection below is the standards used to evaluate American comic books.*

THE COMICS CODE
Code For Editorial Matter

General Standards Part A:

1) Crimes shall never be presented in such a way as to create sympathy for the criminal, to promote distrust of the forces of law and justice, or to inspire others with a desire to imitate criminals.

2) No comics shall explicitly present the unique details and methods of a crime.

3) Policemen, judges, government officials, and respected institutions shall never be presented in such a way as to create disrespect for established authority.

4) If crime is depicted it shall be as a sordid and unpleasant activity.

5) Criminals shall not be presented so as to be rendered glamorous or to occupy a position which creates the desire for emulation.

6) In every instance good shall triumph over evil and the criminal punished for his misdeeds.

7) Scenes of excessive violence shall be prohibited. Scenes of brutal torture, excessive and unnecessary knife and gun play, physical agony, gory and gruesome crime shall be eliminated.

8) No unique or unusual methods of concealing weapons shall be shown.

9) Instances of law enforcement officers dying as a result of a criminal's activities should be discouraged.

10) The crime of kidnapping shall never be portrayed in any detail, nor shall any profit accrue to the abductor or kidnapper. The criminal or the kidnapper must be punished in every case.

11) The letters of the word "crime" on a comics magazine shall never be appreciably greater than the other words contained in the title. The word "crime" shall never appear alone on a cover.

12) Restraint in the use of the word "crime" in titles or subtitles shall be exercised.

General Standards Part B:

1) No comic magazine shall use the word "horror" or "terror" in its title.

2) All scenes of horror, excessive bloodshed, gory or gruesome crimes, depravity, lust, sadism, masochism shall not be permitted.

3) All lurid, unsavory, gruesome illustrations shall be eliminated.

4) Inclusion of stories dealing with evil shall be used or shall be published only where the intent is to illustrate a moral issue and in no case shall evil be presented alluringly nor so as to injure the sensibilities of the reader.

5) Scenes dealing with, or instruments associated with walking dead, torture, vampires and vampirism, ghouls, cannibalism, and werewolfism are prohibited.

322

General Standards Part C:

All elements or techniques not specifically mentioned herein, but which are contrary to the spirit and intent of the Code, and are considered violations of good taste or decency, shall be prohibited.

Dialogue:

1) Profanity, obscenity, smut, vulgarity, or words or symbols which have acquired undesirable meanings are forbidden.

2) Special precautions to avoid references to physical afflictions or deformities shall be taken.

3) Although slang and colloquialisms are acceptable, excessive use should be discouraged and wherever possible good grammar shall be employed.

Religion:

Ridicule or attack on any religious or racial group is never permissible.

Costume:

1) Nudity in any form is prohibited, as is indecent or undue exposure.

2) Suggestive and salacious illustration or suggestive posture is unacceptable.

3) All characters shall be depicted in dress reasonably acceptable to society.

4) Females shall be drawn realistically without exaggeration of any physical qualities.

NOTE: It should be recognized that all prohibitions dealing with costume, dialogue, or artwork applies as specifically to the cover of a comic magazine as they do to the contents.

Marriage and Sex:

1) Divorce shall not be treated humorously nor shall be represented as desirable.

2) Illicit sex relations are neither to be hinted at nor portrayed. Violent love scenes as well as sexual abnormalities are unacceptable.

3) Respect for parents, the moral code, and for honorable behavior shall be fostered. A sympathetic understanding of the problems of love is not a license for moral distortion.

4) The treatment of love-romance stories shall emphasize the value of the home and the sanctity of marriage.

5) Passion or romantic interest shall never be treated in such a way as to stimulate the lower and baser emotions.

6) Seduction and rape shall never be shown or suggested.

7) Sex perversion or any inference to same is strictly forbidden.

Code For Advertising Matter:

These regulations are applicable to all magazines published by members of the Comics Magazine Association of America, Inc. Good taste shall be the guiding principle in the acceptance of advertising.

1) Liquor and tobacco advertising is not acceptable.

2) Advertisement of sex or sex instructions books are unacceptable.

3) The sale of picture postcards, "pin-ups," "art studies," or any other reproduction of nude or semi-nude figures is prohibited.

4) Advertising for the sale of knives, concealable weapons, or realistic gun facsimiles is prohibited.

5) Advertising for the sale of fireworks is prohibited.

6) Advertising dealing with the sale of gambling equipment or printed matter dealing with gambling shall not be accepted.

7) Nudity with meretricious purpose and salacious postures shall not be permitted in the advertising of any product; clothed figures shall never be presented in such a way as to be offensive or contrary to good taste or morals.

8) To the best of his ability, each publisher shall ascertain that all statements made in advertisements conform to the fact and avoid misinterpretation.

9) Advertisement of medical, health, or toiletry products of questionable nature are to be rejected. Advertisements for medical, health or toiletry products endorsed by the American Medical Association, or the American Dental Association, shall be deemed acceptable if they conform with all other conditions of the Advertising Code.

HOW WELL DID YOU UNDERSTAND THIS SELECTION?

1. What types of advertising matter are not acceptable?

2. How did the code require marriage to be depicted?

3. What did the code say about the depiction of love, sex, and romance?

4. How were women supposed to be depicted?

5. What were the code requirement regarding dialogue?

6. How did the code regulate the content of comic books?

7. What standards about crime and punishment did the code create?

8. Does the Comics Code violate the First Amendment to the United States Constitution? Explain?

SELF-TEST

MULTIPLE CHOICE: Circle the correct response. The correct answers are given at the end.

1. The most popular recording artist of the 1950s was
   a. B. B. King.
   b. Bill Haley.
   c. Elvis Presley.
   d. Johnny Cash.

2. What did Dr. Frederic Werthem maintain in *The Seduction of the Innocent?*
   a. That rock 'n' roll had a detrimental impact on American youth.
   b. That comic books had a detrimental impact on American youth.
   c. That love scenes in movies caused American teenagers to become sexually active at a young age.
   d. That blacks and Hispanics did not deserve civil rights.

3. Who authored *On the Road?*
   a. Jack Kerouac.
   b. John Clelon Holmes.
   c. Gregory Corso.
   d. Allen Ginsberg.

4. According to the findings of sexual researcher Alfred Kinsey
   a. 80 percent of women had extramarital affairs.
   b. 90 percent of men engaged in premarital intercourse.
   c. 50 percent of women had at least one lesbian lover.
   d. 25 percent of men had at least one homosexual experience.

5. Which of the following was a Latino civil rights organization?
   a. The NAACP.
   b. The Urban League.
   c. The Hell's Angels.
   d. LULAC.

6. Who is generally regarded as the primary leader of the black civil rights movement?
   a. Dr. Martin Luther King, Jr.
   b. Che Guerrero.
   c. Rev. Ralph Abernathy.
   d. Col. Tom Parker.

7. The Supreme Court decision that desegregated public schools was
   a. *Mendez v. California.*
   b. *Gideon v. Wainwright.*
   c. *Brown v. Board of Education of Topeka, KS.*
   d. *New York Times v. Sullivan.*

8. What desegregated the American armed forces?
   a. Truman's Executive Order 9981.
   b. Eisenhower's decision to integrate the army.
   c. The Supreme Court's decision in *Brown v. Board of Education.*
   d. The Montgomery Bus Boycott.

9. The first black to play for a major league baseball team was
   a. Hank Aaron.
   b. Jackie Robinson.
   c. Willie Mays.
   d. Mickey Mantle.

10. The founder of Playboy Magazine was
    a. Gabriel Jones.
    b. Dr. Alfred Kinsey.
    c. William Gardner.
    d. Hugh Hefner.

Answers: 1-c; 2-b; 3-a; 4-b; 5-d; 6-a; 7-c; 8-a; 9-b; 10-d.

ESSAYS:

1. Discuss social and economic events that shaped Americans society during the Truman and Eisenhower administrations.

2. How did the 1940s and 1950s pave the way for the 1960s?

3. Was society during the 1940s and 1950s conservative, moderate, or liberal? Fully support your choice using historical evidence.

OPTIONAL ACTIVITIES:

1. Interview someone you know who lived through the 1940s and 1950s. Summarize the interview in an oral classroom presentation. How does their perspective differ from that of the textbook chapter?

2. Using the internet, view old television shows from the 1950s. Describe the differences between those programs and modern programs.

3. Research the difference in the way Americans travelled before construction of the interstate highway system.

WEB SITE LISTINGS:

Middle Class Life
Kingwood College Library
   http://kclibrary.nhmccd.edu/decade50.html

"United States Culture and Society in the 1950s," Jessamyn Neuhaus
   http://home.earthlink.net/~neuhausj/1950s/

"The Literature & Culture of the American 1950s," Alan Filreis, University of Pennsylvania
   http://www.english.upenn.edu/~afilreis/50s/home.html

Chapter Twenty-three

KENNEDY-JOHNSON YEARS

Few decades in American History were as troublesome as the 1960s. Americans, in some respects, were seemingly at war with each other. Protests against the Vietnam War, clashes over civil rights, race riots in several cities, and other incidents gave the appearance that the United States was coming apart at the seams. The status quo was being challenged on all fronts and much change would occur during the decade.

Even though turmoil rocked American society throughout most of the 1960s, the decade actually began amid much hope and optimism. In January 1961, John F. Kennedy took the presidential oath of office, becoming the first Catholic elected President and also the youngest person to hold the nation's highest office. His election over Republican Richard Nixon in 1960 provided Americans with a sense of optimism about the future. Kennedy's administration and the "high hopes" of Americans were, however, short-lived. In November 1961, the youthful president was assassinated in Dallas, Texas. Kennedy's assassination cast a dark pall over the nation.

Kennedy's brief domestic program, the New Frontier, had limited success. At Kennedy's request, Congress increased the minimum wage and Social Security benefits. The president also made a limited commitment to black civil rights through support of integration at the University of Alabama, creation of the President's Committee on Equal Employment Opportunity to rid the nation of discrimination in government hiring, and issuance of an executive order forbidding landlords to discriminate against ethnic minorities in government subsidized housing.

Racial tensions, leftover from the 1950s, surfaced during Kennedy's administration. In the spring of 1961, James Farmer, the executive director of the Congress of Racial Equality, sent white and black freedom riders into southern states to provoke confrontation from white racists that would force the Kennedy administration to enforce federal court decisions mandating desegregation of interstate transportation systems. As expected, white mobs attacked the freedom riders while police officers made no attempt to stop the violence, and the Kennedy administration eventually had to act. Clashes over integration also occurred when James Meredith tried to enroll at the all-white University of Mississippi. Mob violence on the Oxford campus forced President Kennedy to dispatch military troops to quell the disturbance and protect Meredith. In Birmingham, Dr. Martin Luther King, Jr., leader of the Civil Rights Movement, was arrested and jailed when he organized a boycott of city businesses to end racial discrimination against blacks in department stores. Later, when Alabama governor George Wallace attempted to stop the integration of the University of Alabama, President Kennedy nationalized the Alabama National Guard in support of black civil rights. After Medgar Evers was murdered in Jackson, Mississippi, Kennedy submitted to Congress civil rights legislation that largely ended Jim Crow segregation in the South. Unfortunately, it took the deaths of four young girls in the bombing of a black church in Birmingham and the assassination of President Kennedy before passage of the Civil Rights legislation could be secured. In 1964, however, liberal Democrats and Republicans overcame opposition by white southern racists to pass Kennedy's legislation and his successor, Lyndon Baines Johnson, signed the Civil Rights Act into law. Kennedy's death, to some degree, galvanized public opinion in favor of civil rights.

Kennedy's assassination and the assassination of his murderer, Lee Harvey Oswald, the next day while in custody of Dallas police, were the first of several assassinations and attempted assassinations that marked the 1960s. Martin Luther King, Jr. and Robert Kennedy, President Kennedy's brother, would both be killed toward the decade's end. Segregationist governor George Wallace was shot and permanently paralyzed while campaigning for the presidency.

President Johnson, capitalizing on the sudden popularity of Kennedy following the assassination, enacted much of the New Frontier into law as part of his domestic program called the Great Society. Two important pieces of civil rights legislation—the Civil Rights Act of 1964 and the 1965 Voting Rights Act—became law during the Johnson administration. American society and politics were forever changed as a result of these actions.

After dispatching Barry Goldwater, the Republican presidential nominee, in a landslide 1964 election that saw Democrats win two Senate seats and 37 House seats, Johnson had sufficient support in Congress to enact Great Society legislation with little Republican help. In 1965, 84 of the 87 bills Johnson submitted to Congress were enacted. The Great Society, in addition to focusing on civil rights, attempted to wage a war on poverty. About 20 percent of all Americans lived below the poverty line in 1964. Johnson created the office of Economics Opportunity to administer antipoverty programs such as the Jobs Corps, urban renewal projects, Neighborhood Youth Corps, Volunteers in Service to America, the Head Start, and other antipoverty initiatives. Despite limited success, the War on Poverty did not achieve its primary objective to eliminate poverty in the United States.

Despite its limited successes, Johnson's Great Society and War on Poverty changed America for the better. Since the time of Roosevelt's New Deal, Congressional Democrats had tried to provide health care to Americans. President Truman, as early as 1945, proposed the creation of a universal health care system for Americans. While Johnson did not go as far as Truman, the Great Society did provide health insurance for the poor and elderly. Medicare and Medicaid became important parts of the War on Poverty and represented the greatest domestic programs since Social Security.

President Johnson was also concerned about the environment. In 1965 Congress passed and Johnson signed into law the Clean Air and the Clean Water Acts. For the first time in American History the federal government could mandate air and water quality standards. As a result of these laws, water and air quality slowly began to improve across America. Johnson also presided over passage of the Wilderness Act of 1964 that added millions of acres of land to the National Park system.

One of the most important agents of social change during the administration of Kennedy and Johnson was the Supreme Court. Chief Justice Earl Warren, a former Republican governor of California appointed by President Eisenhower, presided over one of the most liberal Courts in American History. Under Warren's leadership the Court broadened criminal rights, expanded freedom of speech and the press, outlawed prayer in public schools, extended civil rights, established the one man one vote principle in elections, and broadened sexual freedom.

The Kennedy-Johnson years also witnessed an arms and space race with the Soviet Union. Both the United States and the U.S.S.R. competed with each other in an attempt to build the most destructive conventional and nuclear weapons on earth. Americans were shocked when the Soviets launched *Sputnik I*, the first man-made satellite to orbit the Earth. Americans could not believe the Soviet Union had won the first leg of the race into space. Americans moved quickly to make up lost ground and launched vehicles into space. President Kennedy approved the *Apollo* program and charged it with landing an American on the moon before the 1960s ended. Under both Kennedy and Johnson the United States eventually surpassed the Soviet Union and achieved Kennedy's objective of landing an American on the moon.

Overall, the 1960s was a decade of great achievement wrought by turmoil and bloodshed. Many Americans recall the 1960s as the best of times while others see them as the worst of times. To some degree, both views are accurate.

IDENTIFICATION: Briefly describe each term.

Martin Luther King, Jr.

Great Society

Sheriff "Bull" Connor

"I Have a Dream"

Cesar Chavez

Volunteers in Service to America

Head Start

Medicare/Medicaid

Civil Rights Act of 1964

Congress of Racial Equality

Sit-Ins

Student Non-Violent Coordinating Committee

Southern Christian Leadership Conference

John F. Kennedy

Lyndon B. Johnson

Richard Nixon

Nikita Khrushchev

The New Frontier

Bay of Pigs Fiasco

Cuban Missile Crisis

Robert Kennedy

Apollo Program

John Glenn

Earl Warren

Baker v. Carr

Loving v. Virginia

Estelle v. Griswold

Miranda v. Arizona

Gideon v. Wainwright

James Farmer

J. Edgar Hoover

Freedom Riders

James Meredith

George Wallace

March on Washington

Lee Harvey Oswald

Warren Commission

Freedom Summer

Voter Education Project

Twenty-fourth Amendment

Voting Rights Act of 1965

Mississippi Freedom Democratic Party

War on Poverty

Water Quality Act

Bloody Sunday

Malcolm X

Watts Riot

Stokley Carmichael

Black Panther Party

Proposition 14

Equal Employment Opportunity Commission

THINK ABOUT:

1. Describe how the 1960s were the "best of times and the worst of times."

2. Discuss how President Johnson used emotional feelings sparked by Kennedy's assassination to enact many of Kennedy's initiatives as part of the Great Society.

3. Examine the evolution of the Civil Rights Movement. How did the movement change? What caused the changes?

4. Compare and contrast the New Frontier with the Great Society.

After receiving proof from American U-2 planes that the Soviet Union had placed nuclear warheads in missiles on Cuba, an island nation located approximately 90 miles south of Florida, President John F. Kennedy insisted that the Soviets remove the weapons. When the Soviets ignored Kennedy's request, the young president faced a crisis that put the world at the brink of nuclear war. Fortunately, Kennedy rejected advice from conservatives to take the weapons out with an airstrike and instead placed a naval quarantine around Cuba to prevent the Soviets from bringing additional weapons to the island. On October 22, 1962, Kennedy scheduled airtime so that he could inform the American public by television and radio about the threat to the nation's security. Fortunately, the United States and the Soviet Union averted nuclear war by reaching an agreement under which the Soviets would remove their missiles from Cuba in exchange for American removal of nuclear weapons from Turkey, which were located near the border with the Soviet Union.

October 22, 1962, Washington, D.C.
PRESIDENT JOHN F. KENNEDY

Good evening my fellow citizens:

This Government, as promised, has maintained the closest surveillance of the Soviet military buildup on the island of Cuba. Within the past week, unmistakable evidence has established the fact that a series of offensive missile sites is now in preparation on that imprisoned island. The purpose of these bases can be none other than to provide a nuclear strike capability against the Western Hemisphere.

Upon receiving the first preliminary hard information of this nature last Tuesday morning on 9 A.M., I directed that our surveillance be stepped up. And having now confirmed and completed our evaluation of the evidence and our decision on a course of action, this Government feels obliged to report this new crisis to you in fullest detail.

The characteristics of these new missile sites indicate two distinct types of installations. Several of them include medium range ballistic missiles, capable of carrying a nuclear warhead for a distance of more than 1,000 nautical miles. Each of these missiles, in short, is capable of striking Washington, D.C., the Panama Canal, Cape Canaveral, Mexico City, or any other city in the southeastern part of the United States, in Central America, or in the Caribbean area.

Additional sites not yet completed appear to be designed for intermediate range ballistic missiles-capable of traveling more that twice as far-and thus capable of striking most of the major cities in the Western Hemisphere, ranging as far north as Hudson Bay, Canada, and as far south as Lima, Peru. In addition, jet bombers, capable of carrying nuclear weapons, are now being uncrated and assembled in Cuba, while the necessary air bases are being prepared.

This urgent transformation of Cuba into an important strategic base-by the presence of these large, long-range, and clearly offensive weapons of sudden mass destruction – constitutes an explicit threat to the peace and security of all the Americas, in flagrant and deliberate defiance of the Rio Pact of 1947, the traditions of this Nation and hemisphere, the joint resolution of the 87th Congress, the Charter of the United Nations and my own public warnings to the Soviets on September 4 and 13. This action also contradicts the repeated assurances of Soviet spokesmen, both publicly and privately delivered, that the arms buildup in Cuba would retain its original defensive character, and that the Soviet Union had no need or desire to station strategic missiles, on the territory of any other nation.

The size of this undertaking makes clear that it has been planned for some months. Yet only last month, after I had made clear the distinction between any introduction of ground-to-ground missiles and the existence of defensive antiaircraft missiles, the Soviet Government publicly stated on September 11 that, and I quote, "the armaments and military equipment sent to Cuba are designed exclusively for defensive for defensive purposes," that, and I quote the Soviet Government, "there is no need for the Soviet Government to shift its weapons…for a retaliatory blow to any other country, for instance Cuba," and that, and I quote their government, "the Soviet Union has so powerful rockets to carry these nuclear warheads that there is no need to search for sites for them beyond the boundaries of the Soviet Union." That statement was false.

Only last Thursday, as evidence of this rapid offensive buildup was already in my hand, Soviet Foreign Minister Gromyko told me in my office that he was instructed to make it clear once again, as he said his government had already done, that Soviet assistance to Cuba, and I quote, "pursued solely the purpose of contributing to the defense capabilities of Cuba," that, and I quote him, "training by Soviet specialists of Cuban nationals in handling defensive armaments was by no means offensive, and if it were otherwise," Mr. Gromyko went on, "the Soviet Government would never become involved in rendering such assistance." That statement also was false.

Neither the United States of America nor the world community of nations can tolerate deliberate deception and offensive threats on the part of any nation, large or small. We no longer live in a world where only the actual firing of weapons represents a sufficient challenge to a nation's security to constitute maximum peril. Nuclear weapons are so destructive and ballistic missiles are so swift, that any substantially increased possibility of their use or any sudden change their deployment may well be regarded as a definite threat to peace.

For many years, both the Soviet Union and the United States, recognizing this fact, have deployed strategic nuclear weapons with great care, never upsetting the precarious status quo which insured that these weapons would not be used in the absence of some vital challenge. Our own strategic missiles have never been transferred to the territory of any other nation under a cloak of secrecy and deception; and our history-unlike that of the Soviets since the end of World War II – demonstrates that we have no desire to dominate or conquer any other nation or impose our system upon its people. Nevertheless, American citizens have become adjusted to living daily on the bull's-eye of Soviet missiles located inside the U.S.S.R. or in submarines.

In that sense, missiles in Cuba add to an already clear and present danger – although it should be noted the nations of Latin America have never previously been subjected to a potential nuclear threat.

But this secret, swift, and extraordinary buildup of Communist missiles – in an area well known to have a special and historical relationship to the United States and the nations of the Western Hemisphere, in violation of Soviet assurances, and in defiance of American and hemispheric policy – this sudden, clandestine decision to station strategic weapons for the first time outside of Soviet soil – is a deliberately provocative and unjustified change in the status quo which cannot be accepted by this country, if our courage and our commitments are ever to be trusted again by either friend or foe.

The 1930's taught us a clear lesson: aggressive conduct, if allowed to go unchecked, ultimately leads to war. This nation is opposed to war. We are also true to our word. Our unswerving objective, therefore, must be to prevent the use of these missiles against this or any other country, and to secure their withdrawal or elimination from the Western Hemisphere.

Our policy has been one of patience and restraint, as befits a peaceful and powerful nation, which leads a worldwide alliance. We have been determined not to be diverted from our central concerns by mere irritants and fanatics. But now prematurely or unnecessarily risk the costs of worldwide nuclear war in which even the fruits of victory would be ashes in our mouth – but neither will we shrink from that risk at any time it must be faced.

Acting, therefore, in the defense of our own security and of the entire Western Hemisphere, and under the authority entrusted to me by the Constitution as endorsed by the Resolution of the Congress, I have directed that the following *initial* steps be taken immediately:

First: To halt this offensive buildup, a strict quarantine on all offensive military equipment under shipment to Cuba is being initiated. All ships of any kind bound for Cuba from whatever nation or port will, if found to contain cargoes of offensive weapons, be turned back. This quarantine will be extended, if needed, to other types of cargo and carriers. We are not at this time, however, denying the necessities of life as the Soviets attempted to do in their Berlin blockade of 1948.

Second: I have directed the continued and increased close surveillance of Cuba and its military buildup. The foreign ministers of the OAS, in their communiqué of October 6, rejected secrecy on such matters in this hemisphere. Should these offensive military preparations continue, thus increasing the threat to the hemisphere, further action will be justified. I have directed the Armed Forces to prepare for any eventualities; and I trust that in the interest of both the Cuban people and the Soviet technicians at the sites, the hazards to all concerned of continuing this threat will be recognized.

Third: It shall be the policy of this Nation to regard any nuclear missile launched from Cuba against any nation in the Western Hemisphere as an attack by the Soviet Union on the United States, requiring a full retaliatory response upon the Soviet Union.

Fourth: As a necessary military precaution, I have reinforced our base at Guantanamo, evacuated today the dependents of our personnel there, and ordered additional military units to be on a standby alert basis.

Fifth: We are calling tonight for an immediate meeting of the Organ of Consultation under the Organization of American States, to consider this threat to hemispheric security and to invoke articles 6 and 8 of the Rio Treaty in support of all necessary action. The United Nations Charter allows for regional security arrangements – and the nations of this hemisphere decided long ago against military presence of outside powers. Our other allies around the world have also been alerted.

Sixth: Under the Charter of the United Nations, we are asking tonight that an emergency meeting of the Security Council be convoked without delay to take action against this latest Soviet threat to world peace. Our resolution will call for the prompt dismantling and withdrawal of all offensive weapons in Cuba, under the supervision of U.N. observers, before the quarantine can be lifted.

Seventh and finally: I call upon Chairman Khrushchev to halt and eliminate this clandestine. Reckless, and provocative threat to world peace and to stable relations between our two nations. I call upon him further to abandon this course of world domination, and to join in an historic effort to end the perilous arms race and to transform the history of man. He has an opportunity now to move the world back from the abyss of destruction – by returning to his government's own words that it had no need to station missiles outside its own territory, and withdrawing these weapons from Cuba-by refraining from any action which will widen or deepen the present crisis – and then by participating in a search for peaceful and permanent solutions.

This Nation is prepared to present its case against the Soviet threat to peace, and our own proposals for a peaceful world, at any time and in any forum – in the OAS, in the United Nations, or in any other meeting that could be useful – without limiting our freedom of action. We have in the past made strenuous efforts to limit the spread of nuclear weapons. We have proposed the elimination of all arms and military bases in a fair and effective disarmament treaty. We are prepared to discuss new proposals for the removal of tensions on both sides – including the possibilities of a genuinely independent Cuba, free to determine its own destiny. We have no wish to war with the Soviet Union – for we are a peaceful people who desire to live in peace with all other peoples.

But it is difficult to settle or even discuss these problems in an atmosphere of intimidation. That is why this latest Soviet threat – or any other threat which is made either independently or in response to our actions this week – must and will be met with determination. Any hostile move anywhere in the world against the safety and freedom of peoples to whom we are committed – including in particular the brave people of West Berlin – will be met by whatever action is needed.

Finally, I want to say a few words to the captive people of Cuba, to whom this speech is being directly carried by special radio facilities. I speak to you as a friend, as one who knows of your deep attachment to your fatherland, as one who shares your aspirations for liberty and justice for all. And I have watched and the American people have watched with deep sorrow how your nationalist revolution was betrayed – and how your fatherland fell under foreign domination. Now your leaders are no longer Cuban leaders inspired by Cuban ideals. They are puppets and agents of an international conspiracy which has turned Cuba against your friends and neighbors in the Americas – and turned it into the first Latin American country to become a target for nuclear war – the first Latin American country to have these weapons on its soil.

These new weapons are not in your interest. They contribute nothing to your peace and well-being. They can only undermine it. But this country has no wish to cause you to suffer or to impose any system upon you. We know that your lives and land are being used as pawns by those who deny your freedom. Many times in the past, the Cuban people have risen to throw out tyrants who destroyed their liberty. And I have no doubt that most Cubans today look forward to the time when they will be truly free – free from foreign domination, free to choose their own leaders, free to select their own system, free to own their own land, free to speak and write and worship without fear or degradation. And then shall Cuba be welcomed back to society of free nations and to the associations of this hemisphere.

My fellow citizens: let no one doubt that this is a difficult and dangerous effort on which we have set out. No one can foresee precisely what course it will take or what costs or casualties will be incurred. Many months of sacrifice and self-discipline lie ahead – months in which both our patience and our will will be tested – months in which many threats and denunciations will keep us aware of our dangers. But the greatest danger of all would be to do nothing.

The path we have chosen for the present is full of hazards, as all paths are – but it is the one most consistent with our character and courage as a nation and our commitments around the world. The cost of freedom is always high – but Americans have always paid it. And one path we shall never choose, and that is the path of surrender or submission.

Our goal is not the victory of might, but the vindication of right – not peace at the expense of freedom, but both peace and freedom, here in this hemisphere, and, we hope, around the world. God willing, that goal will be achieved.

Thank you and good night.

HOW WELL DID YOU UNDERSTAND THIS SELECTION?

1. How serious does President Kennedy think the crisis with the Soviet Union is? Explain.

2. What did Kennedy propose to do about the situation? What other choices did he have?

3. Why did Kennedy say the Soviet weapons on Cuba were illegal?

4. How does Kennedy draw upon history to explain the situation?

5. Why does Kennedy include a message to the Cuban people in his speech?

In 1961, President Kennedy established the President's Commission on the Status of Women on the recommendation of Esther Peterson, assistant Secretary of Labor. The commission, chaired by Eleanor Roosevelt, was designed to investigate legal and economic discrimination against women. The findings of the commission contributed to the passage of the Equal Pay Act in 1963.

Spring 1963
Washington, D.C.

PRESIDENT KENNEDY

This report is an invitation to action. When President John F. Kennedy appointed our Commission, he said:…*we have by no means done enough to strengthen family life and at the same time encourage women to make their full contribution as citizens…It is appropriate at this time…to review recent accomplishments, and to acknowledge frankly the further steps that must be taken. This is a task for the entire Nation…*

Certain tenets have guided our thinking. Respect for the worth and dignity of every individual and conviction that every American should have a chance to achieve the best of which he-or she-is capable are basic to the meaning of both freedom and equality in this democracy. They have been, and now are, great levers for constructive social change, here and around the world. We have not hesitated to measure the present shape of things against our convictions regarding a good society and to note discrepancies between American life as it is in 1963 and as it might become through informed and intelligent action.

The human and national costs of social lag are heavy; for the most part, they are also avoidable. That is why we urge changes, many of them long overdue, in the conditions of women's opportunity in the United States…

We believe that one of the greatest freedoms of the individual in a democratic society is the freedom to choose among different life patterns. Innumerable private solutions found by different individuals in search of the good life provide society with basic strength far beyond the possibilities of a dictated plan.

Illumined by values transmitted through home and school and church, society and heritage, and informed by present and past experience, each woman must arrive at her contemporary expression of purpose, whether as a center of home and family, a participant in the community, a contributor to the economy, a creative artist or thinker or scientist, a citizen engaged in politics and public service. Part and parcel of this freedom is the obligation to assume corresponding responsibility.

Yet there are social as well as individual determinants of freedom of choice; for example, the city slum and the poor rural crossroad frustrate natural gifts and innate human powers. It is a bitter fact that for millions of men and women economic stringency all but eliminates choice among alternatives…

Economic expansion is of particular significance to women. One of the ironies of history is that war has brought American women their greatest economic opportunities. In establishing this Commission, the President noted: "In every period of national emergency, women have served with distinction in widely varied capacities but thereafter have been subject to treatment as a marginal group whose skills have been inadequately utilized."

Comparable opportunity-and far more varied choice-could be provided by full employment in a period without war.

The Council of Economic Advisers had estimated that between 1958 and 1962 the country's productive capacity exceeded its actual output by some $170 billion, or almost $1,000 per person in the United States. Had this potential been realized, lower rates of unemployment and an impressive supply of additional goods and services would have contributed to national well-being. The currently unused resources of the American economy include much work that could be done by women…

But while freedom of choice for many American women, as for men, is limited by economic considerations, one of the most pervasive limitations is the social climate in which women choose what they prepare themselves to do. Too many plans recommended to young women reaching maturity and only partially suited to the second half of the twentieth century. Such advice is correspondingly confusing to them.

Even the role most generally approved by counselors, parents, and friends-the making of a home, the rearing of children, and the transmission to them in their earliest years of the values of the American heritage-is frequently presented as it is thought to have been in an earlier and simpler society…

Similarly, women's participation in such traditional occupations as teaching, nursing, and social work is generally approved, with current shortages underscoring the nation's need for such personnel. But means for keeping up to date the skills of women who continue in such professions are few. So, too, are those for bringing up to date the skills of women who withdraw in order to raise families but return after their families are grown.

Commendation of women's entry into certain other occupations is less general, even though some of them are equally in need of trained people. Girls hearing that most women find mathematics and science difficult, or that engineering and architecture are unusual occupations for a woman, are not led to test their interest by activity in these fields.

Because too little is expected of them, many girls who graduate from high school intellectually able to do good college work do not go to college. Both they as individuals and the nation as a society are thereby made losers.

The subtle limitations imposed by custom are, upon occasion, reinforced by specific barriers. In the course of the twentieth century many bars against women that were firmly in place in 1900 have been lowered or dropped. But certain restrictions remain…

Some of these discriminatory provisions are contained in the common law. Some are written into statute. Some are upheld by court decisions. Others take the form of practices of industrial, labor, professional, or governmental organizations that discriminate against women in apprenticeship, training, hiring, wages, and promotion. We have identified a number of outmoded and prejudical attitudes and practices.

Throughout it deliberation, the Commission has kept in mind certain women who have special disadvantages. Among head of families in the United States, 1 in 10 is a woman. At least half of them are carrying responsibility for both earning the family's living and making the family's home. Their problems are correspondingly greater; their resources are usually less.

Seven million nonwhite women and girls belong to minority racial groups. Discrimination based on color is morally wrong and a source of national weakness. Such discrimination currently places an oppressive dual burden on millions of Negro women. The consultation held by the Commission on the situation of Negro women emphasized that in too many families lack of opportunity for men as well as women, linked to racial discrimination, has forced the women to assume too large a share of the family responsibility. Such women are twice as likely as other women to have to seek employment while they have preschool children at home; they are just beginning to gain entrance to the expanding fields of clerical and commercial employment; except for the few who can qualify as teachers or other professionals, they are forced into low-paid service occupations.

Hundreds of thousands of other women face somewhat similar situations: American Indians, for instance, and Spanish –Americans, many of whom live in urban centers but are new to urban life and burned with language problems.

While there are highly skilled members of all these groups, in many of the families of these women the unbroken cycle of deprivation and retardation repeats itself from generation to generation, compounding its individual cost in human indignity and unhappiness and its social cost in incapacity and delinquency. This cycle must be broken, swiftly and at as many points as possible. The Commission strongly urges that in the carrying out of its recommendations, special attention be given to difficulties that are wholly or largely the products of this kind of discrimination...

Eight out of ten women are in paid employment outside the home at some time during their lives, and many of these, and others as well, engage in unpaid work as volunteers.

The population contains 13 million single girls and women 14 and over. A 20-year-old girl, if she remains single, will spend some 40 years in the labor force. If after working for a few years, she marries and has a family, and then goes back into the labor force at 30, she is likely to work for some 23 more years. Particularly during the years when her children are in school but have not yet left home permanently, the work she seeks is apt to be part time. Inflexibility with regard to part time employment in most current hiring systems, alike in government and in private enterprise, excludes the use of much able and available trained womanpower; practices should be altered to permit it...

U.S. President's Commission on the Status of Women, American Women: Report of the Presidents Commission (Washington, DC: Government Printing Office, 1963) pp. 1-7

HOW WELL DID YOU UNDERSTAND THIS SELECTION?

1. According to the Commission's report, what problems did American women face?

2. What does the Commission recommend to solve the problems women face?

3. What particular difficulties does the report say minority women face?

4. What does the Commission conclude is the cause of the various problems American women face?

5. What does the Commission conclude about the educational system and women?

In 1965 Joseph Lee Jones, an African American, filed a lawsuit against Alfred H. Mayer Company in the Eighth Circuit District Court. The basis of this suit was an allegation by Jones that the Mayer Company refused to sell the plaintiff a house in St. Louis County, Missouri because he was black. Jones argued that Mayer's refusal to sell to an African American violated the Civil Rights Act passed during Reconstruction in 1866. This act guaranteed that all citizens could own property in all states. Jones lost the case in the District Court and on appeal. However, the United States Supreme Court decided to hear the case and issued its ruling on September 17, 1968.

…We begin with the language of the statute itself. In plain and unambiguous terms, section 1982 grants to all citizens, without regard to race or color, "the same right" to purchase and lease property 'as is enjoyed by white citizens." …

On its face, therefore, section 1982 appears to prohibit all discrimination against Negroes in the sale or rental of property – discrimination by private owners as well as discrimination by public authorities. Indeed, even the respondents seem to concede that, if section 1982 "means what it says" – to use the words of the respondents' brief – then it must encompass every racially motivated refusal to sell or rent and cannot be confined to officially sanctioned segregation in housing. Stressing what they consider to be the revolutionary implications of so literal a reading of section 1982, the respondents argue that Congress cannot possibly have intended any such result. Our examination of the relevant history, however, persuades us that Congress meant exactly what it said. …

In light of the concern that led Congress to adopt it and the contents of the debates that preceded its passage, it is clear that the Act was designed to do just what its terms suggest: to prohibit all racial discrimination, whether or not under color of law, with respect to the rights enumerated therein – including the right to purchase or lease property. …

Against this background, it would obviously make no sense to assume, without any historical support whatever, that Congress made a silent decision in 1870 to exempt private discrimination from the operation of the Civil Rights Act in 1866. …

The remaining question is whether Congress has power under the Constitution to do what section 1982 purports to do: to prohibit all racial discrimination, private and public, in the sale and rental of property. Our starting point is the Thirteenth Amendment. …

Negro citizens, North and South, who saw in the Thirteenth Amendment a promise of freedom – freedom to "go and come at pleasure" and to "buy and sell when they please" – would be left with "a mere paper guarantee" if Congress were powerless to assure that a dollar in the hands of a Negro will purchase the same thing as a dollar in the hands of a white man. At the very least, the freedom that Congress is empowered to secure under the Thirteenth amendment includes the freedom to buy whatever a white man can buy, the right to live wherever a white man can live. If Congress cannot say that being a free man means at least this much, then the Thirteenth amendment made a promise the nation cannot keep. …

The judgment is

Reversed.

Source: The United States Supreme Court, Jones v. Alfred Mayer Co. ,392 U.S. 409, 1967

HOW WELL DID YOU UNDERSTAND THIS SELECTION?

1. What did the Supreme Court rule in this case?

2. Upon what reasoning did the Court base its reversal of the previous court decisions?

3. What does the Court say about the Thirteenth Amendment?

4. What does it appear that the defense argued about section 1982 of the Civil Rights Act and the Thirteenth Amendment?

Urban riots rocked American cities in the 1960s. Detroit, the Watts section of Los Anglos, and other cities burned as rioters looted and destroyed homes and businesses. In 1967 President Johnson established the National Advisory Commission on Civil Disorders to investigate the riots in hopes of determining their causes and finding ways to prevent future disturbances. The Commission issued its report in 1968

1968, Washington, D.C.
THE KERNER COMMISSION REPORT ON THE CAUSES OF CIVIL DISORDERS

The summer of 1967 again brought racial disorders to American cities, and with them shock, fear and bewilderment to the nation.

The worst came during a two-week period in July, first in Newark and then in Detroit. Each set off a chain reaction in neighboring communities.

On July 28, 1967, the President of the United States established this Commission and directed us to answer three basic questions:

What happened?

Why did it happen?

What can be done to prevent it from happening again?...

This is our basic conclusion: Our nation is moving toward two societies, one black, one white-separate and unequal.

Reaction to last summer's disorders has quickened the movement and deepened the division. Discrimination and segregation have long permeated much of American life; they now threaten the future of every American.

This deepening racial division is not inevitable. The movement apart can be reversed. Choice is still possible. Our principle task is to define that choice and to press fore a national resolution...

Race prejudice has shaped our history decisively; it now threatens to affect our future.

White racism is essentially responsible for the explosive mixture which has been accumulation in our cities since the end of World War II. Among the ingredients of this mixture are:

Pervasive discrimination and segregation in employment, education and housing, which have resulted in the

340

continuing exclusion of great numbers of Negroes from the benefits of economic progress.

Black in-migration and white exodus, which have produced the massive and growing concentrations of impoverished Negroes in our major cities, creating a growing crisis of deteriorating facilities and services and unmet human needs.

The black ghettos, where segregation and poverty converge on the young to destroy opportunity and enforce failure. Crime, drug addiction, dependency on welfare, and bitterness and resentment against society in general and white society in particular are the result....

Yet these facts alone cannot be said to have caused the disorders. Recently, other powerful ingredients have begun to catalyze the mixture:

Frustrated hopes are the residue of the unfulfilled expectations aroused by the greater judicial and legislative victories of the civil rights movement and the dramatic struggle for equal rights in the South.

A climate that tends toward approval and encouragement of violence as a form of protest has been created by white terrorism directed against nonviolent protest; by the open defiance of law and federal authority by state and local officials resisting desegregation; and by some protest groups engaging in civil disobedience who turn their backs on nonviolence, go beyond the constitutionally protected rights of petition and free assembly, and resort to violence to attempt to compel alteration of laws and policies with which they disagree.

The frustrations of powerlessness have led some Negroes to the conviction that there is not effective alternative to violence as a means of achieving redress of grievances, and of "moving the system." These frustrations are reflected in alienation and hostility toward the institutions of law and government and the white society which controls them, and in the reach toward racial consciousness and solidarity reflected in the slogan "Black Power."

A new mood has sprung up among Negroes, particularly among the young, in which self-esteem and enhanced racial pride are replacing apathy and submission to "the system."

The police are not merely a "spark" factor. To some Negroes police have come to symbolize white power, white racism and white repression. And the fact is that many police do reflect and express these white attitudes. The atmosphere of hostility and cynicism is reinforced by a wide-spread belief among Negroes in the existence of police brutality and in a "double standard" of justice and protection-one for Negroes and on for whites....
The major goal is the creation of a true nation – a single society and a single American identity. Toward that goal, we propose the following objectives for national action:

Opening up opportunities to those who are restricted by racial segregation and discrimination and eliminating all barriers to their choice of jobs, education and housing.

Removing the frustration of powerlessness among the disadvantaged by providing the means for them to deal with the problems that affect their own lives and by increasing the capacity of our public and private institutions to respond to these problems.

Increasing communication across racial lines to destroy stereotypes, to halt polarization, end distrust and hostility and create common ground for efforts toward public order and social justice.

We propose these aims to fulfill our pledge of equality and to meet the fundamental needs of a democratic and civilized society – domestic peace and social justice.

Report of the National Advisory Commission on Civil Disorders (Washington, D.C.: Government Printing Office, 1968), pp.1-13.

HOW WELL DID YOU UNDERSTAND THIS SELECTION?

1. What did President Johnson charge the Commission to do?

2. What did the Commission conclude?

3. What did the Commission determine caused the riots?

4. What did the Commission recommend?

5. What role did the Commission say law enforcement played in causing the riots?

President Johnson's top legislative priority in 1964 was passage of the Civil Rights Act that removed several remaining vestiges of Jim Crow in southern states. This law, which Johnson convinced Congress to pass by recalling martyred President Kennedy's commitment to civil rights, outlawed segregation at public facilities, discrimination at work, empowered the Justice Department to sue school systems that refused to integrate, and withheld federal funds from segregated schools. Senator Richard Russell, a Georgia segregationist, coordinated a filibuster against the bill. The filibuster ended when liberal Senator Hubert Humphrey and President Johnson convinced Senator Everett Dirksen, leader of the Republican caucus, to support passage of the legislation. On June 10, 1964, Democrats and Republicans ended the filibuster with a 71-29 cloture vote. Afterwards, the Civil Rights Act of 1964 passed Congress and President Johnson signed it into law. Jim Crow, the legalized system of segregation that engulfed the South, had been mortally wounded.

Civil Rights Act of 1964

Eighty-eighth Congress of the United States of America
At the Second Session
Begun and held at the City of Washington on Tuesday, the seventh day of January, One thousand nine hundred and sixty-four
An Act
To enforce the constitutional right to vote, to confer jurisdiction upon the district courts of the United States to provide injunctive relief against discrimination in public accommodations, to authorize the Attorney General to institute suits to protect constitutional rights to public facilities and public education, to extend the Commission on Civil Rights, to prevent discrimination in federally assisted programs, to establish a Commission on Equal Employment Opportunity, and for other purposes.
Be it enacted by the Senate and House of Representatives of the United States of America in Congress assembled, That this Act may be cited as the "Civil Rights Act of 1964"

TITLE I-VOTING RIGHTS
SEC.101. Section 2004 of the Revised Statutes (42 U.S.C. 1971), as amended by section 131 of the Civil Rights Act of 1957 (71 Stat. 637), and as further amended by section 601 of the Civil Rights Act of 1960 (74 Stat.90), is further amended as follows:
(a) Insert "1" after "(a)" in subsection (a) and add at the end of subsection (a) the following new paragraphs:
"(2) No person acting under color of law shall-

342

"(A) in determining whether any individual is qualified under State law or laws to vote in any Federal election, apply any standard, practice, or procedure different from the standards, practices, or procedures applied under such law or laws to other individuals within the same county, parish, or similar political subdivision who have been found by State officials to be qualified to vote;

"(B) deny the right of any individual to vote in any Federal election because of an error or omission on any record or paper relating to any application, registration, or other act requisite to voting, if such error or omission is not material in determining whether such individual is qualified under State law to vote in such election; or

"(C) employ any literacy test as a qualification for voting in any Federal election unless (i) such test is administered to each individual and is conducted wholly in writing, and (ii) a certified copy of the test and of the answers given by the individual is furnished to him within twenty-five days of the submission of his request made within the period of time during which records and papers are required to be retained and preserved pursuant to title III of the Civil Rights Act of 1960 (42 U.S.C. 1974-74e; 74 Stat. 88): Provided, however, That the Attorney General may enter into agreements with appropriate State or local authorities that preparation, conduct, and maintenance of such tests in accordance with the provisions as are necessary in the preparation, conduct, and maintenance of such tests for persons who are blind or otherwise physically handicapped, meet the purposes of this subparagraph and constitute compliance therewith.

TITLE III- DESEGREGATION OF PUBLIC FACILITIES

Sec. 301 (a) Whenever the Attorney General receives a complaint in writing signed by an individual to the effect that he is being deprived of or threatened with the loss of his right to the equal protection of the laws, on account of his race, color, religion, or national origin, by being denied equal utilization of any public facility which is owned, operated, or managed by or on behalf of any State or subdivision thereof, other than a public school or public college as defined in section 401 of title IV hereof, and the Attorney General believes the complaint is meritorious and certifies that the signer or signers of such complaint are unable, in his judgment, to initiate and maintain appropriate legal proceedings for relief and that the institution of an action will materially further the orderly progress of desegregation in public facilities, the Attorney General is authorized to institute for or in the name of the United States a civil action in any appropriate district court of the United States against such parties and for such relief as may be appropriate, and such court shall have and shall exercise jurisdiction of proceedings instituted pursuant to this section. The Attorney General may implead as defendants such additional parties as are or become necessary to the grant of effective relief hereunder.

(b) The Attorney General may deem a person or persons unable to initiate and maintain appropriate legal proceedings within the meaning of subsection (a) of this section when such person or persons are unable, either directly or through other interested persons or organizations, to bear the expense of the litigation or to obtain effective legal representation; or whenever he is satisfied that the institution of such litigation would jeopardize the personal safety, employment, or economic standing of such person or persons, their families, or their property.

SEC. 302. In any action or proceeding under this title the United States shall be liable for costs, including a reasonable attorney's fee, the same as a private person.

SEC. 303. Nothing in this title shall affect adversely the right of any person to sue for or obtain relief in any court against discrimination in any facility covered by this title.

SEC. 304. A complaint as used in this title is a writing or document within the meaning of section 1001, title 18, United States Code.

TITLE VII-EQUAL EMPLOYMENT OPPORTUNITY
DISCRIMINATON BECAUSE OF RACE, COLOR, RELIGION, SEX, OR NATIONAL ORIGIN
SEC. 703.

(a) It shall be an unlawful employment practice for an employer—

(1) to fail or refuse to hire or to discharge any individual, or otherwise to discriminate against any individual with respect to his compensation, terms, conditions, or privileges or employment, because of such individual's race, color, religion, sex, or national origin; or

(2) to limit, segregate, or classify his employees in any way which would deprive or tend to deprive any individual of employment opportunities or otherwise adversely affect his status as an employee, because of such individual's race, color, religion, sex, or national origin.

(b) It shall be an unlawful employment practice for an employment agency to fail or refuse to refer for employment, or otherwise to discriminate against, any individual because of his race, color, religion, sex, or national origin, or to classify or refer for employment any individual on the basis of his race, color, religion, sex, or national origin.

(c) It shall be an unlawful employment practice for a labor organization—

(1) to exclude or to expel from its membership, or otherwise to discriminate against, any individual because of his race, color, religion, sex, or national origin;

(2) to limit, segregate, or classify its membership, or to classify or fail or refuse to refer for employment any individual, in any way, which would deprive or tend to deprive any individual of employment opportunities, or would limit such employment opportunities or otherwise adversely affect his status as an employee or as an applicant for employment, because of such individual's race, color, religion, sex, or national origin; or

(3) to cause or attempt to cause an employer to discriminate against an individual in violation of this section.

(d) It shall be an unlawful employment practice for any employer, labor organization, or joint labor-management committee controlling apprenticeship or other training or retraining, including on-the-job training programs to discriminate against any individual because of his race, color, religion, sex, or national origin in admission to, or employment in , any program established to provide apprenticeship or other training.

(e) Notwithstanding any other provision of this title, (1) it shall not be an unlawful employment practice for an employer to hire and employ employees, for an employment agency to classify, or refer for employment any individual, for a labor organization to classify its membership or to classify or refer for employment any individual, or for an employer, labor organization, or joint labor-management committee controlling apprenticeship or other training or retraining programs to admit or employ any individual in any such program, on the basis of his religion, sex, or national origin in those certain instances where religion, sex, or national origin is a bona fide occupational qualification reasonably necessary to the normal operation of that particular business, or enterprise, and (2) it shall not be an unlawful employment practice for a school, college, university, or other educational institution or institution of learning to hire and employ employees of a particular religion if such school, college, university, or other educational institution or institution of learning is directed toward the propagation of a particular religion.

(f) As used in this title, the phrase "unlawful employment practice" shall not be deemed to include any action or measure taken by an employer, labor organization, joint labor-management committee, or employment agency with respect to an individual who is a member of the Communist Party of the United States or of any other organization required to register as a Communist-action or Communist-front organization by final order of the Subversive Activities Control Board pursuant to the Subversive Activities Control Act of 1950.

(g) Notwithstanding any other provision of this title, it shall not be an unlawful employment practice for an employer to fail or refuse to hire and employ any individual for any position, for an employer to discharge any individual from any position, or for an employment agency to fail or refuse to refer any individual for employment in any position, or for a labor organization to fail or refuse to refer any individual for employment in any position, if—

(1) the occupancy of such position, or access to the premises in or upon which any part of the duties of such position is performed or is to be performed, is subject to any requirement imposed in the interest of the national security of the United States under any security program in effect pursuant to or administered under any statute of the United States or any Executive order of the President; and

(2) such individual has not fulfilled or has ceased to fulfill that requirement.

(h) Notwithstanding any other provision of this title, it shall not be an unlawful employment practice for an employer to apply different standards of compensation, or different terms, conditions, or privileges of employment pursuant to a bona fide seniority or merit system, or a system which measures earnings by quantity or quality of production or to employees who work in different locations, provided that such differences are not the result of an intention to discriminate because of race, color, religion, sex, or national origin, nor shall it be an unlawful employment practice for an employer to give an to act upon the results of any professionally developed ability test provided that such test, its administration or action upon the results is not designed, intended or used to discriminate because of race, color, religion, sex, or national origin. It shall not be an unlawful employment practice under this title for any employer to differentiate upon the basis of sex in determining the amount of the wages or compensation paid or to be paid to employees of such employer if such differentiation is authorized by the provisions of section 6(d) of the Fair Labor Standards Act of 1938, as amended (29 U..C. 206 (d)).

(i) Nothing contained in this title shall be interpreted to require any employer, employment agency, labor organization, or joint labor-management committee subject to this title to grant preferential treatment to any individual or to any group because of race, color, religion, sex, or national origin of such individual or group on account of an imbalance which may exist with respect to the total number or percentage of persons of any race, color, religion, sex, or national origin employed by an employer, referred or classified for employment by any employment agency or labor organization, admitted to membership or classified by any labor organization, or admitted to, or employed in, any apprenticeship or other training program, in comparison with the total number or percentage of persons of such race, color, religion, sex, or national origin in any community, State, section, or other area, or in the available work force in any community, State, section, or other area.

OTHER UNLAWFUL EMPLOYMENT PRACTICES

SEC. 704.

(a) It shall be an unlawful employment practice for an employer to discriminate against any of his employees or applicants for employment, for an employment agency to discriminate against any individual, or for a labor organization to discriminate against any member thereof or applicant for membership, because he has opposed any practice made an unlawful employment practice by this title, or because he has made a charge, testified, assisted, or participated in any manner in an investigation, proceeding, or hearing under this title.

(b) It shall be an unlawful employment practice for an employer, labor organization, or employment agency to print or publish or cause to be printed or published any notice or advertisement relating to employment by such an employer or membership in or any classification or referral for employment by such a labor organization, or relating to any classification or referral for employment by such an employment agency, indicating any preference, limitation, specification, or discrimination, based on race, color, religion, sex, or national origin, except that such a notice or advertisement may indicate a preference, limitation, specification, or discrimination based on religion…

HOW WELL DID YOU UNDERSTAND THIS SELECTION?

1. How did the 1964 Civil Rights Act expand voting rights for minorities?

2. What remedies were provided by the Civil Rights Act for the desegregation of public services?

3. How did the Civil Rights Act of 1964 end employment discrimination? Explain.

4. Did the 1964 Civil Rights Act improve the work situation for African Americans? Explain.

On November 22, 1963 President John F. Kennedy was assassinated while riding in an open top car as part of a motorcade in Dallas, Texas. Despite heroic efforts by doctors at Parkland Hospital to save the youthful President, bullet wounds to the neck and head took Kennedy's life. Americans, shocked by the assassination, were hesitant to accept the death of their beloved leader without explanation. President Lyndon Johnson, Kennedy's vice president who took the oath of office shortly after Kennedy's death, appointed a commission headed by Chief Justice Earl Warren to investigate the assassination. After conducting an exhaustive investigation the Commission released the results of its findings, which concluded that the assassination of President Kennedy and the wounding of Texas Governor John Connally were the work of a lone assassin firing a rifle from the sixth floor of the Texas School Book Depository. This conclusion did not sit well with many Americans who believed that Warren Commission ignored evidence that Kennedy's assassination was part of a larger conspiracy.

Warren Commission Report

This Commission was created to ascertain the facts relating to the preceding summary of events and to consider the important questions which they raised. The Commission has addressed itself to this task and has reached certain conclusions based on all the available evidence. No limitations have been placed on the Commission's inquiry; it has conducted its own investigation, and all Government agencies have fully discharged their responsibility to cooperate with the Commission in its investigation. These conclusions represent the reasoned judgment of all members of the Commission and are presented after an investigation which has satisfied the Commission that it: has ascertained the truth concerning the assassination of President Kennedy to the extent that a prolonged and thorough search makes this possible.

1. The shots which killed President Kennedy and wounded Governor Connally were fired from the sixth floor window at the southeast corner of the Texas School Book Depository. This determination is based upon the following:

    (a) Witnesses at the scene of the assassination saw a rifle being fired from the sixth floor window of the Depository Building, and some witnesses saw a rifle in the window immediately after the shots were fired.

    (b) The nearly whole bullet found on Governor Connally's stretcher at Parkland Memorial Hospital and the two bullet fragments found in the front seat of the Presidential limousine were fired from the 6.5- millimeter Mannlicher-Carcano rifle found on the sixth floor of the Depository Building to the exclusion of all other weapons.

    (c) The three used cartridge cases found near the window on the sixth floor at the southeast corner of the building were fired from the same rifle which fired the above-described bullet and fragments, to the exclusion of all other weapons.

    (d) The windshield in the Presidential limousine was struck by a bullet fragment on the inside surface of the glass, but was not penetrated.

    (e) The nature of the bullet wounds suffered by President Kennedy and Governor Connally and the location of the car at the time of the shots establish that the bullets were fired from above and behind the Presidential limousine, striking the President and the Governor as follows:

    1. President Kennedy was first struck by a bullet which entered at the back of his neck and exited through the lower front portion of his neck, causing a wound which would not necessarily have been lethal. The President was struck a second time by a bullet which entered the right-rear portion of his head, causing a massive and fatal wound.

    2. Governor Connally was struck by a bullet which entered on the right side of his back and traveled downward through the right side of his chest, exiting below his right nipple. This bullet then passed through his right wrist and entered his left thigh where it caused a superficial wound.

    (f) There is no credible evidence that the shots were fired from the Triple Underpass, ahead of the motorcade, or from any other location.

3. The weight of the evidence indicates that there were three shots fired.

4. Although it is not necessary to any essential findings of the Commission to determine just which shot hit Governor Connally, there is very persuasive evidence from the experts to indicate that the same bullet which pierced the President's throat also caused Governor Connally's wounds. However, Governor Connally's testimony and certain other factors have given rise to some difference of opinion as to this probability but there is no question in the mind of any member of the Commission that all the shots which caused the President's and Governor Connally's wounds were fired from the sixth floor window of the Texas School Book Depository.

5. The shots which killed President Kennedy and wounded Governor Connally were fired by Lee Harvey Oswald. This conclusion is based upon the following:

(a) The Mannlicher-Carcano 6.5-millimeter Italian rifle from which the shots were fired was owned by and in the possession of Oswald.

(b) Oswald carried this rifle into the Depository Building on the morning of November 22, 1963.

(c) Oswald, at the time of the assassination, was present at the window from which the shots were fired.

(d) Shortly after the assassination, the Mannlicher-Carcano rifle belonging to Oswald was found partially hidden between some cartons on the sixth floor and the improvised paper bag in which Oswald brought the rifle to the Depository was found close by the window from which the shots were fired.

(e) Based on testimony of the experts and their analysis of films of the assassination, the Commission has concluded that a rifleman of Lee Harvey Oswald's capabilities could have fired the shots from the rifle used in the assassination within the elapsed time of the shooting. The Commission has concluded further that Oswald possessed the capability with a rifle which enabled him to commit the assassination.

(f) Oswald lied to the police after his arrest concerning important substantive matters.

(g) Oswald had attempted to kill Maj. Gen. Edwin A. Walker (Retired, U.S. Army) on April 10, 1963, thereby demonstrating his disposition to take human life.

6. Oswald killed Dallas Police Patrolman J. D. Tippit approximately 45 minutes after the assassination. This conclusion upholds the finding that Oswald fired the shots which killed President Kennedy and wounded Governor Connally and is supported by the following:

(a) Two eyewitnesses saw the Tippit shooting and seven eyewitnesses heard the shots and saw the gunman leave the scene with revolver in hand. These nine eyewitnesses positively identified Lee Harvey Oswald as the man they saw.

(b) The cartridge cases found at the scene of the shooting were fired from the revolver in the possession of Oswald at the time of his arrest to the exclusion of all other weapons.

(c) The revolver in Oswald's possession at the time of his arrest was purchased by and belonged to Owald.

(d) Oswald's jacket was found along the path of flight taken by the gunman as he fled from the scene of the killing.

7. Within 80 minutes of the assassination and 35 minutes of the Tippit killing Oswald resisted arrest at the theatre by attempting to shoot another Dallas police officer.

8. The Commission has reached the following conclusions concerning Oswald's interrogation and detention by the Dallas police:

(a) Except for the force required to effect his arrest, Oswald was not subjected to any physical coercion by any law enforcement officials. He was advised that he could not be compelled to give any information and that any statements made by him might be used against him in court. He was advised of his right to counsel. He was given the opportunity to obtain counsel of his own choice and was offered legal assistance by the Dallas Bar Association, which he rejected at that time.

(b) Newspaper, radio, and television reporters were allowed uninhibited access to the area through which Oswald had to pass when he was moved from his cell to the interrogation room and other sections of the building, thereby subjecting Oswald to harassment and creating chaotic conditions which were not conducive to orderly interrogation or the protection of the rights of the prisoner.

(c) The numerous statements, sometimes erroneous, made to the press by various local law enforcement officials, during this period of confusion and disorder in the police station, would have presented serious obstacles to the obtaining of a fair trial for Oswald. To the extent that the information was erroneous or misleading, it helped to create doubts, speculations, and fears in the mind of the public which might otherwise not have arisen.

8. The Commission has reached the following conclusions concerning the killing of Oswald by Jack Ruby on November 24, 1963:

(a) Ruby entered the basement of the Dallas Police Department shortly after 11:17 a.m. and killed Lee Harvey Oswald at 11:21 a.m.

(b) Although the evidence on Ruby's means of entry is not conclusive, the weight of the evidence indicates that he walked down the ramp leading from Main Street to the basement of the police department.

(c) There is no evidence to support the rumor that Ruby may have been assisted by any members of the Dallas Police Department in the killing of Oswald.

(d) The Dallas Police Department's decision to transfer Oswald to the county jail in full public view was unsound. The arrangements made by the police department on Sunday morning, only a few hours before the attempted transfer, were inadequate. Of critical importance was the fact that news media representatives and others were not excluded from the basement even after the police were notified of threats to Oswald's life. These deficiencies contributed to the death of Lee Harvey Oswald.

9. The Commission has found no evidence that either Lee Harvey Oswald or Jack Ruby was part of any conspiracy, domestic or foreign, to assassinate President Kennedy. The reasons for this conclusion are:

(a) The Commission has found no evidence that anyone assisted Oswald in planning or carrying out the assassination. In this connection it has thoroughly investigated, among other factors, the circumstances surrounding the planning of the motorcade route through Dallas, the hiring of Oswald by the Texas School Book Depository Co. on October 15, 1963, the method by which the rifle was brought into the building, the placing of cartons of books at the window, Oswald's escape from the building, and the testimony of eyewitnesses to the shooting.

(b) The Commission has found no evidence that Oswald was involved with any person or group in a conspiracy to assassinate the President, although it has thoroughly investigated, in addition to other possible leads, all facets of Oswald's associations, finances, and personal habits, particularly during the period following his return from the Soviet Union in June 1962.

(c) The Commission has found no evidence to show that Oswald was employed, persuaded, or encouraged by any foreign government to assassinate President Kennedy or that he was an agent of any foreign government, although the Commission has reviewed the circumstances surrounding Oswald's defection to the Soviet Union, his life there from October of 1959 to June of 1962 so far as it can be reconstructed, his known contacts with the Fair Play for Cuba Committee and his visits to the Cuban and Soviet Embassies in Mexico City during his trip to Mexico from September 26 to October 3, 1963, and his known contacts with the Soviet Embassy in the United States.

(d) The Commission has explored all attempts of Oswald to identify himself with various political groups, including the Communist Party, U.S.A., the Fair Play for Cuba Committee, and the Socialist Workers Party, and has been unable to find any evidence that the contacts which he initiated were related to Oswald's subsequent assassination of the President.

(e) All of the evidence before the Commission established that there was nothing to support the speculation that Oswald was an agent, employee, or informant of the FBI, the CIA, or any other governmental agency. It has thoroughly investigated Oswald's relationships prior to the assassination with all agencies of the U.S. Government. All contacts with Oswald by any of these agencies were made in the regular exercise of their different responsibilities.

(f) No direct or indirect relationship between Lee Harvey Oswald and Jack Ruby has been discovered by the Commission, nor has it been able to find any credible evidence that either knew the other, although a thorough investigation was made of the many rumors and speculations of such a relationship.

(g) The Commission has found no evidence that Jack Ruby acted with any other person in the killing of Lee Harvey Oswald.

(h) After careful investigation the Commission has found no credible evidence either that Ruby and Officer Tippit, who was killed by Oswald, knew each other or that Oswald and Tippit knew each other. Because of the difficulty of proving negatives to a certainty the possibility of others being involved with either Oswald or Ruby cannot be established categorically, but if there is any such evidence it has been beyond the reach of all the investigative agencies and resources of the United States and has not come to the attention of this Commission.

11. In its entire investigation the Commission has found no evidence of conspiracy, subversion, or disloyalty to the U.S. Government by any Federal, State, or local official.

12. On the basis of the evidence before the Commission it concludes that Oswald acted alone. Therefore, to determine the motives for the assassination of President Kennedy, one must look to the assassin himself. Clues to Oswald's motives can be found in his family history, his education or lack of it, his acts, his writings, and the recollections of those who had close contacts with him throughout his life. The Commission has presented with this report all of the background information bearing on motivation which it could discover. Thus, others may study Lee Oswald's life and arrive at their own conclusions as to his possible motives.

The Commission could not make any definitive determination of Oswald's motives. It has endeavored to isolate factors which contributed to his character and which might have influenced his decision to assassinate President Kennedy. These factors were:

(a) His deep-rooted resentment of all authority which was expressed in a hostility toward every society in which he lived;

(b) His inability to enter into meaningful relationships with people, and a continuous pattern of rejecting his environment favor of new surrounding;

(c) His urge to try to find a place in history and despair at times over failures in his various undertakings;

(d) His capacity for violence as evidenced by his attempt to kill General Walker;

(e) His avowed commitment to Marxism and communism, as he understood the terms and developed his own interpretation of them; this was expressed by his antagonism toward the United States, by his defection to the Soviet Union, by his failure to be reconciled with life in the United States even after his disenchantment with the Soviet Union, and by his efforts, though frustrated, to go to Cuba. Each of these contributed to his capacity to risk all in cruel and irresponsible actions.

13. The Commission recognizes that the varied responsibilities of the President require that he make frequent trips to all parts of the United States and abroad. Consistent with their high responsibilities Presidents can never be protected from every potential threat. The Secret Service's difficulty in meeting its protective responsibility varies with the activities and the nature of the occupant of the Office of President and his willingness to conform to plans for his safety. In appraising the performance of the Secret Service it should be understood that it has to do its work within such limitations. Nevertheless, the Commission believes that recommendations for improvements in Presidential protection are compelled by the facts disclosed in this investigation.

(a) The complexities of the Presidency have increased so rapidly in recent years that the Secret Service has not been able to develop or to secure adequate resources of personnel and facilities to fulfill its important assignment. This situation should be promptly remedied.

(b) The Commission has concluded that the criteria and procedures of the Secret Service designed to identify and protect against persons considered threats to the president, were not adequate prior to the assassination.

1. The Protective Research Section of the Secret Service, which is responsible for its preventive work, lacked sufficient trained personnel and the mechanical and technical assistance needed to fulfill its responsibility.

2. Prior to the assassination the Secret Service's criteria dealt with direct threats against the President. Although the Secret Service treated the direct threats against the President adequately, it failed to recognize the necessity of identifying other potential sources of danger to his security. The Secret Service did not develop adequate and specific criteria defining those persons or groups who might present a danger to the President. In effect, the Secret Service largely relied upon other Federal or State agencies to supply the information necessary for it to fulfill its preventive responsibilities, although it did ask for information about direct threats to the President.

(c) The Commission has concluded that there was insufficient liaison and coordination of information between the Secret Service and other Federal agencies necessarily concerned with Presidential protection. Although the FBI, in the normal exercise of its responsibility, had secured considerable information about Lee Harvey Oswald, it had no official responsibility, under the Secret Service criteria existing at the time of the President's trip to Dallas, to refer to the Secret Service the information it had about Oswald. The Commission has concluded, however, that the FBI took an unduly restrictive view of its role in preventive intelligence work prior to the assassination. A more carefully coordinated treatment of the Oswald case by the FBI might well have resulted in bringing Oswald's activities to the attention of the Secret Service.

(d) The Commission has concluded that some of the advance preparations in Dallas made by the Secret Service, such as the detailed security measures taken at Love Field and the Trade Mart, were thorough and well executed. In other respects, however, the Commission has concluded that the advance preparations for the President's trip were deficient.

  2. Although the Secret Service is compelled to rely to a great extent on local law enforcement officials, its procedures at the time of the Dallas trip did not call for well-defined instructions as to the respective responsibilities of the police officials and others assisting in the protection of the President.

  3. The procedures relied upon by the Secret Service for detecting the presence of an assassin located in a building along a motorcade route were inadequate. At the time of the trip to Dallas, the Secret Service as a matter of practice did not investigate, or cause to be checked, any building located along the motorcade route to be taken by the President. The responsibility for observing windows in these buildings during the motorcade was divided between local police personnel stationed on the streets to regulate crowds and Secret Service agents riding in the motorcade. Based on its investigation the Commission has concluded that these arrangements during the trip to Dallas were clearly not sufficient.

(e) The configuration of the Presidential car and the seating arrangements of the Secret Service agents in the car did not afford the Secret Service agents the opportunity they should have had to be of immediate assistance to the President at the first sign of danger. to the President's safety reacted promptly at the time the shots were fired from the Texas School Book Depository Building.

HOW WELL DID YOU UNDERSTAND THIS SELECTION?

1. What did the Warren Commission conclude about President Kennedy's assassination? Is this conclusion valid? Why or why not?

2. What evidence did the Warren Commission use to support its conclusions? Is this evidence reliable? Why or why not?

3. Who does the Commission conclude was the assassin? What evidence does the Commission use to support this conclusion?

4. What happened to the assassin?

5. Why do so many Americans believe Kennedy's assassination was part of a larger conspiracy? How does the Warren Commission refute conspiracy theories? Is the attempt to refute conspiracy theories successful? Explain.

6. What does the Warren Commission conclude about the Secret Service and its inability to protect President Kennedy?

PRESIDENT JOHNSON'S REMARKS AT THE SIGNING CEREMONY FOR THE AIR QUALITY ACT OF 1967

President Johnson signed the Air Quality Act into law on November 21, 1967. This legislation gave the federal government authority to impose standards on industry that would reduce the amount of pollution pouring into the skies every day. The automobile industry was a particular target of the legislation. The Air Quality Act of 1967 allowed governmental regulators to set standards under which automobile manufacturers would be required to produce cars that emitted much less noxious and poisonous fumes into the atmosphere. President Johnson uttered the following remarks at the signing ceremony held in the East Room of the White House for the Air Quality Act:

I DEEPLY APPRECIATE your patience and I plead for your understanding. But this is the last day that I will have an opportunity to visit with General Westmoreland, Ambassador Bunker, and Mr. Komer, and others.

We started out at 8 o'clock this morning and we have been running a little late. But each one of them is trying to get everything on their agenda reviewed before they leave.

So I am a little behind time, but I am grateful to you for whatever understanding you can give me.

I would like to begin this morning by reading you a little weather report:

"... dirty water and black snow pour from the dismal air to ...the putrid slush that waits for them below."

Now that is not a description of Boston, Chicago, New York, or even Washington, D.C. It is from Dante's "Inferno," a 600-yearold vision of damnation.

But doesn't it sound familiar?

Isn't it a forecast that fits almost any large American city today?

I think those like Secretary Gardner and Senator Muskie, and all you Members of the Congress and the Cabinet who have worked with this subject would agree with that.

Don't we really risk our own damnation every day by destroying the air that gives us life?

I think we do. We have done it with our science, our industry, and our progress. Above all, we have really done it with our own carelessness—our own continued indifference and our own repeated negligence.

Contaminated air began in this country as a big-city problem. But in just a few years, the gray pall of pollution has spread throughout the Nation. Today its threat hangs everywhere—and it is still spreading.

Today we are pouring at least 130 million tons of poison into the air each year. That is two-thirds of a ton for every man, woman, and child that lives in America.

And tomorrow the picture looks even blacker. By 1980, we will have a third more people living in our cities than are living there today. We will have 40 percent more automobiles and trucks. And we will be burning half again as much fuel.

That leaves us, according to my evaluation, only one real choice. Either we stop poisoning our air—or we become a nation in gas masks, groping our way through the dying cities and a wilderness of ghost towns that the people have evacuated.

We make our choice with the bill that we are going to sign very shortly. It is not the first clean air bill—but it is, I think, the best.

I am indebted to all of you who had a part in its fashioning.

Congress passed the Clean Air Act in 1963. I signed it to establish the Government's obligation and to establish the Government's authority to act forcefully against air pollution.

Two years later we amended that act. Standards were set in 1965 to control automobile pollution.

These were important steps. But they were really, as Senator Muskie has reminded us many times, just really baby steps. Today we grow up to our responsibilities. This new Air Quality Act lets us face up to our problem as we have never faced up before.

In the next 3 years, it will authorize more funds to combat air pollution—more funds in the next 3 years to combat air pollution—than we have spent on this subject in the entire Nation's history of 180 years.

It will give us scientific answers to our most baffling problem: how to get the sulphur out of our fuel—and how to keep it out of our air.

351

It will give Secretary Gardner new power to stop pollution before it chokes our children and before it strangles our elderly—before it drives us into a hospital bed.

It will help our States fight pollution in the only practical way—by regional airshed controls—by giving the Federal Government standby power to intervene if and when States rights do not always function efficiently.

It will help our States to control the number one source of pollution—our automobiles.

But for all that it will do, the Air Quality Act will never end pollution. It is a law—and not a magic wand to wave that will cleanse our skies. It is a law whose ultimate power and final effectiveness really rests out there with the people of this land--on our seeing the damnation that awaits us if the people do not act responsibly to avoid it and to curb it.

Last January, in asking Congress to pass this legislation, I had this to say: "This situation does not exist because it was inevitable, nor because it cannot be controlled. Air pollution is the inevitable consequence of neglect. It can be controlled when that neglect is no longer tolerated.

"It will be controlled when the people of America, through their elected representatives, demand the right to air that they and their children can breathe without fear."

So, let us then strengthen that demand from this moment on. Let us seize the new powers of this new law to end a long, dark night of neglect.

Let our children say, when they look back on this day, that it was here that a sleeping giant—it was here that their Nation awoke. It was here that America turned away from damnation, and found salvation in reclaiming God's blessings of fresh air and clean sky.

We are distressed at the condition that we cannot at the moment find the solution for—our men dying on the battlefields.

We are troubled with the economic international uncertainties and deficits here at home. But, there are many things that we can do and that we must do in this 20th century that have not been done in the two centuries that have gone by.

I talked yesterday about some of the protections that this century requires for the consumers of this country. We have 12 measures that we have recommended and most of them are moving along. There is no reason why anyone in this country ought to be permitted to eat dirty, diseased, filthy meat and it is not going to bankrupt the Treasury to bring a stop to that.

There is no reason why anyone in this country should not know how much interest they are paying. So, we can have a truth-in-lending bill. The poorest people are paying the highest interest. We ought to act there. It is not going to bankrupt the Treasury.

There is no reason in the world why a baby ought to be put in a blanket and burned up. We ought to take some steps to protect them from all these casualties.

I feel the same way in this general field. All the Members of Congress whom I am looking at—I would call every one of your names if I had them--some of you tell me you are coming and don't make it—some of you say you won't come here and then you are here. So, when I start calling your names I am embarrassed.

However, I am indebted to everyone—beginning with the first man on the row and going down to attractive Edna Kelly, then, going over here and seeing the Cabinet members and Congressmen who worked on this—for what you are doing to keep our air clean and to keep our water pure, and to give our children a place where they can go and play without having their lungs filled with disease.

I sat with a great person, one of the greatest products of this land. I suffered with him not long ago because he could hardly utter a full sentence without coughing and choking because of the effects of what he had breathed and what had gone into his body from residence here in this town.

Senator Muskie has been shoving me as no other person has, all these years, to do something in the pollution field.

I remember an old man told me when I came to Washington, he said, "Son, you get ready. If you are going to live in this town you are either going to be shoving somebody or somebody is going to be shoving you."

So, when I see influential Senators, chairmen of committees like Senator Randolph and other Members of Congress here this morning, I want to shove you.

It may not cost you $1 billion for the things we are shoving because we are going to have to watch those expenditures with the way things are developing. But we can purify our water. We can clean up our air. We can give protection to our babies and to our old folks.

We can mark how much we are paying on some of these things. We can clean up our diseased meats.

I think actually we will find it is pretty profitable if we deal with this question of disease. I expect we lose more from it than it would cost us to protect ourselves against it.

So, I appeal to you to try to do your best to get us those 12 consumer bills. If you can't pass them just exactly as we recommend, we will understand. Just give us 90 percent this year and we will come back next year—if we are all here—for the other 10 percent.

HOW WELL DID YOU UNDERSTAND THIS SELECTION?

1. How does President Johnson describe air pollution? Is his description accurate? Why or why not?

2. Who or what does Johnson attribute the problem of air pollution to?

3. How does Johnson see the future with passage of the act? Without passage of the act? Explain.

ENGLE V. VITALE

*The Supreme Court under Chief Justice Earl Warren brought about much social change in the 1950s and 1960s in a variety of landmark cases, including Brown v. Board of Education of Topeka, KS that desegregated public schools, gave poor defendants in criminal cases the right to free legal counsel with its ruling in Gideon v. Wainwright, and in Miranda v. Arizona required police to inform suspects of basic constitutional rights before interrogation. No case, however, irritated conservatives more than did the court's ruling in **Engel v. Vitale** upholding the Constitution's separation of church and state. Justice Black wrote the opinion of the court.*

Engle v. Vitale

The respondent Board of Education of Union Free School District No. 9, New Hyde Park, New York, acting in its official capacity under state law, directed the School District's principal to cause the following prayer to be said aloud by each class in the presence of a teacher at the beginning of each school day:

"Almighty God, we acknowledge our dependence upon Thee, and we beg Thy blessings upon us, our parents, our teachers and our Country."

This daily procedure was adopted on the recommendation of the State Board of Regents, a governmental agency created by the State Constitution to which the New York Legislature has granted broad supervisory, executive, and legislative powers over the State's public school system. These state officials composed the prayer which they recommended and published as a part of their "Statement on Moral and Spiritual Training in the Schools," saying: "We believe that this Statement will be subscribed to by all men and women of good will, and we call upon all of them to aid in giving life to our program."

Shortly after the practice of reciting the Regents' prayer was adopted by the School District, the parents of ten pupils brought this action in a New York State Court insisting that use of this official prayer in the public schools was contrary to the beliefs, religions, or religious practices of both themselves and their children. Among other things, these parents challenged the constitutionality of both the state law authorizing the School District to direct the use of prayer in public schools and the School District's regulation ordering the recitation of this particular prayer on the ground that these actions of official governmental agencies violate that part of the First Amendment of the Federal Constitution which commands that "Congress shall make no law respecting an establishment of religion" - a command which was "made applicable to the State of New York by the Fourteenth Amendment of the said Constitution." The New York Court of Appeals, over the dissents of Judges Dye and Fuld, sustained an order of the lower state courts which had upheld the power of New York to use the Regents' prayer as a part of the daily procedures of its public schools so long as the schools did not compel any pupil to join in the prayer over his or his parents' objection. We granted certiorari to review this important decision involving rights protected by the First and Fourteenth Amendments. 3

We think that by using its public school system to encourage recitation of the Regents' prayer, the State of New York has adopted a practice wholly inconsistent with the Establishment Clause. There can, of course, be no doubt that New York's program of daily classroom invocation of God's blessings as prescribed in the Regents' prayer is a religious activity. It is a solemn avowal of divine faith and supplication for the blessings of the Almighty. The nature of such a prayer has always been religious, none of the respondents has denied this and the trial court expressly so found:

"The religious nature of prayer was recognized by Jefferson and has been concurred in by theological writers, the United States Supreme Court and State courts and administrative officials, including New York's Commissioner of Education. A committee of the New York Legislature has agreed.

"The Board of Regents as amicus curiae, the respondents and intervenors all concede the religious nature of prayer, but seek to distinguish this prayer because it is based on our spiritual heritage. . . ."

The petitioners contend among other things that the state laws requiring or permitting use of the Regents' prayer must be struck down as a violation of the Establishment Clause because that prayer was composed by governmental officials as a part of a governmental program to further religious beliefs. For this reason, petitioners argue, the State's use of the Regents' prayer in its public school system breaches the constitutional wall of separation between Church and State. We agree with that contention since we think that the constitutional prohibition against laws respecting an establishment of religion must at least mean that in this country it is no part of the business of government to compose official prayers for any group of the American people to recite as a part of a religious program carried on by government.

It is a matter of history that this very practice of establishing governmentally composed prayers for religious services was one of the reasons which caused many of our early colonists to leave England and seek religious freedom in America. The Book of Common Prayer, which was created under governmental direction and which was approved by Acts of Parliament in 1548 and 1549, set out in minute detail the accepted form and content of prayer and other religious ceremonies to be used in the established, tax-supported Church of England. The controversies over the Book and what should be its content repeatedly threatened to disrupt the peace of that country as the accepted forms of prayer in the established church changed with the views of the particular ruler that happened to be in control at the time. Powerful groups representing some of the varying religious views of the people struggled among themselves to impress their particular views upon the Government and obtain amendments of the Book more suitable to their respective notions of how religious services should be conducted in order that the official religious establishment would advance their particular religious beliefs. Other groups, lacking the necessary political power to influence the Government on the matter, decided to leave England and its established church and seek freedom in America from England's governmentally ordained and supported religion.

It is an unfortunate fact of history that when some of the very groups which had most strenuously opposed the established Church of England found themselves sufficiently in control of colonial governments in this country to write their own prayers into law, they passed laws making their own religion the official religion of their respective

354

colonies. Indeed, as late as the time of the Revolutionary War, there were established churches in at least eight of the thirteen former colonies and established religions in at least four of the other five. But the successful Revolution against English political domination was shortly followed by intense opposition to the practice of establishing religion by law. This opposition crystallized rapidly into an effective political force in Virginia where the minority religious groups such as Presbyterians, Lutherans, Quakers and Baptists had gained such strength that the adherents to the established Episcopal Church were actually a minority themselves. In 1785-1786, those opposed to the established Church, led by James Madison and Thomas Jefferson, who, though themselves not members of any of these dissenting religious groups, opposed all religious establishments by law on grounds of principle, obtained the enactment of the famous "Virginia Bill for Religious Liberty" by which all religious groups were placed on an equal footing so far as the State was concerned. Similar though less far-reaching] legislation was being considered and passed in other States.

By the time of the adoption of the Constitution, our history shows that there was a widespread awareness among many Americans of the dangers of a union of Church and State. These people knew, some of them from bitter personal experience, that one of the greatest dangers to the freedom of the individual to worship in his own way lay in the Government's placing its official stamp of approval upon one particular kind of prayer or one particular form of religious services. They knew the anguish, hardship and bitter strife that could come when zealous religious groups struggled with one another to obtain the Government's stamp of approval from each King, Queen, or Protector that came to temporary power. The Constitution was intended to avert a part of this danger by leaving the government of this country in the hands of the people rather than in the hands of any monarch. But this safeguard was not enough. Our Founders were no more willing to let the content of their prayers and their privilege of praying whenever they pleased be influenced by the ballot box than they were to let these vital matters of personal conscience depend upon the succession of monarchs. The First Amendment was added to the Constitution to stand as a guarantee that neither the power nor the prestige of the Federal Government would be used to control, support or influence the kinds of prayer the American people can say -] that the people's religious must not be subjected to the pressures of government for change each time a new political administration is elected to office. Under that Amendment's prohibition against governmental establishment of religion, as reinforced by the provisions of the Fourteenth Amendment, government in this country, be it state or federal, is without power to prescribe by law any particular form of prayer which is to be used as an official prayer in carrying on any program of governmentally sponsored religious activity.

There can be no doubt that New York's state prayer program officially establishes the religious beliefs embodied in the Regents' prayer. The respondents' argument to the contrary, which is largely based upon the contention that the Regents' prayer is "non-denominational" and the fact that the program, as modified and approved by state courts, does not require all pupils to recite the prayer but permits those who wish to do so to remain silent or be excused from the room, ignores the essential nature of the program's constitutional defects. Neither the fact that the prayer may be denominationally neutral nor the fact that its observance on the part of the students is voluntary can serve to free it from the limitations of the Establishment Clause, as it might from the Free Exercise Clause, of the First Amendment, both of which are operative against the States by virtue of the Fourteenth Amendment. Although these two clauses may in certain instances overlap, they forbid two quite different kinds of governmental encroachment upon religious freedom. The Establishment Clause, unlike the Free Exercise Clause, does not depend upon any showing of direct governmental compulsion and is violated by the enactment of laws which establish an official religion whether those laws operate directly to coerce nonobserving individuals or not. This is not to say, of course, that laws officially prescribing a particular form of religious worship do not involve coercion of such individuals. When the power, prestige and financial support of government is placed behind a particular religious belief, the indirect coercive pressure upon religious minorities to conform to the prevailing officially approved religion is plain. But the purposes underlying the Establishment Clause go much further than that. Its first and most immediate purpose rested on the belief that a union of government and religion tends to destroy government and to degrade religion. The history of governmentally established religion, both in England and in this country, showed that whenever government had allied itself with one particular form of religion, the inevitable result had been that it had incurred the hatred, disrespect and even contempt of those who held contrary beliefs. That same history showed that many people had lost their respect for any religion that had relied upon the support of government to spread its faith. The Establishment Clause thus stands as an expression of principle on the part of the Founders of our Constitution that religion is too personal, too sacred, too holy, to permit its "unhallowed perversion" by a civil magistrate. Another purpose of the Establishment Clause rested upon an awareness of the historical fact that governmentally established religions and religious persecutions go hand in hand. The Founders knew that only a few years after the Book of Common Prayer became the only accepted form of religious services in the established Church of England, an Act of Uniformity was passed to compel all Englishmen to attend those services and to make it a criminal offense to conduct or attend religious gatherings of any other kind - a law which was consistently flouted by dissenting religious groups in England and which contributed to widespread persecutions of people like John Bunyan who persisted in holding "unlawful [religious] meetings . . . to the great disturbance and distraction of the good subjects of this kingdom . . . ." And they knew that similar persecutions had received the sanction of law in several of the colonies in this country soon after the establishment of official religions in those colonies. It was in large part to get completely away from this sort of systematic religious persecution that the Founders brought into being our Nation, our Constitution, and our Bill of Rights with its prohibition against any governmental establishment of religion. The New York laws officially prescribing the Regents' prayer are inconsistent both with the purposes of the Establishment Clause and with the Establishment Clause itself.

It has been argued that to apply the Constitution in such a way as to prohibit state laws respecting an establishment of religious services in public schools is to indicate a hostility toward religion or toward prayer. Nothing, of course, could be more wrong. The history of man is inseparable from the history of religion. And perhaps it is not too much to say that since the beginning of that history many people have devoutly believed that "More things are wrought by prayer than this world dreams of." It was doubtless largely due to men who believed this that there grew up a sentiment that caused men to leave the cross-currents of officially established state religions and religious persecution in Europe and come to this country filled with the hope that they could find a place in which they could pray when they pleased to the God of their faith in the language they chose. And there were men of this same faith in the power of prayer who led the fight for adoption of our Constitution and also for our Bill of Rights with the very guarantees of religious freedom that forbid the sort of governmental activity which New York has attempted here. These men knew that the First Amendment, which tried to put an end to governmental control of religion and of prayer, was not written to destroy either. They knew rather that it was written to quiet well-justified fears which nearly all of them felt arising out of an awareness that governments of the past had shackled men's tongues to make them speak only the religious thoughts that government wanted them to speak and to pray only to the God that government wanted them to pray to. It is neither sacrilegious nor antireligious to say that each separate government in this country should stay out of the business of writing or sanctioning official prayers and leave that purely religious function to the people themselves and to those the people choose to look to for religious guidance.

It is true that New York's establishment of its Regents' prayer as an officially approved religious doctrine of that State does not amount to a total establishment of one particular religious sect to the exclusion of all others - that, indeed, the governmental endorsement of that prayer seems relatively insignificant when compared to the governmental encroachments upon religion which were commonplace 200 years ago. To those who may subscribe to the view that because the Regents' official prayer is so brief and general there can be no danger to religious freedom in its governmental establishment, however, it may be appropriate to say in the words of James Madison, the author of the First Amendment:

"[I]t is proper to take alarm at the first experiment on our liberties. . . . Who does not see that the same authority which can establish Christianity, in exclusion of all other Religions, may establish with the same ease any particular sect of Christians, in exclusion of all other Sects? That the same authority which can force a citizen to contribute three pence only of his property for the support of any one establishment, may force him to conform to any other establishment in all cases whatsoever?"

The judgment of the Court of Appeals of New York is reversed and the cause remanded for further proceedings not inconsistent with this opinion.

Justice Stewart's Dissent

A local school board in New York has provided that those pupils who wish to do so may join in a brief prayer at the beginning of each school day, acknowledging their dependence upon God and asking His blessing upon them and upon their parents, their teachers, and their country. The Court today decides that in permitting this brief non-denominational prayer the school board has violated the Constitution of the United States. I think this decision is wrong.

The Court does not hold, nor could it, that New York has interfered with the free exercise of anybody's religion. For the state courts have made clear that those who object to reciting the prayer must be entirely free of any compulsion to do so, including any "embarrassments and pressures." Cf. *West Virginia State Board of Education v. Barnette*. But the Court says that in permitting school children to say this simple prayer, the New York authorities have established "an official religion."

With all respect, I think the Court has misapplied a great constitutional principle. I cannot see how an "official religion" is established by letting those who want to say a prayer say it. On the contrary, I think that to deny the wish of these school children to join in reciting this prayer is to deny them the opportunity of sharing in the spiritual heritage of our Nation.

The Court's historical review of the quarrels over the Book of Common Prayer in England throws no light for me on the issue before us in this case. England had then and has now an established church. Equally unenlightening, I think, is the history of the early establishment and later rejection of an official church in our own States. For we deal here not with the establishment of a state church, which would, of course, be constitutionally impermissible, but with whether school children who want to begin their day by joining in prayer must be prohibited from doing so. Moreover, I think that the Court's task, in this as in all areas of constitutional adjudication, is not responsibly aided by the uncritical invocation of metaphors like the "wall of separation," a phrase nowhere to be found in the Constitution. What is relevant to the issue here is not the history of an established church in sixteenth century England or in eighteenth century America, but the history of the religious traditions of our people, reflected in countless practices of the institutions and officials of our government.

At the opening of each day's Session of this Court we stand, while one of our officials invokes the protection of God. Since the days of John Marshall our Crier has said, "God save the United States and this Honorable Court." Both the Senate and the House of Representatives open their daily Sessions with prayer. Each of our Presidents, from George Washington to John F. Kennedy, has upon assuming his Office asked the protection and help of God.

The Court today says that the state and federal governments are without constitutional power to prescribe any particular form of words to be recited by any group of the American people on any subject touching religion. One of the stanzas of "The Star-Spangled Banner," made our National Anthem by Act of Congress in 1931, contains these verses:

"Blest with victory and peace, may the heav'n rescued land
Praise the Pow'r that hath made and preserved us a nation!
Then conquer we must, when our cause it is just, And this be our motto 'In God is our Trust.'"

In 1954 Congress added a phrase to the Pledge of Allegiance to the Flag so that it now contains the words "one Nation under God, indivisible, with liberty and justice for all." In 1952 Congress enacted legislation calling upon the President each year to proclaim a National Day of Prayer. Since 1865 the words "IN GOD WE TRUST" have been impressed on our coins.

Countless similar examples could be listed, but there is no need to belabor the obvious. It was all summed up by this Court just ten years ago in a single sentence: "We are a religious people whose institutions presuppose a Supreme Being." *Zorach v. Clauson*.

I do not believe that this Court, or the Congress, or the President has by the actions and practices I have mentioned established an "official religion" in violation of the Constitution. And I do not believe the State of New York has done so in this case. What each has done has been to recognize and to follow the deeply entrenched and highly cherished spiritual traditions of our Nation - traditions which come down to us from those who almost two hundred years ago avowed their "firm Reliance on the Protection of divine Providence" when they proclaimed the freedom and independence of this brave new world.

I dissent.

HOW WELL DID YOU UNDERSTAND THIS SELECTION?

1.What were the facts in this case?

2. What did the court rule?

3. Upon what reasoning did the court base its decision?

4. Why did Justice Stewart dissent?

SELF TEST:

MULTIPLE CHOICE: Circle the correct response. The correct answers are given at the end.

1.   What aspect about John F. Kennedy's religion disturbed some voters in the 1960 presidential election?
a.   He was pro life.
b.   He was pro choice.
c.   He was an atheist.
d.   He was Catholic.

2.   What crisis did Kennedy face as President that brought the world the brink of nuclear war?
a.   The Cuban Missile Crisis.
b.   The Summit meeting with Soviet Premier Khrushev.
c.   The failed Bay of Pigs invasion.
d.   The Vietnam War.

3.   Who was the first American to orbit the earth?
a.   Yuri Gagarin.
b.   John Glenn.
c.   Neil Armstrong.
d.   Ed White.

4.   What did the Supreme Court rule in Estelle v. Griswold?
a.   That racial segregation was illegal.
b.   That criminal suspects must be informed of basic constitutional rights before police can question them.
c.   That Fanny Hill, a sexually explicit novel could be published.
d.   That a Connecticut law outlawing the use of contraceptives was unconstitutional.

5. According to the Warren Commission's findings,
   a. President Kennedy's assassination was orchestrated by Republicans
   b. Was part of a vast right-wing conspiracy.
   c. Was carried out by a protestant hit-man
   d. Was the result of a lone gunman, Lee Harvey Oswald.

6. What did the Civil Rights Act of 1964 do?
   a. Outlawed the separate but equal doctrine.
   b. Required states to undergo due process before denying blacks the right to vote.
   c. Banned segregation at public facilities and racial discrimination in the workplace.
   d. Required segregated school systems to integrate with "all deliberate speed."

7. Legislation passed by Congress that outlawed literacy tests, poll taxes, and other devices   southern states used to prevent African Americans from exercising the franchise was called the
   a. Voting Rights Act of 1965.
   b. Civil Rights Act of 1967.
   c. Clean Voting Act.
   d. Voter Quality Law.

8. The African American leader who severed ties with the Nation of Islam and became more racially tolerant after taking a hajj to Mecca was
   a. Elijah Muhammed.
   b. Muhammed Ali.
   c. Malcolm X.
   d. Spike Lee.

9. Which American city faced perhaps the worst race riot during the long, hot summer of 1967?
   a. New York.
   b. Detroit.
   c. Cleveland.
   d. Newark.

10. White anger helped elect _____ governor of California in 1966.
    a. Pat Brown.
    b. Barry Goldwater.
    c. Ronald Reagan.
    d. Richard Nixon.

Answers: 1-d; 2-a; 3-b; 4-d; 5-d; 6-c; 7-a; 8-c; 9-b; 10-c.

ESSAYS:

1. Describe the changes in civil rights for minorities during the 1960s. Who were the primary leaders of the Civil Rights Movement? What ideology and tactics did they use? How successful was the movement?

2. Discuss the successes and failures of Johnson's Great Society?

3. How effective was Kennedy's presidency? Support your answer with historical evidence.

OPTIONAL ACTIVITIES: (Use your knowledge **and** imagination when appropriate.)

1.   Research the Kennedy assassination. Was it part of a larger conspiracy? Explain.

2.   Interview African American members of the community in which you live about their memories of the Civil Rights Movement.

3.   Read The Autobiography of Malcolm X. Had he lived, what changes do you think Malcolm would have made in the movement he led? Explain.

WEB SITE LISTINGS:

The Sixties
>   http://history.acusd.edu/gen/classes/20th/sixties.html
>   http://kclibrary.nhmccd.edu/decade60.html
>   http://www.ukans.edu/history/VL/USA/ERAS/20TH/1960s.html
>   http://www.hist.umn.edu/~hist20c/internet/1960s.htm

John F. Kennedy
>   **Assassination:**
>>   http://mcadams.posc.mu.edu/home.htm
>   **Biography & resources:**
>>   http://www.ipl.org/div/potus/jfkennedy.html
>   **Cuban Missile Crisis:**
>>   http://www.gwu.edu/~nsarchiv/nsa/cuba_mis_cri/
>>   http://www.yale.edu/lawweb/avalon/diplomacy/forrel/cuba/cubamenu.htm
>>   http://www.mtholyoke.edu/acad/intrel/cuba.htm

Lyndon B. Johnson
>   **Biographical Information:**
>>   http://www.potus.com/lbjohnson.html
>>   http://www.lbjlib.utexas.edu/
>   **Vietnam:**
>>   http://www.cnn.com/US/9702/15/lbj.vietnam/
>   **Great Society:**
>>   http://coursesa.matrix.msu.edu/~hst306/documents/great.html
>>   http://ci.columbia.edu/0715/index.html

Vietnam, Documents
>   http://www.mtholyoke.edu/acad/intrel/vietnam.htm
>   http://coombs.anu.edu.au/~vern/van_kien/docs.html
>   http://www.ford.utexas.edu/library/exhibits/vietnam/vietnam.htm

Civil Rights:
>   http://memory.loc.gov/ammem/aaohtml/exhibit/aopart9b.html
>   http://hitchcock.itc.virginia.edu/BlackLeadership/historicalindex.html
>   **Martin Luther King, Jr.**
>>   http://www.stanford.edu/group/King/
>   **Malcolm X**
>>   http://www.brothermalcolm.net/

Chapter Twenty-four

VIETNAM

For many long years the United States fought against North Vietnam. This conflict, which tore America apart from 1965 until 1974, was largely fought in vain. Thousands of American soldiers served in Vietnam in a conflict the nation ultimately lost. The war itself overshadowed all the successes of the Great Society, and as the war's cost escalated funding for domestic programs decreased. After it became clear in 1968 that the United States could not win the Vietnam War, President Lyndon Johnson decided not to seek a second term. This decision allowed Republican Richard Nixon to defeat Vice President Hubert Humphrey in the 1968 election.

American involvement in Vietnam stretched back at least to World War II when Vietnam, Laos, and Cambodia were part of a larger French colony called Indochina that was invaded by Japan. President Franklin Roosevelt enlisted the support of Ho Chi Minh, a young Vietnamese leader, to fight against Japan. In return for a promise that the United States would support independence for Vietnam after World War II ended, Ho Chi Minh agreed to fight against the Japanese and provide intelligence information to Allied forces operating in Asia. Unfortunately, Roosevelt died before the Second World War ended, and Harry Truman either did not know about the agreement to make Vietnam independent or choose to ignore it. After Japanese forces were defeated, Truman allowed France to reestablish control over Vietnam, Laos, and Cambodia. Ho Chi Minh felt betrayed by the United States. He then began to fight France for Vietnam's independence. Since France was an American ally, during the Cold War, the Soviet Union began to support Ho Chi Minh. Truman and American policy makers then branded Ho Chi Minh as Communist in part because he had been educated in Russia. Ensuring that Ho Chi Minh did not make Vietnam a communist nation became an American objective. Truman, Eisenhower, Johnson, and Nixon all believed that winning in Vietnam would prevent the spread of Communism into other regions of southeast Asia.

In 1954 Ho Chi Minh defeated French forces at the mountain fortress of Bien Bien Phu. That victory resulted in a meeting at Geneva, Switzerland in which Vietnam was temporarily divided into two countries—Communist North Vietnam and "free" South Vietnam. Under terms of this agreement, known are the Geneva Accords, the division of Vietnam was supposed to last only two years. In 1956 free elections were scheduled to unify the two Vietnams. President Eisenhower, afraid that Ho Chi Minh's side would win the elections and make all of Vietnam Communist, decided to call off the elections and keep Vietnam divided. Ho Chi Minh again felt betrayed by the United States and began to wage a guerilla war against the American-supported government.

American involvement in Vietnam gradually escalated. Eisenhower sent approximately one thousand Americans to advise and train the South Vietnamese army. In 1965 President Johnson drastically increased the number of troops in Vietnam to nearly a half-million after telling the American public that North Vietnamese gunboats had attached American ships in the Tonkin Gulf despite hard evidence that no attack had actually occurred. Nevertheless, Johnson persuaded Congress to pass the Gulf of Tonkin Resolution authorizing the President to respond to any attack against American forces. Acting under authority given him in the Gulf of Tonkin Resolution, Johnson began sending thousands of American soldiers to contain Communism in the jungles of Southeast Asia.

In early 1965 Johnson ordered massive and sustained bombing of North Vietnam in Operation Rolling Thunder. In January 1968, despite advanced warnings from the Central Intelligence Agency, American forces were surprised by the Tet Offensive. North Vietnamese and their Viet Cong allies launched attacks on multiple targets throughout South Vietnam. Although American Forces generally repelled most of these attacks, the Tet Offensive eroded support for the war within the American population. After the press, Johnson advisors, and the CIA all concluded that the Vietnam War was unwinnable, public protests against American involvement in the war increased. Johnson then halted Operation Rolling Thunder and ask the North Vietnamese government to engage in negotiations to end the war.

Unfortunately, negotiations between the United States and North Vietnam stalled, and the Vietnam War continued into the administration of Richard Nixon, who largely won the 1968 election by maintaining that he had a plan to end the war with honor. In an effort to pressure North Vietnam to negotiate, Nixon ordered the bombing of Cambodia and Laos. Nixon then reached an agreement to withdraw the American forces from Vietnam. The North Vietnamese, after waiting a respectable amount of time, overran South Vietnam. Americans were evacuated from South Vietnam in 1975, and the two Vietnams were unified under a Communist government.

The American loss in Vietnam affected United States foreign policy for the next two decades. American presidents became hesitant to commit American troops to combat in a situation where victory might not be possible. Congress enacted the War Powers Act in 1973 that required presidents to get congressional permission if American troops were committed to combat for a period longer than sixty days without a declaration of war.

IDENTIFICATION: Briefly describe each term.

Diem Regime

Dwight Eisenhower

John Kennedy

Gulf of Tonkin Incident

Gulf of Tokin Resolution

Lyndon Johnson

Geneva Accords

Dien Bien Phu

Robert McNamara

Operation Rolling Thunder

Richard Nixon

Eugene McCarthy

Vietcong

Hanoi

Ho Chi Minh

Tet Offensive

Hubert Humphrey

General Maxwell Taylor

Peace with Honor

Henry Cabot Lodge

Domino Theory

U.S.S Maddox

James Stockdale

U.S.S.C. Turner

Vo Nguyen Giap

William Westmoreland

Ben Tre

William E. Dupoy

Arthur Goldberg

New Left Movement

Student for a Democratic Society

Tom Hayden

Port Huron Manifesto

University of California at Berkeley

Draft Dodgers

William Fulbright

George Kennan

Black Muslims

Muhammad Ali

Dr. Benjamin Spock

Rev. William Sloane Coffin

Ramsey Clark

Walter Cronkite

Clark Clifford

Robert Kennedy

Catonsville Nine

Daniel Seeger

Christopher H. Pyle

Henry Kissinger

William P. Rogers

Vietnamization

Nixon Doctrine

Laos

Cambodia

Paris Peace Talks

Vietnam Moratorium Committee

Kent State

Jackson State College

My Lai

William Calley

Khmer Rouge

Pentagon Papers

Daniel Ellsberg

Easter Offensive

Christmas Bombing of Hanoi

President Thieu

War Powers Act

THINK ABOUT:

1. By what steps did the United States get involved in the Vietnam War?

2. Explain the "Domino Theory."

3. How did the United States government view their involvement in the Vietnam war?

THE UNITED STATES AND THE WAR IN VIETNAM

Following the French defeat at Dien Bien Phu and withdrawal from Vietnam in 1954, the Eisenhower administration, as part of its attempt to globally contain Communism, increased American military aid to South Vietnam. When Eisenhower left office in 1961, President Kennedy initially continued efforts to stop the spread of Communism in Southeast Asia by increasing the numbers of American military advisors in South Vietnam. After the situation deteriorated in the fall of 1963, however, Kennedy began to rethink America's Vietnam policy. The first hint that President Kennedy might change course in Vietnam came in an interview conducted by CBS news anchor Walter Cronkite, the most trusted man in America, on September 2, 1963..

September 2, 1963
CBS Television Interview with Walter Cronkite
Washington, D.C.

PRESIDENT JOHN F. KENNEDY

MR. CRONKITE: Mr. President, the only hot war we've got running at the moment is of course the one in Viet-Nam, and we have our difficulties here, quite obviously.

PRESIDENT KENNEDY: I don't think that unless a greater effort is made by the Government to win popular support that the war can be won out there. In the final analysis, it is their war. They are the ones who have to win it or lose it. We can help them, we can give them equipment, we can send our men out there as advisers, but they have to win it-the people of Viet-Nam - against the Communists. We are prepared to continue to assist them, but I don't think that the war can be won unless the people support the effort, and, in my opinion, in the last 2 months the Government has gotten out of touch with the people.

The repression against the Buddhists, we felt, were very unwise. Now we can do is to make it very clear that we don't think this is the way to win. It is my hope that this will become increasingly obvious to the Government, that they will take steps to try to bring back popular support for this very essential struggle.

...[I]n the final analysis it is the people and the government itself who have to win or lose this struggle. All we can do is help, and we are making it very clear. But I don't agree with those who say we should withdraw. That would be a great mistake. I know people don't like Americans to be engaged in this kind of an effort. Forty-seven Americans have been killed in combat with the enemy, but this is a very important struggle even though it is far away.

We took all this-made this effort to defend Europe. Now Europe is quite secure. We also have to participate-we may not like it-in the defense of Asia.

Source: CBS Interview, September 2, 1963, *United States Senate Committee on Foreign Relations, Background Information Relating to Southeast Asia and Vietnam*, 90th Congress 1st Session. (Washington, D.C.: Government Printing Office, 1967), pp. 112-114.

HOW WELL DID YOU UNDERSTAND THIS SELECTION?

1. What does Kennedy conclude about the war in Vietnam?

2. What role does Kennedy see for the United States in Vietnam?

3. Is Kennedy's assessment about the Vietnam situation accurate? Explain?

About a month after the Cronkite interview President Kennedy met with Robert McNamara, his secretary of defense and general Maxwell Taylor, Chairman of the Joint Chiefs of Staff, to review the situation in South Vietnam. Following the meeting with Kennedy, they presented a statement on Vietnam to the National Security Council. President Kennedy, the National Security Council, and Henry Cabot Lodge, American ambassador to South Vietnam, endorsed the following recommendations on October 2, 1963.

October 2, 1963
Washington, D.C.
WHITE HOUSE STATEMENT

1. The security of South Viet-Nam is a major interest of the United States as other free nations. We will adhere to our policy of working with the people and government of South Viet-Nam to deny this country to communism and to suppress the externally stimulated and supported insurgency of the Viet-Cong as promptly as possible. Effective performance in the undertaking is the central objective of our policy in South Viet-Nam.
2. The military program in South Viet-Nam has made progress and is sound in principle, though improvements are being energetically sought.
3. Major U.S. assistance in support of this military effort is needed only until the insurgency has been suppressed or until the national security forces of the government of South Viet-Nam are capable of suppressing it. Secretary McNamara and General Taylor reported their judgement that the major part of the U.S. military task can be completed by the end of 1965, although there may be a continuing requirement for a limited number of U.S. training personnel. They reported that by the end of this year, the U.S. program for training Vietnamese should be progressed to the point where 1,000 U.S. military personnel assigned to South Viet-Nam can be withdrawn.
4. The political situation in South Viet-Nam remains deeply serious. The United States has made clear its continuing opposition to any repressive actions in South Viet-Nam. While such actions have not yet significantly affected the military effort, they could do so in the future.
5. It remains the policy of the United States, in South Viet-Nam as in other parts of the world, to support the efforts of the people of that country to defeat aggression and to build a peaceful and free society.

HOW WELL DID YOU UNDERSTAND THIS SELECTION?

1. What role does the statement see the U.S. playing in Vietnam?

2. Was the idea that most American military personnel could be withdrawn from Vietnam by the end of 1965 realistic? Explain.

3. Is there any evidence in the American statement on Vietnam that Kennedy might have withdrawn all American military personnel from Vietnam? Explain.

During the Kennedy administration the number of American advisors in South Vietnam had increased from 2,000 in 1961 to 16,000 by 1963. Despite the increased American presence, the situation in South Vietnam had deteriorated. Following Kennedy's assassination, President Johnson reversed the order to withdraw the American advisors. In 1964 Johnson obtained the authority from Congress to intensify American activity in Vietnam with Operation Rolling Thunder, the sustained bombing of North Vietnam. On April 7, 1965, Johnson defended his policy.

April 7, 1965
Johns Hopkins University, Baltimore, Maryland

PRESIDENT LYNDON B. JOHNSON

My fellow Americans: Last week 17 nations sent their views to some dozen countries having interest in Southeast Asia. We are joining these 17 countries in stating our American policy, which we believe will contribute toward peace in this area.

Tonight I want to review once again with my own people the views of your Government.

Tonight Americans and Asians are dying for a world where each people may choose its own path to change.

This is the principle for which our ancestors fought in the valleys of Pennsylvania. It is the principle for which our sons fight in the jungles of Vietnam.

Vietnam is far from this quiet campus. We have no territory there, nor do we seek any. The war is dirty and brutal and difficult. And some 400 young men – born into an America bursting with opportunity and promise – have ended their lives on Vietnam's steaming soil.

Why must we take this painful road?

Why must this nation hazard its ease, its interest and its power for the sake of a people so far away?

We fight because we must fight if we are to live in a world where every country can shape its own destiny. And only in such a world will our own freedom be finally secure.

This kind of a world will never be built by bombs and bullets. Yet the infirmities of man are such that force must often precede reason – and the waste of war, the works of peace.

We wish this were not so. But we must deal with the world as it is, if it is ever to be as we wish.

The world as it is in Asia is not a serene or peaceful place.

The first reality is the North Vietnam has attacked the independent nation of South Vietnam. Its object is total conquest.

Of course, some of the people of South Vietnam are participating in attack on their own Government. But trained men and supplies, orders and arms, flow in a constant stream from North to South. This support is the heartbeat of the war.

And it is a war of unparalleled brutality. Simple farmers are the targets of assassination and kidnapping. Women and children are strangled in the night because their men are loyal to the Government. Small and helpless villages are ravaged by sneak attacks. Large-scale raids are conducted on towns, and terror strikes in the heart of cities.

The confused nature of this conflict cannot mask the fact that it is the new face of an old enemy. It is an attack by one country upon another. And the object of that attack is a friend to which we are pledged.

Over this war - and all Asia – is another reality: the deepening shadow of Communist China. The rulers in Hanoi are urged on by Peking. This is a regime which has destroyed freedom in Tibet, attacked India and has been condemned by the United Nations for aggressions in Korea. It is a nation which is helping the forces of violence in almost every continent. The contest in Vietnam is part of a wider pattern of aggressive purpose.

Why are these realities our concern? Why are we in South Vietnam?

We are there because we have a promise to keep. Since 1954 every American President has offered support to the people of South Vietnam. We have helped to build and we have helped to defend. Thus, over many years, we have made a national pledge to help South Vietnam defend its independence.

I intend to keep our promise.

To dishonor that pledge, to abandon this small and brave nation to its enemy – and to the terror that must follow – would be an unforgivable wrong.

We are also there to strengthen world order. Around the globe – from Berlin to Thailand - are people whose well-being rests, in part, on the belief they can count on us if they are attacked. To leave Vietnam to its fate would shake the confidence of all these people in the value of American commitment. The result would be increased unrest and instability, or even war.

We are also there because there are great stakes in the balance. Let no one think that retreat from Vietnam would bring an end to conflict. The battle would be renewed in one country and then another. The central lesson of our time is that the appetite of aggression is never satisfied. To withdraw from one battlefield means only to prepare for the next. We must say in Southeast Asia – as we did in Europe – in the words of the Bible: "Hitherto shalt thou come, but no further."

There are those who say that all our efforts there will be futile – that China's power is such it is bound to dominate all Southeast Asia. But there is no end to that argument until all the nations of Asia are swallowed up.

There are those who wonder why we have a responsibility for the defense of freedom in Europe. World War II was fought in both Europe and Asia, and when it ended we found ourselves with continued responsibility for the defense of freedom.

Our objective is the independence of South Vietnam, and its freedom from attack. We want nothing for ourselves – only that the people of South Vietnam be allowed to guide their own country in their own way.

We will do everything necessary to reach that objective. And we will do only what is necessary.

In recent months attacks on South Vietnam were stepped up. Thus it became to increase our response and make attacks by air. This is not a change of purpose. It is a change in what we believe that purpose requires.

We do this in order to slow down aggression.

We do this to increase the confidence of the brave people of South Vietnam who have bravely borne this brutal battle for so many years and with so many casualties.

And we do this to convince the leaders of North Vietnam – and all who seek to share their conquest – of a simple fact:

We will not be defeated.

We will not grow tired.

We will not withdraw, either openly or under the cloak of a meaningless agreement.

We know that air attacks alone will not accomplish all these purposes. But it is our best and prayerful judgement that they are a necessary part of the surest road to peace.

We hope that peace will come swiftly. But that is in the hands of others beside ourselves. And we must be prepared for a long, continued conflict. It will require patience as well as bravery – the will to endure as well as the will to resist.

I wish it were possible to convince others with word of what we now   find it necessary to say with guns and planes: Armed hostility is futile. Our resources are equal to any challenge. Because we fight for values and a principal, rather than territory or colonies, our patience and determination are unending.

Once this is clear, then it should be also be clear that the only path for reasonable men is the path of peaceful settlement.

Such peace demands an independent South Vietnam – securely guaranteed and able to shape its own relationships to all others, free from outside interference, tied to no alliance, a military base for no other country.

These are the essentials of any final settlement.

We will never be second in the search for such a peaceful settlement in Vietnam.

There may be many ways to this kind of peace: in discussion or negotiation with the governments concerned; in large groups or in small ones; in the reaffirmation of old agreements or their strengthening with new ones.

We have stated this position over and over again 50 times and more to friend and foe alike. And we remain ready, with this purpose, for unconditional discussions.

And until that bright and necessary day of peace, we will try to keep conflict from spreading. We have no desire to see thousands die in battle – Asians or Americans. We have no desire to devastate that which the people of North Vietnam have built with toil and sacrifice. We will use our power with restraint and with all the wisdom we can command. But we will use it.

This war, like most wars, is filled with terrible irony. For what do the people of North Vietnam want? They want what their neighbors also desire; food for their hunger, health for their bodies and a chance to learn, progress for their country and an end to the bondage of material misery. And they would find all these things far more readily in peaceful association with others than in the endless course of battle.

These countries of Southeast Asia are homes for millions of impoverished people. Each day these people rise at dawn and struggle through weary hours to wrestle existence from the soil. They are often wracked by disease, plagued by hunger, and death comes early, at the age of 40.

Stability and peace do not come easily in such a land. Neither independence nor human dignity will be won by arms alone. It also requires the works of peace.

The American people have helped generously in these works.

Now there must be a much more massive effort to improve the life of man in the conflict-torn corner of the world.

The first step is for the countries of Southeast Asia to associate themselves in a greatly expanded cooperative effort for development. We would hope that North Vietnam will take its place in the common effort just as soon as peaceful cooperation is possible.

The United Nations is already actively engaged in development in this area. I would hope that the Secretary General of the United Nations could use the prestige of his great office-and his deep knowledge of Asia-to initiate, as soon as possible with the countries of the area a plan for cooperation in increased development.

For our part I will ask the Congress to join in a billion-dollar American investment in this effort when it is underway.

And I hope all other industrialized countries-including Soviet Union- will join in this effort to replace despair with hope and terror with progress.

The task is nothing less than to enrich the hopes and existence of more than a hundred million people. And there is much to be done.

The vast Mekong River can provide food and water and power on a scale to dwarf even our own T.V.A.

The wonders of modern medicine can be spread through villages where thousands die for lack of care.

Schools can be established to train people in the skills needed to manage the process of development.

And these objectives, and more, are within the reach of a cooperative and determined effort.

I also intend to expand and speed up a program to make available our farm surplus to assist in feeding and clothing the needy in Asia. We should not allow people to go hungry and naked while our own warehouses overflow with an abundance of wheat and corn, rice and cotton.

I will very shortly name a special team of patriotic and distinguished Americans to inaugurate our participation in these programs. This team will be headed by Mr. Eugene Black, the very able former president of the World Bank.

In areas still ripped by conflict, development will not be easy. Peace will be necessary for final success. But we cannot wait for peace to begin the job.

This will be a disorderly planet for a long time. In Asia, as elsewhere, the forces of the modern world are shaking old ways and uprooting ancient civilizations. There will be turbulence and struggle and even violence. Great social change, as we see in our own country, does not always come without conflict.

We must also expect that nations will on occasions be in dispute with us. It may be because we are rich or powerful, or because we have made mistakes, or because they honestly fear our intentions. However, no nation need ever fear that we desire their land or to impose our will or to dictate their institutions.

But we will always oppose the effort of one nation to conquer another. We will do this because our own security is at stake.

But there is more to it than that. For our generation has a dream. It is a very old dream. But we have the power and the opportunity to make it real.

For centuries nations have struggled among each other. But we dream of a world where disputes are settled by law and reason. And we will try to make it so.

For most of history men have hated and killed one another in battle. But we dream of an end to war. And we will try to make it so.

For all existence most men have lived in poverty, threatened by hunger. But we dream of a world where all are fed and charged with hope. And we will help to make it so.

The ordinary men and women of North Vietnam and South Vietnam, of China and India, of Russia and America, are brave people. They are filled with the same proportions of hate and fear, of love and hope. Most of them want the same things for themselves and their families. Most of them do not want their sons to die in battle, or see the homes of others destroyed.

This can be their world yet. Man now has the knowledge-always before denied-to make this planet serve the real needs of the people who live on it.

I know this will not be easy. I know how difficult it is for reason to guide passion and love to master hate. The complexities of this world do not bow easily to pure and consistent answers.

But the simple truths are there just the same. We must try to follow them as best we can.

We often say how impressive power is. But I do not find it impressive. The guns and bombs, the rockets and warships are all symbols of human failure. They are necessary symbols. They protect what we cherish. But they are witness to human folly.

A dam built across a great river is impressive.

In the countryside where I was born, I have seen the night illuminated the kitchens warmed and the homes heated where once the cheerless night and the ceaseless cold held sway. And all this happened because electricity came to our town along the humming wires of the Rural Electrification Administration. Electrification of the countryside is impressive.

A rich harvest in a hungry land is impressive.

These-not mighty arms-are the achievements which the American nation believes to be impressive.

And-if we are steadfast-the time may come when all other nations will also find it so.

We may well be living in the time foretold many years ago when it was said: "I call heaven and earth to record this day against you, that I have set before you life and death, blessing, and cursing: therefore choose life, that both thou and thy seed may live."

This generation of the world must choose: destroy or build, kill or aid, hate or understand.

We can do all these things on a scale never dreamed of before.

We will choose life. And so doing we will prevail over the enemies within man, and over the natural enemies of all mankind.

HOW WELL DID YOU UNDERSTAND THIS SELECTION?

1. How does Johnson justify the escalation of American involvement in Vietnam?

2. According to Johnson, what are the American objectives in this conflict?

3. How does he propose to achieve these objectives?

On August 5, 1964 President Johnson addressed Congress about an incident that supposedly happened in the Tonkin Gulf in which North Vietnam attacked American naval vessels. In this address Johnson asks Congress to support his policy of responding to attacks on American forces with military might.

President Johnson's Message to Congress—August 5, 1964

Last night I announced to the American people that the North Vietnamese regime had conducted further deliberate attacks against U.S. naval vessels operating in international waters, and I had therefore directed air actions against gunboats and supporting facilities used in these hostile operations. This air action has now been carried out with substantial damage to the boats and facilities. Two U.S. aircraft were lost in the action.

After consultation with the leaders of both parties in the Congress, I further announced a decision to ask the Congress for a resolution expressing the unity and determination of the United States in supporting freedom and in protecting peace in Southeast Asia.

This latest action of the North Vietnamese regime has given a new and grave turn to the already serious situation in Southeast Asia. Our commitments in those areas are well known to the Congress. They were first made in 1954 by President Eisenhower. They were further defined in the Southeast Asia Collective Defense Treaty approved by the Senate in February 1955.

This treaty with its accompanying protocol obligates the United States and other members to act in accordance with their constitutional processes to meet Communist aggression against any of the parties or protocol states. Our policy in Southeast Asia has been consistent and unchanged since 1954. I summarized it on June 2 in four simple propositions:

1. America keeps her word. Here as elsewhere, we must and shall honor our commitments.
2. The issue is the future of Southeast Asia as a whole. A threat to any nation in that region is a threat to all, and a threat to us.
3. Our purpose is peace. We have no military, political, or territorial ambitions in the area.
4. This is not just a jungle war, but a struggle for freedom on every front of human activity. Our military and economic assistance to South Vietnam and Laos in particular has the purpose of helping these countries to repel aggression and strengthen their independence.

The threat to the free nations of Southeast Asia has long been clear. The North Vietnamese regime has constantly sought to take over South Vietnam and Laos. This communist regime has violated the Geneva accords for Vietnam. It has systematically conducted a campaign of subversion, which includes the direction, training and supply of personnel and arms for the conduct of guerrilla warfare in South Vietnamese territory. In Laos, the North Vietnamese regime has maintained military forces, used Laotian territory for infiltration into South Vietnam, and most recently carried out combat operations – all in direct violation of the Geneva Agreements of 1962.

In recent months, the actions of the North Vietnamese regime have become steadily more threatening.

As President of the United States I have concluded that I should now ask the Congress, on its part, to join in affirming the national determination that all such attacks will be met, and that the United States will continue in its basic policy of assisting the free nations of the area to defend their freedom.

As I have repeatedly made clear, the United States intends no rashness, and seek no wider war. We must make it clear to all that the United States is united in its determination to bring about the end of Communist subversion and aggression in the area. We seek the full and effective restoration of the international agreements signed in Geneva in 1954, with respect to South Vietnam, and again in Geneva in 1962, with respect to Laos.

HOW WELL DID YOU UNDERSTAND THIS SELECTION?

1. How did Johnson say the U.S. respond to the attacks on American naval vessels?

2. What does Johnson say American policy in Southeast Asia is?

3. How does Johnson portray North Vietnam?

4. Given what historians now know about the Gulf of Tonkin incident, what do you think was Johnson's ultimate aim? Explain.

On August 7, 1964 Congress passed a joint resolution supporting President Johnson's use of force against North Vietnam in response to what was likely a fictitious attack on American naval forces operating off the coast of North Vietnam. Johnson used the Gulf of Tonkin Resolution to escalate the war in Vietnam despite maintaining in any address to Congress two days before that the United States had no desire to broaden the conflict.

GULF OF TONKIN RESOLUTION
Joint Resolution of Congress
H.J. RES 1145 August 7, 1964

Resolved by the Senate and House of Representatives of the United States of America in Congress assembled.
That the Congress approves and supports the determination of the President, as Commander in Chief, to take all necessary measures to repel any armed attack against the forces of the United States and to prevent further aggression.
Section 2. The United States regards as vital to its national interest and to world peace the maintenance of international peace and security in Southeast Asia. Consonant with the Constitution of the United States and the Charter of the United Nations and in accordance with its obligations under the Southeast Asia Collective Defense Treaty, the United States is, therefore, prepared as the President determines, to take all necessary steps, including the use of armed forces, to assist any member or protocol state of the Southeast Asia Collective Defense Treaty requesting assistance in defense of its freedom.
Section 3. This resolution shall expire when the President shall determine that the peace and security of the area is reasonably assured by international conditions created by action of the United Nations or otherwise, except that it may be terminated earlier by concurrent resolution of the congress.

HOW WELL DID YOU UNDERSTAND THIS SELECTION?

1. What did Congress do in the Gulf of Tonkin Resolution?

2. What did President Johnson use the authority granted in the Gulf of Tonkin Resolution to do? Did Congress intend for Johnson to broaden the Vietnam War? Why or why not?

In 1973 Congress passed the War Power Act that limited the ability of future presidents to get the United States involved in a prolonged conflict without congressional approval as President Johnson had done in Vietnam.

Public Law 93-148
93rd Congress, H. J. Res. 542
November 7, 1973

Joint Resolution Concerning the war powers of Congress and the President.

Resolved by the Senate and the House of Representatives of the United States of America in Congress assembled.
SECTION 1.
This joint resolution may be cited as the "War Powers Resolution."
SEC. 2 (a)

It is the purpose of this joint resolution to fulfill the intent of the framers of the Constitution of the United States and insure that the collective judgment of both the Congress and the President will apply to the introduction of the United States Armed Forces into hostilities, or into situations where imminent involvement in hostilities is clearly indicate by the circumstances, and to the continued use of such forces in hostilities or in such situations.
SEC. 2 (b)

Under article 1, section 8, of the Constitution, it is specifically provided that the Congress shall have the power to make all laws necessary and proper for carrying into execution, not only its own powers but also all other powers vested by the Constitution in the Government of the United States, or in any department or officer thereof.
SEC.2 (c)

The constitutional powers of the President as Commander-in-Chief to introduce the United States Armed Forces into hostilities, or into situations where imminent involvement in hostilities is clearly indicated by the circumstances, are exercised only pursuant to (1) a declaration of war, (2) specific statutory authorization, or (3) a national emergency created by attack upon the United States, its territories or possessions, or its armed forces.
SEC. 3.

The President in every possible instance shall consult with Congress before introducing United States Armed Forces into hostilities or into situation where imminent involvement in hostilities is clearly indicated by the circumstances, and after every such introduction shall consult regularly with the Congress until United States Armed Forces are no longer engaged in hostilities or have been removed from such situations.
Sec. 4. (a)

In the absence of a declaration of war, in any case in which United States Armed Forces are introduced—
(1) Into hostilities or into situations where imminent involvement in hostilities is clearly indicated by the circumstances:
(2) Into the territory, airspace or waters of a foreign nation, while equipped for combat, except for deployments which relate solely to supply, replacement, repair, or training of such forces; or
(3) (a) the circumstances necessitating the introduction of United States Armed Forces;
   (b) the constitutional and legislative authority under which such introduction took place; and
   (c) the estimate scope and duration of the hostilities or involvement.
Sec. 4. (b)

The President shall provide such other information as the Congress may request in the fulfillment of its constitutional responsibilities with respect to committing the Nation to war and to the use of United States Armed Forces abroad.
Sec. 4 (c)

Whenever United States Armed Forces are introduced into hostilities or into any situation described in subsection (a) of this section, the President shall, so long as such armed forces continue to be engaged in such hostilities or situation, report to the Congress periodically on the status of such hostilities or situation as well as on the scope and duration of such hostilities or situation, but in no event shall he report to the Congress less often than once every six months.

SEC. 5. (a)

Each report submitted pursuant to section 4(a)(1) shall be transmitted to the Speaker of the House of Representatives and to the President pro tempore of the Senate on the same calendar day. Each report so transmitted shall be referred to the Committee on Foreign Affairs of the House of Representatives and to the Committee on Foreign Relations of the Senate for appropriate action. If, when the report is transmitted, the Congress has adjourned sine die or has adjourned for any period in excess of three calendar days, the Speaker of the House of Representatives and the President pro tempore of the Senate, if they deem it advisable (or if petitioned by at least 30 percent of the membership of their respective Houses) shall jointly request the President to convene Congress in order that it may consider the report and take appropriate section pursuant to this section.

SEC. 5. (b)

Within sixty calendar days after a report is submitted or is required to be submitted pursuant to section 4(a)(1), whichever is earlier, the President shall terminate any use of United States Armed Forces with respect to which such report was submitted (or required to be submitted), unless the Congress (1) has declared war or has enacted a specific authorization for such use of United States Armed Forces, (2) has extended by law such sixty-day period, or (3) is physically unable to meet as a result of an armed attack upon the United States. Such sixty-day period shall be extended for not more than an additional thirty days if the President determines and certifies to the Congress in writing that unavoidable military necessity respecting the safety of United States Armed Forces requires the continued use of such armed forces in the course of bringing about a prompt removal of such forces.

SEC. 5 (c)

Notwithstanding subsection (b), at any time the United States Armed Forces are engaged in hostilities outside the territory of the United States, its possessions and territories without a declaration of war or specific statutory authorization, such forces shall be removed by the President if the Congress so directs by concurrent resolution.

HOW WELL DID YOU UNDERSTAND THIS SELECTION?

1. Why did Congress pass the War Power Act?

2. What does the War Power Act require?

3. Is the War Powers Act a necessary law? Why or why not?

4. What possible problems could the United States face in the future as a result of passage of the War Powers Act?

Republican Richard Nixon campaigned for the presidency using the slogan "peace with honor." He told American voters that he had a secret plan to end the Vietnam War in an honorable manner. Nixon's campaign slogan resonated with the public, and he was elected to two terms. Despite a massive bombing campaign designed to "soften up" North Vietnam so that they would be more willing to negotiate an end to the war and to destroy supply routes in neighboring Laos and Cambodia, the peace talks proceeded slowly. Finally, on January 23, 1973, Dr. Henry Kissinger, Secretary of State, initialed an agreement ending the Vietnam War. That evening President Nixon addressed the American public live on television and radio.

January 23, 1973

Good evening. I have asked for the radio and television time tonight for the purpose of announcing that we today have concluded an agreement to end the war and bring peace with honor in Vietnam and Southeast Asia.

The following statement is being issued at this moment in Washington and Hanoi:

At 12:30 Paris time today [Tuesday], January 23, 1973, the agreement on ending the war and restoring peace in Vietnam was initialed by Dr. Henry Kissinger on behalf of the Democratic Republic of Vietnam.

The agreement will be formally signed by the parties participating in the Paris Conference on Vietnam on January 27, 1973, at the International Conference Center in Paris.

The cease-fire will take effect at 2400 Greenwich Mean Time, January 27, 1973. The United States and the Democratic Republic of Vietnam express the hope that this agreement will insure stable peace in Vietnam and contribute to the preservation of lasting peace in Indochina and Southeast Asia.

That concludes the formal statement.

Throughout the years of negotiations, we have insisted on peace with honor. In my addresses to the Nation from this room of January 25 and May 8 (these dates refer to 1972, ed.) I set forth the goals that we considered essential for peace with honor.

In the settlement that has now been agreed to, all the conditions that I laid down then have been met. A cease-fire, internationally supervised, will begin at 7 p.m., this Saturday, January 27, Washington time. Within 60 days from this Saturday, all Americans held prisoners of war throughout Indochina will be released. There will be the fullest possible accounting for all of those who are missing in action.

During the same 60-day period, all American forces will be withdrawn from South Vietnam.

The people of South Vietnam have been guaranteed the right to determine their own future, without outside interference.

By joint agreement, the full text of the agreement and the protocols to carry it out, will be issued tomorrow.

Throughout these negotiations we have been in the closet consultation with President Thieu and other representatives of the Republic of Vietnam. This settlement meets the goals and has the full support of President Thieu and the Government of the Republic of Vietnam, as well as that of our other allies who are affected.

The United States will continue to recognize the Government of the Republic of Vietnam as the sole legitimate government of South Vietnam.

We shall continue to aid South Vietnam within the terms of the agreement and we shall support efforts by the people of Vietnam to settle their problems peacefully among themselves.

We must recognize that ending the war is only the first step toward building the peace. All parties must now see to it that this is a peace that lasts, and also a peace that heals and a peace that that not only ends that war in Southeast Asia, but contributes to the prospects of peace in the whole world.

This will mean that the terms of the agreement must be scrupulously adhered to. We shall do everything that the agreement requires of us and we shall expect the other parties to do everything it requires of them. We shall also expect other interested nations to help insure that the agreement is carried out and peace is maintained.

As this long and very difficult war ends, I would like to address a few special words to each of those who have been parties in the conflict.

First, to the people and Government of South Vietnam: By your courage, by your sacrifice, you have won the precious right to determine your own future and you have developed the strength to defend that right. We look forward to working with you in the future, friends in peace as we have been allies in war.

To the leaders of North Vietnam: as we have ended the war through negotiations, let us now build a peace of reconciliation. For our part we are prepared to make a major effort to help achieve that goal. But just as reciprocity was needed to end the war so, to, will it be needed to build and strengthen the peace.

To the other major powers that have been involved even indirectly: Now is the time for mutual restraint so that the peace we have achieved can last.

And finally, to all of you who are listening, the American people: your steadfastness in supporting our insistence on peace with honor has made peace with honor possible. I know that you would not have wanted that peace jeopardized. With our secret negotiations at the sensitive stage they were in during this recent period, for me to have discussed publicly our efforts to secure peace would not only have violated our understanding with North Vietnam, it would have seriously harmed and possibly destroyed the chances for peace. Therefore, I know now that you can understand why, during these past several weeks, I have not made any public statements about those efforts.

The important thing was not to talk about peace, but to get peace and to get the right kind of peace. This we have done.

Now that we have achieved an honorable agreement, let us be proud that America did not settle for a peace that would have betrayed our allies, that would have abandoned our prisoners of war, or that would have ended the war for us but would have continued the war for the 50 million people of Indochina. Let us be proud of the 2 ½ million young Americans who served in Vietnam, who served with honor and distinction in one of the most selfless enterprises in the history of nations. And let us be proud of those who sacrificed, who gave their lives so that the people of South Vietnam might live in freedom and so that the world might live in peace.

In particular, I would like to say a word to the bravest people I have ever met—the wives, the children, the families of our prisoners of war and the missing in action. When others called on us to settle on any terms, you had the courage to stand for the right kind of peace so that those who died and those who suffered would not have died and suffered in vain, and so that where this generation knew war, the next generation would know peace. Nothing means more to me at this moment than the fact that your long vigil is coming to an end.

Just yesterday, a great American, who once occupied this office, died. In this life President [Lyndon B.] Jonson endured the vilification of those who sought to portray him as a man of war. But there was nothing he cared about more deeply than achieving a lasting peace in the world.

I remember the last time I talked with him. It was just the day after New Year's. He spoke then of his concern with bringing peace, with making it the right kind of peace, and I was grateful that he once again expressed his support for my efforts to gain such a peace. No one would have welcomed this peace more than he.

And I know he would join me in asking for those who died and for those who live, let us consecrate this moment by resolving together to make the peace we had achieved a peace that will last.

Thank you and good evening.

HOW WELL DID YOU UNDERSTAND THIS SELECTION?

1. What does Nixon say were the provisions of the agreement?

2. What does Nixon mean when he uses the phrase "peace with honor?" Did the U.S. truly achieve peace with honor? Explain.

Chaos reigned in South Vietnam during the spring of 1975. Despite the 1973 peace accord that guaranteed the independence of South Vietnam, North Vietnamese forces overran South Vietnam, prompting a massive evacuation of Americans and high risk Vietnamese from Saigon. Henry Kissinger, Secretary of State under the Ford administration, sent a cable to Ambassador Graham Martin containing instructions regarding the evacuation.

FLASH
DE WTE #2378 1190107
Z 29710701Z APR 75
FM: THE WHITE HOUSE

To: Ambassador Graham Martin
From: Henry A. Kissinger

1. The president has met with the National Security Council and has made the following decisions:
    A. If the airport is open for fixed-wing operations today, you are to continue the evacuation of high risk Vietnamese by fixed-wings aircraft. You are also to evacuate by the end of the day all American personnel at Tan Son Nhut as well as all but bare minimum personnel from the embassy.
    B. While you should not say so, this will be the last repeat last day of fixed-wings evacuation from Tan Son Nhut.
    C. If the airport is unusable for fixed-wing aircraft or becomes so during the day as a result of enemy fire, you are immediately to resort to helicopter evacuation of all repeat all Americans, both from the compound and from the embassy compound, fighters cap and suppressive fire will be used as necessary in the event of helicopter evacuation.
2. Admiral Gayler will be receiving identical instructions from defense.
3. Warm regards,
0208

HOW WELL DID YOU UNDERSTAND THIS SELECTION?

1. What were Kissinger's instructions?

2. Why do you think Kissinger told Martin not to say that "this will be the last repeat last day of fixed-wing evacuation…"

After the Vietnam War ended Secretary of State Henry Kissinger prepared a report for President Gerald Ford on the lessons of Vietnam.

Memorandum

The White House
Washington

Memorandum for: The President
From: Henry A. Kissinger
Subject: Lessons of Vietnam

At your request, I have prepared some thoughts on the "lessons of Vietnam" for your consideration and for your background information in dealing with further press questions on the subject.

It is remarkable, considering how long the war lasted and how intensely it was reported and commented, that there are really not very many lessons from our experience in Vietnam that can be usefully applied elsewhere despite the obvious temptation to try. Vietnam represented a unique situation, geographically, ethnically, politically, militarily and diplomatically. We should probably be grateful for that and should recognize it for what it is, instead of trying to apply the "lessons of Vietnam" as universally as we once tried to apply the "lesson of Munich."

The real frustration of Vietnam, in terms of commentary and evaluation, may be that the war has almost universal effects but did not provide a universal catechism.

A frequent temptation of many commentators has been to draw conclusions regarding the tenacity of the American people and the ultimate failure of our will. But I question whether we can accept that conclusion. It was the longest war in American history, the most distant, the least obviously relevant to our nation's immediate concerns, and yet the American people supported our involvement and its general objectives until the very end. The people made enormous sacrifices. I am convinced that, even at the end, they would have been prepared to support a policy that would have saved South Vietnam if such an option had been available to use.

It must not be forgotten that the decisions of American administrations that involved this nation in the war were generally supported not only among the people at large but among the political elements and among the journalists who later came to oppose the war. The American people generally supported and applauded President Eisenhower for a decision to partition Vietnam and to support an anti-Communist government in the South. The American people, and particularly the American media, supported President Kennedy's decision to go beyond the restrictions on American involvement that President Eisenhower had set and they also supported his decision to permit American involvement in the removal of President Diem—although the extent if that involvement was not clear at the time. Many who were later to be labeled as "doves" on Vietnam then insisted that South Vietnam has to be saved and that President Diem's removal was essential to save it. You yourself will remember the strong support that the Tonkin Gulf resolution won on the Hill and the general support for President Johnson's decision to send troops. President Nixon won an outpouring of support for the decision to withdraw American forces at a gradual pace, as well as for the Paris Peace Agreement.

If one could offer any guidelines for the future about the lessons to be drawn regarding domestic support for foreign policy, it would be that American political groups will not long remain comfortable in positions that go against their traditional attitudes. The liberal Democrats could not long support a war against a revolutionary movement, no matter how reactionary the domestic tactics of that movement. They had accepted the heavy commitment to Vietnam because of President Kennedy, whom they regarded as their leader, but they withdrew from it under President Johnson.

One clear lesson that can be drawn, however, is the importance of absolute honesty and objectivity in all reporting, within and from the government as well as from the press. U.S. official reports tended for a long time to be excessively optimistic, with the result that official statements did not make clear to the American people how long and how tough the conflict might turn out to be. After a while the pessimistic reports from journalists began to gain greater credence because such positive trends as did emerge came too slowly to justify optimistic Washington assessments. In Vietnam, the situation was generally worse than some reported and better than others reported. But the pessimistic report, even if they were inaccurate, began to look closer to the mark until almost any government statement could be rejected as biased, not only by the opposition but by an increasingly skeptical public.

Another lesson would be the absolute importance of focusing our own remarks and the public debate on essentials—even if those essentials are not clearly visible every night on the television screen. The Vietnam debate often turned into a fascination with issues that were, at best, peripheral. The "tiger cages" were seen as a symbol of South Vietnamese Government oppression, although that Government was facing an enemy who has assassinated, tortured and jailed an infinitely greater number; the "Phoenix" program became a subject of attack although North Vietnamese and Viet Cong tactics were infinitely more brutal. The My Lai incident tarnished the image of an American Army that had generally - - through not always - - been compassionate in dealing with the civilian population. Even at the end, much of the public discussion focused on President Thieus's alleged failure to gain political support, but it was the Communists who rejected free election and who brought in their reserve divisions because they did not have popular support. And at home, it was argued that your aid request meant American reinvolvement when nothing was further from your mind.

Of equal importance may be dedication to consistency. When the United States entered the war during the 1960's, it did so with excesses that not only ended the career and the life of an allied leader but that may have done serious damage to the American economy and that poured over half a million soldiers into a country where we never had more than 100,000 who were actually fighting. At the end, the excesses in the other direction made it impossible to get from the Congress only about 2 or 3 percent as much money as it had earlier appropriated every year. When we entered, many did so in the name of morality. Before the war was over, many opposed it in the name of morality. But nobody spoke of the morality of consistency, or of the virtue of seeing something through once its cost had been reduced to manageable proportions.

In terms of military tactics, we cannot help draw the conclusion that our armed forces are not suited to this kind of war. Even the Special Forces who had been designed for it could not prevail. This was partly because of the nature of the conflict. It was both a revolutionary war fought at knife-point during the night within the villages and also a main force war in which technology could make a genuine difference. Both sides has trouble devising tactics that would be suitable for each type of warfare. But we and the South Vietnamese had more difficulty with this than the other side. We also had trouble with excesses here: when we made it "our war" we would not let the South Vietnamese fight it. Ironically, we prepared the South Vietnamese for main force warfare after 1954 (anticipating another Korean-type attack), and they faced a political war; they had prepared themselves for political warfare after 1973 only to be faced with a main force invasion 20 years after it had been expected.

Our diplomacy also suffered in the process, and it may take us some time to bring things back to balance. We often found that the United States could not sustain a diplomatic position for more than a few weeks or months before it came under attack from the same political elements that had often advocated that very position. We ended up negotiating with ourselves, constantly offering concession after concession while the North Vietnamese changed nothing in their diplomatic position. It was only in secret diplomacy that we could hold anything approaching a genuine dialogue, and even then the North Vietnamese could keep us under constant public pressure. Our diplomacy often degenerated into frantic efforts to find formulas that would evoke momentary support and would gloss over obvious differences between ourselves and the North Vietnamese. The legacy of this remains to haunt us, making it difficult for us to sustain a diplomatic position for any length of time, no matter how obdurate the enemy, without becoming subject to domestic attack.

In the end, we must ask ourselves whether it was all worth it, or at least what benefits we did gain. I believe the benefits were many, though they have long been ignored, and I fear that we will only now begin to realize how much we need to shore up our positions elsewhere once our position in Vietnam is lost. We may be compelled to support other situations much more strongly in order to repair the damage and to take tougher stands in order to make others believe in us again.

I have always believed, as have many observers, that our decision to save South Vietnam in 1965 prevented Indonesia from falling to Communism and probably preserved the American presence in Asia.

This not only means that we kept our troops. It also means that we kept our economic presence as well as political influences, and that our friends—including Japan—did not feel that they had to provide for their own defense.

When we consider the impact of what is now happening, it is worth remembering how much greater the impact would have been ten years ago when the Communist movement was still widely regarded as a monolith destined to engulf us all. Therefore, in our public statements, I believe we can honorably avoid self-flagellation and that we should not characterize our roles in the conflict as a disgraceful disaster. I believe our efforts, military, diplomatically and politically, were not in vain. We paid a high price but we gained ten years of time and we changed what then appeared to be an overwhelming momentum. I do not believe or soldiers or our people need to be ashamed.

HOW WELL DID YOU UNDERSTAND THIS SELECTION?

1. What is the purpose of Dr. Kissinger's report? Why did he prepare the report for President Ford?

2. What does Kissinger conclude about public support for governmental decisions regarding Vietnam? In his assessment accuate? Why or why not?

3. Summarize the lesson Dr. Kissinger drew from the Vietnam War.

4. Why does Kissinger conclude that the U.S. military could not win the war?

5. What benefits does Kissinger say the U.S .got from the Vietnam War? Do you agree? Why or why not?

6. What affect does Kissinger think the Vietnam War will have in the future for the U.S.? Is he correct? Why or why not?

SELF TEST

MULTIPLE CHOICE: Circle the correct response. The correct answers are given at the end.

1. French Union forces were defeated in 1954 at _____ by the Vietminh
   a. Ngo Diem Die
   b. Dien Bien Phu
   c. Saigon
   d. Hanoi

2. The Vietnamese leader Franklin Roosevelt promised independence for Vietnam in return for help against the Japanese war.
    a. Chiang Kai-Shek
    b. Daio Bao
    c. Mao Tse-tung
    d. Ho Chi Minh

3. Prior to World War II, Vietnam War part of a larger French colony called?
    a. Indochina
    b. The French Union
    c. Saignam
    d. SEATO

4. When campaigning for the President, Richard Nixon called his plan to end the Vietnam war
    a. Total Victory
    b. Unconditional Vietnamese Surrender
    c. Peace with Honor
    d. Win at all Costs

5. _____ was an international agreement that temporarily divided Vietnam into two zones.
    a. The Geneva Accords
    b. The Saigon Plan
    c. The Hanoi Partition
    d. The Kissigner Plan

6. In 1973 Congress passed the _____ that required the President to withdraw American forces from combat situations within 90 days without a formal declaration of war or approval by congress to keep troops in a combat situation.
    a. Non-Combat Act
    b. Dove Act
    c. War Power Act
    d. War Declaration Act

7. Nixon's Secretary of State who negotiated an end to the Vietnam war was
    a. John Foster Duller
    b. Dean Acheson
    c. Henry Stinson
    d. Henry Kissinger

8. Henry Kissinger maintained that an important lesson that could be drawn from the Vietnam War was?
    a. The need for absolute honesty in reporting from both the government and press
    b. The need for absolute Presidential control during war
    c. The need for a public vote prior to sending American forces into a hostile situation
    d. The absolute necessiity for a Congressional declaration of war

9. President Johnson's massive and sustained bombing of North Vietnam in 1965 was called?
    a. Hanoi Hell
    b. Operation Rolling Thunder
    c. Saigon Silliness
    d. Detonate and Destroy

10. _____war a series of massive attacks throughout South Vietnam by North Vietnamese and Viet Cong forces in January 1968 that helped turn American public opinion against the Vietnam war
    a. The Ho Chi minh Advance
    b. The Vietminh Rush
    c. The Tet offensives
    d. The Victory Parade

Answers: 1-B ; 2-D ; 3-A ; 4-C ; 5-A ; 6-C ; 7-D ; 8-A ; 9-B ; 10-C

ESSAYS:

1. What caused the Vietnam War?

2. Was Vietnam really a war the United States could not win? Why or why not? Use historical evidence to support your answer.

3. Had President Kennedy lived would he have ended American involvement in the Vietnam War? Support your answer with historical evidence.

OPTIONAL ACTIVITIES: (Use your knowledge **and** imagination when appropriate.)

1. You are a young college student during the Vietnam War. Write a letter to your father, a Vietnam of War World II, explaining your decision to evade the draft.

2. Interview a Vietnam Veteran about their experiences in the Vietnam War and their treatment by the American public upon returning home.

3. Hold a class debate about the merits of American participation in the Vietnam War.

WEB SITE LISTINGS:

Vietnam War:
>   http://www.fsmitha.com/h2/ch26.htm
>   http://members.aol.com/veterans/warlib6v.htm

John F. Kennedy
>   **Assassination:**
>   http://mcadams.posc.mu.edu/home.htm
>   **Biography & resources:**
>   http://www.ipl.org/div/potus/jfkennedy.html

Lyndon B. Johnson
>   **Biographical Information:**
>   http://www.potus.com/lbjohnson.html
>   http://www.lbjlib.utexas.edu/
>   **Vietnam:**
>   http://www.cnn.com/US/9702/15/lbj.vietnam/

Vietnam, Documents
>   http://www.mtholyoke.edu/acad/intrel/vietnam.htm
>   http://coombs.anu.edu.au/~vern/van_kien/docs.html
>   http://www.ford.utexas.edu/library/exhibits/vietnam/vietnam.htm

Chapter Twenty-five

1968:

The Year that all Hell Broke Loose

1968 was a pivotal year in American History as liberals and conservatives clashed in what appeared to be never ending battle, and violence rocked the nation time and time again. Many Americans were shocked to learn from nightly newscasts that American soldiers massacred hundreds of innocent Vietnamese villagers at My Lai. Thousands of students at Columbia and other colleges and universities rioted and began to protest against what they saw as a unjust war in Vietnam and against social injustice and economic inequality within the United States. Older Americans, along with the conservative establishment, believed the nation war coming apart at the seams.

President Johnson, fearing that public dissatisfaction with the war might undermine his reelection to a second term, unexpectedly announced that he would not seek the presidency in March 1968. Johnson's withdrawal from the race virtually assured the election of conservative Republican candidate Richard Nixon, especially after the National Democratic Party seemingly imploded in chaos after Chicago policeman beat protesters with billy clubs. Footage of the beatings aired on the evening news and destroyed any chance the Democratic presidential nominee had of winning the election. Americans began to view Nixon as the candidate of law and order while Humphrey and Democrats were associated with chaos and disorder.

A few days after Johnson's announcement that he was withdrawing from the 1968 presidential election, James Earl Ray assassinated Civil Rights leader Martin Luther King, Jr in Memphis, Tennessee. King's murder sparked a period of rioting in major cities throughout the country. Two months later Robert Kennedy, former Attorney General and brother to assassinated President John Kennedy, was gunned down by Sirhan Sirhan, a Jordanian nationalist living in California, because of his call for increased military aid to Israel. Many historians speculate that Kennedy, who had just won the California Democratic Primary, might have won the presidency in 1968, ended the Vietnam War early and, in doing so, changed the American political and social climate.

Protests against racism, social injustice, and economic inequality continued throughout 1968. On October 17 Olympic sprinters Tommie Smith and John Carlos provoked controversy when they made a black power salute on international television following their receipt of the gold and bronze medals in the Mexico City Olympics.

In retrospect, 1968 was not a year that advanced liberal reform made the United States a better place to live but one in which conservatism began to dominate American politics and government. Liberals and conservatives alike accepted the notion that the era of big government was over despite the fact that Nixon's administration began a multi-decade period in which government debit spiraled. Johnson's last year in office was the last year the federal budget was balanced until the 1990s under the Clinton Administration. 1968, the year that all hell broke loose, was certainly a watershed year in American history as it marked perhaps the last chance Americans had to creat a society of equality, justice, and happiness for all regardless of race, social status, or economic circumstances.

IDENTIFICATION: Briefly describe each term.

Robert Kennedy

Columbia University

Cicero Wilson

Mark Rudd

Tommie Smith

John Carlos

U.S.S Pueblo

Lyndon Johnson

Tet Offensive

Ho Chi Minh

Nguyen Ngoc Loan

Ben Tre

Robert McNamara

William Westmoreland

Walter Cronkite

My Lai Massacre

William Calley

Hugh Clowers Thompson

Eugene McCarthy

Clarke Clifford
-

Wise Old Man

Martin Luther King, Jr.

G. Edgar Hoover

Poor People March

James Earl Ray

Stokely Carmichael

Hubert Humphrey

George Wallace

Sirhan Sirhan

Richard Nixon

Strom Thurmond

Nelson Rockefeller

Ronald Reagan

Democratic National Convention

Yippies

Abbie Hoffman

Jerry Rubin

COPE

Curtis LeMay

Roger Ailes

THINK ABOUT:

1. What made the year 1968 so violent? Could the violence and turmoil have been prevented? Explain?

2. Why do you think President Johnson decided not to seek a second term?

3. What was the significance of the year 1968 for American History?

4. What effect did events in 1968 have on American government? On American Society?

JOHNSON'S STATE OF THE UNION SPEECH
January 17, 1968

President Lyndon Baines Johnson did not likely know that 1968 would be such a tumultuous year when he delivered the State of Union address before Congress and the nation on January 17th. Although Johnson recognized that the United States faced challenges at home and overseas, the tone of the speech was generally positive. The President detailed the "progress" in the Vietnam War and efforts underway to halt the spread of nuclear weapons before turning to domestic matters. Within the domestic sphere Johnson celebrated the progress and prosperity America had achieved but challenged the nation to do better, especially in housing for the poor and jobs for the unemployment, and urged Congress to pass legislation to combat crime and drugs. Inflation, the federal budget, and the national economy were other issues the President addressed in the speech. Johnson urged Congress to enact measures that would enable the nation's economic expansion to continue into its eighth year and to hold down expenditures so that revenue and spending could be balanced.

I was thinking as I was walking down the aisle tonight of what Sam Rayburn told me many years ago: The Congress always extends a very warm welcome to the president as he comes in.

Thank all of you very, very much.

I have come once again to this Chamber the home of our democracy to give you, as the Constitution requires, "Information on the State of the Union."

I report to you that our country is challenged, at home and abroad:

- that it is our will that is being tried, not our strength; our sense of purpose, not our ability to achieve a better America;
- that we have the strength to meet our every challenge; the physical strength to hold the course of decency and compassion at home; and the moral strength to support the cause of peace in the world.

And I report to you that I believe, with abiding conviction, that this people—nurtured by their deep faith, tutored by their hard lessons, moved by their high aspirations—have the will to meet the trials that these times impose.

Since I reported to you last January:

- Three elections have been held in Vietnam--in the midst of war and under the constant threat of violence.
- A president, a Vice President, a House and Senate, and village officials have been chosen by popular, contested ballot.
- The enemy has been defeated in battle after battle.
- The number of South Vietnams living in areas under Government protection tonight has grown by more than a million since January of last year.

These are all marks of progress. Yet:

- The enemy continues to pour men and material across frontiers and into battle, despite his continuous heavy losses.
- He continues to hope that America's will to persevere can be broken. Well he is wrong. America will persevere.

Our patience and our perseverance will match our power. Aggression will never prevail.

But our goal is peace-and-peace at the earliest possible moment.

Right now we are exploring the meaning of Hanoi's recent statement. There is no mystery about the questions which must be answered before the bombing is stopped.

We believe that any talks should follow the San Antonio formula that I stated last September, which said:

- The bombing would stop immediately if talks would take place promptly and with reasonable hopes that they would be productive.
- And the other side must not take advantage of our restraint as they have in the past. This Nation simply cannot accept anything less without jeopardizing the lives of our men and our allies.

If a basis for peace talks can be established on the San Antonio foundations—and it is my hope and my prayer that they can—we would consult with our allies and with the other side to see if a complete cessation of hostilities—a really true cease-fire—could be made the first order of business. I will report a the earliest possible moment the results of these explorations to the American people.

I have just recently returned from a very fruitful visit and talks with His Holiness the Pope and I share his hope—as he expressed it earlier today—that both sides will extend themselves in an effort to bring an end to the war in Vietnam. I have today assured him that we and our allies will do our full part to bring this about.

Since I spoke to you last January, other events have occurred that have major consequences for world peace.

- The Kennedy Round achieved the greatest reduction in tariff barriers in all the history of trade negotiations.
- In Asia, the nation from Korea and Japan to Indonesia and Singapore worked behind America's shield to strengthen their economies and to broaden their political cooperation.
- In Africa, from which the distinguished Vice President has just returned, he reports to me that there is a spirit of regional cooperation that is beginning to take hold in very practical ways.

These events we all welcomed. Yet since I last reported to you, we and the world have been confronted by a number of crises:

- During the Arab-Israeli war last June the hot line between Washington and Moscow was used for the first time in our history. A cease-fire was achieved without a major power confrontation.

Now the nations of the Middle East have the opportunity to cooperate with Ambassador Jarring's U.N. mission and they have the responsibilities to find the terms of living together in stable peace and dignity, and we shall do all in our power to help them achieve that result.

- Not far from this scene of conflict, a crisis flared on Cyprus involving two people who are America's friends: Greece and Turkey. Our very able representative, Mr. Cyrus Vance, and other helped to ease this tension.

- Turmoil continues on the mainland of China after a year of violent disruption. The radical extremism of their government has isolated the Chinese people behind their own borders. The United States, however, remains willing to permit the travel of journalists to both our countries; to undertake cultural and educational exchanges; and to talk about the exchange of basic food crop materials.

Since I spoke to you last, the United States and Soviet Union have taken several important steps toward the goal of international cooperation.

As you will remember, I met with Chairman Kosygin at Glassboro and we achieved, if not accord, at least a clearer understanding of our respective position after two days of meeting.

Because we believe that nuclear danger must be narrowed, we have worked with the Soviet Union and with other nations to reach an agreement that will halt the spread of nuclear weapons. On the basis of communications from Ambassador Fisher in Geneva this afternoon, I am encouraged to believe that a draft treaty can be laid before the conference in Geneva in the very near future. I hope to be able to present that treaty to the Senate this year for approval.

We achieved, in 1967, a consular treaty with the Soviets, the first commercial air agreement between the two counties, and a treaty banning weapons in outer space. We shall sign, and submit to the Senate shortly, a new treaty with the Soviets and with other for the protection of astronauts.

Serious differences still remain between us, yet in these relations, we have made some progress since Vienna, the Berlin Wall, and the Cuban Missile Crisis.

But despite this progress, we must maintain a military force that is capable of deterring any threat to this Nation's security, whatever the mode of aggression. Our choices must not be confined to total war or to total acquiescence. We have such a military force today. We shall maintain it.

I wish with all of my heart that the expenditures that are necessary to build and to protect our power could all be devoted to the programs of peace. But until world conditions permit, and until pace is assured, America's might and America's bravest sons who wear our Nation's uniform must continue to stand guard for all of us as they gallantly do tonight in Vietnam and other places in the world.

Yet neither great weapons nor individual courage can provide the conditions of peace.

For two decades America has committed itself against the tyranny of want and ignorance in the world that threatens the peace. We shall sustain that commitment.

This year I shall propose:
- That we launch, with other nations, and exploration of the ocean depths to tap its wealth, and its energy, and its abundance.
- That we contribute our fair share to a major expansion of the International Development Association, and to increase the resources of the Asian Development Bank.
- That we adopt a prudent aid program, rooted in the principle of self-help.
- That we renew and extend the food for freedom program.

Our food programs have already helped millions avoid the horrors of famine.

But unless the rapid growth of population in developing countries is slowed, the gap between rich and poor will widen steadily.

Government in the developing countries must take such facts into consideration. We in the United States are prepared to help assist them in those efforts.

But we must also improve the lives of children already born in the villages and towns and cities on this earth. They can be taught by great teachers through space communications and the miracle of satellite television and we are going to bring to bear every resource of mind and technology to help make this dream come true.

Let me speak now about some matters here at home.

Tonight our Nation is accomplishing more for its people than has ever been accomplished before. Americans are prosperous as men have never been in recorded history. Yet there is in the land certain restlessness—a questioning. The total of our nation's annual production is now above $800 billion. For 83 months this Nation has been on a steady upward trend of growth.

All about them, most American families can see the evidence of growing abundance: higher paychecks, humming factories, new cars moving down new highways. More and more families own their own homes, equipped with more than 70 million television sets.

A new college is founded every week. Today more than half of the high school graduates go on to college.

There are hundreds of thousands of fathers and mothers who never complete grammar school-who will see their children graduate from college.

Why, then, this restlessness?

Because when a great ship cuts through the sea, the waters are always stirred and troubled.

And our ship is moving. It is moving through troubled and new waters; it is moving toward new and better shores.

We ask now, not how long can we achieve abundance but how shall we use our abundance? Not, is there abundance enough for all but, how can all share in our abundance?

While we accomplished much, much remains for us to meet and much remains for us to master.

- in some areas, the jobless rate is still three or four times the national average.
- Violence has shown its face in some of our cities.
- Crime increases on our streets.
- Income for farm workers remains far behind that for urban workers; and parity for our farmers who produce our food is still just a hope--not an achievement.
- New housing construction is far less than we need to assure decent shelter for every family.
- Hospital and medical costs are high, and they are rising.
- Many rivers and the air in many cities remain badly polluted. And our citizens suffer from breathing that air.

We have lived with conditions like these for many, many years. But much that we once accepted as inevitable, we now find absolutely intolerable.

In our cities last summer we saw how wide the gulf is for some Americans between the promise and the reality of our society.

We know that we cannot change all of this in a day. It represents the bitter consequences of more than three centuries.

But the issue is not whether we can change this; the issue is whether we will change this.

Well, I know we can. And I believe we will.

This then is the work we should do in the months that are ahead of us in the Congress.

The first essential is more jobs, useful jobs for tens of thousands who can become productive and can pay their own way.

Our economy has created seven and one half million new jobs in the past four years. It is adding more than a million and a half new jobs this year.

Through programs passed by the Congress, job training is being given tonight to more than a million Americans in this country.

This year, the time has come when we must go to those who are last in line--the hard-core unemployed--the hardest to reach.

Employment officials estimate that 500,000 of these persons are now unemployed in the major cities of America. Our objective is to place these 500,000 in private industry jobs within the next three years.

To do this, I propose a $2.1 billion manpower programs in the coming fiscal year--a 25 percent increased over the current year. Most of this increase will be used to start a new partnership between government and private industry to train and to hire the hard-core unemployed persons. I know of no task before us of more importance to us, to the country, or to our future.

Another essential is to rebuild our cities.

Last year the Congress authorized $662 million for the Model Cities programs. I requested the full amount of that authorization to help meet the crisis in the cities of America. But the Congress appropriated only $312 million—less than half.

This year I urge the Congress to honor my request for Model Cities funds to rebuild the centers of American cities by granting us the full amount that you in the Congress authorized—$1 billion.

The next essential is more housing-and more housing now.

Surely a nation that can go to the moon can place a home within the reach of its families.

Therefore we must call together the resources of industry and labor, to start building 300,000 housing units for low-and middle-income families next year--that is three times more than this year. We must make it possible for thousands of families to become homeowners, not rent-payers.

I propose, for the consideration of this Congress, a 10-year campaign to build six million new housing units for low and middle income families. Six million units in the next ten years. We have built 530,000 the last ten years.

Better health for our children—all of our children—is essential if we are to have a better America.

Last year, Medicare, Medicaid, and other new programs that you passed in the Congress brought better health to more than 25 million Americans. American medicine, with the very strong support and cooperation of public resources, has produced a phenomenal decline in the death rate from many of the dread diseases. But it is a shocking fact that, in saving, the lives of babies, America ranks 15th among the nations of the world. And among children, crippling defects are often discovered too late for any corrective action. This is a tragedy that Americans can, and Americans should prevent.

I shall, therefore, propose to the Congress a child health program to provide, over the next five years, for families unable to afford it, access to health services from prenatal care of the mother through the child's first year. When we do that you will find it is the best investment we ever made because we will get these diseases in their infancy and we will find a cure in a great many instances that we can never find by overcrowding our hospitals when they are grown.

Now when we act to advance the consumer's cause I think we help every American. Last year, with very little fanfare the Congress and the executive branch moved in that field. We enacted the Wholesome Meat Act, the Flammable Fabrics Act, the Product Safety Commission, and a law to improve clinical laboratories.

And now, I think, the time has come to complete our unfinished work. The Senate has already passed the truth-in-lending bill, the fire safety, and the pipeline safety laws.

Tonight I plead with the House to immediately act upon all of them. I call upon the Congress to enact, without delay, the remainder of the 12 vital consumer protection laws that I submitted to the Congress last year.

I also urge final action on a measure that is already passed by the House to guard against fraud and manipulation in the Nation's commodity exchange market.

These measures are a pledge to our people to keeps them safe in their homes and at work, and to give them a fair deal in the marketplace. And I think we must do more. I propose:

- New powers for the Federal Trade Commission to stop those who defraud and who swindle our public.
- New safeguards to insure the quality of fish and poultry, and the safety of our community water supplies.
- A major study of automobile insurance.
- Protection against hazardous radiation from television sets and other electronic equipment.

And to give the consumer a stronger voice, I plan to appoint a consumer counsel in the Justice Department—a lawyer for the American consumer—to work directly under the Attorney General, to serve the President's Special Assistance for Consumer Affairs, and to serve the consumers of this land.

This Congress—Democrats and Republicans—can earn the thanks of history. We can make this truly a new day for the American consumer, and by giving him this protection we can live in history as the consumer-conscious Congress. So let us get on with the work. Let us act soon.

We, at every level of the Government, State, Local, Federal, know that the American people have had enough of rising crime and lawlessness in this country.

They recognize that law enforcement is first the duty of local police and local government.

They recognize that the frontline headquarters against crime is in the home, the church, the city hall and the county courthouse and the statehouse—not in the far-removed National Capital of Washington.

But the people also recognize that the National Government can and the National Government should help the cities and the States in their war on crime to the full extent of its resources and its constitutional authority. And this we shall do.

This does not mean a national force. It does mean help and financial support:

- to develop State and local master plans to combat crime,
- to provide better training and better pay for police, and
- to bring the most advanced technology to the war on crime in every city and every country in America.

There is no more urgent business before this Congress than to pass the Safety Streets Act this year that I proposed last year. That law will provide these required funds. They are so critically needed that I have doubled my request under this act to $100 million in fiscal 1969.

And I urge the Congress to stop the trade in mail-order murder, to stop it this year by adopting a proper gun control law.

This year, I will propose a Drug Control Act to provide stricter penalties for those who traffic in LSD and other dangerous drugs with our people.

I will ask for more vigorous enforcement of all of our drug laws by increasing the number of Federal drug and narcotics control officials by more than 30 percent. The time has come to stop the sale of slavery to the young. I also request you to give us funds to add immediately 100 assistant United States attorneys throughout the land to help prosecute our criminal laws. We have increased our judiciary by 40 percent and we have increased our prosecutors by 16 percent. The dockets are full of cases because we don't have assistant district attorneys to go before the Federal judge and handle them. We start these young lawyers at $8,200 a year. And the dockets are clogged because we don't have authority to hire more of them.

I ask the Congress for authority to hire 100 more. These young men will give special attention to this drug abuse, too.

Finally, I ask you to add 100 FBI agents to strengthen law enforcement in the Nation and to protect the individual rights of every citizen.

A moment ago I spoke of despair and frustrated hopes in the cities where the fires of disorder burned last summer. We can and in time will change that despair into confidence, and change those frustrations into achievements. But violence will never bring progress.

We can make progress only by attacking the causes of violence and only where there is civil order founded on justice.

Today we are helping local officials improve their capacity to deal promptly with disorders.

Those who preach disorder and those who preach violence must know local authorities are able to resist them swiftly, to resist them sternly, and to resist them decisively.

I shall recommend other actions:
• To raise the farmers' income by establishing a security commodity reserve that will protect the marker from price-depressing stocks to protect the consumer from food scarcity.
• I shall recommend programs to help farmers bargain more effectively for fair prices.
• I shall recommend programs for new air safety measures.
• Measures to stem the rising costs of medical care.
• Legislation to encourage our returning veterans to devote themselves to careers in community service such as teaching, and being firemen, and joining our police force, and our law enforcement officials.
• I shall recommend programs to strengthen and finance our anti-pollution efforts.
• Fully funding all of the $2.18 billion poverty programs that you in the Congress have just authorized in order to bring opportunity to those who have been left far behind.
• I shall recommend an Educational Opportunity Act to speed up our drive to break down the financial barriers that are separating our young people from college.

I shall also urge the Congress to act on several other vital pending bills--especially the civil rights measures--fair jury trials, protection of Federal rights, enforcement of equal employment opportunity, and fair housing.

The unfinished work of the first session must be completed--the Juvenile Delinquency Act, conservation measures to save the redwoods of California, and to preserve the wonders of our scenic rivers, the Highway Beautification Act—and all the other measures for a cleaner, and for a better, and for a more beautiful America.

Next month we'll begin our 8th year of uninterrupted prosperity. The economic outlook for this year is one of steady growth if we are vigilant.

True, there are some clouds on the horizon. Prices are rising. Interest rates have passed the peak of 1966; and if there is continued inaction on the tax bills, they will climb even higher.

I warn the Congress and the Nation tonight that this failure to act on the tax bill will sweep us into an accelerating spiral of price increases, a slump in homebuilding, and a continuing erosion of the America dollar.

This would be a tragedy for every America family. And I predict that if this happens, they will all let us know about it.

We—those of us in the Executive Branch, in Congress, and the leaders of labor and business—must do everything we can to prevent that kind of misfortune.

Under the new budget, the expenditures for 1969 will increase by $10.4 billion. Receipts will increase by $22.3 billion including the added tax revenues. Virtually all of this expenditures increase represents the mandatory cost of our defense efforts, $3 billion; increased interest, almost $1 billion; or mandatory payments under laws passed by

Congress—such as those provided in the Social Security Act that you passed in 1967, and to Medicare and Medicaid beneficiaries, Veterans, and farmers, of about $4 ½ billion; and the additional $1 billion 600 million next year for the pay increased that you passed in military and civilian pay. That makes up the $10 billion that is added to the budget. With few exceptions, very few, we are holding the fiscal 1969 budget to lasts year's level, outside of those mandatory and required increases.

A Presidential commission composed of distinguished congressional fiscal leaders and other prominent Americans recommended this year that we adopt a new budget approach. I am carrying out their recommendations in this year's budget. This budget, therefore, for the first time accurately covers all Federal expenditures and all Federal receipts, including for the first time in one budget $47 billion from the Social Security, Medicare, highways, and other trust funds.

The fiscal 1969 budget has expenditures of approximately $186 billion, with total estimated revenues, including the tax bill, of about $178 billion.

If the Congress enacts the tax increase, we will reduce the budget deficit by some $12 billion. The war in Vietnam is costing us about $25 billion and we are asking for about $12 billion in taxes, and if we get that $12 billion tax bill we will reduce the deficit from about $20 billion in 1968 to about $8 billion in 1969.

Now, this is a tight budget. It follows the reduction that I made in cooperation with the Congress—a reduction made after you had reviewed every appropriations bill and reduced the appropriations by some $5 or $6 billion and expenditures by $1.5 billion. We conferred together and I recommended to the Congress and you subsequently approval taking 2 percent from payrolls and 10 percent from controllable expenditures. We therefore reduced appropriations almost $10 billion last session and expenditures over $4 billion. Now, that was in the budget last year. I ask Congress to recognize that there are certain selected programs that meet the Nation's most urgent needs and they have increased. We had insisted that decreases in very desirable but less urgent programs be made before we would approve any increases.

So I ask the Congress tonight:
- to hold its appropriations to the budget requests, and
- to act responsibly early this year by enacting the tax surcharge which for the average American individual amounts to about a penny out of each dollar's income.

This tax increases would yield this year about half of the $23 billion per year that we returned to the people in the tax reduction bills of 1964 and 1965.

This must be a temporary measure, which expires in less than two years. Congress can repeal it sooner if the need has passed. But Congress can never repeal inflation.

The leaders of Americans business and the leaders of American labor—those who really have power over wages and prices—must act responsibly, and in their Nation's interest by keeping increases in line with productivity. If our recognized leader do not do this, they and those for whom they speak and all of us are going to suffer very serious consequences.

On January 1st, I outlined a program to reduce our balance of payments deficit sharply this year. We will ask the Congress to help carry out those parts of the program which require legislation. We must restore equilibrium to our balance of payments.

We must also strengthen the international monetary system. We have assured the world that America's full gold stock stands behind our commitment to maintain the price of gold at $35 an ounce. We must back this commitment by legislating now to free our gold reserves.

Americans, traveling more than any other people in history, took $4 billion out of their country last year in travel costs. We must try to reduce the travel deficit that we have of more than $2 billion. We are hoping that we can reduce it by $500 million without unduly penalizing the travel of teachers, students, business people who have essential and necessary travel, or people who have relatives abroad whom they want to see. Even with this reduction of $500 million, the American people will still be traveling more overseas than they did in 1967, 1966, or 1965 or any other year in their history.

If we act together as I hope we can, I believe we can continue our economic expansion which has already broken all past records. And I hope we can continue that expansion in the days ahead.

Each of these questions I have discussed with you tonight is a question of policy for our people. Therefore, each of them should be—and doubtless will be—debated by candidates for public office this year.

I hope those debates will be marked by new proposals and by a seriousness that matches the gravity of the questions themselves.

These are not appropriate subjects for narrow partisan oratory. They go to the heart of what we Americans are all about—all of us, Democrats and Republican.

Tonight I have spoken of some of the goals I should like to see America reach. Many of them can be achieved this year—others by the time we celebrate our Nation's 200th birthday—the bicentennial of our independence.

Several of those goals are going to be very hard to reach. But the State of our Union will be much stronger eight years from now on our 200th birthday if we resolve to reach these goals now. They are more important—much more important—than the identity of the party or the President who will then be in office.

These goals are what the fighting and our alliances are really meant to protect.

Can we achieve these goals?

Of course we can, if we will.

If ever there were a people who sought more than mere abundance, it's our people.

If ever there was a nation that was capable of solving its problems, it's this Nation.

If ever there were a time to know the pride and the excitement and the hope of being an American, it's this time.

So this, my friends, is the State of our Union: seeking, building, tested many times in this past year and always equal to the test.

HOW WELL DID YOU UNDERSTAND THIS SELECTION?

1. What do you think was the most important topic Johnson addressed in the 1968 State of the Union? Support your answer with historical evidence.

2. What were the major domestic proposals Johnson made in the 1968 address?

3. What did Johnson maintain about the Vietnam War? Explain? Was he correct? Why or why not?

4. Does Johnson's speech foreshadow the disastrous events of 1968? Explain and use evidence from within the speech to support your answer.

5. Is Johnson optimistic or pessimistic in the address? Explain using evidence from the speech to support your answer.

PRESIDENT JOHNSON'S ADDRESS TO THE NATION REGARDING THE VIETNAM WAR AND HIS DECISION NOT TO SEEK REELECTION

March 31, 1968

On March 31, 1968, President Johnsons requested television time to address the American public about the Vietnam War. In the speech the president told Americans that the Tet offensive had failed and outlined plans to start peace talks with the North Vietnamese. Johnson also made clear that the war would continue until a negotiated peace had been reached and that the United States would maintain its resolve to win. In order to finance the war Johnson called for increased taxes and decreased spending while maintaining that the war in Vietnam War was vital to America national security. The president also cautioned Americans against division within the nation. At the end of the speech Johnson surprisingly announced that he would not seek reelection to a second term.

Good evening, my fellow Americans. Tonight I want to speak to you of peace in Vietnam and Southeast Asia. No other question so preoccupies our people. No other dream so absorbs the 250 million humans begins who live in that part of the world. No other goal motivates American policy in Southeast Asia.

For years, representatives of our Government and others have traveled the world—seeking to find a basis for peace talks. Since last September, they have carried the offer that I made public at San Antonio. That offer was this:

That the United States would stop its bombardment of North Vietnam when that would lead promptly to productive discussion—and that we would assume that North Vietnam would not take military advantage of our restraint.

Hanoi denounced this offer, both privately and publicly. Even while the search for peace was going on, North Vietnam rushed their preparations for a savage assault on the people, the government, and the allies of South Vietnam. Their attack—during the Tet holidays—failed to achieve its principle objectives. It did not collapse the elected government of South Vietnam or shatter its army—as the Communists had hoped. It did not produce a "general uprising" among the people of the cities as they had predicted. The Communists were unable to maintain control of any of the more than 30 cities that they attacked. And they took very heavy casualties. But they did compel the South Vietnamese and their allies to move certain forces from the countryside into the cities. They caused widespread disruption and suffering. Their attacks, and the battles that followed, made refugees of half a million human begins.

The Communists may renew their attack any day. They are, it appears, trying to make 1968 the year of decision in South Vietnam—the year that brings, if not final victory or defeat, at least a turning point in the struggle.

This much is clear. If they do mount another round of heavy attacks, they will not succeed in destroying the fighting power of South Vietnam and its allies.

But tragically, this is also clear: many men—on both sides of the struggle—will be lost. A nation that has already suffered 20 years of warfare will suffer once again. Armies on both sides will take new casualties. And the war will go on. There is no need for this to be so. There is no need to delay the talks that could bring an end to this long and this bloody war.

Tonight, I renew the offer I made last August—to stop the bombardment of North Vietnam. We ask that talks begin promptly, that they be serious talks on the substance of peace. We assume that during those talks Hanoi will not take advantage of our restraint. We are prepared to move immediately toward peace through negotiations.

So, tonight, in the hope that this action will lead to early talks, I am taking the first step to deescalate the conflict. We are reducing—substantially reducing—the present level of hostilities. And we are doing so unilaterally, and at once.

Tonight, I have ordered our aircraft and our naval vessels to make no attacks on North Vietnam's population, and most of its territory. Thus there will be no attacks around the principal populated areas, or in the food-producing areas of North Vietnam.

Even this very limited bombing of the North could come to an early end if our restraint is matching by restraint in Hanoi. But I cannot in good conscience stop all bombing so long as to do so would immediately and directly endanger the lives of our men and our allies. Whether a complete bombing halt becomes possible in the future will be determined by events. Our purpose in this action is to bring about a reduction in the level of violence that now exists.

It is to save the lives of brave men—and to save the lives of innocent women and children. It is to permit the contending forces to move closer to a political settlement.

And tonight, I call upon the United Kingdom and I call upon the Soviet Union—as cochairmen of the Geneva Conferences, and as permanent members of the United Nations Security Council—to do all they can to move from the unilateral act of de-escalation that I have just announced toward genuine peace in Southeast Asia.

Now, as in the past, the United States is ready to send its representatives to any forum, at any time, to discuss the means of bringing this ugly war to an end. I am designating one of our most distinguished Americans, Ambassador Averell Harriman, as my personal representatives for such talks. In addition, I have asked Ambassador Llewellyn Thompson, who returned from Moscow for consultation, to be available to join Ambassador Harriman at Geneva or any other suitable place—just as soon as Hanoi agrees to a conference.

I call upon President Ho Chi Minh to respond positively, and favorably, to this new step toward peace.

But if peace does not come now through negotiations, it will come when Hanoi understands that our common resolve is unshakable, and our common strength is invincible. Tonight, we and the other allied nations are contributing 600,000 fighting men to assist 700,000 South Vietnamese troops in defending their little country.

Our presence there has always rested on this basic belief: the main burden of preserving their freedom must be carried out by them—by the South Vietnamese themselves. We and our allies can only help to provide a shield behind which the people of South Vietnam can survive and can grow and develop. On their efforts—on their determination and resourcefulness—the outcome will ultimately depend.

That small, beleaguered nation has suffered terrible punishment for more than 20 years. I pay tribute once again tonight to the great courage and endurance of its people. South Vietnam supports armed forces tonight of almost 700,000 men—and I call your attention to the fact that this is the equivalent of more than 10 million in our own population. Its people maintain their firm determination to be free of domination by the North.

The South Vietnamese know that further efforts are going to be required:

- to expand their own armed forces,
- to move back into the countryside as quickly as possible,
- to increase their taxes,
- to select the very best men that they have for civil and military responsibility,
- to achieve a new unity within their constitutional government, and
- to include in the national efforts all those groups who wish to preserve South Vietnam's control over its own destiny.

Last week President Thieu ordered the mobilization of 135,000 additional South Vietnamese. He plans to reach—as soon as possible—a total military strength of more than 800,000 men. To achieve this, the Government of South Vietnam started the drafting of 19-year-olds on March 1st. On May 1st, the government will begin the drafting of 18-year-olds.

Last month, 10,000 men volunteered for military service—that was two and a half times the number of volunteers during the same month last year. Since the middle of January, more than 48,000 South Vietnamese have joined the armed forces and nearly half of them volunteered to do so. All men in the South Vietnamese armed forces have had their tours of duty extended for the duration of the war, and reserves are now being called up for immediate active duty.

President Thieu told his people last week, "We must make greater efforts and accept more sacrifices because, as I have said many times, this is our country. The existence of our nation is at stake, and this is mainly a Vietnamese responsibility." He warned his people that a major national effort is required to root out corruption and incompliance at all levels of government.

We applaud this evidence of determination on the part of South Vietnam. Our first priority will be to support their effort. We shall accelerate the equipment of South Vietnam's armed forces in order to meet the enemy's increased firepower. This will enable them progressively to undertake a larger share of combat operations against the Communist invaders.

On many occasions I have told the American people that we would send to Vietnam those forces that are required to accomplish our mission there. So, with that as our guide, we have previously authorized a force level of approximately 525,000.

Some weeks ago—to help meet the enemy's new offensive we sent to Vietnam about 11,000 additional Marine and airborne troops. They were deployed by air in 48 hours, on an emergency basis. But the artillery, tank, aircraft, medical and other units that were needed to work with and to support these infantry troops in combat could not then accompany them by air on that short notice.

In order that these forces may reach maximum combat effectiveness the Joint Chiefs of Staff have recommended to me that we should prepare to send during the next 5 months support troops totaling approximately 13,500 men. A portion of these men will be made available from our active forces. The balance will come from reserve component units which will be called up for service.

The actions that we have taken since the beginning of the year:
- to reequip the South Vietnamese forces,
- to meet our responsibilities in Korea, as well as our responsibilities in Vietnam,
- to meet price increase and the cost of activation and deploying reserve forces,
- to replace helicopters and provide the other military supplies we need, all of these actions are going to require additional expenditures.

The tentative estimate of those additional expenditures is $2.5 billion in this fiscal year and $2.6 billion in the next fiscal year. These projected increases in expenditures for our national security will bring into sharper focus the Nation's need for immediate action: action to protect the prosperity of the American people and to protect the strength and the stability of our American dollar.

On many occasions I have pointed out that, without a tax bill or decreased expenditures, next year's deficit would again be around $20 billion. I have emphasized the need to set strict priorities in our spending. I have stressed that failure to act and to act promptly and decisively would raise very strong doubts throughout the world about America's willingness to keep its financial house in order. Yet Congress has not acted. And tonight we face the sharpest financial threat in the postwar era—a threat to the dollar's role as the keystone of international trade and finance in the world.

Last week, at the monetary conference in Stockholm, the major industrial countries decided to take a big step toward creating a new international monetary asset that will strengthen the international monetary system. I am very proud of the very able work done by Secretary Fowler and Chairman Martin of the Federal Reserve Board. But to make this system work the United States must bring its balance of payments to—or very close to—equilibrium. We must have a responsible fiscal policy in this country. The passage of a tax bill now, together with expenditure control that the Congress may desire and dictate, is absolutely necessary to protect this Nation's security, to continue our prosperity, and to meet the needs of our people.

What is at stake is seven years of unparalleled prosperity. In those seven years, the real income of the average American, after taxes, rose by almost 30 percent--a gain as large as that of the entire preceding 19 years. So the steps that we must take to convince the world are exactly the steps we must take to sustain our own economic strength here at home. In the past eight months, prices and interest rates have risen because of our inaction. We must, therefore, now do everything we can to move from debate to action, from talking to voting. There is, I believe—I hope there is—in both Houses of the Congress—a growing sense of urgency that this situation must be acted upon and must be corrected.

My budget in January was, we thought, a tight one. It fully reflected our evaluation of most of the demanding needs of this Nation. But in these budgetary matters, the President does not decide alone. The Congress has the power and the duty to determine appropriations and taxes. The Congress is now considering our proposals and they are considering reductions in the budget that we submitted.

As part of a program of fiscal restraint that includes the tax surcharge, I shall approve appropriate reduction in the January budget when and if Congress so decides that that should be done.

One thing is unmistakably clear, however: Our deficit just must be reduced. Failure to act could bring on conditions that would strike hardest at those people that all of us are trying so hard to help. These times call for prudence in this land of plenty. I believe that we have the character to provide it, and tonight I plead with the Congress and with the people to act promptly to serve the national interest, and thereby serve all of our people.

Now let me give you my estimate of the changes for peace:
- the peace that will one day stop the bloodshed in South Vietnam,
- that will permit all the Vietnamese people to rebuild and develop their land,
- that will permit us to turn more fully to our own tasks here at home.

I cannot promise that the initiatives that I have announced tonight will be completely successful in achieving peace any more than the 30 other that we have undertaken and agreed to in recent years.

But it is our fervent hope that North Vietnam, after years of fighting that have left the issue unresolved, will now cease its efforts to achieve a military victory and will join with us in moving toward the peace table. And there may come a time when Vietnamese—on both sides—are able to work out a way to settle their own differences by free political choice rather than by war. As Hanoi considers its course, it should be in no doubt of our intentions. It must not miscalculate pressures within our democracy in this election year.

We have no intention of widening this war. But the United States will never accept a fake solution to this long and arduous struggle and call it peace. No one can foretell the precise terms of an eventual settlement.

Our objective in South Vietnam has never been the annihilation of the enemy. It has been to bring about recognition in Hanoi that its objective—taking over the South by force—could not be achieved. We think that peace can be based on the Geneva Accords of 1954—under political conditions that permits the South Vietnamese—all South Vietnamese—to chart their course free of any outside domination or interference, from us or from anyone else.

So tonight I reaffirm the pledge that we made at Manila--which we are prepared to withdraw our forces from South Vietnam as the other side withdraws its forces to the north, stops the infiltration, and the level of violence thus subsides. Our goal of peace and self-determination in Vietnam is directly related to the future of all of Southeast Asia where much has happened to inspire confidence during the past 10 years. We have done all that we knew how to do to contribute and to help build that confidence. A number of its nations have shown what can be accomplished under conditions of security. Since 1968, Indonesia, the fifth largest nation in the entire world, with a population of more than 100 million people, has had a government that is dedicated to peace with its neighbors and improved conditions for its own people. Political and economic cooperation between nations has grown rapidly.

I think every American can take a great deal of pride in the role that we have played in bringing this about in Southeast Asia. We can rightly judge—as responsible Southeast Asians themselves do—that the progress of the past three years would have been far less likely—if not completely impossible—if America's sons and others had not made their stand in Vietnam.

At Johns Hopkins University, about three years ago, I announced that the United States would take part in the great work of developing Southeast Asia, including the Mekong Valley, for all the people of that region. Our determination to help build a better land—a better land for men on both sides of the present conflict—has not diminished in the least. Indeed, the ravages of war, I think, have made it more urgent than ever.

So, I repeat on behalf of the United States again tonight what I said at Johns Hopkins—that North Vietnam could take its place in this common efforts just as soon as peace comes. Over time, a wider framework of peace and security in Southeast Asia may become possible. The new cooperation of the nations of the area could be a foundation-stone. Certainly friendship with the nations of such a Southeast Asia is what the United States seeks-and that is all the United States seeks.

On day, my fellow citizen, there will be peace in Southeast Asia. It will come because the people of Southeast Asia want it—those whose armies are at war tonight, and those who, though threatened, have thus far been spared. Peace will come because Asians were willing to work for it—and to sacrifice for it—and to die by the thousands for it.

But let it never be forgotten: Peace will come also because America sent her sons to help secure it. It has not been easy—far from it. During the past 4 ½ years, it has been my fate and my responsibility to be Commander in Chief. I have lived—daily and nightly—with the cost of this war. I know the pain that it has inflicted. I know, perhaps better than anyone, the misgivings that it has aroused. Throughout this entire, long period, I have been sustained by a single principle: that what we are doing now, in Vietnam, is vital not only to the security of Southeast Asia, but it is vital to the security of every American.

Surely we have treaties which we must respect. Surely we have commitments that we are going to keep. Resolutions of the Congress testify to the need to resist aggression in the world and in Southeast Asia. But the heart of our involvement in South Vietnam—under three different presidents, three separate administrations—has always been American's own security.

And the larger purpose of our involvement has always been to help the nations of Southeast Asia become independent and stand alone, self-sustaining, as at peace with all others. With such an Asia, our country—and the world—will be far more secure than it is tonight.

I believe that a peaceful Asia is far nearer to reality because of what American has done in Vietnam. I believe that the men who endure the dangers of battle—fighting there for us tonight—are helping the entire world avoid far greater conflicts, far wider wars, far more destruction, than this one. The peace that will bring them home someday will come. Tonight I have offered the first in what I hope will be series of mutual moves toward peace.

I pray that it will not be rejected by the leaders of North Vietnam. I pray that they will accept it as a means by which the sacrifices of their own people may be ended. And I ask your help and your support, my fellow citizens, for this effort to reach across the battlefield toward an early peace.

Finally, my fellow Americans, let me say this: Of those to whom much is given, much is asked. I cannot say and no man could say that no more will be ask of us.

Yet, I believe that now, no less than when the decade began, this generation of Americans is willing to "pay any price, bear any burden, meet any hardship, support any friend, and oppose any foe to assure the survival and the success of liberty." Since those words were spoken by John F. Kennedy, the people of America have kept that compact with mankind's noblest cause.

And we shall continue to keep it. Yet, I believe that we must always be mindful of this one thing, whenever the trials and the tests ahead, the ultimate strength of our country and our cause will lie not in powerful weapons or infinite resources or boundless wealth, but will lie in the unity of our people.

This I believe very deeply. Throughout my entire public career I have followed the personal philosophy that I am a free man, and American, a public servant, and a member of my party, in that order always and only. For 37 years in the service of our Nation, first as a Congressman, as a Senator, and as Vice President, and now as your President, I have put the unity of the people first. I have put it ahead of any divisive partisanship. And in these times as in times before, it is true that a house divided against itself by the spirit of faction, of party, of region, of religion, of race, is a house that cannot stand.

There is division in the American house now. There is divisiveness among us all tonight. And holding the trust that is mine, as President of all the people, I cannot disregard the peril to the progress of the American people and the hope and the prospect of peace for all peoples. So, I would ask all Americans, whatever their personal interests or concern, to guard against divisiveness and all its ugly consequences.

Fifty-two months and 10 days ago, in a moment of tragedy and trauma, the duties of this office fell upon me. I asked then for your help and God's, that we might continue America on its course, binding up our wounds, healing our history, moving forward in new unity, to clear the American agenda and to keep the American commitment for all of our people. United we have kept that commitment. United have enlarged that commitment.

Through all time to come, I think America will be a stronger nation, a more just society, and a land of greater opportunity and fulfillment because of what we have all done together in these years of unparalleled achievement.

Our reward will come in the life of freedom, peace, and hope that our children will enjoy through ages ahead.

What we won when all of our people united just must not now be lost in suspicion, distrust, selfishness, and politics among any of our people.

Believing this as I do, I have concluded that I should not permit the Presidency to become involved in the partisan division that we are developing in this political year.

With American's sons in the fields far away, with America's future under challenge right here at home, with our hopes and the world's hopes for peace in the balance every day, I do not believe that I should devote an hour or a day of my time to any personal partisan causes or to any duties other than the awesome duties of this office--the presidency of your country.

Accordingly, I shall not seek, and I will not accept, the nomination of my party for another term as your President.

But let men everywhere know, however, that a strong, a confident, and a vigilant America stands ready tonight to seek an honorable peace—and stands ready tonight to defend an honored cause—whatever the price, whatever the burden, whatever the sacrifice that duty may require.

Thank you for listening.

Good night and God bless all of you.

HOW WELL DID YOU UNDERSTAND THIS SELECTION?

1. What does Johnson say about the Tet offensive?

2. What does Johnson propose in an effort to end the Vietnam War?

3. What does the President maintain about American resolve?

4. What does Johnson say about why the United States is fighting in Vietnam?

5. How does Johnson characterize the American economy?

6. Why do you think Johnson chose not to seek reelection?

7. Why did the President caution Americans about division? Explain?

NIXON'S ACCEPTANCE SPEECH

Following major defeats for the presidency in 1960 and in the California governor's race in 1962, Richard M. Nixon resurrected his political career by winning the Republican presidential nomination in 1968. Nixon's resurgence came largely because he tied himself to the far right wing of the Republican Party, appealing particularly to white southern racists by embracing Strom Thurmond, the champion of white rights in the South. Careful to avoid mistakes during the campaign, Nixon ran a campaign that focused on law and order and barely defeated Hubert H. Humphrey, his Democratic opponent. Nixon's election signaled an end to big government and represented a repudiation of Lyndon Johnson's policies and programs. White voters seemed to have tired of the permissiveness of American society in the 1960s, of the Civil Rights Movement, and the Vietnam War. They wanted a return to what they perceived to be the normalcy of the 1950s and believed Nixon the candidate that could best achieve that objective.

Mr. Chairman, delegates to this convention, my fellow Americans.

Sixteen years ago I stood before this Convention to accept your nomination as the running mate of one of the greatest Americans of our time – Dwight D. Eisenhower.

Eight years ago, I had the highest honor of accepting your nomination for President of the United States. Tonight, I again proudly accept that nomination for President of the United States.

But I have news for you. This time there is a difference.

This time we are going to win.

We're going to win for a number of reasons: first a personal one. General Eisenhower, as you know, lies critically ill in Walter Reed Hospital tonight. I have talked, however, with Mrs. Eisenhower on the telephone. She tells me that his heart is with us. And she says that there is nothing that he lives more for and there is nothing that would lift him more than for us to win in November and I say let's win this one for Ike.

We are going to win because this great Convention has demonstrated to the nation that the Republican Party has the leadership, the platform and the purpose that America needs. We are going to win because you have nominated as my running mate a statesman of the first rank who will be a great campaigner and one who is fully qualified to undertake the new responsibilities that I shall give to the next Vice President of the United States.

And he is a man who fully shares my conviction and yours, after a period of forty years when power has gone from the cities and the states to the government in Washington, D.C., it's time to have power go back from Washington to the states and to the cities of this country all over America.

We are going to win because at a time that America cries out for the unity that this Administration has destroyed, the Republican Party – after a spirited contest for its nomination – for President and for Vice President stands united before the nation tonight.

I congratulate Governor Reagan. I congratulate Governor Rockefeller. I congratulate Governor Romney. I congratulate all those who have made the hard fight that they have for this nomination. And I know that you will all fight even harder for the great victory our party is going to win in November because we're going to be together in that election campaign.

And a party that can unite itself will unite America.

My fellow Americans, most important – we are going to win because our cause is right.

We make history – not for ourselves but for the ages.

The choice we make in 1968 will determine not only the future of America but the future of peace and freedom in the world for the last third of the Twentieth Century.

And the question that we answer tonight: can America meet this challenge?

For a few moments, let us look at America; let us listen to America to find the answer to that question.

As we look at America, we see cities enveloped in smoke and flame. We hear sirens in the night. We see Americans dying on distant battlefields abroad. We see Americans hating each other, fighting each other, killing each other at home. And as we see and hear these things, millions of Americans cry out in anguish.

Did we come all this way for this? Did American boys die in Normandy, and Korea, and in Valley Forge for this?

Listen to the answer to those questions. It is another voice. It is the quiet voice in the tumult and the shouting. It is the voice of the great majority of Americans, the forgotten Americans – the non-shouters; the non-demonstrators. They are not racists or sick; they are not guilty of the crime that plagues the land. They are black and they are white – they're native born and foreign born – they're young and they're old. They work in America's factories. They run America's businesses. They serve in government. They provide most of the soldiers who died to keep us free. They give drive to the spirit of America. They give lift to the American Dream. They give steel to the backbone of America. They are good people, they are decent people; they work, and they save, and they pay their taxes, and they care.

Like Theodore Roosevelt, they know that this country will not be a good place for any of us to live in unless it is a good place for all of us to live in. This I say to you tonight is the real voice of America. In this year 1968, this is the message it will broadcast to America and to the world.

Let's never forget that despite her faults, America is a great nation. And America is great because her people are great.

With Winston Churchill, we say: "We have not journeyed all this way across the centuries, across the oceans, across the mountains, across the prairies because we are made of sugar candy."

America is in trouble today not because her people have failed but because her leaders have failed. And what America needs are leaders to match the greatness of her people. And this group of Americans, the forgotten Americans, and others know that the great question Americans must answer by their votes in November is this: Whether we shall continue for four more years the policies of the last five years.

And this is their answer and this is my answer to that question. When the strongest nation in the world can be tied down for four years in war in Vietnam with no end in sight; When the richest nation in the world can't manage its own economy; When the nation with the greatest tradition of the rule of law is plagued by unprecedented lawlessness; When a nation that has been known for a century for equality of opportunity is torn by unprecedented racial violence; And when the President of the United States cannot travel abroad or to any major city at home without fear of a hostile demonstration – then it's time for new leadership for the United States of America.

My fellow Americans, tonight I accept the challenge and the commitment to provide that new leadership for America. And I ask you to accept it with me. And let us accept this challenge not as a grim duty but as an exciting adventure in which we are privileged to help a great nation realize its destiny. And let us begin by committing ourselves to the truth – to see it like it is, and tell it like it is – to find the truth, to speak the truth, and to live the truth – that's what we will do.

We've had enough of big promises and little action. The time has come for honest government in the United States of America. And so tonight I do not promise the millennium in the morning. I don't promise that we can eradicate poverty, and discrimination, eliminate all danger of war in the space of four, or even eight years. But, I do promise action – a new policy for peace abroad; a new policy for peace and progress and justice at home.

Look at our problems abroad. Do you realize that we face the stark truth that we are worse off in every area of the world tonight than we were when President Eisenhower left office eight years ago. That's the record. And there is only one answer to such a record of failure and that is a complete housecleaning of those responsible for the failures of that record. The answer is a complete re-appraisal of America's policies in every section of the world.

We shall begin with Vietnam. We all hope in this room that there is a chance that current negotiations may bring an honorable end to that war. And we will say nothing during this campaign that might destroy that chance. But if the war is not ended when the people choose in November, the choice will be clear. Here it is. For four years, America's fighting men have set a record for courage and sacrifice unsurpassed in our history. For four years, this Administration has had the support of the Loyal Opposition for the objective of seeking an honorable end to the struggle. Never has so much military and economic and diplomatic power been used so ineffectively. And if after all of this sacrifice and all of this support there is still no end in sight, then I say the time has come for the American people to turn to new leadership – not tied to the mistakes and the policies of the past. That is what we offer to America.

And I pledge to you tonight that the first priority foreign policy objective of our next Administration will be to bring an honorable end to the war in Vietnam. We shall not stop there – we need a policy to prevent more Vietnams. All of American's peace-keeping intuitions and all of America's foreign commitments must be reappraised. Over the past twenty-five years. America has provided more than one-hundred fifty billion dollars in foreign aid to nations abroad. In Korea and now again in Vietnam, the United States furnished most of the money, most of the arms; most of the men to help the people of those countries defend themselves against aggression.

Now we are a rich country. We are a strong nation. We are a populous nation. But there are two hundred million Americans and there are two billion people that live in the Free World. And I say the time has come for other nations in the Free World to bear their fair share of the burden of defending peace and freedom around this world. What I call for is not a new isolationism. It is a new internationalism in which America enlists its allies and its friends around the world in those struggles in which their interest is as great as ours. And now to the leaders of the Communist world, we say: After an era confrontation, the time has come for an era of negotiation.

Where the world's super powers are concerned, there is no acceptable alternative to peaceful negation. Because this will be a period of negotiation, we shall restore the strength of America so that we shall always negotiation from strength and never from weakness. And as we seek peace through negotiation, let our goals be made clear: We do not seek domination over any country. We believe deeply in our ideas, but we believe they should travel on their own power and not on the power of our arms. We shall never be belligerent but we shall be as firm in defending our system as they are in expanding theirs. We believe this should be an era of peaceful competition, not only in the productivity of our factories but in the quality of our ideas. We extend the hand of friendship to all people, to the Russian people, to the Chinese people, to all people in the world. And we shall work toward the goal of an open world – open skies, open cities, open hearts, open minds.

The next eight years, my friends, this period in which we are entering. I think we will have the greatest opportunity for world peace but also face the greatest danger of world war of any time in our history.

I believe we must have peace. I believe that we can have peace, but I do not underestimate the difficulty of this task. Because you see the art of preserving peace is greater than that of waging war and much more demanding. But I am proud to have served in an Administration which ended one war and kept the nation out of other wars for eight years.

And it is that kind of experience and it is that kind of leadership that America needs today, and that we will give to America with your help.

And as we commit to new policies for America tonight, let us make one further pledge: For five years hardly a day has gone by when we haven't read or heard a report of the American flag being spit on; an embassy being stoned; a library being burned; or an ambassador being insulted some place in the world. And each incident reduced respect for the United States until the ultimate insult inevitably occurred. And I say to you tonight that when respect for the United States of America falls so low that a fourth-rate military power, like North Korea, will seize an American naval vessel on the high seas, it is time for new leadership to restore respect for the United States of America.

My friends, America is a great nation. And it is time we started to act like a great nation around the world. It is ironic to note when we were a small nation – weak militarily and poor economically – America was respected. And the reason was that America stood for something more powerful than military strength or economic wealth.

The American Revolution was a shining example of freedom in action which caught the imagination of the world. Today, too often, America is an example to be avoided and not followed. A nation that can't keep the pace at home won't be trusted to keep the peace abroad. A president who isn't treated with respect at home will not be treated with respect abroad. A nation which can't manage its own economy can't tell others how to manage theirs. If we are to restore prestige and respect for America abroad, the place to begin is at home in the United States of America.

My friends, we live in an age of revolution in America and in the world. And to find the answers to our problems, let us turn to a revolution, a revolution that will never grow old. The world's greatest continuing revolution, the American Revolution. The American Revolution was and is dedicated to progress, but our founders recognized that the first requisite of progress is order.

Now, there is no quarrel between progress and order – because neither can exist without the other. So let us have order in America – not the order that suppresses dissent and discourages change but the order which guarantees the right to dissent and provides the basis for peaceful change. And tonight, it is time for some honest talk about the problem of order in the United States.

Let us always respect, as I do, our courts and those who serve on them. But let us also recognize that some of our courts in their decisions have gone too far in weakening the peace forces as against the criminal forces in this country and we must act to restore that balance. Let those who have the responsibility to enforce our laws and our judges who have the responsibility to interpret them be dedicated to the great principles of Civil Rights. But let them also recognize that the first Civil Right of every American is to be free from domestic violence, and that right must be guaranteed in this country. And if we are to restore order and respect for law in this country there is one place we are going to begin. We are going to have to have a new Attorney General of the United States of America.

I pledge to you that our new Attorney General will be directed by the President of the United States to launch a war against organized crime in this country. I pledge to you that the new Attorney General of the United States will be an active belligerent against the loan sharks and the numbers racketeers that rob the urban poor in our cities. I pledge to you that the new Attorney General will open a new front against the fifth peddlers and the narcotics peddlers who are corrupting the lives of the children of this country.

Because, my friends, let this message come through clear from what I say tonight. Time is running out for the merchants of crime and corruption in American society. The wave of crime is not going to be the wave of the future in the United States of America. We shall re-established freedom from fear in America so that America can take the lead in re-establishing freedom from fear in the world.

And to those who say that law and order is the code word for racism, there are here is a reply: Or goal is justice for every American. If we are to have respect for law in America, we must have laws that deserve respect. Just as we cannot have progress without order, we cannot have order without progress, and so, as we commit to order tonight, let us commit to progress.

And this brings me to the clearest choice among the great issues of this campaign. For the past five years we have been deluged by government programs for the unemployed; programs for the cities; programs for the poor. And we have reaped from these programs and ugly harvest of frustration, violence and failure across the land. And now our opponents will be offering more of the same – more billions for government jobs, government housing, government welfare. I say it is time to quit pouring billions of dollars into programs that have failed in the United States of America. To put it bluntly, we are on the wrong road – and it's time to take a new road, to progress.

Again, we turn to the American Revolution for our answer. The war on poverty didn't begin five years ago in this country. It began when this country began. It's been the most successful war on poverty in the history of nations. There is more wealth in America today, more broadly shared, than in any nation in the world.

We are a great nation, and we must never forget how we became great. America is a great nation today not because of what government did for people – but because of what people did for themselves over a hundred-ninety years in this country.

So it is time to apply the lessons of the American Revolution to our present problem. Let us increase the wealth of America so that we can provide more generously for the aged; and for the needy; and for all those who cannot help themselves. But for those who are able to help themselves – what we need are not more millions on welfare rolls – but more millions on payrolls in the United States of America. Instead of government jobs, and government housing, and government welfare, let government use its tax and credit policies to enlist in this battle the greatest engine of progress ever developed in the history of man – American private enterprise. Let us enlist in this great cause the millions of Americans in volunteer organizations who will bring a dedication to this task that no amount of money could ever buy. And let us build bridges, my friends; build bridges to human dignity across that gulf that separates black America from white America. Black Americans, no more than white Americans, they do not want more government programs which perpetuate dependency. They don't want to be a colony in a nation.

They want the pride, and the self-respect, and the dignity that can only come if they have an equal chance to own their own homes, to own their own businesses, to be managers and executives as well as workers, to have a piece of the action in the exciting ventures of private enterprise. I pledge to you tonight that we shall have new programs which will provide that equal chance. We make a great history tonight. We do not fire a shot heard 'round the world but we shall light the lamp of hope in millions of homes across this land in which there is no hope today. And that great light shining out from America will again become a beacon of hope for all those in the world who seek freedom and opportunity.

My fellow Americans, I believe that historians will recall that 1968 marked the beginning of the American generation in world history. Just to be alive in America, just to be alive at this time is an experience unparalleled in history. Here is where the action is. Think. Thirty-two years from now most Americans living today will celebrate a new year that comes once in a thousand years. Eight years from now, in the second term of the next President, we will celebrate the 200th anniversary of the American Revolution.

And by our decision in this election, we all of us here, all of you listening on television and radio, we will determine what kind of nation America will be on its 200th birthday; we will determine what kind of a world America we live in the year 2000. This is the kind of a day I see for America on that glorious Fourth – eight years from now.

I see a day when Americans are once again proud of their flag. When once again at home and abroad, it is honored as the world's greatest symbol of liberty and justice. I see a day when the President of the United States is respected and his office is honored because it is worthy of respect and worthy of honor. I see a day when every child in this land, regardless of his background, has a chance for the best education our wisdom and schools can provide, and an equal chance to go just as high as his talents will take him. I see a day when life in rural America attracts people to the country, rather than driving them away. I see a day when we can look back on massive breakthroughs in solving the problems of slums and pollution and traffic which are choking our cities to death. I see a day when our senior citizens and millions of others can plan for the future with the assurance that their government is not going to rob them of their savings by destroying the value of their dollars. I see a day when we will again have freedom from fear in America and freedom from fear in the world. I see a day when our nation is at peace and the world is at peace and everyone on earth – those who hope, those who aspire, and those who crave liberty – will look at America as the shining example of hopes realized and dreams achieved.

My fellow Americans, this is the cause I ask you to vote for. This is the cause I ask you to work for. This is the cause I ask you to commit to – not just for victory in November but beyond that to a new Administration. Because the time when one man or a few leaders could save America is gone. We need tonight nothing less than the total commitment and the total mobilization of the American people if we are to succeed.

Government can pass laws. But respect for law can come only from people who take the law into their hearts and their minds – and not into their hands. Government can provide opportunity. But opportunity means nothing unless people are prepared to seize it.

A President can ask for reconciliation in the racial conflict that divides Americans. But reconciliation comes only from the hearts of people. And tonight, therefore, as we make this commitment, let us look into our hearts and let us look down into the faces of our children.

Is there anything in the world that should stand in their way? None of the old hatreds mean anything when we look down into the faces of our children. In their faces is our hope, our love, and our courage.

Tonight, I see the face of a child. He lives in a great city. He is black. Or he is white. His is Mexican, Italian, Polish. None of that matters. What matters, he's an American child. That child in that great city is more important than any politician's promise. He is American. He is a poet. He is a scientist, he is a great teacher, and he is a proud craftsman. He is everything we ever hoped to be and everything we dare to dream to be. He sleeps the sleep of childhood and he dreams of a child. And yet when he awakens, he awakens to a living nightmare of poverty, neglect and despair. He fails in school. He ends up on welfare. For him the American system is one that feeds his stomach and starves his soul. It breaks his heart. And in the end it may take his life on some distant battlefields. To millions of children in this rich land, this is their prospect of the future.

But this is only part of what I see in America. I see another child tonight. He hears to train go by at night and he dreams of faraway places where he'd like to go. But he is helped on his journey through life. A father, who had to go to work before he finished the sixth grade, sacrificed everything he had so that his sons could go to college. A gentle, Quaker mother, with a passionate concern for peace, quietly wept when he went to war but she understood why he had to go. A great teacher, a remarkable football coach, an inspirational minister encouraged him on his way. A courageous wife and loyal children stood by him in victory and also defeat. And in his chosen professional of politics, first there were scores, then hundreds, then thousands, and finally millions worked for his success. And tonight he stands before you – nominated for President of the United States of America.

You can see why I believe so deeply in the American Dream. For most of us the American Revolution has been won; the American Dream has come true. And what I ask you to do tonight is to help me make that dream come true for millions to whom it's an impossible dream today.

One hundred and eight years ago, the newly elected President of the United States, Abraham Lincoln, left Springfield, Illinois, never to return again. He spoke to his friends gathered at the railroad station. Listen to his words: "Today I leave you. I go to assume a greater task than devolved on General Washington. The great God which helped him must help me. Without that great assistance, I will surely fail. With it, I cannot fail."

Abraham Lincoln lost his life but he did not fail. The next president of the United States will face challenges which in some ways will be greater than those of Washington or Lincoln. Because for the first time in our nation's history, an American President will face not only the problem of restoring peace abroad but of restoring peace at home.

My fellow Americans, the long dark night for America is about to end. The time has come for us to leave the valley of despair and climb the mountain so that we may see the glory of the dawn—a new day for America, a new dawn for peace and freedom in the world.

HOW WELL DID YOU UNDERSTAND THIS SELECTION?

1. Does Nixon appeal to the past in the speech? Explain?

2. What does Nixon say is wrong with the United States?

3. What does Nixon promise Americans?

4. How does Nixon say he will change foreign policy? Explain?

5. Is Nixon optimistic or pessimistic? Support your answer with evidence from the speech.

6. What does Nixon say about law and order? About Civil Rights?

7. What does Nixon say about the War Poverty? Are his views correct? Explain.

8. Is Nixon racist? Explain?

Democrats, after enduring an horrific national convention at which police clubbed antiwar protestors, nominated Vice President Hubert Humphrey as their President candidate in the 1968 election. Humphrey began his quest for the nomination carrying the baggage of the Johnson administration. Nearly 80 percent of Democratic primary voters favored Eugene McCarthy or Robert Kennedy, one of the party's anti-war candidates. Many Americans viewed Humphrey as the establishment candidate and refused to support his candidacy as a result of his refusal to denounce Johnson's policy on the Vietnam War. Even Johnson did not ardently support his Vice President, preferring instead Republican Nelson Rockefeller. Humphrey won the Democratic nomination by skipping the primaries, focusing instead on wooing delegates selected through the more traditional convention process. In the general election Humphrey overcame a wide gap in the polls and pulled nearly even with Richard Nixon, his Republican opponent, after changing his position on continuing the Vietnam War. In the end Humphrey barely lost the election to Nixon.

The Acceptance Speech of
Vice President Hubert H. Humphrey
Democratic National Convention
Chicago, Illinois
August 29, 1968

A NEW DAY FOR AMERICA

My fellow Americans, my fellow Democrats:
    I proudly accept the nomination of our party.
    This moment is one of personal pride and gratification. Yet one cannot help but reflect the deep sadness that

we feel over the troubles and the violence which have erupted regrettably and tragically in the streets of this great city, and for the personal injuries which have occurred. Surely we have learned the lesson that violence breeds more violence and that it cannot be condoned—whatever the source.

I know that every delegate to this convention shares tonight my sorrow and my distress for these incidents. And may we, for just one moment, in sober reflection, in serious purpose, may we just quietly and silently – each in our own way – pray for our country. And may we just share for a moment a few of those immortal words of the prayer of St. Francis of Assisi – words which I think may help heal the wounds and lift our hearts. Listen to this immortal saint: "Where there is hatred, let me sow love; where there is injury, pardon; where there is doubt, faith; where there is despair, hope; where there is darkness, light."

Those are the words of a saint. And may those of us of less purity listen to them well. And may America tonight resolve that never, never again shall we see what we have seen.

Yes, I accept your nomination in this spirit that I have spoken; knowing that the months and the years ahead will severely test our America. And as this America is tested once again, we give our testament to America. And I do not think it is sentimental nor is it cheap – that each and every one of us in our own way should once again reaffirm to ourselves and our posterity – that we love this nation – we love America.

This is not the first time that our nation has faced a challenge to its life and its purpose. Each time that we have faced these challenges, we have emerged with new greatness and with new strength. We must make this moment of crisis a moment of creation. As it has been said: "In the worst of times, a great people must do the best of things." And let us do it.

We stand at such a moment now – in the affair of this nation. Because, my fellow Americans, something new, something different has happened. It is the end of an era and is the beginning of a new day.

It is the special genius of the Democratic Party that it welcomes change, not as an enemy but as an ally, not as a force to be suppressed, but as an instrument of progress to be encouraged.

This week our party has debated the great issues before America is this very hall. Had we not raised these issues, troublesome as they were, we would have ignored the reality of change. Had we papered over differences with empty platitudes instead of frank, hard debate, we would deserve the contempt of our fellow citizen and the condemnation of history.

We have heard hard a sometimes bitter debate. But I submit that this is the debate and this is the work of free people, the work of an open convention, and the work of a political party responsive to the needs of this nation. Democracy affords debate, discussion and dissent. But it also requires decision. And we have decided, here, not by edict but by vote – not by forces but by ballot. Majority rule has prevailed, while minority rights are preserved.

There is always the temptation to leave the scene of battle in anger and despair, but those who know the true meaning of democracy accept the decision of today, but never relinquish their rights to change it tomorrow.

In the space of one week, this convention had laid the foundations for a new Democratic Party structure in America. From precinct level to the floor of this convention, we have revolutionized our rules and procedures.
And that revolution is in the proud tradition of our Party. In the tradition of Franklin Roosevelt, who knew that America had nothing to fear but fear itself and it is in the tradition of Harry Truman who let 'em have it and told it like it was. And that's the way we're going to do it for here on out. It is in the tradition of that beloved man, Adlai Stevenson, who talked sense to the American people. And, oh, tonight, how we miss that great, good and gentle man of peace in America. And my fellow Americans, all that we do and all that we ever hope to do, must be in the tradition of John F. Kennedy who said to us: Ask not what your country can do for you, but what can you do for your country." And my fellow Democrats and my fellow Americans, in the spirit of that great man, ask what together we can do for the freedom of man.

And what we are doing is in the tradition of Lyndon B. Johnson who rallied a grief-stricken nation when our leader was stricken by the assassin's bullet and said to you and said to me and said to the entire world: "let us continue." And in the space of five years since that tragic moment, President Johnson has accomplished more of the unfinished business of America than any of his modern predecessors. I do believe that history will surely record the greatness of his contributing to the people of this land. And tonight, to you, Mr. President, I say: Thank you, thank you, Mr. President.

At this convention, too, we have recognized the end of an era and the beginning of a new day. And that new day belongs to the people – to all of the people everywhere in this land of the people – to every man, woman, and child that is a citizen of the Republic.

Within that new day lies nothing less than the promise seen a generation ago by Thomas Wolfe: "To every man his chance, to every man regardless of his birth, his shining golden opportunity. To every man the right to live and to work and to be himself. And to become whatever thing his manhood and his vision can combine to make him. This is the promise of America."

Yes, a new day is here. Across America – throughout the entire world – the forces of emancipation are at work. We hear freedom's rising chorus: "Let me live my own life. Let me live in peace. Let me be free, "say the people. And that cry is heard today in our slums and on our farms and in our cities. It is heard from the old, as well as from the young. It is heard in Eastern Europe and it is heard in Vietnam. And it will be answered by us in how we face the three realities that confront this nation.

The first reality is the necessity for peace in Vietnam and in the world. The second reality is the necessity for peace in our cities and in our nation. The third reality is the paramount necessity for unity in our country. Let me speak first about Vietnam.

There are differences, of course, serious differences, within our party on this vexing, painful issue of Vietnam. And these differences are found even within the ranks of all the Democratic Presidential candidates. Once you have examined the differences, I hope you will recognize the much larger area of agreement.

Let those who believe that our cause in Vietnam has been right – and those who believe it has been wrong – agree here and now: Neither vindication nor repudiation will bring peace or be worthy of our country. The question is what do we do now?

No one knows what the situation in Vietnam will be on January 20, 1969. Every heart in America prays that, by then, we shall have reached a cease-fire in all Vietnam, and be in serious negotiation toward a durable peace. Meanwhile, as a citizen, a candidate, and Vice President, I pledge to you and to my fellow Americans, that I shall do everything within my power to aid the negotiations and to bring a prompt end to this war.

May I remind you of the words of a truly great citizen of the world, Winston Churchill – it was he who said – and we would heed his words well: "Those who use today and the present to stand in judgment of the past, may well lose the future." And if there is one lesson we should have learned, it is that the policies of tomorrow need not be limited by the policies of yesterday.

And my fellow Americans, if it becomes my high honor to serve as President of these states and people, I shall apply that lesson to the search for peace in Vietnam, as to all areas of national policy.

Now, let me ask you, do you remember these words, at another time, in a different place: "Peace and freedom do not come cheap. And we are destined – All of us here today – to live out most, if not all of our lives, in uncertainty and challenge and peril." The words of a prophet? Yes. The words of a President? Yes. The words of the challenge of today? Yes. And the words of John Kennedy to you, me, and posterity.

Last week we witnessed once again in Czechoslovakia the desperate attempt of tyranny to crush out the forces of liberalism by force and brutal power – to hold back change. But in Eastern Europe, as elsewhere, the old era will surely end and, there, as here, a new day will dawn. And to speed this day, we must go far beyond where we've been, beyond containment to communication, beyond differences to dialogue, beyond fear to hope. We must cross the remaining barriers of suspicion and despair. We must halt the arms race before it halts humanity. And is this, is this a vain hope? It is but a dream? I say the record says no.

Within the last few years we have made progress. We have negotiated a Nuclear Test Ban Treaty. We have laid the groundwork for a Nuclear Non-Proliferation Treaty. We have reached agreement on banning weapons in outer space. We have been building patiently stone by stone, each in our own say, the cathedral of peace. And now we must take new initiatives.

Every American, black or white, rich or poor, has the right in this land of ours to a safe and decent neighborhood. And on this there can be no compromise. I put it very bluntly. Rioting, sniping, mugging, traffic in narcotics and disregard for law are the advance guard of anarchy and they must and they will be stopped.

But may I say most respectfully, particularly to some who have spoken before, the answer lies in reasoned, effective action by state, local and federal authority. The answer does not lie in an attack on our courts, our laws or our Attorney General. We do not want a police state, but we need a state of law and order. And neither mob violence nor police brutality has any place in America. And I pledge to use every resource that is available to the president to end for once and for all the fear that is in our cities.

Now let me speak of other rights. Nor can there be any compromise with the right of every American who is able to live in a decent home in the neighborhood of his own choice.

Now can there be any compromise with the right of every American who is anxious and willing to learn to have a good education.

And it is to these rights – the right of law and order, the right of life, the right of liberty, the right of a job, the right of a home in a decent neighborhood, and the right to an education – it is to these rights that I pledge my life and whatever capacity and ability I have.

But we cannot be satisfied with merely repairing that which is old. We must also move beyond the enclosures of our traditional cities to create new cities, to restore our present cities, yes, and we must bring prosperity and modern living and opportunity to our rural areas. We must design and open America, opening new opportunities for new Americans in open land. I say to this audience, we have invested billions to explore outer space where man may live tomorrow. We must also be willing to invest to develop inner space rights here on earth where many live today.

And now that third reality. Essential if the other two are to be achieved, is the necessity, my fellow American, for unit in our country, for tolerance and forbearance, for holding together as a family. And we must make a great decision: are we to be one nation, or are we to be a nation divided between black and white, between rich and poor, between north and south, between young and old.

I take my stand. We are and we must be one nation – united by liberty and justice for all, one nation under God, indivisible, with liberty and justice for all. This is our America.

And just as I've said to you that there can be no compromise on that right of personal security, there can be no compromise on securing of human rights. If America is to make a crucial judgment of leadership, in this coming election, then let that selection be made without either candidate hedging or equivocating. Winning the presidency for me is not worth the price of silence or evasion on that issue of human rights.

And winning the presidency, and listen well, winning the presidency is not worth a compact with extremism. I choose not simply to run for president. I seek to lead a great nation. And either we achieve true justice in our land or we shall doom ourselves at a terrible exhaustion of body and spirit. I base my entire candidacy on the belief which comes from the very depth of my soul, which comes from basic religious conviction that the American people will stand up, that they will stand up for justice and fair play, and that they will respond to the call of one citizenship, one citizenship open to all for all Americans.

So this is the message that I shall take to the people and I ask you to stand with me. And to all of my fellow Democrats now who have labored hard and openly this week at the difficult and sometimes frustrating work of democracy, I pledge myself to the task of leading the Democratic Party to victory in November. And may I say to those who have differed with their neighbor or those who have differed with a fellow Democrat, that all of your goals, that all of you high hopes, that all of your dreams, all of them will come to naught if we lose this election. And many of them can be realized with a victory that can come to us.

And now a word to two good friends, and they are my friends, and they're your friends, and they're fellow Democrats. To my friend, Gene McCarthy and George McGovern, who have given new hope to a new generation of Americans that there can be greater meaning in their lives, that Americans can respond to men of moral concern, to these two good Americans I ask your help for our America. And I ask you to help me in the difficult campaign that lies ahead.

And now I appeal to those thousands, yes, millions of young Americans to join us not simply as campaigners but to continue as vocal, creative and even critical participants in the politics of our times. Never were you needed so much and never could you do so much if you were to help now.

Martin Luther King, Jr. had a dream. Robert F. Kennedy as you saw tonight had a great vision. If America will respond to that dream and that vision, their deaths will not mark the moment when America lost its way, but it will mark the time when America found its conscience. These men have given us inspiration and direction. And I pledge from this platform tonight we shall not abandon their purposes. We shall honor their dreams by our deeds, now and in the days to come.

I am keenly aware of the fears and frustration of the world in which we live. It is all too easy to play on these emotions. But I do not intend to do so.

I do not intend to appeal to fear, but rather to hope.

I do not intend to appeal to frustration, but rather to your faith.

I shall appeal to reason and to your good judgment.

HOW WELL DID YOU UNDERSTAND THIS SELECTION?

1. How did Humphrey describe the Democratic Party?

2. What does Humphrey say about Johnson? Why?

3. What does Humphrey say about the Vietnam War?

4. What does Humphrey mean when he says "… the policies of today need not be limited by the policies of yesterday."

5. What does Humphrey say to young people?

6. Compare and contrast Humphrey's acceptance speech to that of Richard Nixon. How are they alike? How are they different? Which is the most effective? Why?

GEORGE WALLACE'S MADISON SQUARE GARDEN SPEECH

Alabama governor George Wallace sought to tap into discontent among white racists in the 1968 Presidential race by forming the American Independent Party and running as a third party candidate Wallace, whose constituency, according to a Detroit newspaper columnist consisted of Klansman, Neo-Nazis, and other kooks, ran one of the most successful campaigns by a third party in American History, gaining slightly more than 13 percent of the popular vote and getting 46 electoral votes. His appeal was largely to voters in the deep South, who like Wallace, wanted to undo progress made in Civil Rights and who believed that the race riots and general violence rocking the nation were part of a vast Communist conspiracy to destroy America from within. Right wing racists flocked to hear Wallace denounce pointy headed bureaucrats and liberal professors, who along with blacks and foreign immigrants, he saw as part of a sinister plot to destroy America. Ardent conservatives like movie star John Wayne and billionaire Bunker Hunt contributed thousands of dollars to Wallace's campaign in 1968.

Well, thank you very much ladies and gentlemen. Thank you very much for you gracious and kind reception here in Madison Square Garden. I'm sure that the New York Times took note of the reception that we've received here in the great city of New York. I'm very grateful to the people of this city and this state for the opportunity to be on the ballot on November 5, and as you know we're on the ballot in all 50 states in this Union. This is not a sectional movement. It's a national movement, and I am sure that those who are in attendance here tonight, especially of the press, know that our movement is a national movement and that we have an excellent chance to carry the great Empire State of New York.

I have a few friends from Alabama with me and we have a number of others who were with us last week, but we have with us Willie Kirk, past president of Local 52, United Association of Plumbers and Pipefitters.

Well, I want to tell you something. After November 5, you anarchists are through in this country. I can tell you that. Yes, you'd better have your say now, because you are going to be through after November 5, I can assure you that.

I have also with me W.C. Williamson, business manager of Local 52, UAPP, Montgomery, Alabama, and R.H. Low, president of the Mobile Building and Construction Trade Council and business manager of Local 653 Operating Engineers. And you came for trouble, you sure got it.

And we have R.H. Bob Low, president of the MBC. Well why don't you come down after I get through and I'll autograph your sandals for you, you know?

And Charlie Ryan, recording secretary of the Steam Fitters Local 818, New York City. We have been endorsed in Alabama by nearly every local in our state: textiles workers, paper workers, steel workers, rubber workers, you name it. We've been endorsed by the working people of our state.

Regardless of what they might say, your national leaders, my wife carried every labor box in 1966, when she ran for governor of Alabama in the primary and the general election. And I also was endorsed by labor when I was elected governor in 1962.

Now, if you fellows will I can drown listen if you'll sit down, ladies and gentlemen, I can drown that crowd out. If you'll just sit down, I'll drown em out that's all he needs is a good haircut. If he'll go to the barbershop, I think you can cure him. So all you newsmen look up this way now. Here's the main event. I've been wanting to fight the main a long time in Madison Square Garden, so here we are. Listen, that's just a preliminary match up there. This is the main bout right here. So let me say again as I said a moment ago, that we have had the support of the working people of our state. Alabama's a large industrial state, and you could not be elected governor without the support of people in organized labor.

Let me also say this about race, since I'm here in the state of New York, and I'm always asked the question. I am very grateful for the fact that in 1966 my wife received more black votes in Alabama than did either one of her opponents. We are proud to say that they support us now in this race for the presidency, and we would like to have the support of people of all races, color, creeds, religion, and national origins in the state of New York.

Our system is under attack: the property system, the free enterprise system, and local government. Anarchy prevails today in the streets of the large cities of our country, making it unsafe for you to even go to a political rally here in Madison Square Garden, and that is a sad commentary. Both national parties in the last number of years have kowtowed to every anarchist that has roamed the streets. I want to say before I start on this any longer, that I'm not talking about race. The overwhelming majority of all races in this country are against the breakdown of law and order as much as those who are assembled here tonight. It's a few anarchists, a few activists, a few militants, a few revolutionaries, and a few communists. But your day, of course, is going to be over soon. The American people are not going to stand by and see the security of our nation imperiled, and they're not going to stand by and see this nation destroyed, I can assure you that.

The liberals and the left-wingers in both national parties have brought us to the domestic mess we are in now. And also this foreign mess we are in.

You need to read the book, how to Behave in a Crowd. You really don't know how to behave in a crowd, do you?

Yes, the liberals and left-wingers in both parties have brought us to the domestic mess we are in also to the foreign policy mess we find our nation involved in at the present time, personified by the no-win war in Southeast Asia.

Now what are some of the things we are going to do when we have become president? We are going to turn back to you, the people of the states, the right to control our domestic institutions. Today you cannot even go to the school system of the large cities of our country without fear. This is a sad day when in the greatest city in the world, there is fear not only in Madison Square Garden, but in every school building in the state of New York, and especially in the city of New York. Why has the leadership of both national parties kowtowed to this group of anarchists that make it unsafe for your child and for your family? I don't understand it. But I can assure you of this, that there's not ten cents worth of difference with what the national parties say other than our party. Recently they say most of the same things we say. Remember six years ago when this anarchy movement started, Mr. Nixon said: it's a great movement and Mr. Humphrey said, it's a great movement. Now when they try to speak and are heckled down, they stand up and say: we've got to have some law and order in this country. They ought to give you law and order back for nothing, because they have helped to take it away from you, along with the Supreme Court of our country that's made up of Republicans and Democrats.

It's costing the taxpayers of New York and the other states in the Union almost a half billion dollars to supervise the schools, hospitals, seniority and apprenticeship lists of labor unions, and businesses. Every year on the federal level we have passed a law that would jail you without a trial by jury about the sale of your own property. Mr. Nixon and Mr. Humphrey, both three or four weeks ago, called for the passage of a bill on the Federal level that would require you to sell or lease your own property to whomsoever they thought you ought to lease it to. I say that when Mr. Nixon and Mr. Humphrey succumb to the black of a few anarchists in the streets who said we're going to destroy this country if you do not destroy that adage that a man's home is his castle, they are not fit to lead the American people during the next four years in our country. When I become your president, I am going to ask that Congress repeal this so-called open occupancy law and we're going to, within the law, turn back to the people of every state their public school system. Not one dime of you federal money is going to be used to bus anybody any place that you don't want them to be bussed in New York or any other state.

Yes, the theoreticians and the pseudo-intellectuals have just about destroyed not only local government but the school systems of your country. That's all right. Let the police handle it. So let us talk about law and order. We don't have to talk about it much up here. You understand what I'm talking about in, of course, the City of New York, but let's talk about it.

Yes, the pseudo-intellectuals and the theoreticians and some professors and some newspaper editors and some judges and some preachers have looked down their nose long enough at the average man on the street: the pipe-fitter, the communications worker, the fireman, the policeman, the barber, the white collar worker, and said we must write you a guideline about when you go to bed at night and when you get up in the morning. But there are more of us than there are of them because the average citizen of New York and of Alabama and of the other states of our Union are tired of guidelines being written, telling them when to go to bed at night and when to get up in the morning.

I'm talking about law and order. The Supreme Court of our country has hand-cuffed the police, and tonight if you walk out of this building and are knocked in the head, the person who knocks you in the head is out of jail before you get in the hospital, and on Monday morning, they'll try a policeman about it. I can say I'm going to give the total support of the presidency to the policeman and the firemen in this country, and I'm going to say, you enforce the law and you make it safe on the streets, and the President of the United States will stand with you. My election as president is going to put some backbone in the backs of some mayors and governors I know through the length and breadth of this country.

You had better be thankful for the police and the firemen of this country. If it were not for them, you couldn't even ride in the streets, much less walk in the streets, of our large cities. Yes, the Kerner Commissions Report, recently written by Republicans and Democrats, said that you are to blame for the breakdown of law and order, and that the police are to blame. Well, you know, of course, you aren't to blame. They said we have a sick society. Well, we don't have any sick society. We have a sick Supreme Court and some sick politicians in Washington, that's whose sick in our country. The Supreme Court of our country has ruled that you cannot even say a simple prayer in a public school, but you can send obscene literature through the mail, and recently they ruled that a Communist can work in a defense plant. But when I become your president, we're going to take every Communist out of every defense plant in the United States, I can assure you.

HOW WELL DID YOU UNDERSTAND THIS SELECTION?

1. How does Wallace describe his candidacy?

2. What is the main theme of Wallace's speech?

3. What does Wallace say about the Vietnam War?

4. What does Wallace say about law and order?

5. Overall, what does Wallace think is wrong with America?

6. How does Wallace handle protectors in the crowd?

=======

I'VE BEEN TO THE MOUNTAINTOP SPEECH
by Martin Luther King, Jr.

=======

Dr. Martin Luther King, Jr, the foremost leader of Civil Rights Movement, began to shift focus from fighting for African American Civil Rights to fighting against poverty endemic to all races in 1968. He spent the first part of 1968 planning a Poor PeopleS March on Washington D.C. in hopes of confronting an issue that transcended race. King's planning for the Poor Peoples March was interrupted by a strike by sanitation workers in Memphis, Tennessee. Believing that the fight of the Memphis sanitation workers would aid his plans to fight poverty, King agreed to speak to workers and their support-ers. On April 3rd King addressed a large crowd of workers, delivering one of the most elegant orations of his career. In the speech King compared himself to Moses who led the ancient Israelites out of slavery in Egypt but did not himself get to see the Promised Land. This comparison was somewhat prophetic as the next day James Earl Ray assassinated King from across the street as the Civil Rights icon stood on the balcony of his hotel room. The assassination touched off a period of rioting across the country.

Thank you very kindly, my friends. As I listened to Ralph Abernathy and his eloquent and generous introduction and then thought about myself, I wondered who he was talking about. It's always good to have your closest friend and associate to say something good about you, and Ralph Abernathy is the best friend that I have in the world.

I'm delighted to see each of you here tonight in spite of a storm warning. You reveal that you are determined to go on anyhow. Something is happening in Memphis, something is happening in our world. And you know, if I were standing at the beginning of time with the possibility of taking a kind of general and panoramic view of the whole of human history up to now, and the Almighty said to me, "Martin Luther King, which age would you like to live in?" I would take my mental flight by Egypt, and I would watch God's children in their magnificent trek from the dark dungeons of Egypt through, or rather, across the Red Sea, through the wilderness, on toward the Promised Land. And in spite of its magnificence, I wouldn't stop there.

I would move on by Greece, and take my mind to Mount Olympus. And I would see Plato, Aristotle, Socrates, Euripides, and Aristophanes assembled around the Parthenon, and I would watch them around the Parthenon as they discussed the great and eternal issues of reality. But I wouldn't stop there.

I would go on even to the great heyday of the Roman Empire, and I would see development around there, through various emperors and leaders. But I wouldn't stop there.

I would even come up to the early thirties and see a man grappling with the problems of the bankruptcy of his nation, and come with an eloquent cry that "we have nothing to fear but fear itself." But I wouldn't stop there.

Strangely enough, I would turn to the Almighty and say, "If you allow me to live just a few years in the second half of the twentieth century, I will be happy.

Now that's a strange statement to make because the world is all messed up. The nation is sick; trouble is in the land, confusion all around. That's a strange statement. But I know, somehow, that only when it is dark enough can you see the stars. And I see God working in this period of the twentieth century in a way that men in some strange ways are responding. Something is happening in our world. The masses of people are rising up. And wherever they are assembled today, whether they are in Johannesburg, South Africa; Nairobi, Kenya; Accra, Ghana; New York City; Atlanta, Georgia; Jackson, Mississippi; or Memphis, Tennessee, the cry is always the same: "We want to be free."

And another reason I'm happy to live in this period is that we have been forced to a point where we are going to have to grapple with the problems that men have been trying to grapple with through history, but the demands didn't force them to do it. Survival demands that we grapple with them. Men for years now have been talking about war and peace. But now no longer can they just talk about it. It is no longer a choice between violence and nonviolence in this world; its nonviolence or nonexistence. That is where we are today.

And also, in the human rights revolution, if something isn't done and done in a hurry to bring the colored peoples of the world out of their long years of poverty; their long years of hurt and neglect, the whole world is doomed. Now I'm just happy that God has allowed me to live in this period to see what is unfolding. And I'm happy that he's allowed me to be in Memphis.

I can remember, I can remember when Negroes were just going around, as Ralph has said so often, scratching where they didn't itch and laughing when they were not tickled. But that day is all over. We mean business now and we are determined to gain our rightful place in God's world. And that's all this whole thing is about. We aren't engaged in any negative protest and in any negative arguments with anybody. We are saying that we are determined to be men. We are saying, we are saying that we are God's children. And if we are God's children, we don't have to live like we are forced to live.

Now what does all this mean in this great period of history? It means that we've got to stay together. We've got to stay together and maintain unity. You know, whenever Pharaoh wanted to prolong the period of slavery in Egypt, he had a favorite, favorite formula of doing it. What was that? He kept the slaves fighting among themselves. But whenever the slaves get together, that's the beginning of getting out of slavery. Now let us maintain unity.

Secondly, let us keep the issues where they are. The issue is injustice. The issue is the refusal of Memphis to be fair and honest in its dealing with its public servants, who happen to be sanitation workers. Now we've got to keep attention on that. That's always the problem with a little violence. You know what happened the other day, and the press dealt only with the window breaking. I read the articles. They very seldom got around to mentioning the fact that 1,300 sanitation workers are on strike, and that Memphis is not being fair to them, and that Mayor Loeb is in dire need of a doctor. They didn't get around to that.

Now we're going to march again, and we've got to march again in order to put the issue where it is supposed to be and force everybody to see that there are thirteen hundred of God's children here suffering, sometimes going hungry, going through dark and dreary nights wondering how this thing is going to come out. For when people get caught up with that which is right and they are willing to sacrifice for it, there is no stopping point short of victory.

We aren't going to let any mace stop us. We are masters in our nonviolent movement in disarming police forces. They don't know what to do. I've seen them so often. I remember in Birmingham, Alabama, when we were in the majestic struggle there, we would move out of this Sixteenth Street Baptist Church day after day. By the hundreds we would move out, and Bull Connor would tell them to send the dogs forth, and they did come. But we just went before the dogs singing. "Ain't gonna let nobody turn me around." Bull Connor next would say, "Turn the fire hoses on." And as I said to you the other night, Bull Connor didn't know history; he knew a kind of physics that somehow didn't relate to the trans-physics that we knew about. And that was the fact that there was a certain kind of fire that no water could put out. And we went before the fire hoses. We had known water. If we were Baptist or some other denominations, we had been immersed. If we were Methodist or some others, we had been sprinkled. But we knew water. That couldn't stop us.

And we just went on before the dogs and we would look at them, and we'd go on before the water hoses and we would look at it. And we'd go on singing. "Over my head, I see freedom in the air." And then we would be thrown into paddy wagons, and sometimes we were stacked in there like sardines in a can. And they would throw us in, and old Bull would say "Take 'em off." And they did, and we would just go on in the paddy wagon singing. "We shall overcome." And every now and then we'd get in jail, and we'd see the jailers looking through the window being moved by our prayers and being moved by our words and our songs. And there was a power there which Bull Connor couldn't adjust to, and so we ended up transforming Bull into a steer and we went on our struggle in Birmingham. Now we've got to go on in Memphis just like that. I call upon you to be with us when we go out Monday. Now about injunctions. We have an injunction and we're going into court tomorrow morning to fight this illegal, unconstitutional injunction. All we say to America is to be true to what you said on paper. If I lived in China or even Russia, or any totalitarian country, maybe I could understand some of these illegal injunctions. Maybe I could understand the denial of certain basic First Amendment privileges, because they haven't committed themselves to that over there. But somewhere I read of the freedom of assembly. Somewhere I read of the freedom of speech. Somewhere I read of the freedom of press. Somewhere I read that the greatness of America is the right to protest for right. And so just as I say we aren't going to let any dogs or water hoses turn us around, we aren't going to let any injunction turn us around. We are going on. We need all of you.

You know, what's beautiful to me is to see all of these ministers of the Gospel. It's a marvelous picture. Who is it that is supposed to articulate the longings and aspirations of the people more than the preacher? Somewhere the preacher must have a kind of fire shut up in his bones, and whenever injustice is around he must tell it. Somehow the preacher must be an Amos, who said, "When God Speaks, who can but prophesy?" Again with Amos, "Let justice roll down like waters and righteousness like a mighty stream." Somehow the preacher must say with Jesus. "The spirit of the Lord is upon me, because he halt anointed me, and he's anointed me to deal with the problems of the poor."

And I wanted to commend the preachers, under the leadership of these noble men: James Lawson, one who has been in the struggle for many years. He's been to jail for struggling: he's been kicked out of Vanderbilt University for this struggling; but he's still going on, fighting for the rights of this people. Reverend Ralph Jackson, Billy Kyles; I could just go right on down the list, but time will not permit. But I want to thank all of them, and I want you to thank them because so often preachers aren't concerned about anything but themselves. And I'm always happy to see a relevant ministry. It's all right to talk about long white robes over yonder, in all of its symbolism, but ultimately people want some suits and dresses and shoes to wear down here. It's all right to talk about streets flowing with milk and honey, but God has commanded us to be concerned about the slums down here and his children who can't eat three square meals a day. It's all right to talk about the New Jerusalem, but one day God's preacher must talk about the new New York, the new Atlanta, the new Philadelphia, the new Los Angeles, the new Memphis, Tennessee. This is what we have to do.

Now the other thing we'll have to do is this: always anchor our external direct action with the power of economic withdrawal. Now we are poor people, individually we are poor when you compare us with white society in America. We are poor. Never stop and forget that collectively, that means all of us together, collectively we are richer than all the nations in the world, with the exception of nine. Did you every think about that? After you leave the United States, Soviet Russia, Great Britain, West Germany, France, and I could name the others, the American Negro collectively is richer than most nations of the world. We have an annual income of more than thirty billion dollars a year, which is more than all of the exports of the United States and more than the national budget of Canada. Did you know that? That's power right there, if we know how to pool it.

And so, as a result of this, we are asking you tonight to go out and tell your neighbor not to buy Coca-Cola in Memphis. Go by and tell them not to buy Sealtest milk. Tell them not to buy-what is the other bread? - Wonder Bread. And what is the other bread company, Jesse? Tell them not to buy Hart's bread. As Jesse Jackson has said, up to now only the garbage men have been feeling pain. Now we must kind of redistribute that pain. We are choosing these companies because they haven't been fair in their hiring policies, and we are choosing them because they can begin the process of saying they are going to support the needs and the rights of these men who are on strike. And they can move on downtown and tell Mayor Loeb to do what is right

Now not only that, we've got to strengthen black institutions. I call upon you to take your money out of the banks downtown and deposit your money in Tri-State Bank. We want a "bank-in" movement in Memphis. Go by the savings and loan association. I'm not asking you something that we don't do ourselves in SCLS. Judge Hooks and others will tell you that we have an account here in the savings and loan association from the Southern Christian Leadership Conference. We are telling you to follow what we're doing, put your money there. You have six or seven black insurance companies here in the city of Memphis. Take out your insurance there. We want to have an "insurance-in." Now these are some practical things that we can do. We begin the process of building a greater economic base, and at the same time, we are putting pressure where it really hurts. And I ask you to follow through here.

Now let me say as I move to my conclusion that we've got to give ourselves to this struggle until the end. Nothing would be more tragic then to stop at this point in Memphis. We've got to see it through. And when we have our march, you need to be there. If it means leaving work, if it means leaving school, be there. Be concerned about your brother. You may not be on strike, but either we go up together or we go down together. Let us develop a kind of dangerous unselfishness.

One day a man came to Jesus and he wanted to raise some questions about some vital matters of life. At points he wanted to trick Jesus, and show him that he knew a little more than Jesus knew and throw him off base. Now that question could have easily ended up in a philosophical and theological debate. But Jesus immediately pulled that question from midair and places it on a dangerous curve between Jerusalem and Jericho. And he talked about a certain man who fell among thieves. You remember that a Levite and a priest passed by on the other side; they didn't stop to help the man in need. Jesus ended up saying this was the good man; this was the great man because he had the capacity to project the "I" into the "thou," and to be concerned about his brother.

Now, you know, we use our imagination a great deal to try to determine why the priest and the Levite didn't stop. At times we say they were busy going to a church meeting. At other times we would speculate that there was a religious law that one who was engaged in religious ceremonials was not to touch a human body twenty-four hours before the ceremony. And every now and then we begin to wonder whether maybe they were not going down to Jerusalem, or down to Jericho, rather, to organize a Jericho Road Improvement Association. That's possibility. Maybe they felt it was better to deal with the problem from the causal root, rather than to get bogged down with an individual effect.

But I'm going to tell you what my imagination tells me. It's possible that those men were afraid. You see, the Jericho Road is a dangerous road. I remember when Mrs. King and I were first in Jerusalem. We rented a car and drove from Jerusalem down to Jericho. And as soon as we get on that road I said to my wife. "I can see why Jesus used this as the setting for his parable." It's a winding, meandering road. It's really conductive for ambushing. You start out of Jerusalem, which is about twelve hundred miles, or rather, twelve hundred feet above sea level. And by the time you get down to Jericho fifteen or twenty minutes later, your about twenty-two feet below sea level. That's a dangerous road. In the days of Jesus it came to be known as the "Bloody Pass." And you know, it's possible that the priest and the Levite looked over that man on the ground and wondered if the robbers were still around. Or it's possible that they felt that the man on the ground was merely faking and he was acting like he had been robbed and hurt in order to seize them over there, lure them there for quick and easy seizure. And so the first question that the priest asked, that first question that the Levite asked was "If I stop to help this man, what will happen to me?"

But then the Good Samaritan came by, and he reversed the question: "if I do not stop to help this man, what will happen to him?" That's the question before you tonight. Not, "If I stop to help the sanitation workers, what will happen to my job?" Not, "If I stop to help the sanitation workers, what will happen to all of the hours that I usually spend in my office every day and every week as a pastor? "The question is not, "if I stop to help this man in need, what will happen to me?" The question is "If I do not stop to help the sanitation workers, what will happen to them.?" That's the question.

Let us rise up tonight with a greater readiness. Let us stand with a greater determination. And let us move on in these powerful days, these days of challenge, to make America what it ought to be. We have an opportunity to make American a better nation.

And I want to thank God, once more, for allowing me to be here with you. You know, several years ago I was in New York autographing the first book that I had written. And while sitting there autographing books, a demented black women came up. The only question I heard from her was, "Are you Martin Luther King?" And I was looking down writing and I said, "Yes."

The next minute I felt something beating on my chest. Before I knew it I had been stabbed by this demented woman. I was rushed to Harlem Hospital. It was a dark Saturday afternoon. And that blade had gone through, and the X-rays revealed that the tip of the blade was on the edge of my aorta, the main artery. And once that's punctured you're drowned in your own blood, that's the end of you. It came out in the New York Times the next morning that if I had merely sneezed, I would have died.

Well, about four days later, they allow me, after the operation, after my chest had been opened and the blade had been taken out, to move around in the wheelchair of the hospital. They allowed me to read some of the mail that came in, and from all over the states and the world kind letters came in. I read a few, but one of them I will never forget. I had received one from the president and the vice president; I've forgotten what those telegrams said. I'd received a visit and a letter from the governor of New York, but I've forgotten what that letter said.

But there was another letter that came from a little girl, a young girl who was a student at the White Plains High School. And I looked at that letter and I'll never forget it. It said simply, "Dear Dr. King: I am a ninth-grade student at the White Plains High School." She said "While it should not matter, I would like to mention that I'm a white girl. I read in the paper of your misfortune and of your suffering. And I read that if you had sneezed, you would have died. And I'm so happy that you didn't sneeze."

And I wanted to say tonight, I wanted to say tonight that I, too, am happy that I didn't sneeze. Because if I had sneezed, I wouldn't have been around here in 1960, when students all over the South started sitting-in at lunch counters. And I knew that as they were sitting in, they were really standing up for the best in the American dream and taking the whole nation back to those great wells of democracy, which were dug deep by the founding fathers in the Declaration of Independence and the Constitution.

If I had sneezed, I wouldn't have been around here in 1961, when we decided to take a ride for freedom and ended segregation in interstate travel.

If I had sneezed, I wouldn't have been around here in 1962, when Negroes in Albany, Georgia, decided to straighten their backs up. And whenever men and women straighten their backs up, they are going somewhere, because a mean can't ride your back unless it is bent.

If I had sneezed, If I had sneezed, I wouldn't have been here in 1963, when the black people of Birmingham, Alabama, aroused the conscience of this nation and brought into being the Civil Rights Bill.

If I had sneezed I wouldn't have had a chance later that year, in August, to try to tell America about a dream that I had had.

If I had sneezed, I wouldn't have been in Selma, Alabama, to see the great movement there.

If I had sneezed, I wouldn't have been in Memphis to see a community rally around those brothers and sisters who are suffering. I'm so happy that I didn't sneeze.

And they were telling me. Now it doesn't matter now. It really doesn't matter what happens now. I left Atlanta this morning, and as we got started on the plane-there were six of us-the pilot said over the public address system: "We are sorry for the delay, but we have Dr. Martin Luther King on the plane. And to be sure that all of the bags are checked and to be sure that nothing would be wrong on the plane, we have to check out everything carefully. And we've had the plane protected and guarded all night."

And then I got into Memphis. And some began to say that threats, or talk about the threats that were out, or what would happen to me from some of our sick white brothers.

Well, I don't know what will happen now; we've got some difficult days ahead. But it really doesn't matter to with me now, because I've been to the mountaintop. And I don't mind. Like anybody, I would like to live a long life-longevity has its place. But I'm not concerned about that now. I just want to do God's will. And he's allowed me go to up to the mountain. And I've looked over, and I've seen the Promised Land. I may not get there with you. But I want to know tonight, that we, as a people, will get to the Promise Land. And so I'm happy tonight; I'm not worried about anything; I'm not fearing any man. Mine eyes have seen glory of the coming of the Lord.

HOW WELL DID YOU UNDERSTAND THIS SELECTION?

1. Is King's comparison of the Civil Rights Movement to the Hebrew exodus from Egypt valid? Why or why not?

2. What does King say about violence that was part of the Memphis Sanitation Strike?

3. How does King appeal to history? Explain.

4. How does King address poverty?

5. What does King tell his listeners to do to fight injustice?

6. What is King referring to when he uses the words "promised land" toward the end of the speech? Is the speech prophetic? Explain?

ROBERT KENNEDY ON THE DEATH OF MARTIN LUTHER KING

On April 4, 1968 the Reverend Martin Luther King, Jr., leader of the Civil Rights Movement, was tragically assassinated by James Earl Ray in Memphis, Tennessee. Robert F. Kennedy, brother of slain President John F. Kennedy and candidate for the Democratic presidential nomination, had to inform an audience of African Americans assembled to hear him speak in Indianapolis, Indiana that evening. The speech was originally planned as part of a campaign rally for Kennedy. Upon his arrival at the Indianapolis airport Kennedy was informed about King's death and advised not to address the crowd for fear of racial violence. Kennedy refused to heed the advice of local police to cancel the speech and proceeded to address the crowd. Almost immediately he realized the audience did not know about King's death and that he would have to inform them. Historians generally consider that short speech Kennedy made informing the African-American crowd of King's death one of the most extraordinary moments in American political history. Little did Kennedy know at the time that two months later, on June 5th, his life also would be cut short by an assassin's bullet.

Ladies and Gentlemen – I'm only going to talk to you just for a minute or so this evening. Because I have some very sad news for all of you, and I think sad news for all of our fellow citizens, and people who love peace all over the world, and that is that Martin Luther King was shot and was killed tonight in Memphis Tennessee.

Martin Luther King dedicated his life to love and to justice between fellow human beings. He died in the cause of that effort. In this difficult day, in this difficult time for the United States, it's perhaps well to ask what kind of a nation we are and what direction we want to move in.

For those of you who are black – considering the evidence evidently is that there were white people who were responsible – you can be filled with bitterness, and with hatred, and a desire for revenge.

We can move in that direction as a country, in greater polarization – black people amongst blacks, and white among whites, filled with hatred toward one another. Or we can make an effort, as Martin Luther King did, to understand and to comprehend, and replace that violence, that stain of bloodshed that has spread across our land, with an effort to understand, compassion and love.

For those of you who are black and are tempted to be filled with hatred and mistrust of the injustice of such an act, against all white people, I would only say I can also feel in my own heart the same kind of feeling. I had a member of my family killed, but he was killed by a white man.

But we have to make an effort in the United States, we have to make an effort to understand, to get beyond these rather difficult times.

My favorite poet was Aeschylus. He once wrote: "Even in our sleep, pain which cannot forget falls drop by drop upon the heart, until in our own despair, against our will, comes wisdom through the awful grace of God."

What we need in the United States is not division; what we need in the United States is not hatred; what we need in the United States is not violence and lawlessness, but is love and wisdom, and compassion toward one another, and a feeling of justice toward those who still suffer within our country, whether they be white or whether they be black.

So I ask you tonight to return home, to say a prayer for the family of Martin Luther King, yeah that's true, but more importantly to say a prayer for our own country, which all of us love – a prayer for understanding and that compassion of which I spoke. We can do well in this country. We will have difficult times. We've had difficult times in the past. And we will have difficult times in the future. It is not the end of violence; it is not the end of lawlessness; and it's not the end of disorder.

But the vast majority of white people and the vast majority of black people in this country want to live together, want to improve the quality of our life, and want justice for all human beings that abide in our land.

Let us dedicate ourselves to what the Greeks wrote many years ago: to tame the savageness of man and make gentle the life of this world.

Let us dedicate ourselves to that, and say a prayer for our country and for our people. Thank you very much.

Robert F. Kennedy – April 4, 1968

HOW WELL DID YOU UNDERSTAND THIS SELECTION?

1. What does Kennedy ask that crowd to do?

2. What does Kennedy ask the audience to think about?

3. What does Kennedy say about violence?

4. Were Kennedy's words "similar in spirit" to those Dr. King might have uttered? Explain?

On April 11, 1968. President Lyndon Baines Johnson signed into law the Civil Rights Act of 1968. Popularly known as the Fair Housing Act, this law forbade discrimination in the sale and rental of housing within the United States. Neighborhoods that once were closed to blacks were now open; landlords that previously had refused to rent to black tenants could no longer do so. President Johnson held a formal signing ceremony at the White House when he signed the legislation into law. The remarks he made at the signing ceremony are reproduced below.

Members of the Congress, members of the Cabinet, distinguished Americans, and guests. On an April afternoon in the year 1966, I asked a distinguished group of citizens who were interested in human rights to meet me in the Cabinet room in the White House. In their presence that afternoon, I signed a message to the Congress. That message called for the enactment of "the first effective federal law against discrimination in the sale and rental of housing" in the United States of America.

New in the nation—and the record will show very few in that room that afternoon—believed that fair housing would—in our time—become the unchallenged law of this land.

And indeed, this bill has had a long a stormy trip. We did not get it in 1966. We pleaded for it again in 1967. But the Congress took no action that year. We asked for it again this year. And now—at long last this afternoon—its day has come.

I do not exaggerate when I say that the proudest moments of my Presidency have been times such as this when I have signed into law the promise of a century.

I shall never forget that it was more than 100 years ago when Abraham Lincoln issued the Emancipation Proclamation—but it was a proclamation; it was not a fact. In the Civil Rights Act of 1964, we affirmed through law that men equal under God are also equal when they seek a job, when they go to get a meal in a restaurant, or when they seek lodging for the night in any State in the Union.

Now the Negro families no longer suffer the humiliation of being turned away because of their race.

In the Civil Rights Act of 1965, we affirmed through law for every citizen in this land the most basic rights of democracy—the right of a citizen to vote in an election in his country. In the five States where the Act had its greater impact, Negro voter registration has already more than doubled.

Now, with this bill, the voice of justice speaks again.

It proclaims that fair housing for all—all human begins who live in this country—is now a part of the American way of life.

We all know that the roots of injustice run deep. But violence cannot redress a solitary wrong, or remedy a single unfairness.

Of course, all America is outraged at the assassination of an outstanding Negro leader who was at that meeting that afternoon in the White House in 1966. And America is also outraged at the looting and the burning that defiles our democracy.

We just must put out shoulders together and put a stop to both. The time is here. Action must be now.

So, I would appeal to my fellow Americans by saying, the only real road to progress for free people is through the process of law and that is the road that America will travel.

I urge the Congress to enact the measures for social justice that I have recommended in some twenty messages. These messages went to the Congress in January and February of this year. They broke a precedent by being completed and delivered and read and printed. These measures provide more than $78 billion that I have urged the Congress to enact for major domestic programs for all Americans in the fiscal 1969 budget.

This afternoon, as we gather here in this historic room in the White House, I think we can take some heart that democracy's work is being done. In the Civil Rights Act of 1968 America does move forward and the bell of freedom rings out a little louder.

We have come some of the way, not near all of it. There is much yet to do. If Congress sees fit to act upon these twenty messages and some fifteen appropriations bills, I assure you that what remains to do be done will be recommended in ample time for you to do it after you have completed what is already before you.

Thank you very much.

HOW WELL DID YOU UNDERSTAND THIS SELECTION?

1. How does Johnson relate passage of the 1968 Civil Rights Acts to previous Civil Rights legislation?

2. Overall, what does Johnson think the 1968 Civil Rights Act is part of in American history and society?

3. What does Johnson urge Congress to do in the future?

THE NUCLEAR NON-PROLIFERATION TREATY

On July 1, 1968 the United States signed a treaty with the Soviet Union to prevent the spread of nuclear weaponS to countries that did not currently have them. This document, which was the result of prolonged negotiation between the United States and the Soviet Union at the height of the Cold War, was hailed throughout as an event that moved the world a step back from possible nuclear annihilation.

The States concluding this Treaty, hereinafter referred to as "Parties to the Treaty,"

Considering the devastation that would be visited upon all mankind by a nuclear war and the consequent need to make every effort to avert the danger of such a war to take measures to safeguard the security of peoples,

Believing that the proliferation of nuclear weapons would seriously enhance the danger of nuclear war,

In conformity with resolutions of the United Nations General Assembly calling for the conclusion of an agreement on the prevention of wider dissemination of nuclear weapon,

Undertaking to cooperate in facilitating the application of International Atomic Energy Agency safeguards on peaceful nuclear activities,

Expressing their support for research, development and other efforts to further the application, within the framework of the International Atomic Energy Agency safeguards system, of the principle of safeguarding effectively the flow of source and special fissionable materials by use of instruments and techniques at certain strategic points,

Affirming the principle that the benefits of peaceful applications of nuclear technology, including any technological by products which may be derived by nuclear-weapon States from the development of nuclear explosive devices, should be available for peaceful purposes to all Parties of the Treaty, whether nuclear-weapon or non-nuclear weapon States,

Convinced that, in furtherance of this principle, all Parties to the Treaty are entitled in the fullest possible exchange of scientific information for, and to contribute alone or in cooperation with other States to, the further development of the applications of atomic energy for peaceful purposes,

Declaring their intention to achieve at the earliest possible date the cessation of the nuclear arm race and to undertake effective measures in the direction of nuclear disarmament,

Urging the cooperation of all States in the attainment of this objective,

Recalling the determination expressed by the Parties to the 1963 Treaty banning nuclear weapon tests in the atmosphere, in outer space and under water in its Preamble to seek to achieve the discontinuance of all test explosions of nuclear weapon for all time and to continue negotiations to this end.

Desiring to further the easing of international tension and the strengthening of trust between State in order to facilitate the cessation of the manufacture of nuclear weapons, the liquidation of all their existing stockpiles, and the elimination from national arsenals of nuclear weapon and the means of their delivery pursuant to the Treaty on general and complete disarmament under strict and effective international control,

Recalling that, in accordance with the Charter of the United Nations, States must refrain in their international relations from the threat or use of force against the territorial integrity or political independence of any State, or in any other manner inconsistent with the Purposes of the United Nations, and that the establishment and maintenance of international peace inconsistent with the purposes of the United Nations, and that the establishment and maintenance of international peace and security are to be promoted with the least diversion for armaments of the world's human and economic resources.

Have agreed as follows:

Article I

Each nuclear-weapon State Party to the Treaty undertake not to transfer to any recipient whatsoever nuclear weapon or other nuclear explosive devices or control over such weapons or explosives devices directly, or indirectly; and not in any way to assist, encourages, or induce any non-nuclear weapon State to manufacture or otherwise acquire nuclear weapon or other nuclear explosive devices, or control over such weapons or explosives devices.

Article II

Each non-nuclear-weapon State Party to the Treaty undertake not to receive the transfer from any transferor whatsoever of nuclear weapon or other nuclear explosive devices or of control over such weapons or explosive devices directly, or indirectly; not to manufacture or otherwise acquire nuclear weapon or other nuclear devices; and not to seek or receive any assistance in the manufacture of nuclear weapons or other nuclear explosive devices.

Article III

1. Each non-nuclear-weapon State Party to the Treaty undertakes to accept safeguards, as set forth in an agreement to be negotiated and concluded with the International Atomic Energy Agency in accordance with the Statute of the International Atomic Energy Agency and the Agency's safeguard system, for the exclusive purpose of verification of the fulfillment of its obligations assumed under this Treaty with a view to preventing diversion of nuclear energy from peaceful uses to nuclear weapon or other nuclear explosive devices. Procedures for the safeguards required by this article shall be followed with respect to source or special fissionable material whether it is being produced, processed or used in any principal nuclear facility or is outside any such facility. The safeguards required by this article shall be applied to all source or special fissionable material in all peaceful nuclear activities within the territory of such State, under its jurisdiction, or carried out under its control anywhere.

2. Each State Party to the Treaty undertake not to provide: (a) source of special fissionable material, or (b) equipment or material especially designed or prepared for the processing, use or production of special fissionable material, to any non-nuclear-weapon State for peaceful purpose, unless the source or special fissionable material shall be subject to the safeguards required by this article.

3. The safeguards required by this article shall be implemented in a manner designed to comply with article IV of this treaty, and to avoid hampering the economic or technological development of the parties or international cooperation in the field of peaceful nuclear activities, including the international exchange of nuclear material and equipment for the processing, use or production of nuclear material for peaceful purposes in accordance with the provisions of this article and the principle of safeguarding set forth in the Preamble of the Treaty.

4. Non-nuclear-weapon states party to the treaty shall include agreements with the International Atomic Energy Agency to meet the requirements of this article either individually or together with other states in accordance with the statute of the International Atomic Energy Agency. Negotiation of such agreements shall commence within 180 days from the original entry into force of this treaty. For states depositing their instruments of ratification or accession after the 180-day period, negotiation of such agreements shall commence not later than the date of such deposit. Such agreements shall enter into force not later than eighteen months after the date of initiation of negotiations.

Article IV
1. Nothing in this treaty shall be interpreted as affecting the inalienable right of all the Parties to the Treaty to develop research, production and use of nuclear energy for peaceful purposes without discrimination and in conformity with articles I and II of this treaty.

2. All the parties to the treaty undertake to facilitate, and have the right to participate in, the fullest possible exchange of equipment, material and scientific and technological information for the peaceful uses of nuclear energy. Parties to the treaty in a position to do so shall also cooperate in contributing alone or together with other state or international organizations to the further development of the applications of nuclear energy for peaceful purpose, especially in the territories of non-nuclear-weapon States Party to the Treaty, with due consideration for the needs of the developing areas of the world.

Article V
Each party to the treaty undertakes to take appropriate measures to ensure that, in accordance with this treaty, under appropriate international observation and through appropriate international procedures, potential benefits from any peaceful applications of nuclear explosions will be made available to non-nuclear-weapon States Party to the Treaty on a nondiscriminatory basis and that the charge to such parties for the explosive devices used will be as low as possible and exclude any charge for research and development. Non-nuclear-weapon State Party to the Treaty shall be able to obtain such benefits, pursuit to a special international agreement or agreements, through an appropriate international body with adequate representation of non-nuclear-weapon states. Negotiations on this subject shall commence as soon as possible after the treaty enters into force. Non-nuclear-weapon States Party to the Treaty so desiring may also obtain such benefits pursuant to bilateral agreements.

Article VI
Each of the Parties to the Treaty undertakes to pursue negotiations in good faith on effective measures relating to cessation of the nuclear arms race at an early date and to nuclear disarmament, and on a treaty on general and complete disarmament under strict and effective international control.

Article VII
1. Any party to the treaty may propose amendments to this treaty. The text of any proposed amendment shall be submitted to the Depositary Government which shall circulate it to all parties to the treaty. Thereupon, if requested to do so by one-third or more of the parties to treaty, the Depositary Government shall convene a conference, to which they shall invite all the parties to the treaty, to consider such an amendment.

2. Any amendment to this treaty must be approved by a majority of the votes of all the Parties to the Treaty, including the votes of all nuclear weapon States Party to the Treaty and all other parties which, on the date the amendment is circulated, are members of the Board of Governors of the International Atomic Energy Agency. The amendment shall enter into force for each Party that deposits its instrument of ratification of the amendment upon the deposit such instrument of ratification of all nuclear-weapon States Party to the Treaty and all other parties which, on the date the amendment is circulated, are members of the board of Governors of the International Energy Agency. Thereafter, it shall enter into force for any other party upon the deposit of its instrument of ratification of the amendment.

3. Five years after the entry into force of this treaty, a conference of parties to the treaty shall be held in Geneva, Switzerland, in order to review the operation of this treaty with a view to assuring that the purpose of the Preamble and the provisions of the treaty are being realized. At intervals of five years thereafter, a majority of the Parties to the

Treaty may obtain, by submitting a proposal to this effect to the Depositary Government, the convening of further conferences with the same objective of reviewing the operation of the treaty.

Article IX

1. This treaty shall be open to all states for signature. Any state which does not sign the treaty before its entry into force in accordance with paragraph 3 of this article may accede to it at any time.

2. This treaty shall be subject to ratification by signatory states. Instrument of ratification and instrument of accession shall be deposited with the Government of the United States of America, the United Kingdom of Great Britain and Northern Ireland and the Union of Soviet Socialist Republics, which are hereby designated the Depositary Governments.

3. This treaty shall enter into force after its ratification by the state, the government of which are designated Depositaries of the Treaty, and forty other states signatory to this treaty and the deposit of their instruments of ratification. For the purpose of this treaty, a nuclear-weapon state is one which has manufactured and exploded a nuclear weapon or other nuclear explosive device prior to January 1, 1967.

4. For states whose instruments of ratification or accession are deposited subsequent to the entry force of this treaty, it shall enter into force on the date of the deposit of their instrument of ratification or accession.

5. The Depositary Governments shall promptly inform all signatory and acceding states of the date of each signature, the date of deposit of each instrument of ratification or of accession, the date of the entry into force of this treaty, and the date of receipt of any requests for convening a conference or other notices.

6. This treaty shall be registered by the Depositary Government pursuant to article 102 of the charter of the United Nations.

Article X

1. Each party shall in exercising its national sovereignty have the right to withdraw from the treaty if it decides that extraordinary events, related to the subject matter of this treaty, have jeopardized the supreme interests of its country. It shall give notice of such withdrawal to all other parties to the treaty and to the United Nations Security Council three months in advance. Such notice shall include a statement of the extraordinary events it regards as having jeopardized its supreme interest.

2. Twenty-five years after the entry into force of the treaty, a conference shall be convened to decide whether the treaty shall continue in force indefinitely, or shall be extended for an additional fixed period or periods. This decision shall be taken by a majority of the Parties to the Treaty.

Article XI

This treaty, the English, Russian, French, Spanish and Chinese texts of which are equally authentic, shall be deposited in the archives of the Depositary Governments. Duty certified copies of this treaty shall be transmitted by the Depositary Governments to the Governments of the signatory and acceding states.
IN WITNESS WHEREOF the authorized, have signed the treaty.

DONE in triplicate, at the cities of Washington, London and Moscow, this first day of July one thousand sixty-eight.

HOW WELL DID YOU UNDERSTAND THIS SELECTION?

1. What was the treaty designed to accomplish?

2. Why would the Soviet Union and the United States sign the treaty?

3. Over the years has the treaty generally been effective? Explain and support your answer with historical evidence.

4. What are the primary provisions of the treaty?

SELF TEST

MULTIPLE CHOICE: Circle the correct response. The correct answers are given at the end.

1. --------------------------------- was the Democratic presidential candidate assassinated shortly after he won the California Primary.
    a. George Wallace
    b. Herbert Humphrey
    c. Robert Kennedy
    d. Martin Luther King, Jr.

2. The leader of the Civil Rights Movement killed in Memphis, TN in 1968 was
    a. George Wallace
    b. Hubert Humphrey
    c. Robert Kennedy
    d. Martin Luther King, Jr.

3. A student revolt at _____ in New York City captured 1968 in a microcosm.
    a. Columbia University
    b. New York Community and Technical College
    c. New York City College
    d. Radcliff College

4. The American naval vessel captured by North Korea in 1968 was the
   a. U.S.S Colorado
   b. U.S.S Pueblo
   c. U.S.S Minsk
   d. U.S.S Arizona

5. American soldiers massacred Vietnamese civilians at the village of
   a. Saigon
   b. My Lai
   c. Dien Bien Pu
   d. Buena Vista

6. Which one of the following was not one of the groups of LBJ advisor called the "Wise Old Men?"
   a. Robert Kennedy
   b. Clarke Clifford
   c. McGeorge Bundy
   d. Abe Fortas

7. The African American leader _____ told a crowd of people angry over Martin Luther King's assassination to "go home and get your guns."
   a. H. Rap Brown
   b. Stokely Carmichael
   c. Malcolm X
   d. Jesse Jackson

8. Richard Nixon, campaigning for President in 1968, maintained that the violence rocking America stemmed from
   a. Permissive parents who had mollycoddled the young
   b. Greed perpetuated from immersion in a corporate culture
   c. Schools that used corporal punishment
   d. An American culture that stressed individualism

9. George Wallace was the nominee of what political party in 1968?
   a. The Republican Party
   b. The Democratic Party
   c. The Green Party
   d. The American Party

10. The Democratic Party nominated Vice President _____ as its presidential candidate in the 1968 election
   a. Lyndon Johnson
   b. Richard Nixon
   c. Herbert Humphrey
   d. George Wallace

Answers: 1-C; 2-D; 3-A; 4-B; 5-B; 6-A; 7-B; 8-A; 9-D; 10-C

ESSAYS:

1. Explain why 1968 was such a violent year in American History

2. What factors allowed Richard Nixon to win the 1968 presidential election?

3. Why was there so much political activity and unrest among American's youth in 1968?

4. What role did racism play in destabilizing American society in 1968?

OPTIONAL ACTIVITIES:

1. Pretend that you were alive in 1968. Describe your feelings on the following: the Vietnam War; Robert Kennedy's assassination; Martin Luther King's Death; the Tet offensive; Lyndon Johnson's Decision not to seek reelection; the election of Richard Nixon

2. As an 18 year old American male, write a letter to your local draft board explaining why you fled to Canada rather than serve in the American military during the Vietnam War.

3. Stage a mock debate between Hubert Humphrey, George Wallace, Robert Kennedy, Eugene McCarthy, and Richard Nixon.

WEB SITE LISTINGS:

Vietnam War:
        http://www.fsmitha.com/h2/ch26.htm
        http://members.aol.com/veterans/warlib6v.htm

John F. Kennedy
    Assassination:
        http://mcadams.posc.mu.edu/home.htm
    Biography & resources:
        http://www.ipl.org/div/potus/jfkennedy.html

Lyndon B. Johnson
    Biographical Information:
        http://www.potus.com/lbjohnson.html
        http://www.lbjlib.utexas.edu/
    Vietnam:
        http://www.cnn.com/US/9702/15/lbj.vietnam/

The Sixties
        http://history.acusd.edu/gen/classes/20th/sixties.html
        http://kclibrary.nhmccd.edu/decade60.html
        http://www.ukans.edu/history/VL/USA/ERAS/20TH/1960s.html
        http://www.hist.umn.edu/~hist20c/internet/1960s.htm

Chapter Twenty-six

NIXON - FORD- CARTER YEARS

Most Americans were happy to see the tumultuous years of the 1960s end. 1968 had been a particularly violent year, and Americans generally wanted to leave the violence behind and work toward a brighter, more stable future. Unfortunately, many aspects of the 1960s carried over into the 1970s, including the violence. Former presidential candidate George Wallace was seriously wounded in a 1972 assassination attempt. The Cold War continued and despite the signing of treaties with the Soviet Union to place ceilings on the number of nuclear weapon both sides could have, the arms race showed little sign of abating. Americans in general feared atomic Armageddon and lived in constant fear that a regional conflict somewhere in the world would escalate into a nuclear confrontation with the Soviet Union.

Nixon and his Secretary of State Henry Kissinger began the policy of détente that resulted in a relaxation of tension between the United States and the Soviet Union. Nixon and Kissinger were successful with détente largely because of a policy of triangulation in which the United States cozied up to Communist China in order to win concessions from the Soviet Union. In February 1972, Nixon visited the People's Republic of China, beginning a process that ultimately resulted in formal recognition of the Communist government of China. The triangulation strategy was successful. The Soviet Union, fearing a possible alliance between the United States and Red China, agreed to sign the Strategic Arms Limitation Treaty (SALT I) in May 1972. Eventually, more treaties designed to limit the size and number of nuclear weapons would also be negotiated. Détente also resulted in cultural exchange programs between the United States and Communist countries. Athletes, entertainers, and students from the Soviet Union and Communist China visited the United States to study and perform, and Americans in turn visited various Communist nations, including Red China and the Soviet Union.

Nixon and Kissinger, however, upset leaders and people in Third World nations by pursuing policies beneficial to American interests at the expense of the Third World. Efforts to curb revolution, stifle nationalistic movements, and support of dictators in impoverished countries caused many Americans to question the policy and motives of the United States. Some Americans, fearing perhaps another Vietnam type war, questioned whether the United States should interfere in the affairs of other countries to suit American interest. The United States continued its unwavering support of Israel, which upon two occasions caused the Organization of Petroleum Exporting Countries (OPEC), dominated by Middle Eastern Islamic nations hostile to a Jewish state in the Middle East, to impose an oil embargo on the United States. During both embargo periods Americans faced gasoline shortages, which caused long lines at service stations, the imposition of government fuel rationing programs, and increased prices at the pump. Despite the embargos, American policy in the Middle East changed little.

The oil embargos worsened an economic mess Nixon inherited from Lyndon Johnson. When oil prices rose, inflation spirited out of control as manufacturing and transportation companies had to increase prices and workers demanded wage increases to keep pace with rising prices. Compounding America's economic problems was competition from foreign manufacturers, high unemployment, and a decline in the nation's Gross Domestic Product. In an attempt to stimulate exports Nixon then ordered a wage and price freeze that did little to cure American's economic woes.

Nixon's domestic programs had limited success. Congress failed to enact his plan to reform welfare but did expand Medicare, Medicaid, and the Jobs Corps program. Despite opposition from big business, Nixon signed legislation to protect the environment and enhance worker safety. Unlike Lyndon Johnson, Nixon was not committed to Civil Rights for American minorities and ending poverty. Many gains in these areas were rolled back by Republican officials and the Office of Economic Opportunity, the governmental agency that largely oversaw the War on Poverty, was eliminated. Nixon also appointed conservative judges to the Supreme and lower federal courts, which ended the judicial activism that characterized the 1960s.

Nixon faced legal and political problems as a result of the Watergate Scandal that his administration was embroiled in after burglars were apprehended following a break-in at the headquarters of George McGovern, Nixon's Democratic opponent in the 1972 election. Eventually, evidence that Nixon had authorized a cover up of the break-in caused the House of Representatives to draw up charges of impeachment against the president for obstructing justice and abusing power. Facing impeachment, including a trial by the Senate, and likely removal from office if convicted, Nixon resigned on August 8, 1974. Thus far, he is the only American president to resign from office before his term was complete.

Since Nixon's elected Vice President Spiro Agnew had previously resigned over allegations of tax evasion and accepting bribes from business while serving as Maryland's governor, Gerald Ford, former House Minority Leader, who Nixon had named as Agnew's replacement, assumed the presidency. Shortly after becoming president, Ford pardoned Nixon of any crimes he had committed as a result of the Watergate Scandal. Ford's actions, which he believed would help heal the nation's wounds from Watergate, caused many to question his motives and led to allegations of the "Buddy Deal" between Nixon and Ford. Even though both Ford and Nixon denied the existence of a Buddy Deal, a large number of Americans believed that Nixon had named Ford as Agnew's successor in return for an agreement to pardon Nixon once he resigned and Ford became president. Regardless of whether the Buddy Deal existed, Ford's Pardon of Nixon forever linked him to the corruption of Republicans involved in the Watergate break-in and subsequent cover-up.

Ford was unable to tame the inflation and other economic problems inherited from the Nixon administration and as a result, lost to Democrat James Earl Carter in the 1976 election. Although Carter's honesty and hard work restored a degree of integrity to a White House tainted by scandal, his lack of government experience hampered efforts to tame inflation and solve economic problems left over from the Nixon and Ford administrations. In an effort to wean America from its dependence on Middle Eastern oil Carter created the Energy Security Corporation and charged the agency with developing an alternative fuel to power America's automobiles. Despite the expenditure of more than one billion dollars, the Energy Security Corporation's effort to create synthetic fuel was largely a failure. America remained dependent on Middle Eastern oil and as a result, Carter could not end the "stagflation" that gripped the American economy.

Both Ford and Carter continued Nixon's policy of détente. Both presidents attempted to slow down the arms race and negotiated several agreements that improved relations with China and the Soviet Union. Carter was responsible for getting Israel and Egypt to sign the Camp David Accords, which began a peace process in the Middle East that continues to this day. In return for land, Egypt recognized Israel's right to exist as a sovereign nation. The Soviet invasion of Afghanistan in 1979 and the capture of American hostage at the American embassy in Iran created problems for the Carter administration. Carter's seemingly incompetence in securing the release of the hostages caused problems for him during his reelection attempt in 1980 and paved the way for a conservative resurgence with the election of Ronald Reagan.

IDENTIFICATION: Briefly describe each term.

William L. Calley

Richard Nixon

Henry Kissinger

The Silent Majority

The Southern Strategy

John Mitchell

Affirmative Action

Stagflation

George McGovern

Arthur Bremer

Watergate

Dirty Tricks

Thomas Eagleton

OPEC

Nixon Doctrine

Salvador Allende Gossens

Détente

Jimmy Carter

Leonid Brezhnev

SALT I

Kent State

Fragging

VVAW

The Pentagon Papers

Daniel Ellsburg

White House Plumbers

Christmas Bombings

Le Duc Tho

War Powers Act

Gerald Ford

Operation Frequent Wind

Khmer Rogue

G. Gordon Liddy

Bob Woodward

Howard Hunt

Carl Bernstein

James W. McCord

Sam Ervin

John Dean

John Sirica

Archibald Cox

Alexander Butterfield

Spiro Agnew

Saturday Night Massacre

Elliott Richardson

Robert Bork

Leon Jaworski

The United States v. Nixon

Federal Election Campaign Act of 1974

Federal Election Commission

Church Committee Hearings

Project Bluebird

James Schlesinger

WIN

Ronald Reagan

Helsinki Accords

Three Mile Island

The Great Inflation

Panama Canal Treaty

Camp David Accords

Anwar Sadat

Menachem Begin

Ayatollah Rubollah Khomeini

Roe v. Wade

Moral Majority

Proposition 13

Edward Kennedy

Steve Dahl

THINK ABOUT:

1. What were the major problems the United States confronted during the Nixon, Ford and Carter years?

2. Did the United States undergo a permanent economic, political, and spiritual decline in the 1970s? Why or why not? Support your answer with historical evidence.

3. What impact did the following have on American history? The Vietnam War? Watergate? The Iranian Hostage Crisis? The Energy Crisis?

JOHN KERRY "STATEMENT"

By 1970 many Americans were tired of the war in Vietnam and wanted the United States to reach a diplomatic settlement that would "bring our boys home." Even Vietnam military veterans began calling for an end to the conflict. The Vietnam Veterans against the War held its Winter Soldier Investigation, a mock trial in which Vietnam Veterans spoke about human rights violations they had seen in Vietnam. One member of the group, future U.S. Senator and Democratic president candidate John Kerry, was invited to speak to the Senate Foreign Relations Committee on April 23, 1971. Kerry testified that the war was immoral and a violation of American principles.

April 23, 1971
Washington, D.C.
U.S. Senate Committee of Foreign Relations, Legislative Proposals Relating to the War in Southeast Asia

I would like to talk on behalf of all those veterans and say that several months ago in Detroit we had an investigation at which over 150 honorably discharged, and many very highly decorated, veterans testified to war crimes committed in Southeast Asia. These were not isolated incidents but crimes committed on a day-to-day basis with the full awareness of officers at all levels of command. It is impossible to describe to you exactly what did happen in Detroit - the emotions in the room and the feelings of the men who were reliving their experiences in Vietnam. They relived the absolute horror of what this country, in a sense, made them do.

They told stories that at times they had personally raped, cut off ears, cut off heads, taped wires from portable telephones to human genitals and turned up the power, cut off limbs, blown up bodies, randomly shot at civilians, razed villages in fashion reminiscent of Ghengis Khan, shot cattle and dogs for fun, poisoned food stocks, and generally ravaged the countryside of South Vietnam in addition to the normal ravage of war and the normal and very particular ravaging which is done by the applied bombing power of this country.

We call this investigation the Winter Soldier Investigation. The term Winter Soldier is a play on words of Thomas Paines in 1776 when he spoke of the Sunshine Patriots and summertime soldiers who deserted at Valley Forge because the going was rough.

We who have come here to Washington have come here because we feel we have to be winter soldiers now. We could come back to this country, we could be quiet, we could hold our silence, we could not tell what went on in Vietnam, but we feel because of what threatens this country, not the reds, but the crimes which we are committing that threaten it, that we have to speak out....

In our opinion and from our experience, there is nothing in South Vietnam which could happen that realistically threatens the United States of America. And to attempt to justify the loss of one American life in Vietnam, Cambodia or Laos by linking such loss to the preservation of freedom, which those misfits supposedly abuse, is to us the height of criminal hypocrisy, and it is that kind of hypocrisy which we feel has torn this country apart.

We found that not only was it a civil war, an effort by a people who had for years been seeking their liberation from any colonial influence whatsoever, but also we found that the Vietnamese whom we had enthusiastically molded after our own image were hard put to take up the fight against the threat we were supposedly saving them from.

We found most people didn't even know the difference between communism and democracy. They only wanted to work in rice paddies without helicopters strafing them and bombs with napalm burning their villages and tearing their country apart. They wanted everything to do with the war, particularly with this foreign presence of the United States of America, to leave them alone in peace, and they practiced the art of survival by siding with whichever military force was present at a particular time, be it Viet Cong, North Vietnamese or American.

We found also that all too often American men were dying in those rice paddies for want of support from their allies. We saw first hand how monies from American taxes were used for a corrupt dictatorial regime. We saw that many people in this country had a one-sided idea of who was kept free by the flag, and blacks provided the highest percentage of casualties. We saw Vietnam ravaged equally by American bombs and search and destroy missions, as well as by Viet Cong terrorism - and yet we listened while this country tried to blame all of the havoc on the Viet Cong.

We rationalized destroying villages in order to save them. We saw America lose her sense of morality as she accepted very coolly a My Lai and refused to give up the image of American soldiers who hand out chocolate bars and chewing gum.

We learned the meaning of free fire zones, shooting anything that moves, and we watched while America placed a cheapness on the lives of Orientals.

We watched the United States falsification of body counts, in fact the glorification of body counts. We listened while month after month we were told the back of the enemy was about to break. We fought using weapons against "oriental human beings." We fought using weapons against those people which I do not believe this country would dream of using were we fighting in the European theater. We watched while men charged up hills because a general said that hill has to be taken, and after losing one platoon or two platoons they marched away to leave the hill for reoccupation by the North Vietnamese. We watched pride allow the most unimportant baffles to be blown into extravaganzas, because we couldn't lose, and we couldn't retreat, and because it didn't matter how many American bodies were lost to prove that point, and so there were Hamburger Hills and Khe Sanhs and Hill Sis and Fire Base 6s, and so many others.

Now we are told that the men who fought there must watch quietly while American lives are lost so that we can exercise the incredible arrogance of Vietnamizing the Vietnamese.

Each day to facilitate the process by which the United States washes her hands of Vietnam someone has to give up his life so that the United States doesn't have to admit something that the entire world already knows, so that we can't say that we have made a mistake. Someone has to die so that President Nixon won't be, and these are his words, "the first President to lose a war."

We are asking Americans to think about that because how do you ask a man to be the last man to die in Vietnam? How do you ask a man to be the last man to die for a mistake. We are here in Washington to say that the problem of this war is not just a question of war and diplomacy. It is part and parcel of everything that we are trying as human beings to communicate to people in this country—the question of racism which is rampant in the military, and so many other questions such as the use of weapons; the hypocrisy in our taking umbrage at the Geneva Conventions and using that as justification for a continuation of this war when we are more guilty than any other body of violations of those Geneva Conventions; in the use of free fire zones, harassment interdiction fire, search and destroy missions, the bombings, the torture of prisoners, all accepted policy by many units in South Vietnam. That is what we are trying to say. It is part and parcel of everything.

An American Indian friend of mine who lives in the Indian Nation of Alcatraz put it to me very succinctly. He told me how as a boy on an Indian reservation he had watched television and he used to cheer the cowboys when they came in and shot the Indians, and then suddenly one day he stopped in Vietnam and he said, "my God, I am doing to these people the very same thing that was done to my people," and he stopped. And that is what we are trying to say, that we think this thing has to end.

We are here to ask, and we are here to ask vehemently, where are the leaders of our country? Where is the leadership? We're here to ask where are McNamara, Rostow, Bundy, Gilpatrick, and so many others? Where are they now that we, the men they sent off to war, have returned? These are the commanders who have deserted their troops. And there is no more serious crime in the laws of war. The Army says they never leave their wounded. The marines say they never even leave their dead. These men have left all the casualties and retreated behind a pious shield of public rectitude. They've left the real stuff of their reputations bleaching behind them in the sun in this country....

We wish that a merciful God could wipe away our own memories of that service as easily as this administration

436

has wiped away their memories of us. But all that they have done and all that they can do by this denial is to make more clear than ever our own determination to undertake one last mission to search out and destroy the last vestige of this barbaric war, to pacify our own hearts, to conquer the hate and fear that have driven this country these last ten years and more. And more. And so when thirty years from now our brothers go down the street without a leg, without an arm, or a face, and small boys ask why, we will be able to say "Vietnam" and not mean a desert, not a filthy obscene memory, but mean instead where America finally turned and where soldiers like us helped it in the turning.

John Kerry, "Statement," April 23, 1971, Senate Committee on Foreign Relations, *Legislative Proposals Relating to the War in Southeast Asia: Hearings* April 20, 21, 22, 28, 1971 (Washington: Government Printing Office, 1971), pp. 180-210.

HOW WELL DID YOU UNDERSTAND THIS SELECTION?

1. Does Kerry suggest racism played a role in Vietnam? Explain and support your answer with evidence from the text.

2. How does Kerry portray American involvement in the Vietnam War?

3. Where does the term "Winter Soldiers" originate? What does the term mean?

4. What is the purpose of Kerry's statement?

*After the release of the **Pentagon Papers**, Nixon organized a secret unit within the White House to discredit anyone who leaked confidential or damaging information to the press. E. Howard Hunt, a veteran of the CIA, and G. Gordon Liddy, a former FBI agent, headed the new unit called the "plumbers." To ensure Nixon's re-election in 1972, Attorney General John Mitchell organized the Committee to Re-elect the President (CREEP). They engaged in unethical practices against the Democratic Party. Under the direction of Liddy, five men broke into the Democratic National Headquarters at the Watergate complex. The men were arrested and convicted along with Liddy and Hunt. At their sentencing, it became evident that White House aides had assisted the break-in. When it came to light that the president had been complicit in attempting to cover up the break-in, and that tapes of Nixon's conversations existed, the court ordered Nixon to present the tapes. Nixon resisted. What follows are excerpts from recorded conversations between President Nixon and his advisors in 1972-1973.*

June 23, 1972
The White House

HALDEMAN:Now, on the investigation you know the Democratic break-in thing, we're back in the problem area because the FBI is not under control, because [Director Patrick] Gray doesn't exactly know how to control it and they have-their investigation is now leading into some productive areas. They've been able to trace the money-not through the money itself-but through the bank sources-the banker. And it goes in some directions we don't want it to go. Ah, also there have been some (other) things-like an informant came in off the street to the FBI in Miami who was a photographer or has a friend who is a photographer who developed some films through this guy [Bernard] Barker and the alms had pictures of Democratic National Committee letterhead documents and things. So it's things like that that are filtering in. . . . [John] Mitchell came up with yesterday, and John Dean analyzed very carefully last night and concludes, concurs now with Mitchell's recommendation that the only way to solve this . . . is for us to have [CIA Assistant Director Vernon Walters call Pat Gray and just say, "Stay to hell out of this-this is ah, [our] business here. We don't want you to go any further on it." That's not an unusual development, and ah, that would take care of it.
PRESIDENT: What about Pat Gray-you mean Pat Gray doesn't want to?
HALDEMAN: Pat does want to. He doesn't know how to, and he doesn't have any basis for doing it. Given this, he will then have the basis. He'll call [FBI Assistant Director Mark Felt in, and the two of them-and Mark Felt wants to cooperate because he's ambitious-
PRESIDENT: Yeah.
HALDEMAN: He'll call him in and say, "We've got the signal from across the river to put the hold on this." And that will fit rather well because the FBI agents who are working the case, at this point, feel that's what it is.
PRESIDENT: This is CIA? They've traced the money? Who'd they trace it to?
HALDEMAN: Well, they've traced it to a name, but they haven't gotten to the guy yet.
PRESIDENT: Would it be somebody here?
HALDEMAN: Ken Dahlberg.
PRESIDENT: Who the hell is Ken Dahlberg?
HALDEMAN: He gave $25,000 in Minnesota and, ah, the check went directly to this guy Barker.
PRESIDENT: It isn't from the Committee though, from [Maurice] Stans?
HALDEMAN: Yeah. It is. It's directly traceable and there's some more through some Texas people that went to the Mexican bank which can also be traced to the Mexican bank-they'll get their names today.
PRESIDENT: Well, I mean, there's no way-I'm just thinking if they don't cooperate, what do they say? That they were approached by the Cubans? That's what Dahlberg has to say, the Texans too.
HALDEMAN: Well, if they will. But then we're relying on more and more people all the time. That's the problem and they'll [the FBI] . . . stop if we could take this other route.
PRESIDENT: All right.

HALDEMAN: [Mitchell and Dean) say the only way to do that is from White House instructions. And it's got to be to [CIA Director Richard] Helms and to-ah, what's his name?. . . Walters.

PRESIDENT: Walters.

HALDEMAN: And the proposal would be that... (John) Ehrlichman and I call them in, and say, ah-

PRESIDENT: All right, fine. How do you call him in-I mean you just-well, we protected Helms from one hell of a lot of things.

HALDEMAN: That's what Ehrlichman says.

PRESIDENT: Of course; this [Howard] Hunt [business.] That will uncover a lot of things. You open that scab there's a hell of a lot of things and we just feel that it would be very detrimental to have this thing go any further. This involves these Cubans, Hunt, and a lot of hanky-panky that we have nothing to do with ourselves. Well, what the hell, did Mitchell know about this?

HALDEMAN: I think so. I don't think he knew the details, but I think he knew.

PRESIDENT: He didn't know how it was going to be handled though-with Dahlberg and the Texans and so forth? Well who was the asshole that did? Is it [C. Gordon] Liddy? Is that the fellow? He must be a little nuts!

HALDEMAN: He is.

PRESIDENT: I mean he just isn't well screwed on, is he? Is that the problem?

HALDEMAN: No, but he was under pressure, apparently, to get more information, and as he got more pressure, he pushed the people harder.

PRESIDENT: Pressure from Mitchell?

HALDEMAN: Apparently....

PRESIDENT: All right, fine, I understand it all. We won't second-guess Mitchell and the rest. Thank God it wasn't [special White House counsel Charles] Colson.

HALDEMAN: The FBI interviewed Colson yesterday. They determined that would be a good thing to do. To have him take an interrogation, which he did, and the FBI guys working the case concluded that there were one or two possibilities-one, that this was a White House (they don't think that there is anything at the Election Committee) they think it was either a White House operation and they had some obscure reasons for it-non-political, or it was a-Cuban [operation] and (involved] the CIA. And after their interrogation of Colson yesterday, they concluded it was not the White House, but are now convinced it is a CIA thing, so the CIA turnoff would-

PRESIDENT: Well, not sure of their analysis, I'm not going to get that involved. I'm (unintelligible).

HALDEMAN: No, sir, we don't want you to.

PRESIDENT: You call them in.

HALDEMAN: Good deal.

PRESIDENT: Play it tough. That's the way they play it and that's the way we are going to play it.

PRESIDENT: O.K...Just say (unintelligible) very bad to have this fellow Hunt, ah, he knows too damned much. . . . If it gets out that this is all involved the Cuba thing, it would be a fiasco. It would make the CIA look bad, it's going to make Hunt look bad, and it is likely to blow the whole Bay of Pigs thing which we think would be very unfortunate—both for CIA, and for the country, at this time, and for American foreign policy. Just tell him to lay off Don't you [think] so?

HALDEMAN: Yep. That's the basis to do it on. Just leave it at that.

September 15, 1972

PRESIDENT: We are all in it together. This is a war. We take a few shots and it will be over. We will give them a few shots and it will be over. Don't worry. I wouldn't want to be on the other side right now. Would you?

DEAN: Along that line, one of the things I've tried to do, I have begun to keep notes on a lot of people who are emerging as less than our friends because this will be over some day and we shouldn't forget the way some of them have treated us.

PRESIDENT: I want the most comprehensive notes on all those who tried to do us in. They didn't have to do it. If we had had a very dose election and they were playing the other side I would understand this. No—they were doing this quite deliberately and they are asking for it and they are going to get it. We have not used the power in this first four years, as you know. We have never used it. We have not used the Bureau, and we have not used the Justice Department, but things are going to change now. And they are either going to do it right or go.

DEAN: What an exciting prospect.

PRESIDENT: Thanks. It has to be done. We have been (adjective deleted) fools for us to come into this election campaign and not do anything with regard to the Democratic Senators who are running, et cetera. And who the hell are they after? They are after us. It is absolutely ridiculous. It is not going to be that way any more.

March 13, 1973

PRESIDENT: How much of a crisis? It will be-am thinking in terms of-the point is, everything is a crisis. (expletive deleted) it is a terrible lousy thing it will remain a crisis among the upper intellectual types, the soft heads, our own, to – Republicans and the Democrats and the rest. Average people won't think it is much of a crisis unless it affects them. (unintelligible)

DEAN: I think it will pass. I think after the (Senator Sam) Ervin hearings, they are going to find so much - there will be some new revelations. I don't think that the thing will get out of hand. I have no reason to believe it will.

PRESIDENT: As a matter of fact, it is just a bunch of (characterization deleted). We don't object to such damn things anyway. On, and on and on. No, I tell you this it is the last gasp of our hardest opponents. They've just got to have something to squeal about it.

DEAN: It is the only thing they have to squeal-

PRESIDENT: (Unintelligible) They are going to lie around and squeal. They are having a hard time now. They got the hell kicked out of them in the election. There is not a Watergate around in this town, not so much our opponents even the media, but the basic thing is the establishment. The establishment is dying, and so they've got to show that despite the successes we have had in foreign policy and in the election, they've got to show that it is just wrong, just because of this. They are trying to use this as the whole thing.

March 21, 1973

DEAN: So that is it. That is the extent of the knowledge. So where are the soft spots on this? Well, first of all, there is the problem of the continued blackmail which will not only go on now, but it will go on while these people are in prison, and it will compound the obstruction of justice situation. It will cost money. It is dangerous. People around here are not pros at this sort of thing. This is the sort of thing Mafia people can do: washing money, getting dean money, and things like that. We just don't know about those things, because we are not criminals and not used to dealing in that business.

PRESIDENT: That's right.

DEAN: It is a tough thing to know how to do.

PRESIDENT: Maybe it takes a gang to do that.

DEAN: That's right. There is a real problem as to whether we could even do it. Plus there is a real problem in raising money. Mitchell has been working on raising some money. He is one of the ones with the most to lose. But there is no denying the fact that the White House, in Ehrlichman, Haldeman and Dean, are involved in some of the early money decisions.

PRESIDENT: How much money do you need?

DEAN: I would say these people are going to cost over a million dollars over the next two years.

PRESIDENT: We could get that. On the money, if you need the money you could get that. You could get a minion dollars. You could get it in cash. I know where it could be gotten. It is not easy, but it could be done. But the question is who the hell would handle it? Any ideas on that?

DEAN: That's right. Well, I think that is something that Mitchell ought to be charged with.

PRESIDENT: I would think so too.

From *Hearings before the Committee on The Judiciary*, House of Representatives, 93rd Congress, 2nd Session (Government Printing Office, Washington, D.C., 1974).

440

HOW WELL DID YOU UNDERSTAND THIS SELECTION?

1. Was Nixon guilty of criminal activity? Support your answer with evidence from the recorded conversation.

2. Why might Nixon have had a recording system installed in the White House?

3. How did Nixon and his advisors propose to handle the scandal?

4. What particular crimes did Nixon and his aides commit?

PRESIDENTIAL TELEVISION ADDRESS

By spring of 1973, largely due to excellent reporting by Carl Bernstein and Bob Woodward, the Watergate Scandal had escalated to the point that Nixon's presidency was threatened. In an attempt to prevent the scandal from broadening, President Nixon spoke to the American public in a televised address. Nixon apparently hoped to stop the investigation of criminal activity within his administration by talking directly to the American people, explaining actions taken by his administration to deal with the scandal. The text of Nixon's address appears below.

April 30, 1973, Washington, D.C.
PRESIDENT RICHARD M. NIXON

I want to talk to you tonight from my heart on a subject of deep concern to every American.

In recent months, members of my Administration and officials of the Committee for the Re-election of the President – including some of my closest friends and most trusted aides – have been charged with involvement in what has come to be known as the Watergate Affair. These include charges of illegal activity during and proceeding the 1972 Presidential election and charges that responsible officials participated in efforts to cover that illegal activity.

The inevitable result of these charges has been to raise serious questions about the integrity of the White House itself. Tonight I wish to address those questions.

Last June 17, while I was in Florida trying to get a few day's rest after my visit to Moscow, I first learned from news reports of the Watergate break-in. I was appalled at this senseless, illegal action, and I was shocked to learn that employees of the Re-election Committee were apparently among those guilty. I immediately ordered an investigation by appropriate government authorities. On September 15, as you will recall, indictments were brought against seven defendants in the case.

As the investigations went forward, I repeatedly asked those conducting the investigation whether there was any reason to believe that members of my Administration were in any way involved. I received repeated assurances that there were not. Because of these continuing reassurances – because I believed the reports I was getting, because I had

441

faith in the persons from whom I was getting them - I discounted the stories in the press that appeared to implicate members of my Administration or other officials of the campaign committee.

Until March of this year, I remained convinced that the denials were true and that the charges of involvement by members of the White House staff were false. The comments I made by my Press Secretary on my behalf, were based on the information provided to us at the time we made those comments. However, new information then came to me which persuaded me that there was a real possibility that some of these charges were true, and suggesting further that there had been an effort to conceal the facts both from the public, from you, and from me.

As a result, on March 21, I personally assumed the responsibility for coordinating intensive new inquiries into the matter, and I personally ordered those conducting the investigations to get all the facts and to report them directly to me, right here in this office.

I again ordered that all persons in the Government or at the Re-election Committee should cooperate fully with the FBI, the prosecutors and the Grand Jury. I also ordered that anyone who refused to cooperate in telling the truth would be asked to resign from government service. And, with ground rules adopted that would preserve the basic constitutional separation of powers between the Congress and the Presidency, I directed that members of the White House staff should appear and testify voluntarily under oath before the Senate Committee investigating Watergate.

I was determined that we should get to the bottom of the matter, and that the truth should fully brought out – no matter who was involved.

At the same time, I was determined not to take precipitate action, and to avoid, if at all possible, any action that would appear to reflect on innocent people. I wanted to be fair. But I knew that in the final analysis, the integrity of this office – public faith in the integrity of this office – would have to take priority over all personal considerations.

Today, in one of the most difficult decisions of my Presidency, I accepted the resignations of two of my closest associates in the White House – Bob Haldeman, John Ehrlichman – two of the finest public servants it has been my privilege to know.

I want to stress that in accepting these resignations, I mean to leave no implication whatever of personal wrongdoing on their part, and I leave no implication tonight of implication on the part of others who have been charged in this matter. But in matters as sensitive as guarding the integrity of our democratic process, it is essential not only that rigorous legal and ethical standards be observed, but also that the public, you, have the total confidence that they are both being observed and enforced by those in authority and particularly by the President of the United States. They agree with me that this move was necessary in order to restore that confidence.

Because Attorney General Kleindienst – through a distinguished public servant, my personal friend for 20 years, with no personal involvement whatever in this matter – has been a close personal and professional associate of some of those who are involved in this case, he and I both felt that it was also necessary to name a new Attorney General.

The Counsel to the President, John Dean, has also resigned.

As the new Attorney General, I have today named Elliot Richardson, a man of unimpeachable integrity and rigorously high principle. I have directed him to do everything necessary to ensure that the Department of Justice has the confidence and trust of every law abiding person in this country.

I have given him absolute authority to make all decisions bearing upon the prosecution of the Watergate case and related matters. I have instructed him that if he should consider it appropriate, he has the authority to name a special supervising prosecutor for matters arising out of the case.

Whatever may appear to have been the case before – whatever improper activities may yet be discovered in connection with this whole sordid affair – I want the American people, I want you to know beyond the shadow of a doubt that during my terms as President, justice will be pursued fairly, fully, and impartially, no matter who is involved. This office is a sacred trust and I am determined to be worthy of that trust.

Looking back at history of this case, two questions arise:

How could it have happened?

Who is to blame?

Political commentators have correctly observed that during my 27 years in politics, I have always previously insisted on running my own campaigns for office.

But 1972 presented a very different situation. In both domestic and foreign policy, 1972 was a year of crucially important decisions, of intense negotiations, of vital new directions, particularly in working toward the goal which has been my overriding concern throughout my political career – the goal of bringing peace to America and peace to the world.

That is why I decided, as the 1972 campaign approached, that the Presidency should come first and politics second. To the maximum extent possible, therefore, I sought to delegate campaign operations, and to remove the day-to-day campaign decisions from the President's office and from the White House. I also, as you recall, severely limited the number of my own campaign appearances.

Who, then, is to blame for what happened in this case?

For specific criminal actions by specific individuals, those who committed those actions, must, of course, beat the liability and pay the penalty.

For the fact that alleged improper actions took place within the White House or within my campaign organization, the easiest course would be for me to blame those to whom I delegated the responsibility to run the campaign. But that would be cowardly thing to do.

I will not place the blame on subordinates – on people whose zeal exceeded their judgement, and who may have done wrong in a cause they deeply believed to be right.

In any organization, the men at the top must bear the responsibility. That responsibility, therefore, belongs here, in this office. I accept that. And I pledge to you tonight, from this office, that I will do everything in my power to ensure that the guilty are brought to justice, and that such abuses are purged from our political processes in the years to come, long after I have left this office....

....I love America. I deeply believe that America is the hope of the world, and I know that in the quality and wisdom of the leadership America gives lies the only hope for millions of people all over the world, that they can live their lives in peace and freedom. We must be worthy of that hope, in every sense of the word. Tonight, I ask for your prayers to help me in everything that I do throughout the days of my Presidency to be worthy of their hopes and of yours.

God bless America and God bless each and every one of you.

HOW WELL DID YOU UNDERSTAND THIS SELECTION?

1. How does Nixon explain the Watergate Scandal to the American public? Is his explanation credible? Why or why not? Use historical evidence to support your answer.

2. Who does Nixon blame the Watergate Scandal on?

3. Based on your knowledge of the Watergate Scandal, is Nixon telling the American people the truth? Why or why not? Support your answer with historical evidence?

On August 8, 1974, President Nixon resigned rather than face impeachment over the Watergate Scandal. Nixon's resignation, however, did not mean that Watergate had ended. Special Prosecution Leon Jawoski continued the investigation. His task was to determine whether enough evidence existed to indict Nixon on criminal charges for ordering the break-in of the Democratic National Headquarters and for involvement in the cover-up. On August 9, 1974, Carl B. Feldbaum and Peter M. Kreindler, attorneys working for the Justice Department, sent Jaworski the following memorandum discussing the case against Nixon.

DEPARTMENT OF JUSTICE
MEMORANDUM
TO : Leon Jaworski, Special Prosecutor
DATE: August 9, 1974
FROM : Carl B Feldbaum and Peter M. Kreindler
SUBJECT: Factors to be Considered in Deciding Whether to Prosecute Richard M. Nixon for Obstruction of Justice

In our view there is clear evidence that Richard M. Nixon participated in a conspiracy to obstruct justice by concealing the identity of those responsible for the Watergate break-in and other criminal offenses. There is a presumption (which in the past we have operated upon) that Richard M. Nixon, like every citizen, is subject to the rule of law. Accordingly, one begins with the premise that if there is sufficient evidence, Mr. Nixon should be indicted and prosecuted. The question then becomes whether the presumption for proceeding is outweighed by the factors mandating against indictment and prosecution.

The factors which mandate against indictment and prosecution are:

1. His resignation has been sufficient punishment.

2. He has been subject to an impeachment inquiry with resulting articles of impeachment which the House Judiciary Committee unanimously endorsed as to Article I (the Watergate cover-up).

3. Prosecution might aggravate political divisions in the country.

4. As a political matter, the times call for conciliation rather than recrimination.

5. There would be considerable difficulty in achieving a fair trial because of massive pre-trial publicity.

The factors which mandate in favor of indictment and prosecution are:

1. The principle of equal justice under law requires that every person, no matter what his past position or office, answer to the criminal justice system for his past offenses. This is a particularly weighty factor if Mr. Nixon's aides and associates, who acted upon his orders and what they conceived to be his interests, are to be prosecuted for she same offenses.

2. The country will be further divided by Mr. Nixon unless there is a final disposition of charges of criminality outstanding against him so as to forestall the belief that he was driven from his office by erosion of his political base. This final disposition may be necessary to preserve the integrity of the criminal justice system and the legislative process, which together marshalled the substantial evidence of Mr. Nixon's guilt.

3. Article I, Section 3, clause 7 of the Constitution provides that a person removed from office by impeachment and conviction "shall nevertheless be liable and subject to Indictment, Trial, Judgment, and Punishment, according to Law." The Framers contemplated that a person removed from office because of abuse of his public trust still would have to answer to the criminal justice system for criminal offenses.

4. It cannot be sufficient retribution for criminal offenses merely to surrender the public office and trust which has been demonstrably abused. A person should not be permitted to trade in the abused office in return for immunity.

5. The modern nature of the Presidency necessitates massive public exposure of the President's actions through the media. A bar to prosecution on the grounds of such publicity effectively would immunize all future Presi-dents for their actions, however criminal. Moreover, the courts may be the appropriate forum to resolve ques-tions of pre-trial publicity in the context of an adversary proceeding.

(National Archives and Records Administration: Records of the Watergate Special Prosecution Force, Record Group 460.)

HOW WELL DID YOU UNDERSTAND THIS SELECTION?

1.   What factors did Feldbaum and Kreindler think warranted prosecution of Nixon? What factors did they cite as reasons not to prosecute Nixon?

2.   Based on what you know about Watergate, should Nixon have been prosecuted on criminal charges? Support your answer with historical evidence.

3.   What does the Constitution say regarding criminal prosecution of individuals who have undergone impeach-ment? Explain?

Gloria Steinem, a leader of the Women's Movement in the 1970s, testified before the Senate Subcommittee on Constitutional Amendment in support of the Equal Rights Amendment that would ensure the rights of American women would not be abridged or denied because of sex. The ERA, which was eventually sent to state legislatures for ratification, was not approved by the required number of states. In fact, several state legislatures rescinded their approval of the ERA once conservative Republicans gained control of the legislature.

Washington, D.C.

I hope this committee will hear the personal, daily injustices suffered by many women-professionals and day laborers, women housebound by welfare as well as suburbia. We have all been silent for too long. We won't be silent anymore.

The truth is that all our problems stem from the same sex-based myths. We may appear before you as white radicals or the middle-aged middleclass or black soul sisters, but we are all sisters in fighting against these outdated myths. Like radical myths, they have been reflected in our laws. Let me list a few:

That Women are Biologically Inferior to Men

In fact, an equally good case can be made for the reverse. Women live longer than men, even when the men are not subject to business pressures.

However, I don't want to prove the superiority of one sex to another; That would only be repeating a male mistake. ...

What we do know is that the difference between two races or two sexes is much smaller than the differences to be found within each group. Therefore, in spite of the slide show on female inferiority's that I understand was shown to you yesterday, the law makes much more sense when it treats individuals, not groups bundled together by some condition of birth....

That Women Are Already Treated Equally in This Society

I'm sure there has been ample testimony to prove that equal pay for equal work, equal chance for advancement, and equal training or encouragement is obscenely scarce in every field, even those - like food and fashion industries-that are supposedly "feminine."

A deeper result of social and legal injustice, however, is what sociologists refer to as "Internalized Aggression." Victims of aggression absorb the myth of their own inferiority, and come to believe that their group is in fact second class.

Women suffer this second class treatment from the moment they are born. They are expected to be rather than achieve, to function biologically rather than learn. A brother; whatever his intellect, is more likely to get the family's encouragement and education money, while girls are often pressured to conceal ambition and intelligence, to a Uncle Tom."

Teachers, parents, and the Supreme Court may exude a protective, well-meaning rationale, but limiting the individual's ambition is doing no one a favor. Certainly not this country. It needs all the talent it can get.

That American Women Hold Great Economic Power

51% of all shareholders in this country are women. That's a favorite malechauvinist statistic. However; the number of shares they hold is so small that the total is only 18% of all shares. Even those holdings are often controlled by men.

Similarly, only 5% of all the people in the country who receive $10,000 a year or more, earned or otherwise, are women. And that includes all the famous rich widows.

The constantly - repeated myth of our economic power seems less testimony to our real power than to the resentment of what little power we do have.

That Children Must Have full-time Mothers

American mothers spend more time with their homes and children than those of any other society we know about....

The truth is that most American children seem to be suffering from too much Mother; and too little Father.

Part of the program of Women's Liberation is a return of fathers to their children.

As for the psychic health of the children, studies show that the quality of time spent by parents is more important than the quantity. The most damaged children were not those whose mothers worked, but those whose mothers preferred to work but stayed home out of a role-playing desire to be a "good mother"

That the Women's Movement Is Not Political, Won't Last, or Is Somehow Not "Serious"

We are 51 % of the population, we are essentially united on these issues across boundaries of class or race or age, and we may well end by changing this society more than the civil rights movement. That is an apt parallel. We, too, have our right wing and left wing, our separatists, gradualists, and Uncle Toms. But we are changing our own consciousness, and that of the country....

I had deep misgivings About discussing this topic when National Guardsmen are occupying our campuses, the country is being turned against itself in a terrible polarization, and America is enlarging an already inhuman and unjustifiable wan But it seems to me that much of the trouble this country is in has to do with the Masculine Mystique; with the myth that masculinity somehow depends on the subjugation of other people. It is a bipartisan problem: both our past and current Presidents seem to be victims of this myth, and to behave accordingly.

Women are not more moral than men. We are only uncorrupted by power. But we do not want to imitate men, to join this country as it is, and I think our very participation will change it. Perhaps women elected leaders-and there will be many more of them-will not be so likely to dominate black people or yellow people or men; anybody who looks different from us.

After all, we won't have our masculinity to prove.

Testimony of Gloria Steinem, U.S. Congress, Senate Committee on the Judiciary, Subcommittee on Constitutional Amendment, 91st Congress, 2nd Session, 1970, pp. 335-337.

HOW WELL DID YOU UNDERSTAND THIS SELECTION?

1. What myths does Steinem address in her testimony?

2. What does Steinem think is the difference between men and women?

3. What does Steinem think is the greatest problems women face in 1970s America?

4. Do you agree with Steinem's statement? Why or why not?

Since its creation, the Central Intelligence Agency attempted to develop or acquire techniques to control human behavior. Over the years the agency tested various truth serums and psychedelic drugs such as LSD in attempts to gain the upper hand over the Soviet Union during the Cold War. In 1977 documents surfaced about a top-secret CIA effort to develop various methods that could be used to control human behavior. This program, code named MK-ULRRA, was an attempt to develop "chemical, biological, and radiological materials capable of employment in a clandestine operation to control human behaviors." Following the Watergate Scandal, distrust of government among Americans was at an all-time high. Consequently, the U.S. Senate investigated the CIA's MK-ULTRA programs. The following are excerpts from Senate hearings regarding the matter.

WEDNESDAY, AUGUST 3, 1977

U.S. SENATE, SELECT COMMITTEE ON INTELLIGENCE, AND SUBCOMMITTEE ON HEALTH AND SCIENTIFIC RESEARCH OF THE COMMITTEE ON HUMAN RESOURCES
Washington, D.C.

The committees met, pursuant to notice, at 9:07 a.m. in room 1202, Dirksen Senate Office Building, Senator Daniel K. Inouye (chairman of the Select Committee on Intelligence) presiding.

Present: Senators Inouye (presiding), Kennedy, Goldwater, Bayh, Hathaway, Huddleston, Hart, Schweiker, Case, Garn, Chafee, Lugar and Wallop.

Also present: William G. Miller, staff director, Select Committee on Intelligence; Dr. Lawrence Horowitz, staff director, Subcommittee on Health and Scientific Research; and professional staff members of both committees.

Senator INOUYE. The Senate Select Committee on Intelligence is meeting today and is joined by the Subcommittee on Health and Scientific Research chaired by Senator Edward Kennedy of Massachusetts and Senator Richard Schweiker of Pennsylvania. Senator Hathaway and Senator Chafee are members of both committees. We are to hear testimony from the Director of Central Intelligence, Adm. Stansfield Turner, and from other Agency witnesses on issues concerning new documents supplied to the committee in the last week on drug testing conducted by the Central Intelligence Agency.

It should be made clear from the outset that in general, we are focusing on events that happened over 12 or as long as 25 years ago. It should be emphasized that the programs that are of greatest concern have stopped and that we are reviewing these past events in order to better understand what statutes and other guidelines might be necessary to prevent the recurrence of such abuses in the future. We also need to know and understand what is now being done by the CIA in the field of behavioral research to be certain that no current abuses are occurring.

I want to commend Admiral Turner for his full cooperation with this committee and with the Subcommittee on Health in recognizing that this issue needed our attention. The CIA has assisted our committees and staffs in their investigative efforts and in arriving at remedies which will serve the best interests of our country.

The reappearance of reports of the abuses of the drug testing program and reports of other previously unknown drug programs and projects for behavioral control underline the necessity for effective oversight procedures both in the executive branch and in the Congress. The Select Committee on Intelligence has been working very closely with President Carter, the Vice President, and Admiral Turner and his associates in developing basic concepts for statutory guidelines which will govern all activities of the intelligence agencies of the United States.

In fact, it is my expectation that the President will soon announce his decisions on how he has decided the intelligence agencies of the United States shall be organized. This committee will be working closely with the President and Admiral Turner in placing this new structure under the law and to develop effective oversight procedures.

448

It is clear that effective oversight requires that information must be full and forthcoming. Full and timely information is obviously necessary if the committee and the public is to be confident that any transgressions can be dealt with quickly and forcefully.

One purpose of this hearing is to give the committee and the public an understanding of what new information has been discovered that adds to the knowledge already available from previous Church and Kennedy inquiries, and to hear the reasons why these documents were not available to the Church and Kennedy committees. It is also the purpose of this hearing to address the issues raised by any additional illegal or improper activities that have emerged from the files and to develop remedies to prevent such improper activities from occurring again.

Finally, there is an obligation on the part of both this committee and the CIA to make every effort to help those individuals or institutions that may have been harmed by any of these improper or illegal activities. I am certain that Admiral Turner will work with this committee to see that this will be done.

I would now like to welcome the most distinguished Senator from Massachusetts, the chairman of the Health Subcommittee, Senator Kennedy.

Senator KENNEDY. Thank you very much, Mr. Chairman. We are delighted to join together in this very important area of public inquiry and public interest.

Some 2 years ago, the Senate Health Subcommittee heard chilling testimony about the human experimentation activities of the Central Intelligence Agency. The Deputy Director of the CIA revealed that over 30 universities and institutions were involved in an "extensive testing and experimentation" program which included covert drug tests on unwitting citizens "at all social levels, high and low, native Americans and foreign." Several of these tests involved the administration of LSD to "unwitting subjects in social situations."

At least one death, that of Dr. Olson, resulted from these activities. The Agency itself acknowledged that these tests made little scientific sense. The agents doing the monitoring were not qualified scientific observers. The tests subjects were seldom accessible beyond the first hours of the test. In a number of instances, the test subject became ill for hours or days, and effective follow up was impossible.

Other experiments were equally offensive. For example, heroin addicts were enticed into participating in LSD experiments in order to get a reward — heroin.

Perhaps most disturbing of all was the fact that the extent of experimentation on human subjects was unknown. The records of all these activities were destroyed in January 1973, at the instruction of then CIA Director Richard Helms. In spite of persistent inquiries by both the Health Subcommittee and the Intelligence Committee, no additional records or information were forthcoming. And no one — no single individual — could be found who remembered the details, not the Director of the CIA, who ordered the documents destroyed, not the official responsible for the program, nor any of his associates.

We believed that the record, incomplete as it was, was as complete as it was going to be. Then one individual, through a Freedom of Information request, accomplished what two U.S. Senate committees could not. He spurred the agency into finding additional records pertaining to the CIA's program of experimentation with human subjects. These new records were discovered by the agency in March. Their existence was not made known to the Congress until July.

The records reveal a far more extensive series of experiments than had previously been thought. Eighty-six universities or institutions were involved. New instances of unethical behavior were revealed.

The intelligence community of this Nation, which requires a shroud of secrecy in order to operate, has a very sacred trust from the American people. The CIA's program of human experimentation of the fifties and sixties violated that trust. It was violated again on the day the bulk of the agency's records were destroyed in 1973. It is violated each time a responsible official refuses to recollect the details of the program. The best safeguard against abuses in the future is a complete public accounting of the abuses of the past.

I think this is illustrated, as Chairman Inouye pointed out. These are issues, are questions that happened in the fifties and sixties, and go back some 15, 20 years ago, but they are front page news today, as we see in the major newspapers and on the television and in the media of this country; and the reason they are, I think, is because it just continuously begins to trickle out, sort of, month after month, and the best way to put this period behind us, obviously, is to have the full information, and I think that is the desire of Admiral Turner and of the members of this committee.

The Central Intelligence Agency drugged American citizens without their knowledge or consent. It used university facilities and personnel without their knowledge. It funded leading researchers, often without their knowledge.

These institutes, these individuals, have a right to know who they are and how and when they were used. As of today, the Agency itself refuses to declassify the names of those institutions and individuals, quite appropriately, I might say, with regard to the individuals under the Privacy Act. It seems to me to be a fundamental responsibility to notify those individuals or institutions, rather. I think many of them were caught up in an unwitting manner to do research for the Agency. Many researchers, distinguished researchers, some of our most outstanding members of our scientific community, involved in this network, now really do not know whether they were involved or not, and it seems to me that the whole health and climate in terms of our university and our scientific and health facilities are entitled to that response.

So, I intend to do all I can to persuade the Agency to, at the very least, officially inform those institutions and individuals involved.

Two years ago, when these abuses were first revealed, I introduced legislation, with Senator Schweiker and Senator Javits, designed to minimize the potential for any similar abuses in the future. That legislation expanded the jurisdiction of the National Commission on Human Subjects of Biomedical and Behavioral Research to cover all federally funded research involving human subjects. The research initially was just directed toward HEW activities, but this legislation covered DOD as well as the CIA.

This Nation has a biomedical and behavioral research capability second to none. It has had for subjects of HEW funded research for the past 3 years a system for the protection of human subjects of biomedical research second to none, and the Human Experimentation Commission has proven its value. Today's hearings and the record already established underscore the need to expand its jurisdiction.

The CIA supported that legislation in 1975, and it passed the Senate unanimously last year. I believe it is needed in order to assure all our people that they will have the degree of protection in human experimentation that they deserve and have every right to expect.

Senator INOUYE. Thank you very much. Now we will proceed with the hearings. Admiral Turner?

The following outline of methods and substances used by the CIA in experimenting with so-called "brainwashing techniques was one of the many secret documents revealed during the MK-ULTRA hearings.

5 May 1955
A portion of the Research and Development Program of TSS/Chemical Division is devoted to the discovery of the following materials and methods:

1. Substances which will promote illogical thinking and impulsiveness to the point where the recipient would be discredited in public.

2. Substances which increase the efficiency of mentation and perception.

3. Materials which will prevent or counteract the intoxicating effect of alcohol.

4. Materials which will promote the intoxicating effect of alcohol.

5. Materials which will produce the signs and symptoms of recognized diseases in a reversible way so that they may be used for malingering, etc.

6. Materials which will render the indication of hypnosis easier or otherwise enhance its usefulness.

7. Substances which will enhance the ability of individuals to withstand privation, torture and coercion during interrogation and so-called "brainwashing".

8. Materials and physical methods which will produce amnesia for events preceding and during their use.

9. Physical methods of producing shock and confusion over extended periods of time and capable of surreptitious use.

10. Substances which produce physical disablement such as paralysis of the legs, acute anemia, etc.

11. Substances which will produce "pure" euphoria with no subsequent let-down.

12. Substances which alter personality structure in such a way that the tendency of the recipient to become dependent upon another person is enhanced.

13. A material which will cause mental confusion of such a type that the individual under its influence will find it difficult to maintain a fabrication under questioning.

14. Substances which will lower the ambition and general working efficiency of men when administered in undetectable amounts.

15. Substances which will promote weakness or distortion of the eyesight or hearing faculties, preferably without permanent effects.

16. A knockout pill which can surreptitiously be administered in drinks, food, cigarettes, as an aerosol, etc., which will be safe to use, provide a maximum of amnesia, and be suitable for use by agent types on an ad hoc basis.

17. A material which can be surreptitiously administered by the above routes and which in very small amounts will make it impossible for a man to perform any physical activity whatever.

The development of materials of this type follows the standard practice of such ethical drug houses as [deleted]. It is a relatively routine procedure to develop a drug to the point of human testing. Ordinarily, the drug houses depend upon the services of private physicians for the final clinical testing. The physicians are willing to assume the responsibility of such tests in order to advance the science of medicine. It is difficult and sometimes impossible for TSS/CD to offer such an inducement with respect to its products. In practice, it has been possible to use the outside cleared contractors for the preliminary phases of this work. However, that part which involves human testing at effective dose levels presents security problems which cannot be handled by the ordinary contractor.

The proposed facility [deleted] offers a unique opportunity for the secure handling of such clinical testing in addition to the many advantages outline in the project proposal. The security problems mentioned above are eliminated by the fact that the responsibility for the testing will rest completely with the physician and the hospital.

451

[deleted] will allow TSS/CD personnel to supervise the work very closely to make sure that all tests are conducted according to the recognized practices and embody adequate safeguards.

Source: Government Printing Office: Joint Hearings before the Select Committee on Intelligence, 95th Congress 1st Session, August 3, 1977)

HOW WELL DID YOU UNDERSTAND THIS SELECTION?

1. What was the MK-ULRA Program? Why did the CIA undertake this program?

2. Did the program violate individual rights? Why or why not?

3. Was development of this program constitutionally justified? Why or why not?

CAMP DAVID ACCORDS, 1978

President Jimmy Carter was determined to make progress toward peace in the Middle East between Arabs and Israelis who seemed to be perpetually at war. He persuaded Israeli leader Menachem Begin and Egyptian leader Anwar al-Sadat to meet secretly at Camp David, the presidential retreat in Maryland. After twelve days of negotiations the two leaders signed two agreements known collectively as the Camp David Accords. The first agreement extended formal Egyptian diplomatic recognition of Israel's right to exist as a nation in return for control of the Sinai Peninsula being given to Egypt. The second document was a framework for peace in the Middle East. It established a format for conducting negotiations for establishing a Palestinian state on the West Bank of the Jordan River and in the Gaza Strip. Both agreements are reproduced below.

Preamble

The search for peace in the Middle East must be guided by the following:
*   The agreed basis for a peaceful settlement of the conflict between Israel and its neighbors is United Nations Security Council Resolution 242, in all its parts.
*   After four wars during 30 years, despite intensive human efforts, the Middle East, which is the cradle of civilization and the birthplace of three great religions, does not enjoy the blessings of peace. The people of the Middle East yearn for peace so that the vast human and natural resources of the region can be turned to the pursuits of peace and so that this area can become a model for coexistence and cooperation among nations.
*   The historic initiative of President Sadat in visiting Jerusalem and the reception accorded to him by the parliament, government and people of Israel, and the reciprocal visit of Prime Minister Begin to Ismailia, the peace proposals made by both leaders, as well as the warm reception of these missions by the peoples of both countries, have created an unprecedented opportunity for peace which must not be lost if this generation and future generations are to be spared the tragedies of war.

- The provisions of the Charter of the United Nations and the other accepted norms of international law and legitimacy now provide accepted standards for the conduct of relations among all states.

- To achieve a relationship of peace, in the spirit of Article Two of the United Nations Charter, future negotiations between Israel and any neighbor prepared to negotiate peace and security with it are necessary for the purpose of carrying out all the provisions and principles of Resolutions 242 and 338.

- Peace requires respect for the sovereignty, territorial integrity and political independence of every state in the area and their right to live in peace within secure and recognized boundaries free from threats or acts of force. Progress toward that goal can accelerate movement toward a new era of reconciliation in the Middle East marked by cooperation in promoting economic development, in maintaining stability and in assuring security.

- Security is enhanced by a relationship of peace and by cooperation between nations which enjoy normal relations. In addition, under the terms of peace treaties, the parties can, on the basis of reciprocity, agree to special security arrangements such as demilitarized zones, limited armaments areas, early warning stations, the presence of international forces, liaison, agreed measures for monitoring and other arrangements that they agree are useful.

Framework

Taking these factors into account, the parties are determined to reach a just, comprehensive, and durable settlement of the Middle East conflict through the conclusion of peace treaties based on Security Council resolutions 242 and 338 in all their parts. Their purpose is to achieve peace and good neighborly relations. They recognize that for peace to endure, it must involve all those who have been most deeply affected by the conflict. They therefore agree that this framework, as appropriate, is intended by them to constitute a basis for peace not only between Egypt and Israel, but also between Israel and each of its other neighbors which is prepared to negotiate peace with Israel on this basis. With that objective in mind, they have agreed to proceed as follows:

A. West Bank and Gaza

1. Egypt, Israel, Jordan and the representatives of the Palestinian people should participate in negotiations on the resolution of the Palestinian problem in all its aspects. To achieve that objective, negotiations relating to the West Bank and Gaza should proceed in three stages:

   a. Egypt and Israel agree that, in order to ensure a peaceful and orderly transfer of authority, and taking into account the security concerns of all the parties, there should be transitional arrangements for the West Bank and Gaza for a period not exceeding five years. In order to provide full autonomy to the inhabitants, under these arrangements the Israeli military government and its civilian administration will be withdrawn as soon as a self-governing authority has been freely elected by the inhabitants of these areas to replace the existing military government. To negotiate the details of a transitional arrangement, Jordan will be invited to join the negotiations on the basis of this framework. These new arrangements should give due consideration both to the principle of self-government by the inhabitants of these territories and to the legitimate security concerns of the parties involved.

   b. Egypt, Israel, and Jordan will agree on the modalities for establishing elected self-governing authority in the West Bank and Gaza. The delegations of Egypt and Jordan may include Palestinians from the West Bank and Gaza or other Palestinians as mutually agreed. The parties will negotiate an agreement which will define the powers and responsibilities of the self-governing authority to be exercised in the West Bank and Gaza. A withdrawal of Israeli armed forces will take place and there will be a redeployment of the remaining Israeli forces into specified security locations. The agreement will also include arrangements for assuring internal and external security and public order. A strong local police force will be established, which may include Jordanian citizens. In addition, Israeli and Jordanian forces will participate in joint patrols and in the manning of control posts to assure the security of the borders.

   c. When the self-governing authority (administrative council) in the West Bank and Gaza is established and inaugurated, the transitional period of five years will begin. As soon as possible, but not later than the third year after the beginning of the transitional period, negotiations will take place to determine the final status of the West Bank and Gaza and its relationship with its neighbors and to conclude a peace treaty between Israel and Jordan by the end of the transitional period. These negotiations will be conducted among Egypt, Israel, Jordan and the elected representatives of the inhabitants of the West Bank and Gaza. Two separate but related committees will be convened, one committee, consisting of representatives of the four parties which will negotiate and agree on the final status of the West Bank and Gaza, and its relationship with its neighbors, and the second committee, consisting of representatives of Israel and representatives of Jordan to be joined by the elected representatives of the inhabitants of the West Bank and Gaza, to negotiate the peace treaty between Israel and Jordan, taking into account the agreement reached in the final status of the West Bank and Gaza. The negotiations shall be based on all the provisions and principles of UN Security Council Resolution 242. The negotiations will resolve, among other matters, the location of the boundaries and the nature of the security arrangements. The solution from the negotiations must also recognize the legitimate right of the Palestinian peoples and their just requirements. In this way, the Palestinians will participate in the determination of their own future through:

    i. The negotiations among Egypt, Israel, Jordan and the representatives of the inhabitants of the West Bank and Gaza to agree on the final status of the West Bank and Gaza and other outstanding issues by the end of the transitional period.

    ii. Submitting their agreements to a vote by the elected representatives of the inhabitants of the West Bank and Gaza.

    iii. Providing for the elected representatives of the inhabitants of the West Bank and Gaza to decide how they shall govern themselves consistent with the provisions of their agreement.

    iv. Participating as stated above in the work of the committee negotiating the peace treaty between Israel and Jordan.

d. All necessary measures will be taken and provisions made to assure the security of Israel and its neighbors during the transitional period and beyond. To assist in providing such security, a strong local police force will be constituted by the self-governing authority. It will be composed of inhabitants of the West Bank and Gaza. The police will maintain liaison on internal security matters with the designated Israeli, Jordanian, and Egyptian officers.

e. During the transitional period, representatives of Egypt, Israel, Jordan, and the self-governing authority will constitute a continuing committee to decide by agreement on the modalities of admission of persons displaced from the West Bank and Gaza in 1967, together with necessary measures to prevent disruption and disorder. Other matters of common concern may also be dealt with by this committee.

f. Egypt and Israel will work with each other and with other interested parties to establish agreed procedures for a prompt, just and permanent implementation of the resolution of the refugee problem.

B. Egypt-Israel

1. Egypt-Israel undertake not to resort to the threat or the use of force to settle disputes. Any disputes shall be settled by peaceful means in accordance with the provisions of Article 33 of the U.N. Charter.

2. n order to achieve peace between them, the parties agree to negotiate in good faith with a goal of concluding within three months from the signing of the Framework a peace treaty between them while inviting the other parties to the conflict to proceed simultaneously to negotiate and conclude similar peace treaties with a view the achieving a comprehensive peace in the area. The Framework for the Conclusion of a Peace Treaty between Egypt and Israel will govern the peace negotiations between them. The parties will agree on the modalities and the timetable for the implementation of their obligations under the treaty.

C. Associated Principles

1. Egypt and Israel state that the principles and provisions described below should apply to peace treaties between Israel and each of its neighbors - Egypt, Jordan, Syria and Lebanon.

2. Signatories shall establish among themselves relationships normal to states at peace with one another. To this end, they should undertake to abide by all the provisions of the U.N. Charter. Steps to be taken in this respect include:

a. full recognition;

b. abolishing economic boycotts;

c. guaranteeing that under their jurisdiction the citizens of the other parties shall enjoy the protection of the due process of law.

3. Signatories should explore possibilities for economic development in the context of final peace treaties, with the objective of contributing to the atmosphere of peace, cooperation and friendship which is their common goal.
4. Claims commissions may be established for the mutual settlement of all financial claims.
5. The United States shall be invited to participated in the talks on matters related to the modalities of the implementation of the agreements and working out the timetable for the carrying out of the obligations of the parties.
6. The United Nations Security Council shall be requested to endorse the peace treaties and ensure that their provisions shall not be violated. The permanent members of the Security Council shall be requested to under-write the peace treaties and ensure respect or the provisions. They shall be requested to conform their policies an actions with the undertaking contained in this Framework.

For the Government of Israel:
    Menachem Begin
For the Government of the Arab Republic of Egypt
    Muhammed Anwar al-Sadat
Witnessed by
    Jimmy Carter, President of the United States of America

Framework for the Conclusion of a Peace Treaty between Egypt and Israel

In order to achieve peace between them, Israel and Egypt agree to negotiate in good faith with a goal of concluding within three months of the signing of this framework a peace treaty between them:

It is agreed that:

• The site of the negotiations will be under a United Nations flag at a location or locations to be mutually agreed.
• All of the principles of U.N. Resolution 242 will apply in this resolution of the dispute between Israel and Egypt.
• Unless otherwise mutually agreed, terms of the peace treaty will be implemented between two and three years after the peace treaty is signed.

The following matters are agreed between the parties:

1. the full exercise of Egyptian sovereignty up to the internationally recognized border between Egypt and mandated Palestine;
2. the withdrawal of Israeli armed forces from the Sinai;
3. the use of airfields left by the Israelis near al-Arish, Rafah, Ras en-Naqb, and Sharm el-Sheikh for civilian purposes only, including possible commercial use only by all nations;
4. the right of free passage by ships of Israel through the Gulf of Suez and the Suez Canal on the basis of the Constantinople Convention of 1888 applying to all nations; the Strait of Tiran and Gulf of Aqaba are international waterways to be open to all nations for unimpeded and nonsuspendable freedom of navigation and overflight;
5. the construction of a highway between the Sinai and Jordan near Eilat with guaranteed free and peaceful passage by Egypt and Jordan; and
6. the stationing of military forces listed below.

Stationing of Forces

No more than one division (mechanized or infantry) of Egyptian armed forces will be stationed within an area lying approximately 50 km. (30 miles) east of the Gulf of Suez and the Suez Canal.

Only United Nations forces and civil police equipped with light weapons to perform normal police functions will be stationed within an area lying west of the international border and the Gulf of Aqaba, varying in width from 20 km. (12 miles) to 40 km. (24 miles).

In the area within 3 km. (1.8 miles) east of the international border there will be Israeli limited military forces not to exceed four infantry battalions and United Nations observers.

Border patrol units not to exceed three battalions will supplement the civil police in maintaining order in the area not included above.

The exact demarcation of the above areas will be as decided during the peace negotiations.

Early warning stations may exist to insure compliance with the terms of the agreement.

United Nations forces will be stationed:

1. in part of the area in the Sinai lying within about 20 km. of the Mediterranean Sea and adjacent to the international border, and
2. in the Sharm el-Sheikh area to insure freedom of passage through the Strait of Tiran; and these forces will not be removed unless such removal is approved by the Security Council of the United Nations with a unanimous vote of the five permanent members.

After a peace treaty is signed, and after the interim withdrawal is complete, normal relations will be established between Egypt and Israel, including full recognition, including diplomatic, economic and cultural relations; termination of economic boycotts and barriers to the free movement of goods and people; and mutual protection of citizens by the due process of law.

Interim Withdrawal

Between three months and nine months after the signing of the peace treaty, all Israeli forces will withdraw east of a line extending from a point east of El-Arish to Ras Muhammad, the exact location of this line to be determined by mutual agreement.

For the Government of the Arab Republic of Egypt:
Muhammed Anwar al-Sadat
For the Government of Israel:
Menachem Begin
Witnessed by:
Jimmy Carter, President of the United States of America

HOW WELL DID YOU UNDERSTAND THIS SELECTION?

1. Basically, what do the Camp David Accords do?

2. What does Israel get? What did Egypt do?

3. What has been the historical significance of the Camp David Accords? Explain and support your answer with historical evidence.

SELF TEST

MULTIPLE CHOICE: Circle the correct response. The correct answers are given at the end.

1. Richard Nixon once described himself as a/an
    a. Outgoing friendly sort of man
    b. Introvert in an extrovert's business
    c. Very unpleasant man
    d. As basically a lazy unprepared man

2. _____ a presidential candidate who promoted racial segregation was wounded and left paralyzed in an assassination attempt in Wheaton, Maryland by Arthur Bremen.
    a. Richard Nixon
    b. Edmund Mushie
    c. Robert Kennedy
    d. George Wallace

3. Which one of the following was not an American response to the 1973 Energy Crisis?
    a. Americans were asked to voluntarily turn down thermostats.
    b. President Nixon asked American companies to stay open for fever hours.
    c. Congress set a national maximum highway speed limit of 65 miles per hour.
    d. Congress and the President approved construction of the Trans-Alaskan pipeline.

4. National Guardsmen open fire on a group of students protesting against the Vietnam War at _____ in Ohio
    a. Ohio State University
    b. The University of Dayton
    c. The University of Cincinnati
    d. Kent State University

5. _____ staged the Winter Soldiers Investigation in January 1971 as a mock war crimes trial in which Vietnam Veterans described war crimes they had witnessed while in the military.
    a. The Vietnam Veterans Against the War (VVAW)
    b. Americans Against Violence
    c. The Students Non-Violent Coordinating Committee
    d. The Leftist League

6. President Richard Nixon resigned as a result of a break-in at the Democratic national headquarters in a scandal that became known as _____
    a. Watergate
    b. The Iran-Contra Scandal
    c. Whitewater
    d. Irangate

7. _____ replaced Richard Nixon as President after his resignation due to the Watergate Scandal
    a. Jimmy Carter
    b. Gerald Ford
    c. Ronald Reagan
    d. Bill Clinton

8. The Georgia Governor elected president in 1976 was
   a. Richard Nixon
   b. Gerald Ford
   c. Jimmy Carter
   d. Ronald Reagan

9. The 1978 agreement between Egypt and Israel in which Israel returned the Sinai Peninsula to Egypt in return for Egypt's diplomatic recognition of Israel's right to exist was called the
   a. Begin-Sadat Treaty
   b. Camp David Accords
   c. Israeli-Egyptian Accord
   d. The Yom Kippur Agreement

10. The moderate Republican congressman who ran as an independent in the 1980 presidential election was
   a. Ronald Reagan
   b. George H.W. Bush
   c. Rick Perry
   d. John Anderson

Answers: 1-B; 2-D; 3-C; 4-D; 5-A; 6-A; 7-B; 8-C; 9-B; 10-D

ESSAYS:

1. Discuss the significance of Nixon's foreign policy success in China and the Soviet Union.

2. Examine the economic challenges facing the U.S. in the 1970s. How did each administration attempt to solve them?

3. Explain the increase in white ethnic resistance to the new militancy of women, homosexuals, and racial and ethnic minorities during the 1970s.

OPTIONAL ACTIVITIES: (Use your knowledge **and** imagination when appropriate.)

1. This chapter includes several events that place the U.S. in conflict with Arab nations. Create a time-line that plots American involvement in the Middle East. Highlight American activities there that elicited a negative response from Arab countries.

2. Create a chart comparing and contrasting the foreign policy approaches of Nixon and Carter. Evaluate the relative success of each president's approach.

2. This chapter notes that many groups in the U.S. exhibited "new militancy." Select one of these groups (African Americans, women, Asian-Americans, Hispanics, Native Americans, gays & lesbians, etc.), and create a poster presentation that outlines the group's demands and lists their strategy for achieving their goals.

WEB SITE LISTINGS:

The Seventies:
>   http://www.super70s.com/Super70s/Timeline/
>   http://www.nostalgiacentral.com/seventies.htm
>   http://kclibrary.nhmccd.edu/decade70.html

Vietnam War:

http://www.fsmitha.com/h2/ch26.htm
http://members.aol.com/veterans/warlib6v.htm

Nixon:

http://www.archives.gov/nixon/
http://www.pbs.org/wgbh/amex/presidents/37_nixon/index.html

Pentagon Papers:
http://www.gwu.edu/~nsarchiv/NSAEBB/NSAEBB48/
http://www.mtholyoke.edu/acad/intrel/pentagon/pent1.html

Watergate:
http://www.realhistoryarchives.com/collections/conspiracies/watergate.htm
http://www.archives.gov/exhibit_hall/american_originals/nixon2.html
http://www.archives.gov/exhibit_hall/american_originals/contemp.html

Three Mile Island:
http://www.pbs.org/wgbh/amex/three/

SALT Talks
http://dosfan.lib.uic.edu/acda/treaties/salt1.htm

Détente:
http://www.pbs.org/wgbh/amex/china/
http://www.gwu.edu/~nsarchiv/nsa/publications/DOC_readers/kissinger/nixzhou/

Ford:

http://www.americanpresident.org/history/geraldford/
http://www.pbs.org/wgbh/amex/presidents/38_ford/index.html
Nixon Pardon:
http://www.watergate.info/ford/pardon.shtml

Carter:

http://www.jimmycarterlibrary.org/
http://www.pbs.org/wgbh/amex/presidents/39_carter/index.html
http://odur.let.rug.nl/~usa/H/1990/ch8_p21.htm

Iran Hostage Crisis:
http://www.jimmycarterlibrary.org/documents/hostages.phtml
http://www.jimmycarterlibrary.org/documents/r_ode/index.phtml

SALT II Talks:
http://dosfan.lib.uic.edu/acda/treaties/salt2-1.htm

Chapter Twenty-seven

"CHIMES OF FREEDOM": Protest, American Culture, and the Counterculture of the 1960s and 1970s

Born from the post World War II prosperity Americans enjoyed during the 1950s, the 1960s, and the 1970s were decades in which the babyboom generation began to assert itself by finding fault with American society. In what may have been youthful naivety, teenagers and young adults tried to remake the American social system, solve humanities' problems, change the economy, and, for some, create a utopian society. Older Americans who had lived through the hard economic times of the Great Depression, endured death, destruction, and collective sacrifice of the Second World War, and experienced the fear of Armageddon as a result of the Cold War between the United States and the Soviet Union, realized that the development and use of nuclear weapons might destroy all life on Earth. They desired above all else, a safe, homogeneous, and predictable life. Their desire, however, was difficult to achieve.

Nightly news broadcasts on televisions, that by the 1960s had become a fixture in practically every house, and daily newspapers read by millions of suburbanites were filled with stories about violent crime that seemed to increase rapidly each year, Cold War events that held the potential for nuclear annihilations, and dire predictions of gloom and doom that collectively created a relatively high anxiety level within the American population. Even though the United States prospered economically during the decades following World War II, the nation's increased wealth did not give Americans the safety, security, and peace of mind most desired.

Americans in general felt they were not part of what television had dubbed the "rat race." Throughout life they had been told that wealth, prosperity, and material possessions would bring the individual happiness and security. Despite achieving economic success as evidenced by a suburban house, nice clothes, and a new car, Americans did not feel very secure or happy. Tensions between husbands and wives, parents and children, and young and old were often present within households. These tensions translated over into everyday life and caused young people especially to feel uncomfortable, unsafe, and insecure. As they aged, Americans began to question whether the rat race their parents were part of and that they were about to join was worth the sacrifice of quality personal time with family for material gain.

460

Teenaged children of parents trapped in the rate race began to question the lifestyle and values of parents and grandparents. Many realized that they, like their elders, were unhappy residing in a "Leave it to Beaver" fantasy world that did not exist in reality. Life for them didn't resemble that of Ward, June, Wally, and Theodore Cleaver on the popular television show. Domestic tension sometimes produced rebellion among American youth. This rebellion often culminated in open rejection of their parents' values. Teenagers and young adults disparaged materialism and the culture they had grown up in. Rather than accepting the homogenization and conformity of the 1950s, young people wanted to do their own thing and embraced individualism that was different for each person.

For Americans of earlier generations the counterculture movement of the 1960s and 1970s appeared to be a rejection of all they held dear. Males began to grow their hair long and wore unkempt beards, women wore revealing mini-skirts, and both sexes smoked marijuana, experimented with LSD and other drugs, wore gaudy jewelry, and made love without benefit of matrimony. Older Americans wondered about the nation's future as the United States appeared to be disintegrating before their eyes.

Teenagers and young people who participated in the counterculture movement were also concerned about America's future. Some began to question traditional religion and wonder why a God that they had been taught was loving and good could allow so many evil things to happen in the world. A few youth embraced Eastern religions and others turned toward cults that arose within the United States in their search for goodness, spiritual fulfillment, peace, love, and harmony.

In politics and academia, the counterculture movement manifests itself as the "New Left." Historians, political scientists, economists, sociologists, and others were not content to focus on organizing workers into labor unions and challenging Jim Crow Laws as their liberal ancestors had done in the 1930s, 40s, and 50s. Rather, leftists of the 1960s, and 1970s focused on larger, more philosophical issues that included class, race, gender roles, the morality of capitalism, family structure, and the ownership of private property. A particular target of the New Left was the Vietnam War, which was generally viewed as an immoral American misadventure in militarism. Young liberals also questioned traditional economic and political power structures, including American and European colonial domination of developing nations in Asia, Africa, and Latin America, corporate welfare within the United Sates, and exploitation of nature by capitalism.

In general, protestors in the 1960s and 1970s desired a more authentic life that seemed real. Rather than embracing the artificial world created by technology of the scientific and industrial revolutions, young Americans sometimes sought a more natural life, arguing that less was actually more. By the end of 1970, the counter cultural movement had largely ran its course. Aside from a few leftover hippies and New Leftist in academia, most protestors had, like their predecessors of earlier decades, embraced capitalism and materialism.

IDENTIFICATION: Briefly describe each term

New Left

Counterculture

Rachel Carson

Earth Day

Clean Air Act of 1970

Endangered Species Act of 1973

Safe Drinking Water Act of 1974

Abalone Alliance

Love Canal

Superfund Law

Three Mile Island

Black Power

Malcolm X

Civil Rights Act of 1964

Voting Rights Act of 1965

Sidney Portier

Star Trek

Black Nationalists

Black Panthers

Roots

Crystal City

César Chávez

Chicanismo

Red Power

American Indian Movement

Wounded Knee

The Weather Underground

All in the Family

Betty Friedan

President's Commission on the Status of Women

Equal Pay Act of 1963

Title VII of the Civil Rights Act

National Organization for Women

National Women's Political Caucus

Title IX

Schultz v. Wheaton Glass Co.

Corning Glass v. Brennan

Equal Rights Amendment

Phyllis Schlafly

Roe v. Wade

John O'Keefe

Gay Liberation Movement

Highlander Folk School

Bob Dylan

The Beatles

Hippies

LSD

The Pranksters

L. Ron Hubbard

Apollo II

Woodstock

Altamont Concert

Jerry Falwell

THINK ABOUT:

1. What likely caused the Counterculture movement to develop in the 1960s and 1970s?

2. What changes were made within American society as a result of events that occurred during the 1960s and 1970s? Explain.

3. How did conservatives react to the countercultural movement of the 1960s and 1970s? Explain and support your answers with historical evidence.

In 1963, Congress amended the Fair Labor Standards Act of 1938 to include a section prohibiting sex-based wage discrimination for workers who do essentially the same job and who hold similar qualifications at the same place of employment. Violations of the Equal Pay Act, as the amendment was called, would eventually be enforced by the Equal Employment Opportunity Commission. Over the years the Equal Pay Act has been amended several times. The main section of the original act appears below.

1) No employer having employees subject to any provisions of this section shall discriminate, within any establishment in which such employees are employed, between employees on the basis of sex by paying wages to employees in such establishment at a rate less than the rate at which he pays wages to employees of the opposite sex in such establishment for equal work on jobs the performance of which requires equal skill, effort, and responsibility, and which are performed under similar working conditions, except where such payment is made pursuant to (i) a seniority system; (ii) a merit system; (iii) a system which measures earnings by quantity or quality of production; or (iv) a differential based on any other factor other than sex: Provided, That an employer who is paying a wage rate differential in violation of this subsection shall not, in order to comply with the provisions of this subsection, reduce the wage rate of any employee.

(2) No labor organization, or its agents, representing employees of an employer having employees subject to any provisions of this section shall cause or attempt to cause such an employer to discriminate against an employee in violation of paragraph (1) of this subsection.

(3) For purposes of administration and enforcement, any amounts owing to any employee which have been withheld in violation of this subsection shall be deemed to be unpaid minimum wages or unpaid overtime compensation under this chapter.

(4) As used in this subsection, the term "labor organization" means any organization of any kind, or any agency or employee representation committee or plan, in which employees participate and which exists for the purpose, in whole or in part, of dealing with employers concerning grievances, labor disputes, wages, rates of pay, hours of employment, or conditions of work.

HOW WELL DID YOU UNDERSTAND THIS SELECTION?

1. What is the primary purpose of the Equal Pay Act?

2. Why did Congress find it necessary to add the Equal Pay Act to the Fair Labor Standards Act?

3. Under what conditions does the Equal Pay Act allow female workers holding essentially the same qualifications doing the same job with similar responsibilities at the same place of employment to receive less wages than male workers doing the same job with the same qualifications?

Working women generally faced discrimination due to their sex on the job. Gender barriers often made it difficult or impossible for women to advance into higher ranking and higher paying jobs. The gender discrimination led women to call for an amendment to the U.S. Constitution that would prevent the denial of rights to any individual because of their gender. A version of the Equal Rights Amendment had been written by women's rights advocate Alice Paul and introduced into every congressional session since 1923. In 1972 a version of the ERA passed both houses of Congress and was sent to the states for ratification, which was to occur over a seven-year period. Hawaii ratified the ERA on the day the Amendment passed Congress. Within three days five more states had ratified the ERA and within five years 35 of the required 38 states had passed the amendment. Unfortunately the three additional states needed for approval did not materialize despite an extension of the ratification date to 1982 by Congress. Since 1982 the ERA has been introduced into every session of Congress but has not passed. Blow is the text of the Equal Rights Amendment:

Section 1. Equality of Rights under the law shall not be denied or abridged by the United States or any state on account of sex.

Section 2. The Congress shall have the power to enforce, by appropriate legislation, the provisions of this article.

Section 3. This amendment shall take effect two years after the date of ratification.

HOW WELL DID YOU UNDERSTAND THIS SELECTION?

1. What does the ERA do?

2. Is the ERA needed? Why or why not?

3. Why did the required number of states not ratify the ERA?

Few rulings by the U.S. Supreme Court have caused as much controversy as **Roe v. Wade** *that legalized abortion in 1973. This case arose after Norma McCorvey, a high school dropout living in Dallas, Texas, became pregnant for a third time. McCorvey, who had put one child up for adoption and given the other to her mother, did not want to bear a third child. After being unable to secure a legal adoption in Texas, she agreed to allow Linda Coffee and Sarah Weddington to file suit against Texas alleging that the states' anti-abortion law was unconstitutional because it violated privacy rights guaranteed by the Constitution. On January 22, 1973, the Supreme Court, in a seven to two decision, held that the Constitution's right to privacy allowed women to terminate pregnancy during the first two trimesters. Justice Harry Blackmun wrote the opinion for the Court. Afterwards, abortion became more common within the United States and remains a controversial issue today.*

This Texas federal appeal and its Georgia companion, *Doe v. Bolton*, present constitutional challenges to state criminal abortion legislation. The Texas statutes are typical of those that have been in effect in many States for approximately a century. The Georgia statutes, in contrast, have a modern cast and are a legislative product that, to an extent at least, obviously reflects the influences of recent attitudinal change, of advancing medical knowledge and techniques, and of new thinking.

The Texas statutes make it a crime except with respect to "an abortion procured or attempted by medical advice for the purpose of saving the life of the mother."

Roe alleged that she was unmarried and pregnant and that she was unable to get a "legal" abortion in Texas because her life did not appear to be threatened by the continuation of her pregnancy. On the merits, the District Court held that the "fundamental right of women to choose whether to have children is protected by the Ninth Amendment, through the Fourteenth Amendment," and that the Texas criminal abortion statutes were void on their face because they were both unconstitutionally vague and constituted an overbroad infringement of the plaintiffs' Ninth Amendment rights. Because the district court denied injunctive relief requested, Roe appealed.

Restrictive criminal abortion laws like Texas in effect in a majority of states today derive from statutory changes effected, for the most part, in the latter half of the 19th century. The court then reviewed, in some detail, "ancient attitudes," "the Hippocratic Oath" which forbids abortion, "the common law," "the English statutory law," and "the American law." Subsequently, it described the position of the American Medical Association, and the American Public Health Association, and the American Bar Association. Thus, at common law, at the time of the adoption of our Constitution, and throughout the major portion of the 19th century, a woman enjoyed a substantially broader right to terminate a pregnancy than she does in most States today.

Three reasons have been advanced to explain historically the enactment of criminal abortion laws in the 19th century and to justify their continuance.

It has been argued occasionally that these laws were the product of a Victorian social concern to discourage illicit sexual conduct. Texas, however, does not advance this justification and it appears that no court or commentator has taken the argument seriously.

A second reason is that when most criminal abortion laws were first enacted, the procedure was a hazardous one for the women. But medical data indicates that abortion in early pregnancy, this is, prior to the end of the first trimester, although not without its risk, is now relatively safe.

The third reason is that the State's interest—some phrase it in terms of duty—in protecting parental life. Some of the argument for this justification rest on the theory that a new human life is present from the moment of conception. Only when the life of the pregnant mother herself is at stake, balanced against life she carries within her, should the interest of the embryo or fetus not prevail. In assessing the State's interest, recognition may be given to the less rigid claim that as long as at least potential life is involved, the State may assert interest beyond the protection of the pregnant woman alone.

It is with these interests, and the weight to be attached to them, that this case is concerned.

The Constitution does not explicitly mention any rights of privacy. But the court has recognized that a right of personal privacy, or a guarantee of certain areas or zones of privacy, does exist under the Constitution. In varying contexts the Court or individual Justices have indeed found at least the roots of that right in the First Amendment,

Stanley v. Georgia; in the Fourth and Fifth Amendments, *Terry v. Ohio, Katz v. United States*; in the penumbras of the Bill of Rights, Griswold; in the Ninth Amendment, (id. Goldberg, J., concurring); or in the concept of liberty guaranteed by the first section of the Fourteenth Amendment, see Meyer. These decisions make it clear that only personal rights that can be deemed "fundamental: or "implicit in the concept of ordered liberty," are included in this guarantee of personal privacy. They also make it clear that the right has some extension to activities relating to marriage, Loving; procreation, Skinner; contraception, Eisenstaedt; family relationship, *Prince v. Massachusetts*; and child rearing and education, Pierce."

This right of privacy, whether it be founded in the Fourteenth Amendment's concept of person liberty as we feel it is, or in the Ninth Amendment's reservation of rights to the people, is broad enough to encompass a woman's decision whether or not to terminate her pregnancy. The detriment that the State would impose upon the pregnant woman by denying this choice altogether is apparent. Specific and direct harm medically diagnosable even in early pregnancy may be involved. Psychological harm may be imminent. Mental and physical health may be taxed by child care. There is also the distress, for all concerned, associated with the unwanted child, and there is the problem of bringing a child into a family already unable, psychologically and otherwise, to care for it. In other case, as in this one, the additional difficulties and continuing stigma of unwed motherhood may be involved. All these are factors the woman and her responsible physician necessarily will consider in consultation.

On the basis of element such as these, appellants and some amici argue that she is entitled to terminate her pregnancy at whatever time, in whatever way, and for whatever reason she alone chooses. With this we do not agree. The Court's decision recognizing rights of privacy also acknowledge that some state regulation in areas protected by that right is appropriate. A state may properly assert important interests in safeguarding health, in maintaining medical standards, and in protecting potential life. At some point in pregnancy, these respective interests become sufficiently compelling to sustain regulations of the factors that govern the abortion decision. In fact, it is not clear to us that the claim that one has an unlimited right to do with someone's body as one pleases bears a close relationship to the right of privacy previously articulated in the Court's decisions. The Court has refused to recognize an unlimited right of this kind in the past. *Jacobson v. Massachusetts*, (vaccination); *Buck v. Bell* (sterilization).

Where certain "fundamental rights" are involved, the Court has held that regulation limiting these rights may be justified only by a "compelling state interest," and that legislative enactments must be narrowly drawn to express only the legitimate state interests at stake.

The appellee and certain amici argued that the fetus is a "person" within the language and meaning of the Fourteenth Amendment. If so, appellant's case of course, collapses, for the fetus' right to life is then guaranteed specifically by the Amendment.

The Constitution does not define "person" in so many words. The Court then listed each provision in which the word appears. But in nearly all these instances, the use of the word is such that it has application only postnatally. None indicates, with any assurance, that it has any possible pre-natal application.

All this, together with our observation that throughout the major portion of the 19th century prevailing legal abortion practices were far freer than today, persuades us that the word "person" as used in the Fourteenth Amendment, does not include the unborn. Thus, we pass on to other considerations.

The pregnant woman cannot be isolated in her privacy. She carries an embryo and, later, a fetus. The situation therefore is inherently different from marital intimacy, or bedroom possession of obscene material, or marriage, or procreation, or education, with which Eisenstadt, Griswold, Stanley, Loving, Skinner, Pierce, and Meyer were concerned.

Texas urges that, apart from the Fourteenth Amendment, life begins at conception and is present throughout pregnancy, and that, therefore, the State has a compelling interest in protecting that life from and after conception. We need not resolve the difficult question of when life begins. When those trained in medicine, philosophy, and theology are unable to arrive at any consensus, the judiciary, at this point in the development of man's knowledge, is not in a position to speculate as to the answer.

We do not agree that, by adopting one theory of life, Texas may override the rights of the pregnant women that are at stake. We repeat, however, that the state does have an important and legitimate interest in preserving and protecting the health of the pregnant women and that it has still another important and legitimate interest in protecting the potentiality of human life. These interests are separate and distinct. Each grows in substantiality as the woman approaches term and, at a point during pregnancy, each becomes "compelling."

With respect to the interest in the health of the mother, the "compelling" point, in the light of present medical knowledge, is at approximately the end of the first trimester. This is so because of the now established medical fact that until the end of the trimester mortality in abortion is less than mortality in normal childbirth. It follows that, from and after this point, a state may regulate the abortion procedure to the extent that the regulation reasonably relates to the preservation and protection of maternal health. Example of permissible state regulation in this area are requirements as to the qualifications of the person who is to perform the abortion; as to facility in which the procedure is to be preformed, and the like.

This means on the other hand, that, for the period of pregnancy prior to this "compelling" point, the attending physician, in consultation with his patient, is free to determine, without regulation by the state, that in his medical judgment the patient's pregnancy should be terminated. If that decision is reached, the judgment may be effectuated by an abortion free of interference by the state.

With respect to the interest in potential life, the "compelling" point is at viability which "is usually placed at about seven months (28 weeks) but may occur earlier, even at 24 weeks." This is so because the fetus then presumably has the capability of meaningful life outside the mother's womb. State regulation protective of fetal life after viability thus has both logical and biological justifications. If the state is interested in protecting fetal life after viability, it may go as far as to proscribe abortion during that period except when it is necessary to preserve the life or health of the mother.

Measured against these standards, the Texas statue sweeps too broadly and therefore, cannot survive the constitutional attack made upon it here.

In Doe procedural requirements contained in one of the modern abortion statutes are considered. That opinion and this one are to be read together.

This holding, we feel, is consistent with the relative weights of the respective interests involved, with the lessons and example of medical and legal history, with the lenity of the common law, and with the demands of the profound problems of the present day.

HOW WELL DID YOU UNDERSTAND THIS SELECTION?

1. What does Justice Blackmun cite as reasons criminal abortion laws were enacted?

2. What was the ruling in *Roe v. Wade* based on? Explain?

3. What restriction did the Court place on abortion?

4. How does the Court reject the idea that a fetus is a person?

Minorities faced discrimination across America when seeking employment. In an attempt to remedy this situation, Congress enacted Title VII of the Civil Rights Act of 1964. This law, sections of which are reprinted below, generally forbade employers to refuse to hire or discharge an employee due to race, color, religion, sex or other ethnic origin, defined illegal employment practices, and created the Equal Employment Opportunity Commission to investigate employment law violations.

UNLAWFUL EMPLOYMENT PRACTICES

(a) Employer practices

It shall be an unlawful employment practice for an employer -

(1) to fail or refuse to hire or to discharge any individual, or otherwise to discriminate against any individual with respect to his compensation, terms, conditions, or privileges of employment, because of such individual's race, color, religion, sex, or national origin; or

(2) to limit, segregate, or classify his employees or applicants for employment in any way which would deprive or tend to deprive any individual of employment opportunities or otherwise adversely affect his status as an employee, because of such individual's race, color, religion, sex, or national origin.

(b) Employment agency practices

It shall be an unlawful employment practice for an employment agency to fail or refuse to refer for employment, or otherwise to discriminate against, any individual because of his race, color, religion, sex, or national origin, or to classify or refer for employment any individual on the basis of his race, color, religion, sex, or national origin.

(c) Labor organization practices

It shall be an unlawful employment practice for a labor organization-

(1) to exclude or to expel from its membership, or otherwise to discriminate against, any individual because of his race, color, religion, sex, or national origin;

(2) to limit, segregate, or classify its membership or applicants for membership, or to classify or fail or refuse to refer for employment any individual, in any way which would deprive or tend to deprive any individual of employment opportunities, or would limit such employment opportunities or otherwise adversely affect his status as an employee or as an applicant for employment, because of such individual's race, color, religion, sex, or national origin; or

(3) to cause or attempt to cause an employer to discriminate against an individual in violation of this section.

(d) Training programs

It shall be an unlawful employment practice for any employer, labor organization, or joint labor-management committee controlling apprenticeship or other training or retraining, including on-the-job training programs to discriminate against any individual because of his race, color, religion, sex, or national origin in admission to, or employment in, any program established to provide apprenticeship or other training.

(e) Businesses or enterprises with personnel qualified on basis of religion, sex, or national origin; educational institutions with personnel of particular religion

Notwithstanding any other provision of this subchapter, (1) it shall not be an unlawful employment practice for an employer to hire and employ employees, for an employment agency to classify, or refer for employment any individual, for a labor organization to classify its membership or to classify or refer for employment any individual, or for an employer, labor organization, or joint labor-management committee controlling apprenticeship or other training or retraining programs to admit or employ any individual in any such program, on the basis of his religion, sex, or national origin in those certain instances where religion, sex, or national origin is a bona fide occupational qualification reasonably necessary to the normal operation of that particular business or enterprise, and (2) it shall not be an unlawful employment practice for a school, college, university, or other educational institution or institution of learning to hire and employ employees of a particular religion if such school, college, university, or other educational institution or institution of learning is, in whole or in substantial part, owned, supported, controlled, or managed by a particular religion or by a particular religious corporation, association, or society, or if the curriculum of such school, college, university, or other educational institution or institution of learning is directed toward the propagation of a particular religion.

(f) Members of Communist Party or Communist-action or Communist-front organizations

As used in this subchapter, the phrase "unlawful employment practice" shall not be deemed to include any action or measure taken by an employer, labor organization, joint labor¬ management committee, or employment agency with respect to an individual who is a member of the Communist Party of the United States or of any other organization required to register as a Communist¬-action or Communist-¬front organization by final order of the Subversive Activities Control Board pursuant to the Subversive Activities Control Act of 1950.

(g) National security

Notwithstanding any other provision of this subchapter, it shall not be an unlawful employment practice for an employer to fail or refuse to hire and employ any individual for any position, for an employer to discharge any individual from any position, or for an employment agency to fail or refuse to refer any individual for employment in any position, or for a labor organization to fail or refuse to refer any individual for employment in any position, if-

> (1) the occupancy of such position, or access to the premises in or upon which any part of the duties of such position is performed or is to be performed, is subject to any requirement imposed in the interest of the national security of the United States under any security program in effect pursuant to or administered under any statute of the United States or any Executive order of the President; and
>
> (2) such individual has not fulfilled or has ceased to fulfill that requirement.

(h) Seniority or merit system; quantity or quality of production; ability tests; compensation based on sex and authorized by minimum wage provisions

Notwithstanding any other provision of this subchapter, it shall not be an unlawful employment practice for an employer to apply different standards of compensation, or different terms, conditions, or privileges of employment pursuant to a bona fide seniority or merit system, or a system which measures earnings by quantity or quality of production or to employees who work in different locations, provided that such differences are not the result of an intention to discriminate because of race, color, religion, sex, or national origin, nor shall it be an unlawful employment practice for an employer to give and to act upon the results of any professionally developed ability test provided that such test, its administration or action upon the results is not designed, intended or used to discriminate because of race, color, religion, sex or national origin. It shall not be an unlawful employment practice under this subchapter for any employer to differentiate upon the basis of sex in determining the amount of the wages or compensation paid or to be paid to employees of such employer if such differentiation is authorized by the provisions of section 206(d) of Title 29 [section 6(d) of the Labor Standards Act of 1938, as amended].

(i) Businesses or enterprises extending preferential treatment to Indians

Nothing contained in this subchapter shall apply to any business or enterprise on or near an Indian reservation with respect to any publicly announced employment practice of such business or enterprise under which a preferential treatment is given to any individual because he is an Indian living on or near a reservation.

(j) Preferential treatment not to be granted on account of existing number or percentage imbalance

Nothing contained in this subchapter shall be interpreted to require any employer, employment agency, labor organization, or joint labor-¬management committee subject to this subchapter to grant preferential treatment to any individual or to any group because of the race, color, religion, sex, or national origin of such individual or group on account of an imbalance which may exist with respect to the total number or percentage of persons of any race, color, religion, sex, or national origin employed by any employer, referred or classified for employment by any employment agency or labor organization, admitted to membership or classified by any labor organization, or admitted to, or employed in, any apprenticeship or other training program, in comparison with the total number or percentage of persons of such race, color, religion, sex, or national origin in any community, State, section, or other area, or in the available work force in any community, State, section, or other area.

(k) Burden of proof in disparate impact cases

> (1) (A) An unlawful employment practice based on disparate impact is established under this subchapter only if-
>
> (i) a complaining party demonstrates that a respondent uses a particular employment practice that causes a disparate impact on the basis of race, color, religion, sex, or national origin and the respondent fails to demonstrate that the challenged practice is job related for the position in question and consistent with business necessity; or

(ii) the complaining party makes the demonstration described in subparagraph (C) with respect to an alternative employment practice and the respondent refuses to adopt such alternative employment practice.

(B) (i) With respect to demonstrating that a particular employment practice causes a disparate impact as described in subparagraph (A)(i), the complaining party shall demonstrate that each particular challenged employment practice causes a disparate impact, except that if the complaining party can demonstrate to the court that the elements of a respondent's decision making process are not capable of separation for analysis, the decision making process may be analyzed as one employment practice.

(ii) If the respondent demonstrates that a specific employment practice does not cause the disparate impact, the respondent shall not be required to demonstrate that such practice is required by business necessity.

(C) The demonstration referred to by subparagraph (A)(ii) shall be in accordance with the law as it existed on June 4, 1989, with respect to the concept of "alternative employment practice".

(2) A demonstration that an employment practice is required by business necessity may not be used as a defense against a claim of intentional discrimination under this subchapter.

(3) Notwithstanding any other provision of this subchapter, a rule barring the employment of an individual who currently and knowingly uses or possesses a controlled substance, as defined in schedules I and II of section 102(6) of the Controlled Substances Act other than the use or possession of a drug taken under the supervision of a licensed health care professional, or any other use or possession authorized by the Controlled Substances Act or any other provision of Federal law, shall be considered an unlawful employment practice under this subchapter only if such rule is adopted or applied with an intent to discriminate because of race, color, religion, sex, or national origin.

(l) Prohibition of discriminatory use of test scores

It shall be an unlawful employment practice for a respondent, in connection with the selection or referral of applicants or candidates for employment or promotion, to adjust the scores of, use different cutoff scores for, or otherwise alter the results of, employment related tests on the basis of race, color, religion, sex, or national origin.

(m) Impermissible consideration of race, color, religion, sex, or national origin in employment practices

Except as otherwise provided in this subchapter, an unlawful employment practice is established when the complaining party demonstrates that race, color, religion, sex, or national origin was a motivating factor for any employment practice, even though other factors also motivated the practice.

(n) Resolution of challenges to employment practices implementing litigated or consent judgments or orders

(1) (A) Notwithstanding any other provision of law, and except as provided in paragraph (2), an employment practice that implements and is within the scope of a litigated or consent judgment or order that resolves a claim of employment discrimination under the Constitution or Federal civil rights laws may not be challenged under the circumstances described in subparagraph (B).

(B) A practice described in subparagraph (A) may not be challenged in a claim under the Constitution or Federal civil rights laws-

(i) by a person who, prior to the entry of the judgment or order described in subparagraph (A), had-

(I) actual notice of the proposed judgment or order sufficient to apprise such person that such judgment or order might adversely affect the interests and legal rights of such person and that an opportunity was available to present objections to such judgment or order by a future date certain; and

(II) a reasonable opportunity to present objections to such judgment or order; or

(ii) by a person whose interests were adequately represented by another person who had previously challenged the judgment or order on the same legal grounds and with a similar factual situation, unless there has been an intervening change in law or fact.

(2) Nothing in this subsection shall be construed to-

(A) alter the standards for intervention under rule 24 of the Federal Rules of Civil Procedure or apply to the rights of parties who have successfully intervened pursuant to such rule in the proceeding in which the parties intervened;

(B) apply to the rights of parties to the action in which a litigated or consent judgment or order was entered, or of members of a class represented or sought to be represented in such action, or of members of a group on whose behalf relief was sought in such action by the Federal Government;

(C) prevent challenges to a litigated or consent judgment or order on the ground that such judgment or order was obtained through collusion or fraud, or is transparently invalid or was entered by a court lacking subject matter jurisdiction; or

(D) authorize or permit the denial to any person of the due process of law required by the Constitution.

OTHER UNLAWFUL EMPLOYMENT PRACTICES

(a) Discrimination for making charges, testifying, assisting, or participating in enforcement proceedings

It shall be an unlawful employment practice for an employer to discriminate against any of his employees or applicants for employment, for an employment agency, or joint labor-¬management committee controlling apprenticeship or other training or retraining, including on—the-job training programs, to discriminate against any individual, or for a labor organization to discriminate against any member thereof or applicant for membership, because he has opposed any practice made an unlawful employment practice by this subchapter, or because he has made a charge, testified, assisted, or participated in any manner in an investigation, proceeding, or hearing under this subchapter.

(b) Printing or publication of notices or advertisements indicating prohibited preference, limitation, specification, or discrimination; occupational qualification exception

It shall be an unlawful employment practice for an employer, labor organization, employment agency, or joint labor-¬management committee controlling apprenticeship or other training or retraining, including on¬-the-¬job training programs, to print or publish or cause to be printed or published any notice or advertisement relating to employment by such an employer or membership in or any classification or referral for employment by such a labor organization, or relating to any classification or referral for employment by such an employment agency, or relating to admission to, or employment in, any program established to provide apprenticeship or other training by such a joint labor¬-management committee, indicating any preference, limitation, specification, or discrimination, based on race, color, religion, sex, or national origin, except that such a notice or advertisement may indicate a preference, limitation, specification, or discrimination based on religion, sex, or national origin when religion, sex, or national origin is a bona fide occupational qualification for employment.

EQUAL EMPLOYMENT OPPORTUNITY COMMISSION

There is hereby created a Commission to be known as the Equal Employment Opportunity Commission, which shall be composed of five members, not more than three of whom shall be members of the same political party. Members of the Commission shall be appointed by the President by and with the advice and consent of the Senate for a term of five years. Any individual chosen to fill a vacancy shall be appointed only for the unexpired term of the member whom he shall succeed, and all members of the Commission shall continue to serve until their successors are appointed and qualified, except that no such member of the Commission shall continue to serve (1) for more than sixty days when the Congress is in session unless a nomination to fill such vacancy shall have been submitted to the Senate, or (2) after the adjournment sine die of the session of the Senate in which such nomination was submitted. The President shall designate one member to serve as Chairman of the Commission, and one member to serve as Vice Chairman. The Chairman shall be responsible on behalf of the Commission for the administrative operations of the Commission, and, except as provided in subsection (b) of this section, shall appoint, in accordance with the provisions of Title 5 [United States Code] governing appointments in the competitive service, such officers, agents, attorneys, administrative law judges [originally, hearing examiners], and employees as he deems necessary to assist it in the performance of its functions and to fix their compensation in accordance with the provisions of chapter 51 and subchapter III of chapter 53 of Title 5 [United States Code], relating to classification and General Schedule pay rates: Provided, That assignment, removal, and compensation of administrative law judges [originally, hearing examiners] shall be in accordance with sections 3105, 3344, 5372, and 7521 of Title 5 [United States Code].

(g) Powers of Commission

The Commission shall have power-

(1) to cooperate with and, with their consent, utilize regional, State, local, and other agencies, both public and private, and individuals;

(2) to pay to witnesses whose depositions are taken or who are summoned before the Commission or any of its agents the same witness and mileage fees as are paid to witnesses in the courts of the United States;

(3) to furnish to persons subject to this subchapter such technical assistance as they may request to further their compliance with this subchapter or an order issued thereunder;

(4) upon the request of (i) any employer, whose employees or some of them, or (ii) any labor organization, whose members or some of them, refuse or threaten to refuse to cooperate in effectuating the provisions of this subchapter, to assist in such effectuation by conciliation or such other remedial action as is provided by this subchapter;

(5) to make such technical studies as are appropriate to effectuate the purposes and policies of this subchapter and to make the results of such studies available to the public;

(6) to intervene in a civil action brought under section 2000e-5 of this title [section 706] by an aggrieved party against a respondent other than a government, governmental agency or political subdivision.

ENFORCEMENT PROVISIONS

(a) Power of Commission to prevent unlawful employment practices

The Commission is empowered, as hereinafter provided, to prevent any person from engaging in any unlawful employment practice as set forth in section 2000e-2 or 2000e-3 of this title [section 703 or 704].

(b) Charges by persons aggrieved or member of Commission of unlawful employment practices by employers, etc.; filing; allegations; notice to respondent; contents of notice; investigation by Commission; contents of charges; prohibition on disclosure of charges; determination of reasonable cause; conference, conciliation, and persuasion for elimination of unlawful practices; prohibition on disclosure of informal endeavors to end unlawful practices; use of evidence in subsequent proceedings; penalties for disclosure of information; time for determination of reasonable cause

Whenever a charge is filed by or on behalf of a person claiming to be aggrieved, or by a member of the Commission, alleging that an employer, employment agency, labor organization, or joint labor ¬management committee controlling apprenticeship or other training or retraining, including on-¬the-¬job training programs, has engaged in an unlawful employment practice, the Commission shall serve a notice of the charge (including the date, place and circumstances of the alleged unlawful employment practice) on such employer, employment agency, labor organization, or joint labor-¬management committee (hereinafter referred to as the "respondent") within ten days, and shall make an investigation thereof. Charges shall be in writing under oath or affirmation and shall contain such information and be in such form as the Commission requires. Charges shall not be made public by the Commission. If the Commission determines after such investigation that there is not reasonable cause to believe that the charge is true, it shall dismiss the charge and promptly notify the person claiming to be aggrieved and the respondent of its action. In determining whether reasonable cause exists, the Commission shall accord substantial weight to final findings and orders made by State or local authorities in proceedings commenced under State or local law pursuant to the requirements of subsections (c) and (d) of this section. If the Commission determines after such investigation that there is reasonable cause to believe that the charge is true, the Commission shall endeavor to eliminate any such alleged unlawful employment practice by informal methods of conference, conciliation, and persuasion. Nothing said or done during and as a part of such informal endeavors may be made public by the Commission, its officers or employees, or used as evidence in a subsequent proceeding without the written consent of the persons concerned. Any person who makes public information in violation of this subsection shall be fined not more than $1,000 or imprisoned for not more than one year, or both. The Commission shall make its determination on reasonable cause as promptly as possible and, so far as practicable, not later than one hundred and twenty days from the filing of the charge or, where applicable under subsection (c) or (d) of this section, from the date upon which the Commission is authorized to take action with respect to the charge.

(1) If within thirty days after a charge is filed with the Commission or within thirty days after expiration of any period of reference under subsection (c) or (d) of this section, the Commission has been unable to secure from the respondent a conciliation agreement acceptable to the Commission, the Commission may bring a civil action against any respondent not a government, governmental agency, or political subdivision named in the charge. In the case of a respondent which is a government, governmental agency, or political subdivision, if the Commission has been unable to secure from the respondent a conciliation agreement acceptable to the Commission, the Commission shall take no further action and shall refer the case to the Attorney General who may bring a civil action against such respondent in the appropriate United States district court. The person or persons aggrieved shall have the right to intervene in a civil action brought by the Commission or the Attorney General in a case involving a government, governmental agency, or political subdivision. If a charge filed with the Commission pursuant to subsection (b) of this section is dismissed by the Commission, or if within one hundred and eighty

days from the filing of such charge or the expiration of any period of reference under subsection (c) or (d) of this section, whichever is later, the Commission has not filed a civil action under this section or the Attorney General has not filed a civil action in a case involving a government, governmental agency, or political subdivision, or the Commission has not entered into a conciliation agreement to which the person aggrieved is a party, the Commission, or the Attorney General in a case involving a government, governmental agency, or political subdivision, shall so notify the person aggrieved and within ninety days after the giving of such notice a civil action may be brought against the respondent named in the charge (A) by the person claiming to be aggrieved or (B) if such charge was filed by a member of the Commission, by any person whom the charge alleges was aggrieved by the alleged unlawful employment practice. Upon application by the complainant and in such circumstances as the court may deem just, the court may appoint an attorney for such complainant and may authorize the commencement of the action without the payment of fees, costs, or security. Upon timely application, the court may, in its discretion, permit the Commission, or the Attorney General in a case involving a government, governmental agency, or political subdivision, to intervene in such civil action upon certification that the case is of general public importance. Upon request, the court may, in its discretion, stay further proceedings for not more than sixty days pending the termination of State or local.

HOW WELL DID YOU UNDERSTAND THIS SELECTION?

1. What does the Title VII of the 1964 Civil Rights forbid?

2. What are some examples of illegal hiring practices?

3. How does the law protect individuals who have complained about employment practices?

4. What is the purpose of the Equal Employment Opportunity Commission?

5. What power does the law give the EEOC?

In 1972, after decades of activity by feminists to break the "glass ceiling," Congress enacted the landmark Title IX, Education Amendment Act that prohibits gender discrimination in college admission, hiring, and athletics. This important legislation made it easier for women to earn college degrees and accounted for a slow but steady increase in the number of women earning professional and advanced graduate degrees. In 1960, for example, less than 2 percent of adult American women held a degree higher than a Bachelor of Arts or Science. About 4.5 percent of males, in contrast, held Master's or other advanced degrees. By 2010, largely as a result of Title IX, slightly more than 10 percent of women held advanced or professional degrees in comparison to 11 percent of males holding similar degrees. Clearly, enactment of Title IX helped American women achieve nearly educational parity with their male counterparts.

Section 1681. Sex

(a) Prohibition against discrimination; exceptions. No person in the United States shall, on the basis of sex, be excluded from participation in, be denied the benefits of, or be subjected to discrimination under any education program or activity receiving Federal financial assistance, except that:

(1) Classes of educational institutions subject to prohibition

In regard to admissions to educational institutions, this section shall apply only to institutions of vocational education, professional education, and graduate higher education, and to public institutions of undergraduate higher education;

(2) Educational institutions commencing planned change in admissions

In regard to admissions to educational institutions, this section shall not apply (A) for one year from June 23, 1972, nor for six years after June 23, 1972, in the case of an educational institution which has begun the process of changing from being an institution which admits only students of one sex to being an institution which admits students of both sexes, but only if it is carrying out a plan for such a change which is approved by the Secretary of Education or (B) for seven years from the date an educational institution begins the process of changing from being an institution which admits only students of one sex to being an institution which admits students of both sexes, but only if it is carrying out a plan for such a change which is approved by the Secretary of Education, whichever is the later;

(3) Educational institutions of religious organizations with contrary religious tenets

This section shall not apply to any educational institution which is controlled by a religious organization if the application of this subsection would not be consistent with the religious tenets of such organization;

(4) Educational institutions training individuals for military services or merchant marine

This section shall not apply to an educational institution whose primary purpose is the training of individuals for the military services of the United States, or the merchant marine;

(5) Public educational institutions with traditional and continuing admissions policy

In regard to admissions this section shall not apply to any public institution of undergraduate higher education which is an institution that traditionally and continually from its establishment has had a policy of admitting only students of one sex;

(6) Social fraternities or sororities; voluntary youth service organizations

This section shall not apply to membership practices --

(A) of a social fraternity or social sorority which is exempt from taxation under section 501(a) of Title 26, the active membership of which consists primarily of students in attendance at an institution of higher education, or

(B) of the Young Men's Christian Association, Young Women's Christian Association; Girl Scouts, Boy Scouts, Camp Fire Girls, and voluntary youth service organizations which are so exempt, the membership of which has traditionally been limited to persons of one sex and principally to persons of less than nineteen years of age;

(7) Boy or Girl conferences

This section shall not apply to--

(A) any program or activity of the American Legion undertaken in connection with the organization or operation of any Boys State conference, Boys Nation conference, Girls State conference, or Girls Nation conference; or

(B) any program or activity of any secondary school or educational institution specifically for--

(i) the promotion of any Boys State conference, Boys Nation conference, Girls State conference, or Girls Nation conference; or

(ii) the selection of students to attend any such conference;

(8) Father-son or mother-daughter activities at educational institutions

This section shall not preclude father-son or mother-daughter activities at an educational institution, but if such activities are provided for students of one sex, opportunities for reasonably comparable activities shall be provided for students of the other sex; and

(9) Institutions of higher education scholarship awards in "beauty" pageants

This section shall not apply with respect to any scholarship or other financial assistance awarded by an institution of higher education to any individual because such individual has received such award in any pageant in which the attainment of such award is based upon a combination of factors related to the personal appearance, poise, and talent of such individual and in which participation is limited to individuals of one sex only, so long as such pageant is in compliance with other nondiscrimination provisions of Federal law.

(b) Preferential or disparate treatment because of imbalance in participation or receipt of Federal benefits; statistical evidence of imbalance.

Nothing contained in subsection (a) of this section shall be interpreted to require any educational institution to grant preferential or disparate treatment to the members of one sex on account of an imbalance which may exist with respect to the total number or percentage of persons of that sex participating in or receiving the benefits of any federally supported program or activity, in comparison with the total number or percentage of persons of that sex in any community, State, section, or other area: Provided, that this subsection shall not be construed to prevent the consideration in any hearing or proceeding under this chapter of statistical evidence tending to show that such an imbalance exists with respect to the participation in, or receipt of the benefits of, any such program or activity by the members of one sex.

(c) Educational institution defined.

For the purposes of this chapter an educational institution means any public or private preschool, elementary, or secondary school, or any institution of vocational, professional, or higher education, except that in the case of an educational institution composed of more than one school, college, or department which are administratively separate units, such term means each such school, college or department.

Section 1682. Federal administrative enforcement; report to Congressional committees

Each Federal department and agency which is empowered to extend Federal financial assistance to any education program or activity, by way of grant, loan, or contract other than a contract of insurance or guaranty, is authorized and directed to effectuate the provisions of section 1681 of this title with respect to such program or activity by issuing rules, regulations, or orders of general applicability which shall be consistent with achievement of the objectives of the statute authorizing the financial assistance in connection with which the action is taken. No such rule, regulation, or order shall become effective unless and until approved by the President. Compliance with any requirement adopted pursuant to this section may be effected (1) by the termination of or refusal to grant or to continue assistance under such program or activity to any recipient as to whom there has been an express finding on the record, after opportunity for hearing, of a failure to comply with such requirement, but such termination or refusal shall be limited to the particular political entity, or part thereof, or other recipient as to whom such a finding has been made, and shall be limited in its effect to the particular program, or part thereof, in which such noncompliance has been so found, or (2) by any other means authorized by law: Provided, however, that no such action shall be taken until the department or agency concerned has advised the appropriate person or persons of the failure to comply with the requirement and has determined that compliance cannot be secured by voluntary means. In the case of any action terminating, or refusing to grant or continue, assistance because of failure to comply with a requirement imposed pursuant to this section, the head of the Federal department or agency shall file with the committees of the House and Senate having legislative jurisdiction over the program or activity involved a full written report of the circumstances and the grounds for such action. No such action shall become effective until thirty days have elapsed after the filing of such report.

Section 1683. Judicial Review

Any department or agency action taken pursuant to section 1682 of this title shall be subject to such judicial review as may otherwise be provided by law for similar action taken by such department or agency on other grounds. In the case of action, not otherwise subject to judicial review, terminating or refusing to grant or to continue financial assistance upon a finding of failure to comply with any requirement imposed pursuant to section 1682 of this title, any person aggrieved (including any State or political subdivision thereof and any agency of either) may obtain judicial review of such action in accordance with chapter 7 of title 5, United States Code, and such action shall not be deemed committed to unreviewable agency discretion within the meaning of section 701 of that title.

Section 1684. Blindness or visual impairment; prohibition against discrimination

No person in the United States shall, on the ground of blindness or severely impaired vision, be denied admission in any course of study by a recipient of Federal financial assistance for any education program or activity; but nothing herein shall be construed to require any such institution to provide any special services to such person because of his blindness or visual impairment.

Section 1685. Authority under other laws unaffected

Nothing in this chapter shall add to or detract from any existing authority with respect to any program or activity under which Federal financial assistance is extended by way of a contract of insurance or guaranty.

Section 1686. Interpretation with respect to living facilities

Notwithstanding anything to the contrary contained in this chapter, nothing contained herein shall be construed to prohibit any educational institution receiving funds under this Act, from maintaining separate living facilities for the different sexes.

Section 1687. Interpretation of "program or activity"

For the purposes of this title, the term "program or activity" and "program" mean all of the operations of --

     (l)(A) a department, agency, special purpose district, or other instrumentality of a State or of a local government; or

(B) the entity of such State or local government that distributed such assistance and each such department or agency (and each other State or local government entity) to which the assistance is extended, in the case of assistance to a State or local government;

     (2)(A) a college, university, or other postsecondary institution, or a public system of higher education; or

(B) a local educational agency (as defined in section2854(a)(10) of this title, system of vocational education, or other school system;

     (3)(A) an entire corporation, partnership, or other private organization, or an entire sole proprietorship --

          (i) if assistance is extended to such corporation, partnership, private organization, or sole proprietorship as a whole; or

          (ii) which is principally engaged in the business of providing education, health care, housing, social services, or parks and recreation; or

(B) the entire plant or other comparable, geographically separate facility to which Federal financial assistance is extended, in the case of any other corporation, partnership, private organization, or sole proprietorship; or

     (4) any other entity which is established by two or more of the entities described in paragraph (l), (2) or (3);

any part of which is extended Federal financial assistance, except that such term does not include any operation of an entity which is controlled by a religious organization if the application of section 1681 if this title to such operation would not be consistent with the religious tenets of such organization.

Section 1688. Neutrality with respect to abortion

Nothing in this chapter shall be construed to require or prohibit any person, or public or private entity, to provide or pay for any benefit or service, including the use of facilities, related to an abortion. Nothing in this section shall be construed to permit a penalty to be imposed on any person or individual because such person or individual is seeking or has received any benefit or service related to a legal abortion.

HOW WELL DID YOU UNDERSTAND THIS SELECTION?

1. What does Title IX do?

2. What exceptions does Title IX make?

3. What legal remedies did the law allow if discrimination occurred?

4. What educational institutions were required to abide by the law? What types did not have to comply?

THE ENDANGERED SPECIES ACT OF 1973

Publication of Rachael Carson's **Silent Spring** *in 1962 awakened Americans to the effect pollution and economic development had on wildlife and the natural environment as the nation's most pressing problem. Faced with public pressure to do something to clean up the environment, Congress enacted laws designed to undo some of the damage done to the natural world. One of the most important of these laws was the Endangered Species Act of 1973. This law not only attempted to save animals and plants threatened by extinction but protected as well the habitat endangered wildlife needed for survival. Excerpts from the Endangered Species Act are printed below.*

Findings, Purposes, and Policy

Sec. 2 (a) Findings- the Congress finds and declares that –

(1) Various species of fish, wildlife, and plants in the United States have been rendered extinct as a consequence of economic growth and development untendered by adequate concern and conservation;

(2) Other species of fish, wildlife, and plants have been so depleted in numbers that they are danger of threatened with extinction;

(3) These species of fish, wildlife, and plants are of aesthetic, ecological, educational, historical, recreational, and scientific value to the Nation and its people;

(4) The United States has pledged itself as a sovereign state in the international community to conserve to the extent practicable the various species of fish or wildlife and plants facing extinction, pursuant to

(a) Migratory bird treaties with Canada and Mexico;

(b) The Migratory and Endangered Bird Treaty with Japan;

(c) The Convention on Nature Protection and Wildlife preservation in the Western Hemisphere;

(d) The International Convention for the Northwest Atlantic Fisheries;

(e) The International Convention for the High Seas Fisheries of the North Pacific Ocean;

(f) The convention on International Trade in Endangered Species of Wild Fauna and Flora; and

(g) Other international agreements; and

479

(5) Encouraging the States and other interested parties, through Federal financial assistance and a system of incentives, to develop and maintain conservation program which meet national and international standards is a key to meeting the Nation's international commitments and to better safeguarding, for the benefits of all citizens, the Nation's heritage in fish, wildlife, and plants.

(b) Purposes.—the purposes of this Act are to provide a means whereby the ecosystem upon which endangered species and threatened species depend may be conserved, to provide a program for the conservation of such endangered species and threatened species, and to take such steps as may be appropriate to achieve the purposes of the treaties and conventions set forth in subsection (a) of this section.

(c) Policy.—(1) it is further declared to be the policy of Congress that all Federal departments and agencies shall seek to conserve endangered species and threatened species and shall utilize their authorities in furtherance of the purposes of this Act.

(2) It is further declared to be the policy of Congress that Federal agencies shall cooperate with State and local agencies to resolve water resource issues in concert with conservation of endangered species.

PROHIBITED ACTS

Sec. 9. (a) GENERAL.—(1) Except as provided in sections 6(g)(2) and 10 of this Act, with respect to any endangered species of fish or wildlife listed pursuant to section 4 of this Act it is unlawful for any person subject to the jurisdiction of the United States to—

(a) Import any such species into, or export any such species from the United States;

(b) Take any such species within the United States or the territorial sea of the United States;

(c) Take such species upon the high seas;

(d) Possess, sell, deliver, carry, transport, or ship, by any means whatsoever, any such species taken in violation of subparagraphs(b) and (c);

(e) Deliver, receive, carry, transport, or ship in interstate or foreign commerce, by any means whatsoever and in the course of a commercial activity such species;

(f) Sell or offer for sale in interstate or foreign commerce any such species; or

(g) Violate any regulation pertaining to such species or to any threatened species of fish or wildlife listed pursuant to section 4 of this Act and promulgated by the Secretary pursuant to authority provided by this act.

(2) Except as provided in sections 6(g)(2) and 10 of this act, with respect to any endangered species of plants listed pursuant to section 4 of this act, it is unlawful for any person subject to the jurisdiction of the United States to—

(a) Import any such species into, or export any such species from, the United States;

(b) Remove and reduce to possession any such to possession any such species from areas under Federal jurisdiction; maliciously damage or destroy any such species on any such area; or remove, cut, dig, or damage or destroy any such species on any other area in knowing violation of any law or regulation of any State or in the course of any violation of a State criminal trespass law.

(c) Deliver; receive, carry, transport, or ship in interstate or foreign commerce, by any means whatsoever and in the course of a commercial activity, any such species;

(d) Sell or offer for sale in interest or foreign commerce any such species or to any threatened

(e) Violate any regulation pertaining to such species or to any threatened species of plants listed pursuant to section 4 of this act and promulgated by the Secretary pursuant to authority provide by this act.

ENDANGERED PLANTS

SEC. 12. The Secretary of the Smithsonian Institution, in conjunction with other affected agencies, is authorized and directed to review (1) species of plants which are now or may become endangered or threatened and (2) methods of adequately conserving such species, and to report to Congress, within one year after the date of the enactment of this act, the result of such review including recommendations for new legislation or the amendment of existing legislation.

HOW WELL DID YOU UNDERSTAND THIS SELECTION?

1.   What basically does the Endangered Species Act do?

2.   What do you think is the law's purpose? Explain?

3.   Why was the Endangered Species Act needed? Explain?

4.   What do you think might have happened had Congress not have enacted the Endangered Species Act?

REORGANIZATION PLAN NO. 3 OF 1970 (Creation of the EPA)

Republican President Richard Nixon, who personally believed that the environmental activism that characterized the 1960s and 1970s would be short-lived, succumbed to pressures from the left and created the EPA (Environmental Protection Agency) in 1970. The EPA's creation was achieved when Nixon sent to Congress the Reorganization Plan Number Three. Below are remarks Nixon sent to Congress on July 9, 1970, the day he sent the Reorganization Plan Number Three to Capitol Hill.

July 9, 1970

To the Congress of the United States:

As concern with the condition of our physical environment has intensified, it has become increasingly clear that we need to know more about the total environment--land, water, and air. It also has become increasingly clear that only by reorganizing our Federal efforts can we develop that knowledge, and effectively ensure the protection, development and enhancement of the total environment itself.

The Government's environmentally-related activities have grown up piecemeal over the years. The time has come to organize them rationally and systematically. As a major step in this direction, I am transmitting today two reorganization plans: one to establish an Environmental Protection Agency, and one to establish, with the Department of Commerce, a National Oceanic and Atmospheric Administration.

Environmental Protection Agency (EPA)

Our national government today is not structured to make a coordinated attack on the pollutants which debase the air we breathe, the water we drink, and the land that grows our food. Indeed, the present governmental structure for dealing with environmental pollution often defies effective and concerted action.

Despite its complexity, for pollution control purposes the environment must be perceived as a single, interrelated system. Present assignments of departmental responsibilities do not reflect this interrelatedness.

Many agency missions, for example, are designed primarily along media lines--air, water, and land. Yet the sources of air, water, and land pollution are interrelated and often interchangeable. A single source may pollute the air with

481

smoke and chemicals, the land with solid wastes, and a river or lake with chemical and other wastes. Control of the air pollution may produce more solid wastes, which then pollute the land or water. Control of the water-polluting effluent may convert it into solid wastes, which must be disposed of on land.

Similarly, some pollutants--chemicals, radiation, pesticides--appear in all media. Successful control of them at present requires the coordinated efforts of a variety of separate agencies and departments. The results are not always successful.

A far more effective approach to pollution control would:
- Identify pollutants.
- Trace them through the entire ecological chain, observing and recording changes in form as they occur.
- Determine the total exposure of man and his environment.
- Examine interactions among forms of pollution.
- Identify where in the ecological chain interdiction would be most appropriate.

In organizational terms, this requires pulling together into one agency a variety of research, monitoring, standard-setting and enforcement activities now scattered through several departments and agencies. It also requires that the new agency include sufficient support elements--in research and in aids to State and local anti-pollution programs, for example--to give it the needed strength and potential for carrying out its mission. The new agency would also, of course, draw upon the results of research conducted by other agencies.

Components of the EPA

Under the terms of Reorganization Plan No.3, the following would be moved to the new Environmental Protection Agency:
- The functions carried out by the Federal Water Quality Administration (from the Department of the Interior).
- Functions with respect to pesticides studies now vested in the Department of the Interior.
- The functions carried out by the National Air Pollution Control Administration (from the Department of Health, Education, and Welfare).
- The functions carried out by the Bureau of Solid Waste Management and the Bureau of Water Hygiene, and portions of the functions carried out by the Bureau of Radiological Health of the Environmental Control Administration (from the Department of Health, Education, and Welfare).
- Certain functions with respect to pesticides carried out by the Food and Drug Administration (from the Department of Health, Education, and Welfare).
- Authority to perform studies relating to ecological systems now vested in the Council on Environmental Quality.
- Certain functions respecting radiation criteria and standards now vested in the Atomic Energy Commission and the Federal Radiation Council.
- Functions respecting pesticides registration and related activities now carried out by the Agricultural Research Service (from the Department of Agriculture).

With its broad mandate, EPA would also develop competence in areas of environmental protection that have not previously been given enough attention, such, for example, as the problem of noise, and it would provide an organization to which new programs in these areas could be added.

In brief, these are the principal functions to be transferred:

Advantages of Reorganization

This reorganization would permit response to environmental problems in a manner beyond the previous capability of our pollution control programs. The EPA would have the capacity to do research on important pollutants irrespective of the media in which they appear, and on the impact of these pollutants on the total environment. Both by itself and together with other agencies, the EPA would monitor the condition of the environment--biological as well as physical. With these data, the EPA would be able to establish quantitative "environmental baselines"--critical if we are to measure adequately the success or failure of our pollution abatement efforts.

As no disjointed array of separate programs can, the EPA would be able--in concert with the States- -to set and enforce standards for air and water quality and for individual pollutants. This consolidation of pollution control authorities would help assure that we do not create new environmental problems in the process of controlling existing ones. Industries seeking to minimize the adverse impact of their activities on the environment would be assured of consistent standards covering the full range of their waste disposal problems. As the States develop and expand their own pollution control programs, they would be able to look to one agency to support their efforts with financial and technical assistance and training.

In proposing that the Environmental Protection Agency be set up as a separate new agency, I am making an exception to one of my own principles: that, as a matter of effective and orderly administration, additional new independent agencies normally should not be created. In this case, however, the arguments against placing environmental protection activities under the jurisdiction of one or another of the existing departments and agencies are compelling.

In the first place, almost every part of government is concerned with the environment in some way, and affects it in some way. Yet each department also has its own primary mission--such as resource development, transportation, health, defense, urban growth or agriculture--which necessarily affects its own view of environmental questions.

In the second place, if the critical standard-setting functions were centralized within any one existing department, it would require that department constantly to make decisions affecting other departments--in which, whether fairly or unfairly, its own objectivity as an impartial arbiter could be called into question.

Because environmental protection cuts across so many jurisdictions, and because arresting environmental deterioration is of great importance to the quality of life in our country and the world, I believe that in this case a strong, independent agency is needed. That agency would, of course, work closely with and draw upon the expertise and assistance of other agencies having experience in the environmental area.

Roles and Functions of the EPA

The principal roles and functions of the EPA would include:
- The establishment and enforcement of environmental protection standards consistent with national environmental goals.
- The conduct of research on the adverse effects of pollution and on methods and equipment for controlling it, the gathering of information on pollution, and the use of this information in strengthening environmental protection programs and recommending policy changes.
- Assisting others, through grants, technical assistance and other means in arresting pollution of the environment.
- Assisting the Council on Environmental Quality in developing and recommending to the President new policies for the protection of the environment.

One natural question concerns the relationship between the EPA and the Council on Environmental Quality, recently established by Act of Congress.

It is my intention and expectation that the two will work in close harmony, reinforcing each other's mission. Essentially, the council is a top-level advisory group (which might be compared with the Council of Economic Advisers), while the EPA would be an operating, "line" organization. The Council will continue to be a part of the Executive Office of the President and will perform its overall coordinating and advisory roles with respect to all Federal programs related to environmental quality.

The Council, then, is concerned with all aspects of environmental quality--wildlife preservation, parklands, land use, and population growth, as well as pollution. The EPA would be charged with protecting the environment by abating pollution. In short, the Council focuses on what our broad policies in the environmental field should be; the EPA would focus on setting and enforcing pollution control standards. The two are not competing, but complementary--and taken together, they should give us, for the first time, the means to mount an effectively coordinated campaign against environmental degradation in all of its many forms.

National Oceanic and Atmospheric Administration

An On-Going Process

The reorganization which I am here proposing afford both the Congress and the Executive Branch an opportunity to re-evaluate the adequacy of existing program authorities involved in these consolidations. As these two new organizations come into being, we may well find that supplementary legislation to perfect their authorities will be necessary. I look forward to working with the Congress in this task.

In formulating these reorganization plans, I have been greatly aided by the work of the President's Advisory Council on Executive Organization (the Ash Council), the Commission on Marine Science, Engineering and Resources (the Stratton Commission, appointed by President Johnson), my special task force on oceanography headed by Dr. James Wakelin, and by the information developed during both House and Senate hearings on proposed NOAA legislation.

Many of those who have advised me have proposed additional reorganizations, and it may well be that in the future I shall recommend further changes. For the present, however, I think the two reorganizations transmitted today represent a sound and significant beginning. I also think that in practical terms, in this sensitive and rapidly developing area, it is better to proceed a step at a time-- and thus to be sure that we are not caught up in a form of organizational indigestion from trying to rearrange too much at once.

As we see how these changes work out, we will gain a better understanding of what further changes--in addition to these--might be desirable.

Ultimately, our objective should be to insure that the nation's environmental and resource protection activities are so organized as to maximize both the effective coordination of all and the effective functioning of each.

The Congress, the Administration and the public all share a profound commitment to the rescue of our natural environment, and the preservation of the Earth as a place both habitable by and hospitable to man. With its acceptance of the reorganization plans, the Congress will help us fulfill that commitment.

Richard Nixon

The White House

July 9, 1970

HOW WELL DID YOU UNDERSTAND THIS SELECTION?

1. Why did President Nixon say in this message to Congress that the EPA and NOAA were needed?

2. What did Nixon say an effective approach to pollution control would involve?

3. What basically would the role and function of the EPA be?

4. Why do you think President Nixon created the EPA?

On June 20, 1969 President Kennedy's goal of landing a man on the moon was accomplished. Aapproximately 600 million people worldwide watched on television as astronaut Neil Armstrong announced that "the Eagle has landed." Americans took great pride in this achievement by Armstrong and other members of the Apollo 11 crew. Many Americans believed the lunar landing demonstrated that the United States was superior to the Soviet Union, America's rival and chief enemy during the Cold War. Some Americans, however, saw the Lunar landing as an attempt to bring racism, sexism, capitalistic injustice, and human failures into the wider universe. The selection that follows is the first of three sections of NASA's official report on the Apollo 11 mission.

The purpose of the Apollo 11 mission was to land men on the lunar surface and to return them safely to earth. The crew were Neil A. Armstrong, Commander; Michael Collins, Command Module Pilot; and Edwin E. Aldrin, Jr., Lunar Module Pilot.

The space vehicle was launched from Kennedy Space Center, Florida, at 8:32:00 a.m.,EST., July 16, 1969. The activities during earth orbit checkout, translunar injection, transposition and docking, spacecraft ejection, and translunar coast were similar to those of Apollo 10. Only one midcourse correction, performed at about 27 hour's elapsed time, was required during translunar coast.

The spacecraft was inserted into lunar orbit at about 76 hours, and the circularization maneuver was performed two revolution later. Initial checkout of lunar module systems was satisfactory, and after a planned rest period, the Commander and Lunar Module Pilot entered the lunar module to prepare for descent.

The two spacecraft were undocked at about 100 hours, followed by separation of the command and service modules from the lunar module. Descent orbit insertion was performed at approximately 101-1/2 hours, and powered descent to the lunar surface began about 1 hour later. Operation of the guidance and descent propulsion system was nominal. The lunar module was maneuvered manually approximately 1100 feet downrange from the nominal landing point during the final 2-1/2 minutes of descent. The spacecraft landed in the Sea of Tranquillity at 102:42:40. The landing coordinates were 0 degree 41 minutes 15 seconds' north latitude and 23 degrees 26 minutes east longitude referenced to lunar map ORB-IT-6(100), first edition, December 1967. During the first 2 hours on the surface, the two crewmen preformed a post landing checkout of all lunar module systems. Afterwards, they ate their first meal on the moon and elected to perform the surface operations earlier than planned.

Considerable time was deliberately devoted to checkout and donning of the back-mounted portable life support and oxygen purge system. The Commander regressed through the forward hatch and deployed an equipment module in the descent stage. A camera in the module provided live television coverage of the Commander descending the ladder to the surface, with first contact made at 109:25:15 (9:56:15 p.m. est., July 20, 1969). The Lunar Module Pilot regressed soon thereafter, and both crewmen used the initial period on the surface to become acclimated to the reduced gravity and unfamiliar surface conditions. A contingency sample was taken from the surface, and the television camera was deployed so that most of the lunar module was included in its view field. The crew activated the scientific experiments, which included a solar wind detector, a passive seismometer, and a laser retro-reflector. The Lunar Module Pilot evaluated his ability to operate and move about, and was able to translate rapidly and with confidence. Forty-seven pounds of lunar surface material were collected to be returned for analysis. The surface exploration was concluded in the allotted time of 2-1/2 hours, and the crew reentered the lunar module at 111 ½ hours.

Ascent preparation was conducted efficiently, and the ascent stage lifted off the surface at 124-1/4 hours. A nominal firing of the ascent engine placed the vehicle into a 45-by-9 mile orbit. After rendezvous sequence similar to that of Apollo 10, the two spacecraft were docked at 128 hours. Following transfer of the crew, the ascent stage was jettisoned, and the command and service modules were prepared for trans-earth injection.

The return flight started with a 150-second firing of the service propulsion engine during the 31st lunar revolution at 135-1/2 hours. As in translunar flight, only one midcourse correction was required, and passive thermal control was exercised for most of transearth coast. Inclement weather necessitated moving the landing point 215 miles downrange. The entry phase was normal, and the command module landed in the Pacific Ocean at 195-1/4 hours. The landing coordinates, as determined from the onboard computer, were 13 degrees 19 minutes north latitude and 169 degrees 09 minutes west longitude.

After landing, the crew donned biological isolation garments. They were then retrieved by helicopter and taken to the primary recovery ship, USS Hornet. The crew and lunar material samples were placed in the Mobile Quarantine Facility for transport to the Lunar Receiving Laboratory in Houston. The command module was taken aboard the Hornet about 3 hours after landing.

With the completion of Apollo 11, the national objective of landing men on the moon and returning them safely to earth before the end of the decade had been accomplished.

1.0 MISSION DESCRIPTION

The Apollo 11 mission accomplished the basic mission of the Apollo Program; that is, to land two men on the lunar surface and return them safely to earth. As a part of this first lunar landing, three basic experiments packages were deployed, lunar material samples were collected, and surface photographs were taken. Two of the experiments were a part of the early Apollo scientific experiments package which was developed for deployment on the lunar surface.

The Apollo 11 space vehicle was launched on July 16, 1969, at 8:32 a.m. e.s.t., as planned. The spacecraft and S-IVB were inserted into 100.78-by99.2 mile earth parking orbit. After a 2-1/2 hour checkout period, the spacecraft/S-IVB combination was injected into the translunar phase of the mission. Trajectory parameters after the translunar injection firing were nearly perfect, with the velocity within 1.6 ft/sec of that planned. Only one of the four options for midcourse corrections during the translunar phase was exercised. This correction was made with the service propulsion system at approximately 26-1/2 hours and provide a 20.9 ft/sec velocity change. During the remaining periods of free-attitude flight, passive thermal control was used to maintain spacecraft temperatures within desired limits. The commander and lunar module pilot transferred to the lunar module during the translunar phase to make an initial inspection and preparations for system checks shortly after lunar orbit insertion.

The spacecraft was inserted into a 60- by 169.7-mile lunar orbit at approximately 76 hours. Four hours later, the lunar orbit circularization maneuver was preformed to place the spacecraft in a 65.7- by 53.8-mile orbit. The Lunar Module Pilot entered the lunar module at about 81 hours for initial power-up and systems checks. After the planned sleep period was completed at 93-1/2 hours, the crew donned their suits, transferred to the lunar module, and made final preparations for descent to the lunar surface. The lunar module was undocked on time at about 100 hours. After the exterior of the lunar module was inspected by the Command Module Pilot; a separation maneuver was preformed with the service module reaction control system.

The descent or orbit insertion maneuver was preformed with the descent propulsion system at 101-1/2 hours. Trajectory parameters following this maneuver were as planned, and the powered descent initiation was on time at 102-1/2 hours. The maneuver lasted approximately 12 minutes, with engine shutdown occurring almost simultaneously with the lunar landing in the Sea of Tranquility. The coordinates of the actual landing point was 0 degree 41 minutes 15 seconds north latitude and 23 degrees 26 minutes east longitude, compared with the planned landing point of 0 degree 43 minutes 53 seconds north latitude and 23 degree 38 minutes 51 seconds east longitude. These coordinates are referenced to Lunar Map ORB-II-6 east longitude. These coordinates are referenced to Lunar Map ORB-II-6(100), first edition, dated December 1967.

A 2-hour post landing checkout was completed, followed by a partial power-down of the spacecraft. A crew rest period was planned to precede the extravehicular activity to explore the lunar surface. However, the crew elected to perform the extravehicular portion of the mission prior to the sleep period because they were not overly tired and was adjusting easily to the 1/6 gravity. After the crew donned their portable life support systems and completed the required checkouts, the Commander egressed at about 109 hours. Prior to descending the ladder, the Commander deployed the equipment module in the descent stage. The television camera located in the module operated satisfactorily and provided live television coverage of the commander's descent to the lunar surface. The commander collected the contingency lunar material samples, and approximately 20 minutes later, the Lunar Module Pilot egressed and dual exploration of the lunar surface began.

During this exploration period, the television camera was deplored and the American flag was raised on the lunar surface. The solar wind experiment was also deployed for later retrieval. Both crewmen evaluated their mobility on the lunar surface, deployed the passive seismic material, and obtained photographic documentation of their activities and the conditions around them. The crewmen reentered the lunar module after about 2 hours 14 minutes of exploration.

Approximately 4-1/2 hours after lunar module ascent, the command module preformed a docking maneuver, and the two spacecraft were docked. The ascent stage was jettisoned in lunar orbit and the command and service modules were prepared for transearth injection at 135-1/2 hours.

The activities during transearth coast were similar to those during translunar flight. The service module was separated from the command module 15 minutes before reaching the entry interface at 400 000 feet altitude. After an automatic entry sequence and landing system deployment, the command module landed in the Pacific Ocean at 195-1/2 hours. The post landing procedures involving the primary recovery ship, USS Hornet, and the crew and samples were placed in quarantine.

After reaching the Manned Spacecraft Center, the spacecraft, crew, and samples entered the Lunar Receiving Laboratory quarantine area for continuation of the postlanding observation and analyses. The crew and spacecraft were released from quarantine on August 10, 1969, after no evidence of abnormal medical reaction was observed.

HOW WELL DID YOU UNDERSTAND THIS SELECTION?

1. What was the purpose of the Apollo 11 mission? Did the mission accomplish its purpose? Explain?

2. What scientific experiments did the crew conduct on the lunar surface?

3. Did the mission encounter problems? Explain?

4. Was the Apollo mission and program worth its high cost? Explain and defend your answer with historical evidence.

MULTIPLE CHOICE: Circle the correct response. The correct answers are given at the end.

1. What did the New Left do?
    a. Work within the Republican Party to defeat liberal Democrats throughout the 1960s.
    b. Question existing power structures
    c. Glorify the advantages of being left-handed
    d. Provide the primary opposition for the 1960s and 1970s counterculture movement

2. What did Rachel Carson's book Silent Spring do?
    a. Criticize the environmental movement as being comprised of hippies who were against industrial progress.
    b. Convince Republicans to vote in favor of Medicare
    c. Urge President Nixon to create the Environmental Protection Agency (the EPA)
    d. Argued that chemical pesticides killed birds and left their eggshells dangerously thin.

3. What did Black Nationalists generally believe?
    a. That African American freedom when black lived under black leaders, were served by black institutions, and supported black businesses
    b. That African American could become as economically prosperous as whites if the Federal Government ended racial segregation within the United States
    c. That Marin Luther King's use of non-violence would eventually create a society in which blacks could achieve equality with whites.
    d. That African Americans should return to Africa, their continent of origin

4. Who was the only Latino leader recognized as a national leader by the mainstream Civil Rights and antiwar movement within the United States?
    a. Guan Valdez
    b. Juan Cornejo
    c. Bert Corna
    d. César Chávez

5. The high-water mark of Native American activism was
    a. Founding of the American Indian Movement by Dennis Banks in 1964
    b. Getting the United Nations to recognize Native American sovereignty
    c. The siege at Wounded Knee in 1973
    d. The occupational of Alcatraz

6. Who wrote the Feminine Mystique?
    a. Phyllis Schlafly
    b. Hugh Hefner
    c. Betty Friedan
    d. Anita Bryant

7. What did the Supreme Court ruling in Roe v. Wade allow?
    a. Abortion during the first two trimesters of pregnancy
    b. Women to purchase birth control pills with a doctor's prescription
    c. Uncontested divorce if both parties agreed
    d. Custody of minor children in divorce cases to be given to women

8. Which one of the following is not associated with the Beatles?
   a. Beginning of a trend in which men wore long hair
   b. The election of Richard Nixon as President in 1968
   c. "I want to hold your hand," a song that sold over three million copies
   d. Beatlemania.

9. Who invented LSD?
   a. Timothy Leary
   b. George Harrison
   c. Bob Dylan
   d. Albert Hoffman

10. Who wrote Dianetics: The Modern Science of Mental Health
    a. Martin Luther King, Jr.
    b. Malcolm X
    c. L. Ron Hubbard
    d. Phyllis Schofley

Answers: 1-B ; 2-D; 3-A ; 4-D ; 5-C ; 6-C ; 7-A ; 8-B ; 9-D ; 10-C

ESSAYS:

1. Describe the Counterculture Movement of the 1960s and 1970s. What were its successes and failures?

2. What impact did the Environmental Movement have on American policy and American society?

3. How important were young people to the changes in American society during the 1960s and 1970s? Support your answer with historical evidence.

4. What were the most significant successes of the 1960s and 1970s? What was the greatest failure of the time period?

5. What did the Women's Movement achieve in the 1960s and 1970s?

6. Discuss the successes and failure of African American during the 1960s and 1970s.

OPTIONAL ACTIVITIES:

1. Write a poem or song that defines the 1960s and 1970s

2. Stage a mock demonstration on your campus protesting the Vietnam War.

3. Hold a class debate between hippies and squares regarding the issues of the 1960s and 1970s.

WEB SITE LISTINGS:

The Sixties
http://history.acusd.edu/gen/classes/20th/sixties.html
http://kclibrary.nhmccd.edu/decade60.html
http://www.ukans.edu/history/VL/USA/ERAS/20TH/1960s.html
http://www.hist.umn.edu/~hist20c/internet/1960s.htm

The Seventies:
http://www.super70s.com/Super70s/Timeline/
http://www.nostalgiacentral.com/seventies.htm
http://kclibrary.nhmccd.edu/decade70.html

Nixon:
http://www.archives.gov/nixon/
http://www.pbs.org/wgbh/amex/presidents/37_nixon/index.html

Pentagon Papers:
http://www.gwu.edu/~nsarchiv/NSAEBB/NSAEBB48/
http://www.mtholyoke.edu/acad/intrel/pentagon/pent1.html

Watergate:
http://www.realhistoryarchives.com/collections/conspiracies/watergate.htm
http://www.archives.gov/exhibit_hall/american_originals/nixon2.html
http://www.archives.gov/exhibit_hall/american_originals/contemp.html

Three Mile Island:
http://www.pbs.org/wgbh/amex/three/

SALT Talks
http://dosfan.lib.uic.edu/acda/treaties/salt1.htm

Détente:
http://www.pbs.org/wgbh/amex/china/
http://www.gwu.edu/~nsarchiv/nsa/publications/DOC_readers/kissinger/nixzhou/

Ford:
http://www.americanpresident.org/history/geraldford/
http://www.pbs.org/wgbh/amex/presidents/38_ford/index.html
Nixon Pardon:
http://www.watergate.info/ford/pardon.shtml

Carter:
http://www.jimmycarterlibrary.org/
http://www.pbs.org/wgbh/amex/presidents/39_carter/index.html
http://odur.let.rug.nl/~usa/H/1990/ch8_p21.htm

SALT II Talks:
http://dosfan.lib.uic.edu/acda/treaties/salt2-1.htm

Chapter Twenty-eight

THE RISE OF CONSERVATISM: Ronald Reagan to George Herbert Walker Bush 1981-1992

Americans, after the Iranian hostage humiliation and the economic woes of the late 1970s, turned their concerns into hope with the arrival of Ronald Reagan on the national political scene. Reagan, whose own political career was born out of his experiences in the film industry—from hero on the screen to hero in California as its governor—portrayed himself as a new leader for the nation. His own conversion from the Democratic Party's allegiance to Republican conservatism signaled the country to follow him into a new age of American history.

With the economy stagnating, Reagan called for "supply-side economics," which revised the tax system, providing major cuts for the wealthy and corporations while cutting many areas in domestic spending, including many social programs. "Reaganomics" was based on the idea that the free market would boost the economy and that the government's role was to step back from the "big government" of the Democrats and let capitalism run the economy. In 1985, the Gramm Rudman Act created automatic cuts in federal budget spending. The philosophy was toward the idea of small government but, in reality, a large national deficit grew. Poverty increased and the stress produced a rise in crime, including an increase in drug use, both of which contributed to epidemics of AIDs and crack/cocaine use, homelessness, and a flood of illegal immigrants from Asia and Latin America.

Reagan's foreign policy began with a strong stand against those who opposed American positions, especially the Soviet Union. He promised that democracy would be the guiding principle of his administration and that all communist countries would be on his list of the "evil empire." His famous "Mr. Gorbachev, Tear Down this Wall" speech increased his popularity, and the Berlin Wall did come down during his administration. However, other attempts to show American dominance on the international scene were not as successful. The U.S. intervened on the tiny island of Grenada, but intervention into Lebanon was a disaster. The latter added to U.S. problems in the Middle East. Reagan's pro-Israel policies caused Palestinians and their supporters to look upon the U.S. as unfriendly to their dream of a Palestinian state. Reagan eventually met with the Soviet leader Mikhail Gorbachev, and as their friendship grew, Reagan's own positions in foreign affairs changed.

Reagan's own charisma held on to his popularity even in the face of national scandals like the Iran-Contra fiasco. The image of the tall, smiling, fatherly figure calling the U.S. to noble goals kept his popularity strong even after he left office. The nation mourned when he died in 2004.

In 1988, Reagan ended his second term, and his vice president, George Herbert Walker Bush, ran against Michael Dukakis, former governor of Massachusetts. Bush campaigned successfully claiming that the Democrats were "soft" on crime and communism. The now infamous ad claiming that Dukakis let a murderer, Willy Horton, out of jail only to "let him kill again" raised the fear that social reforms had made the U.S. a dangerous place in which to live.

Bush's own tenure as president concentrated on foreign affairs. Domestic programs, in the Reagan tradition, continued to be cut. Meanwhile, the U.S. invaded Panama and fought a war in Iraq when Saddam Hussein invaded Kuwait and claimed it as part of Iraqi territory. While Bush triumphed in the success of his "100 Day War," there were many scandals in the savings and loan industry (in which his son, Neil, was involved), and the federal deficit, growing since Reagan's time in office, kept increasing. Rising health-care costs kept many Americans uninsured. Despite the publicity of Ryan White's death, funding for AIDs and cancer research were limited. Racial unrest came to national attention when Rodney King was severely beaten, and riots erupted against the treatment of blacks by police.

During the last years of his office, Bush was forced to face some of his original grandiose promises such as "no new taxes." Economic problems caused the American public to increasingly see him as unconcerned with the problems in the daily lives of most Americans, and this perception haunted him in the election of 1992.

IDENTIFICATION: Briefly describe each term.

Reaganomics

Strategic Defense Initiative ("Star Wars")

Sandra Day O'Connor

Reagan Doctrine

Bombing of U.S. Marine headquarters in Lebanon

Iran-Contra Scandal

Walter Mondale

Geraldine Ferraro

Mikhail Gorbachev

Glastnost and *Perestroika*

AIDS

Crack and cocaine epidemic

Simpson-Mazzoli Act of 1987

Michael Dukakis

Saving and Loan Crisis

The Exxon Valdez

Thomas – Hill hearings

"Year of the Woman"

American Disabilities Act

Collapse of the Soviet Union

Persian Gulf War/ Desert Storm

"Liberal"

"Conservative"

Willy Horton

Gramm Rudman Act

Illegal Immigration

Trickle Down Economics

Federal or National Deficit

"Evil Empire"

Grenada

Palestinians

Lebanon Crisis

"Soft on Crime"

Panama

Kuwait

100 Days of War

The Heritage Foundation/ Cato Institute

Rodney King

"a thousand points of light"

"No new taxes"

THINK ABOUT:

1.   Some people have argued that Ronald Reagan's push for greater defense expenditures coupled with a vigorous anti-Soviet policy caused the collapse of the Soviet Union. If Reagan had not pushed his policies with such vehemence, would the disintegration of the Soviet Union have occurred anyhow? Was the basic cause of this collapse American pressure or internal problems and issues?

2.   When questioned about many inconsistencies in the politics of his administration, Ronald Reagan pleaded "I can't remember." How did this effect his popularity? Why did his position work/not work in assessing his success?

3.   In the election of 1988, the issues pertaining to national needs were blurred by "dirty campaigning." Comment on this statement: How often has this type of campaigning been part of the U.S. political scene?

4.   President George H. W. Bush declared the Persian Gulf War over on the 100th day of its "mission." What was the strategy for doing this and was it effective?

Most political observers agree that Ronald Reagan possessed extraordinary skill in expressing his views and rallying support for them. Reagan had clear ideas, many of which conflicted with the direction of American government and policies since the New Deal. He wanted to end the "welfare state," cut taxes, restore a laissez faire economy, and, at the same time, build a larger and stronger new military machine. He hoped to bring about a "new American revolution," to alter American political life. Here in his State of the Union Address in 1985, he outlines that revolution and attempts to build support for his strong ideas.

Mr. Speaker, Mr. President, distinguished members of the Congress, honored guests and fellow citizens. I come before you to report on the state of our union. And I am pleased to report that, after four years of united effort, the American people have brought forth a nation renewed-stronger, freer and more secure than before.

Four years ago, we began to change-forever, I hope-our assumptions about government and its place in our lives. Out of that change has come great and robust growth-in our confidence, our economy and our role in the world . . . .

Four years ago, we said we would invigorate our economy by giving people greater freedom and incentives to take risks, and letting them keep more of what they earned.

We have begun well. But it's only a beginning. We are not here to congratulate ourselves on what we have done, but to challenge ourselves to finish what has not yet been done.

We are here to speak for millions in our inner cities who long for real jobs, safe neighborhoods and schools that truly teach. We are here to speak for the American farmer, the entrepreneur and every worker in industries fighting to modernize and compete. And, yes, we are here to stand, and proudly so, for all who struggle to break free from to-talitarianism; for all who know in their hearts that freedom is the one true path to peace and human happiness . . . .

We honor the giants of our history- not by going back, but forward to the dreams their vision foresaw. My fellow citizens, this nation is poised for greatness. The time has come to proceed toward a great new challenge-a Second American Revolution of hope and opportunity; a revolution carrying us to new heights of progress by pushing back frontiers of knowledge and space; a revolution of spirit that taps the soul of America, enabling us to summon greater strength than we have ever known; and, a revolution that carries beyond our shores the golden promise of human freedom in a world at peace.

Let us begin by challenging conventional wisdom: There are no constraints on the human mind, no walls around the human spirit, no barriers to our progress except those we ourselves erect. Already, pushing down tax rates has freed our economy to vault forward to record growth. In Europe, they call it "the American Miracle." Day by day, we are shattering accepted notions of what is possible . . . .

We stand on the threshold of a great ability to produce more, do more, be more. Our economy is not getting older and weaker, it's getting younger and stronger; it doesn't need rest and supervision, it needs new challenge, greater freedom. And that word-freedom-is the key to the Second American Revolution we mean to bring about.

Let us move together with an historic reform of tax simplification for fairness and growth. Last year, I asked then-Treasury Secretary Regan to develop a plan to simplify the tax code, so all taxpayers would be treated more fairly, and personal tax rates could come further down.

We have cut tax rates by almost 25 percent, yet the tax system remains unfair and limits our potential for growth. Exclusions and exemptions cause similar incomes to be taxed at different levels. Low income families face steep tax barriers that make hard lives even harder. The Treasury Department has produced an excellent reform plan whose principles will guide the final proposal we will ask you to enact.

One thing that tax reform will not be is a tax increase in disguise. We will not jeopardize the mortgage interest deduction families need. We will reduce personal tax rates as low as possible by removing many tax preferences. We will propose a top rate of no more than 35 percent, and possibly lower. And we will propose reducing corporate rates while maintaining incentives for capital formation . . . .

Tax simplification will be a giant step toward unleashing the tremendous pent-up power of our economy. But a Second American Revolution must carry the promise of opportunity for all. It is time to liberate the spirit of enterprise in the most distressed areas of our country.

This government will meet its responsibility to help those in need. But policies that increase dependency, break up families and destroy self-respect are not progressive, they are reactionary. Despite our strides in civil rights, blacks, Hispanics and all minorities will not have full and equal power until they have full economic powers . . . .

Let us resolve that we will stop spreading dependency and start spreading opportunity; that we will stop spreading bondage and start spreading freedom. There are some who say that growth initiatives must await final action on deficit reductions. The best way to reduce deficits is through economic growth. More business will be started, more investments made, more jobs created and more people will be on payrolls paying taxes. The best way to reduce government spending is to reduce the need for spending by increasing prosperity . . . .

To move steadily toward a balanced budget we must also lighten government's claim on our total economy. We will not do this by raising taxes. We must make sure that our economy grows faster than growth in spending by federal government. In our fiscal year 1986 budget, overall government program spending will be frozen at the current level; it must not be one dime higher than fiscal year 1985. And three points are key:

First, the social safety net for the elderly, needy, disabled and unemployed will be left intact. Growth of our major health care programs, Medicare and Medicaid, will be slowed, but protections for the elderly and needy will be preserved.

Second, we must not relax our efforts to restore military strength just as we near our goal of a fully equipped, trained and ready professional corps. National security is government's first responsibility, so, in past years, defense spending took about half the federal budget. Today it takes less than a third. . . . You know, we only have a military industrial complex until a time of danger. Then it becomes' the arsenal of democracy. Spending for defense is investing in things that are priceless: peace and freedom.

Third, we must reduce or eliminate costly government subsidies. For example, deregulation of the airline industry has led to cheaper airfares, but on Amtrak taxpayers pay about $35 per passenger every time an Amtrak train leaves the station. It's time we ended this huge federal subsidy . . . .

In the long run, we must protect the taxpayers from government. And I ask again that you pass, as 32 states have now called for, an amendment mandating the federal government spend no more than it takes in. And I ask for the authority used responsibly by 43 governors to veto individual items in appropriations bills. . . .

Nearly 50 years of government living beyond its means has brought us to a time of reckoning. Ours is but a moment in history. But one moment of courage, idealism and bipartisan unity can change American history forever. . . .

Every dollar the federal government does not take from us, every decision it does not make for us, will make our economy stronger, our lives more abundant, our future more free . . . .

There is another great heritage to speak of this evening. Of all the changes that have swept America the past four years, none brings greater promise than our rediscovery of the value of faith, freedom, family, work and neighborhood.

We see signs of renewal in increased attendance in places of worship: renewed optimism and faith in our future; love of country rediscovered by our young who are leading the way. We have rediscovered that work is good in and of itself; that it ennobles us to create and contribute no matter how seemingly humble our jobs. We have seen a powerful new current from an old and honorable tradition, American generosity . . . .

I thank the Congress for passing equal access legislation giving religious groups the same right to use classrooms after school that other groups enjoy. But no citizen need tremble, nor the world shudder, if a child stands in a classroom and breathes a prayer. We ask you again-give children back a right they had for a century-and-a-half or more in this country.

The question of abortion grips our nation. Abortion is either the taking of human life, or it isn't; and if it is-and medical technology is increasingly showing it is-it must be stopped . . . .

Of all the changes in the past 20 years, none has more threatened our sense of national well-being than the explosion of violent crime. One does not have to have been attacked to be a victim. The woman who must run to her car after shopping at night is a victim; the couple draping their door with locks and chains are victims; as is the tired, decent cleaning woman who can't ride a subway home without being afraid.

We do not seek to violate rights of defendants, but shouldn't we feel more compassion for victims of crime than for those who commit crime? For the first time in 20 years, the crime index has fallen two years in a row; we've convicted over 7,400 drug offenders, and put them, as well as leaders of organized crime, behind bars in record numbers.

But we must do more. I urge the House to follow the Senate and enact proposals permitting use of all reliable evidence that police officers acquire in good faith. These proposals would also reform the habeas corpus laws and allow, in keeping with the will of the overwhelming majority of Americans, the use of the death penalty where necessary.

There can be no economic revival in ghettos when the most violent among us are allowed to roam free. It is time we restored domestic tranquility. And we mean to do just that . . . .

Tonight I have spoken of great plans and great dreams. They are dreams we can make come true. Two hundred years of American history should have taught us that nothing is impossible . . . . Anything is possible in America if we have the faith, the will and the heart.

History is asking us, once again, to be a force for good in the world. Let us begin-in unity, with justice and love. Thank you and God bless you.

HOW WELL DID YOU UNDERSTAND THIS SELECTION?

1. What did President Reagan believe he had accomplished by 1985?

2. How did Reagan expect to reduce deficits? Did it work?

3. What conservative programs did Reagan advocate in his State of the Union address? What arguments did he use to support these programs?

4. How do you evaluate his "great plans and great dreams"?

REMARKS AT THE BRANDENBURG GATE
President Reagan, West Berlin, Germany, June 12, 1987

Ronald Reagan believed that communism was the evil of the modern political world. On June 12, 1987, he stood at the Brandenburg Gate in Berlin and called out: "Mr. Gorbachev, Tear Down this Wall." It took until November 1989 to get the Berliners to press the Soviet government to open the gates in the wall and when they did, many East Germans climbed the wall. The crowd that had gathered began to tear the wall down. Reagan was seen as a hero for the Free World.

Note: The President spoke at 2:20 p.m. at the Brandenburg Gate. This speech was delivered to the people of West Berlin, yet it was also audible on the East side of the Berlin wall. In his opening remarks, he referred to West German Chancellor Helmut Kohl. Prior to his remarks, President Reagan met with West German President Richard von Weizsacker and the Governing Mayor of West Berlin Eberhard Diepgen at Schloss Bellevue, President Weizsacker's official residence in West Berlin. Following the meeting, President Reagan went to the Reichstag, where he viewed the Berlin Wall from the East Balcony.

Thank you very much.

Chancellor Kohl, Governing Mayor Diepgen, ladies and gentlemen: Twenty-four years ago, President John F. Kennedy visited Berlin, speaking to the people of this city and the world at the City Hall. Well, since then two other presidents have come, each in his turn, to Berlin. And today I, myself, make my second visit to your city.

We come to Berlin, we American presidents, because it's our duty to speak, in this place, of freedom. But I must confess, we're drawn here by other things as well: by the feeling of history in this city, more than 500 years older than our own nation; by the beauty of the Grunewald and the Tiergarten; most of all, by your courage and determination. Perhaps the composer Paul Lincke understood something about American presidents. You see, like so many presidents before me, I come here today because wherever I go, whatever I do: Ich hab noch einen Koffer in Berlin. [I still have a suitcase in Berlin.]

Our gathering today is being broadcast throughout Western Europe and North America. I understand that it is being seen and heard as well in the East. To those listening throughout Eastern Europe, a special word: Although I cannot be with you, I address my remarks to you just as surely as to those standing here before me. For I join you, as I join your fellow countrymen in the West, in this firm, this unalterable belief: Es gibt nur ein Berlin. [There is only one Berlin.]

Behind me stands a wall that encircles the free sectors of this city, part of a vast system of barriers that divides the entire continent of Europe. From the Baltic, south, those barriers cut across Germany in a gash of barbed wire, concrete, dog runs, and guard towers. Farther south, there may be no visible, no obvious wall. But there remain armed guards and checkpoints all the same—still a restriction on the right to travel, still an instrument to impose upon ordinary men and women the will of a totalitarian state. Yet it is here in Berlin where the wall emerges most clearly; here, cutting across your city, where the news photo and the television screen have imprinted this brutal division of a continent upon the mind of the world. Standing before the Brandenburg Gate, every man is a German, separated from his fellow men. Every man is a Berliner, forced to look upon a scar.

President von Weizsacker has said, "The German question is open as long as the Brandenburg Gate is closed." Today I say: As long as the gate is closed, as long as this scar of a wall is permitted to stand, it is not the German question alone that remains open, but the question of freedom for all mankind. Yet I do not come here to lament. For I find in Berlin a message of hope, even in the shadow of this wall, a message of triumph.

In this season of spring in 1945, the people of Berlin emerged from their air-raid shelters to find devastation. Thousands of miles away, the people of the United States reached out to help. And in 1947 Secretary of State—as you've been told—George Marshall announced the creation of what would become known as the Marshall Plan. Speaking precisely 40 years ago this month, he said: "Our policy is directed not against any country or doctrine, but against hunger, poverty, desperation, and chaos."

In the Reichstag a few moments ago, I saw a display commemorating this 40th anniversary of the Marshall Plan. I was struck by the sign on a burnt-out, gutted structure that was being rebuilt. I understand that Berliners of my own generation can remember seeing signs like it dotted throughout the western sectors of the city. The sign read simply: "The Marshall Plan is helping here to strengthen the free world." A strong, free world in the West, that dream became real. Japan rose from ruin to become an economic giant. Italy, France, Belgium —virtually every nation in Western Europe saw political and economic rebirth; the European Community was founded.

In West Germany and here in Berlin, there took place an economic miracle, the Wirtschaftswunder. Adenauer, Erhard, Reuter, and other leaders understood the practical importance of liberty—that just as truth can flourish only when the journalist is given freedom of speech, so prosperity can come about only when the farmer and businessman enjoy economic freedom. The German leaders reduced tariffs, expanded free trade, lowered taxes. From 1950 to 1960 alone, the standard of living in West Germany and Berlin doubled.

Where four decades ago there was rubble, today in West Berlin there is the greatest industrial output of any city in Germany—busy office blocks, fine homes and apartments, proud avenues, and the spreading lawns of parkland. Where a city's culture seemed to have been destroyed, today there are two great universities, orchestras and an opera, countless theaters, and museums. Where there was want, today there's abundance—food, clothing, automobiles—the wonderful goods of the Ku'damm. From devastation, from utter ruin, you Berliners have, in freedom, rebuilt a city that once again ranks as one of the greatest on earth. The Soviets may have had other plans. But my friends, there were a few things the Soviets didn't count on—Berliner Herz, Berliner Humor, ja, und Berliner Schnauze. [Berliner heart, Berliner humor, yes, and a Berliner Schnauze.]

In the 1950s, Khrushchev predicted: "We will bury you." But in the West today, we see a free world that has achieved a level of prosperity and well-being unprecedented in all human history. In the Communist world, we see failure, technological backwardness, declining standards of health, even want of the most basic kind—too little food. Even today, the Soviet Union still cannot feed itself. After these four decades, then, there stands before the entire world one great and inescapable conclusion: Freedom leads to prosperity. Freedom replaces the ancient hatreds among the nations with comity and peace. Freedom is the victor.

And now the Soviets themselves may, in a limited way, be coming to understand the importance of freedom. We hear much from Moscow about a new policy of reform and openness. Some political prisoners have been released. Certain foreign news broadcasts are no longer being jammed. Some economic enterprises have been permitted to operate with greater freedom from state control.

Are these the beginnings of profound changes in the Soviet state? Or are they token gestures, intended to raise false hopes in the West, orto strengthen the Soviet system without changing it? We welcome change and openness; for we believe that freedom and security go together, that the advance of human liberty can only strengthen the cause of world peace. There is one sign the Soviets can make that would be unmistakable, that would advance dramatically the cause of freedom and peace.

General Secretary Gorbachev, if you seek peace, if you seek prosperity for the Soviet Union and Eastern Europe, if you seek liberalization: Come here to this gate! Mr. Gorbachev, open this gate! Mr. Gorbachev, tear down this wall!

I understand the fear of war and the pain of division that afflict this continent— and I pledge to you my country's efforts to help overcome these burdens. To be sure, we in the West must resist Soviet expansion. So we must maintain defenses of unassailable strength. Yet we seek peace; so we must strive to reduce arms on both sides.

Beginning 10 years ago, the Soviets challenged the Western alliance with a grave new threat, hundreds of new and more deadly SS-20 nuclear missiles, capable of striking every capital in Europe. The Western alliance responded by committing itself to a counter-deployment unless the Soviets agreed to negotiate a better solution; namely, the elimination of such weapons on both sides. For many months, the Soviets refused to bargain in earnestness. As the alliance, in turn, prepared to go forward with its counter-deployment, there were difficult days—days of protests like those during my 1982 visit to this city—and the Soviets later walked away from the table.

But through it all, the alliance held firm. And I invite those who protested then— I invite those who protest today—to mark this fact: Because we remained strong, the Soviets came back to the table. And because were mained strong, today we have within reach the possibility, not merely of limiting the growth of arms, but of eliminating, for the first time, an entire class of nuclear weapons from the face of the earth.

As I speak, NATO ministers are meeting in Iceland to review the progress of our proposals for eliminating these weapons. At the talks in Geneva, we have also proposed deep cuts in strategic offensive weapons. And the Western allies have likewise made far-reaching proposals to reduce the danger of conventional war and to place a total ban on chemical weapons.

While we pursue these arms reductions, I pledge to you that we will maintain the capacity to deter Soviet aggression at any level at which it might occur. And in cooperation with many of our allies, the United States is pursuing the Strategic Defense Initiative—research to base deterrence not on the threat of offensive retaliation, but on defenses that truly defend; on systems, in short, that will not target populations, but shield them. By these means we seek to increase the safety of Europe and all the world. But we must remember a crucial fact: East and West do not mistrust each other because we are armed; we are armed because we mistrust each other. And our differences are not about weapons but about liberty. When President Kennedy spoke at the City Hall those 24 years ago, freedom was encircled, Berlin was under siege. And today, despite all the pressures upon this city, Berlin stands secure in its liberty. And freedom itself is transforming the globe.

In the Philippines, in South and Central America, democracy has been given a rebirth. Throughout the Pacific, free markets are working miracle after miracle of economic growth. In the industrialized nations, a technological revolution is taking place—a revolution marked by rapid, dramatic advances in computers and telecommunications.

In Europe, only one nation and those it controls refuse to join the community of freedom. Yet in this age of redoubled economic growth, of information and innovation, the Soviet Union faces a choice: It must make fundamental changes, or it will become obsolete.

Today thus represents a moment of hope. We in the West stand ready to cooperate with the East to promote true openness, to break down barriers that separate people, to create a safe, freer world. And surely there is no better place than Berlin, the meeting place of East and West, to make a start. Free people of Berlin: Today, as in the past, the United States stands for the strict observance and full implementation of all parts of the Four Power Agreement of 1971. Let us use this occasion, the 750th anniversary of this city, to usher in a new era, to seek a still fuller, richer life for the Berlin of the future. Together, let us maintain and develop the ties between the Federal Republic and the Western sectors of Berlin, which is permitted by the 1971 agreement.

And I invite Mr. Gorbachev: Let us work to bring the Eastern and Western parts of the city closer together, so that all the inhabitants of all Berlin can enjoy the benefits that come with life in one of the great cities of the world.

To open Berlin still further to all Europe, East and West, let us expand the vital air access to this city, finding ways of making commercial air service to Berlin more convenient, more comfortable, and more economical. We look to the day when West Berlin can become one of the chief aviation hubs in all central Europe.

With our French and British partners, the United States is prepared to help bring international meetings to Berlin. It would be only fitting for Berlin to serve as the site of United Nations meetings, or world conferences on human rights and arms control or other issues that call for international cooperation.

There is no better way to establish hope for the future than to enlighten young minds, and we would be honored to sponsor summer youth exchanges, cultural events, and other programs for young Berliners from the East. Our French and British friends, I'm certain, will do the same. And it's my hope that an authority can be found in East Berlin to sponsor visits from young people of the Western sectors.

One final proposal, one close to my heart: Sport represents a source of enjoyment and ennoblement, and you may have noted that the Republic of Korea—South Korea—has offered to permit certain events of the 1988 Olympics to take place in the North. International sports competitions of all kinds could take place in both parts of this city. And what better way to demonstrate to the world the openness of this city than to offer in some future year to hold the Olympic games here in Berlin, East and West? In these four decades, as I have said, you Berliners have built a great city. You've done so in spite of threats—the Soviet attempts to impose the East-mark, the blockade. Today the city thrives in spite of the challenges implicit in the very presence of this wall. What keeps you here? Certainly there's a great deal to be said for your fortitude, for your defiant courage. But I believe there's something deeper, something that involves Berlin's whole look and feel and way of life—not mere sentiment. No one could live long in Berlin without being completely disabused of illusions. Something instead, that has seen the difficulties of life in Berlin but chose to accept them, that continues to build this good and proud city in contrast to a surrounding totalitarian presence that refuses to release human energies or aspirations. Something that speaks with a powerful voice of affirmation, that says yes to this city, yes to the future, yes to freedom. In a word, I would submit that what keeps you in Berlin is love—love both profound and abiding.

Perhaps this gets to the root of the matter, to the most fundamental distinction of all between East and West. The totalitarian world produces backwardness because it does such violence to the spirit, thwarting the human impulse to create, to enjoy, to worship. The totalitarian world finds even symbols of love and of worship an affront. Years ago, before the East Germans began rebuilding their churches, they erected a secular structure: the television tower at Alexander Platz. Virtually ever since, the authorities have been working to correct what they view as the tower's one major flaw, treating the glass sphere at the top with paints and chemicals of every kind. Yet even today when the sun strikes that sphere—that sphere that towers over all Berlin—the light makes the sign of the cross. There in Berlin, like the city itself, symbols of love, symbols of worship, cannot be suppressed.

As I looked out a moment ago from the Reichstag, that embodiment of German unity, I noticed words crudely spray-painted upon the wall, perhaps by a young Berliner: "This wall will fall. Beliefs become reality." Yes, across Europe, this wall will fall. For it cannot withstand faith; it cannot withstand truth. The wall cannot withstand freedom.

And I would like, before I close, to say one word. I have read, and I have been questioned since I've been here about certain demonstrations against my coming. And I would like to say just one thing, and to those who demonstrate so. I wonder if they have ever asked themselves that if they should have the kind of government they apparently seek, no one would ever be able to do what they're doing again.

Thank you and God bless you all.

HOW WELL DID YOU UNDERSTAND THIS SELECTION?

1. Why did Reagan issue this challenge to Mikhail Gorbachev when he is Russian and the "wall" was in Berlin, Germany?

2. How different were the economies of East and West Berlin? Why?

3. How did Reagan compare NATO to the Soviet Union?

4. How good was Reagan's threat that the U.S. would "maintain the capacity to deter Soviet aggression at any level"?

5. What did the Berlin Wall symbolize?

In the (first) Bush administration, tensions with countries who did not support the increasing U.S. hegemony increased. Bush said that the Panamanians were being denied democracy by the military dictatorship of General Manuel Noriega. He informed the American public that their fellow citizens had been killed. He felt he had no choice but to send U.S. troops into the area and preserve the shaky democratic government that Panamanians had set up. These kinds of ventures had an effect on the long term image of the U.S. in Central and South America.

My fellow citizens, last night I ordered U.S. military forces to Panama. No President takes such action lightly. This morning I want to tell you what I did and why I did it.

For nearly 2 years, the United States, nations of Latin America and the Caribbean have worked together to resolve the crisis in Panama. The goals of the United States have been to safeguard the lives of Americans, to defend democracy in Panama, to combat drug trafficking, and to protect the integrity of the Panama Canal treaty. Many attempts have been made to resolve this crisis through diplomacy and negotiations. All were rejected by the dictator of Panama, General Manuel Noriega, an indicted drug trafficker.

Last Friday, Noriega declared his military dictatorship to be in a state of war with the United States and publicly threatened the lives of Americans in Panama. The very next day, forces under his command shot and killed an unarmed American serviceman; wounded another; arrested and brutally beat a third American serviceman; and then brutally interrogated his wife, threatening her with sexual abuse. That was enough.

General Noriega's reckless threats and attacks upon Americans in Panama created an imminent danger to the 35,000 American citizens in Panama. As President, I have no higher obligation than to safeguard the lives of American citizens. And that is why I directed our Armed Forces to protect the lives of American citizens in Panama and to bring General Noriega to justice in the United States. I contacted the bipartisan leadership of Congress last night and informed them of this decision, and after taking this action, I also talked with leaders in Latin America, the Caribbean, and those of other U.S. allies.

At this moment, U.S. forces, including forces deployed from the United States last night, are engaged in action in Panama. The United States intends to withdraw the forces newly deployed to Panama as quickly as possible. Our forces have conducted themselves courageously and selflessly. And as Commander in Chief, I salute every one of them and thank them on behalf of our country.

Tragically, some Americans have lost their lives in defense of their fellow citizens, in defense of democracy. And my heart goes out to their families. We also regret and mourn the loss of innocent Panamanians.

The brave Panamanians elected by the people of Panama in the elections last May, President Guillermo Endara and Vice Presidents Calderon and Ford, have assumed the rightful leadership of their country. You remember those horrible pictures of newly elected Vice President Ford, covered head to toe with blood, beaten mercilessly by so-called "dignity battalions." Well, the United States today recognizes the democratically elected government of President Endara. I will send our Ambassador back to Panama immediately.

Key military objectives have been achieved. Most organized resistance has been eliminated, but the operation is not over yet: General Noriega is in hiding. And nevertheless, yesterday a dictator ruled Panama, and today constitutionally elected leaders govern.

I have today directed the Secretary of the Treasury and the Secretary of State to lift the economic sanctions with respect to the democratically elected government of Panama and, in cooperation with that government, to take steps to effect an orderly unblocking of Panamanian Government assets in the United States. I'm fully committed to implement the Panama Canal treaties and turn over the Canal to Panama in the year 2000. The actions we have taken and the cooperation of a new, democratic government in Panama will permit us to honor these commitments. As soon as the new government recommends a qualified candidate — Panamanian — to be Administrator of the Canal, as called for in the treaties, I will submit this nominee to the Senate for expedited consideration.

I am committed to strengthening our relationship with the democratic nations in this hemisphere. I will continue to seek solutions to the problems of this region through dialog and multilateral diplomacy. I took this action only after reaching the conclusion that every other avenue was closed and the lives of American citizens were in grave danger. I hope that the people of Panama will put this dark chapter of dictatorship behind them and move forward together as citizens of a democratic Panama with this government that they themselves have elected.

The United States is eager to work with the Panamanian people in partnership and friendship to rebuild their economy. The Panamanian people want democracy, peace, and the chance for a better life in dignity and freedom. The people of the United States seek only to support them in pursuit of these noble goals. Thank you very much.

HOW WELL DID YOU UNDERSTAND THIS SELECTION?

1. Who was General Noriega and why did the Bush administration feel he should be overthrown (with U.S. help)?

2. After military operations were successful, what measures did Bush use to stabilize the situation?

3. Have Bush's actions achieved his goals for Panama? Are these the same as, he claims, the goals of the Panamanians?

4. What happened to Noriega?

President George H. W. Bush carried on the Reagan plan to spread U.S. democracy across the world, thus hoping to defeat communism's influence. His program, a New World Order, called for American leadership in all global matters so that the goal of democratic government would be available across the globe.

Note: This speech has often been cited as the US administration's principal policy statement on the new order in the Middle East following the expulsion of Iraqi forces from Kuwait.

... Tonight I come to this House to speak about the world – the world after war.

The recent challenge could not have been clearer. Saddam Hussein was the villain, Kuwait the victim. To the aid of this small country came nations from North America and Europe, from Asia and South America, from Africa and the Arab world, all united against aggression.

Our uncommon coalition must now work in common purpose to forge a future that should never again be held hostage to the darker side of human nature.

Tonight in Iraq, Saddam walks amidst ruin. His war machine is crushed. His ability to threaten mass destruction is itself destroyed. His people have been lied to, denied the truth. And when his defeated legions come home, all Iraqis will see and feel the havoc he has wrought. And this I promise you: for all that Saddam has done to his own people, to the Kuwaitis, and to the entire world, Saddam and those around him are accountable.

All of us grieve for the victims of war, for the people of Kuwait and the suffering that scars the soul of that proud nation. We grieve for all our fallen soldiers and their families, for all the innocents caught up in this conflict. And, yes, we grieve for the people of Iraq, a people who have never been our enemy. My hope is that one day we will once again welcome them as friends into the community of nations.

Our commitment to peace in the Middle East does not end with the liberation of Kuwait. So tonight let me outline four key challenges to be met.

First, we must work together to create shared security arrangements in the region. Our friends and allies in the Middle East recognize that they will bear the bulk of the responsibility for regional security. But we want them to know that just as we stood with them to repel aggression, so now America stands ready to work with them to secure the peace.

This does not mean stationing US ground forces on the Arabian Peninsula, but it does mean American participation in joint exercises involving both air and ground forces. It means maintaining a capable US naval presence in the region, just as we have for over 40 years. Let it be clear: our vital national interests depend on a stable and secure Gulf.

Second, we must act to control the proliferation of weapons of mass destruction and the missiles used to deliver them. It would be tragic if the nations of the Middle East and Persian Gulf were now, in the wake of war, to embark on a new arms race. Iraq requires special vigilance. Until Iraq convinces the world of its peaceful intentions – that its leaders will not use new revenues to re-arm and rebuild its menacing war machine – Iraq must not have access to the instruments of war.

And third, we must work to create new opportunities for peace and stability in the Middle East. On the night I announced Operation Desert Storm, I expressed my hope that out of the horrors of war might come new momentum for peace. We have learned in the modern age geography cannot guarantee security and security does not come from military power alone.

All of us know the depth of bitterness that has made the dispute between Israel and its neighbours so painful and intractable. Yet, in the conflict just concluded, Israel and many of the Arab states have for the first time found themselves confronting the same aggressor. By now, it should be plain to all parties that peacemaking in the Middle East requires compromise. At the same time, peace brings real benefits to everyone. We must do all that we can to close the gap between Israel and the Arab states – and between Israelis and Palestinians. The tactics of terror lead nowhere. There can be no substitute for diplomacy.

A comprehensive peace must be grounded in United Nations Security Council Resolutions 242 and 338 and the principle of territory for peace. This principle must be elaborated to provide for Israel's security and recognition, and at the same time for legitimate Palestinian political rights. Anything else would fail the twin tests of fairness and security. The time has come to put an end to Arab-Israeli conflict.

The war with Iraq is over. The quest for solutions to the problem in Lebanon, in the Arab-Israeli dispute, and in the Gulf must go forward with new vigour and determination. And I guarantee you: no one will work harder for a stable peace in the region than we will.

Fourth, we must foster economic development for the sake of peace and progress. The Persian Gulf and Middle East form a region rich in natural resources with a wealth of untapped human potential. Resources once squandered on military might must be redirected to more peaceful ends. We are already addressing the immediate economic consequences of Iraq's aggression. Now the challenge is to reach higher—to foster economic freedom and prosperity for all people of the region.

By meeting these four challenges, we can build a framework for peace. I've asked Secretary of State Baker to go to the Middle East to begin the process. He will go to listen, to probe, to offer suggestions, and to advance the search for peace and stability. I have also asked him to raise the plight of the hostages held in Lebanon. We have not forgotten them, and we will not forget them.

To all the challenges that confront this region of the world, there is no single solution, no solely American answer. But we can make a difference. America will work tirelessly as a catalyst for positive change.

But we cannot lead a new world abroad if, at home, it's politics as usual on American defense and diplomacy. It's time to turn away from the temptation to protect unneeded weapons systems and obsolete bases. It's time to put an end to micro-management of foreign and security assistance programs, micro-management that humiliates our friends and allies and hamstrings our diplomacy. It's time to rise above the parochial and the pork barrel, to do what is necessary, what's right and what will enable this nation to play the leadership role required of us.

The consequences of the conflict in the Gulf reach far beyond the confines of the Middle East. Twice before in this century, an entire world was convulsed by war. Twice this century, out of the horrors of war hope emerged for enduring peace. Twice before, those hopes proved to be a distant dream, beyond the grasp of man.

Until now, the world we've known has been a world divided – a world of barbed wire and concrete block, conflict and cold war.

Now, we can see a new world coming into view. A world in which there is the very real prospect of a new world order. In the words of Winston Churchill, a "world order" in which "the principles of justice and fair play ... protect the weak against the strong ..." A world where the United Nations, freed from cold war stalemate, is poised to fulfil the historic vision of its founders. A world in which freedom and respect for human rights find a home among all nations.

The Gulf war put this new world to its first test, and, my fellow Americans, we passed that test.

For the sake of our principles, for the sake of the Kuwaiti people, we stood our ground. Because the world would not look the other way, Ambassador [Saud Nasir] al-Sabah, to-night, Kuwait is free.

Tonight as our troops begin to come home, let us recognize that the hard work of freedom still calls us forward. We've learned the hard lessons of history. The victory over Iraq was not waged as "a war to end all wars." Even the new world order cannot guarantee an era of perpetual peace. But enduring peace must be our mission ...

HOW WELL DID YOU UNDERSTAND THIS SELECTION?

1. Why did Bush call the military force during Desert Storm an "uncommon coalition"?

2. What phrases did Bush use to inspire the public to support the war against Iraq?

3. What were Bush's goals in the "new world order" he proposed? Which were achieved? Which were not?

4. What would Bush consider "positive change" in the world?

When Saddam Hussein of Iraq invaded Kuwait, which he claimed was historically part of Iraq, the Bush administration called for a coalition of nations to stop him. Previously, the U.S. had supported Hussein in his confrontations with Iran but now the fear that he would dominate the area and its oil led the U.S. to move to "protect" Kuwait. These quotations show the various sides in the controversy.

"I can tell you this: If I'm ever in a position to call the shots, I'm not going to rush to send somebody else's kids into a war."
George Bush
Man of Integrity (1988)

"By God, we will make the fire eat up half of Israel if it tries to do anything against Iraq."
Saddam Hussein
April 2, 1990

"Obviously, I didn't think—and nobody else did—that the Iraqis were going to take all of Kuwait. Every Kuwaiti and Saudi, every analyst in the Western world was wrong too. That does not excuse me. But people who now   claim that all was clear were not heard from at the time."
Ambassador Glaspie

"Remember, George, this is no time to go wobbly."
Margaret Thatcher
August 3, 1990

"A line has been drawn in the sand . . .Withdraw from Kuwait unconditionally and immediately, or face the terrible consequences."
George Bush

"'Operation Desert Shield' will provide air cover for the Savings-and-Loan bank scandal and the budget deficit."
Peter Hart, a Democrat pollster
November, 1990

"We are not intimidated by the size of the armies, or the type of hardware the U.S. has brought."
Saddam Hussein
November 12, 1990

"I do not believe the President requires any additional authorization from the Congress before committing U.S. forces to achieve our objectives in the Gulf."
Secretary of Defense Dick Cheney
December 3, 1990

"Allah is on our side. That is why we will beat the aggressor."
Saddam Hussein
December 12, 1990

"Our firm view is that the president has no legal authority, none whatsoever, to commit American troops to war in the Persian Gulf or anywhere else without congressional authorization."
Senator George J. Mitchell (D., Me)
December 14, 1990

"As I report to you, air attacks are under way against military targets in Iraq . . . I've told the American people before that this will not be another Vietnam. And I repeat this here tonight. Our troops will have the best possible support in the entire world, and they will not be asked to fight with one hand tied behind their back."
President George Bush
Address to the nation
January 16, 1991

"Our objectives are clear. Saddam Hussein's forces will leave Kuwait. The legitimate government of Kuwait will be restored to its rightful place and Kuwait once again will be free. Iraq will eventually comply with all relevant United Nations resolutions..."
President George Bush
Address to the nation
January 16, 1991

"Fight them with your faith in God, fight them in defense of every free honorable woman and every innocent child, and in defense of the values of manhood and the military honor . . . Fight them because with their defeat you will be at the last entrance of the conquest of all conquests. The war will end with . . . dignity, glory, and triumph for your people, army, and nation."
Saddam Hussein
Radio Broadcast
January 19, 1991

"Our strategy to go after the Army is very, very simple. First we are going to cut it off, and then we're going to kill it."
General Colin L. Powell, USA
Chairman of the Joint Chiefs of Staff,
news conference
January 23, 1991

"If anyone tells you America's best days are behind her, they're looking the wrong way."
George Bush
January 28, 1991

"Achieving our goals will require sacrifice and time, but we will prevail. Make no mistake about that."
George Bush
February 1, 1991

"Bush said he had no dispute with Iraqi people. It certainly looks different from Baghdad."
A resident of Baghdad
February 1, 1991

"Iraqis will never forget that on 8 August 1990 Kuwait became part of Iraq legally, constitutionally and actually. It continued to do so until last night, when withdrawal began."
Saddam Hussein
February 26 1991

"The Iraqi forces are conducting the Mother of all Retreats."
Dick Cheney
February 27, 1991

"More than 200 ships from 13 nations conducted over 10,000 flawless intercepts, which formed a steel wall around the waters leading to Iraq. And these operations continue today. Thanks to these superb efforts not one cargo hold, not one crate, not even one pallet of seaborne contraband even touched Saddam Hussein's shores. The result: Iraq lost 90% of its imports, 100% of its exports, and had its gross national product cut in half."
General Norman Schwarzkopf
Speech at U.S. Naval Academy
May 23, 1991

These have been compiled from various sources, including Reuters, *Triumph in the Desert* , and *George Bush's War*.

HOW WELL DID YOU UNDERSTAND THIS SELECTION?

1. Who were the major players on the scene when the war began? Who were the major players when the war ended?

2. Did the U.S. gain prestige around the world because it "saved" Kuwait?

3. What attitudes of the leading figure may have contributed to the situation in the Middle East today?

4. The issue presented by the U.S. to invade Iraq was Saddam Hussein's invasion of Kuwait. Were there other reasons?

One problem that seemed to worsen in the 1980s was the issue of homelessness. The cuts in social welfare programs loosened the already precarious "safety nets" designed to help the most vulnerable members of society. During the 1980s the characteristics of homeless people seemed to change from single people to families headed by women. Homeless people are often ignored by the political system, but this seemed even more true in the 1980s.

You see them now in every American city - the homeless people, who sleep by night in doorways, under highway bridges, in tents, on steaming grates, in bus stations. By day they wander warily from park bench to soup kitchen to abandoned building to public library or museum, watching the long hours slip away into nothingness. On frigid winter nights, they jam into emergency shelters that more closely resemble concentration camps than warm havens. These hundreds of thousands, if not millions, of homeless represent a national epidemic - the most severe housing crisis since the Depression. It is a problem that most agree will only get dramatically worse, growing far faster than the remedies.

Wide disagreement exists over the number of homeless, with the most frequently cited national figures ranging from a low of 250,000 (estimated by the Department of Housing and Urban Development in 1984) to four million (a 1982 estimate by the Community for Creative Non-Violence, an advocacy group located in Washington, D.C.). In a report to the National Governors' Association, New York Gov. Mario Cuomo gave the following estimates for 1983: 20,000 to 25,000, Chicago; 12,000 to 15,000, Baltimore; 2,500, Denver; 8,000 to 10,000, San Francisco; 2,000, Boston; 7,700, St. Louis:; 22,000, Houston.

One difficulty in accurately counting the homeless population is that the number changes constantly in response to such factors as national economic policy, unemployment rates, availability of social services, availability of low-rent housing, season of the year, weather, day of the month. In addition, definitions of homelessness vary, as do counting methodologies. However, as Congressman Bruce Vento (D. Minn.) says, "We shouldn't be diverted by an argument about numbers. The obvious fact is that we have a growing number of homeless."

The real issue is not the precise number of homeless, but the gravity of their situation. The Department of Health and Human Services reports: 'They [the homeless live brutal, debilitating, stressful lives of great hardship." In New York City alone, some 25 to 50 homeless people are thought to die on the streets during each of the winter months. The causes are violence; weather related illnesses (pneumonia, frostbite, gangrene, stroke, heart failure); alcohol-induced illnesses, among others.

Public awareness of the plight of the homeless has heightened. Yet grave misconceptions still abound as to who the homeless are, why they are on the streets, and what is needed to remedy their situation. Some communities acknowledge the problem by shipping the homeless out of town.

Elsewhere, homelessness has become the latest fashion fad: In the spring of 1983, Bloomingdale's department store in New York City opened in its second floor boutique a new display called "Street Couture." The clothing was designed to mimic the dress of the homeless poor: disheveled, wrinkled, patched, and mismatched. A jacket with torn sleeves listed for $190. An employee insisted that the "street look" sells. "Bag ladies are in," she explained.

The insensitivity continues on a daily basis in every city by those who more easily tell a joke about the homeless on the streets than acknowledge the homeless as human beings. D.C. homeless advocates Mary Ellen Hombs and Mitch Snyder offer the following as an example:

"In all of the years that Red and Willie [two homeless men] have spent on the down town [Washington, D.C.] heat grates, millions of people have walked or driven by them, but only a handful have stopped to talk, to see if they could be of any help. Some furtively scan the scene; others stare in amazement. For most, expressions do not change. Red and Willie, their pain and their loneliness, are invisible. If not invisible, then surely untouchable."

Dr. Michael Vergare, a psychiatrist with the Albert Einstein Medical Center in Philadelphia, suggests, "We struggle to comprehend how, in this day and age when so many people are so well off, we have people who cannot find shelter."

John Philips, AIA, 1985 chairman of AIA's housing committee says, "The epidemic of homelessness to some Americans, maybe to many, is so unthinkable that they refuse to recognize the visible homeless although the homeless are all around .... We must acknowledge that homelessness is a major social crisis today."

Often the homeless are identified by their tattered appearance; bizarre behavior; belongings carried in plastic bags or cardboard boxes tied with string or stuffed into shopping carts; swollen, ulcerated legs; apparent aimlessness. But, as Hombs and Snyder describe, "There are also those who have been able to maintain a reasonably good personal appearance and whose behavior betrays no apparent sign of disorder," which allows them to more easily find food, daytime shelter in libraries or museums, and public washroom facilities and to escape threats, violence, and harassment.

Generally, a homeless person is someone who has no stable residence, which is defined as a place to sleep and receive mail. This person is usually destitute and has either minimal or no resources or income. In addition, a homeless person is not likely receiving any government assistance.

Perhaps the first step in understanding the homeless is to dispel the myth that the homeless are on the streets by choice, having voluntarily rejected any available assistance. "It is an overstatement to say even a small minority of these people live on the streets by choice. There is no evidence that people live on the streets by choice," says Robert Hayes, founder and legal counsel of the National Coalition for the Homeless, headquartered in New York City. "It is essential to see the homeless as suffering individuals," Hayes adds, and to illustrate his point offers the following examples:

Alice is an elderly woman who has lived her entire life in quite a normal way. She raised children, then moved out of her home town to the Midwest. Her husband died. Then her rent went up dramatically. She first moved to a cheap hotel, an SRO (single-room-occupancy hotel). She lost that suddenly, at the age of 73, for the first time in her life, Alice could not find a place to live. She wound up in a train terminal. She became confused, and suddenly people were describing her as a "bag lady. "

Joey is a six-year-old boy in New York City. He's been homeless for three years-half of his life. He's been shunted from welfare hotels to what we euphemistically call "barrack shelters" in New York -refugee camps where cots and cribs are lined up on large, open rooms with common sleeping areas. When 1 first met Joey, he was a little fellow He was playful and had that glint in his eyes. And that glint was, to me, something that 1 thought would get him through. But he's six now. The glint's gone. Joey has struggled. Joey has suffered. But most of all, he's lost his playfulness, his right to that commodity that every child should have - his childhood.

Hayes maintains that "if people are offered safe, decent, humane shelters, they will go in off the streets."

A barometer of the problem's seriousness in the incidence of hunger, since hunger is considered the handmaiden of homelessness. In a survey of 181 food pantries and soup kitchens in 12 states, the National Governors' Association found a "dramatic increase" in the numbers seeking emergency food aid between February 1982 and February 1983. In that single year, demand in over half of the programs surveyed rose by 50 percent or more.

In a survey of 25 major cities, the U.S. Conference of Mayors found that hunger and homelessness rose sharply during 1985. Demand rose an average of 28 percent for emergency food and an average of 25 percent for shelter. In fact, the survey of cities ranging in size from New York to Charleston, S. C., found that "in none of the cities surveyed has the economic recovery lessened the problems of homelessness." There are also indications of a growing disparity between the have and have nots. For example, in Chicago "there has been no significant shift in the economic status of the city's poor and near poor." In Salt Lake City, "the national economic recovery has not alleviated the problems of low-income people. In fact, it appears that there are more people in need and that they are worse off, than previously."

Hayes reports, "What we saw in most parts of the country was a 20 to 30 percent increase during 1985 in the number of people seeking help I don't know any place that had spare beds."

Hayes noted last year, "In understanding homelessness, we have to start out by realizing that here we are in 1985 in a period without precedence in the history of the United States. By that I mean, sure there have been a lot of homeless folks in this country over the past few hundred years, but always mass homelessness in this country has been accompanied by system-wide economic dislocations - serious depressions or recessions. But something peculiar is happening because maybe [homelessness was understandable] in the 1930s, maybe even in 1982 or 1983 when there were serious economic problems. But in 1985, it does not seem so simple to understand. It seems that something fairly severe has to be undertaken because the old systems of dealing with mass homelessness in this country aren't working in the 1980s."

What makes the '80s feel like the '30s is the make-up of the homeless population. Now, as in the Depression, the homeless represent a broad cross section of American society - the young and old, single people and families, the mentally and physically disabled, and the ablebodied. The most dramatic change in the last 10 years has been a sharp increase in the number of women, children, young men, and families.

The New York State Department of Social Services reports: "Increasingly, the problem of homelessness is affecting people and families who are in most respects like other poor people, except that they cannot find or afford housing. The homeless transient, the wandering loner who may be alcoholic or mentally disabled, is no longer typical of the great majority of people without shelter. More and more, those sleeping in emergency shelters include parents and children whose primary reason for homelessness is poverty or family disruption. They have arrived in shelters not from the streets but from some dwelling (typically not their own) where they are no longer welcome or where they can no longer afford to stay."

The homeless population is now vastly different from the homogeneous skid row population of the post-World War II era, the majority of whom were older white men suffering from alcoholism and/or drug addiction. Since many cities and states had anti-vagrancy laws (until the 1970s), most skid rowers were actually not homeless, but sheltered - in jails, if not seedy hotels, flophouses, or missions,. But, regardless, many were considered the derelicts of society, as often the homeless are today. Now, though, according to the U.S. General Accounting Office (GAO), the average age of homeless persons is 34. Single women make up 13 percent of the homeless population, minorities 44 percent, and families 21 percent, the GAO reported in 1985. The U.S. Conference of Mayors reported in 1985 that the most significant recent change in the homeless population was the growing number of families with children; the number of young single adults also increased. It is especially poignant to see young children as miniature bag people dragging their toys in plastic bags.

A microcosm of the homeless population is found in Los Angeles County, where the number of homeless in not only large-HUD estimated 33,800 as of July '84- but is thought to be increasing rapidly. The compositional changes in that population parallel shifts in the national homeless population. For example- single males who had became homeless 12 months prior to a survey of homeless shelters (conducted over a six month period ending in May '84) were younger and better educated, and more likely to be non-white, recently unemployed, and veterans than those homeless for more than 12 months. Increased numbers of families with children, single women, and youths were visible throughout the county.

"A whole new wave of homeless people in the U.S. is made up of the young and ablebodied who have little chance of winning a place in a tight [employment] market and consequently no ability to win the competition for housing in a tighter and tighter housing market;" Hayes suggests, Marita Dean, of the Washington D.C., office of Catholic Charities, reported in 1984: We're seeing people now that no agency ever saw before, people who never had to beg before. They're frightened, so you help them this month, but they're not going to be any better off next month."

In addition to its demographic diversity, the homeless population varies significantly in duration of homelessness. Vergare and his associate, Dr. Anthony Arce, have suggested three groupings: the chronic, who are homeless for more than 30 continuous days - although many, if not most, have been homeless for months or years; the episodic, who tend to alternate for varying periods of time between being domiciled and homeless, with homelessness usually lasting less then 30 days; and the situational, for whom homelessness is the temporary result of an acute life crisis.

What looms ahead? One clue may be the number of people doubling up (living with one or two other persons or families). The National Coalition for the Homeless estimated at the end of 1985 that there were as many as 10 to 20 million doubling up, with as many as 500,000 in New York City alone. Seattle's Mayor Charles Royer noted in May 1985, "For every homeless person in Seattle, there are 10 others who are at risk and who need some kind of housing assistance."

A recent needs assessment in New York State found "disturbing information - the numbers of homeless people were far larger than imagined. But even more distressing was the consensus among service providers of the tremendous number of persons and families doubling up," says Nancy Travers, assistant commissioner, New York State Department of Social Services. She suggests that if New York State continued providing shelter to the homeless at the level it did in 1984, "it would take 20 years to meet the needs of the homeless. Clearly this is a housing problem of a scale that is hard to imagine."

Meanwhile, the numbers keep growing. In its Dec. 16, 1985, issue, *Newsweek* reported: "Across the frost belt last week, cities set records in sheltering the homeless: New York, Boston, Philadelphia have emergency policies requiring police and city employees to round up the homeless and take them to shelters after the temperature turns frigid. But the hundreds of shelter beds - in the case of New York City, 23,000 - come nowhere close to meeting the need."

Source: Subcommittee on Housing and Community Development. January 26, 1988.

HOW WELL DID YOU UNDERSTAND THIS SELECTION?

1. How does this reading define a homeless person?

2. What examples are given of homeless people that might not fit your stereotype?

3. How does the homeless population differ from the "skid row" population of the post-World War II era?

4. What problems did the report foresee in the future? Have those predictions come to pass in the last 12 years since the report was written?

Ryan White got AIDS virus from the blood-clotting medicine he took for his hemophilia. He died in 1990, at age eighteen. This is part of his testimony before the Presidential Commission on AIDS, given in 1988. The issue of AIDS was just beginning to become part of the public awareness.

I came face to face with death at thirteen years old. I was diagnosed with AIDS: a killer. Doctors told me I'm not contagious. Given six months to live and being the fighter that I am, I set high goals for myself. It was my decision to live a normal life, go to school, be with my friends, and enjoy day-to-day activities. It was not going to be easy.

The school I was going to said they had no guidelines for a person with AIDS . . . . We began a series of court battles for nine months, while I was attending classes by telephone. Eventually, I won the right to attend school, but the prejudice was still there. Listening to medical facts was not enough. People wanted one hundred percent guarantees. There are no one hundred percent guarantees in life, but concessions were made by Mom and me to help ease the fear. We decided to meet everyone halfway . . . . Because of the lack of education on AIDS, discrimination, fear, panic, and lies surrounded me. (1) I became the target of Ryan White jokes. (2) Lies about me biting people. (3) Spitting on vegetables and cookies. (4) Urinating on bathroom walls. (5) Some restaurants threw away my dishes. (6) My school locker was vandalized inside and folders were marked FAG and other obscenities.

I was labeled a troublemaker, my mom an unfit mother, and I was not welcome anywhere. People would get up and leave, so they would not have to sit anywhere near me. Even at church, people would not shake my hand.

This brought in the news media, TV crews, interviews, and numerous public appearances. I became known as the AIDS boy. I received thousands of letters of support from all around the world, all because I wanted to go to school . . . . It was difficult, at times, to handle, but I tried to ignore the injustice, because I knew the people were wrong. My family and I held no hatred for those people because we realized they were victims of their own ignorance. We had great faith that, with patience, understanding, and education, my family and I could be helpful in changing their minds and attitudes . . . .

Financial hardships were rough on us, even though Mom had a good job at G.M. The more I was sick, the more work she had to miss. Bills became impossible to pay. My sister, Andrea, was a championship roller skater who had to sacrifice too.. There was no money for her lessons and travel. AIDS can destroy a family if you let it, but luckily for my sister and me, Mom taught us to keep going. Don't give up, be proud of who you are, and never feel sorry for yourself.

HOW WELL DID YOU UNDERSTAND THIS SELECTION?

1. How did Ryan White contract AIDS?

2. Why did both students and adults react to Ryan White the way they did?

3. What caused the attitudes towards Ryan to gradually change?

4. In what ways have public views about AIDS changed since 1988?

SELF TEST

MULTIPLE CHOICE: Circle the correct response. The correct answers are given at the end.

1. Part of President Reagan's supply-side economics was a push to
   a. lower military expenditures
   b. increase taxes on the rich
   c. cut domestic social program expenditures
   d. increase the power of federal government agencies

2. The first woman to be on a major party ticket as a vice presidential candidate in 1984 was
   a. Janet Reno
   b. Sandra Day O'Connor
   c. Hillary Rodham
   d. Geraldine Ferraro

3. The people who profited most from the economic policies of the 1980s were
   a. wealthy businessmen
   b. skilled workers
   c. black inner-city residents
   d. small farmers

4. One result of Reagan's economic policies was that the national debt
   a. stayed the same because of reductions in the budget for social welfare programs
   b. declined a bit due a combination of budget cuts and tax increases
   c. declined substantially as a result of prosperity and increased federal revenues
   d. doubled due to a combination of tax cuts and increased defense expenditures

5. Like the 1880s, the 1980s was an era characterized by
   a. government regulation of all aspects of the economy
   b. powerful union movements asserting workers' demands
   c. an emphasis on personal wealth and greed
   d. a strong idealistic push for community involvement

6. The main reason for the dramatic changes in the Soviet Union from the late 1980s to early 1990s was
   a. the reforms launched by Soviet leader Mikhail Gorbachev
   b. the brilliant diplomacy instituted by Ronald Reagan
   c. the fears caused by the American Strategic Defense Initiative
   d. the constant worries about an imminent western invasion

7. What led some people to wonder if President Bush was trustworthy in keeping his promises?
   a. his attempt to end all affirmative action
   b. his characterization of the Soviet Union as an "evil empire"
   c. the breaking of his, "Read my lips, no new taxes" pledge
   d. his belated embrace of a pro-choice stance on abortion

8. The American public supported the Persian Gulf War for all these reasons EXCEPT
   a. It seemed a matter of the forces of democracy against an evil dictatorship.
   b. There were genuine fears that the Soviet Union would seize control of the region.
   c. People worried that Saddam Hussein would have too much control over oil production.
   d. Some people wanted to see America demonstrating that it could use its military might.

9. Bush based his attack on Iraq in 1991 on
   a. his alliance with the Soviet Union
   b. his fear that Saddam Hussein might have weapons of mass destruction
   c. Hussein's denial of the United Nations ultimatum
   d. his plan to rule in the Middle East.

10. In the election of 1992, one of the Democrat's slogans was
    a. Down with Republicanism
    b. It's the Economy, Stupid
    c. Let's Work with the Communists
    d. Youth Should Rule.

Answers: 1-c; 2-d; 3-a; 4-d; 5-c; 6-a; 7-c; 8-b; 9-c; 10-b.

ESSAYS:

1. What kind of leader were U.S. voters looking for in 1980? Why did Ronald Reagan win an overwhelmingly large percentage of the popular vote as well as the votes in the Electoral College?

2. From Reagan to G.H.W. Bush, international policies and changes looked for "a new world order." What did this mean and how has it affected the U.S. role in the world today?

3. Reagan pressed the idea that capitalism and democracy would regulate the economy (supply side economics). Did this work for the U.S. in the long run?

4. What were the reasons for Reagan's changing attitude toward the Soviet Union.

OPTIONAL ACTIVITIES: (Use your knowledge **and** imagination when appropriate.)

1. Ronald Reagan died in 2004 and was hailed as a hero; the nation took days to mourn. Consider what makes a hero in the American political scene.

2. Ask someone who voted for Reagan and/or Bush what they remember of the issues and campaigns from that period.

3. Many of the members of the present Bush administration (George W) were members of his father's administration. What issues and solutions have they carried with them?

WEB SITE LISTINGS:

Official Site of Ronald Reagan Presidential Library:
> http://www.reagan.utexas.edu/

White House home page – source on recent presidents:
> http://www.whitehouse.gov

History of AIDS:
> http://www.library.ucsf.edu/collres/archives/ahpl

Iran/Contra:
> http://www.Realhistoryarchives.com/collections/conspiracies/irancontra.htm

House Judiciary Impeachment Report:
> http://www.house.gov/judiciary/report5

Document Center including Documents on Poverty, Crime, Terrorism, Impeachment and War:
> http://www.lib.umich.edu/govdocs/usterror.html
> > /impeach.html
> > /census2/
> > /iraqwar.html

Recent and Older Supreme Court Decisions:
> http://www.findlaw.com/casecode/supreme.html

Recent Elections:
> http://www.pbs.org/newshour/election98
> > /election2000

Best Sources for Current Events:
> http://www.nytimes.com
> http://www.cnn.com

Chapter Twenty-nine

A DIVIDED AMERICA:
William Jefferson Clinton to George W. Bush to Barack Obama

Reading the political environment of 1992, Bill Clinton gained the Democratic nomination for the presidency by positioning himself as a New Democrat. His middle of the road approach convinced many voters that the supposed liberalism of the Democratic Party was a misreading of its goals and ideals and that it would not give way to big government and massive expenditures. Here he predicted the future and during his administration, the budget was balanced and the national deficit paid off.

In an opposite direction from the Reagan and Bush administrations, Clinton put together an aggressive domestic program. Now that the Soviet Union was on the decline and competition with great communist leaders was over (i.e., the end of the Cold War), the U.S. could turn its attention toward internal reforms. Tax cuts for the middle class, support for education, universal health care, and reduction or even eradication of the national deficit seemed to be mandates. The election campaign against George H.W. Bush had pointed out Bush's lack of understanding of the needs of most of the American public, and Clinton made it his goal to associate with his average supporters. Stories of his difficult childhood and rise above the trials of an abusive home to become a Rhodes Scholar and Yale graduate were the products of the American dream.

The Clinton White House, even with 44 percent of the national vote, had as many detractors as supporters and the image of the president as "Bubba," the pot smoking, draft dodging, philandering good ol' boy was hard to escape. Almost everywhere the new president turned to change the system, personal attacks followed him, causing defeats to many of his major proposals. Health-care legislation failed in the face of the charge of socialized medicine, which would be mediocre at best. (The U.S. is the only modern industrial nation that does not have a national health-care system.) He did manage some smaller successes in the Family and Medical Leave Act, which Bush had vetoed twice. On the front against crime, gun control laws were stiffened and funding for 100,000 new police across the country was enacted. The cabinet became a multicultural unit that was more representative of the U.S. population.

After 12 years of Republican control, reduction of major cost areas in order to balance the budget was difficult to achieve. Clinton was adamant that some move to reduce the budget had to be made and when the Republicans added tax cuts for the wealthy while cutting funds for Medicare, Clinton vetoed the bill, shutting down the government for three weeks. Some accused Clinton as irresponsible, but the Republicans finally came to the compromise table. In 1996, Clinton won reelection.

The tensions between the Republicans and Clinton increased, and finally the rift broke open with the charges against Clinton that he had had several affairs with women. These charges finally came to fruition for the Republicans with the revelations of his relationship with a White House intern, Monica Lewinsky. An investigation found that Clinton had lied about his actions and thus obstructed justice. Impeachment charges were brought and although the American public thought these charges specious and political, the Senate held a trial. Republicans fell short of the two-thirds majority needed to convince so the matter died, at least legally. Clinton had had to spend so much time defending himself that his major concerns and programs were not accomplished.

Internationally, Clinton was hesitant about American involvement. Chaos in Somalia had caused Bush to send American troops to the area and hoping to stabilize the situation, Clinton sent more soldiers to help the U.N. Peacekeeping Force. In October 1995, 18 Americans were killed and 87 wounded. Gradually, Clinton withdrew American troops. On another front, Clinton struggled with what to do about the genocide in Rwanda but did not send troops. Closer to home, he threatened an invasion of Haiti, which caused some political concessions to American interests, including replacing the president with a man more favorable to U.S. policies. In the Balkans, "ethnic cleansing" caused great concern in the Western world, and Clinton involved Americans in a NATO effort to bomb the area to stop the slaughter.

Tensions in the Middle East, formed since the establishment of Israel in 1948, continued to draw U.S. attention. Clinton invited leaders from Israel and the Palestinian Liberation Organization to Washington to create some form of truce that would benefit each side. An agreement was made but stability in the region remained elusive. Radical Islamic movements arose to support the PLO and U.S. favoritism for Israel increased their hostility to the U.S. In 1993, Muslim extremists bombed the basement of the World Trade Center; in 1998, they bombed American embassies in Kenya and Tanzania; and, in 2000, they blew a huge hole in the side of the *U.S. Cole*, stationed in Yemen. The Saudi terrorist Osama bin Ladin was linked to these attacks, but the mysterious figure could not be found. Several terrorists have been brought to trial for these actions.

Clinton left office almost as popular as when he entered it. His Vice President, Al Gore of Tennessee, seemed to be on a good track to follow him to the White House. The Republicans nominated George Walker Bush, son of the 41st President. The country was bitterly divided, politically as well as geographically. The coasts were seen as "liberal" and supported Gore; the center of the country championed Bush's message of a return to the times of Ronald Reagan, to conservative morality and to small government. The popular vote went to Gore by 500,000 votes but the electoral vote was unclear because of flawed counting problems in Florida. The Florida vote was counted and recounted and finally the Supreme Court decided, by a 5 to 4 decision, to give Florida to Bush. The Electoral College vote was 271 for Bush and 267 for Gore. It was the first time in American History that the Court ruled on a presidential election.

Following the policies of his father, George Walker Bush concentrated on foreign affairs. Most of his major appointments went to men who had served in the first Bush White House. Claiming a return to the days of Reagan, Bush led a government that cut funding for many domestic programs while spending billions on war in Iraq and Afghanistan. The 9/11 attacks in New York and Washington, D.C. nine months after Bush took office justified American mobilization of forces to search out Osama bin Laden and his terrorist allies in Afghanistan. Not long after this, the war frontier moved to Iraq where, Bush claimed, Saddam Hussein had "weapons of mass destruction," which could be used against the U.S. Although UN inspectors found no cache of such weapons and the link to Osama bin Laden went unproved, Bush grew weary of the search and decided that action against Iraq was necessary. When the first phase, "shock and awe,"—bombings—was unsuccessful in toppling Hussein, ground troops were committed to the battle. This has been the major effort of the Bush administration.

On the domestic scene, many programs were cut, and the national debt kept growing. For instance, Bush's program of "No Child Left Behind" has been woefully underfunded. Support for the unemployed, students, and the elderly were all limited to provide for defense spending. Although statistics showed a strong economy, many have lost their jobs, outsourcing has become a standard in American industry, there is a crisis in the mortgage industry, and scandals have dented the Bush claim to integrity. Reaching deep into what conservative Americans believe, Bush has led a coalition against the legalization of gay marriage and made this an issue of "national morality."

In 2004, Bush stood for reelection against Massachusetts Senator John Kerry. Using a similar strategy from the 2000 election, which was devised by his trusted advisor Karl Rove, Bush ignored the population's call for a new direction in Iraq and concentrated on domestic issues, condemning the Democrats for supporting gay marriage, abortion, and socialized medicine. He pressed for tax rebates for the "little people" and pointed to the so-called strong economy. He painted Kerry as an out of touch intellectual and bashed Kerry's military record. Although the Electoral College vote was again very close, with problems in Ohio surfacing this time, Bush did win the popular vote and claimed he had "political capital" to do what he wished.

On the national level, scandals in both parties sullied the reputation of the national government. The president's approval rate plummeted due to inconclusive results in Iraq. There is increasing hostility to U.S. policies around the world. Disasters such as Hurricane Katrina's devastation of New Orleans continue to convince many that the president does not care about the day to day problems of average Americans. The field for candidates in the 2008 election widens and the direction for the U.S. continues to be reassessed by its citizens.

IDENTIFICATION: Briefly describe each term.

Newt Gingrich and the Contract for America

Ross Perot

Kenneth Starr

H.U.D.

Janet Reno and Elian Gonzales

Oklahoma Bombing

Monica Lewinsky

Yitzak Rabin and Yasser Arafat

Alan Greenspan

Impeachment

Black Hawk Down

Ethnic Cleansing/Genocide in Africa

Bosnia

NAFTA/GAT

Madeline Albright

Health Care Reform

Dayton Accords

Saddam Hussein

UN Coalition Forces

Condoleeza Rice

Donald Rumsfeld

Karl Rove

No Child Left Behind

Osama bin Laden

Tony Blair

Antiballistic Missile Treaty

Constitutional Amendment

Hillary Clinton

General David Petraeus

John Roberts

Illegal Immigration

Butcher of Baghdad

Stem Cell Research

UN Security Council

WMD

Pre-emptive Strike

"Shock and Awe"

Homeland Security Act

Patriot Act

May 19, 2003

Partial Birth Abortion Act of 2003

"W"

Global Warming

Kyoto Protocol

"An Inconvenient Truth"

THINK ABOUT:

1. In the election of 1992, Ross Perot ran as a third party candidate. How successful have third party candidates been on the national level, and why?

2. There have been two impeachment trials in U.S. history pertaining to the presidency.
    a. Why have both of these attempts failed to convict the president?
    b. What other officials are liable to impeachment charges?

3. In both the elections of 2000 and 2004, Democratic candidates have been labeled "liberal intellectual." What is a "liberal intellectual" and why has this characterization been so effective in U.S. elections?

4. What does the Bush administration mean by "faith based initiatives"?

5. The war in Iraq has become a divisive issue in American politics. What are the positions of each side in the political conversation of today?

African-American fury exploded in the 1992 riots in South Central Los Angeles. After the acquittal of four white police officers accused of beating Rodney King, enraged residents erupted into violence, destroying sections of the city. The riots led to 38 deaths, 3,700 burned-out buildings, and more than $500 million in damages. Congresswoman Maxine Waters, who represented the district, testified about the underlying causes of the riots.

The riots in Los Angeles and in other cities shocked the world. They shouldn't have. Many of us have watched our country-including our government-neglect the problems, indeed the people, of our inner-cities for years-even as matters reached a crisis stage.

The verdict in the Rodney King case did not cause what happened in Los Angeles. It was only the most recent injustice-piled upon many other injustices-suffered by the poor, minorities and the hopeless people living in this nation's cities. For years, they have been crying out for help. For years, their cries have not been heard.

I recently came across a statement made more than 25 years ago by Robert Kennedy, just two months before his violent death. He was talking about the violence that had erupted in cities across America. His words were wise and thoughtful:

> There is another kind of violence in America, slower but just as deadly, destructive as the shot or bomb in the night .... This is the violence of institutions; indifference and inaction and slow decay. This is the violence that afflicts the poor, that poisons relations between men and women because their skin is different colors. This is the slow destruction of a child by hunger, and schools without books and homes without heat in winter.

What a tragedy it is that America has still, in 1992, not learned such an important lesson.

I have represented the people of South Central Los Angeles in the U. S. Congress and the California State Assembly for close to 20 years. I have seen our community continually and systematically ravaged by banks who would not lend to us, by governments which abandoned us or punished us for our poverty, and by big businesses who exported our jobs to Third-World countries for cheap labor.

In LA, between 40 and 50 percent of all African-American men are unemployed. The poverty rate is 32.9 percent. According to the most recent census, 40,000 teenagers-that is 20 percent of the city's 16 to 19 year olds-are both out of school and unemployed ....

We have created in many areas of this country a breeding ground for hopelessness, anger and despair. All the traditional mechanisms for empowerment, opportunity and self-improvement have been closed.

We are in the midst of a grand economic experiment that suggests if we "get the government off people's backs," and let the economy grow, everyone, including the poor, will somehow be better off .... The results of this experiment have been devastating. Today, more than 12 million children live in poverty, despite a decade of "economic growth," the precise mechanism we were told would reduce poverty. Today, one in five children in America lives in poverty ....

While the budget cuts of the eighties were literally forcing millions of Americans into poverty, there were other social and economic trends destroying inner-city communities at the same time.

I'm sure everyone in this room has read the results of the Federal Reserve Board's study on mortgage discrimination that demonstrates African Americans . . . are twice as likely as whites of the same income to be denied mortgages ....

In law enforcement, the problems are longstanding and well documented as well.

Is it any wonder our children have no hope? The systems are failing us. I could go on and on .... We simply cannot afford the continued terror and benign neglect that has characterized the federal government's response to the cities since the late 1970s.

Source: Maxine Waters, "Testimony before the Senate Banking Committee," Congressional Record (1992).

HOW WELL DID YOU UNDERSTAND THIS SELECTION?

1. According to Maxine Waters, why shouldn't the 1992 Los Angeles riots have shocked the world?

2. Why was South Central Los Angeles (and other such areas) "a breeding ground for hopelessness, anger and despair"?

3. What government policies of the 1980s did she believe worsened the situation?

4. Do you feel these problems have been solved since then? Can you think of current events that would illustrate similar concerns?

REMARKS BY VICE PRESIDENT ALBERT GORE
GLACIER NATIONAL PARK
Tuesday, September 2, 1997

Even before his vice presidency, Al Gore had discussed problems of Global Warming, a crisis for the 21ˢᵗ century that endangered the lives of humans as well as all the plants and animals around the globe. His crusade has taken him to many places, but his appearance on the edge of the melting glacier is particular informative.

I thank all of you for joining me here in Glacier National Park — one of the greatest glories of America's park system. The rich landscape we see all around us — the deep valleys and dramatic summits — date back more than a billion years, when Ice Age glaciers cut through this terrain, shaping and sculpting what is now one of the largest wild areas in the United States.

The Blackfeet Indians called this land "the Backbone of the World" — and there is no question that, for the two million people who visit this park each year, Glacier connects us to the very core of our nature. It's a place where stunning summits overlook a million acres of wilderness; where the most rugged rock formations rub against meadows of bear grass blossoms; where grizzly bear, and elk, and bighorn sheep roam free.

It's easy to understand why Glacier means so much to the families that come here. It is a land that seems almost untouched by time, undamaged by man's heavy hand. To look out on Glacier's alpine beauty is to want to preserve it and protect it — for our children, and for our children's children.

That's a responsibility President Clinton and I have taken very seriously — not just here in Glacier, but in all of America's special places. That's why we prevented oil and gas drilling in the Arctic Refuge. That's why we preserved 1.7 million precious acres in Utah by creating the Grand Staircase/Escalante National Monument. That's why we protected 1.4 million acres of the unique California desert. That's why we're restoring the Florida Everglades.

That's why we're protecting Yellowstone National Park from the dangers of mining on its borders. That's why we're putting record resources into our parks and rivers and wilderness preserves. To President Clinton and me, preserving America's special places isn't just good public policy — it's a moral obligation.

I have come here today because Glacier National Park faces a grave threat to its heritage — and it's one that can't be met with a simple restoration plan. The 50 glaciers in this park —which date back to the last Ice Age, 10,000 years ago — are melting away at an alarming rate. Over the last century, we have lost nearly three-quarters of all the glaciers in this park. Grinnell Glacier has retreated by over 3,100 feet.

Jackson Glacier has lost about 75% of its surface area. If this trend continues, in about thirty years, there won't be any glaciers left at all. To borrow a phrase from a well-known pop musician, this could become be the Park Formerly Known as Glacier.

What's happening at Glacier National Park is strong evidence of global warming over the past century — the disruption of our climate because of greenhouse gas emissions into the atmosphere, all over the world. The overwhelming evidence shows that global warming is no longer a theory — it's a reality. Greenhouse gases keep rising at record rates. The last few decades have been the warmest of this century — and the ten warmest years in this century have all occurred since 1980.

More than 2,000 scientists from all over the world on a special panel on climate change found that the evidence shows, and I quote, "a discernable *human* influence on global climate."

If we stay on our present course, scientists predict that average global temperatures will rise by 2 to 6 degrees Fahrenheit in the next century. That may not sound like much. But keep in mind that the difference in temperature between today and the last ice age, when all the glaciers in this park were formed, is only about *nine* degrees Fahrenheit. That's why, if we fail to act, scientists believe the human impact of global warming will be severe:

Infectious diseases could spread, affecting families and children in regions that had been too cold for tropical viruses to survive. Farmers and rural communities could be in jeopardy, since farms depend on a stable climate to be productive. Back in 1988, when we faced both record temperatures and droughts, the United States lost a third of its grain supply. We could face greater floods, droughts, and heat waves. Some see the unusually severe flooding in the Midwest, the Dakotas, and around the country — those "hundred-year floods" that seem to be happening every couple of years now — as early evidence of this.

As we see here at Glacier, the impact on our natural heritage and special places could be just as strong.

Our seas could rise by one to three feet, flooding thousands of miles of Florida, Louisiana, and other coastal areas. A sea level rise of just one foot could place a third of the Florida Everglades completely underwater; it would also threaten our coral reefs, and endanger the countless varieties of fish that live in them. With warmer temperatures, we could lose important parts of our forests. Some have predicted that the Northeast could lose all of its sugar maples; and in New Hampshire's White Mountains, many of the trees could stop changing colors with the seasons.

Scientists aren't the only ones who are concerned. The President of the Reinsurance Association of America, Frank Nutter, says that significant, perhaps permanent changes in our climate could bankrupt the insurance industry in years to come. Strong words from an industry that's all about calculating risk. This spring, John Browne, the CEO of British Petroleum, acknowledged the importance of taking, and I quote, "precautionary action now."

My purpose today is not to be alarmist — nor is it to say that we need radical changes in the way we live and work. But it's time to face the facts: Global warming is *real*. We helped to cause it — and by taking reasonable, common-sense steps, we can help to reduce it.

What we need is an approach that is prudent and *balanced*. On one hand, we must recognize that energy consumption has led to enormous increase in our standard of living throughout this century, and we want to continue those increases. On the other hand, we see all around us today glaciers that have survived for 10,000 years, now facing the prospect of melting away in a single century. We've seen people struck by severe heat waves — more than 400 in Chicago just two years ago — and many others who have lost homes, jobs, even their lives to increasingly heavy storms.

We need to understand our role in climate change — and we need to act to address it.

As one ecologist recently told President Clinton and me at the White House, simply by *slowing* the rate of climate change, we can make it much easier for our environment to evolve and adapt to it.

Thanks to President Clinton, we're already working to develop new energy technologies, to shrink greenhouse emissions in ways that also grow the economy. Let me give you just a few examples: First of all, after a decade of declining budgets, President Clinton is working to restore our commitment to the Energy Department's research into renewable energy and energy efficiency.

We need help from Congress to do that — and quite frankly, there are some on Capitol Hill who still cling to the old programs, and the old industry   subsidies. If we really want to move forward in this area, and capture these new energy markets for America — if we want to keep up with nations like Germany and Japan, which are already establishing an edge in these technologies — Congress has to join us in meeting the challenge.

Our efforts reach beyond Washington as well. The President has asked some of the nation's leading experts from academia and industry to conduct an intensive review of all our energy research and development programs, and to   report back by October 1st with their recommendations — so we can start to shape a national energy strategy for the next century.

We're working with the auto industry through our Partnership for a New Generation of Vehicles — to try to *triple* the fuel efficiency of cars with no loss in comfort or safety. We're working with the building industry through our Partnership for Advancing Technologies in Housing, to make homes cheaper, more energy-efficient, and more environmentally-friendly.

But we know that America's efforts alone will never be good enough. Because winds circle the earth within a few weeks, greenhouse gases don't respect national borders. Any real solution to global warming must be an *international* solution — including developing nations as well as industrialized ones.

This December, when the nations of the world meet in Kyoto, Japan on this issue, the United States will work to achieve realistic, binding limits on the emissions of greenhouse gases.

We will emphasize approaches that are flexible and market-based, to give industry the opportunity to develop the most cost-effective solutions.

We will continue our efforts in research and development. We will work with industry, with environmental groups, with *all* who share a stake in this problem here at home. And we will ask all nations, developed and developing, to join with us to meet this challenge.

We don't have all the answers today. But we know we must reverse the trend of global warming. We must safeguard our precious natural resources, and put a premium on public health and safety.

You see, thirty years from now, I want my grandchildren to live in a world that is safer from disease, freer from droughts and floods, able to grow the food they need for their children and families.

But just as importantly, I want them to understand that God created only one earth — and that its parks and forests and wilderness preserves can never be replicated. Our responsibility to this land is one of the most profound and sacred responsibilities we have. It is really a responsibility to each other — and to future generations.

Ultimately, that's why we came here today, to the very Crown of this Continent. We've got to start facing up to that responsibility — not just for the sake of these glaciers, but for the sake of our children. Here in the shadow of these glorious mountains, let us resolve to make that start — let us protect this land for its rightful inheritors — and let us fulfill our obligation to the millions of families who have yet to enjoy it.

HOW WELL DID YOU UNDERSTAND THIS SELECTION?

1. What do the Blackfeet Indians call the glacial system? Why does Gore provide this image for his audience?

2. How old is the glacier system? What does Gore say is happening to it in 1997?

3. Gore says that there are natural weather cycles affecting changes. He credits the sudden changes in our environment to human causes. This has created an international argument about Global Warming. What are the points that each side make in this argument?

4. Why is Global Warming important to human beings?

In 1998, after having won reelection in 1996, a confident President Clinton delivered his annual State of the Union address. Despite the shadow of impending scandal, the president continued to pursue his agenda. He had been particularly adept at occupying the middle ground in American politics and demonstrated his ability to continue to do that in this speech.

January 27, 1998

. . . Community means living by the defining American value-the ideal heard round the world that we are all created equal. Throughout our history, we haven't always honored that ideal and we've never fully lived up to it. Often it's easier to believe that our differences matter more than what we have in common. It may be easier, but it's wrong.

What we have to do in our day and generation to make sure that America becomes truly one nation-what do we have to do? We're becoming more and more and more diverse. Do you believe we can become one nation? The answer cannot be to dwell on our differences, but to build on our shared values. We all cherish family and faith, freedom and responsibility. We all want our children to grow up in a world where their talents are matched by their opportunities.

I've launched this national initiative on race to help us recognize our common interests and to bridge the opportunity gaps that are keeping us from becoming one America. Let us begin by recognizing what we still must overcome. Discrimination against any American is un-American.

We must vigorously enforce the laws that make it illegal. I ask your help to end the backlog at the Equal Employment Opportunity Commission. Sixty thousand of our fellow citizens are waiting in line for justice, and we should act now to end their wait.

We also should recognize that the greatest progress we can make toward building one America lies in the progress we make for all Americans, without regard to race. When we open the doors of college to all Americans, when-we rid all our streets of crime, when there are jobs available to people from all our neighborhoods, when we make sure all parents have the child care they need, we're helping to build one nation.

We, in this chamber and in this government, must do all we can to address the continuing American challenge to build one America. But we'll only move forward if all our fellow citizens-including every one of you at home watching tonight-is also committed to this cause.

We must work together, learn together, live together, serve together. On the forge of common enterprise Americans of all backgrounds can hammer out a common identity. We see it today in the United States military, in the Peace Corps, in AmeriCorps. Wherever people of all races and backgrounds come together in a shared endeavor and get a fair chance, we do just fine. With shared values and meaningful opportunities and honest communication and citizen service, we can unite a diverse people in freedom and mutual respect. We are many; we must be one.

In that spirit, let us lift our eyes to the new millennium. How will we mark that passage? It just happens once every thousand years. This year, Hillary and I launched the White House Millennium Program to promote America's creativity and innovation, and to preserve our heritage and culture into the 21st century. Our culture lives in every community, and every community has places of historic value that tell our stories as Americans. We should protect them. I am proposing a public/private partnership to advance our arts and humanities, and to celebrate the millennium by saving American's treasures, great and small.

And while we honor the past, let us imagine the future. Think about this-the entire store of human knowledge now doubles every five years. In the 1980s, scientists identified the gene causing cystic fibrosis-it took nine years. Last year, scientists located the gene that causes Parkinson's Disease-in only nine days. Within a decade, "gene chips" will offer a road map for prevention of illnesses throughout a lifetime. Soon we'll be able to carry all the phone calls on Mother's Day on a single strand of fiber the width of a human hair. A child born in 1998 may well live to see the 22nd century.

Tonight, as part of our gift to the millennium, I propose a 21st Century Research Fund for path-breaking scientific inquiry-the largest funding increase in history for the National Institutes of Health, the National Science Foundation, the National Cancer Institute.

We have already discovered genes for breast cancer and diabetes. I ask you to support this initiative so ours will be the generation that finally wins the war against cancer, and begins a revolution in our fight against all deadly diseases.

As important as all this scientific progress is, we must continue to see that science serves humanity, not the other way around. We must prevent the misuse of genetic tests to discriminate against any American. And we must ratify the ethical consensus of the scientific and religious communities, and ban the cloning of human beings.

We should enable all the world's people to explore the far reaches of cyberspace. Think of this-the first time I made a State of the Union speech to you, only a handful of physicists used the World Wide Web. Literally, just a handful of people. Now, in schools, in libraries, homes and businesses, millions and millions of Americans surf the Net every day. We must give parents the tools they need to help protect their children from inappropriate material on the Internet. But we also must make sure that we protect the exploding global commercial potential of the Internet. We can do the kinds of things that we need to do and still protect our kids.

For one thing, I ask Congress to step up support for building the next generation Internet. It's getting kind of clogged, you know. And the next generation Internet will operate at speeds up to a thousand times faster than today.

Even as we explore this inner space in a new millennium we're going to open new frontiers in outer space. Throughout all history, humankind has had only one place to call home---our planet Earth. Beginning this year, 1998, men and women from 16 countries will build a foothold in the heavens-the international space station. With its vast expanses, scientists and engineers will actually set sail on an unchartered sea of limitless mystery and unlimited potential.

And this October, a true American hero, a veteran pilot of 149 combat missions and one, five-hour space flight that changed the world, will return to the heavens. Godspeed, John Glenn.

John, you will carry with you America's hopes. And on your uniform, once again, you will carry America's flag, marking the unbroken connection between the deeds of America's past and the daring of America's future. Nearly 200 years ago, a tattered flag, its broad stripes and bright stars still gleaming through the smoke of a fierce battle, moved Francis Scott Key to scribble a few words on the back of an envelope-the words that became our national anthem. Today, that Star Spangled Banner, along with the Declaration of Independence, the Constitution and the Bill of Rights, are on display just a short walk from here. They are America's treasures and we must also save them for the ages.

I ask all Americans to support our project to restore all our treasures so that the generations of the 21st century can see for themselves the images and the words that are the old and continuing glory of America; an America that has continued to rise through every age, against every challenge, of people of great works and greater possibilities, who have always, always found the wisdom and strength to come together as one nation-to widen the circle of opportunity, to deepen the meaning our freedom, to form that "more perfect union." Let that be our gift to the 21st century.

God bless you, and God bless the United States.

Bill Clinton, "Let us Strengthen our Nation for the 21st Century," The 1998 State of the Union, January 27, 1998 (Vital Speeches of the Day, February 15, 1999).

HOW WELL DID YOU UNDERSTAND THIS SELECTION?

1. What issues did President Clinton consider to be most important in his 1998 State of the Union address?

2. How did his views of what was most important differ from those of President Reagan thirteen years earlier?

3. Why does the president speak of and introduce John Glenn?

4. What unspoken issue existed at this time? How might it affect the president's program?

ADDRESSING THE NATION - William Jefferson Clinton
August 17, 1998

William Jefferson Clinton is only the second U.S. President to be impeached. His trial centered on supposed lies about his behavior in adulterous situations. His defense was that these were personal offenses and that his public duties were never compromised. Much of the nation felt the same and Clinton (as was Andrew Johnson) was acquitted.

After testifying for five and a half hours before Ken Starr's grand jury, President Clinton gave the following nationally-televised address.

Good evening.

This afternoon in this room, from this chair, I testified before the Office of Independent Counsel and the grand jury.

I answered their questions truthfully, including questions about my private life, questions no American citizen would ever want to answer.

Still, I must take complete responsibility for all my actions, both public and private. And that is why I am speaking to you tonight.

As you know, in a deposition in January, I was asked questions about my relationship with Monica Lewinsky. While my answers were legally accurate, I did not volunteer information.

Indeed, I did have a relationship with Ms. Lewinsky that was not appropriate. In fact, it was wrong. It constituted a critical lapse in judgment and a personal failure on my part for which I am solely and completely responsible.

But I told the grand jury today and I say to you now that at no time did I ask anyone to lie, to hide or destroy evidence or to take any other unlawful action.

I know that my public comments and my silence about this matter gave a false impression. I misled people, including even my wife. I deeply regret that.

I can only tell you I was motivated by many factors.   First, by a desire to protect myself from the embarrassment of my own conduct.

I was also very concerned about protecting my family. The fact that these questions were being asked in a politically inspired lawsuit, which has since been dismissed, was a consideration, too.

In addition, I had real and serious concerns about an independent counsel investigation that began with private business dealings 20 years ago, dealings, I might add, about which an independent federal agency found no evidence of any wrongdoing by me or my wife over two years ago.

The independent counsel investigation moved on to my staff and friends, then into my private life. And now the investigation itself is under investigation.

This has gone on too long, cost too much and hurt too many innocent people.

Now, this matter is between me, the two people I love most — my wife and our daughter — and our God. I must put it right, and I am prepared to do whatever it takes to do so.
Nothing is more important to me personally. But it is private, and I intend to reclaim my family life for my family. It's nobody's business but ours.

Even presidents have private lives. It is time to stop the pursuit of personal destruction and the prying into private lives and get on with our national life.

Our country has been distracted by this matter for too long, and I take my responsibility for my part in all of this. That is all I can do.

Now it is time — in fact, it is past time — to move on.

We have important work to do — real opportunities to seize, real problems to solve, real security matters to face.

And so tonight, I ask you to turn away from the spectacle of the past seven months, to repair the fabric of our national discourse, and to return our attention to all the challenges and all the promise of the next American   century.

Thank you for watching. And good night.

HOW WELL DID YOU UNDERSTAND THIS SELECTION?

1. How much does the public have a right to know about a public official's or candidate's personal life?

2. What did Clinton say were his motives for being misleading?

3. What standards should we use to judge a public official or candidate?

4. Whom does Clinton say should be concerned about his "critical lapse of judgment"? Is he right?

"DON'T ASK, DON'T TELL"

When President Clinton first took office, he attempted to fulfill his promise to gays to end the policy forbidding gays in the military. This position created enormous controversy. As a result, Clinton agreed to a compromise policy known as "Don't Ask, Don't Tell" that permitted homosexuals in the military provided that they did not announce their sexual preference.

U.S. Code – Title 10, Section 654
Policy Concerning Homosexuality in the Armed Forces

(13) The prohibition against homosexual conduct is a long-standing element of military law that continues to be necessary in the unique circumstances of military service.

(14) The armed forces must maintain personnel policies that exclude persons whose presence in the armed forces would create an unacceptable risk to the armed forces' high standards of morale, good order and discipline, and unit cohesion that are the essence of military capability.

(15) The presence in the armed forces of persons who demonstrate a propensity or intent to engage in homosexual acts would create an unacceptable risk to the high standards of morale, good order and discipline, and unit cohesion that are the essence of military capability.

(b) Policy. - A member of the armed forces shall be separated from the armed forces under regulations prescribed by the Secretary of Defense if one or more of the following findings is made and approved in accordance with procedures set forth in such regulations:

(1) That the member has engaged in, attempted to engage in, or solicited another to engage in a homosexual act or acts unless there are further findings, made and approved in accordance with procedures set forth in such regulations, that the member has demonstrated that

(A) such conduct is a departure from the member's usual and customary behavior;

(B) such conduct, under all the circumstances, is unlikely to recur;

(C) such conduct was not accomplished by use of force, coercion, or intimidation;

(D) under the particular circumstances of the case, the member's continued presence in the armed forces is consistent with the interests of the armed forces in proper discipline good order, and morale; and

(E) the member does not have a propensity or intent to engage in homosexual acts.

(2) That the member has stated that he or she is a homosexual or bisexual, or words to that effect, unless there is a further finding, made and approved in accordance with procedures set forth in the regulations, that the member has demonstrated that he or she is not a person who engages in, attempts to engage in, has a propensity to engage in, or intends to en age in homosexual acts.

(3) That the member has married or attempted to marry a person known to be of the same biological sex.

PENTAGON ISSUES NEW GUIDELINES FOR GAYS IN MILITARY

August 13, 1999, Web Posted at: 4:12 p. m. EDT (2012 GMT) From staff and wire reports

WASHINGTON-The U.S. military Friday issued new directives intended to end abuses of the "don't ask, don't tell" policy toward gays and lesbians in the armed forces.

The revised specifications require that troops receive anti-gay harassment training throughout their military careers, starting with boot camp.

"I've made it clear there is no room for harassment or threats in the military," Defense Secretary William Cohen said in issuing the new directives.

The guidelines also mandate that any investigation into the sexual orientation of a soldier be handled at a more senior level of the military justice system than before.

The revisions follow the beating death last month of a soldier at Fort Campbell, Kentucky, who was rumored to be gay. Barry Winchell was bludgeoned to death in his barracks.

The Army conducted a hearing this week to determine whether the murder case against Pvt. Calvin Glover, 18, of Sulphur, Oklahoma, will go to a general court-martial. The decision is expected in about two weeks.

Some activists have charged that gay harassment and investigation of gays have surged to record levels in the military, despite the "don't ask, don't tell" policy.

Last year, 1,145 people were discharged from the armed forces for homosexuality, according to a Pentagon report. In 1997, the total was 997, the highest number since 1987. The number of discharges hit a low of 617 in 1994, the year the "don't ask, don't tell" policy took effect.

Pentagon officials have defended the policy, contending that roughly 80 percent of the discharges occur because the individual has come forward.

The new guidelines do not make any major changes in the procedures that have been followed since 1994, but try to spell them out more clearly, the officials said.

Michelle Benecke, a former Army officer now with the Service members Legal Defense Network, said she "seriously doubts"' the new guidelines will be an adequate response to the problem.

Still, officials said it is hoped that the intended clarifications—and mandatory anti-gay harassment, training —will end what they claim are a relatively small number of abuses.

Under the policy, those who are openly homosexual are still barred from serving in the in the military.

Gays can remain in the services so long as they do not discuss their sexual orientation openly. Commanders and investigators are not permitted to ask troops about their sexual orientation.

The policy was a compromise developed after Congress rejected an earlier proposal by President Clinton for an outright ban on discrimination based on sexual orientation.

Source: CNN, August 13, 1999. Correspondent David Ensor and the Associated Press contributed to this report.

HOW WELL DID YOU UNDERSTAND THIS SELECTION?

1. Why was the government policy called, "Don't Ask, Don't Tell"? What behavior would lead to the "separation" of a homosexual member of the armed forces from the services?

2. What event caused a revision of the policy?

3. What were the "new guidelines"? Do you think these guidelines will be more effective?

RALPH NADER ELECTION NIGHT SPEECH
November 7, 2000

The election of 2000 had many unusual aspects. Ralph Nader, the Green Party candidate, was hailed both as an alternative to the traditional bi-party system and as a spoiler that kept Al Gore out of the presidency. Here he states his case for his actions.

First, let me thank all these people who worked on the campaign. What we know for sure is that we're coming out of this election day with the third-largest party in America, replacing the Reform Party. Building a long-term progressive reform movement. That's really quite an achievement, it took lot of people from all over the country to do that, so, great staff, working day and night here in Washington, and above all it took a commitment by people to no longer settle for the least of the worst or the lesser of two evils, where at the end of the day you're still stuck with worst and evil.

To try to challenge the entrenched two-party system, this is really a lot what the campaign was about. The two parties raised these statutory barriers to get on the ballot, and they campaign with most of the money by raising   corrupt soft money, and corporate money and PAC money — all of which we rejected, because we wanted to set an example of what is necessary for real reform of our corrupt campaign system. And of course you're up against (the   fact that) most of the coverage on the horse race was between these two horses. They're tired and hollow, and have forgotten even to eat their oats in order to reinvigorate themselves. And then, the two parties control the debate commission which is really a private company. And they exclude Third Party candidates, so really it's a quite amazing and varied system of rigging the election for the two major parties. . . . It's why the two major parties can't regenerate themselves because their excluding all kinds of competition, and instead, imitating themselves.

535

The Republican and Democratic parties take more money from the same sources, they morph into one corporate party with two heads, and (then Americans) presume that it really matters for the State Department, or Defense Department or Treasury Department, or Department of Commerce, Labor, Agriculture, or the health and safety regulatory agencies—whether Gore or Bush is in the White House (but it isn't) because they don't make the decisions. The decisions are made by the people we trip over in Washington D.C. every day: 22,000 corporate lobbyists, and 9,000 political action committees pumping money into both Republican and Democratic coffers.

This is what we expected was gonna happen, and we took 'em on. And the important thing here is we've reached a take-off stage in the Green Party, and that this is the last time that the two parties in a national election will have a monopoly power to exclude significant Third-Party members from the debate. . . .

Going around the country you get the feeling that there are millions of people who are really ready for a new progressive political movement, and it takes a lot of work to get them together, and to believe that they can do it, because of the dominance of the two-party duopoly.

But we have now seen enormous talent come out from all over the country, not just in local state Green parties, like Medea Benjamin in California, but we've seen seasoned citizen activists, who recognize that the civil society has been crowded out in Washington increasingly the last 20 years by the two corporate powers, and we have to heed Thomas Jefferson's wisdom, that when our country is taken away from us, we have to go into political arena and mobilize new political civic energy throughout the United States in order to come back and take our government back from the corporate supremacists who think that there's nothing they can't control, there's nothing that they can't commercialize, there's nothing that they cannot daunt. And we're going to prove them wrong.

Most members of the press misread the distinction of this Green Party's mobilization. They said "Well, it's just another Green Party, and makes a valiant effort, election's over and then it recedes, and their leaders go back to their business in Texas or elsewhere." ...
Right after the election the Green Party moves and locks arms with all those neighborhood and citizen groups all over the United States who are fighting for a more just America. Who are fighting for the environment, fighting to establish missions against poverty, and enforcing the civil rights laws and civil liberties laws. Missions that say to the American people, that the choice is the sovereignty of the people, or the sovereignty of global corporations over the United States of America, and that's an easy choice to decide on whose side we're going to be.

Also it's important to note that in our country you cannot fire a citizen. . . . . The Green Party is going to give an authenticity . . . . Standing with labor, living wage issues. You know? There's no Republican parties, no Democratic parties in those struggles. The two parties after election, they take a few days off, they relax, and then they turn themselves into money-raising machines for the duration. While the Green Party turns itself into a civic force.

We had some funny mention moments — and I don't mean going on Saturday Night Live, or David Letterman — we had some funny moments when MasterCard was foolish enough to sue us. Saying that we violated their trademark registration on the word "priceless." They put a price on "priceless!"

So all these moments will be recalled with pleasure, because we really performed I think all of us in a very exemplary manner. There's a lot of content behind David Broder — the Washington Post political editor — who this Sunday wrote a column that said "Who ran the best campaign in the presidential campaign year?" And he said hands-down, it was the Green Party and the Nader/LaDuke campaign.

Bush came in second and Gore third. And I tell you — anyone who knows Dave Broder knows that he does not deal out praise very liberally. . . . But I think it reflects that we really practiced what we preached in order to preach what we practiced. Not just in the way we raised our funds, but in the way we comported ourselves, focusing on one important issue after another, which the media systemically ignored, as it continues to pepper us with this horse race question.

It's really quite unique in the sense that having received one percent of the national media coverage, and having raised less than one percent of the money, and having been excluded from the debates, that the majority of the   coverage was on the horse race. "Are you gonna be a spoiler?" And I would say "Well, you can't spoil a system spoiled to the core."

It'd be so predictable that the reporters would say "I know you've been asked about this one thousand times" — I felt like having a recorded announcement, but then that would have been too much like the corporations. . . . It really didn't give us a chance to raise the subject matter that the press over the years have been reporting on. Corporate crime, corporate welfare, the problem of labor and the living wage, WTO and NAFTA — all these things that are reported on in the major press — the Gore, Bush campaigns ignored all these issues uniformly in their lookalike status, and still the press was obsessed with the horse-race question.

So one of our goals after the election, is to, in a very kindly way, give some of the media an invitation to learn about what the criteria are for newsworthiness for a Third-Party candidacy. We attracted the largest mass paid political rallies by far of any presidential candidate; Madison Square Garden, to Boston Garden, to Target Center, all the huge arenas we filled with Green Party enthusiasts. That's one criteria.

Another is our 37-year record on weekends and during weekdays of fighting for the American people for safer cars, and food and air and water, and trying to make the government more accountable and the corporations more   responsive.

And the third criteria is that we have all kinds of people organized all over the country working their hearts out and their minds out for our effort. And the fourth criteria is that we were above the screen in the polls, they thought that was an important criteria. So we had the agenda, we had the rallies, we had the record, we had the polls rising. And still it wasn't newsworthy. So you see, a lot of these journalists are caught in a trap, a kind of time warp, and we've got to liberate them as well.

I want to thank people for voting for us. The people who have yet to vote out in the West Coast and Alaska and Hawaii, they can certainly build our reservoir of voters so we can build more after this election day with a great second leap forward in 2002, with all kinds of great people running for local, state and federal office. Building not only an exemplary election record, not just building a unifying force in civil society, but above all, building a deeper democracy. That's what it's really all about, building a deep democracy, so we can really put some reality into this hollow phrase, "a government of, by and for the people."

HOW WELL DID YOU UNDERSTAND THIS SELECTION?

1.   What is the Green Party and what was Nader's platform? Why does Nader say the program was misrepresented?

2.   Nader says that the Democrats and Republicans take funding from the same sources so there is no difference between them. How would you assess this charge?

3. What is the system of lobbying? How effective is it?

4. Did Nader "spoil" Gore's victory?

On election night, 2000, the scoreboard for Al Gore and George W. Bush, flip flopped until no one was sure who had won enough electoral votes. Gore earned the popular vote by some 500,000 ballots, but irregularities in a number of states, particularly Florida, made the final election unclear. Weeks went by with Florida counting and recounting the votes. The Governor of Florida, Jeb Bush (brother to George W), set up a special commission to determine the vote. Finally the Bush team sued to stop the counting and the issue ended up in the U.S. Supreme Court. On December 11, the Court voted 7 to 2 to stop counting. This has been the only time in U.S. history that the Court has intervened in a presidential election.

SUPREME COURT OF THE UNITED STATES
GEORGE W. BUSH, ET AL., PETITIONERS v. ALBERT GORE, JR., ET AL.
No. 00-949
[December 12, 2000]
PER CURIAM.
ON WRIT OF CERTIORARI TO THE FLORIDA SUPREME COURT

I

On December 8, 2000, the Supreme Court of Florida ordered that the Circuit Court of Leon County tabulate by hand 9,000 ballots in Miami-Dade County. It also ordered the inclusion in the certified vote totals of 215 votes identified in Palm Beach County and 168 votes identified in Miami-Dade County for Vice President Albert Gore, Jr., and Senator Joseph Lieberman, Democratic Candidates for President and Vice President. The Supreme Court noted that petitioner, Governor George W. Bush asserted that the net gain for Vice President Gore in Palm Beach County was 176 votes, and directed the Circuit Court to resolve that dispute on remand. The court further held that relief would require manual recounts in all Florida counties where so-called "undervotes" had not been subject to manual tabulation. The court ordered all manual recounts to begin at once. Governor Bush and Richard Cheney, Republican Candidates for the Presidency and Vice Presidency, filed an emergency application for a stay of this mandate. On December 9, we granted the application, treated the application as a petition for a writ of certiorari, and granted certiorari.

On November 8, 2000, the day following the Presidential election, the Florida Division of Elections reported that petitioner, Governor Bush, had received 2,909,135 votes, and respondent, Vice President Gore, had received 2,907,351 votes, a margin of 1,784 for Governor Bush. Because Governor Bush's margin of victory was less than "one-half of a percent . . . of the votes cast," an automatic machine recount was conducted under §102.141(4) of the election code, the results of which showed Governor Bush still winning the race but by a diminished margin. Vice President Gore then sought manual recounts in Volusia, Palm Beach, Broward, and Miami-Dade Counties, pursuant to Florida's election protest provisions. Fla. Stat. §102.166 (2000). A dispute arose concerning the deadline for local county canvassing boards to submit their returns to the Secretary of State (Secretary). The Secretary declined to waive the November 14 deadline imposed by statute. §§102.111, 102.112. The Florida Supreme Court, however, set the deadline at November 26. We granted certiorari and vacated the Florida Supreme Court's decision, finding considerable uncertainty as to the grounds on which it was based. On December 11, the Florida Supreme Court issued a decision on remand reinstating that date.

On November 26, the Florida Elections Canvassing Commission certified the results of the election and declared Governor Bush the winner of Florida's 25 electoral votes. On November 27, Vice President Gore, pursuant to Florida's contest provisions, filed a complaint in Leon County Circuit Court contesting the certification. Fla. Stat. §102.168 (2000). He sought relief pursuant to §102.168(3)(c), which provides that "[r]eceipt of a number of illegal votes or rejection of a number of legal votes sufficient to change or place in doubt the result of the election" shall be grounds for a contest. The Circuit Court denied relief, stating that Vice President Gore failed to meet his burden of proof. He appealed to the First District Court of Appeal, which certified the matter to the Florida Supreme Court.

Accepting jurisdiction, the Florida Supreme Court affirmed in part and reversed in part. The court held that the Circuit Court had been correct to reject Vice President Gore's challenge to the results certified in Nassau County and his challenge to the Palm Beach County Canvassing Board's determination that 3,300 ballots cast in that county were not, in the statutory phrase, "legal votes."

The Supreme Court held that Vice President Gore had satisfied his burden of proof under §102.168(3)(c) with respect to his challenge to Miami-Dade County's failure to tabulate, by manual count, 9,000 ballots on which the machines had failed to detect a vote for President ("undervotes"). Noting the closeness of the election, the Court explained that "[o]n this record, there can be no question that there are legal votes within the 9,000 uncounted votes sufficient to place the results of this election in doubt." A "legal vote," as determined by the Supreme Court, is "one in which there is a 'clear indication of the intent of the voter.'" The court therefore ordered a hand recount of the 9,000 ballots in Miami-Dade County. Observing that the contest provisions vest broad discretion in the circuit judge to "provide any relief appropriate under such circumstances," Fla. Stat. §102.168(8) (2000), the Supreme Court further held that the Circuit Court could order "the Supervisor of Elections and the Canvassing Boards, as well as the necessary public officials, in all counties that have not conducted a manual recount or tabulation of the undervotes . . . to do so forthwith, said tabulation to take place in the individual counties where the ballots are located."

The Supreme Court also determined that both Palm Beach County and Miami-Dade County, in their earlier manual recounts, had identified a net gain of 215 and 168 legal votes for Vice President Gore. Rejecting the Circuit Court's conclusion that Palm Beach County lacked the authority to include the 215 net votes submitted past the November 26 deadline, the Supreme Court explained that the deadline was not intended to exclude votes identified after that date through ongoing manual recounts. As to Miami-Dade County, the Court concluded that although the 168 votes identified were the result of a partial recount, they were "legal votes [that] could change the outcome of the election." The Supreme Court therefore directed the Circuit Court to include those totals in the certified results, subject to resolution of the actual vote total from the Miami-Dade partial recount.

The petition presents the following questions: whether the Florida Supreme Court established new standards for resolving Presidential election contests, thereby violating Art. II, §1, cl. 2, of the United States Constitution and failing to comply with 3 U. S. C. §5, and whether the use of standardless manual recounts violates the Equal Protection and Due Process Clauses. With respect to the equal protection question, we find a violation of the Equal Protection Clause.

II

A

The closeness of this election, and the multitude of legal challenges which have followed in its wake, have brought into sharp focus a common, if heretofore unnoticed, phenomenon. Nationwide statistics reveal that an estimated 2% of ballots cast do not register a vote for President for whatever reason, including deliberately choosing no candidate at all or some voter error, such as voting for two candidates or insufficiently marking a ballot... In certifying election results, the votes eligible for inclusion in the certification are the votes meeting the properly established legal requirements.

This case has shown that punch card balloting machines can produce an unfortunate number of ballots which are not punched in a clean, complete way by the voter. After the current counting, it is likely legislative bodies nationwide will examine ways to improve the mechanisms and machinery for voting.

B

The individual citizen has no federal constitutional right to vote for electors for the President of the United States unless and until the state legislature chooses a statewide election as the means to implement its power to appoint members of the Electoral College. U. S. Const., Art. II, §1. This is the source for the statement in McPherson v. Blacker, 146 U. S. 1, 35 (1892), that the State legislature's power to select the manner for appointing electors is plenary; it may, if it so chooses, select the electors itself, which indeed was the manner used by State legislatures in several States for many years after the Framing of our Constitution. History has now favored the voter, and in each of the several States the citizens themselves vote for Presidential electors. When the state legislature vests the right to vote for President in its people, the right to vote as the legislature has prescribed is fundamental; and one source of its fundamental nature lies in the equal weight accorded to each vote and the equal dignity owed to each voter. The State, of course, after granting the franchise in the special context of Article II, can take back the power to appoint electors...

The right to vote is protected in more than the initial allocation of the franchise. Equal protection applies as well to the manner of its exercise. Having once granted the right to vote on equal terms, the State may not, by later arbitrary and disparate treatment, value one person's vote over that of another...It must be remembered that "the right of suffrage can be denied by a debasement or dilution of the weight of a citizen's vote just as effectively as by wholly prohibiting the free exercise of the franchise." Reynolds v. Sims, 377 U. S. 533, 555 (1964).

There is no difference between the two sides of the present controversy on these basic propositions. Respondents say that the very purpose of vindicating the right to vote justifies the recount procedures now at issue. The question before us, however, is whether the recount procedures the Florida Supreme Court has adopted are consistent with its obligation to avoid arbitrary and disparate treatment of the members of its electorate.

Much of the controversy seems to revolve around ballot cards designed to be perforated by a stylus but which, either through error or deliberate omission, have not been perforated with sufficient precision for a machine to count them. In some cases a piece of the card — a chad — is hanging, say by two corners. In other cases there is no separation at all, just an indentation.

The Florida Supreme Court has ordered that the intent of the voter be discerned from such ballots. For purposes of resolving the equal protection challenge, it is not necessary to decide whether the Florida Supreme Court had the authority under the legislative scheme for resolving election disputes to define what a legal vote is and to mandate a manual recount implementing that definition. The recount mechanisms implemented in response to the decisions of the Florida Supreme Court do not satisfy the minimum requirement for non-arbitrary treatment of voters necessary to secure the fundamental right. Florida's basic command for the count of legally cast votes is to consider the "intent of the voter." This is unobjectionable as an abstract proposition and a starting principle. The problem inheres in the absence of specific standards to ensure its equal application. The formulation of uniform rules to determine intent based on these recurring circumstances is practicable and, we conclude, necessary.

The law does not refrain from searching for the intent of the actor in a multitude of circumstances; and in some cases the general command to ascertain intent is not susceptible to much further refinement. In this instance, however, the question is not whether to believe a witness but how to interpret the marks or holes or scratches on an inanimate object, a piece of cardboard or paper which, it is said, might not have registered as a vote during the machine count.

The factfinder confronts a thing, not a person. The search for intent can be confined by specific rules designed to ensure uniform treatment.

The want of those rules here has led to unequal evaluation of ballots in various respects…As seems to have been acknowledged at oral argument, the standards for accepting or rejecting contested ballots might vary not only from county to county but indeed within a single county from one recount team to another.

The record provides some examples. A monitor in Miami-Dade County testified at trial that he observed that three members of the county canvassing board applied different standards in defining a legal vote. 3 Tr. 497, 499 (Dec. 3, 2000). And testimony at trial also revealed that at least one county changed its evaluative standards during the counting process. Palm Beach County, for example, began the process with a 1990 guideline which precluded counting completely attached chads, switched to a rule that considered a vote to be legal if any light could be seen through a chad, changed back to the 1990 rule, and then abandoned any pretense of a per se rule, only to have a court order that the county consider dimpled chads legal. This is not a process with sufficient guarantees of equal treatment.

An early case in our one person, one vote jurisprudence arose when a State accorded arbitrary and disparate treatment to voters in its different counties. Gray v. Sanders, 372 U. S. 368 (1963). The Court found a constitutional violation. We relied on these principles in the context of the Presidential selection process in Moore v. Ogilvie, 394 U. S. 814 (1969), where we invalidated a county-based procedure that diluted the influence of citizens in larger counties in the nominating process. There we observed that "[t]he idea that one group can be granted greater voting strength than another is hostile to the one man, one vote basis of our representative government."

The State Supreme Court ratified this uneven treatment. It mandated that the recount totals from two counties, Miami-Dade and Palm Beach, be included in the certified total. The court also appeared to hold sub silentio that the recount totals from Broward County, which were not completed until after the original November 14 certification by the Secretary of State, were to be considered part of the new certified vote totals even though the county certification was not contested by Vice President Gore. Yet each of the counties used varying standards to determine what was a legal vote. Broward County used a more forgiving standard than Palm Beach County, and uncovered almost three times as many new votes, a result markedly disproportionate to the difference in population between the counties.

In addition, the recounts in these three counties were not limited to so-called undervotes but extended to all of the ballots. The distinction has real consequences. A manual recount of all ballots identifies not only those ballots which show no vote but also those which contain more than one, the so-called overvotes. Neither category will be counted by the machine. This is not a trivial concern. At oral argument, respondents estimated there are as many as 110,000 overvotes statewide. As a result, the citizen whose ballot was not read by a machine because he failed to vote for a candidate in a way readable by a machine may still have his vote counted in a manual recount; on the other hand, the citizen who marks two candidates in a way discernable by the machine will not have the same opportunity to have his vote count, even if a manual examination of the ballot would reveal the requisite indicia of intent. Furthermore, the citizen who marks two candidates, only one of which is discernable by the machine, will have his vote counted even though it should have been read as an invalid ballot. The State Supreme Court's inclusion of vote counts based on these variant standards exemplifies concerns with the remedial processes that were under way.

That brings the analysis to yet a further equal protection problem. The votes certified by the court included a partial total from one county, Miami-Dade. The Florida Supreme Court's decision thus gives no assurance that the recounts included in a final certification must be complete. Indeed, it is respondent's submission that it would be consistent with the rules of the recount procedures to include whatever partial counts are done by the time of final certification, and we interpret the Florida Supreme Court's decision to permit this…This accommodation no doubt results from the truncated contest period established by the Florida Supreme Court in Bush I, at respondents' own urging. The press of time does not diminish the constitutional concern. A desire for speed is not a general excuse for ignoring equal protection guarantees.

In addition to these difficulties the actual process by which the votes were to be counted under the Florida Supreme Court's decision raises further concerns. That order did not specify who would recount the ballots. The county canvassing boards were forced to pull together ad hoc teams comprised of judges from various Circuits who had no previous training in handling and interpreting ballots. Furthermore, while others were permitted to observe, they were prohibited from objecting during the recount.

The recount process, in its features here described, is inconsistent with the minimum procedures necessary to protect the fundamental right of each voter in the special instance of a statewide recount under the authority of a single state judicial officer. Our consideration is limited to the present circumstances, for the problem of equal protection in election processes generally presents many complexities.

The question before the Court is not whether local entities, in the exercise of their expertise, may develop different systems for implementing elections. Instead, we are presented with a situation where a state court with the power to assure uniformity has ordered a statewide recount with minimal procedural safeguards. When a court orders a statewide remedy, there must be at least some assurance that the rudimentary requirements of equal treatment and fundamental fairness are satisfied.

Given the Court's assessment that the recount process underway was probably being conducted in an unconstitutional manner, the Court stayed the order directing the recount so it could hear this case and render an expedited decision. The contest provision, as it was mandated by the State Supreme Court, is not well calculated to sustain the confidence that all citizens must have in the outcome of elections. The State has not shown that its procedures include the necessary safeguards. The problem, for instance, of the estimated 110,000 overvotes has not been addressed, although Chief Justice Wells called attention to the concern in his dissenting opinion.

Upon due consideration of the difficulties identified to this point, it is obvious that the recount cannot be conducted in compliance with the requirements of equal protection and due process without substantial additional work. It would require not only the adoption (after opportunity for argument) of adequate statewide standards for determining what is a legal vote, and practicable procedures to implement them, but also orderly judicial review of any disputed matters that might arise. In addition, the Secretary of State has advised that the recount of only a portion of the ballots requires that the vote tabulation equipment be used to screen out undervotes, a function for which the machines were not designed. If a recount of overvotes were also required, perhaps even a second screening would be necessary. Use of the equipment for this purpose, and any new software developed for it, would have to be evaluated for accuracy by the Secretary of State, as required by Fla. Stat. §101.015 (2000).

The Supreme Court of Florida has said that the legislature intended the State's electors to "participat[e] fully in the federal electoral process," as provided in 3 U. S. C. §5...That statute, in turn, requires that any controversy or contest that is designed to lead to a conclusive selection of electors be completed by December 12. That date is upon us, and there is no recount procedure in place under the State Supreme Court's order that comports with minimal constitutional standards. Because it is evident that any recount seeking to meet the December 12 date will be unconstitutional for the reasons we have discussed, we reverse the judgment of the Supreme Court of Florida ordering a recount to proceed.

Seven Justices of the Court agree that there are constitutional problems with the recount ordered by the Florida Supreme Court that demand a remedy...The only disagreement is as to the remedy. Because the Florida Supreme Court has said that the Florida Legislature intended to obtain the safe-harbor benefits of 3 U. S. C. §5, JUSTICE BREYER's proposed remedy — remanding to the Florida Supreme Court for its ordering of a constitutionally proper contest until December 18-contemplates action in violation of the Florida election code, and hence could not be part of an "appropriate" order authorized by Fla. Stat. §102.168(8) (2000).

* * *

None are more conscious of the vital limits on judicial authority than are the members of this Court, and none stand more in admiration of the Constitution's design to leave the selection of the President to the people, through their legislatures, and to the political sphere. When contending parties invoke the process of the courts, however, it becomes our unsought responsibility to resolve the federal and constitutional issues the judicial system has been forced to confront.

The judgment of the Supreme Court of Florida is reversed, and the case is remanded for further proceedings not inconsistent with this opinion.

Pursuant to this Court's Rule 45.2, the Clerk is directed to issue the mandate in this case forthwith.
It is so ordered.

HOW WELL DID YOU UNDERSTAND THIS SELECTION?

1. Why was there a controversy in the 2000 Presidential Election?

2. On what grounds did the U.S. Supreme Court get to rule on the election procedures in states?

3. What is a "chad"?

4. How relevant is the Electoral College in today's political elections?

LEGISLATION IN A TIME OF TERROR

These two short sections of very long laws show a trend to reinterpret rights traditionally held to be protected by the Constitution. Although "privacy" itself is not specifically mentioned in the 18th century document, the right to it has long been believed to be an American tradition.

(Pre 9/11)

The Omnibus Counter Terrorism Act — 1995

Domestic Terror:

...the President , the Secretary of State, or the Attorney General may designate any group as a "terrorist organization." ... the President shall be controlling and shall not be subject to review by any court: and no question concerning the validity of the issuance of such designation may be raised by a defendant in a criminal prosecution."

Passed 41 days after 9/11

The Patriot Act, October 26, 2001

Section 105: The Director of the United States Secret Service shall take appropriate actions to develop a national network of electronic crime task forces, based on the New York Electronic Crimes Task Force model, throughout the United States, for the purpose of preventing, detecting, and investigating various forms of electronic crimes, including potential terrorist attacks against critical infrastructures and financial payment systems.

Section 106: (The President has the power) when the United States is engaged in military hostilities or has been attacked by a foreign country or foreign nationals, confiscate any property, subject to the jurisdiction of the United States, or any foreign person, foreign organization, or foreign country that he determines has planned, authorized ordered, or engaged in such hostilities or attacks against the United States, and all right, title, and interest in any property so confiscated ... (and) shall vest, when, as, and upon the terms directed by the President, in such agency or person as the as the President shall designate from time to time, and upon such terms and conditions as the President may prescribe, such interest of an for the benefit of the United States, and such designated agency or person may perform any and all acts incident to the accomplishment or furtherance of these purposes.

HOW WELL DID YOU UNDERSTAND THIS SELECTION?

1.   Does the so-called "war on terror" require a change in the access to rights of citizens?

2.   Do any of these recent laws change the perception of citizen rights addressed in the Bill of Rights (the first 10 amendments to the U.S. Constitution)?

3.   How specific and limited are these powers granted to the Executive Branch of the government?

4.   How much personal liberty is appropriate in the age where individuals can inflict harm on others with suicide bombs, etc.?

ULTIMATUM TO SADDAM HUSSEIN

On March 2003, President George W. Bush addressed the nation concerning Saddam Hussein.

My fellow citizens, events in Iraq have now reached the final days of decision. For more than a decade, the United States and other nations have pursued patient and honorable efforts to disarm the Iraqi regime without war. That regime pledged to reveal and destroy all of its weapons of mass destruction as a condition for ending the Persian Gulf War in 1991.

Since then, the world has engaged in 12 years of diplomacy. We have passed more than a dozen resolutions in the United Nations Security Council. We have sent hundreds of weapons inspectors to oversee the disarmament of Iraq. Our good faith has not been returned. The Iraqi regime has used diplomacy as a ploy to gain time and advantage. It has uniformly defied Security Council resolutions demanding full disarmament....

Intelligence gathered by this and other governments leaves no doubt that the Iraq regime continues to possess and conceal some of the most lethal weapons ever devised. This regime has already used weapons of mass destruction against Iraq's neighbors and against Iraq's people. The regime has a history of reckless aggression in the Middle East. It has a deep hatred of America and our friends and it has aided, trained and harbored terrorists, including operatives of Al Qaeda. The danger is clear: Using chemical, biological or, one day, nuclear weapons obtained with the help of Iraq, the terrorists could fulfill their stated ambitions and kill thousands or hundreds of thousands of innocent people in our country or any other.

The United States and other nations did nothing to deserve or invite this threat, but we will do everything to defeat it. Instead of drifting along toward tragedy, we will set a course toward safety. Before the day of horror can come, before it is too late to act, this danger will be removed. The United States of America has the sovereign authority to use force in assuring its own national security. That duty falls to me as commander of chief by the oath I have sworn, by the oath I will keep. Recognizing the threat to our country, the United States Congress voted overwhelmingly last year to support the use of force against Iraq.

America tried to work with the United Nations to address this threat because we wanted to resolve the issue peacefully. We believe in the mission of the United Nations...One reason the U.N. was founded after the Second World War was to confront aggressive dictators actively and early, before they can attack the innocent and destroy the peace.

Last September, I went to the U.N. General Assembly and urged the nations of the world to unite and bring an end to this danger. On November 8th, the Security Council unanimously passed Resolution 1441, finding Iraq in material breach of its obligations and vowing serious consequences if Iraq did not fully and immediately disarm. Today, no nation can possibly claim that Iraq has disarmed. And it will not disarm so long as Saddam Hussein holds power.

For the last four and a half months, the United States and our allies have worked within the Security Council to enforce that council's longstanding demands. Yet some permanent members of the Security Council have publicly announced that they will veto any resolution that compels the disarmament of Iraq. These governments share our assessment of the danger, but not our resolve to meet it. Many nations, however, do have the resolve and fortitude to act against this threat to peace, and a broad coalition is now gathering to enforce the just demands of the world.

The United Nations Security Council has not lived up to its responsibilities, so we will rise to ours. In recent days, some governments in the Middle East have been doing their part. They have delivered public and private messages urging the dictator to leave Iraq so that disarmament can proceed peacefully. He has thus far refused.

All the decades of deceit and cruelty have now reached an end. Saddam Hussein and his sons must leave Iraq within 48 hours. Their refusal to do so will result in military conflict commenced at a time of our choosing....

Many Iraqis can hear me tonight in a translated radio broadcast, and I have a message for them: If we must begin a military campaign, it will be directed against the lawless men who rule your country and not against you. As our coalition takes away their power, we will deliver the food and medicine you need. We will tear down the apparatus of terror and we will help you to build a new Iraq that is prosperous and free... The tyrant will soon be gone. The day of your liberation is near...

And all Iraqi military and civilian personnel should listen carefully to this warning: In any conflict, your fate will depend on your actions. Do not destroy oil wells, a source of wealth that belongs to the Iraqi people. Do not obey any command to use weapons of mass destruction against anyone, including the Iraqi people. War crimes will be prosecuted, war criminals will be punished and it will be no defense to say, "I was just following orders." Should Saddam Hussein choose confrontation, the American people can know that every measure has been taken to avoid war and every measure will be taken to win it.

Americans understand the costs of conflict because we have paid them in the past. War has no certainty except the certainty of sacrifice. Yet the only way to reduce the harm and duration of war is to apply the full force and might of our military, and we are prepared to do so...In desperation, he and terrorist groups might try to conduct terrorist operations against the American people and our friends. These attacks are not inevitable. They are, however, possible...

And this very fact underscores the reason we cannot live under the threat of blackmail. The terrorist threat to America and the world will be diminished the moment that Saddam Hussein is disarmed. Our government is on heightened watch against these dangers. Just as we are preparing to ensure victory in Iraq, we are taking further actions to protect our homeland…

Should enemies strike our country, they would be attempting to shift our attention with panic and weaken our morale with fear. In this, they would fail. No act of theirs can alter the course or shake the resolve of this country. We are a peaceful people, yet we are not a fragile people. And we will not be intimidated by thugs and killers…

We are now acting because the risks of inaction would be far greater. In one year, or five years, the power of Iraq to inflict harm on all free nations would be multiplied many times over. With these capabilities, Saddam Hussein and his terrorist allies could choose the moment of deadly conflict when they are strongest. We choose to meet that threat now where it arises, before it can appear suddenly in our skies and cities.

The cause of peace requires all free nations to recognize new and undeniable realities. In the 20th century, some chose to appease murderous dictators whose threats were allowed to grow into genocide and global war. In this century, when evil men plot chemical, biological and nuclear terror, a policy of appeasement could bring destruction of a kind never before seen on this earth. Terrorists and terrorist states do not reveal these threats with fair notice in formal declarations.

And responding to such enemies only after they have struck first is not self defense. It is suicide. The security of the world requires disarming Saddam Hussein now… As we enforce the just demands of the world, we will also honor the deepest commitments of our country. Unlike Saddam Hussein, we believe the Iraqi people are deserving and capable of human liberty, and when the dictator has departed, they can set an example to all the Middle East of a vital and peaceful and self-governing nation…

Free nations have a duty to defend our people by uniting against the violent, and tonight, as we have done before, America and our allies accept that responsibility.

Good night, and may God continue to bless America.

Source: Office of the Press Secretary, Address to the Nation, March 17, 2003.

HOW WELL DID YOU UNDERSTAND THIS SELECTION?

1. What are President Bush's main justifications for military action in Iraq?

2. How does he relate his actions to terrorism?

3. What is his attitude towards the United Nations? Countries opposed to America's position?

4. What are his implicit promises to the Iraqi people?

5. To what extent have the president's justifications and promises proven to be accurate?

*Landing dramatically on the **USS Abraham Lincoln**, May 1, 2003, President Bush proudly announced the end of "major combat operations" in Iraq. He called this a victory for freedom over despotism and linked the terror attacks of 9/11, the Taliban in Afghanistan, and other incidents to the regime of Saddam Hussein. "From Pakistan to the Philippines to the Horn of Africa," Bush said, terrorists would be hunted down. In 2007, the war in Iraq continued.*

Admiral Kelly, Captain Card, officers and sailors of the USS Abraham Lincoln, my fellow Americans: Major combat operations in Iraq have ended. In the Battle of Iraq, the United States and our allies have prevailed. And now our coalition is engaged in securing and reconstructing that country.

In this battle, we have fought for the cause of liberty, and for the peace of the world. Our nation and our coalition are proud of this accomplishment — yet it is you, the members of the United States military, who achieved it. Your courage — your willingness to face danger for your country and for each other — made this day possible. Because of you, our nation is more secure. Because of you, the tyrant has fallen, and Iraq is free.

Operation Iraqi Freedom was carried out with a combination of precision, and speed, and boldness the enemy did not expect, and the world had not seen before. From distant bases or ships at sea, we sent planes and missiles that could destroy an enemy division, or strike a single bunker. Marines and soldiers charged to Baghdad across 350 miles of hostile ground, in one of the swiftest advances of heavy arms in history. You have shown the world the skill and the might of the American Armed Forces.

This nation thanks all of the members of our coalition who joined in a noble cause. We thank the Armed Forces of the United Kingdom, Australia, and Poland, who shared in the hardships of war. We thank all of the citizens of Iraq who welcomed our troops and joined in the liberation of their own country. And tonight, I have a special word for Secretary (Donald) Rumsfeld, for General (Tommy) Franks, and for all the men and women who wear the uniform of the United States: America is grateful for a job well done.

The character of our military through history — the daring of Normandy, the fierce courage of Iwo Jima, the decency and idealism that turned enemies into allies — is fully present in this generation. When Iraqi civilians looked into the faces of our servicemen and women, they saw strength, and kindness, and good will. When I look at the members of the United States military, I see the best of our country, and I am honored to be your commander in chief.

In the images of fallen statues, we have witnessed the arrival of a new era. For a hundred years of war, culminating in the nuclear age, military technology was designed and deployed to inflict casualties on an ever-growing scale. In defeating Nazi Germany and imperial Japan, Allied Forces destroyed entire cities, while enemy leaders who started the conflict were safe until the final days. Military power was used to end a regime by breaking a nation. Today, we have the greater power to free a nation by breaking a dangerous and aggressive regime. With new tactics and precision weapons, we can achieve military objectives without directing violence against civilians. No device of man can remove the tragedy from war. Yet it is a great advance when the guilty have far more to fear from war than the innocent.

In the images of celebrating Iraqis, we have also seen the ageless appeal of human freedom. Decades of lies and intimidation could not make the Iraqi people love their oppressors or desire their own enslavement. Men and women in every culture need liberty like they need food, and water, and air. Everywhere that freedom arrives, humanity rejoices. And everywhere that freedom stirs, let tyrants fear.

We have difficult work to do in Iraq. We are bringing order to parts of that country that remain dangerous. We are pursuing and finding leaders of the old regime, who will be held to account for their crimes. We have begun the search for hidden chemical and biological weapons, and already know of hundreds of sites that will be investigated. We are helping to rebuild Iraq, where the dictator built palaces for himself, instead of hospitals and schools. And we will stand with the new leaders of Iraq as they establish a government of, by, and for the Iraqi people. The transition from dictatorship to democracy will take time, but it is worth every effort. Our coalition will stay until our work is done. And then we will leave — and we will leave behind a free Iraq.

HOW WELL DID YOU UNDERSTAND THIS SELECTION?

1. Bush announced that "major combat operations have ended" on May 1, 2003. What gave him the confidence that this was so?

2. Who have been members of the "coalition of freedom"?

3. What "zing" phrases did Bush use in this speech to convince the public that "we have prevailed"?

4. Why does Bush associate the 9/11 attacks with Iraq?

One of the traditional hallmarks of the U.S. Constitution is the separation of church and state. As the conservative religious right increased its presence in American politics, there were demands that federal funds be released to groups that helped youth, couples and the "needy." Many of these organizations were connected to "faith-based groups." The Bush administration founded the Compassionate Capital Fund to cross the line and provide funding for groups which had not been eligible before because of their religious connections.

President Bush today announced $42,957,597 in 145 grants to organizations that provide services and support through soup kitchens, homeless shelters, drug treatment centers, job training programs, and other compassionate programs. Faith-based and community-based organizations will receive the federal funding from the Compassion Capital Fund, which is in its third year of existence.

"The Compassion Capital Fund provides local and faith-based groups with important resources to help those most in need," HHS Secretary Tommy G. Thompson said. "By further empowering organizations to perform works of mercy in their neighborhoods, we are continuing our goal of putting compassion in action."

Today's announcement consists of two sets of grants. The first totals $38 million. $6.9 million — the first installment of a three-year grant award — will go to 14 new intermediary organizations, including the Metropolitan Council on Jewish Poverty in New York; Cherokee Nation in Oklahoma; the Governor's Office for Faith-Based and Community Initiatives in Ohio; and Mission West Virginia, Inc. $31.1 million will be used for 31 second and third-year continuation awards from the Compassion Capital Fund Demonstration Program. The intermediaries will assist grass-root, faith and community-based organizations so they may increase their effectiveness, enhance their ability to provide social services and create collaborations to better serve those in need.

The second set of grants totals $4.9 million under the Compassion Capital Fund Targeted Capacity Building Program. They will be given to 100 organizations that work on priority issues such as at-risk youth, homelessness, healthy marriages and serving people in rural communities. Organizations include Hope Partnership for Education in Pennsylvania; Prevent Child Abuse in Minnesota; the Community Partnership for the Homeless in Texas; EnFamilia in Florida; and Lutheran Social Services of South Dakota.

"The grants we are announcing today give what President Bush calls the 'armies of compassion' the resources they need to serve the poor, the hungry, the homeless and the addicted," said Dr. Wade F. Horn, HHS assistant secretary for children and families. "Faith-based and community-based groups know the problems and solutions in their neighborhoods. Now they will have more resources with which to improve the lives of children and families around the country."

Since the program's inception three years ago, $99.5 million will be given to a total of 1,906 organizations through the Compassion Capital Fund, which is run by HHS' Administration for Children and Families. One hundred and ninety-seven organizations have received grants and 1,709 grass-roots faith and community-based organizations have or will receive sub-awards by Sept. 30, 2004. A complete list of grantees for today's awards is below.

Compassion Capital Fund Demonstration Program

Year One Grantees – First Installment	City	State	Award
Cherokee Nation	Tahlequah	OK	724,080
Developing Resources for Education in America, Inc.	Jackson	MS	440,893
Empower New Haven, Inc.	New Haven	CT	473,077

Governor's Office of Faith-Based & Community Initiative	Columbus	OH	750,000
High County Consulting LLC Faith Initiative of Wyoming	Cheyenne	WV	371,941
Indiana Youth Institute	Indianapolis	IN	649,013
Institute for Contemporary Studies	Oakland	CA	366,179
Metropolitan Council on Jewish Poverty	New York	NY	525,645
Mission West Virginia, Inc.	St. Albans	WV	359,240
New Detroit	Detroit	MI	536,705
New Futures for Youth, Inc.	Little Rock	AR	324,000
North Hills Community Outreach	Allegheny	PA	234,000
The University of Texas at Brownsville/Texas Southmost	Brownsville	TX	586,229
Wichita State University	Wichita	KS	526,766
Sub-Total			**$6,867,768**

Year Two Grantees – Second Installment

Citizens Committee for New York City	New York City	NY	410,984
Foundation for Community Empowerment	Dallas	TX	761,700
Greater Minneapolis Council of Churches	Minneapolis	MN	700,000
Holy Redeemer Institutional Church of God in Christ	Milwaukee	WI	824,471
Kentucky River Foothills Development Council, Inc.	Richmond	KY	750,000
Louisiana Association of Nonprofit Organizations	Baton Rouge	LA	527,660
National Center for Neighborhood Enterprise	Washington	D.C.	655,680
Northwest Leadership Foundation	Tacoma	WA	974,260
United Way of Tucson & Southern Arizona	Tucson	AZ	903,924
We Care America, Inc.	Washington	D.C.	936,868
Sub-Total			**$7,445,547**

Year Three Grantees – Third Installment

Associated Black Charities	Baltimore	MD	1,500,000
Black Ministerial Alliance	Boston	MA	2,000,000
Catholic Charities of Central New Mexico	Albuquerque	NM	1,000,000
Christian Community Health Fellowship	Chicago	IL	1,128,330
CJH Educational Grant Services, Inc.	Raleigh	NC	1,116,440
Clemson University	Clemson	SC	792,350
Community Tech Centers' Network	Boston	MA	1,499,770
Emory University	Atlanta	GA	1,499,999
Institute for Youth Development	Sterling	VA	2,500,000
JVA Consulting, LLC	Denver	CO	1,008,547
Mennonite Economic Development	Lancaster	PA	1,000,000
Montana State University	Bozeman	MT	614,555
Northside Ministerial Alliance	Kalamazoo	MI	895,000
Nueva Esperanza, Inc.	Philadelphia	PA	2,466,470
Operation Blessing International	Virginia Beach	VA	500,000
S.V.D.P. Management, Inc.	San Diego	CA	673,041
Southeast Asia Resource Center	Washington	D.C.	682,240
National Center for Faith-Based Initiatives	W. Palm Beach	FL	525,000
University of Hawaii	Honolulu	HI	600,000
University of Nebraska	Lincoln	NE	1,171,742
Volunteers of America	Arlington	VA	563,000
Sub-Total			**$23,736,484**
CCF Demonstration Program			**$38,049,799**

Compassion Capital Fund Targeted Capacity-Building Program

One-Year Grants	City	State	Amount
1st Choice Pregnancy Resource Center	Texarkana	TX	50,000
Action Network	Gualala	CA	50,000
America On Track	Santa Ana	CA	50,000
Big Brothers, Big Sisters of Metropolitan Detroit	Southfield	MI	50,000
Blue Grass Regional Mental Health	Lexington	KY	50,000
Bluegrass Healthy Marriages Partnership	Lexington	KY	50,000
Boys & girls Club of Sella, AZ	Sella	AZ	50,000
Boys & Girls Clubs of the Black Hills	Hill City	SD	50,000
Center for Family Relations	San Antonio	TX	50,000
Central Council Tingit Haida	Juneau	AK	50,000
Child and Family Resource Council	Grand Rapids	MI	50,000
Church Triumphant, Inc.	Bryant	AR	50,000
Churches United Inc. of the Greater Des Moines Area	Des Moines	IA	50,000
Community Action Resource	Tillamook	OR	50,000
Community Marriage Builders, Inc.	Evansville	IN	50,000
Community Marriage Initiative, Inc.	Amherst	NH	50,000
Community Ministry of Montgomery County, Inc.	Rockville	MD	50,000
Community Partnership for the Homeless, Inc.	Austin	TX	50,000
Dame La Mano Crisis Pregnancy Center	El Paso	TX	50,000
Delaware Ecumenical Council on Children and Families	New Castle	DE	50,000
Downtown Learning Center, Inc.	Brooklyn	NY	50,000
East End Community Services Corporation	Dayton	OH	50,000
Easter Seals – UPC	Bloomington	IL	49,940
EnFamilia, Inc.	Homestead	FL	50,000
Evangelical Children's Home	St. Louis	MO	49,810
Families Are Relationships (FAR) Foundation	Dallas	TX	50,000
Family Addiction Community Treatment	Gallipolis	OH	50,000
Family Life Council of Greater Greensboro, Inc.	Greensboro	NC	50,000
Family Support Council	Dalton	GA	50,000
Fins Up Foundation, Inc.	New York	NY	50,000
First Christian Church of Cheyenne	Cheyenne	WY	50,000
Florence Criffenton Home and Services	Helena	MT	50,000
Friends Outside in Santa Clara County	San Jose	CA	50,000
Friendship House of Christian Service	Billings	MT	50,000
Glenwood, Inc.	Birmingham	AL	49,996
Grand Futures Prevention Coalition	Craig	CO	50,000
Gwinnett Children's Shelter, Inc.	Buford	GA	50,000
HAWC Community Health Center	Reno	NV	50,000
Heritage Community Services, Inc.	Charleston	SC	50,000
Homeless Resource Network, Inc	Columbus	GA	50,000
Hope Partnership for Education	Philadelphia	PA	50,000
Hospice of South Central Indiana	Columbus	IN	45,540
Human Resources Agency of New Britain, Inc.	New Britain	CT	49,982
Iowa Family Policy Center	Pleasant Hill	IA	50,000
Kanawha Institute for Social Research & Action, Inc.	Dunbar	WV	50,000
Kanawha Valley Collective, Inc.	Charleston	WV	50,000
Kanu o ka "Aina Learning 'Ohana	Kamuela	HI	48,350
Kaw Nation of Oklahoma	Kaw City	OK	50,000
Kenaitze Indian Tribe	Kenai	AK	49,419
Kids' Harbor, inc.	Camdenton	MO	44,045

Learning Institute of Family Education (LIFE)	Detroit	MI	50,000
Life Builders Counseling Center	Mesquite	TX	50,000
Los Angeles Mission, Inc.	Los Angeles	CA	50,000
Lourdes Hospital @ Pasco dba Lourdes Counseling Center	Richland	WA	49,746
Loving Shepherd International Services & Foundation	Bluffton	IN	50,000
Lutheran Social Services of South Dakota	Sioux Falls	SD	50,000
Marriage Alliance of Central Virginia	Forest	VA	49,020
Marriage Builders Alliance of Richmond	Richmond	VA	49,500
Martin Temple Community Foundation, Inc.	Chicago	IL	37,000
Miami Urban Ministries of the United Methodist Church,	Miami	FL	50,000
Oakland Livingston Human Service Agency	Howell	MI	50,000
Ohio County Together We Care, Inc.	Hartford	KY	49,967
Old South Baton Rouge Community Revitalization Corp	Baton Rouge	LA	49,948
Opportunitics Industrialization Center of Greater Milwaukee	Milwaukee	WI	50,000
Orange County Marriage Resource Center	Anaheim	CA	50,000
Palmetto Family Council	Columbia	SC	50,000
Panhandle Community Services	Gering	NE	50,000
Portland Impact, Inc.	Portland	OR	49,403
Prevent Child Abuse	St Paul	MN	50,000
Redeemed Incorporated, FL	Quincy	FL	50,000
Rehabilitation Enterprise of North East Wyoming	Sheridan	WY	48,484
Restorative Counseling Services, Inc.	Oklahoma City	OK	50,000
S.A.V.E. (Survivors Against Violent Environments)	Nashville	TN	50,000
Samaritan House, Inc.	Newport	OR	39,200
Sanctuary Zone, Inc.	Estancia	NM	50,000
Seacoast Interfaith Hospitality Network	N. Hampton	NH	49,832
Sioux Empire Marriages Savers	Sioux Falls	SD	50,000
South Baton Rouge Church of Christ	Baton Rouge	LA	50,000
St. Charles Health Council, Inc.	St. Charles	VA	50,000
St. Joseph Center	Venice	CA	50,000
The Center for Community Excellence and Social Justice	Denver	CO	49,996
The Children's Council	Lancaster	SC	40,009
The DreamTree Project Inc.	Taos	NM	49,397
The East of the River-Clergy, Police Community Partners	Washington	DC	50,000
The House of Acts	Vallejo	CA	49,916
The Interfaith Association of Snohomish County	Everett	WA	50,000
The Parenting Center	Fort Worth	TX	50,000
Tunica County Community Development Coalition	Tunica	MS	50,000
Twin City Mission	Bryan	TX	49,928
United Migrant Opportunity Services, Inc.	Milwaukee	WI	49,370
United Way of Johnson County	Franklin	IN	25,000
Victory House of Lehigh Valley	Bethlehem	PA	50,000
Volunteers of America	Lewellen	NE	35,000
Volunteers of America, Utah	Salt Lake City	UT	50,000
Young Women's Christian Association	Belleville	IL	50,000
Youth and Shelter Services, Inc.	Ames	IA	50,000
Youth Employment Partnerships, Inc.	Richmond	CA	50,000
Youth Extended Services	McLouth	KS	50,000
Youth Opportunities Unlimited, INC.	Marks	MS	50,000
YWCA of Greater Memphis	Memphis	TN	50,000
CCF Targeted Capacity Building			**$4,907,798**
TOTAL GRANTS			**$42,957,597**

HOW WELL DID YOU UNDERSTAND THIS SELECTION?

1. What groups are eligible for these grants?

2. This is a new program under the Bush administration. Why has it not been tried before?

3. Where does the funding come from for these "initiatives"?

4. What do opponents of this program say?

Nancy Pelosi of California became the first woman to become Speaker of the House of Representatives. The Democratic congressional victory in 2006 seemed to call upon Congress to change directions in many of the programs the Bush administration had put into place, especially the war in Iraq. Pelosi outlined the hopes the Democrats could deliver a new direction for the nation.

"This is a war that each passing day confirms what I have said before and I will say again. This war in Iraq is a grotesque mistake; it is not making America safer, and the American people know it." - Speaker Nancy Pelosi

Our brave men and women in uniform are fighting a war of choice in which we sent our young people into harm's way without leveling with the American people. They were sent into war without intelligence about what they were going to confront, without the equipment to protect them, and without a plan for what would happen after the fall of Baghdad. Disagreement with the policies that sent our troops to Iraq, and which keep them in danger today, in no way diminishes the respect and admiration which we have for them.

Democrats strongly support our troops; we have the finest armed forces in the world and they are doing a great job. Sadly, the level of their sacrifice has never been matched by the level of the Administration's planning, and the American people agree this war is not making America safer.

The American people are outraged at the Bush Administration's misplaced priorities, and Congress is committed to bringing our troops home safely and soon. The House and the Senate are holding a series of hearings examining the war in Iraq, focusing on the recently released National Intelligence Estimate and the Government Accountability Office reports on Iraq, and featuring testimony by retired Marine General James Jones, General David Petraeus, and U.S. Ambassador in Iraq Ryan Crocker. In May, Congress voted to require these reports from the GAO, General Jones, and the White House to look at the political and military situation in Iraq.

While the President continues to stay the course and ask Americans to pay for his failed strategy, Democrats will continue to push for a new direction in Iraq to protect our troops and make America more secure. The situation on the ground is worsening, and the Iraqi government has failed to meet the benchmarks set in law. The American people want Congress to bring our troops home, refocus our efforts to fighting terrorism, and hold the Bush Administration accountable.

Source: Web site of Pelosi, Speaker of the House collection of speeches

HOW WELL DID YOU UNDERSTAND THIS SELECTION?

1. Who is Nancy Pelosi and what is the significance of her role in Congress?

2. What does Pelosi charge the Bush administration of doing in calling for the war in Iraq?

3. Pelosi describes the American public as "outraged." Why does she say this?

4. Why has the war in Iraq split the country? How?

PRESIDENT BARACK OBAMA'S INAUGURAL ADDRESS, 2009

Barack Obama's inauguration as the nations forty-fourth President marked one of the most significant events in this country since the civil war. In the midst of a worldwide economic crisis and the increasing pace of globalization, his election was of interest to more than just the people of the United States. President Obama's inaugural address set the stage for his first years in office.

My fellow citizens: I stand here today humbled by the task before us, grateful for the trust you've bestowed, mindful of the sacrifices borne by our ancestors.

I thank President Bush for his service to our nation—(applause)—as well as the generosity and cooperation he has shown throughout this transition.

Forty-four Americans have now taken the presidential oath. The words have been spoken during rising tides of prosperity and the still waters of peace. Yet, every so often, the oath is taken amidst gathering clouds and raging storms. At these moments, America has carried on not simply because of the skill or vision of those in high office, but because we, the people, have remained faithful to the ideals of our forebears and true to our founding documents.

So it has been; so it must be with this generation of Americans.

That we are in the midst of crisis is now well understood. Our nation is at war against a far-reaching network of violence and hatred. Our economy is badly weakened, a consequence of greed and irresponsibility on the part of some, but also our collective failure to make hard choices and prepare the nation for a new age. Homes have been lost, jobs shed, businesses shuttered. Our health care is too costly, our schools fail too many—and each day brings further evidence that the ways we use energy strengthen our adversaries and threaten our planet.

These are the indicators of crisis, subject to data and statistics. Less measurable, but no less profound, is a sapping of confidence across our land; a nagging fear that America's decline is inevitable, that the next generation must lower its sights.

Today I say to you that the challenges we face are real. They are serious and they are many. They will not be met easily or in a short span of time. But know this America: They will be met. (Applause.)

On this day, we gather because we have chosen hope over fear, unity of purpose over conflict and discord. On this day, we come to proclaim an end to the petty grievances and false promises, the recriminations and worn-out dogmas that for far too long have strangled our politics. We remain a young nation. But in the words of Scripture, the time has come to set aside childish things. The time has come to reaffirm our enduring spirit; to choose our better history; to carry forward that precious gift, that noble idea passed on from generation to generation: the God-given promise that all are equal, all are free, and all deserve a chance to pursue their full measure of happiness. (Applause.)

In reaffirming the greatness of our nation we understand that greatness is never a given. It must be earned. Our journey has never been one of short-cuts or settling for less. It has not been the path for the faint-hearted, for those that prefer leisure over work, or seek only the pleasures of riches and fame. Rather, it has been the risk-takers, the doers, the makers of things—some celebrated, but more often men and women obscure in their labor—who have carried us up the long rugged path towards prosperity and freedom.

For us, they packed up their few worldly possessions and traveled across oceans in search of a new life. For us, they toiled in sweatshops, and settled the West, endured the lash of the whip, and plowed the hard earth. For us, they fought and died in places like Concord and Gettysburg, Normandy and Khe Sahn.

Time and again these men and women struggled and sacrificed and worked till their hands were raw so that we might live a better life. They saw America as bigger than the sum of our individual ambitions, greater than all the differences of birth or wealth or faction.

This is the journey we continue today. We remain the most prosperous, powerful nation on Earth. Our workers are no less productive than when this crisis began. Our minds are no less inventive, our goods and services no less needed than they were last week, or last month, or last year. Our capacity remains undiminished. But our time of standing pat, of protecting narrow interests and putting off unpleasant decisions—that time has surely passed. Starting today, we must pick ourselves up, dust ourselves off, and begin again the work of remaking America. (Applause.)

For everywhere we look, there is work to be done. The state of our economy calls for action, bold and swift. And we will act, not only to create new jobs, but to lay a new foundation for growth. We will build the roads and bridges, the electric grids and digital lines that feed our commerce and bind us together. We'll restore science to its rightful place, and wield technology's wonders to raise health care's quality and lower its cost. We will harness the sun and the winds and the soil to fuel our cars and run our factories. And we will transform our schools and colleges and universities to meet the demands of a new age. All this we can do. All this we will do.

Now, there are some who question the scale of our ambitions, who suggest that our system cannot tolerate too many big plans. Their memories are short, for they have forgotten what this country has already done, what free men and women can achieve when imagination is joined to common purpose, and necessity to courage. What the cynics fail to understand is that the ground has shifted beneath them, that the stale political arguments that have consumed us for so long no longer apply.

The question we ask today is not whether our government is too big or too small, but whether it works—whether it helps families find jobs at a decent wage, care they can afford, a retirement that is dignified. Where the answer is yes, we intend to move forward. Where the answer is no, programs will end. And those of us who manage the public's dollars will be held to account, to spend wisely, reform bad habits, and do our business in the light of day, because only then can we restore the vital trust between a people and their government.

Nor is the question before us whether the market is a force for good or ill. Its power to generate wealth and expand freedom is unmatched. But this crisis has reminded us that without a watchful eye, the market can spin out of control. The nation cannot prosper long when it favors only the prosperous. The success of our economy has always depended not just on the size of our gross domestic product, but on the reach of our prosperity, on the ability to extend opportunity to every willing heart -- not out of charity, but because it is the surest route to our common good. (Applause.)

As for our common defense, we reject as false the choice between our safety and our ideals. Our Founding Fathers— (applause)—our Founding Fathers, faced with perils that we can scarcely imagine, drafted a charter to assure the rule of law and the rights of man—a charter expanded by the blood of generations. Those ideals still light the world, and we will not give them up for expedience sake. (Applause.)

And so, to all the other peoples and governments who are watching today, from the grandest capitals to the small village where my father was born, know that America is a friend of each nation, and every man, woman and child who seeks a future of peace and dignity. And we are ready to lead once more. (Applause.)

Recall that earlier generations faced down fascism and communism not just with missiles and tanks, but with the sturdy alliances and enduring convictions. They understood that our power alone cannot protect us, nor does it entitle us to do as we please. Instead they knew that our power grows through its prudent use; our security emanates from the justness of our cause, the force of our example, the tempering qualities of humility and restraint.

We are the keepers of this legacy. Guided by these principles once more we can meet those new threats that demand even greater effort, even greater cooperation and understanding between nations. We will begin to responsibly leave Iraq to its people and forge a hard-earned peace in Afghanistan. With old friends and former foes, we'll work tirelessly to lessen the nuclear threat, and roll back the specter of a warming planet.

We will not apologize for our way of life, nor will we waver in its defense. And for those who seek to advance their aims by inducing terror and slaughtering innocents, we say to you now that our spirit is stronger and cannot be broken—you cannot outlast us, and we will defeat you. (Applause.)

For we know that our patchwork heritage is a strength, not a weakness. We are a nation of Christians and Muslims, Jews and Hindus, and non-believers. We are shaped by every language and culture, drawn from every end of this Earth; and because we have tasted the bitter swill of civil war and segregation, and emerged from that dark chapter stronger and more united, we cannot help but believe that the old hatreds shall someday pass; that the lines of tribe shall soon dissolve; that as the world grows smaller, our common humanity shall reveal itself; and that America must play its role in ushering in a new era of peace.

To the Muslim world, we seek a new way forward, based on mutual interest and mutual respect. To those leaders around the globe who seek to sow conflict, or blame their society's ills on the West, know that your people will judge you on what you can build, not what you destroy. (Applause.)

To those who cling to power through corruption and deceit and the silencing of dissent, know that you are on the wrong side of history, but that we will extend a hand if you are willing to unclench your fist. (Applause.)

To the people of poor nations, we pledge to work alongside you to make your farms flourish and let clean waters flow; to nourish starved bodies and feed hungry minds. And to those nations like ours that enjoy relative plenty, we say we can no longer afford indifference to the suffering outside our borders, nor can we consume the world's resources without regard to effect. For the world has changed, and we must change with it.

As we consider the role that unfolds before us, we remember with humble gratitude those brave Americans who at this very hour patrol far-off deserts and distant mountains. They have something to tell us, just as the fallen heroes who lie in Arlington whisper through the ages.

We honor them not only because they are the guardians of our liberty, but because they embody the spirit of service—a willingness to find meaning in something greater than themselves.

And yet at this moment, a moment that will define a generation, it is precisely this spirit that must inhabit us all. For as much as government can do, and must do, it is ultimately the faith and determination of the American people upon which this nation relies. It is the kindness to take in a stranger when the levees break, the selflessness of workers who would rather cut their hours than see a friend lose their job which sees us through our darkest hours. It is the firefighter's courage to storm a stairway filled with smoke, but also a parent's willingness to nurture a child that finally decides our fate.

Our challenges may be new. The instruments with which we meet them may be new. But those values upon which our success depends—honesty and hard work, courage and fair play, tolerance and curiosity, loyalty and patriotism— these things are old. These things are true. They have been the quiet force of progress throughout our history.

What is demanded, then, is a return to these truths. What is required of us now is a new era of responsibility—a recognition on the part of every American that we have duties to ourselves, our nation and the world; duties that we do not grudgingly accept, but rather seize gladly, firm in the knowledge that there is nothing so satisfying to the spirit, so defining of our character than giving our all to a difficult task.

This is the price and the promise of citizenship. This is the source of our confidence—the knowledge that God calls on us to shape an uncertain destiny. This is the meaning of our liberty and our creed, why men and women and children of every race and every faith can join in celebration across this magnificent mall; and why a man whose father less than 60 years ago might not have been served in a local restaurant can now stand before you to take a most sacred oath. (Applause.)

So let us mark this day with remembrance of who we are and how far we have traveled. In the year of America's birth, in the coldest of months, a small band of patriots huddled by dying campfires on the shores of an icy river. The capital was abandoned. The enemy was advancing. The snow was stained with blood. At the moment when the outcome of our revolution was most in doubt, the father of our nation ordered these words to be read to the people:

"Let it be told to the future world . . . that in the depth of winter, when nothing but hope and virtue could survive . . . that the city and the country, alarmed at one common danger, came forth to meet [it]."

America: In the face of our common dangers, in this winter of our hardship, let us remember these timeless words. With hope and virtue, let us brave once more the icy currents, and endure what storms may come. Let it be said by our children's children that when we were tested we refused to let this journey end, that we did not turn back nor did we falter; and with eyes fixed on the horizon and God's grace upon us, we carried forth that great gift of freedom and delivered it safely to future generations.

Thank you. God bless you. And God bless the United States of America. (Applause.)

HOW WELL DID YOU UNDERSTAND THIS SELECTION?

1. If you had to summarize President Obama's speech in one sentence, what would you say?

2. What were the three most important things that the president said in his inaugural speech?

3. What are some of the things the president said about America's role in the world?

SELF TEST

MULTIPLE CHOICE: Circle the correct response. The correct answers are given at the end.

1. In the election of 1992, the Bush campaign was defeated by
   a. a lack of success in Iraq
   b. economic problems
   c. the passage of new taxes
   d. all of these
   e. none of these.

2. A new and predominant force in U.S. Presidential Elections since the late 1990s has been
   a. the liberal Democrats
   b. moderate Republicans
   c. right wing conservatives
   d. left wing conservatives.

3. Clinton's effort to make his cabinet more reflective of the American public included
   a. appointing another woman to the U.S. Supreme Court
   b. reappointing Bush's cabinet
   c. excluding Jews from the cabinet
   d. appointing his wife to the cabinet.

4. Two major Clinton programs which did not succeed were
   a. farm subsidy and welfare reform
   b. military spending increases and job training programs
   c. health care reform and the issue of homosexuals in the military
   d. the repeal of pro choice legislation and decreased educational spending.

5. On the international scene, Clinton was
   a. very aggressive
   b. totally an isolationist
   c. tempered in U.S. involvement
   d. followed Bush's example.

6. The "Liberal Agenda," according to George W. Bush in the 2000 presidential election included
   a. marriages for homosexuals
   b. big government
   c. socialized medicine
   d. all of the above
   e. a and c but not b.

7. The election of 2000 was extraordinary because
   a. Joe Lieberman of Connecticut was the first Jewish politician to run for Vice President
   b. the former first lady, Hillary Rodham Clinton, ran for the Senate in New York
   c. the voting standards across the country were confusing
   d. all of these
   e. a and c.

8. The Bush administration's first problem in early 2001
    a. the controversial result of the election
    b. too many women in the cabinet
    c. news of 9/11
    d. having an older man, Dick Cheney, as Vice President.

9. Since the 9/11 attacks, Bush has linked
    a. Saddam Hussein with Al Qaeda
    b. Afghanistan with Muslim moderates
    c. OPEC with terrorism
    d. illegal immigration with terrorism.

10. One of the major supporters of Bush has been
    a. moderates
    b. the religious right
    c. educators
    d. the Hollywood film industry.

11. Reminiscent of Ronald Reagan's policies, Bush's foreign policy can be described as his crusade against
    a. the Soviet Union
    b. African nations
    c. the "axis of evil"
    d. the Middle East.

12. On the domestic scene, Bush would like to see
    a. higher taxes
    b. more funding for social programs
    c. a Constitutional amendment for the extension of presidential terms
    d. a Constitutional amendment defining marriage.

13. In the 2004 presidential election, Bush's campaign characterized the Democratic candidate, John Kerry, as
    a. lying about his service in Viet Nam
    b. "flip flopping" on issues
    c. a liberal intellectual
    d. all of these
    e. none of these.

14. The war in Iraq was justified by the Bush administration as a war against terror and
    a. Muslims
    b. weapons of mass destruction
    c. Shia conservatives
    d. Sunni sheiks.

15. According to the Democrats, their victories in the 2006 mid term elections showed
    a. the war in Iraq was going well
    b. more troops should be sent to Iraq
    c. a new direction in the war was demanded by the American public
    d. nuclear bombs should be used to end the war.

ESSAYS:

1. Describe the impact on American life and society in the last twenty years of our history relative to:
    a. the drug epidemic
    b. the changing lives and status of women
    c. the AIDs epidemic
    d. the problems of the poor and minorities
    e. illegal immigration.

2. Compare and contrast the ideologies of the Democratic Party and the Republican Party. Why have third parties been so ineffective on the national level?

3. What issues are most likely to decide elections? Refer to the past elections of 2000 and 2004.

4. What qualities of leadership do Americans look for in their presidential candidates?

OPTIONAL ACTIVITIES: (Use your knowledge **and** imagination when appropriate.)

1. View the film, "The War Room," and discuss the modernization of political campaigns.

2. Write a two to three page speech as if YOU were running for president. What issues would you want to include as basic to the success of your campaign and the nation?

3. Education is always an issue in a political campaign. How much public funding should go to educating post high school students? Why?

4. Bill Clinton remains a popular figure in American politics. He claims to have found his "home" and is frequently in the news. What causes is he presently supporting and why?

WEB SITE LISTINGS:

White House home page – source on recent presidents:
    http://www.whitehouse.gov

House Judiciary Impeachment Report:
    http://www.house.gov/judiciary/report5

Document Center including Documents on Poverty, Crime, Terrorism, Impeachment and War:
    http://www.lib.umich.edu/govdocs/usterror.html

Recent and Older Supreme Court Decisions:
    http://www.findlaw.com/casecode/supreme.html

Recent Elections:
    http://www.pbs.org/newshour/election98
                            /election2000
9/11:
    http://911digitalarchive.org
    http://www.911ashistory.org

Iraq War 2003 Links to Many Sources:
    http://www.library.umass/edu/subject/iraqwar